THE CONCEPT OF ABUSE IN EU COMPETITION LAW

The objective(s) of Article 102 TFEU, what exactly makes a practice abusive and the standard of harm under Article 102 TFEU have not yet been settled. This lack of clarity creates uncertainty for businesses and, coupled with the current state of economics in this area, raises an important question of legitimacy. Using law and economic approaches, this book inquires into the possible objectives of Article 102 TFEU and proposes a modern approach to interpreting 'abuse'. In doing so, this book establishes an overarching concept of 'abuse' that conforms to the historical roots of the provision, to the text of the provision itself, and to modern economic thinking on unilateral conduct. This book therefore inquires into what Article 102 TFEU is about, what it can be about and what it should be about regarding both objectives and scope.

The book demonstrates that the separation of exploitative abuse from exclusionary abuse is artificial and unsound. It examines the roots of Article 102 TFEU and the historical context of the adoption of the Treaty, the case law, policy and literature on exploitative abuses and, where relevant, on exclusionary abuses. The book investigates potential objectives, such as fairness and welfare, as well as the potential conflict between such objectives. Finally, it critically assesses the European Commission's modernisation of Article 102 TFEU, before proposing a reformed approach to 'abuse' which is centred on three necessary and sufficient conditions: exploitation, exclusion and a lack of an increase in efficiency.

The Concept of Abuse in EU Competition Law

Law and Economic Approaches

Pınar Akman

·HART·
PUBLISHING

OXFORD AND PORTLAND, OREGON
2012

Published in the United Kingdom by Hart Publishing Ltd
16C Worcester Place, Oxford, OX1 2JW
Telephone: +44 (0)1865 517530
Fax: +44 (0)1865 510710
E-mail: mail@hartpub.co.uk
Website: http://www.hartpub.co.uk

Published in North America (US and Canada) by
Hart Publishing
c/o International Specialized Book Services
920 NE 58th Avenue, Suite 300
Portland, OR 97213-3786
USA

Tel: +1 503 287 3093 or toll-free: (1) 800 944 6190
Fax: +1 503 280 8832
E-mail: orders@isbs.com
Website: http://www.isbs.com

British Library Cataloguing in Publication Data
Data Available

ISBN: 978-1-84946-109-2

Typeset by Hope Services, Abingdon
Printed and bound in Great Britain by
CPI Group (UK) Ltd, Croydon CR0 4YY

Acknowledgements

This book is a culmination of my thinking in the area of abuse of a dominant position. The origins of the book can be traced back to my doctoral research, which I conducted at the University of East Anglia from 2004 to 2007. I must, therefore, first thank those who supported me throughout my PhD. Professor Morten Hviid and Dr Michael Harker were great supervisors and have had to discuss the subject matter of this book with me more than anyone else without showing any signs of boredom. The thesis was examined by Professor Richard Whish and Professor Brenda Sufrin, whom I must thank for their greatly appreciated comments. I am grateful to Professor Alastair Mullis, who gave me the idea and the opportunity to do a PhD in the UK; his constant support over the years has always made a difference. Similarly, I thank Gareth Thomas, who has been instrumental in my staying in the UK after the PhD to continue with this research. I also thank Dr Andrew Scott, who supervised my thesis (albeit briefly) in the very early days. Last but not least, my thanks go to my former colleagues at the University of Ankara Law School, particularly at the Department of Commercial Law headed by Professor Sabih Arkan, for all their support at the time.

I am grateful to various people and institutions that have made this experience possible and/or more enjoyable. Various parts of the book have benefited from discussions and comments from Professor Morten Hviid, Professor Bruce Lyons and Dr Michael Harker. Dr Daithí Mac Síthigh has provided continuous support and encouragement throughout the process. I must thank my colleagues at the ESRC Centre for Competition Policy, and particularly Professor Catherine Waddams, for the support I have received over the years and for the endless opportunities that they have provided to enhance my research. Financially, I am grateful to the Overseas Research Students Awards Scheme, the University of East Anglia and the Economic and Social Research Council for providing funding for the research underlying various parts of this book. I must also thank Hart Publishing and in particular Rachel Turner and Richard Hart for the friendly, professional and flexible approach.

I must express my deepest gratitude to my parents Nihal and Nuri Yücel Akman for not only injecting a passion for law in me, but also for helping me in every way they could in everything that I have ever done (which has included anything from career advice to packing suitcases throughout the years). I am extremely privileged to be their daughter.

Finally, I am indebted to my husband Peter, who has not only given me the idea and the encouragement to write this book, but has had to live with the ups and downs of what it entailed. Although Article 102 TFEU is a subject he claims not to like, he spent days on this book, giving me comments which have improved it immensely. I am very lucky to have his continuous personal and professional support, as well as his Irish charm around. He never ceases to amaze me.

Pınar Akman
Norwich, 12 July 2011

Note to the Reader

The Treaties of Rome refer to the European Economic Community (EEC) Treaty and the European Atomic Energy Community (EURATOM) Treaty, both of which came into force on 1 January 1958. The Maastricht Treaty – Treaty on European Union TEU (1993) – brought the EEC, EURATOM and the European Coal and Steel Community (ECSC) under one umbrella, namely the European Union and renamed the EEC as the European Community (EC). The EC Treaty was renumbered by the Treaty of Amsterdam which entered into force on 1 May 1999. The Treaty of Lisbon which entered into force on 1 December 2009 amended and renumbered the TEU. With the Treaty of Lisbon, the EU has replaced and succeeded the EC. The EC Treaty was renamed the Treaty on the Functioning of the European Union (TFEU).

In this book, the most recent numbering is used and the old provision numbers in quotations are replaced by the new numbers within square brackets. When referring to the rule now found in Protocol 27 on the Internal Market and Competition, unless the reference is made to this provision in the current time, the book uses Article 3(1)(g) EC as the reference. The one exception to this is found in chapter eight where the reference is made to Article 3(f) EEC since the issue therein is the particular text which the drafters agreed on in 1957.

The Treaty of Lisbon has also renamed the Court of First Instance (CFI) as the General Court (GC). In this book, reference is made to the GC even if at the relevant time the court was called the CFI. The GC and the Court of Justice (ECJ) make up the Court of Justice of the European Union (CJEU).

The law is stated as of 1 July 2011.

Contents

Table of Cases

Canada

European Union

Decisions

South Africa

United Kingdom

United States of America

Table of Legislation

European Union

Directives

Regulations

France

Germany

South Africa

United Kingdom

United States of America

International Instruments

Introduction

I PURPOSE OF THE BOOK

The reader of this book is invited to put to one side her preconceptions of the prohibition of 'abuse' of a dominant position in Article 102 TFEU (hereafter Article 102), in particular those directly resulting from the judgments of the Court of Justice (ECJ). Fortunately, this is not asking for too much; after all, the ECJ is not legally bound by precedent.[1] Thus, a completely fresh approach to 'abuse' in Article 102 *can* legally be adopted. This book seeks to show that such a new approach is in fact necessary: the approach that has been adopted by the EU authorities to date is far from desirable or appropriate and sometimes is even far from rational. In proposing a new approach, this book on occasions, adopts interpretations that do not conform to the interpretations or the (so far accepted) underlying assumptions of the EU authorities; hence this 'health warning' is provided at the outset.

Article 102 prohibits the 'abuse' of a dominant position on the internal market, insofar as it may affect trade between Member States.[2] Article 102 itself is silent on its precise objective(s) and the test of 'abuse' is not stipulated therein. The purpose of this book is to inquire into the possible objectives of Article 102 and to propose a modern approach to interpreting 'abuse'. In doing so, this book aims to establish an overarching concept of 'abuse' that conforms to the historical roots of the provision, to the text of the provision itself, and to modern economic thinking on unilateral conduct.

The subject of inquiry is important for several reasons. First, Article 102 merely provides examples of abusive conduct and does not define 'abuse'; when exactly the conduct of a dominant undertaking becomes abusive beyond the examples and what triggers the application of the provision and the standard of harm are

[1] On the ECJ not being bound by precedent, see A Arnull, 'Owning up to Fallibility: Precedent and the Court of Justice' (1993) 30 *Common Market Law Review* 247, 248, 262.

[2] The text of Art 102 reads: '[a]ny abuse by one or more undertakings of a dominant position within the internal market or in a substantial part of it shall be prohibited as incompatible with the internal market insofar as it may affect trade between Member States. Such abuse may, in particular, consist in: (a) directly or indirectly imposing unfair purchase or selling prices or other unfair trading conditions; (b) limiting production, markets or technical development to the prejudice of consumers; (c) applying dissimilar conditions to equivalent transactions with other trading parties, thereby placing them at a competitive disadvantage; (d) making the conclusion of contracts subject to acceptance by the other parties of supplementary obligations which, by their nature or according to commercial usage, have no connection with the subject of such contracts'.

not clear.[3] This is aggravated by the fact that the ECJ has adopted a 'teleological' approach to the interpretation of Treaty provisions by applying the rules against the wider backdrop of the Treaty tasks and activities.[4] On occasions, the ECJ has gone as far as ignoring clear words of the Treaty if that construction would ensure an interpretation which best accords with the broad objectives of the Treaty.[5] The resulting ambiguity and lack of clarity inevitably create uncertainty for businesses that might be subject to the provision.

Secondly, the economics of unilateral conduct is not as robust and developed as the economics of, for example, hard-core cartels.[6] This means that in the case of unilateral conduct, establishing whether or not any given practice is 'good' or 'bad' is not a straightforward or simple exercise. The uncertainty of the law and the current state of economics in this area raise an important question of legitimacy. That is, if it is not known *ex ante* by those who are subject to this legal provision, what exactly makes their conduct abusive (and why), and if the economics that should inform the answer to this question is also not robust, then it becomes questionable how legitimate the enforcement of the law actually is.

Thirdly, the European Commission (Commission) has recently completed a 'reform' of its approach to Article 102. This reform can be seen as the outcome of the various criticisms directed at the application of the provision over the years. Specifically, the application in question has been criticised for not being based on sound economic analysis and economic effects, for protecting competitors instead of competition and for being inefficient due to its failure to deliver from a 'welfare' perspective.[7] The current thinking of the Commission and the EU courts on

[3] The ECJ held in *Continental Can* that the list of practices in Art 102 is not exhaustive; Case 6/72 *Europemballage Corp and Continental Can Co Inc v Commission* [1973] ECR 215, [26].

[4] A Jones and B Sufrin, *EU Competition Law: Text, Cases and Materials* 4th edn (Oxford, OUP, 2011) 101.

[5] Jones and Sufrin, ibid. On the interpretative methodology of the ECJ, see in general E Rousseva, *Rethinking Exclusionary Abuses in EU Competition Law* (Oxford, Hart Publishing, 2010) 53 *et seq.*

[6] A 'hard-core cartel' is an anticompetitive agreement, anticompetitive concerted practice or anticompetitive arrangement by competitors to fix prices, make rigged bids, establish output restrictions or share or divide markets by allocating customers, suppliers, territories or lines of commerce; 'Recommendation of the OECD Council Concerning Effective Action Against Hard Core Cartels' adopted by the Council on 25.3.1998 available at www.oecd.org/dataoecd/39/4/2350130.pdf, [2(a)]. There is a consensus that such conduct is devoid of procompetitive benefits; see 'Defining Hard Core Cartel Conduct – Effective Institutions, Effective Penalties' report prepared by ICN Working Group on Cartels, ICN 4th Annual Conference (Bonn, 6–8 June 2005) 14. On the current state of economics of unilateral conduct being less clear-cut, see M Motta, 'The European Commission's Guidance Communication on Article 82' (2009) 30 (12) *European Competition Law Review* 593, 595; I Lianos, '"Judging" Economists: Economic Expertise in Competition Law Litigation: A European View' in I Lianos and I Kokkoris (eds), *The Reform of EC Competition Law* (The Netherlands, Kluwer Law International, 2010) 244–45.

[7] For various criticisms, see among others, EM Fox, 'Monopolization and Dominance in the United States and the European Community: Efficiency, Opportunity, and Fairness' (1986) 61 *Notre Dame Law Review* 981; P Jebsen and R Stevens, 'Assumptions, Goals and Dominant Undertakings: The Regulation of Competition under Article 86 of the European Union' (1996) 64 *Antitrust Law Journal* 443; B Sher, 'The Last of Steam-Powered Trains: Modernising Article 82' (2004) 25(5) *European Competition Law Review* 243; J Kallaugher and B Sher, 'Rebates Revisited: Anti-Competitive Effects

Article 102 has been suggested to be irreconcilable with the modern understanding of Article 101TFEU (hereafter Article 101) and EU merger control, leading to the proposition that Article 102 is the 'last of the steam-powered trains'.[8] The Commission's reform has culminated in a guidance document on the Commission's enforcement priorities in applying Article 102 to abusive exclusionary conduct.[9] The outcome of the reform, however, is far from satisfactory as the fundamental question of what the objective of the law and its enforcement is still remains unanswered. Moreover, the reform process has focused on 'exclusionary' practices and left 'exploitative' practices outside its scope. This presents an important problem and a contradiction: former Commissioner Kroes, under whose mandate the review was undertaken, expressed the reasoning for focusing on exclusionary abuse as it being 'wise in [their] enforcement policy to give priority to so-called exclusionary abuses, since exclusion is often at the basis of later exploitation of customers'.[10] This focus on 'exclusionary' conduct to the exclusion of 'exploitative' abuse is paradoxical as it raises the question why the emphasis is not on exploitative abuse if exclusionary abuses are problematic *because* they ultimately exploit consumers.[11] This paradox follows from the fact that the *main* objection to an undertaking with market power is its ability to *exploit* its position in a way that would not be possible for an undertaking on a competitive market.[12] The reform of the Commission is also incomplete in that it has only provided a general test of abuse for price-based exclusionary practices, thereby creating an artificial separation between price-based conduct and non-price-based conduct.

All in all, an overarching and all-encompassing concept of 'abuse' still does not exist. This means that there is still a gap in the law and its enforcement that has to be filled for the sake of legitimacy and legal certainty. This book therefore inquires into what Article 102 *is* about, what it *can* be about and what it *should* be about regarding both objectives and scope. By providing an overarching concept of 'abuse', it is hoped that this book will contribute to remedying this deficiency concerning legitimacy and legal certainty.

and Exclusionary Abuse under Article 82' (2004) 25(5) *European Competition Law Review* 263; D Waelbroeck, 'Michelin II: A Per Se Rule Against Rebates by Dominant Companies?' (2005) 1(1) *Journal of Competition Law and Economics* 149; C Ahlborn and AJ Padilla, 'From *Fairness* to *Welfare*: Implications for the Assessment of Unilateral Conduct under EC Competition Law' in CD Ehlermann and M Marquis (eds), *European Competition Annual 2007: A Reformed Approach to Article 82 EC* (Oxford, Hart Publishing, 2008); Jones and Sufrin (n 4) 363–64.

[8] Sher (n 7) 243–44. The term 'EU courts' in this study refers collectively to the ECJ and the General Court (GC).

[9] 'Guidance on the Commission's Enforcement Priorities in Applying Article 82 of the EC Treaty to Abusive Exclusionary Conduct by Dominant Undertakings' [2009] OJ C45/7.

[10] N Kroes, 'Tackling Exclusionary Practices to Avoid Exploitation of Market Power: Some Preliminary Thoughts on the Policy Review of Article 82' in B Hawk (ed), *International Antitrust Law and Policy: Fordham Corporate Law Institute Annual Proceedings 2005* (New York, Juris Publishing, 2006) 384.

[11] See BR Lyons, 'The Paradox of the Exclusion of Exploitative Abuse' in *The Pros and Cons of High Prices* (Swedish Competition Authority, 2007) 65.

[12] Jones and Sufrin (n 4) 359.

II SCOPE AND OUTLINE

This book is concerned with the prohibition of abuse of a dominant position in Article 102. As regards jurisdiction, the scope of the book is limited to the law of the European Union. On occasions, however, where necessary, reference is also made to national laws within and outside the European Union. This book is intended to be a research monograph aimed at displaying and promoting research that can inform the practice and making of law and policy in the area of abuse of a dominant position. It is not intended as a textbook and therefore does not deal with all of the issues that might be relevant for a general understanding of the prohibition of abuse of a dominant position. Substantively, the scope of the book is limited to the concept of 'abuse'. As such, it does not concern itself directly with 'dominance', although establishing dominance is an essential part of an assessment under Article 102.[13]

This book is divided into four parts, with each part being comprised of two chapters.

Part I is concerned with the theoretical and historical foundations of the subject of inquiry. Chapter one discusses 'welfare' and other possible objectives of competition law and policy. This has been chosen as the first inquiry of the study as the Commission – which sought to adopt a 'more economic approach' during the 'reform' process – appears to favour 'consumer welfare' as the objective of Article 102.[14] By looking at welfare and other possible objectives, chapter one establishes that, regarding objectives, the best starting point seems to be the acceptance that both process and outcome matter in competition law and policy.[15] In the context of Article 102, this would suggest that the objective of Article 102 should be conceptualised as preventing both the distortion of competition (process) and the consumer harm (outcome) that might result from the practice. This would be the case particularly if 'consumer welfare' is accepted as the objective of the provision. In fact, the thesis of this book is that this approach implies the fusion of 'exclusionary' and 'exploitative' abuse: it is harm to custom-

[13] The ECJ has defined 'dominance' as 'a position of economic strength enjoyed by an undertaking which enables it to prevent effective competition being maintained on the relevant market by affording it the power to behave to an appreciable extent independently of its competitors, its customers and ultimately of its consumers'; Case 85/76 *Hoffmann-La Roche & Co AG v Commission* [1979] ECR 461, [38].

[14] See 'Guidance' (n 9); 'DG Competition Discussion Paper on the Application of Article 82 of the Treaty to Exclusionary Abuses' (Brussels, December 2005) ec.europa.eu/competition/antitrust/art82/discpaper2005.pdf [4]. See also N Kroes, 'Preliminary Thoughts on Policy Review of Article 82' speech at the Fordham Corporate Law Institute (New York, 23 September 2005) 2; N Kroes, 'Exclusionary Abuses of Dominance – The European Commission's Enforcement Priorities' speech at the Fordham University Symposium (New York, 25 September 2008) 2; P Lowe, 'The Commission's Current Thinking on Article 82' BIICL Annual Trans-Atlantic Antitrust Dialogue (15 May 2008) 2, 3.

[15] The assessment of both process and outcome is suggested in J Farrell and ML Katz, 'The Economics of Welfare Standards in Antitrust' (2006) 2(2) *Competition Policy International* 3. See ch 1 this volume, section III.D for a discussion.

ers (exploitation) that is linked to harm to competition (exclusion) that Article 102 seeks to prevent.[16]

Chapter two establishes the historical roots of Article 102, the historical context in which the provision was adopted and the implications these have for a modern application of Article 102. This task is undertaken because the predominant literature claims that Article 102 historically has 'ordoliberal' roots.[17] Based on ordoliberal arguments, some suggest that Article 102 cannot be applied with a 'consumer welfare' standard as the provision in question protects the 'institution of competition' and not necessarily a certain outcome that would result from the protection of the competitive process.[18] This is because, for ordoliberalism, the main objective of competition policy is the protection of 'economic freedom of action' of market participants.[19] It has indeed been argued by certain commentators that the Commission has gone too far by adopting a consumer welfare standard; for them, it has departed from the jurisprudence of the EU courts, something which it cannot do.[20] Chapter two therefore examines the *travaux préparatoires* (preparatory works) of the nego-

[16] One commentator has remarked that, for a model based on consumer or total welfare, there is no 'exclusionary' violation and that the only type of violation is 'exploitation'; see EM Fox, 'What is Harm to Competition? Exclusionary Practices and Anticompetitive Effect' (2002) 70 *Antitrust Law Journal* 371, 372. More recently, Pardolesi and Arnaudo have also suggested the same: R Pardolesi and L Arnaudo, 'Single-Firm Conduct: A Discipline in Search of Itself (Try with Google?)' Working Paper (2010) available at: papers.ssrn.com/sol3/papers.cfm?abstract_id=1541928. This is not the proposal of this study; by contrast, this study argues that exploitation and exclusion must *both* be present for a violation of Art 102 to occur.

[17] See, eg, DJ Gerber, *Law and Competition in Twentieth Century Europe: Protecting Prometheus* (Oxford, OUP, 1998) 264; L Lovdahl Gormsen, 'Article 82 EC: Where Are We Coming From and Where Are We Going To?' (2005) 2(2) *The Competition Law Review* 5, 10; KJ Cseres, *Competition Law and Consumer Protection* (The Hague, Kluwer Law International, 2005) 82; G Marenco, 'The Birth of Modern Competition Law in Europe' in A von Bogdandy PC Mavroidis and Y Mény (eds), *European Integration and International Co-ordination: Studies in Honour of Claus-Dieter Ehlermann* (The Hague, Kluwer Law International, 2002) 303; E Rousseva, 'Modernizing by Eradicating: How the Commission's New Approach to Article 81 EC Dispenses with the Need to Apply Article 82 EC to Vertical Restraints' (2005) 42 *Common Market Law Review* 587, 590–91. Focusing on Art 101 regarding the influence of ordoliberalism, see G Monti, 'Article 81 and Public Policy' (2002) 39(5) *Common Market Law Review* 1057.

[18] See, eg, DJ Gerber, 'The Future of Article 82: Dissecting the Conflict' in CD Ehlermann and M Marquis (eds), *European Competition Law Annual 2007: A Reformed Approach to Article 82 EC* (Oxford, Hart Publishing, 2008) 37, 50–51; T Eilmansberger, 'How to Distinguish Good from Bad Competition under Article 82 EC: In Search of Clearer and More Coherent Standards for Anti-competitive Abuses' (2005) 42 *Common Market Law Review* 129, 133; H Schweitzer, 'The History, Interpretation and Underlying Principles of Section 2 Sherman Act and Article 82 EC' in CD Ehlermann and M Marquis (eds), *European Competition Annual 2007: A Reformed Approach to Article 82 EC* (Oxford, Hart Publishing, 2008) 119, 161.

[19] W Möschel, 'Competition Policy from an Ordo Point of View' in A Peacock and H Willgerodt (eds), *German Neo-Liberals and the Social Market Economy* (London, Macmillan, 1989) 149, 151. *Cf* F Maier-Rigaud, 'On the Normative Foundations of Competition Law: Efficiency, Political Freedom and the Freedom to Compete' (5th Academic Society for Competition Law (ASCOLA) Conference on the Goals of Competition Law, Bonn, May 2010) available at: www.iask.de/micro/paper/ascola.pdf (forthcoming in the ASCOLA Competition Law series by Edward Elgar).

[20] See statement by B Heitzer, President of the Bundeskartellamt on European Competition Day (Paris 18–19 November 2008) available at: www.bundeskartellamt.de/wDeutsch/download/pdf/Diskussionsbeitraege/081127_ECD_Paris.pdf; H Schweitzer, 'Recent developments in EU Competition Law (2006–2008): Single-firm Dominance and the Interpretation of Article 82' (2009) (2) *European Review of Contract Law* 175, 184; L Lovdahl Gormsen, 'Why the European Commission's Enforcement Priorities on Article 82 EC should be Withdrawn' (2010) 31 *European Competition Law Review* 45, 50, 51.

tiations of the Treaties of Rome, as well as other archival evidence relating to the early period of enforcement, to establish whether Article 102 can be applied with a welfare standard. Chapter two shows that – in contrast to the conventional wisdom – Article 102 was *not* envisaged as an ordoliberal rule and that its objective can be based on welfare. It further shows that Article 102 was intended to prohibit 'exploitative' conduct (ie, conduct that harms the trading partners of the dominant undertaking) as opposed to 'exclusionary' conduct (ie, conduct that harms the [competitive position of the] competitors of the dominant undertaking).[21] Chapter two also provides a definition of 'exploitative' abuse that is based on some early understandings of abuse. Similarly, chapter two finds efficiency to have been one of the main concerns of the drafters of the provision. It thus argues that efficiency should be incorporated into the concept of 'abuse'.[22] Based on the premises established in Part I, the remainder of the book seeks to find the correct interpretation of 'abuse' in Article 102, one which aims to prevent 'exploitation' as well as to protect efficiency at the same time.

Part II examines two specific, potential objectives of Article 102: 'welfare' (chapter three) and 'fairness' (chapter four). Since the Commission is propagating a 'consumer welfare' standard for Article 102, chapter three investigates the particular role that 'welfare' has played in the enforcement of Article 102 and provides a critical look at the standard of harm in the application of Article 102 by the Commission and the EU courts. Chapter three also provides a comparison between Article 101(3) TFEU (hereafter Article 101(3)) and Article 102, since it has been suggested that the former sets 'consumer welfare' as the standard for EU competition rules.[23] Chapter three finds that it is difficult to argue that there is a

[21] According to the ECJ '[t]he concept of abuse is an objective concept relating to the behaviour of an undertaking in a dominant position which is such as to influence the structure of a market where, as a result of the very presence of the undertaking in question, the degree of competition is weakened and which, through recourse to methods different from those which condition normal competition in products or services on the basis of the transactions of commercial operators, has the effect of hindering the maintenance of the degree of competition still existing in the market or the growth of that competition'; *Hoffmann-La Roche* (n 13) [91]. Without recourse to the *travaux préparatoires*, on the basis of a textual analysis and a comparison with the US Sherman Act Section II, Joliet had also reached the conclusion that Art 102 does not apply to exclusionary practices; see R Joliet, *Monopolization and Abuse of Dominant Position* (La Haye, Martinus Nijhoff, 1970) 250.

[22] See Whish, noting that the finding from the *travaux préparatoires* concerning efficiency provides a solid foundation for contemporary policy; R Whish, *Competition* Law 6th edn (Oxford, OUP, 2009) 193.

[23] According to Art 101(1), all agreements between undertakings, decisions by associations of undertakings and concerted practices which may affect trade between Member States and which have as their object or effect the prevention, restriction or distortion of competition within the internal market are prohibited as incompatible with the internal market. According to Art 101(3): '[t]he provisions of paragraph 1 may, however, be declared inapplicable in the case of: – any agreement or category of agreements between undertakings, – any decision or category of decisions by associations of undertakings, – any concerted practice or category of concerted practices, which contributes to improving the production or distribution of goods or to promoting technical or economic progress, while allowing consumers a fair share of the resulting benefit, and which does not: (a) impose on the undertakings concerned restrictions which are not indispensable to the attainment of these objectives; (b) afford such undertakings the possibility of eliminating competition in respect of a substantial part of the products in question'. For the argument that Article 101(3) sets a consumer welfare standard see, eg,

'consumer welfare' standard that is adopted in the decisional practice since there does not appear to be a unified and coherent test applied by the EU authorities in finding behaviour to constitute an 'abuse'. In particular, the jurisprudence of the ECJ does not seem to welcome such an approach either. Therefore, chapter four considers 'fairness' as a potential objective of Article 102. This is done because certain 'unfair' conduct is explicitly prohibited in various examples in Article 102, a fact which suggests that 'fairness' might be an objective more so than 'welfare'. Chapter four finds that although there is a 'fairness' element in Article 102, it is practically undefined. Consequently, the chapter looks into other related areas of law, such as contract law and consumer law, seeking insights into 'fairness' from these disciplines. It finds that there is an inherent difficulty with defining and operationalising 'fairness' and that, even when a definition is provided, a significant element of vagueness and arbitrariness remains. This is important since a stand alone 'fairness' objective can clash with other goals, such as 'welfare' and 'efficiency'. Chapter four therefore advocates an understanding of 'fairness' simply as 'exploitation' and not as a stand alone objective.

Part III of this book seeks to achieve two aims: first, to support further the findings of chapter four by showing that the concept of 'fairness' does not *function* effectively on its own; and secondly, to demonstrate the clash between stand alone 'fairness' objectives and 'welfarist' objectives. This is done by an examination of two practices that are prohibited in Article 102: 'unfair pricing' (chapter five) and 'discrimination' (chapter six). The examination of these two practices also highlights the problems with prohibiting 'exploitation' without separate harm to competition for competition law purposes. As such, chapter five establishes the various problems with the prohibition of 'unfair pricing', some of which are of such a degree that the first best option is suggested to be the removal of this particular prohibition from Article 102. However, since a Treaty amendment to realise this is unlikely to be obtained, chapter five also proposes a new method of interpreting 'unfair pricing' that is more rational and operational than the current approach. Chapter six turns to the prohibition of 'discrimination' in Article 102, an issue which demonstrates an important tension between the objectives of 'fairness' and 'welfare'. This is because discrimination – particularly price discrimination – is a ubiquitous business practice with ambiguous effects on welfare. Moreover, chapter six shows that a *prohibition* of discrimination can be objectionable not only for making everyone worse off, but because it can also lead to 'unfairness' itself; all depends on one's understanding of 'fairness'. As with chapter five, chapter six also offers an approach that can reconcile the law and economics concerning the prohibition of 'discrimination'.

Part IV of this study focuses on modernising the approach to Article 102, particularly the concept of 'abuse' therein. Chapter seven assesses the reform process of the Commission, while chapter eight presents this book's proposal for a

J Bourgeois and J Bocken, 'Guidelines on the Application of Article 81(3) of the EC Treaty or How to Restrict a Restriction' (2005) 32(2) *Legal Issues of Economic Integration* 111, 119. For a detailed discussion, see ch 3 this volume, section II.

modern approach to Article 102. Chapter seven aims, therefore, to establish fully the position over which this study's proposal is sought to be an improvement. Chapter seven provides the highlights of the documents that have been adopted in the reform process and critically assesses the 'reformed' approach. It establishes that, by leaving out exploitative conduct and by limiting the general test for abuse to price-based exclusionary conduct, the reform has fallen short of providing a comprehensive and workable concept of 'abuse'. Similarly, chapter seven finds that it is not possible to suggest unequivocally that the Commission has adopted a 'consumer welfare' standard as it advocates. Chapter eight in turn sets out to provide an overarching concept of 'abuse' on the basis of the main findings of this study. The chapter proposes that there are three *necessary and sufficient* conditions for a given practice to be found abusive under Article 102. These cumulative conditions are: (i) exploitation; (ii) exclusion; and (iii) a lack of an increase in efficiency. Chapter eight details why and how these make up the necessary and sufficient conditions under a modern approach to the concept of 'abuse'. It is argued therein that, although this approach does require departure from some of the principles established in the jurisprudence, it brings the application of the provision closer to the true nature of Article 102 itself. By adopting an interpretation that is loyal to the provision itself and that is in line with current economic thinking, this proposal presents a plausible alternative to the current approach.

III METHODOLOGY

With the exception of chapter two, which contains an historical analysis that involves archival research, this book adopts a traditional legal approach which comprises the analysis of the relevant case law, decisional practice, legislation, policy documents and literature. Although the book is in the area of competition law, it adopts an interdisciplinary approach by which it has recourse to contract law, consumer law, industrial economics and behavioural economics. Incorporating contract law and behavioural economics is particularly important for the inquiry due to doctrines of 'fairness' in the former and insightful explanations of 'fairness' in the latter, both of which provide means to interpret 'exploitation' and 'abuse' in Article 102. This approach is also a contribution to the literature since competition law has traditionally been conceived without sufficient reference to contract law or behavioural economics, even though both of these can provide useful guidance.

I

Theoretical and Historical Foundations

1

Welfare and Objectives of Competition Law and Policy

I INTRODUCTION

This chapter introduces the potential objectives that competition law and policy may pursue. As has been noted, 'competition law appears to be one of those fields of law the purpose of which is not self-explanatory'.[1] Starting in the late 1990s and early 2000s, the Commission in particular has arguably been modernising its approach to EU competition rules with a more economic approach that embraces a 'consumer welfare' standard as its objective.[2] This development implies that the objectives of the law and policy in this area are still in flux and are yet to be agreed on by policy makers and enforcers, while the provisions continue to be applied to sanction the practices of undertakings. In some ways, this lack of consensus regarding objectives might be due to this area of law being heavily reliant on economics and to the relevant economics being subject to change as knowledge improves. However, in other ways, it also represents an anomaly since it begs the question of how legitimate enforcement of these provisions can be when one takes into account the impact on legal certainty of this apparent lack of consensus concerning objectives. This seems to be a particular problem in the area of abuse of a dominant position since as current economic understanding stands, the effects of unilateral conduct on competition are far less established and clear-cut in comparison with the effects of, for example, hard-core cartel behaviour. Thus, acknowledging the current emphasis on 'welfare' due to the 'more economic approach' of the Commission, this chapter sets out the relevant concepts of welfare and the potential conflicts between different welfare concepts. Hence, this chapter explains the potential implications of adopting a 'consumer welfare' standard as opposed to a 'total welfare' standard and discusses the trade-offs that

[1] H Vedder, 'Competition Law and Consumer Protection: How Competition Law can be used to Protect Consumers Even Better – Or Not?' [2006] *European Business Law Review* 83, 83.

[2] See, eg, Commission, 'Guidelines on the Application of Article 81(3) of the Treaty' [2004] OJ C101/97, [13]; N Kroes, 'Preliminary Thoughts on Policy Review of Article 82' speech given to the Fordham Corporate Law Institute (New York, 23 September 2005) 3; 'DG Competition Discussion Paper on the Application of Article 82 of the Treaty to Exclusionary Abuses' (Brussels, December 2005) available at: ec.europa.eu/competition/antitrust/art82/discpaper2005.pdf [4], [54], [55], [88].

it might be necessary to make between different types of efficiency. In this context, it also discusses whether welfare is the only value that matters when it comes to establishing the objectives.

Although 'welfare' in the application of Article 102 will be discussed in detail in chapter three and 'fairness' as an alternative objective under Article 102 is dealt with separately in chapter four, within the scope of a discussion of the general objectives of competition law and policy, this chapter also elaborates on the possible necessity of making trade-offs between efficiency and distributional concerns. It must be noted that this potential trade-off will become more important if the focus of EU competition policy shifts to broader objectives than pure economic efficiency-based objectives. For example, the current Commissioner for Competition Policy, Joaquín Almunia, whose office term started in 2010 after the adoption of the Treaty of Lisbon, has expressed his mandate as that of strengthening the social market economy, enhancing its *efficiency* and *fairness*.[3] Therefore, whether or not *efficiency* and *fairness* can be enhanced simultaneously requires discussion and thus, following the brief introduction in this chapter, this becomes one of the recurrent themes of this book.

This chapter is organised as follows. Section II introduces welfare economics, different understandings of welfare and different concepts of efficiency, as well as the potential trade-offs between these. Section III discusses the general objectives of competition law and policy, with a brief discussion of different influential schools of thought, before moving on to a particular comparison of 'total welfare' and 'consumer welfare' as standards for competition law and policy. It also discusses the potential conflict between efficiency and distributional concerns and whether welfare is all that matters in terms of objectives. Section IV concludes.

II WELFARE ECONOMICS, DIFFERENT UNDERSTANDINGS OF WELFARE AND EFFICIENCY

A In General

The 'welfare' of an individual or a community can be defined as its 'well-being'.[4] Welfare economics is concerned with the effect of economic policies on the level of welfare of individuals or groups of people; the analysis is used to compare the relative merits of two situations by assessing the level of welfare in each.[5] Welfare economics focuses on using resources optimally to achieve the maximum well-

[3] See the 'Mandate' of Commissioner Almunia at: ec.europa.eu/commission_2010-2014/almunia/about/mandate/index_en.htm.

[4] CM Price, *Welfare Economics in Theory and Practice* (London, Macmillan, 1977) 3.

[5] ibid.

being for the individuals in society.[6] However, agreement cannot always be reached on what is optimal. Welfare economics' propositions are logical deductions from a set of definitions and assumptions, but the assumptions of welfare economics are arguably fundamentally different from those of positive economics. While there may be controversy regarding whether the assumptions of a model in positive economics conform to reality or whether they are appropriate for the circumstances, the morality or ethics of the assumptions is not an issue in positive economics. Contrarily, the assumptions of welfare economics are ethical assumptions or value judgements with which anyone may legitimately disagree. A second difficulty with welfare economics is that 'economic welfare' is not an observable variable. The economic welfare status of an individual is formally represented by her 'utility' level, a term generally used synonymously with 'happiness' or 'satisfaction'.[7] Apart from the imponderability of utility – even if utility were measurable – there would still be a problem of how to weight individuals, that is how to decide which individual's welfare is more important to society; no objective way exists for solving this problem of interpersonal comparisons.[8]

Since such interpersonal comparisons are not possible without any absolute measure of welfare, to proceed from individual effects to community implications some distributional judgements are necessary so that community welfare can be derived from that of the individuals who comprise it.[9] In cases where it is possible to increase the welfare of every individual, thus raising community welfare, one can draw clear conclusions, whereas it is more difficult in other cases. One approach to the problem would be to construct a social-welfare function relating the overall welfare of the community to all the factors which might affect it. This can only be achieved by incorporating distributional judgements and these may present considerable difficulties since under democratic government it is virtually impossible to gain consensus about the distribution of income, let alone to obtain the information in a way that it can be quantified and incorporated in a model to relate community welfare to individual welfare. However, what may be feasible is to identify and analyse a particular aspect of the social-welfare function, for example, that community welfare would rise if that of every member were to increase. As such, Vilfredo Pareto's work is based on the contention that distributional judgements are best avoided altogether since it is difficult to obtain consensus about them, they do not lend themselves easily to incorporation in an analytical framework and particular assumptions would limit the applicability of conclusions based on them. According to the 'Pareto principle' an improvement in community welfare occurs only if it involves an increase in the utility of at least one

[6] The rest of this paragraph draws mainly on RE Just, DL Hueth and A Schmidtz, *The Welfare Economics of Public Policy: A Practical Approach to Project and Policy Evaluation* (Cheltenham, Edward Elgar, 2004) 3–4.

[7] ibid. The disadvantage of using 'utility' as a synonym for 'welfare' is that it implies that it results from the consumption of 'useful' goods rather than from more trivial pursuits which give pleasure; Price (n 4) 4.

[8] ibid.

[9] This paragraph draws mainly on Price, ibid, 6–7.

individual and a decrease in the utility of none. Such a change is an increase in efficiency and Pareto defined the position of maximum *efficiency* (not necessarily welfare) as one in which no one could be made better off without someone becoming worse off.[10] Following Pareto, most of the conventional theory of welfare economics rests on the assumed value judgement that if one person is better off and no one is worse off, welfare is increased.[11] It should be noted at this point that the literature following Pareto seems to equate 'efficiency' with 'welfare' even though the Pareto principle was originally expressed as a measurement of 'efficiency' and not necessarily 'welfare'. Different types of efficiency are discussed later in section II.B.

In practice, most economic decisions involve combinations of loss and gain; changes which incur only benefits for all members of society are usually undertaken without needing specific economic analysis.[12] The narrowness of the Pareto test which effectively allows any individual to veto a change which would benefit the rest of society makes it of limited use for policy purposes.[13] In contrast, according to the 'Kaldor-Hicks criterion', if a change in policy would result in some persons being better off and some worse off, and the gainers *could* compensate the losers in such a way that on balance everybody was better off, then welfare would be increased by implementing that change.[14] Under this notion of efficiency, only hypothetical compensation is involved, not actual compensation.[15] If the compensation were actually paid, there would be no need for the Kaldor-Hicks test since the Pareto principle alone would be sufficient as everyone would be made better off or at least no one worse off. Thus, the hypothetical nature of the compensation test is both the strength and the weakness of the Kaldor-Hicks criterion.[16] Possible objections to the Kaldor-Hicks test as a conclusive criterion of social welfare are that, first, it allows for the coercive imposition of losses on individuals, and secondly, by balancing gains against losses in terms of money, it assumes that one unit of the currency has the same value whomever owns it or may receive it, though arguably such an assumption must in many circumstances be false.[17]

[10] Price, ibid, 7.

[11] DM Winch, *Analytical Welfare Economics* (Harmondsworth, Penguin, 1971) 27.

[12] Price (n 4) 19.

[13] AI Ogus, *Regulation: Legal Form and Economic Theory* 2nd edn (Oxford, Hart Publishing, 2004) 24.

[14] Winch (n 11) 143. The two most widely used 'willingness to pay' welfare measurements proposed by Hicks are the 'compensating variation' and the 'equivalent variation'. The motivation for the Hicksian measurements is that an observable alternative for measuring the intensities of preferences of an individual for one situation versus another is the amount of money the individual is willing to pay or willing to accept to move from one situation to another. The 'compensating variation' is the amount of money which, when taken away from an individual after an economic change, leaves the person just as well off as before. 'Equivalent variation' is the amount of money paid to an individual which, if an economic change does not happen, leaves the individual just as well off as if the change had occurred. 'Compensating variation' focuses on the initial level of welfare that the consumer held prior to price and/or income changes. 'Equivalent variation' focuses on the subsequent level of welfare that the consumer would obtain with the price and/or income changes. See Just, Hueth and Schmidtz (n 6) 9, 123.

[15] YK Ng, *Welfare Economics: Towards a More Complete Analysis* (Hampshire, Palgrave Macmillan, 2004) 48.

[16] ibid.

[17] Ogus (n 13) 25.

It should be noted that the compensation test requires only the existence of an 'ordinal' utility measure, namely one in which an individual can *rank* states according to her well-being, but cannot say by *how much* her welfare varies in different situations.[18] Thus, it is not a 'cardinal' measure. If utility were measurable in cardinal terms and different individuals' welfare could be compared, then it would be possible to aggregate the total utility experienced by each member of the community to know the community welfare in different cases.[19] However, such interpersonal comparisons are not possible without an absolute measure of welfare.[20] It is indeed this impossibility that leads to having tests such as the Pareto and the Kaldor-Hicks, which can arguably measure the change in efficiency or welfare without having to make distributional judgements.

What must be noted is that excluding redistribution from the analysis by concentrating on efficiency does not mean that redistribution is not a concern in economics; efficiency and redistribution are treated separately in economics by the two welfare theorems. The 'first welfare theorem' states that, under certain conditions, a market economy leads to a Pareto-efficient allocation of the scarce resources of society.[21] The 'second welfare theorem' states that, under certain conditions, every Pareto optimum can be attained by a market economy, provided that it starts from the appropriate distribution of resources.[22] Thus, as long as the conditions hold, in that there are no market failures, the role of the government can be limited to the redistribution of the ownership of resources and of the entitlements of income, leaving the whole process of the allocation of resources and the production of goods and services to the market.[23] As such, the government can bring about the Pareto optimum that yields the most desirable distribution of welfare over the individuals.[24] If the conditions are not fulfilled, namely if there is a market failure (for example, because competition is not perfect, the market for the product does not exist, producers and consumers are not perfectly informed and so on), then these may hamper the realisation of a Pareto-efficient allocation and can be seen as reasons for government intervention.[25]

One basic principle of economics that must be borne in mind is that resources tend to gravitate towards their most valuable uses if voluntary exchange, namely a market, is permitted.[26] By the process of voluntary exchange, resources are shifted

[18] Price (n 4) 5.

[19] ibid 6. The so-called 'marginalist' or 'material' welfare school believed that measuring utility across individuals was possible and essential to policy making, while the so-called 'ordinalist' welfare school believed that such interpersonal comparisons of utility were impossible; see H Hovenkamp, 'Antitrust Policy After Chicago' (1985) 84 *Michigan Law Review* 213, 236–37 for a discussion.

[20] Price (n 4) 6.

[21] H van den Doel and B van Velthoven, *Democracy and Welfare Economics* 2nd edn (Cambridge, CUP, 1993) 33.

[22] ibid.

[23] ibid 33–34. Throughout this study the terms 'product(s)' and 'good(s)' are used to cover 'services' as well, unless specified otherwise.

[24] ibid 34.

[25] ibid.

[26] RA Posner, *Economic Analysis of Law* 4th edn (Boston, Little, Brown and Company, 1992) 10.

to those uses in which the value to consumers (measured by their 'willingness to pay') is highest.[27] When resources are used such that their value is highest, it may be said that they are being employed efficiently.[28] Put by Adam Smith, every individual in the society, by intending her own gain and thus participating in the industry in a manner so that its produce may be of the greatest value, is led by an 'invisible hand' to promote an end which was not a part of her intention – the public interest.[29] By pursuing her own interest, she frequently promotes that of the society more effectually than when she really intends to promote it.[30] Therefore, policy-making is usually aimed at the realisation of greater efficiency and economic efficiency can be expressed in terms of 'consumer surplus', 'producer surplus' and 'total surplus'.[31] Following the general usage in the economics literature, 'welfare' and 'surplus' will be used as synonyms throughout this study.[32]

Introducing the concept to the English-speaking world for the first time, Marshall defined 'consumer surplus' as the excess of the price which a consumer would be willing to pay rather than go without the relevant product, over that which she actually does pay.[33] More recently, economists have defined it as the area under the demand curve and above the price line.[34] Thus, 'consumer surplus' is the aggregate measure of the surplus of all consumers.[35] Likewise, the surplus of an individual producer is the profit it makes by selling the product in question; 'producer surplus' is therefore the sum of all profits made by producers in the industry.[36] The efficiency of a given market can be measured by the sum of 'consumer surplus' and 'producer surplus' which is called 'total surplus'. As such, the combination of the surpluses provides the degree of social 'welfare'.[37] A graph demonstrating these concepts can be found in section II.B.

Economists usually assume that each economic actor maximises something: consumers maximise utility; firms maximise profits; politicians maximise votes and so on.[38] Thus, the concept of 'wealth maximisation' is at the centre of both the descriptive and normative aspects of the theory of 'law and economics'.[39] As such, 'wealth maximisation' is achieved when goods and other resources are in the

[27] ibid 11.

[28] ibid.

[29] A Smith, *An Inquiry into the Nature and Causes of the Wealth of Nations* E Cannan (ed) (Chicago, The University of Chicago Press, 1976) 477.

[30] ibid 477–78.

[31] KJ Cseres, *Competition Law and Consumer Protection* (The Hague, Kluwer Law International, 2005) 17–18.

[32] For the same approach see, eg, M Motta, *Competition Policy: Theory and Practice* (Cambridge, CUP, 2004) 18 *et seq*. There are arguably differences between these concepts since 'welfare' is a broader concept than 'surplus'; BY Orbach, 'The Antitrust Consumer Welfare Paradox' (2010) 7(1) *Journal of Competition Law & Economics* 133.

[33] A Marshall, *Principles of Economics: An Introductory Volume* 8th edn (London, Macmillan and Co, 1920) 124.

[34] Just, Hueth and Schmidtz (n 6) 100.

[35] Motta (n 32) 18.

[36] ibid.

[37] Cseres (n 31) 18.

[38] R Cooter and T Ulen, *Law and Economics* 4th edn (Boston, Pearson Addison Wesley, 2004) 15.

[39] RM Dworkin, 'Is Wealth a Value?' (1980) 9 *Journal of Legal Studies* 191, 191.

hands of those who value them most, and someone values a good more only if she is both willing *and* able to pay more in money (or in the equivalent of money) to have it.[40] Resources are efficiently allocated in a system of wealth maximisation when there is no reallocation that would increase the wealth of society.[41] An individual maximises her own wealth when she increases the value of the resources she owns; whenever she is able, for example, to purchase something she values for any sum less than the most she would be willing to pay for it.[42] Society maximises its wealth when all the resources of that society are so distributed that the sum of all such individual valuations is as high as possible.[43]

It has been argued that there are many conceptual difficulties with this idea of individual and social wealth maximisation.[44] One criticism directed to the root of the whole idea is that it is unclear why social wealth is a worthy goal and once social 'wealth' is divorced from 'utility', it loses plausibility as a component of value.[45] This has been countered by Posner who argued that wealth is conducive to happiness, freedom, self-expression and other uncontroversial goods.[46] Yet, 'wealth maximisation' has also been criticised, for example by Dworkin, on the grounds that for most people there is a difference between the sum they would be willing to pay for something that they do not have and the sum they would take in exchange for it if they already have it.[47] Sometimes the former sum is greater. If many people were often in that position, then social wealth maximisation would be inherently unstable. In these circumstances, wealth maximisation would be a cyclic standard.[48] The second case is perhaps more common: someone will ask for more to give up something that she owns than she would pay to acquire it. If many people are in that position with respect to many goods, then wealth maximisation will not be path-independent; the final distribution that achieves a wealth maximisation will be different even given the same initial distribution, depending on the order in which intermediate transfers are made. In cases where these two tests conflict, the standard of social wealth maximisation is indeterminate.[49] It should be pointed out that there is a good deal of evidence from behavioural economics that people do indeed put different values on the same object depending on whether they are acquiring it or giving it up.[50] Although this so-called 'endowment effect' does not mean that Pareto optimal trades will not take place, it implies that there are fewer mutually advantageous exchanges

[40] ibid.
[41] RA Posner, 'The Value of Wealth: A Comment on Dworkin and Kronman' (1980) 9 *Journal of Legal Studies* 243, 243.
[42] Dworkin (n 39) 191.
[43] ibid 192.
[44] ibid.
[45] ibid 194, 200.
[46] Posner (n 41) 244.
[47] Dworkin (n 39) 192.
[48] ibid.
[49] ibid.
[50] See D Kahneman, JL Knetsch and RH Thaler, 'Experimental Tests of the Endowment Effect and the Coase Theorem' in CR Sunstein (ed), *Behavioural Law and Economics* (Cambridge, CUP, 2000).

possible since there will be a discrepancy between the buyer's and the seller's valuation of the same product.[51]

Perhaps more importantly, wealth maximisation as a moral maxim has also been criticised for being fundamentally incomplete due to the reliance on prices.[52] The principle of wealth maximisation purports to provide a general invocation to actions: actions are right or obligatory to the extent that they promote wealth. However, wealth maximisation can say nothing of rights and liberties, or of duties and responsibilities in the absence of a system of fixed relative prices.[53] Wealth maximisation requires a fixed set of relative prices. The prices of goods depend, among other things, on the relative demand for them. The demand for goods depends in turn on the distribution of wealth, and the distribution of wealth is a function of what individuals are entitled to.[54] Therefore, the system of wealth maximisation must presuppose a set of initial entitlements in order to get started; these initial entitlements cannot, by hypothesis, be accounted for on wealth-maximising grounds.[55] The system of wealth maximisation therefore cannot provide a basis for an initial assignment of entitlements.[56] Since an individual's wealth is defined by her willingness *and* ability to pay, the principle of wealth maximisation necessarily favours those who already have money or the resources with which to earn it and are therefore able to pay more than others to have a new legal rule defined in the way that is favourable to them.[57] The principle of wealth maximisation thus gives an additional advantage to those who are already advantaged. It must be noted that the principle of wealth maximisation has been argued to be fully equivalent to the Kaldor-Hicks test.[58] For example, Posner uses the terms as synonyms.[59] However, it has also been suggested that the concept of 'consumer wealth maximisation' is really the same as the concept known as 'Pareto optimality' and over the long run, a series of Kaldor-Hicks transactions may ultimately bring us closer to the Pareto optimal ideal without the transaction costs incurred by compensating third parties.[60] Hence, some disparity on the meaning of the concepts and the usage of terms is apparent.

Indeed, what can be seen from the above is that there is a certain amount of dispute in terms of both the meaning and the appropriateness of some fundamental concepts surrounding the discussion on welfare and wealth maximisation. For

[51] ibid 227.

[52] JL Coleman, 'Efficiency, Utility and Wealth Maximization' (1980) 8 *Hofstra Law Review* 509, 524.

[53] ibid 524.

[54] ibid.

[55] ibid 534–35.

[56] ibid 525.

[57] AT Kronman, 'Wealth Maximization as a Normative Principle' (1980) 9 *Journal of Legal Studies* 227, 240. See similarly Hovenkamp (n 19) 248 and Coleman (n 52) 524 on allocative efficiency being a poor guide to policy-making for ignoring the starting distribution.

[58] Kronman, ibid, 236.

[59] Posner (n 41) 13.

[60] MC Grauer, 'The Use and Misuse of the Term "Consumer Welfare": Once More to the Mat on the Issue of Single Entity Status for Sports Leagues under Section 1 of the Sherman Act' (1989) 64 *Tulane Law Review* 71, 75.

example, it is not always clear whether 'wealth maximisation' refers to Kaldor-Hicks or Pareto efficiency or whether 'wealth maximisation' is an appropriate goal for policy-making at all. Moreover, although the efficiency models are helpful in allowing one to compare different states of the world, both the Pareto and the Kaldor-Hicks principles are themselves based on certain value judgements which may or may not be acceptable. Furthermore, there is a lack of consensus in finding them – specifically the Kaldor-Hicks test – apt for basing policy or legal decisions on, mainly because the tests exclude distributive issues. Thus, the tests are neither perfect nor easily accepted by all. Consequently, carrying such welfare-based ideas over into the area of competition law and policy as the concepts underlying the supposed goals is not without problems. Yet, these concepts provide useful indicators for comparison between different states of the world within the confines of the various judgements underlying them and can be used for policy making as such so long as no better substitute exists. The following subsection therefore examines the different types of 'efficiency' and possible trade-offs that may have to be made between them in competition law and policy.

B Different Types of Efficiency and Efficiency Trade-Offs in Competition Policy

i Different Types of Efficiency

'Economic efficiency' is usually understood in one of three ways: 'productive', 'allocative' or 'dynamic' efficiency. 'Productive efficiency' occurs when a given set of products is being produced at the lowest possible cost (given current technology, input prices and so on).[61] 'Allocative efficiency' relates to the difference between the cost of producing the marginal product and the valuation of that product by consumers.[62] If the cost of producing one more unit is different from the amount that consumers are willing to pay for that extra unit, then there is allocative *inefficiency*. Finally, 'dynamic (or innovation) efficiency' refers to the extent to which a firm introduces *new* products or processes of production.[63]

In case of so-called 'perfect competition', the market price of a product would be equal to the marginal cost of producing the product, delivering both productive and allocative efficiency.[64] In case of 'monopoly' (that is, there is a single seller

[61] S Bishop and M Walker, *The Economics of EC Competition Law: Concepts, Application and Measurement* 3rd edn (London, Sweet & Maxwell, 2010) 25.

[62] ibid.

[63] Motta (n 32) 55. If lack of competition gives rise to slack or inefficiency in production and this leads to welfare losses, this is known as 'X-efficiency'; see Bishop and Walker (n 61) 25. For the concept of 'X-inefficiency', see H Leibenstein, 'Allocative Efficiency vs. X-Efficiency' (1966) 56 *American Economic Review* 392. Using empirical data, Leibenstein demonstrates that in many instances what can be gained by increasing allocative efficiency is trivial, while the potential gain from increasing X-efficiency is frequently significant; ibid.

[64] Bishop and Walker (n 61) 23, 25. 'Marginal cost' is the change in total cost as a result of producing the last unit; D Begg, S Fischer and R Dornbusch, *Foundations of Economics* 2nd edn (Maidenhead, McGraw-Hill, 2003) 40. The lowest possible price an undertaking can profitably charge is the price which

in the market), the reduction in output and increase in price compared with that under perfect competition leads to a 'deadweight loss' which is the cost to society of a market not operating efficiently.[65] In the context of a monopoly, allocative inefficiency is the welfare loss resulting from prices being too high by being above marginal costs.[66] In other words, allocative inefficiency results from there being a difference between the marginal cost of production and the valuation of the marginal consumer.[67] Where the monopolist does not use the most efficient technology available, this leads to productive inefficiency.[68] Both allocative and productive inefficiency refer to static (rather than dynamic) properties of 'market power', which is usually defined as the difference between the prices charged by a firm and its marginal costs of production.[69]

As shown in Figure 1, the deadweight loss from a monopoly represents the lost consumer surplus which is not turned into producer profits; some consumers who would have paid the competitive price are deprived of the product and will

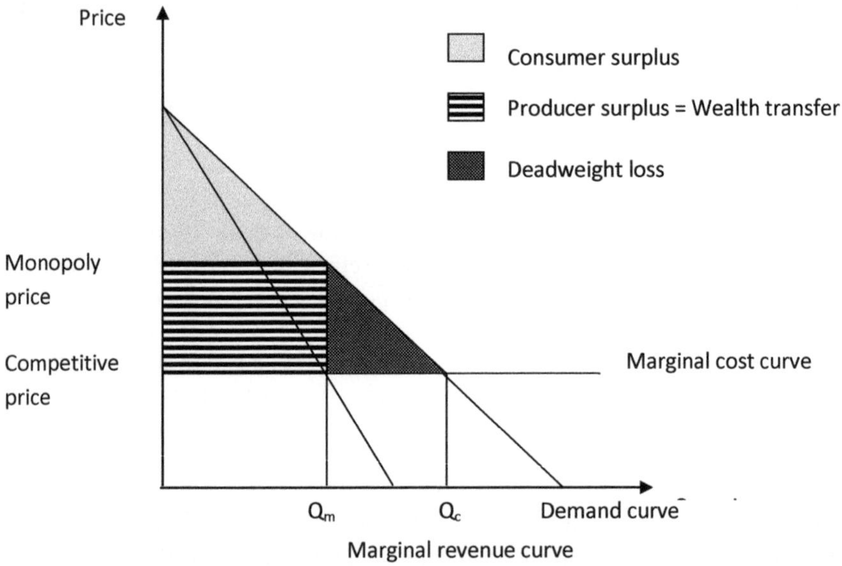

Figure 1: Welfare Effects of Monopoly

equals the marginal cost of production and thus in perfect competition, price equals marginal cost; Motta (n 32) 40, 41, fn 1. 'Perfect competition' bears little relation to reality due to the assumptions underlying the paradigm, namely that there are many buyers and sellers of the product, the quantity bought by any buyer or seller is too small relative to the total quantity that changes in these quantities leave market prices unchanged, the product is homogeneous, all buyers and sellers have perfect information and there is free entry into and exist out of the market; Bishop and Walker (n 61) 17.

65 Bishop and Walker, ibid, 27–28.
66 Motta (n 32) 40, 41.
67 Bishop and Walker (n 61) 28.
68 Motta (n 32) 55.
69 ibid 41, 55.

spend their money on other things, as a result of which consumer surplus is not maximised.[70] In economics, allocative efficiency is a fundamental concept and its recognition – that is a situation where resources move to their most valued uses – is one of the main goals of economic policy.[71] Moreover, the increase in price due to the monopoly leads to a 'wealth transfer' from consumers to the monopolist since those who are able to make a purchase pay a higher price compared with that under perfect competition.

ii Efficiency Trade-Offs in Competition Policy

Efficiency trade-offs are bound to be made in competition policy so long as a practice does not increase or decrease all types of efficiencies simultaneously. One can think of two major trade-offs: the trade-off between allocative and productive efficiency, and the trade-off between static and dynamic efficiency.

The trade-off between allocative and productive efficiency occurs since on the one hand, a higher number of firms entails more competition in the market and lower prices, increasing consumer surplus and allocative efficiency.[72] On the other hand, it also entails a duplication of fixed costs, representing a loss in terms of (static) productive efficiency.[73] This can also be thought of conversely: when a firm with some market power reduces costs, increasing its productive efficiency and its market power, this may lead to decreased allocative efficiency by a reduction in output and increased prices, but also to production cost savings. This can be conceptualised in the context of mergers. For example, Williamson's trade-off model demonstrates that a merger leading to an increase in market power increasing prices and causing a loss in allocative efficiency may nevertheless lead to an increase in welfare due to cost savings.[74] In that model, a *relatively modest* cost reduction is usually sufficient to offset relatively large price increases even if the elasticity of demand is quite high.[75] Thus, a merger which yields non-trivial real efficiencies must produce substantial market power and result in relatively large price increases for the net economic effect to be negative.[76] It must be noted that this model treats the distribution of surplus as a matter of indifference.[77] As such, the transfer of wealth from consumers to producers is neglected. Nevertheless, for example, Farrell and Shapiro show that even though increasing concentration,

[70] A Jones and B Sufrin, *EU Competition Law: Text, Cases and Materials* 4th edn (Oxford, OUP, 2011) 9.

[71] Cseres (n 31) 177.

[72] Motta (n 32) 51.

[73] ibid.

[74] OE Williamson, 'Economies as an Antitrust Defense: The Welfare Trade-Offs' (1968) 58 *American Economic Review* 18.

[75] ibid 22–23. 'Elasticity of demand' is the percentage change in the quantity demanded divided by the corresponding percentage change in the price; Begg, Fischer and Dornbusch (n 64) 41.

[76] Williamson (n 74) 23.

[77] ibid 27.

a merger can make *consumers* better off if certain conditions are fulfilled.[78] In their model, a merger can do this only if it permits the merging firms to exploit economies of scale or if the participants learn from it. Thus, distribution of surplus can be included in the assessment. The issue of whether this should be a concern for competition law and policy is left for section III.C.

It must also be remembered that even though allocative efficiency more directly benefits consumers (as it implies prices at marginal costs), one would expect productive efficiency to benefit consumers as well.[79] This is because reductions in marginal cost feed through into reductions in price, even under monopoly.[80] A more detailed examination of this will again be carried out under section III.C along with the issue of distribution.

The second efficiency trade-off is the one between dynamic and static efficiency. Competition tries to correct static as well as dynamic inefficiency.[81] Although static models focus on prices and quantities emphasising, particularly, price competition between firms, this may be inappropriate in a dynamic environment since in many dynamic environments firms compete not on prices but on innovation.[82] Any trade-off between static and dynamic efficiencies is a significant concern as dynamic economies evolve and in a dynamic economy, competition in product or process innovation may have a more significant effect on welfare, either positive or negative, in the long run than does any likely variation in price.[83] Dynamic efficiency is thus concerned with the optimisation of consumption and investment in a dynamic environment of technological progress and it is said to have the most welfare-increasing effects of the three types of efficiency since competition today is the competition of continuing and speedy product developments, and this is relatively more important than price competition.[84]

The pioneer of the preference for dynamic efficiency over static efficiency is Schumpeter, who saw competition as a 'gale of creative destruction' and argued that 'the fundamental impulse that sets and keeps the capitalist engine in motion' came from the new consumers' goods, the new methods of production, the new markets and so on.[85] Accordingly, any system that at *every* given point of time fully utilises its possibilities to the best advantage may yet in the long run be inferior to a system that does so at *no* given point of time since the latter's failure to do so may be a condition for the level or speed of long-run performance.[86] Schumpeter went further in his argument by asserting that large-scale establishment has come

[78] J Farrell and C Shapiro, 'Horizontal Mergers: An Equilibrium Analysis' (1990) 80(1) *American Economic Review* 107, 113.

[79] Bishop and Walker (n 61) 32.

[80] ibid.

[81] Cseres (n 31) 19.

[82] Bishop and Walker (n 61) 45.

[83] Cseres (n 31) 19.

[84] ibid.

[85] JA Schumpeter, *Capitalism, Socialism and Democracy* 5th edn (London, George Allen & Unwin, 1976) 83.

[86] ibid.

to be the most powerful engine of economic progress and the long-run expansion of total output; in this respect, perfect competition is not only impossible, but inferior, and has no title to being set up as a model of ideal efficiency.[87] Hence, it is arguably a mistake to base the theory of government regulation of industry on the principle that big business should be made to work as that industry would work in perfect competition.[88]

This line of thinking is based on the premise that in many dynamic markets, rather than competing *in* the market, firms compete *for* the market.[89] In such cases, firms spend considerable amounts of money in the research and development stage in order to be the first one to innovate and win the right to earn monopoly profits thereafter.[90] The lower the expected profits from bringing a new product to the market, the less likely a firm is to invest in the first place. As such, rather than representing an inefficient market structure that harms consumers, monopoly can be seen as a necessary market structure that ensures that consumers benefit from firms undertaking risky innovative activities.[91] In such a case, competition to *obtain* a monopoly is an important form of competition.[92] Moreover, such innovation-oriented markets are usually characterised by high fixed costs (of research and development) and low marginal costs of production in which case price must be substantially above marginal cost to cover total costs.[93]

It has been argued in the literature that current competition law enforcement concentrates mostly on promoting allocative efficiency in output markets and as such it has its priorities in the wrong order; the promotion of productive and dynamic efficiency should be the first economic goal of competition policy.[94] This is arguably because, of the three types of efficiency, dynamic efficiency provides the greatest enhancement of social wealth, followed by productive efficiency, with allocative efficiency ranking last.[95] It has also been suggested that the losses to society from allocative inefficiency are likely to be smaller than the losses from

[87] ibid 106. *Cf* FM Scherer, 'Antitrust, Efficiency, and Progress' (1987) 62 *New York University Law Review* 998, 1014 where the author argues that the Schumpeterian view may be correct in isolated cases, but more commonly, loosely structured oligopolies are likely to be at least as progressive as industries dominated by one firm or a few and relatively small technology-oriented enterprises often prove to be more dynamic innovator than giant firms. Motta suggests that the link between market structure and innovation is not clear-cut; Motta (n 32) 57.

[88] Schumpeter (n 85) 106.

[89] Bishop and Walker (n 61) 46.

[90] ibid.

[91] ibid. See also, RA Posner, *Antitrust Law* 2nd edn (Chicago, The University of Chicago Press, 2001) 20 for the argument that since there is not a clear theoretical prediction concerning the relation between market structure and innovation, it is an empirical question whether monopoly retards or advances innovation.

[92] RA Posner, 'Antitrust in the New Economy' (2001) 68 *Antitrust Law Journal* 925, 929; Motta (n 32) 64.

[93] Bishop and Walker (n 61) 46; Posner (n 92) 926; R O'Donoghue and AJ Padilla, *The Law and Economics of Article 82 EC* (Oxford, Hart Publishing, 2006) 607.

[94] JF Brodley, 'The Economic Goals of Antitrust: Efficiency, Consumer Welfare, And Technological Progress' (1987) 62 *New York University Law Review* 1020, 1025. Similarly, see Scherer (n 87) 1002, 1018.

[95] Brodley, ibid, 1026.

productive and dynamic inefficiency.[96] As for measurability, the only efficiency that appears reasonably measurable is productive efficiency, and then only after the fact.[97] In advance of a transaction, none of the three types of efficiencies appears measurable.[98] Allocative efficiency imposes severe measurement problems: in theory it is possible to measure allocative efficiency in output markets if one knows the relevant economic variables – elasticity of demand and either the output reduction or the price increase caused by the monopoly. In practice, estimates of elasticity of demand are hazardous and output as well as price changes have multiple causes, making it difficult to connect them to a particular trade-restraining conduct.[99]

Although the ideal solution is to eliminate the allocative inefficiency while still achieving the productive and dynamic efficiencies, if that is not possible, competition law must face the serious question of whether and under what circumstances the realisation of productive and dynamic efficiencies justifies a loss of allocative efficiency.[100] As such, it has been asserted that competition law enforcement should give priority to advancing dynamic and productive efficiencies in view of their cardinal importance in increasing social wealth; most certainly it should not pursue allocative efficiency alone.[101]

To summarise, the foregoing discussions demonstrate that different types of efficiency may lead to inevitable trade-offs between them in competition law and policy. These trade-offs – and especially the choice between viewing competition and markets from a static or dynamic perspective – can lead to different outcomes in terms of policy and the decisions reached. Both static and dynamic efficiencies should be taken into account when assessing the efficiency of the market or the undertaking. Surely, the real difficulty is to ascertain what weight to ascribe to each type of efficiency. What is important to recognise is that not only lower prices, but also innovation, should be seen as aspects of the expected results of competition with a long-term perspective. Thus, the following section examines the potential objectives of competition law and policy, including consumer welfare and total welfare.

[96] DJ Neven, 'Working Paper' in CD Ehlermann and LL Laudati (eds), *European Competition Law Annual 1997: Objectives of Competition Policy* (Oxford, Hart Publishing, 1998) 114; Scherer (n 87) 999. Harberger's study in 1954 seeking to measure the overall deadweight loss attributable to monopolies found the relevant value to be around one-tenth of one per cent of gross national product or two dollars per capita at 1953 income and price levels; A Harberger, 'Monopoly and Resource Allocation' (1954) 44 *American Economic Review* 77, 84. *Cf* Posner (n 91) 17 criticising Harberger's and similar studies for being incapable of properly measuring the costs of monopoly by ignoring the monopoly profits invested in attempts to monopolise, ie, for rent-seeking purposes.

[97] Brodley (n 94) 1028.

[98] ibid 1028.

[99] ibid 1030.

[100] ibid 1032.

[101] ibid. See also FM Scherer, 'Efficiency, Fairness and the Early Contributions of Economists to the Antitrust Debate' (1990) 29 *Washburn Law Journal* 243, 254.

III OBJECTIVES OF COMPETITION LAW AND POLICY

A In General

A quick survey of suggested goals of competition law and policy reveals a wide variety of alternatives: the maximisation of consumer welfare, economic efficiency, the dispersion of economic and political power, the unclogging of markets, the protection of easy entry into business and the protection of small businesses' welfare are just a few examples.[102] The general discussion of what the goals of competition law and policy are and should be has mostly taken place in the United States. Thus, the propositions and arguments regarding the objectives stemming from the US may not always serve the needs of Europe due to political, economical and cultural differences.[103] Therefore, these should be treated as insights, rather than definitive solutions when considered in the context of EU competition rules.

Broadly speaking, there are two camps (with other camps in between closer to one or the other) regarding objectives – those who think that welfare-based objectives, such as the efficient allocation of resources, have to be the overriding or exclusive goal of competition law and policy, and those who would permit competition law and policy to consider additional values unrelated to efficiency. An interesting debate considering the objectives of American antitrust laws has taken place in the US based on the legislative history.[104] Whereas Bork interpreted the legislative intent of the US antitrust laws as aiming exclusively at 'consumer welfare' meaning 'efficiency',[105] reading the same legislative history, Lande contended that the sole goal of antitrust is not to enhance economic efficiency; according to him, increased economic efficiency is not even the primary goal of antitrust laws.[106] To Lande, the main purpose of the antitrust laws is to prevent firms from acquiring and using market power to force consumers to pay more for their goods and services: US Congress was primarily concerned that corporations would use market power 'unfairly' to extract wealth from consumers.[107] Congress arguably

[102] H Hovenkamp, 'Distributive Justice and the Antitrust Laws' (1982) 51 *George Washington Law Review* 1, 1. According to Fox, there are four major historical goals of antitrust: dispersion of economic power, freedom and opportunity to compete on the merits, satisfaction of consumers and protection of the competition process as the market governor; EM Fox, 'The Modernization of Antitrust: A New Equilibrium' (1981) 66 *Cornell Law Review* 1140, 1180, 1182.

[103] For the argument that the current European competition policy may be the best policy for increasing aggregate wealth in Europe and an objective of wealth maximisation as understood in the US may not be well-suited for Europe, see BH McDonnell and DA Farber, 'Are Efficient Antitrust Rules Always Optimal?' (2003) 48(3) *The Antitrust Bulletin* 807, 808–09, 814–15.

[104] For a similar study of the EU competition rules, see this volume, ch 2 section V.

[105] RH Bork, 'Legislative Intent and the Policy of the Sherman Act' (1966) 9 *Journal of Law and Economics* 7, 7, 16.

[106] RH Lande, 'Chicago's False Foundation: Wealth Transfers (Not Just Efficiency) Should Guide Antitrust' (1989) 58 *Antitrust Law Journal* 631, 631.

[107] ibid.

gave consumers the property right (or entitlement) to purchase competitively priced goods and therefore declared that higher-than-competitive prices constitute 'unfair' takings or extractions of consumers' property.[108] As such, Congress determined that consumers should have the property right that is today termed 'consumer surplus'.[109] Although the idea that consumers have a 'right' to the consumer surplus is debateable, these two different perspectives at two ends of the spectrum could be linked to different schools of thought in antitrust. These are the 'Harvard School' and the 'Chicago School' which has more recently been subjected to qualifications by the 'post-Chicago School'. These schools will be discussed in turn.

i The Harvard School

The Harvard School emerged around the 1950s and was influenced by the 'structure-conduct-performance' (S-C-P) paradigm according to which the structure of a certain industry determines companies' conduct which in turn determines market performance.[110] The S-C-P paradigm was developed by the economist Bain and suggested that certain industry structures, particularly high concentration accompanied by high entry barriers, dictate that firms in that industry will engage in certain types of conduct which would then lead to poor economic performance.[111] Those arguing for the S-C-P paradigm suggested that the emphasis on anticompetitive conduct should be minimised; antitrust should rather go after monopoly *performance* by altering industry *structures*.[112]

Arguably, for the Harvard School, competition was an *aim* in itself and not a tool to attain beneficial economic results; market power was always harmful and as such it should be illegal.[113] The main goals of competition policy were accordingly the achievement of desirable results, the creation and promotion of competitive processes, the prescription of fair conduct norms and the restriction of the power of large firms.[114] Efficiency and progress were considered the most important economic *results* which can be substantially influenced by competition policy.[115] Thereafter, stability of employment and a 'fair' distribution of income were stated to be the desired results for the whole economy. As such, the Harvard School was arguably sympathetic to far-reaching government intervention and extended the scope of liability based on competition law.[116] Yet, it must also be

[108] ibid 632.
[109] ibid 637.
[110] Cseres (n 31) 42–43.
[111] H Hovenkamp, *Federal Antitrust Policy: The Law of Competition and Its Practice* 3rd edn (Minnesota, Thomson/West, 2005) 43.
[112] ibid and references therein.
[113] RJ Van den Bergh and PD Camesasca, *European Competition Law and Economics: A Comparative Perspective* (Antwerpen, Intersentia-Hart, 2001) 32.
[114] C Kaysen and DF Turner, *Antitrust Policy: An Economic and Legal Analysis* (Cambridge, MA, Harvard University Press, 1971) 11 *et seq*. See similarly Cseres (n 31) 56.
[115] Van den Bergh and Camesasca (n 113) 31.
[116] ibid 34.

pointed out that it has been remarked that the Harvard School scholars (in particular, Areeda and Turner and their contemporaries) also discouraged consideration of non-efficiency objectives such as the dispersion of political power and the preservation of opportunities for smaller firms to compete, although they did not define efficiency identically to the Chicago School.[117] Similarly, the view that the Harvard School is sympathetic to government intervention unlike the Chicago School has also been challenged with the argument that Harvard School scholars also tended to share the view that the social costs of enforcing competition rules on dominant firms too aggressively exceeded the costs of enforcing them too weakly.[118] The argument is that over time, the Harvard School scholars became increasingly non-interventionist, based on their concerns about the administrability of various antitrust rules and the costs of likely errors by generalist judges and juries trying to implement them.[119]

ii The Chicago School

The Chicago School which was developed in the 1960s and 1970s saw the market process as a free play of economic forces which produces a perfectly competitive market structure without government intervention; thus, government intervention was rejected due to inefficiencies it may cause.[120] The School emphasised the promotion of efficiency, the promotion of economic interests of producers and consumers and the efficiency of competitive markets.[121] Moreover, most markets were believed to be competitive, even if they contained relatively few sellers and where monopoly existed, it tended to be self-correcting.[122] The argument is that the monopolist's profits would attract new entry into the market and the Chicago School scholars also argued that 'natural' barriers to entry were 'more imagined than real'.[123]

The Chicago School sought to apply price theory to competition law which consists of several theoretical assumptions about how competitive markets and firms behave.[124] These assumptions are mainly that firms are profit maximisers

[117] WE Kovacic, 'The Intellectual DNA of Modern US Competition Law for Dominant Firm Conduct: The Chicago/Harvard Double Helix' (2007) 1(1) *Columbia Business Law Review* 1, 35.

[118] ibid 36.

[119] AI Gavil, WE Kovacic and JB Baker, *Antitrust Law in Perspective: Cases, Concepts and Problems in Competition Policy* 2nd edn (Minnesota, Thomson/West, 2008) 66. For a recent article arguing that the US Sherman Act Section II doctrine is governed by a 'total welfare' standard and this standard can be traced back to the Harvard School, see AJ Meese, 'Debunking the Purchaser Welfare Account of Section 2 of the Sherman Act: How Harvard Brought Us to a Total Welfare Standard and Why We Should Keep It' (2010) 85 *New York University Law Review* 659.

[120] Cseres (n 31) 46.

[121] ibid.

[122] Hovenkamp (n 111) 62. For the argument that the Chicago School's attitude towards concentrations of power shifted from broad hostility to broad acceptance over the years, see R Van Horn, 'Chicago's Shifting Attitude Toward Concentrations of Business Power (1934–1962)' (2011) 34 *Seattle University Law Review* 1527.

[123] Hovenkamp, ibid, 62.

[124] Gavil, Kovacic and Baker (n 119) 68.

and markets left unfettered by regulation will lead to productive and allocative efficiency.[125] Profit maximising firms and efficient markets will in turn maximise consumer welfare.[126] Through the lens of price theory, the Chicago School argued, few of the accepted prohibitions of the 1950s and 1960s were objectionable and many prohibited types of conduct appeared to be driven by the desire to maximise profits by achieving greater efficiencies; thus, the School questioned many traditional prohibitions and argued for a narrower focus on cartels and horizontal mergers of truly substantial competitors.[127]

Other than the assumption that the best policy tool currently available for maximising economic efficiency in the real world is the neoclassical price theory model, Chicago School competition policy is predicated on the assumption that the pursuit of economic efficiency should be the exclusive goal of antitrust enforcement policy.[128] The principle of 'potential Pareto efficiency' (that is, Kaldor-Hicks efficiency) or wealth maximisation which guides the Chicago School analysis, identifies a policy as 'efficient' if total gains experienced by all those who gain from the policy are greater than the total losses experienced by all those who lose. The identity of the gainers and losers is irrelevant. If a policy produces bigger gains to businesses than it does losses to consumers, the Chicago School would approve the policy as efficient.[129] However, it would also approve a policy that produced larger gains to consumers than losses to businesses.[130] For this reason, the Chicago School ideologist can argue that she is not taking sides in any political dispute about how wealth or entitlements ought to be distributed to conflicting interest groups.[131]

Arguably, the claim that the market efficiency model is non-political can be neither verified nor falsified in any general way.[132] Moreover, since the Chicago School is not taking sides in any political debate on how welfare should be distributed among different interest groups, its identification of 'consumer welfare' with economic efficiency is a contradiction in itself, and as such it is not about '*consumer* welfare' but 'total welfare'.[133] Indeed, as Bork famously put it 'the whole task of antitrust can be summed up as the effort to improve allocative efficiency without impairing productive efficiency so greatly as to produce either no gain or a net loss in consumer welfare'.[134] As such, consumer welfare is greatest when

125 ibid 66.

126 ibid.

127 ibid 67.

128 Hovenkamp (n 19) 226; FH Easterbrook, 'The Limits of Antitrust' (1984) 63(1) *Texas Law Review* 1, 13.

129 Hovenkamp, ibid, 231.

130 ibid.

131 ibid 231–32.

132 ibid 233.

133 Lande (n 106) 638; EM Fox and LA Sullivan, 'Antitrust – Retrospective and Prospective: Where Are We Coming From? Where Are We Going?' (1987) 62 *New York University Law Review* 936, 946, 959; Cseres (n 31) 49; SC Salop, 'Question: What is the Real and Proper Antitrust Welfare Standard? Answer: The *True* Consumer Welfare Standard' (2010) 22(3) *Loyola Consumer Law Review* 336, 336.

134 RH Bork, *The Antitrust Paradox: A Policy at War with Itself* (New York, Basic Books Inc, 1978) 91.

society's economic resources are allocated so that consumers are able to satisfy their wants as fully as technological constraints permit; consumer welfare, in this sense, is merely another term for the wealth of the nation.[135] Therefore, for the Chicago School, 'consumer welfare' actually meant 'total welfare'. In fact, due to this confusion created by Bork's usage of the term, one commentator has called the 'consumer welfare' standard, the '*true* consumer welfare' standard to emphasise the focus on *consumers*.[136]

iii The Post-Chicago School

A third school, namely the 'post-Chicago School', has grown out of the criticism of several aspects of the Chicago School. The post-Chicago School added an overlay of strategic thinking to the analysis and although it recognised the importance of efficiency and free markets, it saw that markets were not automatically effective.[137] The distinctive nature of this school is its concern with strategic conduct and this approach has been gaining influence since the mid-1980s.[138]

The post-Chicago School scholars moved away from deductive reasoning on the basis of the neoclassical model, towards more reliance on how markets actually function, based on use of empirical data.[139] The post-Chicago School – in contrast to the Chicago School – works on the premise that markets function imperfectly and this is because firms rarely have complete information about markets, rivals, etc in the market and they assign different values to additional information.[140] Although consumer welfare – understood as allocative efficiency – is the exclusive goal of competition policy under the post-Chicago School as well, by refusing to assume that markets function perfectly, this school suggests the scrutiny of a wider variety of conduct by enforcement agencies than the Chicago School would examine.[141]

The post-Chicago scholars question the Chicago views that markets self-correct, entry is commonly easy, firms cannot successfully coordinate and government intervention can rarely succeed.[142] One body of post-Chicago commentary explains how practices like exclusive dealing, tying and other vertical restraints can under some circumstances facilitate the acquisition or maintenance of market power on grounds other than efficiency.[143] Other post-Chicago commentators explain how

[135] ibid 90.

[136] Salop (n 133) 336. See also Meese (n 119) using the term 'purchaser welfare' for similar reasons.

[137] For a detailed explanation of the school, see Cseres (n 31) 56–61.

[138] Gavil, Kovacic and Baker (n 119) 69.

[139] E Rousseva, *Rethinking Exclusionary Abuses in EU Competition Law* (Oxford, Hart Publishing, 2010) 41.

[140] ibid 42.

[141] MS Jacobs, 'An Essay on the Normative Foundations of Antitrust Economics' (1995) 74 *North Carolina Law Review* 219, 222–23. *Cf* Cseres (n 31) 57 who argues that post-Chicago is not exclusively concerned with maximisation of efficiency as the goal of competition policy.

[142] Gavil, Kovacic and Baker (n 119) 70.

[143] Kovacic (n 117) 23 and references therein.

firms can use price and non-price strategies to diminish economic performance by deterring entry and expansion by rivals.[144]

The difference in viewpoint between Chicago and post-Chicago follows in part because the new economic models, derived from game theory and empirical research, often identify situations under which business conduct can benefit firms by harming competition.[145] Hence, to the question of how best to promote allocative efficiency, the Chicago School would suggest very limited government intervention, whereas the post-Chicago School would encourage more aggressive intervention.[146] Arguably, the greatest success of the post-Chicago School has been in the persuading of competition authorities in the US and Europe to take seriously the claims of anticompetitive harm from exclusion.[147]

B Consumer Welfare and Total Welfare as Standards for Competition Law and Policy

It has been suggested that the choice between the 'total welfare' or the 'consumer welfare' standard can make all the difference in a world of competition policy.[148] How efficiency arguments will be evaluated is indicated by the welfare standard which a legal system adopts and the adoption of one of the welfare standards determines the goals to be pursued by competition policy and the choices made by decision-makers. Making explicit trade-offs between wealth transfers and efficiencies is therefore essential in order to provide clear-cut decisions.[149]

For competition law and policy, most economists adopt the criterion of 'total welfare' which weights the welfare of all members of society equally, including both producers and consumers.[150] The important implication is that a loss of consumer surplus due to higher prices or lower quality can be compensated by a bigger increase in producer profits. However, it has been argued that most major competition authorities operate under legislation and guidelines that reject this standard and no major competition authority seems to apply it consistently.[151]

[144] ibid 23–24 and references therein. Kovacic argues that it is wrong to attribute the modern US antitrust policy to purely the Chicago or post-Chicago Schools, to the exclusion of the Harvard School and also to argue that the post-Chicago School shares no common value with the Chicago School. He calls the intellectual DNA of modern US antitrust doctrine a 'double helix' that consists of two intertwined chains of ideas – one drawn from the Chicago School and the other drawn from the Harvard School; ibid 14.

[145] Gavil, Kovacic and Baker (n 119) 70.

[146] Jacobs (n 141) 259.

[147] Gavil, Kovacic and Baker (n 119) 70.

[148] Cseres (n 31) 38.

[149] ibid 252.

[150] BR Lyons, 'Could Politicians be More Right than Economists? A Theory of Merger Standards' Revised Centre for Competition and Regulation Working Paper CCR 02-1 (15 May 2002) 1. *Cf* Meese (n 119) arguing that the US courts when applying Sherman Act Section II have consistently employed total welfare as the operative standard.

[151] ibid.

Instead, they overwhelmingly focus on consumers, along with industrial customers, to the exclusion of the firm whose conduct is in question.[152] Under the consumer welfare model, the most frequent guide to whether conduct harms competition is whether a price increase or output restriction is likely.[153]

It has been claimed that 'the term consumer welfare is the most abused term in modern antitrust analysis'.[154] If consumer welfare is to serve as an operational principle of competition law, it must arguably refer to the direct and explicit economic benefits received by the consumers of a particular product as measured by its price and quality.[155] As such, consumer welfare adds a distributional thrust to competition law since it refers to the direct and immediate welfare of the *consumers* of a specific product.[156]

In contrast, the consumer welfare criterion has been argued to lack any foundation in welfare economics, precisely because of this distributional aspect as well.[157] This is because whereas in welfare economics equal gains will yield equal increases in utility and these will have equal effects on social welfare, under the consumer welfare standard, utility transferred from consumers to producers will not improve total social welfare, although it will make someone better off.[158] By not counting the impacts of profits flowing to shareholders, some of the welfare consequences are deliberately omitted from the calculus.[159] What distinguishes one person from another in welfare economics is her marginal utility of income; the consumer welfare standard treats the impact on social welfare of a unit of currency transferred from a consumer to a producer differently from the impact on social welfare of an extra unit of currency accruing to the same producer from efficiencies.[160]

As the consumer welfare approach considers wealth transfers from consumers to producers as being rather harmful than neutral, in the competition law and policy and context, it is more critical of efficiency claims.[161] This means that a consumer welfare-based policy will take into account only certain efficiencies, namely the ones that are of direct benefit to consumers. Vis-à-vis the total welfare standard, the consumer welfare standard seems to have a number of shortcomings: it lacks a firm basis in welfare economics and its enforcement before competition authorities confront private companies with a highly complicated

[152] ibid.

[153] F Engelsing, P Marsden and D Möller (primary authors), 'A Bundeskartellamt/Competition Law Forum Debate on Reform of Article 82: A "Dialectic" on Competing Approaches' (2006) 2 (Special Issue) *European Competition Journal* 211, 221.

[154] Brodley (n 94) 1032.

[155] ibid 1033.

[156] ibid 1020–21.

[157] See M Duhamel and PGC Townley, 'An Effective and Enforceable Alternative to the Consumer Surplus Standard' (2003) 26(1) *World Competition* 3, 17; Cseres (n 31) 20.

[158] Cseres, ibid, 20.

[159] Duhamel and Townley (n 157) 19.

[160] ibid.

[161] Cseres (n 31) 21.

burden of proof.[162] It has also been suggested that the dividing line between that which is consumer welfare and that which has wider welfare implications is far from clear.[163] Thus, there is no bright line test to separate out consumer welfare from 'citizen welfare'. Nonetheless, it must be borne in mind that in most cases consumer welfare and total welfare move together; maximising consumer welfare would maximise total welfare as well.[164] Instances where the choice between the two standards would call for different policy prescriptions will be discussed below.[165]

'Total welfare', on the other hand, is a concept that takes into account the welfare effects on all markets.[166] Unlike the consumer welfare model, it views redistribution in the form of wealth transfers from consumers to producers as neutral. Efficiency is the underlying concept of the total welfare view; competition policy based on the total welfare approach will first of all focus on efficiencies and does not require firms to pass on efficiency benefits directly to consumers.[167] In terms of allocative efficiency, it is irrelevant whether producers or consumers take the surplus produced by attaining efficiencies. This criterion is easier to satisfy because the only requirement is that firms gain more than consumers lose.[168] It must be noted that although the concept of 'total welfare' completely overlooks the issue of income distribution among consumers and producers, as pointed out above, this is not because economists think that it is an irrelevant issue, but rather because it is a different issue.[169] The welfare measure is a summarising measure of how efficient a given industry works and does not address the question of how equal income is distributed which can be dealt with by other measures; the rationale is that in principle it is possible to operate redistribution schemes that make both consumers and producers better off.[170] Competition policy that requires the achieved benefits to be passed on to consumers is arguably not based on efficiency analysis, but on 'fairness' considerations.[171] Therefore, competition policy based on the use of consumer welfare criterion might be driven rather by fairness considerations, like the distribution of resources, than the efficiency criterion.[172] The role of 'fairness' as a potential objective under Article 102 as opposed to 'welfare' is discussed in chapter four.

To conceptualise the implications of the choice between the two welfare standards, one can think of at least five settings in which the application of the two

[162] KJ Cseres, 'The Controversies of the Consumer Welfare Standard' (2007) 3(2) *The Competition Law Review* 121, 122.

[163] P Evans, 'Assessing Consumer Detriment' (2007) 28(1) *European Competition Law Review* 26, 27.

[164] Bishop and Walker (n 61) 30; JB Baker, 'Competition Policy as a Political Bargain' (2005) 73(2) *Antitrust Law Journal* 483, 521.

[165] See text after n 172.

[166] Cseres (n 31) 21.

[167] ibid.

[168] ibid.

[169] Motta (n 32) 18. See text around n 21 above for the two welfare theorems.

[170] Motta, ibid.

[171] Cseres (n 31) 21.

[172] ibid 22.

standards would yield different conclusions. The first setting would be where an agreement among competitors reduces competition, resulting in higher prices, while the ensuing allocative efficiency loss is less than the productive efficiency benefits that arise from fixed cost savings.[173] The same scenario can also occur when a dominant undertaking reduces its costs, increasing its productive efficiency which may increase its market power enabling it to increase prices. This would be found harmful under the consumer welfare standard, but not necessarily under the total welfare standard so long as the increase in producer surplus outweighs the decrease in consumer surplus.

The second instance would be exclusionary conduct of a dominant undertaking or a group of undertakings acting collectively that harms competitors which could under some circumstances lead to lower consumer prices, perhaps by preventing free-riding or ending double marginalisation.[174] This would be beneficial under a consumer welfare standard, but under a total welfare standard it could be either beneficial or harmful: the welfare benefit would include production efficiency gains from any reduction in marginal cost and an allocative efficiency gain generated by the expansion of output associated with lower prices. That benefit would have to be compared with the welfare loss to the excluded rivals (their lost producer surplus). Thus, the total welfare standard would call for a more interventionist approach to exclusion than the consumer welfare standard.[175]

The third setting would be an agreement among end consumers to exercise monopsony power in an input market due to which consumer prices decline. Hence, conduct would be beneficial under the consumer welfare test, but the agreement also creates an allocative efficiency loss, both because output is reduced and because sellers may be led to invest less in the future than they would have invested in a competitive market.[176] Thus, conduct would be harmful under a total welfare standard. It must be noted that such conduct may be harmful under a consumer welfare standard as well if one includes dynamic considerations in the test, rather than taking mere price as the criterion.

The fourth setting would be practices that facilitate price discrimination: the result could be an allocative efficiency gain along with a reduction in consumer surplus.[177] Such practices would be considered harmful under a consumer welfare standard, but not necessarily under a total welfare standard.[178] One must bear in mind though, in this case, some consumers who may not have been able to make a purchase (at the uniform price) may be able to do so as a result of price discrimination. If this is seen as a benefit to consumers independent of the price the

[173] Baker (n 164) 516–17.
[174] ibid 517.
[175] ibid, fn 126.
[176] ibid 518.
[177] ibid.
[178] ibid.

consumers are paying, then conduct may not be harmful under the consumer welfare standard either.[179]

A final situation in which total and consumer welfare effects may diverge occurs when courts adopt a competition policy rule that imposes no apparent injury on consumers, but adversely affects the incentives of producers.[180] A court that viewed objectives of competition policy solely in consumer welfare terms might find no grounds for intervention when one monopolist dislodges another by predatory tactics. It has been argued that to withhold remedies in such a situation (for example, a monopoly has been achieved by valuable invention, a second firm steals the invention, registers it as a patent, then excludes the first firm from the market) changes innovation and production incentives in two ways, both unfavourable.[181] It weakens the incentive to innovate by making investment in innovation riskier and consequently more costly.[182] It strengthens the incentive to monopolise by socially unproductive means such as theft of technology.[183] However, it must again be noted that if in such a case the consumer welfare standard is used in a dynamic long-run sense, then such conduct may be found harmful under the consumer welfare standard as well.

A potential danger with the consumer welfare standard if it is not understood properly is that the pursuit of consumer welfare in an entirely static framework can lead to sub-optimal outcomes.[184] If one took literally the objective of maximising consumer welfare, this would lead to pricing at marginal costs, with firms exiting the industry in the long-run or having to be subsidised to cover fixed costs which would mean that the market be replaced by across-the-board regulation.[185] Problems can also arise particularly when the pursuit of consumer welfare leads to an attitude or belief that any profits earned by firms must be at the cost of consumer welfare. Such an attitude is not reasonable in a dynamic framework in which firms innovate and invest to the ultimate benefit of consumers.[186] A short-run consumer welfare standard can be damaging to firms' incentives to invest and innovate.[187] Firms invest and innovate in the expectation that they will be able to earn profits from doing so. The return to successful investments must compensate firms for the risk taken in investing.[188] If profitability is treated with too much suspicion, regulators may be tempted to remove the rewards of risky investment by forcing firms that have successfully taken risks to reduce prices. If this is done consistently, firms will be deterred from investing or innovating. Thus, consumer

[179] For an assessment of price discrimination from a 'welfare' as well as a 'fairness' point of view see this volume, ch 6.

[180] Brodley (n 94) 1034.

[181] ibid.

[182] ibid 1034–35.

[183] ibid 1035.

[184] Bishop and Walker (n 61) 31; Motta (n 32) 19.

[185] Motta, ibid, 21.

[186] Bishop and Walker (n 61) 31–32; R Ahdar, 'Consumers, Redistribution of Income and the Purpose of Competition Law' (2002) 23(7) *European Competition Law Review* 341, 352.

[187] Bishop and Walker, ibid, 32; Ahdar, ibid, 352.

[188] Bishop and Walker, ibid.

welfare needs to be maximised within a dynamic, not static, framework.[189] As such, it has also been suggested that it seems reasonable to place the burden of proof on those who would defend the use of the consumer welfare standard, rather than a total welfare standard that accounts for the well-being of *all* of an economy's members. Arguably, it is far from clear that this burden has been carried out.[190]

The preference for the consumer welfare standard over the total welfare standard is not without its problems from a legal perspective either. Although for some products the interests of users might arguably warrant greater weight than those of sellers, for other products – such as products produced by disadvantaged minorities and sold to the very rich – a reversal might be indicated.[191] For example, the breakup of a cartel of artist-merchants who handcraft porcelain will bestow its distributional benefits only on the rich who shop in this market, thus arguably increasing inequality.[192] A general case that user interests greatly outweigh seller interests is not easy to make and possibly reflects a failure to appreciate that profits ramify through the system in ways – such as taxes, dividends and retained earnings – that greatly weaken the notion that monolithic producer interests exist and are favoured.[193] When the market is not a final goods market, the consumer welfare standard favours buying firms over selling firms and there is no evidence that the wealth distribution of shareholders varies systematically according to a firm's place in the value chain.[194]

It has indeed been argued that it would not be wise for competition policy to adopt a consumer welfare standard since the standard casts consumers as those who count and producers as those who do not; 'consumer welfare' by definition does not take into account the gains made by the firms.[195] However, in today's advanced economies consumers often own firms (partly or fully), directly or through pension and investment funds. Accordingly, dividends are distributed to a vast number of citizens who would be hurt if profits were reduced.[196] Using a consumer welfare standard entails treating all consumers as equally deserving at the margin, yet treating the same people unequally in their role as workers and capital owners.[197] While it may not be unusual to attribute different social values to money flowing to different individuals on the basis of different social marginal

[189] Bishop and Walker, ibid; Motta (n 32) 19. See Schumpeter (n 85) 83 for the argument that the dynamic framework is what matters for progress.

[190] K Heyer, 'Welfare Standards and Merger Analysis: Why not the Best?' (2006) 2(2) *Competition Policy International* 29, 32.

[191] OE Williamson, 'Economies as an Antitrust Defense Revisited' (1977) 125 *University of Pennsylvania Law Review* 699, 711.

[192] KG Elzinga, 'The Goals of Antitrust: Other than Competition and Efficiency, What Else Counts?' (1977) 125 *University of Pennsylvania Law Review* 1191, 1195.

[193] Williamson (n 191) 711.

[194] J Farrell and ML Katz, 'The Economics of Welfare Standards in Antitrust' (2006) 2(2) *Competition Policy International* 3, 11–12. For the implications of treating 'customers' as 'consumers', see P Akman, '"Consumer" versus "Customer": The Devil in the Detail' (2010) 37(2) *Journal of Law and Society* 315.

[195] Heyer (n 190) 54; Motta (n 32) 21.

[196] Motta, ibid; Farrell and Shapiro (n 78) 114.

[197] Farrell and Katz (n 194) 11.

utilities of income, treating the money flowing to the same individual differently is rather odd.[198] Although social and private value can conflict, the contribution of any individual's well-being to total welfare is not determined by her role in society (as a consumer, producer, or consumer-producer).[199]

Based on US competition law and policy, Brodley argues that the law has long recognised that there is an inherent tension between the immediate interests of consumers and the incentives to motivate producers. Consumers desire a low price, while producers seek high profits.[200] Competition law recognises that if inter-firm rivalry is the engine of economic progress, and if such rivalry is to be vigorous, the economic reward must be sufficient to draw forth the effort. Thus, whatever future benefits accrue to consumers generally through innovation and production efficiencies, the need to maintain producer incentives may require the consumers of a particular product to pay higher prices in the short run.[201] Under this suggested approach, activities that increase social wealth but impair the immediate consumer interest would be permitted only when the contemplated action meets three conditions. First, the projected activity must increase total social wealth by realising significant production or innovation efficiencies. Secondly, the activity must be necessary to achieve such efficiencies and among reasonably available alternatives, be least harmful in its effects on consumers.[202] Thirdly, the activity must not permanently suppress inter-firm rivalry, but must allow for the eventual reestablishment of competition.[203]

Brodley's approach is indeed very similar to the approach under Article 101(3) which will be dealt with separately in chapter three, section II. What must nevertheless be said is that there is a certain vagueness in the test which could cause problems in implementation. For example, when is an increase in production or dynamic efficiency 'significant'? Especially with innovation efficiencies, such quantification may be impossible due to the uncertainty inherent in the process of innovation. Similarly, the third condition of the test – that is that the activity must not permanently suppress inter-firm rivalry – is problematic since it has to be determined when inter-firm rivalry will be deemed to be suppressed permanently and how this condition can be applied to already dominant undertakings increasing their productive efficiency.

To summarise, both consumer welfare and total welfare are candidates for being standards of harm in competition law and policy. The crucial difference between the two welfare standards is the existence or lack of concern for the trans-

[198] Duhamel and Townley (n 157) 18–19.

[199] ibid 19.

[200] Brodley (n 94) 1036.

[201] ibid 1037.

[202] ibid.

[203] ibid 1038. The first condition precludes conduct that injures the consumer interest unless the social gain rests on the achievement of significant production or innovation efficiencies – the kinds of efficiencies that appear indispensable to economic progress. According to Brodley, conduct that increases only allocative or pricing efficiency would not justify even temporary harm to the consumer interest.

fer of wealth from consumers to producers and how efficiency gains of otherwise allegedly anticompetitive practices are to be treated. Although in most cases a practice may decrease/increase both consumer and total welfare, in cases where consumer and total welfare standards have different implications, namely when consumer welfare and producer welfare change in opposite directions, the choice between the standards would directly affect the decision on the case. The issue of wealth transfers and efficiency gains are dealt with in turn.

C Triangles, Rectangles and Trapezoids: Whose Interest Matters More?

One important aspect of the question of what the welfare standard of competition law and policy should be is whether the standard should have anything to say about wealth transfers from consumers to producers or whether its focus should be limited to welfare losses from allocative inefficiency as a result of which some consumers are left out of the market. The broader question is whether competition law and policy should be exclusively concentrated on efficiency or whether it should take into account distributional issues as well. As such, this is a clear example of 'efficiency' and 'welfare' goals being challenged by and having to be weighed against 'fairness' goals if the surplus of consumers is to be favoured over the surplus of producers for fairness concerns. 'Fairness' as a separate objective is left for discussion in chapter four.

It has been argued that while academics may find this issue intriguing, the dispute of triangles versus rectangles has little importance for those outside the university.[204] According to Calvani, a debate about shapes is irrelevant to antitrust enforcement since virtually all cases worthy of prosecution have both wealth transfers and welfare losses.[205] Nonetheless, this debate is directly related to the choice between the 'total welfare' and the 'consumer welfare' standard since the preference for one over the other and how the standard is applied will inevitably have implications in terms of including (excluding) distributional concerns in (from) competition policy. Two specific occasions that the choice would directly matter are, first, deciding whether an increase in efficiencies accruing (partly or completely) to producers as profits could outweigh harm to consumers and secondly, whether an increase in allocative efficiency benefiting some consumers could outweigh harm to other consumers. Thus, the question is not one of merely triangles (deadweight loss) versus rectangles (wealth transfer). It is also about determining how trapezoids, namely the sum of triangles and rectangles will be treated in competition policy.

[204] T Calvani, 'Rectangles and Triangles: A Response to Mr Lande' (1989) 58 *Antitrust Law Journal* 657, 657.

[205] ibid 657. According to Calvani, the real debate of very significant import is between those who share an economics perspective and the proponents of an antitrust policy that has nothing to do with competition, ie, the so-called 'populist antitrust'. As such, one should direct attention to that debate and not to academic disputes among sects within the economics school of thought; ibid 659.

As explained above, while the total welfare approach views redistribution in the form of wealth transfers from consumers to producers as neutral, the consumer welfare standard views such wealth transfers as harmful.[206] Within the neoclassical market efficiency model (the price theory of the Chicago School), for example, evidence that a particular practice distributes wealth in a certain way or that a rule increases the opportunities for small business is generally irrelevant because the model does not take such values into account.[207] The model purports to distinguish only the efficient from the inefficient, without reference to distributional consequences. Cseres asserts that despite the argument of economists that distribution should not be a concern of competition policy, no democratic government would impose such legal rules on the basis of simple derivations from analytical models.[208] Similarly, seeing competition policy as a political bargain between consumers and producers, Baker notes that absent such a bargain governmental policy would fluctuate between pro-producer and pro-consumer regulatory regimes, redistributing wealth between interest groups, but not achieving the efficiency gains available from protecting competition.[209] Thus, he suggests that present-day enforcers and courts should be concerned more about the possibility that competition rules might systematically transfer rents from consumers to firms, by allowing firms to adopt practices that generate allocative efficiency benefits while reducing consumers' surplus. This is because any policy that threatens to undermine consumer confidence that competition is the superior regulatory option would tend to undermine consumer political support for the political bargain in favour of competition policy.[210]

In any case, even if we were to accept that wealth distribution considerations are an appropriate focus of competition policy, the question of whether this would provide clear support for use of a consumer welfare standard should be answered.[211] Farrell and Katz have argued that there are at least three rationales for antitrust enforcement's use of total welfare as a measure of social welfare even in the presence of distributional concerns.[212] The first is to view the use of total welfare as a response to uncertainty about distributional effects. If enforcers do

[206] Cseres (n 31) 252. See above, text to n 161.

[207] Hovenkamp (n 19) 215.

[208] Cseres (n 31) 313. It has been argued that a rule is purposefully distributive only if we adopt it instead of an alternative believed to be more efficient, because the one we adopt distributes wealth in a way we find more attractive; Hovenkamp (n 102) 2–3.

[209] Baker (n 164) 483–84.

[210] ibid 519. He proposes a standard in between the consumer welfare and total welfare standard; enforcers and courts should seek to maximise total welfare, subject to the constraint that consumers and producers sufficiently share the efficiency gains, at least on average, so that neither group thinks it can do better by reneging on the political bargain; ibid 518.

[211] Heyer (n 190) 48.

[212] Farrell and Katz (n 194) 10. The authors argue that the antitrust enforcement process involves multiple steps and multiple decision makers. Hence, a full discussion of what standard is or should be applied must specify by whom and how it fits in the overall process. They contend that for several reasons, it may be optimal to have specific agents within the broader system act to maximise a different objective (eg, consumer surplus) even when the ultimate goal of antitrust policy is to maximise total surplus; ibid 4.

not or cannot undertake a case-by-case determination of relative deservingness, then it may be best simply to assume that all affected parties are equally deserving. Secondly, if outcome *A* yields greater total welfare than outcome *B*, then in principle it is possible to design a system of wealth transfers, starting from *A* such that at least one person ends better off than in *B* and no one is worse off.[213] The third rationale concerns the division of labour among public policies.[214] If antitrust enforcement focuses on total welfare, other public policies can redistribute that surplus in accord with notions of 'fairness'. Competition law and policy is poorly suited as a redistribution vehicle in comparison with various tax and subsidy schemes.[215] Its principal shortcoming is that antitrust enforcement does not – and without a fundamental change in the nature of analysis cannot – take a comprehensive view of distribution.[216] It would become necessary to examine the relative income distributions among consumers, workers and firm owners, and in many instances data would be lacking. Consumer welfare can provide a very poor approximation to a welfare measure that weights impacts using ordinary notions of distributional preferences. One reason is that rich and poor consumers may be differentially affected by an antitrust decision; distributional concerns would suggest weighting the impact on the poor more heavily, but a consumer welfare standard insists that they count equally.[217]

In contrast, it has also been argued that use of the consumer welfare standard might lead to higher average level of total welfare. Indeed, there appears to be an emerging literature, specifically regarding merger control, arguing that although total welfare may be adopted as the standard, in terms of enforcement, a total welfare maximising outcome might be more likely to be achieved by the use of a consumer welfare standard under various conditions.[218]

The discussion of which standard to adopt is usually interwoven with the discussion of how to make the trade-offs between wealth transfers (that is, distributional effects) and efficiency gains. On the one hand, it has been argued that policies which offer only minor efficiency gains and have undesirable effects on equity should tend not to be implemented.[219] On the other, it has been asserted that if measures making for efficiency are to have a fair chance, it is extremely desirable that they should be freed from distributive complications as much as

[213] ibid 10.

[214] ibid 11.

[215] ibid. See also Williamson (n 191) 734 and Motta (n 32) 21, fn 57. Similarly, C Ahlborn and AJ Padilla, 'From *Fairness* to *Welfare*: Implications for the Assessment of Unilateral Conduct under EC Competition Law' in CD Ehlermann and M Marquis (eds), *European Competition Law Annual 2007: A Reformed Approach to Article 82 EC* (Oxford, Hart Publishing, 2008) 98.

[216] Farrell and Katz (n 194) 11.

[217] ibid.

[218] See, eg, Lyons (n 150); DJ Neven and LH Röller, 'Consumer Surplus vs Welfare Standard in a Political Economy Model of Merger Control' (2005) 23 *International Journal of Industrial Organization* 829; R Pittman, 'Consumer Surplus as the Appropriate Standard for Antitrust Enforcement' (2007) 3(2) *Competition Policy International* 205; A Majumdar, 'The Role of a Consumer Harm Test in Competition Policy' (2008) 20(2) *Loyola Consumer Law Review* 144.

[219] A Fels and G Edwards, 'Working Paper' in CD Ehlermann and LL Laudati (eds), *European Competition Law Annual 1997: Objectives of Competition Policy* (Oxford, Hart Publishing, 1998) 58.

possible.[220] Moreover, competition policy need not concern itself directly with increasing the purchasing power of the poor because it accomplishes this indirectly when it prohibits cartels and monopolies in the single-minded pursuit of efficiency.[221] As stated by Okun: '[w]e can't have our cake of market efficiency and share it equally'.[222]

When efficiency is compared with equity as a reference for antitrust policy-making, the virtue of efficiency is its relative objectivity.[223] Efficiency is the linchpin of economics; arguably, it is closer to the concept of atom in chemistry or energy in physics than to the political theorist's 'state' or the theologian's 'grace'.[224] Interspersing any equity considerations that conflict with efficiency into competition policy should arguably be done with trepidation: equity does not have the objective or predictive characteristics of efficiency and while it may seem tolerant, even humanitarian, to call for more equity at the expense of efficiency, those who do so seldom are the ones who suffer the loss in real wealth.[225] Nonetheless, it has been argued that efficiency is not to be pursued as the goal of goals; from the perspective of political economy, a viable competitive market system, appropriately seasoned with competition policy, is only a means, not an end.[226]

It has been argued that lawyers and policymakers tend to think in a more nuanced way.[227] Lawyers study legal traditions and become familiar with the underlying values of a certain legal system. They take wider public interests into account in cases where economists would be solely concerned with efficiency arguments.[228] Admittedly, as put by Fox and Sullivan, '[l]aw is not economics'.[229] Moreover, both including and excluding wealth transfers as a concern in competition policy is ultimately a *value* decision to be taken by policymakers.[230] Furthermore, merely the fact that efficiency is more objective and predictable, and thus more operational as a criterion may not be deemed sufficient grounds for it to trump all other concerns. However, the context in which these criteria are to be used should not be lost sight of; competition law sets the rules of and limits to business conduct and imposes sanctions upon their breach. Thus, the objectivity and predictability of the rule is desirable since the undertakings should be able to determine with sufficient certainty *ex ante* that their conduct will not breach the law. Thus, the choice of values and standards has more than philosophical implications.

220 JR Hicks, 'The Foundations of Welfare Economics' (1939) 49(196) *The Economic Journal* 696, 712.
221 Elzinga (n 192) 1194–95.
222 AM Okun, *Equality and Efficiency: The Big Tradeoff* (Washington, DC, The Brookings Institution, 1975) 2.
223 Elzinga (n 192) 1212.
224 ibid.
225 ibid 1213.
226 ibid 1212.
227 Cseres (n 31) 314.
228 ibid.
229 Fox and Sullivan (n 133) 957.
230 Hovenkamp (n 19) 237.

As for the treatment of increases in productive efficiency, it must be pointed out that, even in the case of a monopolist, price *will* decrease when marginal cost decreases.[231] Thus, the claim that a monopolist will 'pocket the cost savings' and not pass any of them on to consumers is based on the incorrect assertion that only competition forces a firm to pass along cost savings. Profit maximisation by the firm causes it to pass along at least some of the cost savings in terms of a lower price, even if the firm is a monopolist. Even if only part of the cost savings is passed on to consumers, efficiency gains still benefit consumers and the economy.[232] A gain in productive efficiency increases the amount of output the economy can produce. Arguably, welfare losses from allocative inefficiency caused by monopoly are typically smaller than those resulting from productive inefficiency.[233] Hence, while a monopolist obviously has more pricing discretion than a firm in a perfectly competitive market, this does not exempt a monopoly from the fundamental profit maximisation 'discipline'.[234] All firms, even monopolists, are price takers in the sense that market forces determine the price that will maximise profits.[235]

A caveat must be stated here. One argument for ignoring the profits of the monopolist is that the monopolist would spend the wealth transferred from consumers for 'rent-seeking' purposes. As such, the allocative inefficiency and the deadweight loss arguably underestimate the costs of the monopoly; potential monopolies will invest resources in lobbying or attempting to organise monopolies.[236] The resources put into monopolisation and defence against monopolisation would be a function of the wealth transfer; the larger the potential transfer, the larger the socially wasteful investment.[237] An opportunity to obtain the

[231] JA Hausman and GK Leonard, 'Efficiencies from the Consumer Viewpoint' (1999) 7(3) *George Mason Law Review* 707, 708; Bishop and Walker (n 61) 32. If the monopolist lowers its price (by a small amount), three effects result. First, the monopolist achieves lower revenue on its existing unit sales; secondly, it sells more units because of the lower price; and thirdly, its total costs increase because of extra production. At the profit maximising optimum, the net effect of these three terms is zero – they cancel each other out. However, if the last term, which is the cost of the extra production, becomes smaller due to efficiencies, the total net effect becomes positive because the added revenue from the price decrease exceeds the added production cost. Thus, the monopolist can increase its profits by reducing its price, causing marginal revenue and marginal cost to be equal once again. Authors argue that a lower bound of 50% of cost savings will be passed on to consumers, regardless of the specific shape of the demand curve so long as it is convex. The proportion of pass-through will be considerably larger than 50% in many situations given the shapes of demand curves that have been found empirically, ie, with convex demand curves; Hausman and Leonard (n 231) 708–09, 727.

[232] Hausman and Leonard, ibid 710.

[233] ibid.

[234] K Kiljanski, '"Pass-on" in Merger Efficiency Defence' (2003) 26(4) *World Competition* 651, 677.

[235] WJ Kolasky, 'What Is Competition? A Comparison of US and European Perspectives' [2004] (Spring/Summer) *The Antitrust Bulletin* 29, 43. The profit maximisation discipline argument is obviously based on the monopolist being productively efficient, namely that it is not leading the 'quiet monopoly life' and is not faced with a problem of managerial slack. If there is managerial inefficiency, then the managers may not be taking the most efficient decisions which would maximise profits; see Motta (n 32) 47.

[236] G Tullock, 'The Welfare Costs of Tariffs, Monopolies, and Theft' (1967) 5(3) *Western Economic Journal* 224, 231–32.

[237] ibid 232.

lucrative wealth transfer as monopoly profits would attract resources into efforts by sellers to monopolise and by consumers to avoid being charged monopoly prices.[238] Posner thus argues that consumers' wealth is not actually transferred to the shareholders of the monopoly; it is dissipated in the purchase of 'inputs' into the activity of becoming a monopolist.[239]

Nonetheless, Posner himself notes that there is no justification for using competition laws to attain objectives unrelated or antithetical to efficiency, such as promoting a more equal distribution of income or wealth.[240] Moreover, the theory of rent-seeking has not been free from criticism either. The assumptions underlying the theory have been questioned and it has been argued that although some resources may be invested in obtaining a monopoly and should be seen as an additional cost of the monopoly, it is unlikely that the resources expended will match all or nearly all of the profits to be earned.[241] Further, Posner's presumption that rent-seeking activities never create socially valuable results is also questionable since, for example, advertising outlays – seen as rent-seeking activities by Posner – might increase information available to consumers as well as their perceived value of the good.[242] Thus, the actual amount of the inefficient distortions rent-seeking activities may cause is an empirical issue.[243] All in all, the criticism of the theory appears to be directed more at its *quantification*, rather than the underlying argument, namely that the monopolist would invest resources in rent-seeking which could be used more productively for other purposes and this should also be seen as a cost of the monopoly to the society.

It has been argued that the trade-off between efficiency and distribution is difficult since efficiency gains are (to some degree) measurable, whereas distributional impacts are (partly) qualitative in nature.[244] As such, 'this is a mathematical problem in need of ethical resolution *via* an unavoidable value judgement'.[245] Thus, a model framing this trade-off is the 'balancing weights' approach accepted by, for example, the Canadian Federal Court of Appeal in the *Propane* case.[246] The balancing weights approach essentially requires the ratio of gains to losses to be calculated.[247] The question for the relevant judicial body is whether there is evidence that would cause it to believe that the distributional impacts of, for example, a merger would be so egregious that the losses of losers should be accorded a premium in excess of the actual ratio relative to the gains of gainers.[248]

238 Posner (n 91) 14.

239 RA Posner, 'The Social Costs of Monopoly and Regulation' (1975) 83(4) *The Journal of Political Economy* 807, 821.

240 Posner (n 91) 2.

241 FM Fisher, 'The Social Costs of Monopoly and Regulation: Posner Reconsidered' (1985) 93(2) *The Journal of Political Economy* 410, 415–16. See also Motta (n 32) 44–45.

242 Motta, ibid, 45.

243 ibid.

244 Duhamel and Townley (n 157) 11.

245 ibid.

246 *Canada (Commissioner of Competition) v Superior Propane Inc* (CA) 2003 FCA 53, [2003] 3 FC 529.

247 Duhamel and Townley (n 157) 11.

248 ibid.

Obviously, making this method operational would require information regarding the income characteristics of gainers and losers.[249] The advantage of the method is that based on the facts of the specific case being considered, it treats distributional impacts as severe when they are severe and treats them as negligible when they are negligible.[250] Nonetheless, the approach raises the problem of how to determine the appropriate weights assigned to different social groups and the problem of predictability, as well as the inevitable risk of subjectivity.[251]

Regarding the issue of allocative efficiency gains for some consumers that lead to harm to other consumers, the determinant should be the effect on consumers in aggregate; if the aggregate effects on consumers is neutral or positive, then harm to some consumers should not be a concern for competition policy purposes.[252] This is because accepting otherwise would require the competition authority/court to engage in social planning by deciding which consumers are more deserving and which are less deserving when deciding cases. Given the division of labour between different policies and institutions, it is highly disputable that the competition authority/court would be the best placed institution to undertake such a task on a case-by-case basis. This should be dealt with under social and income policies. The issue of efficiencies and their relevance in terms of the standard applied by the Commission and the EU courts will be dealt with in chapter three with emphasis being placed on Article 101(3) and its implications for Article 102 since the former arguably sets the welfare standard as that of 'consumer welfare' in EU competition law.[253]

To conclude, it is no easy task to decide whether the standard should be 'consumer welfare' or 'total welfare', whether wealth transfers or allocative inefficiency is more important and whether productive efficiency gains can trump allocative efficiency losses. At some level, the choice is ultimately arbitrary; this is because no matter which of the alternatives is preferred, there will be advantages and disadvantages and thus there is no right or wrong. There seem to be strong enough arguments for the adoption of both the consumer welfare standard and the total welfare standard. As for distribution, the proposition that competition policy is not the best tool for distributional purposes appears to be stronger than

[249] ibid.

[250] ibid 12. See also TW Ross and RA Winter, 'The Efficiency Defense in Merger Law: Economic Foundations and Recent Canadian Developments' (2005) 72 *Antitrust Law Journal* 471 for a discussion of this approach.

[251] Cseres (n 31) 317.

[252] This is in line with the ECJ judgment in Case C-238/05 *Asnef-Equifax, Servicios de Informacion sobre Solvencio y Credito v AUSBANC* [2006] ECR I-11125, [70] where it was held that under Art 101(3), it is the beneficial nature of the effect on all consumers in the relevant markets that must be taken into consideration, not the effect on each member of that category of consumers. See similarly Commission, 'Guidelines on the Application of Article 81(3) of the Treaty' [2004] OJ C101/97, [87].

[253] For the argument that Article 101(3) sets the standard as 'consumer welfare' see, eg, J Bourgeois and J Bocken, 'Guidelines on the Application of Article 81(3) of the EC Treaty or How to Restrict a Restriction' (2005) 32(2) *Legal Issues of Economic Integration* 111; Cseres, *Competition Law* (n 31) 252–53; G Monti, 'Article 81 and Public Policy' (2002) 39(5) *Common Market Law Review* 1057, 1064–65; Lyons (n 150) 2, fn 2. Efficiencies in the context of Art 102 are also discussed in this volume, chs 7 and 8.

the opposite argument. Although there would generally be no harm in competition policy contributing to the achievement of the distributional goals of the society, in instances where this would require the dismissal of possible efficiency benefits that could ultimately benefit the whole society, the case is much less clear. Thus, the authority should assess both the magnitude and the probability of efficiencies and should be able to prove that it is unlikely for efficiencies to benefit the society at all before allowing distributional concerns to offset them. This assessment should be done in a dynamic framework and thus should consider dynamic efficiency gains as potential benefits to the society, albeit in the long run. Following on from the discussion thus far, the next section questions whether welfare is all that matters when it comes to objectives of competition law and policy.

D Is Welfare All That Matters?

Regarding the objectives other than efficiency and consumer welfare, the most important question appears to be whether competition law and policy should protect competitors. It has been argued that competition policy is in fact 'in trouble' because defining 'competition' is avoided: does 'competition' mean a maximum number of industry participants, or does it follow from maximising efficiency as the Chicago School argues?[254] As such, the essential tension is whether one should protect competitors or competition and the incessant discussion of 'competition versus competitors' is merely a manifestation of the struggle between efficiency and distributional goals.[255]

It has been suggested that it would be misleading to accept unconditionally such overly simplistic positions that competitors should never be the focus of competition policy worries and that if inefficient competitors were driven out of the market, even then consumers would be better off overall.[256] The argument is that subject to exceptional cases such as natural monopolies, there can be no effective competition without competitors.[257] This understanding of competition is surely a different one from the Schumpeterian one according to which it is not price competition, but competition *for* the market that matters and this latter type of competition 'acts not only when in being but also when it is merely an ever-present threat'.[258] Thus, even if there are no competitors, the threat of

[254] R Dibadj, 'Saving Antitrust' (2004) 75 *University of Colorado Law Review* 745, 814–15.

[255] ibid 815. *Cf* Amato who appears to view the protection of competitors as a type of economic efficiency concept as well; G Amato, *Antitrust and the Bounds of Power* (Oxford, Hart Publishing, 1997) 110–12.

[256] G Drauz, 'Unbundling *GE/Honeywell*: The Assessment of Conglomerate Mergers under EC Competition Law' in B Hawk (ed), *International Antitrust Law & Policy: Fordham Corporate Law 2001* (New York, Juris Publishing, 2002) 197.

[257] ibid.

[258] Schumpeter (n 85) 85.

competition disciplines before it attacks.[259] As such, it has been contended that competition laws are intended to protect competition, not competitors.[260]

Clearly everything hinges on what one means by 'competition' and rather oddly there does not seem to be any consensus on this term that essentially underlies the whole body of competition law and policy. If 'competition' is understood as an outcome that is represented by, for example, low prices, then the number of competitors on the market is irrelevant in terms of establishing the existence of 'competition'. If, however, 'competition' is understood as a process, then the number of competitors may indeed be relevant to establish whether there is competition on the market. Bringing these two aspects together somewhat, Fox has suggested that the most appropriate focus for competition economics should be as follows: protecting the process of competition among a significant number of rivals in free and open markets, with special regard for long-run consumer interests.[261]

One important distinction that has to be made while considering the objectives of competition policy is indeed to decide whether competition is and should be about the *process* or the *outcome* or both. It has been argued that the primary purpose of competition policy is to perpetuate and preserve a system of governance for a competitive, free enterprise economy: efficiency and consumer welfare constitute ancillary benefits that are expected to flow from a system of economic freedom.[262] As such, competition law and policy is primarily concerned with process and only secondarily with outcomes. It calls for a dispersion of power, buttressed by built-in checks and balances, to guard against the abuse of power and to preserve not only individual freedom, but also more importantly, a free *system*.[263]

Similarly, it has been argued that the goals of consumer welfare, producer welfare and welfare of competitors are all welfarist objectives in that each is a function only of economic agents' utility levels, not of the process by which those utilities are obtained or of other aspects of the outcome.[264] However, whether competition law allows particular conduct depends not just on the consequences of that conduct, but also on characteristics of the conduct itself.[265] A crucial

[259] ibid.

[260] DG Goyder, *EC Competition Law* 4th edn (Oxford, OUP, 2003) 9; RD Joffe, 'Antitrust Law and Proof of Consumer Injury' (2001) 75 *St John's Law Review* 615, 616.

[261] Fox (n 102) 1174–75.

[262] W Adams and J Brock, 'Antitrust and Efficiency: A Comment' (1987) 62 *New York University Law Review* 1116, 1116.

[263] ibid. In the same vein, Fox and Sullivan argue that antitrust laws protect not an outcome, but a process – competition. According to this view, antitrust laws set 'fair' rules of the game. They give rights of access and opportunity. The antitrust laws preserve and foster dynamic interactions among those in the market. Unlike the Chicago School argument, they deal not with aggregate national wealth, but with the expectations and behaviour of the people who participate in the markets. Aggregate outcomes or wealth of the nation as a concept is static and outcome-oriented, while the antitrust laws are dynamic and process-oriented; Fox and Sullivan (n 133) 959.

[264] Farrell and Katz (n 194) 5.

[265] ibid. Authors argue that for this reason, the current approach for determining the legality of firm conduct under US competition policy is neither the total surplus effects nor the consumer surplus effects; ibid.

element of competition law and policy is that it examines not only consequences (the change in consumer or total welfare) but also the process (the nature of the acts) that generates the consequences.[266] Specifically, antitrust prohibits firms from harming consumers and/or efficiency *through anticompetitive actions*.[267] Thus, in antitrust both consequences and process count; it is incomplete and potentially misleading to say that antitrust protects consumer welfare, total welfare or rivals' profits since conduct can violate the antitrust laws only if it harms 'competition'.[268] As the concept of harming competition is often hard to interpret, and too naïve an interpretation would prohibit many beneficial agreements, the law has evolved towards prohibiting only acts that both (a) hurt competition in an ordinary (and sometimes vague) sense and (b) hurt efficiency and/or consumer surplus.[269] The debate over 'the standard' is the debate over the standard applied in the second prong. As such, one suggestion is that there is a strong case for using total welfare, together with appropriate non-welfarist 'process criteria' as the overall objective of antitrust policy and arguably even the process element earns its place through the view that competition promotes total welfare.[270] However, according to this view, although total welfare is the appropriate ultimate objective of antitrust enforcement, this view does not imply that day-to-day antitrust enforcement should be based on seeking in the instance to evaluate a welfarist measure. Since it is impossible to predict long-run effects with certainty, it could easily be consistent with a long-run welfarist view to adhere to well-chosen non-welfarist principles, for example, 'protecting competition'.[271] Indeed, with minor exceptions, even merger policy does *not* seek to *maximise* a welfare measure, but only tries to ensure that such a measure *does not fall* as a result of a merger.[272]

Accepting an objective that has a process element in addition to an outcome element might have the implication that competitors will also be protected as part of the 'process' of competition. This would thus mean that something other than

[266] ibid 6. See similarly D Zimmer, 'On Fairness and Welfare: The Objectives of Competition Policy (Comment)' in CD Ehlermann and M Marquis (eds), *European Competition Law Annual 2007: A Reformed Approach to Article 82 EC* (Oxford, Hart Publishing, 2008) 104.

[267] Farrell and Katz (n 194) 6.

[268] ibid 8. See also GJ Werden, 'Consumer Welfare and Competition Policy' in J Drexl, W Kerber and R Pozsun (eds) *Competition Policy and the Economic Approach* (Cheltenham, Edward Elgar, 2011) 28–29 arguing that although promoting consumer welfare is the ultimate goal of competition law it does not follow that effects on 'consumer welfare' should be the test for legality. He suggests the test to be the effect on the *competitive process* which is presumed to promote consumer welfare; ibid 31, 36, 37.

[269] Farrell and Katz (n 194) 8.

[270] ibid 28. *Cf* Baker (n 164) 483–84 where the author views antitrust as a political bargain between consumers and producers and suggests an intermediate position between a total welfare and a consumer welfare standard: antitrust enforcers and courts should seek to maximise total welfare, subject to the constraint that consumers and producers sufficiently share the efficiency gains, at least on average, so that neither group thinks it can do better by reneging on the political bargain.

[271] Farrell and Katz (n 194) 9, fn 16.

[272] ibid 9. In the same vein, see J Vickers, 'A Reformed Approach to Article 82 EC and the US Practice: An Overall Appreciation' in CD Ehlermann and M Marquis (eds), *European Competition Law Annual 2007: A Reformed Approach to Article 82 EC* (Oxford, Hart Publishing, 2008) 241.

welfare does count: what is important to note is that if this is done on its own, rather than in addition to examining the outcome, it can result in protecting the competitors for their own sake. Therefore, if one is to count the process as an element worth protecting, this should be done alongside an assessment of the outcome if one wishes to avoid protecting certain undertakings for their own sake.[273]

IV CONCLUSION

As the discussions above demonstrate, there is a variety of views on both the potential means and ends of competition law and policy. The proposition that competition law and policy is not just about the outcomes but also the process, appears to be the best starting point among various suggestions regarding objectives and should be kept in mind when assessing objectives. This is because competition law should always be about *competition* and should not lose sight of the aim of protecting competition whatever the ultimate aim. In other words, even if the ultimate objective is to enhance the welfare of society or consumers, competition law should have a say in this by protecting 'competition' – albeit potential competition or the threat of competition. This is because competition law is not the only tool one has in law and policy that can be used to achieve the various desired goals of the society. The expertise of competition law and policy belongs to the area of *anti*competitive behaviour; namely behaviour 'against competition'.

When the objective is 'consumer welfare', this becomes particularly important. Competition law is not consumer law; consumer law can attack all types of behaviour merely because they are harmful to consumers' interests as the purpose of consumer law is the protection of 'consumers'. Competition law cannot and should not go as far as attacking all types of conduct that may be detrimental to consumers unless the conduct is *anticompetitive* and harmful to competition. If consumer welfare is accepted as the objective of competition law, then the detriment to consumers that competition law seeks to avoid should be understood as harm related to an *anticompetitive* act. Thus, for example, although consumer protection may prohibit the use of certain additives in food products by undertakings to avoid consumer harm, this would not fall under the scope of competition law as such usage would not be an act of or against *competition*. Hence, even if the 'process' matters only because of the expected 'outcome', it should still be part of the assessment. Indeed, the process should not be protected for its own sake since doing so may in effect be tantamount to protecting competitors for their own sake. This is why *both* process *and* outcome should matter. Competition law should attack practices that distort competition *and* thus are detrimental to consumer or total welfare (or any other ultimate goal) as determined by policy.

[273] For the argument that 'competition' *can* be protected as a value in itself, see O Andriychuk, 'Rediscovering the Spirit of Competition: On the Normative Value of the Competitive Process' (2010) 6(3) *European Competition Journal* 575.

This should be the dividing line between competition law and consumer law. In the context of Article 102, this would suggest that the objective of Article 102 should be conceptualised as preventing both the distortion of competition and the consumer harm that might result from the conduct of dominant undertakings. The thesis of this book is that this implies the fusion of 'exclusionary' and 'exploitative' abuse: it is harm to trading partners (exploitation) that is linked to harm to competition (exclusion) that Article 102 seeks to prevent.

Finally, if the ultimate aim is some measure of welfare, then for competition law to interfere, the authority must be able to prove a (likely) *decrease* in the chosen welfare standard. The example of Farrell and Katz on merger policy can be generalised to the whole of competition policy: competition policy is not and should not be expected to be about *maximising* some measure of welfare; it is and should be about ensuring that welfare does not *decrease* as a result of anti-competitive behaviour. Put in the context of Article 102, '[f]ailure to maximize consumer well-being cannot be the litmus test of abuse'.[274] This is because 'it would certainly seem wrong for conduct to be considered abusive if consumers would probably do no worse with that conduct than with what the firm would reasonably do if the conduct were prohibited'.[275] Moreover, asking competition policy to actually *maximise* welfare would be asking it to save the world. 'Competition policy can't save the world'.[276] It should not have to do so either.

Building on the concepts discussed in the current chapter, the next chapter investigates the historical roots of Article 102 and the implications of these roots for the correct understanding of the provision and its aims.

[274] Vickers (n 272) 4.

[275] ibid.

[276] J Faull, 'Panel Discussion 1, Competition Policy Objectives' in CD Ehlermann and LL Laudati (eds), *European Competition Law Annual 1997: Objectives of Competition Policy* (Oxford, Hart Publishing, 1998) 12.

2

The Historical Roots of Article 102 TFEU

I INTRODUCTION

After a discussion of welfare and some other potential objectives of competition law and policy in chapter one, this chapter seeks to place Article 102 in the correct historical context within which it belongs. This is important because in the predominant literature, Article 102 has been characterised as a product of 'ordoliberalism', namely the 'Freiburg School' of economic thought that emerged in Germany in the 1930s.[1] This placement has important implications for what the provision *is* and *can be*. This is because for ordoliberalism, the objective of competition policy is the protection of economic freedom and this would imply that if ordoliberal, then Article 102 *cannot* have the objective of 'consumer welfare' or any other efficiency-based objective since for ordoliberals, efficiency is only a possible *outcome* of competition and not an aim. More importantly, the objective of protecting economic freedom may not always result in welfare-enhancing outcomes, and for these instances one must establish whether welfare or economic freedom is to be given priority. Given that the Commission has been rethinking its approach to Article 102 and suggesting that the aim is to enhance consumer welfare with an effects-based approach, whether or not the legal provision itself *can* be applied with such an objective becomes crucial. In fact, it has been suggested by some prominent authors that Article 102 *cannot* be applied with a consumer welfare standard and *cannot* make consumer harm the test of harm.[2] Thus,

[1] See DJ Gerber, *Law and Competition in Twentieth Century Europe Protecting Prometheus* (Oxford, OUP, 1998) 264; L Lovdahl Gormsen, 'Article 82 EC: Where Are We Coming From and Where Are We Going To?' (2005) 2(2) *The Competition Law Review* 5, 10; P Lowe, 'Consumer Welfare and Efficiency – New Guiding Principles of Competition Policy?' (13th International Conference on Competition and 14th European Competition Day, Munich, March 2007) 2; E Rousseva, 'Modernizing by Eradicating: How the Commission's New Approach to Article 81 EC Dispenses with the Need to Apply Article 82 EC to Vertical Restraints' (2005) 42 *Common Market Law Review* 587, 590–91; KJ Cseres, *Competition Law and Consumer Protection* (The Hague, Kluwer Law International, 2005) 82; G Marenco, 'The Birth of Modern Competition Law in Europe' in A von Bogdandy, PC Mavroidis and Y Mény (eds), *European Integration and International Co-ordination: Studies in Honour of Claus-Dieter Ehlermann* (The Hague, Kluwer Law International, 2002) 303.

[2] T Eilmansberger, 'How to Distinguish Good from Bad Competition under Article 82 EC: In Search of Clearer and More Coherent Standards for Anti-competitive Abuses' (2005) 42 *Common Market Law Review* 129, 129, 133; DJ Gerber, 'The Future of Article 82: Dissecting the Conflict' in CD Ehlermann and M Marquis (eds), *European Competition Law Annual 2007: A Reformed Approach*

this chapter furthers the discussion of the potential and existent objectives of EU competition law and policy, with a particular focus on Article 102.

It must be noted that the proposition that Article 102 has ordoliberal foundations has *not* been reached by an examination of the actual drafting process of the provision. Gerber, who has been prominent in the association of the provision with ordoliberalism, particularly in the beginning of the 2000s, has not investigated the official records of the drafting process of the Treaty. As far as this author understands the documents have been publicly available since the late 1980s in line with the 30-year rule.[3] It should also be mentioned that the alleged influence of ordoliberalism on Article 102 has rather been based on the general historical context, the people involved in the integration process and the application of this provision by the Commission and the EU courts *after* the Treaties were signed.[4]

Thus, this chapter first provides an examination of the potential objectives of EU competition law and policy in section II. In section III, ordoliberalism and ordoliberal competition policy is discussed. Section IV provides insights from the period preceding the Treaties of Rome in Germany and in Europe, including a brief discussion of the context in which the European Coal and Steel Community (ECSC) was established. Section V provides some actual evidence from the *travaux préparatoires* of the Treaties of Rome regarding the competition provisions. This is complemented with insights from the early Commission interpretation of Article 102 and some early understandings of the concepts of 'dominance' and 'abuse'. Section VI establishes the implications of the historical insights for Article 102 and its application today and in the future. In doing this, the chapter seeks to defy the common position that Article 102 is an ordoliberal product, to prove that it *can* be applied with a welfare standard and to provide a basis for an interpretation of Article 102 that is not only in line with its historical context, but is also operational. Section VII concludes.

II OBJECTIVES OF EU COMPETITION LAW AND POLICY

There has never been a comprehensive discussion of the goals of EU competition law, which arguably came into existence mainly for political reasons such as the

to Article 82 EC (Oxford, Hart Publishing, 2008) 50–51; H Schweitzer, 'The History, Interpretation and Underlying Principles of Section 2 Sherman Act and Article 82 EC' in CD Ehlermann and M Marquis (eds), *European Competition Law Annual 2007: A Reformed Approach to Article 82 EC* (Oxford, Hart Publishing, 2008) 119, 161.

[3] See Gerber (n 1) 343 stating that the records were not available at the time of his writing. Under 'Council Regulation (EEC, EURATOM) No 354/83 concerning the opening to the public of the historical archives of the European Economic Community and the European Atomic Energy Community' [1983] OJ L43/1 and amending this, Council Regulation (EC, EURATOM) No 1700/2003 [2003] OJ L243/1 the non-confidential documents of EU institutions must be made available after the expiry of a period of 30 years starting from the date of the creation of the document.

[4] See, eg, Lovdahl Gormsen (n 1); Gerber (n 1). See Gerber, ibid, 263 where the influence of ordoliberalism at the European level is explained by reference to the people who were involved in the process of unification.

establishment of a common market.[5] Arguably, lack of clarity about the goals to be achieved will inevitably lead to inconsistent decisions.[6] It has been commented that Articles 101 and 102 are not only concerned with competition matters, but are seeking to implement a broader range of industrial, social and political policies.[7] These purposes make it significantly more difficult for businesses to plan their affairs to ensure compliance with EU competition law.[8] In some cases, the rules have been applied to protect or favour small or medium-sized enterprises, keep markets open, protect competitors, protect consumers in a 'non-technical' sense or allow cooperative enterprises that will advance technology.[9]

The three core aims of EU competition law are suggested to be protecting economic freedom, integrating the market and promoting efficiency.[10] It is generally assumed that the objective of EU competition law is to guarantee 'effective competition' for the benefits that it delivers to consumers and in order to encourage the optimal allocation of resources, industrial efficiency, innovation and progress.[11] However, the Treaty does not refer to this and what 'effective competition' actually means remains unclear.[12] The Commission's XVth Report on Competition Policy in 1985 described the concept of 'effective competition' as preserving 'the freedom and right of initiative of the individual economic operators'. As such, it is supposed to foster the spirit of enterprise and create an environment within which European industry can grow and develop in the most efficient manner and at the same time take account of social goals.[13] This statement has been argued to put the emphasis on individual liberty and the freedom of economic action.[14]

One common proposition regarding the competition rules of the TFEU and particularly Article 102 is that their intellectual foundation lies in ordoliberalism.[15] Although this common explanation is challenged later in this study regarding Article 102 and ordoliberalism is dealt with separately below,[16] since one of the goals of EU competition law and policy is argued to be 'protection of economic freedom', the issue will be briefly discussed here in the context of goals.

[5] RJ Van den Bergh, 'The Difficult Reception of Economic Analysis in European Competition Law' in A Cucinotta, R Pardolesi and RJ Van den Bergh (eds), *Post-Chicago Developments in Antitrust Law* (Cheltenham, Edward Elgar, 2002) 36. The 'common market' has become the 'internal market' with the Treaty of Lisbon.

[6] RJ Van den Bergh and PD Camesasca, *European Competition Law and Economics A Comparative Perspective* (Antwerpen, Intersentia-Hart, 2001) 69. On 'public policy' objectives in competition law and particularly Art 101, see C Townley, *Article 81 EC and Public Policy* (Oxford, Hart Publishing, 2009).

[7] P Jebsen and R Stevens, 'Assumptions, Goals and Dominant Undertakings: The Regulation of Competition under Article 86 of the European Union' (1996) 64 *Antitrust Law Journal* 443, 446.

[8] ibid 460.

[9] A Jones and B Sufrin, *EU Competition Law: Text, Cases and Materials* 4th edn (Oxford, OUP, 2011) 44.

[10] G Monti, 'Article 81 and Public Policy' (2002) 39(5) *Common Market Law Review* 1057, 1059–64.

[11] S Bishop and M Walker, *The Economics of EC Competition Law: Concepts, Application and Measurement* 3rd edn (London, Sweet & Maxwell, 2010) 20; Cseres (n 1) 244.

[12] Cseres, ibid.

[13] Commission, 'Introduction' in 'XVth Annual Report on Competition Policy' (1985).

[14] Van den Bergh (n 5) 44; Cseres (n 1) 245.

[15] See literature in n 1 above.

[16] See section III.

When following the 'economic freedom' model, one examines a practice's possible effects on the competitive *structure* of the market, primarily as evidenced by possible harm to or limitation of the 'freedom of manoeuvre' of the other market players.[17] This model assumes that a dominant firm is able to alter the market structure from the competitive norm and so has a 'special responsibility' not to harm the structure of the market any further.[18] This approach is based on the belief that competition in dominated markets will only have optimal results if the competitors are protected from the constraints which follow from the dominance of one firm.[19] It has been argued that European authorities have shown a continuing interest in preserving rivalry as such by protecting firms against the results of intensive competition.[20] Consequently, they have been criticised for 'protecting competitors, not competition'.[21]

Leaving aside protection of economic freedom, the most important goal of EU competition law and policy so far has perhaps been 'market integration'. Market integration is both a political and an economic objective of EU competition policy.[22] The goal of market integration played an essential role in including competition rules in the founding Treaty.[23] Broader transborder trade was intended to create a mutual interest in common prosperity. Arguably it was, of course, also designed to increase that prosperity directly by allowing for a greater scale of productions.[24] Competition policy has been seen as one of the funda-

[17] F Engelsing, P Marsden and D Möller (primary authors) 'A Bundeskartellamt/Competition Law Forum Debate on Reform of Article 82: A "Dialectic" on Competing Approaches' (2006) 2 (Special Issue) *European Competition Journal* 211, 216.

[18] ibid. On 'special responsibility', see below, text around n 78.

[19] 'Bundeskartellamt/Competition Law Forum Debate' (n 17) 216.

[20] DJ Gifford and RT Kudrle, 'European Union Competition Law and Policy: How much Latitude for Convergence with the United States?' (2003) 48(3) *The Antitrust Bulletin* 727, 740. Authors argue that the protection of business from the rigor of competitive pressures by the Commission echoes similar protections accorded by the US courts to business during the 1960s at which time efficiency had not yet attained the pre-eminent status it currently possesses in the US; ibid 741–43.

[21] See, eg, Gifford and Kudrle, ibid, 759 arguing that the decisional standards employed in European competition law have appeared to protect business firms from the rigors of a competitive marketplace. Similarly, see D Geradin, 'Limiting the Scope of Article 82 EC: What can the EU Learn from the U.S. Supreme Court's Judgment in *Trinko* in the Wake of *Microsoft*, *IMS*, and *Deutsche Telekom*? (2004) 41 *Common Market Law Review* 1519, 1532; Jones and Sufrin (n 9) 363–64. For the argument that this criticism is too harsh, see Cseres (n 1) 293.

[22] A Schaub, 'Working Paper' in CD Ehlermann and LL Laudati (eds), *European Competition Law Annual 1997: Objectives of Competition Policy* (Oxford, Hart Publishing, 1998) 126.

[23] Cseres (n 1) 246. Neven argues that the market integration objective does not necessarily promote market integration; by insisting that a restriction on parallel imports is practically a per se restriction of competition, the Commission tends to confuse symptoms with causes. The existence of price differentials between Member States may well be a symptom of market power in those markets, but it is by no means clear that, conditional on the existence of market power, parallel trade enhances economic efficiency; DJ Neven, 'Working Paper' in CD Ehlermann and LL Laudati (eds), *European Competition Law Annual 1997: Objectives of Competition Policy* (Oxford, Hart Publishing, 1998) 117.

[24] Gifford and Kudrle (n 20) 751. Although the authors argue that the benefits of competition per se played a much smaller role in the designers' overall thinking for a number of reasons that provide considerable contrast with the situation in the US at the time, this proposition does not seem in total conformity with the discussions of the drafters during negotiations; see below, section V.

mental means for achieving and preserving the unity of the market.[25] In this sense, competition law in the EU plays a negative as well as a positive role in the process of market integration: on the one hand, it has the task of preventing measures that attempt to isolate one domestic market from another;[26] on the other, it plays a positive role by encouraging transborder trade and creating a level playing field for firms. The fact that competition law was appointed the 'motor of market integration' significantly affected the way competition policy has been perceived in the EU.[27]

The important point is that market integration may at times conflict with efficiency and consumer welfare – arguably the other core aims of EU competition law and policy.[28] A policy oriented towards market integration does not always promote the interests of consumers.[29] For instance, the prohibition of absolute territorial protection is clearly directed at market integration, although economic analysis shows that such a vertical agreement may have outcomes enhancing allocative efficiency and thereby consumer welfare. Thus, the goal of market integration eventually may come at the expense of inefficiencies in the organisation of production or distribution.[30] It has been noted that in the EU the sacred market integration goal has precedence over other competition aims, like consumer welfare or other efficiency arguments.[31] As a general rule, market integration is arguably the most important factor which is set aside only in limited circumstances and efficiency considerations may justify exemption only if the economic gains are greater than the restriction of competition.[32] However, given that in the current time frame markets have largely been integrated, this raises the question of whether competition rules should still be used as a *direct* mechanism to ensure market integration or whether one can now rely on the *indirect* mechanism, namely protecting the process of effective competition in order to create a market structure which contributes to the objective of market integration.[33] Such conflicts between goals have to be identified in order to see how the Commission balances the conflicting interests and to see whether and in what way consumer interests play a role in the Commission's 'conflict management'.[34]

The potential conflict between the goal of market integration (and other non-efficiency goals) and the efficiency-related goals is important since, according to the Commission, the objective of Articles 101 and 102 is to protect competition on the market as a means of enhancing consumer welfare and of ensuring an

[25] Cseres (n 1) 246.

[26] ibid.

[27] ibid. Also, see in general DJ Gerber, 'The Transformation of European Community Competition Law?' (1994) 35(1) *Harvard International Law Journal* 97.

[28] Monti (n 10) 1064; Neven (n 23) 118; Cseres (n 1) 255; Van den Bergh (n 5) 35; M Motta, *Competition Policy: Theory and Practice* (Cambridge, CUP, 2004) 23.

[29] Cseres (n 1) 82.

[30] Van den Bergh (n 5) 35. See similarly Neven (n 23) 117.

[31] Cseres (n 1) 276.

[32] Monti (n 10) 1094.

[33] Schaub (n 22) 126–27.

[34] Cseres (n 1) 255.

efficient allocation of resources.[35] Competition and market integration serve these ends since the creation and preservation of an open single market promotes an efficient allocation of resources throughout the Union for the benefit of consumers. Hence, it has been argued that the welfare standard for EU competition law is 'consumer welfare' and not 'total welfare'.[36] The former Director General of the Commission's Directorate-General for Competition (DG Competition), Lowe had also remarked that '[c]ompetition is not an end in itself, but an instrument designed to achieve a certain public interest objective, consumer welfare'.[37] Nonetheless, it has also been suggested that although European competition law is increasingly acknowledging the relevance of consumer welfare, it is neither the starting point nor the overriding interest in European competition analysis, unlike in American antitrust law.[38] The great difference between the European and American competition analysis is the treatment of efficiencies: efficiencies play a less significant role in the European assessment of consumer welfare and competition analysis. In Europe, efficiencies are considered as long as they benefit consumers directly and in the short term, whereas in the US efficiencies which would benefit the consumers in the long-run would be considered even if there are no direct short-term benefits.[39] Thus, the US arguably adopts a more dynamic approach to consumer welfare than the EU.

After this brief introduction of the potential objectives, the next section elaborates on ordoliberalism which – according to many – is the school of thought that historically influenced EU competition law and policy.

[35] See Commission, 'Guidelines on the Application of Article 81(3) of the Treaty' [2004] OJ C101/97, [13]; 'DG Competition Discussion Paper on the Application of Article 82 of the Treaty to Exclusionary Abuses' (Brussels, December 2005) available at: ec.europa.eu/comm/competition/antitrust/art82/discpaper2005.pdf, [4], [54]. The expression is rather different in the 'Guidance on the Commission's Enforcement Priorities in Applying Article 82 of the EC Treaty to Abusive Exclusionary Conduct by Dominant Undertakings' [2009] OJ C45/7 where the Commission states the aim of its enforcement activity under Art 102 as ensuring that 'dominant undertakings do not impair effective competition by foreclosing their competitors in an anti-competitive way, thus having an adverse impact on consumer welfare'; [19]. For the argument that the underlying assumptions of EU competition law do not make efficiency the sole or even principle criterion, see Jebsen and Stevens (n 7) 513.

[36] Bishop and Walker (n 11) 32; Van den Bergh (n 5) 42.

[37] P Lowe, 'Preserving and Promoting Competition: A European Response' 2006 (2) (Summer) EC *Competition Policy Newsletter* 1, 1.

[38] Cseres (n 1) 20. See also I Haracoglou, 'Competition Law, Consumer Policy and the Retail Sector: The Systems' Relation and the Effects of a Strengthened Consumer Protection Policy on Competition Law' (2007) 3(2) *The Competition Law Review* 175, 180. For the argument that the interpretation of Art 102 should not be reduced to only one criterion, that of the welfare of the consumer, but aim in the long run to protect competition as a process, see V Mertikopoulou, 'DG Competition's Discussion Paper on the Application of Article 82 of the EC Treaty to Exclusionary Abuses: The Proposed Economic Reform from a Legal Point of View' (2007) 28(4) *European Competition Law Review* 241, 251.

[39] Cseres, ibid, 20, 289. See US Department of Justice and the Federal Trade Commission 2010 'Horizontal Merger Guidelines' Section 10 and fn 15. Efficiencies in the context of Art 102 are discussed in detail in chs 3, 7 and 8 of this volume.

III ORDOLIBERALISM AND ORDOLIBERAL COMPETITION POLICY

In Germany in the 1930s and 1940s, the scholars of a group called the 'Freiburg School' (the 'ordoliberal' school) tried to use law to protect market processes from distortion either by the public power of the state or by the private economic power of large firms.[40] Arguably, in the turn-of-the-century debates about competition law in Germany, parties seeking political support within the new industrial proletariat pictured it as a tool for assuring 'fairness' to the 'common man', while others sought 'fairness' for small and medium-sized enterprises.[41] One leading commentator argues that the structure of Articles 101 and Article 102 closely track ordoliberal thought and bear little resemblance to anything to be found in other European competition laws at the time of the adoption of the Treaties of Rome.[42] As such, the concept of prohibiting abuse of a dominant position was an important new development that was arguably closely associated with ordoliberal and German competition law thought and very different from the discourse of US law.[43] Since the predominant view in the literature appears to be that Article 102 is intellectually grounded in 'ordoliberalism',[44] ordoliberal competition policy deserves a closer look for a better understanding of its implications.

Competition policy of ordoliberalism focuses on the legitimisation of 'economic freedom' in order to prevent this freedom from destroying its own prerequisites; a law against restraints of competition from this point of view effects limits that are inherent in private law and can be considered as a continuation of private law by other means.[45] The actual goal of competition policy for ordoliberals lies in the protection of individual economic freedom of action as a value in itself or vice versa, in the restraint of undue economic power.[46] Economic efficiency as a

[40] DJ Gerber, 'Fairness in Competition Law: European and US Experience' (Conference on Fairness and Asian Competition Laws, Kyoto, 5 March 2004) available at: kyotogakuen.ac.jp/~o_ied/information/fairness_in_competition_law.pdf 7–8.

[41] Gerber (n 1) 419.

[42] ibid 264.

[43] ibid.

[44] See, eg, the references in n 1. This predominant view is challenged in section V. There are nuances in the literature on *how* Art 102 is associated with ordoliberalism. See, eg, Lovdahl Gormsen (n 1) 11 *et seq* and Lowe (n 1) 2 who argue that the *jurisprudence* of the Commission and the EU courts have been influenced by ordoliberalism.

[45] W Möschel, 'Competition Policy from an Ordo Point of View' in A Peacock and H Willgerodt (eds), *German Neo-Liberals and the Social Market Economy* (London, Macmillan, 1989) 149.

[46] ibid 146. *Cf* Maier-Rigaud who argues that ordoliberals never attached intrinsic value to economic freedom; freedom to compete was seen as an *outcome* of 'complete competition', ie, the result of an appropriate market order. According to this view, for ordoliberals the ultimate goal was to establish 'complete competition', and for *neoliberals* protecting the freedom to compete was the ultimate goal. The intrinsic value lay not in the freedom to compete as such, but in the political, human freedom for ordoliberalism; see F Maier-Rigaud, 'On the Normative Foundations of Competition Law: Efficiency, Political Freedom and the Freedom to Compete' (5th Academic Society for Competition Law (ASCOLA) Conference on the Goals of Competition Law, Bonn, May 2010) available at: www.iask.de/micro/paper/ascola.pdf 7, 10, 11, 12 (forthcoming in the ASCOLA Competition Law series by Edward Elgar).

generic term for growth, encouragement and development of technical progress and for allocative efficiency is but an indirect and derived goal; it results generally from the realisation of individual freedom of action in a market system.[47] What matters is that legal principles, as they have been developed in constitutional law with respect to the exercise of governmental power, must be developed with respect to the acquisition and exercise of economic power in a manner which remains consistent with the economic system.[48] Since substantial economic power could be used to subvert the freedom of the less powerful, most ordoliberals consequently favour decentralisation not only of government, but also of private enterprise.[49]

The fundamental problem in the twentieth century for ordoliberals was that the further concentration of economic power in state hands and the direct control of economic life by central state departments curtailed people's freedom more and more.[50] Moreover, according to them, the danger existed that private power groups may once again use their freedom to restrict the independence and freedom of workers, employees, tradesmen or competitors.[51] It had to be established which economic system will guarantee freedom and at the same time prevent the misuse of the rights endowed by freedom.[52] The reference to the 'danger of private groups' using their freedom to restrict others' freedom relates to the Weimar period and is in fact a good pointer that ordoliberal ideas have to be considered in the historical context of their development which is not necessarily similar to the adoption of European-level competition rules in the 1950s.[53]

Ordoliberals all accepted the market economy as indispensable for a modern free society. However, there was an academic debate among them regarding the reason for this, namely whether making economic decisions through the market was preferred because of its efficiency or for its expression of freedom.[54] Ordoliberals would have a bias in favour of the expression of freedom, even if it

[47] Möschel (n 45) 146. For an explanation of different efficiency concepts, see ch 1 this volume, section II.B.

[48] Möschel, ibid, 151.

[49] H Willgerodt and A Peacock, 'German Liberalism and Economic Revival' in A Peacock and H Willgerodt (eds), *Germany's Social Market Economy: Origins and Evolution* (London, Macmillan, 1989) 6, 8.

[50] W Eucken, 'What Kind of Economic and Social System?' in A Peacock and H Willgerodt (eds), *Germany's Social Market Economy: Origins and Evolution* (London, Macmillan, 1989) 36.

[51] ibid.

[52] ibid 37.

[53] Competition did not appear to be a problem in Germany until after the increasing industrialisation from 1871. The number of cartels then increased and the growing movement towards concentration persisted until the First World War. The First World War gave an additional impetus to cartelisation because of governmental rationing policy. The Cartel Ordinance of 1923 stabilised this development by generally sanctioning cartels. Nonetheless, the National Socialists encouraged cartels as a method of planning production. This development occurred despite the fact that socio-political and economic implications of restraints of competition were fully detected and articulated. The main ideas of ordoliberalism had thus been established before the First World War and conditions in the Weimar years constituted an essential background of experience; Möschel (n 45) 143–46. For a further discussion on Germany, see section IV.A below.

[54] Willgerodt and Peacock (n 49) 6.

were demonstrably less efficient. Their conception of efficiency included the continuing possibility of choice for the individual.[55] It must be pointed out that such a concept of efficiency is fundamentally different from the traditional understanding of efficiency in economics which – as explained in chapter one – mainly refers to fully and optimally utilising the resources available in an economy.[56] Although one could possibly include choice as an element of 'consumer welfare' (interpreted as a broader concept than 'consumer surplus'), including it in 'efficiency' as such cannot be easily operationalised once the traditional concept of efficiency in economics is accepted. This is because it does not seem possible to draw universal conclusions about 'choice' in any given market structure.[57] The inclusion of 'choice' in 'consumer welfare' will be returned to in chapter seven.

The ordoliberal competition policy differentiated between two types of competition, namely '*Leistungswettbewerb*' and '*Behinderungswettbewerb*'. '*Leistungswettbewerb*' means conduct that makes a firm's products more attractive to consumers, typically by improving their characteristics or lowering their prices.[58] Conversely, '*Behinderungswettbewerb*' refers to conduct designed to impede a rival's capacity to perform.[59] Ordoliberals believed that *Leistungswettbewerb* was consistent with the competitive model because under competitive conditions, performance improvement is the only means for a firm to improve its profits. Where a firm used its power to impede the performance of a rival, however, it would be interfering with the competitive process and thus the state should prevent such conduct.[60] In the English-speaking world, some commentators such as Gerber have used the terms 'performance competition' and 'impediment competition' to

[55] ibid 7.

[56] For an explanation of different efficiency concepts, see ch 1 this volume, section II.B.

[57] For a study on the determinants of product variety in different market structures, see K Lancaster, 'The Economics of Product Variety: A Survey' (1990) 9(3) *Marketing Science* 189.

[58] Gerber (n 1) 253.

[59] ibid.

[60] ibid. Nonetheless, the general ordoliberal approach towards monopolies does not seem to be that clear. One ordoliberal has argued that if three conditions were fulfilled then a policy to combat monopolies was not necessary. These conditions are: (i) the entrepreneur must be aware that he can, by his policy on price, quality and marketing, put his competitors' backs against the wall and they can do the same to him; (ii) there must be no agreements on prices or on quality between these producers; and (iii) entry to the industry must remain open – everyone must have the opportunity to compete with the existing firms on the same terms; FA Lutz, 'Observations on the Problem of Monopolies' in A Peacock and H Willgerodt (eds), *Germany's Social Market Economy: Origins and Evolution* (London, Macmillan, 1989) 163. Moreover, '[t]he oldest argument used by classicists against monopolies was always that they reduced production to below the level which would occur if they were in perfect competition and that, by this reduction in supply, a rise in prices which "exploited" the consumer was made possible. This is undoubtedly true for the monopolised industry itself. But it seems that the argument is not enough if the national economy is taken as a whole. For one can object that, although fewer factors of production are used in the monopolised industries than would be the case under conditions of perfect competition, these factors are taken up by other industries where they produce more than would otherwise be the case'; ibid 156. Thus, to prove that monopolies create damage, it has to be argued that these factors cannot be taken up by other industries or that the beneficial effect on total production is less than if total production was entirely conducted under the conditions of perfect competition; ibid 156–57. In the course of its dynamic development, competition itself will throw up monopoly situations from time to time which, like soap bubbles, will rise to the surface, last for a while and then burst under pressure from subsequent competition; ibid 161.

signify these concepts respectively.[61] However, it is worth mentioning that '*Leistungswettbewerb*' has not always been translated into English as 'performance competition'. For example, Berghahn translates it as 'competition based on efficiency' which significantly differs from 'performance competition', a term that is not self-explanatory.[62] Berghahn's translation would imply that efficiency was a major objective for ordoliberals as well, whereas 'performance competition' does not necessarily have the same implication since 'performance' unlike 'efficiency' is not an economic benchmark. This is an important point since it might be that due to linguistic issues the English-speaking world might not have an accurate opinion of the ordoliberals, to the extent that it is based on translated works.

In any case, the main concern of Eucken – one of the founders of ordoliberalism – was 'complete competition', that is competition in which no firm in a market has power to coerce other firms in that market.[63] If there is competition on the supply side, as well as on the demand side, and if the economic planning of both sides is based on such competition, then the market form of complete competition is achieved.[64] Two indicators suggested by Eucken to understand whether complete competition exists on a market were: first, that the price is not forced on the market by way of a market strategy, but taken from the market and secondly, that certain measures would indicate that complete competition does not exist as they cannot be implemented under complete competition (such as obstructions to purchasers or suppliers dealing with competitors, loyalty rebates, predatory pricing).[65]

It has been rightly suggested that, although Eucken does not link 'complete competition' to a particular market structure and despite his criticism of neoclassical economics of perfect competition, the concept of 'complete competition' does have an underlying structural assumption of polypoly and can best be understood as the real world adaptation of the model of 'perfect competition'.[66]

[61] See, eg, Gerber (n 1) 253.

[62] VR Berghahn, *The Americanisation of West German Industry 1945–1973* (Leamington Spa, Berg, 1986) 157.

[63] DJ Gerber, 'Constitutionalizing the Economy: German Neo-Liberalism, Competition Law and the "New" Europe' (1994) 42 *American Journal of Comparative Law* 25, 43; C Ahlborn and C Grave, 'Walter Eucken and Ordoliberalism: An Introduction from a Consumer Welfare Perspective' (2006) 2(2) *Competition Policy International* 197, 200. For an explanation of the use of the term 'complete competition' and not 'perfect competition', see Gerber (n 1) 245, n 52.

[64] W Eucken, 'The Competitive Order and its Implementation' (trans C Ahlborn and C Grave) reprinted in (2006) 2(2) *Competition Policy International* 219, 230.

[65] Möschel (n 45) 146.

[66] Ahlborn and Grave (n 63) 200. The authors also refer to another ordoliberal, Möschel, in this context who has noted that: 'the scholars of ordoliberalism have also used economic models for the description of their ideas, for instance, the model of perfect competition as it was developed in the traditional theory of competition. Such models, however, served only for the description of general effects of a market system, illustrating them in what might be called a chemically pure form. That did not imply, however, that those partly unreal premises were to be integrated as goals into practical competition policy. Any attempts to disprove or ridicule the ordoliberal concepts of competition as unrealistic miss the point'; Möschel (n 45) 146. For the model of 'perfect competition', see ch 1 this volume, text to fn 64 and fn 64.

Under ordoliberal policy, a firm or group of firms that had power over price or the power to hinder the performance of its rivals was structurally inconsistent with the complete competition standard.[67] Competition law had to provide a means of requiring that firms divest themselves of components of their operations or otherwise eliminate their monopoly situations.[68] Competition law would 'enforce' competition by creating and maintaining the conditions under which it would flourish.[69] The model of 'complete competition' provided the substantive standards for competition law, requiring that law be used to prevent the creation of monopolistic power, abolish existing monopoly positions where possible and, where not possible, control the conduct of monopolies.[70] This broad conception of economic power has been argued to distinguish German and EU competition law from that of the US.[71] Moreover, this concept was apparently perceived as a far more significant interference with private property than firms in Europe had experienced, except in wartime, and thus highly controversial.[72]

Eucken also argued that 'avoidable monopolies' were to be broken up and 'unavoidable monopolies' were to be regulated.[73] Thus, monopolies had to be prohibited because their very existence distorted the competitive order.[74] In cases of natural monopoly or where the monopoly was based on a legal right or where divestiture would be impractical or entail economic waste, competition law was to provide a standard of conduct: economically powerful firms were supposed to act *as if* they were subject to competition; as if they did not have market power.[75] They would not be allowed to use their power in ways harmful to competitors or to society in general.[76] In practice, this would mean that every form of 'impediment competition' by embargos, loyalty rebates, predatory pricing and so on, is prohibited.[77] This perception might have inspired the 'special responsibility' of dominant undertakings as imposed by the ECJ. According to the ECJ, irrespective of the reasons for which an undertaking has a dominant position, such an

[67] Gerber (n 1) 251.

[68] ibid 252.

[69] Gerber (n 63) 50.

[70] ibid 50–51.

[71] ibid 51.

[72] Gerber (n 1) 252.

[73] Eucken (n 64) 241. By 'unavoidable monopolies' Eucken seems to mean natural monopolies, such as a railway or a gas supplier, where the optimum operating size is so important that the quantity supplied by one undertaking is sufficient for the whole market and several businesses would not be able to sell at prices covering their costs; ibid 238.

[74] Gerber (n 1) 251–52.

[75] ibid 252. For the argument that *as if* competition was not a proposition uniformly accepted by ordoliberals, see Schweitzer (n 2) 135. However, it should be mentioned that Gerber also notes that 'not all ordoliberals were enthusiastic about the "as-if" standard'; Gerber (n 1) 252, fn 71. See Mestmäcker noting that Gerber has misinterpreted Böhm's position by suggesting that the *as if* standard applies to all kinds of exclusionary conduct; EJ Mestmäcker, 'The Development of German and European Competition Law with Special Reference to the EU Commission's Article 82 Guidance of 2008' in LF Pace (ed), *European Competition Law: The Impact of the Commission's Guidance on Article 102* (Cheltenham, Edward Elgar, 2011) 43.

[76] Gerber (n 1) 252. See also, M Vatiero, 'The Ordoliberal Notion of Market Power: An Institutionalist Reassessment' (2010) 6(3) *European Competition Journal* 689, 692 *et seq.*

[77] Eucken (n 64) 242.

undertaking has 'a special responsibility not to allow its conduct to impair genuine undistorted competition on the common market'.[78] In essence, the 'special responsibility' means that dominant undertakings, simply by virtue of the market power they hold, are not allowed to perform certain acts on the market that other non-dominant undertakings are allowed to.[79] The understanding behind both concepts appears to be the same, that is, the dominant undertaking must refrain from acting in accordance with the power it has. Therefore, it has to 'look out' for its competitors and consumers.[80]

Finally, Eucken argued that price discrimination should be prohibited in the competitive order since under complete competition the same prices become established for the same goods.[81] According to him, most difficult was the implementation of the fundamental principle within the scope of determining price levels: the price is to be *fixed* in such a way that offer and demand are in equilibrium at this price, and at the same time, the marginal costs are just covered.[82] From these remarks, it becomes clear that Eucken's 'complete competition' was indeed 'perfect competition'.

For the purposes of this study, a couple of points must be made. First, for ordoliberals, efficiency does not appear to be an aim, but rather an expected *result* of competition. Secondly, monopoly itself was deemed harmful and had to be prohibited where possible. Thirdly, the ordoliberal objective of competition was much closer to 'perfect competition' than, for example, 'workable competition'.[83] Since the ideal was 'perfect competition', on markets where competition was not perfect (for instance, markets with monopolies), the state had to actively intervene to establish a market order of 'ordered regulated competition', as only state interventions in the market could remove market disruptions and maintain the general societal interest.[84] These points raise two questions regarding Article 102:

[78] Case 322/81 *NV Nederlandsche Banden-Industrie Michelin v Commission* [1983] ECR 3461, [57]. In Case 6/72 *Europemballage Corp and Continental Can Co Inc v Commission* [1973] ECR 215, [27] the ECJ held that there need not be a causal link between the dominant position and its abuse.

[79] Rousseva (n 1) 592.

[80] See Case T-228/97 *Irish Sugar plc v Commission* [1999] ECR II-2969, [189], upheld on appeal in Case C-497/99 *Irish Sugar plc v Commission* [2001] ECR I-5333.

[81] Eucken (n 64) 243. Although price discrimination is not consistent with 'perfect competition', modern economics shows that it is possible and sometimes even necessary in competitive markets. See, eg, WJ Baumol and DG Swanson, 'The New Economy and Ubiquitous Competitive Price Discrimination: Identifying Defensible Criteria of Market Power' (2003) 70 *Antitrust Law Journal* 661, 662; JC Cooper, L Froeb, DP O'Brien and S Tschantz, 'Does Price Discrimination Intensify Competition? Implications for Antitrust' (2005) 72 *Antitrust Law Journal* 327, 357. On 'price discrimination' under Art 102, see ch 6, this volume.

[82] Eucken (n 64) 243.

[83] For the definition of 'perfect competition', see ch 1 this volume, text to fn 64 and fn 64. Since 'perfect competition' does not exist in reality, the concept of 'workable competition' has been developed seeking for competitive outcomes in the absence of perfect competition. On 'workable competition', see JM Clark, 'Toward a Concept of Workable Competition' (1940) 20 *American Economic Review* 241; SH Sosnick, 'A Critique of Concepts of Workable Competition' (1958) 72 *Quarterly Journal of Economics* 380.

[84] N Goldschmidt and A Berndt, 'Leonhard Miksch (1901–1950): A Forgotten Member of the Freiburg School' (2005) 64(4) *American Journal of Economics and Sociology* 973, 977–78.

(i) what the significance of efficiency was for the drafters of the competition rules of the Treaty, and (ii) if the drafters were as closely associated with ordoliberalism as argued, since they had a *tabula rasa*, why they did not envisage a rule prohibiting the dominant position itself, but only its 'abuse'. Indeed, these two points will demonstrate the crucial differences between Article 102 and ordoliberalism, examination of which is left for section V. Fourthly, for ordoliberals, 'a duty to deal' or 'obligation to contract' had to be introduced for monopolists in order to achieve a result analogous to competition within the context of the *as if* standard.[85] As will be seen below, some remarks in the *travaux préparatoires* demonstrate that this idea was not totally shared by the German drafters of Article 102.[86] Moreover, the 'abuse' concept of Article 102 itself has been linked to the ordoliberal *as if* approach in the literature and this has been understood to mean that undertakings with market power were required to compete on the merits rather than 'abuse' their power to gain an unfair advantage over rivals.[87] However, as will be seen below, this is not the 'abuse' concept of the drafters of Article 102, since they were mainly concerned with the *trading partners* who dealt with the dominant undertakings, not their rivals.[88]

It must be made clear that if Article 102 is ordoliberal in its foundations, then it becomes questionable whether its objective can be the maximisation of 'consumer welfare' or any other welfare for that matter. As expressed by one of the scholars of the Freiburg School, American antitrust law currents which are directly based on wealth maximisation, on (Richard Posner's) constrained utilitarianism, on (Oliver Williamson's) trade-off and transaction costs approach, as well as property-rights doctrines (as far as these can be traced to the Kaldor-Hicks criterion) are incompatible with the ordoliberal system of values.[89] This is because ordoliberalism treats individuals as ends in themselves and not as the means of another's welfare.[90] This implies that no one's welfare could be preferred over or sacrificed for anyone else's welfare. The actual basis of ordoliberal competition is deduced from an appreciation of law and justice based on contract which is contrary to the various concepts of utilitarianism.[91] Thus, the problem is to find an economic system in which individuals are more than just a means to an end or just a tiny part of the machine.[92]

Interestingly, another ordoliberal, Lutz, has argued that welfare economics' finding – based on static assumptions – that monopolistic competition prevents an optimal allocation of the factors of production, loses its impact once the market is seen in dynamic terms.[93] According to him, the argument of welfare

[85] Eucken (n 64) 237, 243.
[86] See below, text around n 220.
[87] Gerber (n 1) 307.
[88] See below, text around n 244.
[89] Möschel (n 45) 149. For the 'Kaldor-Hicks' test, see ch 1 this volume, text to fn 14.
[90] Möschel, ibid.
[91] ibid 148.
[92] Eucken (n 50) 37.
[93] Lutz (n 60) 162.

economics loses weight 'because imperfect or monopolistic competition is probably more effective in raising living standards than perfect competition'.[94] However, it is not that clear what ordoliberals' general opinion of welfare maximisation was since Böhm – one of the founders of the School – has actually emphasised that consumer interests are the sole directly justifiable economic interests and that the essential function of competition is to 'place the entrepreneur's pursuit of profit in the direct service of the consumer'.[95]

Lutz's view therefore confuses one to the extent that it does not seem in total conformity with the hostility of ordoliberals towards monopolies – demonstrated specifically by Eucken's previous statements. Similarly, Böhm's argument begs the question of how consumer interests are to be served if the protection of economic freedom is the main objective of competition law. These different opinions may mean that ordoliberals were not completely unified in their approach towards monopolies and/or that their opinions evolved over time. It has indeed been pointed out in the literature that ordoliberal teachings do not constitute a completely standardised product; 'disagreement on matters of detail is common and that on more important questions is not rare'.[96] The diversity of views among ordoliberals has actually been interpreted as proof of them being 'liberal'.[97] However, this creates another problem for associating Article 102 with ordoliberalism: ordoliberal authors did not always share the same view on everything, including monopolies. In any case, it has rightly been argued that since pursuing 'economic freedom' does not always coincide with consumer welfare, a competition policy that protects economic freedom may in certain circumstances lead to consumer harm.[98] It is possible that ordoliberals were *against* monopolies and *for* all of those against the monopolies which would include not only the competitors and trading partners of the monopolies, but also consumers. As such, they may have failed to realise that the interests of the competitors and trading partners of monopolies might not always be aligned with the interests of consumers. A mechanism of differentiating consumer harm from competitor harm and a method to deal with this difference appear not to exist in the ordoliberal propositions.

Finally, it is noteworthy that – perhaps apart from Lutz – ordoliberals do not seem to acknowledge the incentives to compete and to become a monopoly as a spur to competition in dynamic terms. Rather the opposite; Eucken's 'complete competition' is – in his words – entirely different from the 'battle for a monopoly'.[99]

[94] ibid. According to Lutz, under certain circumstances a policy to combat monopolies is not necessary; ibid 163 and see above, n 60.

[95] F Böhm, 'The Non-State ("Natural") Laws Inherent in a Competitive Economy' in W Stützel et al (eds), *Standard Texts on the Social Market Economy* (Stuttgart, Gustav Fischer, 1982) 107, 109.

[96] HM Oliver, 'German Neoliberalism' (1960) 74(1) *The Quarterly Journal of Economics* 117, 117. For the argument that views of ordoliberals on monopolies differ, although predominantly they did not want to leave them to their own resources, see H Witkowski, *Zur Missbrauchsaufsicht über Preise marktbeherrschender Unternehmen* (Frankfurt, Peter Lang, 1981) 181–82. See also Mestmäcker (n 75) 42 noting that there were differences in opinion among individual ordoliberal scholars.

[97] Witkowski, ibid, 159.

[98] Ahlborn and Grave (n 63) 214.

[99] Eucken (n 64) 228.

According to him, complete competition has rightly been compared to a race; it is not a battle man-to-man, but a race run in parallel.[100] This 'race run in parallel' clearly demonstrates the ordoliberals' concern with not harming 'competitors' which is another reason why one might find ordoliberalism conflict with 'consumer welfare' since harming rivals may in certain circumstances result in benefits to consumers, for example, in the form of low prices. Therefore, if EU competition law would preferably serve efficiency more than other goals, then Article 102 interpreted from an ordoliberal viewpoint would not be an appropriate tool since that approach is not grounded in efficiency. Indeed, it has been argued that if 'welfare' is to be accepted as the goal of Article 102, then one must, for example, abandon the 'special responsibility' of dominant undertakings.[101]

The next section provides some historical insights from the period leading to the Treaties of Rome in order to critically analyse the ordoliberal influence argument and to put the competition rules in the correct historical context within which they belong.

IV INSIGHTS FROM THE PERIOD LEADING TO THE TREATIES OF ROME

A Germany

Given that the predominant argument in the literature is that EU competition rules have ordoliberal origins, Germany is a good starting point for the inquiry into the history of these rules. Unlike the US, where the organisation of capitalism since the late nineteenth century and the concentration movement led to the creation of trusts and an oligopolistic arrangement of the market, German industry moved in the direction of cartels and syndicates.[102] Thus, a high degree of cartelisation existed well before 1933 when the Hitler government issued a decree proclaiming the comprehensive introduction of cartels.[103] Although cartels were conceived at the time of the Great Depression of the 1870s as a protectionist measure against foreign competition, they had lost their raison d'être with the onset of the boom of the 1890s.[104] By this time, horizontal agreements had become such a well-established habit in many branches of the industry that some entrepreneurs could no longer imagine operating on the competitive principle.[105] However, nothing promoted and strengthened the cartel habit more than a

[100] ibid 229.

[101] C Ahlborn and AJ Padilla, 'From *Fairness* to *Welfare*: Implications for the Assessment of Unilateral Conduct under EC Competition Law' in CD Ehlermann and M Marquis (eds), *European Competition Law Annual 2007: A Reformed Approach to Article 82 EC* (Oxford, Hart Publishing, 2008) 57.

[102] Berghahn (n 62) 20.

[103] ibid.

[104] ibid.

[105] ibid.

decision of the German Supreme Court rendered in 1897 that found cartel agreements legally binding.[106] This was the *Saxon Wood Pulp* case in which the Court virtually equated 'public interest' with the general economic consequences of cartels and found that cartels were generally beneficial.[107] There existed around 700 cartels just before the First World War and in 1930 there were still over 3000 horizontal market agreements.[108]

At the end of the Second World War, for the Americans, the aim of the destruction of the Third Reich was synonymous with the idea of smashing those elements of Nazism which were not merely incompatible with American notions of political democracy but also with American notions of running a capitalist economy.[109] The German cartel system was indeed partly blamed for having produced developments which culminated in the notion of a Nazi closed-space economy as an alternative to the American 'open door' concept which reinforced Washington's determination to ban all horizontal agreements which limited competition.[110] These agreements were seen as dysfunctional to the liberal-capitalist world trading system envisaged by the US.[111] For the Allies in 1945, a central issue being the destruction of German war potential, at the very least industrial giants such as IG Farben had to be broken up.[112] Therefore, 'the demand that cartels be eradicated appears in all basic declarations concerning the structure of the postwar European economy which were drafted by Washington'.[113] Thus, *at the insistence of the Americans*, all German cartel agreements were declared null and void at the end of the Second World War and a strict ban was promulgated which imposed heavy penalties on violations of the ban.[114] In contrast, arguably neither the British nor the French shared the American aversion to cartels.[115]

Realising that Allied anti-cartel legislation would sooner or later have to be replaced by West German regulations, the *Verwaltung für Wirtschaft* (Administration for Economy) was urged to start from Chapter 5 of the Havana Charter when making their preparations for a German Bill.[116] The Havana Charter, which had been adopted in March 1948 and was part of the American attempt to establish a world trading system, recommended a liberalisation of world trade.[117] Referring to Article 46 of the Havana Charter relating to restrictive practices, the Stuttgart *Wirtschaftszeitung* apparently wrote at the time that '[t]hese principles of a future "global" economic order originate in the main from American legal and economic

[106] ibid 20–21.
[107] Gerber (n 1) 91, 92.
[108] Berghahn (n 62) 21.
[109] ibid 39.
[110] ibid 100–01.
[111] ibid 101.
[112] Gerber (n 1) 268.
[113] Berghahn (n 62) 101.
[114] ibid.
[115] ibid.
[116] ibid 157.
[117] ibid.

thought'.[118] The Charter urged the signatories to adopt anti-cartel legislation, but there was no similar suggestion to curb concentration.[119]

This was basically also Ludwig Erhard's view.[120] As early as 1946, Erhard – the then economics minister, later Chancellor – had criticised Allied decartelisation policy arguing that the policy gave the impression that it had the weakening of Germany industry as its sole aim.[121] Arguably, this was because '[o]nly large-scale enterprises would be able to compete successfully in this world market, and this is why Erhard also opposed in 1950 a far-reaching deconcentration of industry'.[122] Thus, cartel agreements and concentrations were seen differently from the beginning, regarding the national competition law in Germany. Concentrations were deemed to be *necessary* for the success of Germany on the world markets.

West Germany's industrial élites found it difficult after 1945 to abandon certain traditional forms of organisation and, aware of this German resistance, Americans were reluctant to hand over the implementation and supervision of decartelisation to the Germans.[123] Instead, they policed the ban on cartels.[124] Similarly, a circle of experts who emerged in the south completed a draft of a decartelisation law in 1947.[125] Thus, the impetus for enacting competition law came from two sources: (i) on the formal level, such a law was a requirement for the US occupation officials to return full sovereignty to the new German state;[126] and (ii) on the other level, the requirement was not that necessary, because all major political parties recognised the need for such legislation and supported the enactment of such a statute.[127]

Among the authors of the draft Bill were Franz Böhm, Walter Bauer and Bernhard Pfister, who had been meeting under the chairmanship of Paul Josten – the former head of the *Reichswirtschaftsministerium* (Ministry of Economics) Cartel Department.[128] Previous legislation – namely the 1923 Cartel Ordinance – had merely outlawed the 'abuse of power' exercised by cartels; the Josten committee set to work on legislation that would establish a general ban on cartels.[129] Yet, when the Josten circle submitted a draft to Erhard in 1949, the draft was filed away: the Josten draft had been overtaken by preceding events before it reached some kind of official status.[130] The draft contained a total ban on cartels, a proposal for a supervisory authority and empowering of the executive to split up

[118] ibid 101 referring to *Wirtschaftszeitung* (16 April 1949).
[119] ibid 157.
[120] ibid.
[121] ibid 157–58.
[122] ibid 159.
[123] ibid 155.
[124] ibid.
[125] ibid 156.
[126] Gerber (n 1) 270.
[127] ibid.
[128] Berghahn (n 62) 156.
[129] JC Van Hook, *Rebuilding Germany: The Creation of the Social Market Economy, 1945–1957* (Cambridge, CUP, 2004) 243.
[130] Berghahn (n 62) 156.

enterprises which had a dominant position.[131] This proposal does indeed seem to be an ordoliberal product, but as will be seen below, it has been ultimately *rejected* at the German level. Thus, the acceptance of similar ideas at the European level influenced by the German national model is unlikely as well. The fact that the European prohibition on dominant positions does not involve the requirement of splitting up the undertakings, but only a regulation of conduct, is the most basic evidence of this. It is also debatable how strong the ordoliberal influence could have been at the European level when it had not succeeded at the German level.

The counterproposal to the Josten Bill (offered by Günther, Risse and Sievert) which became the basis for the official government Bill of 1952, did not seek to criminalise economic power as such, but rather to prohibit 'unreasonable restrictions on trade'.[132] This meant that some arrangements, if proven to benefit the consumer, could be permitted and licensed by the envisioned cartel authority.[133] However, Erhard asked Günther and Risse to draft a Bill that maintained the general prohibition on cartels; to Erhard, maintaining the overall principle of prohibition represented the issue of cardinal importance.[134] Still, the government Bill was, as Gerber puts it, 'less consistently ordoliberal' than the Josten draft since industry representatives had achieved a number of important exemptions that 'significantly weakened' the draft.[135]

Over 20 drafts were considered after the Josten draft.[136] The efforts of Erhard and his supporters to elevate free competition to the core of the social market economy resulted in the much criticised anti-cartel law of 1957.[137] Despite calling for an outright prohibition of cartels, the law also included many exemptions that rendered it inadequate to combat the wave of reconcentration that characterised the West German economy during the late 1950s and early 1960s.[138]

The Americans placed great emphasis on both decartelisation and deconcentration of German industry, but as the Cold War developed, the need for Germany to contribute to European economy and defence outweighed the priority Americans had earlier attached to social reforms that could temporarily hinder an economic recovery.[139] Erhard and the social market economists took up where the Americans left off, but in time Erhard also had to face the criticism that such industrial reforms might forestall economic efficiency and growth.[140] Thus, Erhard eventually made important concessions at the behest of West Germany's federation of German industry which secured the passage of a weakened law in 1957.[141] Since Erhard repeatedly characterised a strong anti-cartel law as the

[131] ibid 156.
[132] Van Hook (n 129) 247–48.
[133] ibid 248.
[134] ibid 249.
[135] Gerber (n 1) 275.
[136] ibid 274.
[137] Van Hook (n 129) 233.
[138] ibid 233.
[139] ibid 234.
[140] ibid.
[141] ibid; Gerber (n 1) 276.

foundation of the social market economy, historians have concluded that the law, with its many exceptions, represented a *failure*.[142] Whatever real effect the anti-cartel law had, was therefore arguably due to American influences.[143] Thus, 'Germany did not differ much from cases such as France, The Netherlands and Italy, where [American] pressures had led to the proposal of antitrust legislation in 1947–1950'.[144]

It is important to emphasise the nuances in Erhard's attitude towards industrial organisation not only because it makes his rejection of the Josten draft more plausible, 'but also because it seems wise, more generally, not to see him as the "ordo-liberal" that he has often been portrayed as'.[145] Although his experiences in the Third Reich had turned him into an opponent of cartels, he was not a dogmatic economics professor or a purist neoliberal who disliked large-scale industry and had hankerings after the ideal of a *mittelständische* capitalism.[146] His close relation with his brother-in-law (Karl Guth) who belonged to the *Reichsgruppe Industrie* and with various prominent industrials during the Second World War, also makes it implausible that he saw himself as the executor of the ideas of Eucken and Röpke.[147] Arguably,

> [i]t seems rather more that there are quite a few striking affinities between his economic philosophy and the consumer-orientated ideology of competition and production cherished by the Americans. This would also seem to apply to Erhard's views on the question of accumulation of economic power. He was conscious of how concentration affected open competition; but he always hoped that it would be possible to contain these dangers through legislation and by setting a legal framework for the operation of a capitalist economy similar to that of the US. The task of the government was not a constant intervention into the economy but to introduce such a framework and to see to it subsequently that the market was not put out of action by a dense network of cartels and monopolies.[148]

It is worthwhile at this point mentioning the views of Erhard on the subject matter as expressed by himself. According to Erhard

> [t]he purpose of all economic activity is to meet consumer needs and thus to contribute to the well-being of the community. Since this purpose is inalienable and independent of passing phenomena and theories, it is only the means and methods to be used to this end that should really be discussed.[149]

[142] Van Hook, ibid, 288.
[143] See ibid 268 and sources cited there.
[144] Y Karagiannis, 'Preference Heterogeneity and Equilibrium Institutions: The Case of European Competition Policy' (PhD thesis, European University Institute, Florence, 2007) 187.
[145] Berghahn (n 62) 158, 159.
[146] ibid 158.
[147] ibid.
[148] ibid.
[149] L Erhard, 'Confusion of Thoughts on the Question of the Economic Order' Article in *Die Neue Zeitung* of 23 June 1947 in L Erhard, *The Economics of Success* (trans JA Arengo-Jones and DJS Thomson, London, Thames and Hudson, 1963) 11.

Moreover, as opposed to some ordoliberal comments on the market price, Erhard has noted that '[t]he market price, which is the only right one for the national economy, simply cannot be defined; it is the natural result of the equilibrium created by prices in a free market'.[150]

Interestingly, on the proposal that the German legislation on *cartels* adopts the 'abuse' principle, Erhard stated his views rather clearly, rejecting such a principle since in his words '[i]f we leave aside any criminal or moral offences, which must be punished in some other way, I would like to ask where, in the view of those who support this principle, abuse is to begin and end and by what criteria we are to judge abuse'.[151] This is because

> [a]buses lie not in the actions and behaviour of the cartels but in their very existence and derive from the fact that the establishment of a cartel limits and even kills competition and that, as soon as prices are fixed, they cease to perform their essential function as a sort of steering-wheel for the national economy.[152]

Thus, the implications of the developments in Germany for the EU competition rules can be described as follows. Germany might have had a different agenda at the EU negotiations than at home: the vague 'abuse' principle was obviously not a problem when it came to the prohibition of conduct by dominant undertakings at the EU level. One – if not the – plausible explanation for this can be that it was in the German *national* interest not to restrict the large German undertakings' conduct excessively at the *supranational* level. This also implies that direct inferences cannot be drawn from the national discussions of the cartel law in Germany for the position of the German delegation at the negotiations of the Treaties of Rome. Moreover, even at the German level, ordoliberalism which has arguably affected the EU rules due to their impact at the German level appears not to have been successful at the end of the day since the German Act Against Restraints of Competition (1957) is far from an ordoliberal product.[153] Therefore, it is unlikely that they will have been influential at the EU level because of an influence at the national level. That the EU competition rules do not reflect ordoliberalism will be further demonstrated by the findings in section V which rely on evidence from the negotiations of the Treaties of Rome. Before that, the next subsection will briefly examine the situation at the European level preceding the adoption of the Treaties of Rome.

[150] L Erhard, 'Ten Theses in Defence of the Anti-Cartel Legislation' 10 July 1952 in L Erhard, *The Economics of Success* (trans JA Arengo-Jones and DJS Thomson, London, Thames and Hudson, 1963) 133. For the contrasting view of Eucken, see above, text to n 82.

[151] L Erhard, 'The Aims of the Law Against Restrictions on Competition' speech in the German Federal Parliament, 24 March 1955 in L Erhard, *The Economics of Success* (trans JA Arengo-Jones and DJS Thomson, London, Thames and Hudson, 1963) 172–73.

[152] Erhard, ibid, 173.

[153] For the argument that efficiency arguments and consumer benefits were dominant in the discussions surrounding the adoption of the German Act and that the Act shows scarce traces of ordoliberal thought and no traces of neoliberal thought, see Maier-Rigaud (n 46) 15, 21.

B Europe

At this point, it should be noted that the negotiations of the Treaties of Rome had not been a smooth process, and to understand this period and the role of the actors in it, one should also have an understanding of the historical period leading up to it. The positions of the delegations negotiating the Treaty establishing the European Coal and Steel Community (ECSC Treaty) and the competition rules in that Treaty are directly relevant for putting Articles 101 and 102 in the appropriate context also because the former set of rules can be seen as the beginning of a tradition of competition in Europe that is continued by the latter.

By 1949 it became increasingly clear that efforts to integrate Europe at a political level kept running into major problems – the psychological and other obstacles to receiving the West Germans as equal partners so soon after the Second World War were too great.[154] However, it had also become clear by 1950 that western Germany was moving towards the resumption of an independent role in the comity of the free world and the German economy was reviving.[155] In these circumstances, economic integration appeared to be the only way forward.[156] The major step in this direction was the ECSC Treaty signed in Paris in 1951. The ECSC was seen by many of its supporters as part of larger plans for uniting Europe that were discussed seriously at the highest levels of government at the time.[157]

Proposed by the French foreign minister Robert Schuman, the ECSC aimed at pooling Franco-German coal and steel resources under a single High Authority.[158] Schuman's plan was a drastic change in the French policy towards Germany, but it was clear that France could not prevent the growth of a strong Germany and trying to delay that would weaken France's own position.[159] The plan was thus the new framework within which German development could proceed along channels that were more acceptable for France, but that also promised mutual benefits.[160] The plan was drafted by Jean Monnet and it represented an attempt to re-stabilise relations between France and Germany after the Second World War and to bind them within a limited framework of peaceful cooperation to prevent rivalry over coal production.[161] The aim was to create a common market for iron, steel and coal in Western Europe by removing all the customs duties, tariffs, quotas and other market restrictions.[162] On the French side, the stimulus was the

[154] Berghahn (n 62) 109.

[155] W Diebold, *The Schuman Plan: A Study in Economic Cooperation 1950–1959* (New York, Council of Foreign Relations, 1959) 9–10.

[156] Berghahn (n 62) 109.

[157] Gerber (n 1) 335–36.

[158] P Craig and G de Burca, *EU Law: Text, Cases and Materials* 4th edn (Oxford, OUP, 2008) 5.

[159] Diebold (n 155) 11.

[160] ibid 11–12.

[161] Craig and de Burca (n 158) 5.

[162] J Goyder and A Albors-Llorens, *Goyder's EC Competition Law* 5th edn (Oxford, OUP, 2009) 26.

traditional feeling of weakness vis-à-vis the West German industrial potential.[163] In fact, arguably it is 'an unquestionable fact that, together with the [US] Treasury and Justice Departments, France was among the very few active promoters of the de-cartelisation and de-concentration of German industry'.[164] Approval comes from Erhard indeed according to whom '[n]ot the least of the factors that will contribute to a fruitful development of German industry is the practical efficiency of larger and freer markets, such as are inherent in all European plans'.[165] This is in conformity with the view above,[166] namely that it was in the German interest not to restrict their undertakings excessively at the European level, making the vague 'abuse' prohibition acceptable, perhaps even desirable when it came to competition rules.

The ECSC included the governments of France, Germany, Italy and the Benelux. The Treaty included provisions on competition, including one regulating mergers (Articles 65 and 66 ECSC). Interestingly, Article 4 ECSC prohibited 'exploitation' of consumers and – to this author's knowledge – this is the first prohibition of exploitation at the European level in competition rules. The competition provisions of the ECSC Treaty were arguably heavily tilted towards the American position but retained an element of the European tradition.[167] Thus, Washington was concerned to reduce French fears of the rapidly unfolding German industrial potential by partial deconcentration.[168] Yet, at the same time, they tried to ensure that the newly-created undertakings were large and viable enough to act as motors of European productivity and European competition within an open system.[169] It has in fact been claimed that the ECSC competition provisions were drafted by a US antitrust professor from Harvard, namely Robert Bowie, on a request by Jean Monnet.[170] It has also been pointed out that

> many of the Founding Fathers of Europe were in some way or another influenced by the American antitrust experience. Some, such as Jean Monnet and Ludwig Erhard, were directly and willingly advised by American lawyers and officials. Others, like Robert Schuman and Konrad Adenauer, had to take into account [US] preferences for a competitive political-economic order. Still others, such as Robert Marjolin and Hans von der Groeben, had a thorough knowledge of American history and policies . . . Though it is impossible to be certain about what European politicians actually thought about [US] antitrust, a few points must have been obvious to them.[171]

[163] Berghahn (n 62) 111–12.
[164] Karagiannis (n 144) 179.
[165] Erhard (n 150) 136.
[166] See above, text after n 152.
[167] Berghahn (n 62) 148–49. See also Gerber (n 1) 338.
[168] Berghahn, ibid, 149.
[169] ibid.
[170] Gerber (n 1) 338 and for an interview with Robert Bowie on this, see F Duchêne, 'Robert R Bowie, Interview with F Duchêne, Washington, 12 May 1987' Historical Archives of the European Union available at: www.eui.eu/HAEU/OralHistory/pdf/INT490.pdf.
[171] Karagiannis (n 144) 149.

It was indeed Jean Monnet who proposed the anti-cartel rule and Monnet called for a strong competition law because it was necessary to achieve the broader integration goals of the Community whose appeal was also useful to help convince the French that German companies would not acquire too much power.[172] Thus, the proposal for the first set of competition rules at the supranational European level emanated from the French, not the (arguably) ordoliberal Germans. The position of Bowie drafting the rules created an *incentive* for Germany to enter the ECSC as well, since the Americans had agreed to give up on their regulatory competence over the German iron and steel industry if the ECSC became a reality.[173] One commentator also notes that '[i]t was an open secret that the group at the American embassy in Paris run by Tommy Tomlinson and supervised by Ambassador David Bruce had been acting as Monnet's personal staff in matters relating to the anti-cartel and anti-concentration provisions of the draft treaty'.[174] Thus, not only were the French the source of the proposal for competition rules, there was also significant American influence on the substance of the provisions. Germans seem to have been at the receiving end of all this rather than behind it.

Indeed, some authors have already noted this and its implications. For example, according to Karagiannis, the story of the negotiations of the ECSC Treaty shows that European competition policy did *not* emanate from Germany, but from the French *Commissariat Général du Plan*.[175] Moreover, Monnet's proposal was not based on any kind of French antitrust tradition, but on France's pressing need to secure continuing control of the Ruhr once the Americans left.[176] Germany was actually reluctant to accept Monnet's proposals as evidenced by the near breakdown of the Paris negotiations towards the end of 1950 and the beginning of 1951.[177] In fact, it was Monnet who lobbied vigorously for the adoption of a memorandum proposing pro-competitive measures including the prohibition of cartel agreements, while the German plan was to preserve the existing structure of the relevant market insofar as possible and the six big German producers which faced reorganisation were given the promise of cooperation of the federal government in implementing the plan.[178] Arguably, Monnet's memorandum of 28 September 1950 was met with angry comments on all sides, although all Monnet was trying to do was to attempt to apply the equitable trade principles of the Havana Charter.[179] Moreover, the Germans were particularly upset since the anti-cartel

[172] Gerber (n 1) 337–38. See also interview with George Ball confirming that it was Jean Monnet; F Duchêne, 'George Ball, Under-Secretary of State in the Kennedy and Johnson Administrations, Interview with F Duchêne, Library Place, Princeton, 10 August 1987' Historical Archives of the European Union available at: www.eui.eu/HAEU/OralHistory/pdf/INT488.pdf.

[173] Gerber (n 1) 338.

[174] J Gillingham, *Coal, Steel, and the Rebirth of Europe, 1945–1955* (Cambridge, CUP, 1991) 259.

[175] Karagiannis (n 144) 212.

[176] ibid.

[177] ibid. See also Gillingham (n 174) 266, 269.

[178] Gillingham, ibid, 258, 259.

[179] ibid 259.

and anti-concentration provisions were directed merely against them as it was only the German companies in the Ruhr that were privately owned of all the negotiating states' companies.[180] Karagiannis has thus suggested that the competition proposals did not result from the existence of or operate like a focal point; they actually polarised the negotiations to the point of almost causing an early end to the process of European integration.[181] Perhaps even more importantly for the argument that any German influence was of an ordoliberal nature, it has indeed been noted that the German draft for the ECSC Treaty deliberately precluded the High Authority from exercising social responsibilities and emphasised that the primary function of the High Authority would be the promotion of *efficiency*.[182]

Diebold has also argued that there had been serious disagreements on the subject of cartels and the different schools of thought about how to deal with them cut across national lines.[183] More importantly, the failure to agree was due to a more fundamental difficulty in that there were doubts about German willingness to accept the Treaty at all and the French insisted on certain measures as conditions before it entered into an agreement with the Germans.[184] Diebold in fact argues that the competition provision was left blank when the draft Treaty was turned over to the governments since the issues called for diplomacy on a greater scale than the other questions affecting the Treaty.[185]

It is worth noting that although Gerber claims that France at the time had no significant competition law,[186] Karagiannis argues that like other European countries, France

> had an old arsenal of laws and judicial decisions that could have been used to protect competition. In particular, the Law of March 2 (17), 1791 abolished the corporatist industrial organisation of the *Ancien Régime* and established legally protected freedom of trade and industry (ie freedom of entry into markets).[187]

This conceptualisation of competition indeed sounds similar to the German view at the time, and would imply that the ordoliberal position was not uniquely German. Moreover, according to Karagiannis,

> [t]he Law of May 4, 1793 'on maximum prices' fixed the maximum price of a long series of goods, against the eventuality of abusive, monopolistic pricing. The Law of July 26, 1793 'contre les accapareurs' even went as far as to threaten offenders with the penalty of death. With less severe penalties, that law went on to become Articles 419 and 420 of the Code Pénal of 1810, which outlawed price-fixing agreements.[188]

[180] ibid 268.
[181] Karagiannis (n 144) 213.
[182] Gillingham (n 174) 241.
[183] Diebold (n 155) 67.
[184] ibid 67.
[185] ibid 66, 67.
[186] Gerber (n 1) 185, 193, 338.
[187] Karagiannis (n 144) 168.
[188] ibid 168.

Among other things, this suggests that the prohibition of 'unfair pricing' in Article 102 might be the result of French influence more than or as much as of German influence. Moreover, it thus appears that France did have laws against distortions of competition and arguably '[re]garding abusive cartels, the French courts adopted consistently an effects-based test, with particular emphasis on consumer welfare'.[189] In fact, it has been suggested that the above-mentioned 1923 Cartel Ordinance which in Germany had established a system for controlling abusive pricing was very hard to implement and can hardly be considered as the origin of any kind of competition policy tradition.[190] In fact, it has been noted that there was no general acceptance of the idea that competition was good and cartels and concentrations were bad in Germany; people of a wide range of political opinions agreed that markets should be organised for stability and efficiency rather than be left to the chaos of atomistic competition.[191]

Importantly, the dominant view that the emergence of a European competition policy reflected German ordoliberal preferences ignores Monnet's fight for the insertion of Articles 65 and 66 in the ECSC Treaty and Monnet's 1952 declaration according to which the Treaty, which is the first European competition law, has a mandate to dissolve cartels, prohibit restrictive practices and prevent undue concentration of economic power.[192] It also ignores the fact that Germany used all its formal and informal power to *block* the implementation of the ECSC competition rules and the adoption of the Article 66 Regulations.[193] Karagiannis thus concludes that 'strong German and weak French preferences for competition policy is as common an assumption as it is unjustified'.[194] Diebold also argues that the Germans had all along *opposed* and to some degree *resisted* deconcentration and decartelisation.[195] Another commentator notes that Adenauer, the German chancellor, decided not to get involved in a war of words over the competition rules of the draft Treaty since 'he recognized that on the terrain of ideology the Germans would continue to lose until Americans had learned to love cartels'.[196] Strikingly, it has been argued that in January 1951, Hallstein – representing Germany in the negotiations – told Monnet that the Federal Republic could not accept the Treaty as written and would sign only under protest that the clauses on deconcentration and decartelisation had been *imposed*, rather than freely negotiated.[197] This was indeed the event that brought the negotiations to the verge of a complete breakdown and shows clearly that is was *not* the Germans striving to insert competition rules into the Treaty. In fact, it was only the American threat of imposing their

[189] ibid.
[190] ibid 174. For the Ordinance see above, text around n 129.
[191] Diebold (n 155) 351.
[192] Karagiannis (n 144) 223.
[193] ibid 224.
[194] ibid.
[195] Diebold (n 155) 73.
[196] Gillingham (n 174) 271.
[197] ibid 275.

own decartelisation scheme that made the Germans finally agree to the Treaty.[198] The following section examines the actual negotiations and the drafting history of the competition provisions of the Treaties of Rome to provide further insights and put the competition rules into the correct context.

V THE HIGHLIGHTS OF THE HISTORY OF THE COMPETITION RULES IN THE TREATIES OF ROME[199]

A Back to Basics: From Messina to the 'Spaak Report'

The Messina Conference was the first step taken to widen the scope of the European integration which had been initiated with the creation of the ECSC. The conference of the foreign ministers of the six founding states – France, Germany, Italy and Benelux ('the Six') – in Messina in June 1955 resulted in the Messina declaration according to which the formation of a common European market without customs and quantitative restrictions was the aim of the Six in the realm of economic policy.[200] They considered that the accomplishment of this market required the study of certain matters among which 'the development of rules for the protection of free competition within the Common Market, especially for the elimination of all forms of nationality-based discrimination' was counted. Hence, the protection of competition was given primary importance from the early days of action.

After Messina and another conference, in Noordwijk, the foreign ministers of the Six held another meeting in Brussels in February 1956. The minutes of this conference include an exposé by Paul-Henri Spaak and a discussion of the findings of the Intergovernmental Committee which was appointed at the Messina Conference to prepare the future conferences and draft the Treaties.[201] According

[198] ibid 280.

[199] Except for subsection F, this section mainly relies on the author's previous publication: P Akman, 'Searching for the Long-Lost Soul of Article 82EC' (2009) 29(2) *Oxford Journal of Legal Studies* 267. The research in this section is mainly based on a special archival fond on the negotiations of the Treaties of Rome at the Historical Archives of the EU in Florence. The fond, entitled 'CM3/NEGO', covers the negotiations period of 1955–57 and consists of 418 dossiers, comprising 815 microfiches. However, the research was not limited to this period or this fond. The original language of the documents studied was mainly German and on a few occasions French. All translations are the author's own. As far as she is aware, the author has covered all the documents in German in fond CM3/NEGO.

[200] *Tagung der Aussenminister der Mitgliedstaaten der Montangemeinschaft, Entschliessung der Aussenminister der Mitgliedstaaten der Montangemeinschaft anlässlich ihrer Tagung in Messina am 1 und 2 Juni 1955* (Meeting of the Foreign Ministers of the Member States of the ECSC, Resolution of the Foreign Ministers of the Member States of the ECSC on the occasion of their Meeting in Messina on 1–2 June 1955).

[201] According to the Messina declaration, the Intergovernmental Committee was to consist of government delegates assisted by experts under the chairmanship of a leading political figure. This figure was chosen to be Paul-Henri Spaak of Belgium. Under the Intergovernmental Committee, specialised Working Groups were formed to conduct the drafting of the provisions.

to these minutes, the goal of a common market was to achieve the optimal growth of production facilities through the use of the most advanced methods of which the rival countries that already possessed a large market availed themselves.[202] As such, it is striking that from early on, the drafters of the Treaty had in mind an idea close to what one could today call 'productive efficiency' as the goal of the common market. This is not surprising, however, as will be seen more clearly from the concerns expressed in the 'Spaak Report'.

B The 'Spaak Report'

i An Overview

As one of the first steps to the drafting of the Treaties, the Heads of Delegations (chaired by Spaak) prepared a report which comprised a programme they unanimously recommended to the governments.[203] According to some commentators, the 'Spaak Report' is a seminal document and the most important of the various *travaux préparatoires* on which the subsequent Treaties of Rome are based.[204]

The Spaak Report explained the situation of Europe very clearly:

> While on the one hand the United States, in almost every sector, are producing one-half of the world's goods, and on the other the Communist countries, numbering a third of the world population, are increasing their production annually by ten or fifteen per cent, Europe, which once had a monopoly in the manufacturing industries and could count on its overseas possessions for considerable resources, now finds its external position weakening, its influence declining and its capacity for progress diminished by internal divisions.[205]

The concerns that ultimately led to the need for integration and creation of the European Communities became even more obvious as the Report went on:

> The expansion which has undoubtedly taken place in the last few years leaves no room for complacency. It is largely due to the rapid adoption of production techniques which until recently could not, owing to circumstances be developed in Europe. In its present economic state, Europe cannot maintain this rate of expansion by its own resources. . . . [S]triking examples could be quoted of the effect of the division of European markets seen in relation to the potentialities of the modern world. There is not a single motor-car factory in Europe large enough to use on an economic basis the most

[202] *Entwurf des Protokolls der Konferenz der Aussenminister der Mitgliedstaaten der E.G.K.S. (Brüssel, den 11 und 12 Februar 1956) Exposé der Präsidenten und Erörterung der Arbeitsergebnisse des von der Messina-Konferenz eingesetzten Regierungsausschuss* (Draft Protocol of the Conference of the Foreign Ministers of the Member States of the ESCS, 11–12 February 1956, Brussels, Exposé of the President and Discussion of the Work of the Intergovernmental Committee appointed at the Messina Conference) 11.

[203] Intergovernmental Committee of the Messina Conference, 'Report by the Heads of Delegations to the Foreign Ministers' ('Spaak Report') 21 April 1956 (Provisional English Text) 6. Although the report is called the 'Spaak Report', it was actually authored by Hans von der Groeben, Pierre Uri and Albert Hupperts.

[204] Goyder and Albors-Llorens (n 162) 32.

[205] Spaak Report (n 203) 5.

> powerful American machine-tools. No country in continental Europe can build heavy transport aircraft without outside help.[206]

Although these paragraphs are not concerned with competition policy, they are nonetheless very important as they set the scene for what is to follow and demonstrate clearly why the Six are there, apart from the obvious aim of avoiding war: they are there because more than ten years after the Second World War, Europe's economy is still falling behind that of the US and the USSR, and no country in Europe is able to compete on its own.

The authors of the Spaak Report seem also to have been aware that the creation of the common market alone will not solve all the problems. They realised that in the economic conditions of the time, broader markets and more open competition would not alone suffice to ensure the most rational distribution of activities and the optimum rate of economic expansion.[207] It was therefore desirable to consider what steps should be taken to ensure that the merging of the markets would lead to the most rational distribution of activity, a general raising of the standard of living and a more rapid rate of expansion.[208] The policy for the common market – which included competition rules – was to serve these ends by providing the legal framework. Although the first and the last of these ends can be expressed as 'efficiency' in economic terms, it is not that easy to identify the second, namely 'raising the standard of living', with 'consumer welfare' as it may as well refer to 'total welfare' (and thus include also the welfare of producers). This will be discussed further in section VI.

ii The Common Market and the Goal of Efficiency

According to the Spaak Report, the purpose of a European common market was to create a large area committed to a common economic policy, constituting a powerful complex of industries and ensuring a continual gain in economic strength and stability, a more rapid rise in living standards and the development of harmonious relations between its component states.[209] To achieve these aims, the markets should be merged, since in this way, by more extensive division of labour, it would be possible to *avoid wasteful use of resources* and, by greater certainty of supplies, do away with *production at uneconomic costs.* The common market would give full play to the *efficiency* of management and men; the pooling of resources will ensure equality of opportunity.

As is obvious from the emphasised parts of the above remarks, for the drafters, efficiency was indeed important and the aim of the whole common market project was to avoid wasteful use of resources and do away with production at uneconomic costs. It is clear that the drafters were well aware of the cause of the problem as the wasteful use of resources (in the context of labour) and production at

[206] ibid 5.
[207] ibid 10.
[208] ibid 43.
[209] ibid 8.

uneconomic costs (namely, productive inefficiency), and the solution envisaged was increased efficiency. Furthermore, it was realised that in many industrial sectors, national markets did not allow firms to develop to their *optimum size* unless they enjoyed a virtual monopoly.[210] Thus, the advantage of a wider market was seen as making large-scale production possible without the necessity for monopoly. By combining markets, large enough outlets that permitted the use of the most advanced production techniques could be created. Put in economic terms, this shows the concern of the drafters with the national firms' not being able to reach the 'minimum *efficient* scale' of production.[211]

Moreover, it is explicitly stated in the Report that in a wider market, it would no longer be possible to maintain outmoded methods of production with their twofold effects of high prices and low wages; commercial trusts, instead of remaining static would have to pursue a dynamic investment policy in order to step up production, improve quality and modernise their methods: they had to make progress or fail.[212]

Thus, not only were the drafters concerned about the productive inefficiency of the commercial trusts of the time for their consequences of *high prices* and *low wages*, they were also aware of 'dynamic efficiency' and its requirements. First, this points out that the trusts were condemned for their *productive inefficiency*, namely the 'quiet monopoly life' which led to high prices and low wages due to outmoded methods of competition. Secondly, unlike the arguments that were made concerning the legislative history of the US Sherman Act,[213] monopolies were *not* condemned for the extortionate profits they earned at the expense of consumers or for stealing consumers' wealth. This could have been because if their production costs were so high as to cause productive inefficiency, then they might not have been making extortionate profits; their high costs would have reduced both producer and consumer surplus. Thus, this leaves unanswered the question of what the stance of the drafters would be on monopolies which were productively efficient but did not pass on the efficiency benefits to the consumers. This will be returned to in section VI.

Thirdly, although there is mention of high prices, which can be taken as a reference to 'allocative inefficiency', since this was expressed as a result of high production costs, the general problem with monopolies in the Spaak Report appears to have been their productive inefficiency, rather than their allocative inefficiency. Finally, the concern with high prices and low wages does not totally reflect the ordoliberal approach since the ordoliberals contemplated the instance of workers

[210] ibid 8.

[211] There are 'economies of scale' when unit costs of production fall with the total quantity produced; Motta (n 28) 2. 'Minimum efficient scale' refers to the lowest output at which all scale economies are achieved; D Begg, S Fischer and R Dornbusch, *Foundations of Economics* 2nd edn (Maidenhead, McGraw-Hill, 2003) 47.

[212] Spaak Report (n 203) 8.

[213] See RH Lande, 'Wealth Transfers as the Original and Primary Concern of Antitrust: The Efficiency Interpretation Challenged' (1982) 34 *Hastings Law Journal* 65, 88, 93, 94 and RH Bork, 'Legislative Intent and the Policy of the Sherman Act' (1966) 9 *Journal of Law and Economics* 7, 11.

having 'just as strong an interest in the monopoly . . . as the entrepreneur' and possibly agreeing to higher prices so long as wages were increased.[214] Thus, ordoliberals did not see the interests of consumers as identical or always in conformity with the interests of workers.

iii The Problem of Monopolies

Regarding monopolies, the Spaak Report first drew attention to discrimination and suggested that action against discrimination would have to be included in the measures taken to preclude the *creation* of monopolies within the market.[215] The Treaty should contain general provisions ensuring that monopoly positions *or* abusive practices did not lead to frustration of the common market. In this connection, steps should be taken to prevent: (i) any distribution of markets by agreement among enterprises since this would be tantamount to setting up cartels; (ii) agreements to restrict production or limit technical progress since such agreements would run counter to efforts to bring about greater productivity; and (iii) monopoly or partial domination of the market for a product by a single enterprise since this would do away with one of the essential advantages of a large market, namely that of reconciling the use of mass production methods and the maintenance of competition.[216]

Apart from the similarity between these suggestions and the final versions of Articles 101 and 102, it is noteworthy that the Spaak Report suggested measures to preclude the *creation* of monopolies and *domination* of the market by a single enterprise. Moreover, provisions were recommended to ensure that monopoly positions *or* abusive practices did not frustrate the market.[217] From these expressions, at first glance, it appears that the recommendation was actually the prohibition of *domination* of a market per se. Such an approach would be much closer to ordoliberalism than a provision merely prohibiting 'abuse' of a dominant position. However, in the same section on monopolies, concerning discrimination it is stated that after the complete removal of obstacles to trade at the final stage of the transition period, discrimination would be possible only where supply undertakings enjoyed a monopoly position.[218] From this one can infer that the authors of the Report envisaged the creation of monopoly situations and allowed for it, since if they had actually intended to prohibit the domination of the market, they would not have also prohibited certain conduct (ie, discrimination) by monopolists.

Finally, the Report recognised that competition was not a sphere in which general solutions could be laid down from the outset for all cases likely to arise.[219] One

[214] Eucken (n 64) 240.
[215] Spaak Report (n 203) 44.
[216] ibid 45.
[217] The consequent counting of the steps in terms of 'agreements' versus 'monopoly or partial domination' gives one the impression that what is meant by 'abusive practices' is the *agreements* between enterprises that restrict competition and not the practices of monopolies.
[218] Spaak Report (n 203) 44.
[219] ibid 46.

particular caveat made was that no attempt should be made to lay down hard-and-fast rules concerning acceptance or refusal of orders or dates of delivery, any more than buyers could be expected to increase their demand and give up their traditional commercial relations. In other words, no 'duty to deal' was to be envisaged unlike the ordoliberal suggestion mentioned above and some subsequent EU court decisions.[220] All in all, it is unclear from this section on monopolies in the Spaak Report what exactly was recommended to the foreign ministers. Perhaps one can interpret this as the first sign of the tension surrounding the competition rules which were to be subject to fierce negotiations in the following stages.

iv 'Fair' Competition

The Spaak Report also referred to 'fair competition': ensuring that undertakings observe the rules of 'fair competition' was one of the practical measures necessary for the establishment and operation of the common market.[221] Moreover, it was argued that in the interests of *producers* themselves and in order to afford them the necessary security, there had to be some direct method of enforcing the rules of 'fair competition'.

This reference to 'fair competition' can be understood in one of two ways. Either it can be interpreted as meaning competition 'fair' to competitors; namely, the opposite of 'unfair competition' which was already regulated in, for example, Germany at the time and thus may be seen as the reflection of ordoliberalism.[222] Alternatively, it can be interpreted within the context of the preceding paragraphs and their emphasis on 'efficiency' and be understood as competition based on the efficiency of undertakings. What is valid in both cases is that this 'fair competition' is deemed necessary in the interests of producers themselves to afford them the necessary security. It is clear that producers would include any producer including monopolies and would *not* include consumers.

The recommendation of the Report was that there be *direct* enforcement of the rules of 'fair competition' and, for that, an organ be created with powers independent from the governments responsible to the whole group.[223] Indeed, later in the Report it is explicitly stated that

[220] See above, text to n 86. For cases where a duty to deal has been imposed on dominant undertakings see, eg, Cases 6 and 7/73 *Istituto Chemioterapico Italiano Spa and Commercial Solvents Corp v Commission* [1974] ECR 223; Case 27/76 *United Brands Co and United Brands Continental BV v Commission* [1978] ECR 207.

[221] Spaak Report (n 203) 17.

[222] 'Unfair competition' law deals with conduct between competitors and seeks to prevent dishonest and fraudulent rivalry in trade and commerce and the emphasis is on the prevention of 'unfair' behaviour by market participants in trade; RW de Vrey, *Towards a European Unfair Competition Law* (Leiden, Martinus Nijhoff Publishers, 2006) 2–3.

[223] See Spaak Report (n 203) 17 where it is stated that '[i]n view of the need for rapid inspection and prompt decisions, the roundabout procedure adopted in intergovernmental relations or organisations would not meet the case. Moreover, it is difficult to see how supervision over the fulfilment of obligations, or the application of saving clauses could be subject to a vote by the governments . . . For both these reasons it appears indispensable to create an organ with independent powers responsible to the whole group'.

> [o]ne of the essential guarantees which must be given to enterprises is that there will be no unfair competition as a result of artificial advantages being given to their competitors. Any assistance given by governments must therefore be very closely examined. . . . As a general rule, whatever form assistance may take, it will be incompatible with a common market if it is prejudicial to fair competition and the distribution of activity by favouring particular enterprises or branches of production.[224]

Thus, it is quite clear that 'fair competition' in the Spaak Report was not about competition conducted in fairness to 'competitors', but referred to undertakings not being disadvantaged in competition due to certain advantages given to their competitors by their governments.Thus, the main concern was 'state aid' by governments which could hamper competition. This implies that the 'fairness' element of competition meant lack of distortion of competition between undertakings that could result from the granting of advantages by the State.

C Drafting of the Competition Rules

After the Spaak Report, the drafting of the competition rules was subject to fierce negotiations with numerous different versions of the provisions going back and forth between delegations.[225] It is probably fair to say that the two extreme positions were those of Germany and France with the other four located in between them, usually closer to one or the other.

In the first draft of the competition rules after the Spaak Report that the author was able to detect, the rules for undertakings consisted of two paragraphs: one on the prohibition of discrimination and the other on monopolies.[226] The rule on monopolies read:

> Paragraph 2 Monopolies
>
> Insofar as trade between Member States can be affected, incompatible with the common market are:
>
> 1. The differential treatment of sellers or buyers who compete with one another, when setting prices or conditions for similar transactions, as a result of agreements or

[224] ibid 46–47.

[225] The bulk of the negotiations of the Treaties was carried out from the base – the meetings of the specialised working groups – to the top – the meetings of the heads of delegations and the ministers of foreign affairs, so that very little was ultimately left for the ministers to negotiate; A Bredimas, *Methods of Interpretation and Community Law* (Amsterdam, North-Holland Publishing, 1978) 58. Hence, although the working groups are not the 'legislator' in the usual sense since as a matter of fact they have formulated the provisions, their intent effectively reflects the legislative intent. As far as this author is aware, Art 102 has been adopted identically as drafted by the Common Market Group.

[226] One of the peculiarities of the negotiations was the drafting of a separate provision on discrimination which was to be one of the rules for undertakings apart from the prohibition of cartels and (abuse of) dominant positions. It appears that some of the most intense discussions were related to this provision with Germany arguing against such a prohibition and France arguing for it. The development of the discrimination provision will not be examined in detail here as it is outside the scope of this study.

under the use of a dominant position, if a disadvantage accrues to them by way of this in comparison with their rivals.

2. The monopolies or abusive practices of the following type:
   a division of markets through agreements between undertakings,
   b agreements which aim at the restriction of production or limitation of technical progress,
   c the full or partial domination of a product market by a single undertaking (1).

. . .

(1) The question arises, whether the case under (c) must be the subject of a specific test, since here it is not a matter of abusive practices but plainly of an existing position.[227]

The similarity of this first version with the recommendations of the Spaak Report is obvious and the question whether to prohibit the dominant position itself or the abuse of it arose as well. Thus, the prohibition of a dominant position *per se* rather than its abuse had been envisaged at the beginning of the negotiations, but was subsequently rejected.

It is understood from the minutes of one meeting of the Common Market Group that, during the negotiations, whereas the German delegation suggested differential treatment of agreements and monopolies, the French delegation proposed that they be subject to the same test.[228] Thus, the French version of the article found incompatible with the common market all cartels, monopolies and abusive practices which had the object of hindering competition or could have this result.[229] The German delegation's suggestion was that an outright prohibition should *not* be adopted for monopolies and oligopolies; rather, they should be subject to the control of abuse.[230]

In another meeting of the Common Market Group during which the draft competition provisions were further discussed, the German representative Alfred

[227] *Regierungskonferenz für den Gemeinsamen Markt und Euratom Brüssel, den 7. Juli 1956 Mar. Com. 4 (rev) Entwurf von Artikeln für die Ausarbeitung eines Vertrages über die Gründung eines Gemeinsamen Europäischen Marktes* (Intergovernmental Conference for the Common Market and EURATOM, 7 July 1956, Draft Articles for the Preparation of a Treaty on the Foundation of a Common European Market) *(MAE 153 d/56 hn)* 4. The omitted parts of this provision are not relevant for this study since they relate to the procedure concerning the application of the provision.

[228] *Extrait du procès-verbal des réunions des 3–5 septembre 1956 du Groupe du marché commun de la conference intergouvernementale pour le marché commun et l'euratom (MAE 252/56), Premiere lecture des articles 40 a 43 du projet d'articles (Doc.Mar.Com. 17)* (Extract of the Minutes of the Meetings of Common Market Group of the Intergovernmental Conference for the Common Market and EURATOM on 3–4 September 1956, Premier Reading of Articles 40 to 43 of the Draft Articles). At the time, the draft arts of the Treaty relating to competition were numbered from Art 40 to Art 43. The single provision envisaged by the French delegation regulating both cartels and monopolies, also included an exemption clause from the prohibition for individual instances.

[229] *Regierungskonferenz für den Gemeinsamen Markt und Euratom, Brüssel, den 4. September 1956 Mar. Com. 37 Arbeitsgruppe für den Gemeinsamen Markt, Bestimmungen, die den Artikel 42 des Dokuments Mar.Com.17 ersetzen, Vorschlag der französischen Delegation* (Intergovernmental Conference for the Common Market and EURATOM, 4 September 1956, Common Market Group, Rules to replace Article 42 of Document Mar.Com.17, the Proposal of the French Delegation).

[230] Premier Reading of Arts 40 to 43 of the draft Articles (n 228) 3.

Müller-Armack (associated with ordoliberalism by some),[231] drew attention to the fact that a too detailed and too rigid regulation of the mode of competition could have the consequence of removing all competition.[232] Accordingly, competition itself was not the consequence of a very complicated legal discipline nor could it only be ensured by law. On the contrary, the most immediate and direct source of competition lay in the fact of a very vast market. On the issue of monopolies, Müller-Armack went even further: after declaring that it was necessary to distinguish clearly between monopolies and oligopolies on one side and the cartels on the other, he argued that monopolies and oligopolies were *not* necessarily incompatible with a system of competition.[233] It was necessary to remove not the monopolies themselves, but the abuses to which certain monopolistic situations could lead.[234] To this end, he proposed the deletion or at least revision of the subparagraph of the draft provision prohibiting 'the full or partial domination of a product market by a single undertaking'.[235]

Therefore, it was an arguably ordoliberal German who argued against the prohibition of dominance per se and proposed that merely *abuse* be prohibited. He did *not* defend the ordoliberal view that monopolies are inherently harmful to competition and should be prohibited as such. It was the French delegation that asked for a prohibition of monopolies identical to that of cartels. The proposal of Müller-Armack was opposed by the Italian and (to a stronger extent) French delegations. Indeed, the representative of France – Donnedieu de Vabres – replied to Müller-Armack by stating that it was inconceivable for him to separate the system relating to the monopolies from that relating to cartels.[236] In any event, he noted that they were ready to study the proposal of the German delegation as soon as he knew their notion of 'abuse'.[237]

A synoptic table of the draft articles found in the *travaux préparatoires* clearly shows the positions of the delegations. The French and the Belgo-Dutch drafts treated agreements and monopolies on the same footing; the French draft banned both in principle while the Belgo-Dutch text subjected both to the control of

[231] He was a professor of economics and founder of the term 'social market economy'. It has been argued that although authors such as Müller-Armack shared important common ground with ordoliberals, there also existed certain differences between them, especially regarding the 'social market economy' of Müller-Armack; see VJ Vanberg, 'The Freiburg School: Walter Eucken and Ordoliberalism', Walter Eucken Institut, Freiburg Discussion Papers on Constitutional Economics 04/11, 2.

[232] *Secretariat Mémento interne Groupe du Marché Commun 3 et 4 septembre 1956 Fascicule 5 Bruxelles, 7 septembre 1956* (Internal Memorandum of the Common Market Group, 3–4 September 1956, Fascicule 5, Brussels, 7 September 1956). In the introduction, it is stated that the President of the Common Market Group summarised the decisions of the Committee of the Chiefs of Delegation which are relevant for the Common Market Group and subject to approval of the Group the minutes of the meeting of 19 and 20 July 1956. This is followed with a discussion of the above-mentioned Premier Reading of Articles 40 to 43 of the Draft Articles (n 228) 2.

[233] Internal Memorandum, ibid, 4.

[234] ibid 5.

[235] ibid.

[236] ibid 5.

[237] ibid 5.

abuse.[238] In contrast, the German draft envisaged the prohibition of agreements and subjected the monopolies to the control of 'abuse'.

This matter was further elaborated on in a Note proposed by the president of the Common Market Group – namely, Hans von der Groeben, who was arguably another follower of ordoliberalism.[239] According to the Note, the abusive use of a market dominating position was to be handled with a uniform principle regardless of whether this position had resulted from the production scale of an undertaking or created through a cartel agreement of many undertakings.[240] Moreover, there were factual differences between cartels and monopolies for which allowance had to be made during the formulation of the relevant rules. For example, cartels had the quality to restrict or prevent competition and were to be prohibited to the extent that these effects were intended or realised. In contrast, in the case of monopolies, the more complete the monopoly, the less competition there was that could be distorted or eliminated. Therefore, regarding monopolies, it was not the distortion of competition, but only the *abuse* of the market dominating position that could be prohibited. Furthermore, cartels could take many forms, such as the partition of supply and sales markets, which was not so in the case of monopolies. Finally, the sanction of voidness for the transactions should be stipulated only for cartel agreements. Therefore, for monopolies, only the abusive use of the market dominating position and not its emergence could be the subject of a sanction which would be applicable in all cases.[241] From a suggestion of von der Groeben it is understood that an 'undertaking in a dominant position' meant an undertaking that was not exposed to any (substantial) competition in the whole or a substantial part of the common market.[242] Thus, the lack of competition due to the existence of a dominant undertaking was accepted by the drafters, contrary to the ECJ's later holding in *Continental Can*.[243]

Importantly for the purposes of this study, the Note of von der Groeben went on to consider the issues of 'exclusion' and 'unfair competition' stating that

[238] *Conference Intergouvernementale pour le Marche Commun et L'Euratom Bruxelles, le 18 Septembre 1956 Tableau Synoptique des Projets D'Articles Soumis par Les Délégations Concernant Les Regles de Concurrence Applicables Aux Entreprises* (Intergovernmental Conference for the Common Market and EURATOM, 18 September 1956, Synoptic Table of Draft Articles submitted by Delegations regarding the Rules of Competition applying to Undertakings).

[239] *Regierungskonferenz für den Gemeinsamen Markt und Euratom, Brüssel den 20. Oktober 1956 Mar. Com. 88 Arbeitsgruppe für den Gemeinsamen Markt, Aufzeichnung über die Diskriminierungen, Kartelle und Monopole betreffende Vorschriften, die der President der Arbeitsgruppe der zweiten Lesung zugrunde zu legen vorschlägt* (Intergovernmental Conference for the Common Market and EURATOM, 20 October 1956, Brussels, Common Market Group, Note on the Rules concerning Discrimination, Cartels and Monopolies that the President of the Group proposed for the Second Reading).

[240] Mar.Com. 88 (n 239) 4.

[241] ibid 4–5.

[242] ibid 7.

[243] See *Continental Can* (n 78) [24] and [26] where the ECJ held that Art 3(1)(g) EC requires, a fortiori, that competition must not be eliminated and abuse may occur if a dominant undertaking strengthens such positions in such a way that the degree of dominance reached substantially fetters competition. Art 3(1)(g) EC has been repealed by the Treaty of Lisbon but its content can be found in Protocol 27 which forms an integral part of the TFEU and TEU.

> [i]t has been proposed within the scope of the rules for cartels and monopolies, to announce, among others, cartel or monopoly situations or practices as incompatible with the common market when they have the aim or could have the effect of hindering the exercise of competition in that they facilitate the absorption or domination of the market for a certain product by a single or a group of undertaking(s). This proposal requires illumination. The proposed rule appears perhaps to be directed at practices by which the rival undertakings are excluded out of the market. Such practices, however, consist in not the restriction, but rather the strengthening of competition and therefore are to be combated only when it is a matter of unfair competition. However, if rules applying to unfair competition are to be included in the Treaty, for systematic reasons, they should be separated from the rules on the maintenance of competition.[244]

This paragraph demonstrates that the intention of the drafters of the competition rules – or at least of their president – was not to prohibit the practices by which rivals are excluded out of the market: 'exclusionary abuses' were not intended to be covered under the prohibition of abuse of a dominant position.[245] Exclusionary practices were to be combated only when they constituted 'unfair competition' and if 'unfair competition' was to be regulated in the Treaty, this was to be done separately from the rules on competition. Hence, the drafters of the competition rules of the Treaty were well aware of the difference between 'protecting competitors' and 'protecting competition' since harming rivals by acts of 'unfair competition' was not seen as identical to harming competition.

Until the signature of the Treaties of Rome on 25 March 1957, several drafts of the competition rules were negotiated between the delegations. The final provisions appear to be a compromise between the delegations, with the Germans having their way more than any other delegation.

At the signature of the Treaty, the Foreign Minister of France, Christian Pineau, stated clearly the intention of the Six:

> [N]o one should make a mistake over our intentions. The six States without doubt want to increase their production capacity and enhance their economic development by their unification. Therewith, they do not want to seclude themselves from the rest of the World and erect insurmountable barriers around themselves.[246]

Thus, the wish to increase production capacity was not directed at maintaining or providing Europe's self-sufficiency; they did not want to close themselves vis-à-vis the rest of the world by increasing their production capacity. 'Production capacity' in this sense referred to the '*ability* to produce' that the merging of the markets would provide, rather than the size of the production facilities. This interpretation also conforms to the Spaak Report according to which at the time, there was a lack of outlets and the existing ones were not able to reach the efficient

[244] Mar.Com. 88 (n 239) 5.

[245] *cf* Schweitzer (n 2) 136.

[246] *Rede des Aussenministers Frankreichs, seiner Exzellenz Herrn Pineau, anlässlich der Unterzeichung der Verträge zur Gründung der Europäischen Wirtschaftsgemeinschaft und der Europäischen Atomgemeinschaft* (*Rom, den 25 März 1957*) (speech of Christian Pineau, Foreign Minister of France on the occasion of the signature of the Treaties founding the European Economic Community and the European Atom Community, 25 March 1957) (MAE 871 d/57 lö/hn).

minimum scale.[247] The markets had to be merged since in that way it would be possible to avoid wasteful use of resources and do away with production at uneconomic cost.[248] As such, it is confirmed that the concerns expressed in the Spaak Report reflected the main intentions of the Six in the drafting process that followed. Therefore, if there is one objective which has survived through the negotiations without any change, it appears to have been the aim for *efficiency*.

D The First Signs of Struggle: Proposal for Regulation 17

Although the legislative history ends with the finalisation of the Treaty, this subsection examines some documents from the subsequent period since the political figures are largely the same as those involved in the drafting of the provisions. As such, they provide further insight into the intentions of the drafters. Moreover, they demonstrate how the competition rules were interpreted shortly after their enactment and what the general position on them was.

First, the minutes of the conference of the Ministers of the Six in November 1960 are noteworthy.[249] The conference was held in order to discuss the content of the proposal of the Commission for the first implementation Regulation on Articles 101 and 102, which became to be known as 'Regulation 17'.[250]

The remarks of van der Schueren (Belgium) are particularly notable as they demonstrate the positive attitude towards cartels in the early years. According to the draft Regulation, the Commission was to reach its decisions concerning the application of Article 101(3) within three years of the receipt of application. Van der Schueren expressed his concern that this would mean that the existent cartels could stay in the dark for a period of three years. As a result, it was to be feared that they flinch from conducting any business during this period of time which – especially in the area of investments – would come at formidable cost. Such refrainment was not desirable and could under circumstances protract adjustments and specialisations necessary within the scope of the common market.[251]

The comments of van der Schueren clearly show that the main concern was investments and specialisations which can be coined as 'dynamic efficiency'. That this view was not limited to just one Member State was later on demonstrated by van Alphen de Veer (Netherlands): he stated that the dominant view in his country was that there existed also good or at least acceptable cartels. According to him, except for some nuances, this view was shared in different countries of the Community.[252]

[247] See text around n 211.
[248] See text around n 210.
[249] *Entwurf eines Protokolls über die Ministertagung am 29 November 1960 in Luxemburg (Erster Teil)* (Draft Protocol of the Ministers' Meeting, 29 November 1960. Luxembourg, Part I) [R/1220 d/60 (Teil I) mue/us].
[250] Council Regulation 17/62 Implementing Articles 85 and 86 EC-Treaty [1962] OJ 13/204.
[251] Ministers' Meeting, Part I (n 249) 8–9.
[252] ibid 29.

However, in this context, van der Schueren's argument met with opposition from Müller-Armack as the latter asserted that if the former's proposal[253] was followed, then the Community would, at least at the beginning, control only abusive practices.[254] Such an approach would contradict Article 101 which prohibits all cartels apart from the exemption in Article 101(3).[255] Moreover, Müller-Armack recognised that although one must proceed step-by-step, 'one cannot base one's self on a foundation as shaky as abuse'.[256] This last statement is striking: a German, claimed to be associated with ordoliberalism, found the concept of 'abuse' too 'shaky' a foundation on which to base the prohibition of cartel agreements, although he had proposed that the provision on dominant positions prohibit their 'abuse'.

Nonetheless, a positive attitude towards cartels and dominant companies was apparent in the statements of other ministers as well. For example, Elvinger (Luxembourg) argued that, since the competition rules took considerable space in the Treaty and for its drafters it was clear that each integration movement inevitably resulted in mergers under single undertakings, the effects of such mergers should be monitored in so far as they were proved to run contrary to the common interest.[257] The agreements should not be condemned as such since the borderline between good and harmful agreements was certainly not very clear in all cases.[258] Interestingly, Elvinger quoted in this context the opinion of Schumpeter that giant companies eventually become the most powerful drive for progress, especially for the long-term expansion of production. A dynamic and realistic conception was to be set against the static view of unimpeded competition.[259] From these remarks, it is clear that there was awareness of 'dynamic competition' and competition economics in the first years of application of the rules.

The issue of 'fair competition' was also brought up at this conference. Van Alphen de Veer pointed out that, in the system of the prevailing order of economic life in the Community States (which was characterised by production through single undertakings), free competition had to be granted a pre-eminent position, so that a higher standard of living could be reached.[260] However, in his view, this free competition could lead to, or be used as a means to a situation that was not desirable from a moral and economic standpoint.[261] Therefore, uncon-

[253] Van der Schueren proposed the following: '[a]ssuming that Article [101] should not inhibit the undertakings, but should much more gradually result in the adherence to a certain competition order, one can take the following procedure into consideration in the first period of time. The authorization procedure provided for in Article [101] (3) could be used by the cartels which would like an authorization and could prove that their activity complies with the criteria laid out in the Treaty. No sanctions would apply to those cartels that do not apply for this authorisation'; Ministers' Meeting, Part I (n 249) 9.

[254] ibid 12.

[255] ibid.

[256] ibid.

[257] ibid 13.

[258] ibid 14.

[259] ibid 15.

[260] ibid 29.

[261] ibid.

trolled competition was not compatible with a modern economic policy. He further stated that certain rules targeting competition restrictions had also been accepted in the US in the form of 'fair trade laws'.[262]

In van Alphen de Veer's statements, one observes – as far as the author has tracked – for the first time the view that competition could be restricted for purposes of 'fairness' and moral values. What is striking is that this was done by reference to the US and its 'fair trade laws', and not to Germany or its *Gesetz gegen den unlauteren Wettbewerb* (Act Against Unfair Competition) which regulates 'unfair competition'. One could argue, therefore, that the US laws at the time, and the perception of competition law there, influenced the early formulations of EU competition policy more than it has been acknowledged. One reason for the reference to the US when it comes to 'unfair competition' may be that although ordoliberals did care for the fairness of competition, they did not actually offer specific solutions as to how this could be reconciled with free competition. This tension can be seen in the arguments of the prominent authors of the Freiburg School who argued that 'free competition' must not be stopped on the erroneous grounds of alleged unfair practice, although it must not be allowed to degenerate into truly 'unfair competition' either, without offering any specific methods to separate one from the other.[263]

Perhaps most important for the purposes of this study are the views of von der Groeben, who was not only the chief drafter of the competition rules of the Treaty, but was also the first Commissioner of the European Commission responsible for competition policy. During the discussions of the draft Regulation, von der Groeben clarified the two principles that guided the Commission in the preparation of the Regulation: (i) loyalty to the Treaty and to the execution of the Treaty's terms; and (ii) the desire to accomplish a workable competition policy.[264] Faced with the criticism that the proposed Regulation – which was originally intended to apply *only* to Article 101 – did not strike the correct balance between Articles 101 and 102, von der Groeben countered by arguing that, if this equilibrium appeared insufficient to some governments, then the question to be asked was 'what terms could be proposed for the concrete use of Article 102?' In response to the proposal of Cattani (Italy) to envisage administrative fines and penalty payments for breach of Article 102, von der Groeben remarkably argued that it would not be possible to proceed against a dominant position with punitive proceedings as long as no sufficiently detailed rules were devised for the conduct of market dominating positions.[265] Indeed, on a different occasion, von der Groeben noted that the Commission intended to propose special rules for Article 102 to facilitate

[262] ibid.

[263] F Böhm, W Eucken and H Grossmann-Doerth, 'The Ordo Manifesto of 1936' in A Peacock and H Willgerodt (eds), *Germany's Social Market Economy: Origins and Evolution* (London, Macmillan, 1989) 24–25.

[264] Ministers' Meeting, Part I (n 249) 31.

[265] ibid 38. However, it appears that criminal proceedings were not envisaged for Art 101 either since the norms relating to that were also not yet sufficiently worked out; ibid.

the use of that provision.[266] This last argument clearly demonstrated that, at the early stages, even for the people who actually drafted the provision, Article 102 was not perceived as a fully enforceable provision as such. This surely explains why for many years, it was feared that Article 102 would remain a 'dead letter'.[267]

Müller-Armack, in similar vein to von der Groeben, reminded the conference of the multiple difficulties evoked in the German legislation as a result of the concern to counteract the abuse of a dominant position.[268] According to him, the use of national law in Germany led to very humble achievements and 'herein arises the infirmity of the abuse concept'.[269] Moreover, he did not believe that the experience gained in Germany gave him the ability to offer a proposal for improving the Commission's proposal on this issue.

The statements of von der Groeben and Müller-Armack are puzzling for the purposes of understanding Article 102. This is because the two people who seemed to have been mostly prominent in drafting the rule do not seem to have been pleased with the rule at all. Thus, this begs the question of why the Treaty ended up having an 'abuse' prohibition if the concept was infirm and shaky even to its authors. The seemingly plausible answer is that the 'abuse' prohibition was offered to avoid, and as an alternative to, an outright prohibition of dominant positions. When seen in the context of the negotiations, where France was pushing for an outright prohibition of both cartels and dominant positions, a provision prohibiting merely the abuse of the latter was perhaps the only compromise that could be reached. Thus, the abuse prohibition was actually more pro-business and less restrictive of freedom than the only other alternative, namely the outright prohibition of dominant positions. From this, one can infer that – at least under the argument that prevailed during the negotiations – the existence of powerful undertakings were *necessary* for expanding production and gaining the strength to compete with the rest of the world; the simple prohibition of the 'abuse' of such powerful positions was deemed sufficient.

Nevertheless, expressed elsewhere, according to von der Groeben, Article 102 made sufficient allowance for the requirements of technical development and optimal business growth, and technical progress only seldom called for a market dominant position.[270] It also remained true that new concentrations were unwanted if they completely eliminated competition, rendered possible mono-

[266] '*Entwurf einer Verordnung gemaess Artikel 87 des Vertrages: Mitteilung von Herrn von der Groeben*' (Draft Regulation under Article 87 of the Treaty: Communication from Mr von der Groeben) (Brussels, 25 October 1960) (BAC71/1988-107) 6–7.

[267] See I Samkalden and IE Druker, 'Legal Problems Relating to Article 86 of the Rome Treaty' (1966) 3 *Common Market Law Review* 158, 162.

[268] *Entwurf eines Protokolls über die Ministertagung am 29 November 1960 in Luxemburg (Teil II)* (Draft Protocol of the Ministers' Meeting, 29 November 1960, Luxembourg, Part II) [R/1220 d/60 (Teil II) las/bs] 46.

[269] Ministers' Meeting, Part II (n 268) 46.

[270] Document 115, 'Beratung über den Bericht des Binnenmarktausschusses im Europäischen Parlament, 19.10.1961' (Deliberation on the Report of the Internal Market Committee in the European Parliament) 196 in R Schulze and T Hören (eds), *Dokumente zum Europäischen Recht Band 3 Kartellrecht (bis 1957)* (Berlin, Springer-Verlag, 2000).

poly profits in this way and more or less abolished the freedom and independence of other undertakings.[271] This expresses the paradox that while on the one hand powerful undertakings were necessary to increase production and compete on the world markets, on the other such undertakings were unwanted if they eliminated competition.

During the discussion of the draft Regulation at the European Parliament, von der Groeben stated the aim of the Treaty was bringing about a constant and well-balanced economic expansion and an accelerated elevation of the standard of living.[272] According to him, the reason the Treaty protected competition was because competition had an important role to play on the common market as a steering instrument and every distortion of competition threatened to distort the optimal supply of goods.[273] Von der Groeben also made clear that their opinion on the advantages of competition on the common market was *not* about perfect/complete competition and they did not think this model was possible in reality.[274] They were more convinced that competition could fulfil its functions even on imperfect markets and an imperfect market with competition was always better than an imperfect market without competition.[275] Moreover, competition was not an end in itself; given the federalist structure of the Community, it was an appropriate and practical means to achieve the objectives of Treaty, namely a fast growth, a better use of production forces and a faster integration of the national economies.[276] Distressed at a comment that he had given the impression that the consumer simply did not exist for the European Commission, von der Groeben explained that they wanted to secure the consumer a supply as low-priced/advantageous as possible.[277] They believed that competition resulted in the highest degree of satisfaction of the consumer's needs as possible and enabled her the free choice of consumption.[278] This was in accordance with the fact that competition was not an end in itself, but a means to achieve certain objectives set out in the Treaty.[279]

According to von der Groeben, the competition law of the Community intended to (and could only) protect honest performance/efficiency-competition, and not to encourage dishonest or unfair competition.[280] Directly related to the purposes of this study, von der Groeben remarked that freedom and fairness of competition called for one another; a competition policy that had the objective of protecting competition from distortions had to aim at also harmonising the unfair competition laws of the Member States through approximation of the laws

[271] ibid.
[272] ibid 192.
[273] ibid 193.
[274] ibid 194.
[275] ibid.
[276] ibid 195.
[277] ibid 258.
[278] ibid 259.
[279] ibid.
[280] ibid 196.

or the conclusion of conventions.[281] It must be noted that, in accordance with the above *travaux préparatoires*, the harmonisation of unfair competition laws was seen as a separate issue from the protection of competition regulated under Articles 101 to 109.

E Early Commission Interpretation

In a speech before the European Parliament in 1965, von der Groeben elaborated on competition policy in a way which throws light on the understanding of the Commission at the time and during the following years. His comments illustrate the positive take on mergers and the paradox that mergers were necessary to increase Europe's competitiveness, while abuse of a dominant position was prohibited by Article 102. Von der Groeben explained that, for the undertakings, it was a matter of matching the growing internal and international competition: '[t]hey accept competition as the source of our wealth as well as the guarantor of their economic freedom'.[282] The undertakings required that competition was conducted 'fairly', that it was not distorted artificially by state aid, differential taxation and different commercial laws; they required that equality of opportunity was established and ensured.[283] According to the Commissioner, especially great was the worry with the superiority of large, financially strong undertakings from third countries; thus, merging into larger undertakings was considered as a necessity and all artificial obstacles to mergers had to be abolished.[284] The Commission was of the view that these concerns of business were justified; they added up to the establishment of a system of undistorted competition, which would help to advance the living and employment conditions of the people. The basic duty of the Community thus consisted in accomplishing such an economic order that would optimally advance wealth and economic freedom, and thereby also serve the consumer.[285]

Von der Groeben argued that such an economic order did not arise automatically, but rather only through the legal order and the embodiment of competition that was characterised by a number of rules and attitudes.[286] Competition policy thus did not mean fighting a battle with one's own resources against all, but rather the laying and realisation of legal rules, to enable 'workable competition' and to protect undertakings from unfair competition. According to the Commissioner, only this type of competition had the effect of promoting wealth and freedom on

[281] ibid 196.

[282] H von der Groeben, 'Die Wettbewerbspolitik als Teil der Wirtschaftspolitik im Gemeinsamen Markt' Rede vor dem Europäischen Parlament (Strassburg am 16 Juni 1965) ('Competition Policy as Part of the Economic Policy in the Common Market' speech before the European Parliament (Strasbourg, 16 June 1965)) 3.

[283] ibid.

[284] ibid 4.

[285] ibid 3.

[286] ibid 4.

which the success of the market economy rested. Competition policy was therefore general economic policy and was not to be separated from it. Moreover, the distortions of competition impaired the competitive positions of the disadvantaged, and deceptively secured the positions of the beneficiaries; the distortions led to dependence on the state and infringed the basic principles of equal treatment, fairness and reward for real commercial performance.[287]

Furthermore, it depended first and foremost on the undertakings themselves, whether competition could deploy their productive powers for the benefit of all market participants and the collectivity, and whether commercial opportunities that the market economy offered them would be realised.[288] Accordingly, even mergers were desired, so long as they were economically necessary – which the Commissioner defined as those 'increasing productivity' – since such accumulations of economic performance power boosted simultaneously the competitiveness and the resistance of the merged undertakings at the European and international level.[289] The following passage from this speech demonstrates the Commissioner's policy clearly:

> Growth of undertakings: yes. Competition under large ones, if it is effective competition: yes. Monopolisation however, that is mergers that make competition non-workable, that challenge the freedom of choice and activity of the consumer, supplier and buyer: no. To the extent that competition becomes non-workable, uncontrolled market power accrues to the merged undertakings. This can in many ways be employed to obtain private commercial advantages, without the need for reducing costs or increasing performances of them.[290]

According to the Commissioner, 'workable competition' meant practically active, effective competition.[291] Therefore, it was essential that the entry to the concerned market stayed open, that the movement of supply and demand reflected itself in the price, that production and sales were not artificially restricted and the freedom of action and freedom of choice of suppliers, buyers and consumers was not challenged. Moreover, competition policy was not pursued as the goal itself, but rather in order to reach the maximum possible productivity, fulfilment of demand, wealth and economic freedom for all people in the common market.[292] Furthermore, competition provided a basis for a division of income and fortune commensurate with social justice that must be complemented with an effective social and income policy.[293]

Certain parts of these remarks of von der Groeben are perhaps some of the most significant expressions of ordoliberalism in the history of EU competition policy. The concept of an economic order, its realisation through the legal order,

[287] ibid 5.
[288] ibid 10.
[289] ibid 13.
[290] ibid 18–19.
[291] ibid 19.
[292] ibid 20–21.
[293] ibid 21.

the concern with fairness and economic freedom are surely reflections of an ordoliberal view. However, it must be borne in mind that these remarks concerned competition *policy* as opposed to *law*. Put differently, this is how the Commission interpreted and applied the competition rules after their enactment at the time. It does not necessarily mean that this is what the law *is* or *should be* once it is accepted that the negotiations demonstrate that Article 102 was not a classic ordoliberal provision as its drafters did not follow ordoliberal thought whilst drafting the provision. The tone of these remarks by von der Groeben is also strikingly different from those during the negotiations of the competition rules and the discussion of the draft Regulation 17. The latter show a stance much more pro-business than the former, which must also carry the experience of the first couple of years.

Furthermore, some of von der Groeben's remarks, such as that competition policy is not an aim in itself, is not actually ordoliberal either. For ordoliberals, competition *was* an aim in itself and not necessarily a tool to attain beneficial economic results.[294] In von der Groeben's speech, there is constant reference to (increasing) productivity, along with 'fairness' and economic freedom. It is noteworthy that the monopolisation that he opposed was one which may be 'employed to obtain private commercial advantages, without the need for reducing costs or increasing performances'.[295] The concern with productive efficiency is again obvious. Thus, it is not clear what the position of the Commissioner would have been in the case, for example, of a merger leading to a dominant position which would reduce the costs of the merging undertakings and increase their productive efficiency, but simultaneously increase prices. What is clear is that the Commissioner saw mergers as a *necessity* and unlike most ordoliberals was not against accumulation of power per se. The concern with enhancing welfare and efficiency, as well as trying to ensure protection of freedom demonstrates the inherently contradictory paradigm in which the Commission was perhaps operating at the time.

It must also be emphasised that, although the freedom of choice of the consumer was seen as an inherent part of EU competition policy and therefore one of its aims, distributional concerns were not perceived in the same manner. Competition was assumed to provide a basis for a division of income and fortune commensurate with social justice which *must* be *complemented* with an effective social and income policy. Hence, competition itself was not expected to automatically result in or bring about this division or redistribution of income. The implication seems to be that competition was to provide the consumers with the choice between different products, but not necessarily the 'fair' price, which raises questions about the meaning of Article 102(a) that prohibits 'unfair pricing'. The discussion of fairness and unfair pricing is left for chapters four and five respectively. The next subsection provides some particular insights into the early understandings of dominance and abuse at the Commission.

[294] Cseres (n 1) 103.
[295] See text to n 290.

F Early Understandings of Dominance and Abuse

According to a group of professors who were consigned to prepare a 'Study on the Instrument of Article 86 of the Treaty' for the Commission, a dominant position on a given market existed if one or more undertakings, by means of an autonomous strategy could substantially influence the decisions of other market participants, so that practicable and adequately effective competition on this market could not develop or be maintained.[296] Market dominance could not be defined merely by using the market share of an undertaking or other quantitative elements of a given market structure.[297] Market dominance was in the first place a commercial potency, namely the ability to behave differently than in a competitive situation.[298] An undertaking that could at discretion exclude competing undertakings from the market could already possess a dominant position and determine the behaviour of the other undertakings decisively, even if its own market share was low.[299] It has also been suggested that it could be deduced from the examples in Article 102 that an abusive exploitation of a dominant position was to be understood/assumed if an undertaking in a dominant position unfairly disadvantaged trading partners or consumers.[300]

In response to the expert group, a Note from the Director General for Competition (Verloren van Themat) to the Commissioner (von der Groeben) argued that if the expert group wanted to treat every restriction of practicable and sufficiently effective competition as abuse under Article 102, they could not be agreed with.[301] This was first because this interpretation went against the letter of the provision, which required not only exploitation, but *abusive* exploitation and, secondly, it appeared from the point of the objectives of Article 102 undesirable to define both the dominant position and its abusive exploitation by using the same criteria and with it to renounce a specific appraisal of the abusive behaviour of an undertaking in a dominant position.[302] Moreover, the existence of a dominant position was not identical to the absence of practicable and sufficiently effective competition.[303] Therefore, concerning the assessment of whether a dominant position existed, the development of the market had also to be considered.[304]

[296] *Vermerk für Herrn Generaldirektor Verloren van Themaat, Artikel 85 und 86: Unternehmenskonzentration 1965* (Note for Director-General Mr Verloren van Themaat, Articles 85 and 86: Concentration of Undertakings 1965) (BAC71/1988-174) [12].

[297] ibid [15].

[298] ibid.

[299] ibid.

[300] ibid [17].

[301] *Vermerk für Herrn von der Groeben, Die Ergebnisse der Untersuchungen über die Anwendung von Artikel 85 und 86 auf die Konzentration 1965* (Note for Mr von der Groeben, The Findings of the Research into the Use of Articles 85 and 86 on Concentrations 1965) (BAC71/1988-174) [43].

[302] ibid. In the German and French texts, Art 102 literally prohibits 'abusive exploitation'; see below n 324.

[303] Note for Mr von der Groeben (n 301) [36].

[304] ibid [37].

According to the Director General, from the examples of abuse named in Article 102, it could be deduced that an abuse existed if the undertaking in a dominant position unfairly disadvantaged its trading partners or consumers.[305] It was sufficient, if in a certain case, a disadvantage that could not be explained or justified by commercial considerations could be objectively proven.[306] The harm to consumers mentioned in Article 102(b) could – other than restriction of production, distribution or technical development – also be caused by further restriction of the consumers' choice by a certain behaviour pattern over the situation resulting from the dominant position.[307] The exploitative abuse of a dominant position thus essentially existed if and in so far as the dominant undertaking drew advantages from its position that were only based on the fact of market dominance.[308]

Similarly, according to von der Groeben himself, the question of whether abuse existed was to be judged not by moral, but by objective commercial and legal criteria.[309] An important indication whether an action was abusive was whether this action was only possible for the undertaking due to its dominant position and therefore it would have been impossible/unfeasible were the undertaking exposed to effective competition.[310] An abusive exploitation in the sense of Article 102 was an objective wrongdoing; since it was merely about the appraisal of objective relations of the dominant undertaking with other market participants, it would be mistaken to associate a subjective condemnation of any kind with the concept of abusive exploitation of a dominant position.[311] Since the dominant undertaking could cause harm without the affected being able to avoid such harm by the rules of competition, the dominant undertaking's behaviour had to be judged by stricter standards than other undertakings.[312] These standards were defined authoritatively by Article 102.[313]

The above statements are helpful in establishing a definition for 'exploitative abuse' which, as the drafting history shows, is the only type of abuse intended to be prohibited under Article 102 that reflects the original thinking behind the provision. Thus, the definition of 'exploitative abuse' seems to be the dominant undertaking receiving advantages that would not be possible *but for* its dominance.[314] Put differently, if the dominant undertaking is able to advantage itself to

[305] ibid [45].

[306] ibid.

[307] ibid [47].

[308] W Fikentscher, '*Rechtsgutachten "Untersuchung über die Mittel des Artikel 86 des EWG-Vertrags"*' (Legal Opinion "Research into the Instrument of Article 86 EC") 26.3.1964 (BAC71/1988-166) 24.

[309] *Vermerk für die Kommission (Mitteilung von Herrn von der Groeben)* (Note for the Commission – Report from Mr von der Groeben) (BAC 26/1969-78) 8.

[310] ibid 8.

[311] Note for Director-General Mr Verloren van Themaat (n 296) [17].

[312] ibid [18].

[313] ibid.

[314] This definition is somewhat similar to the ECJ's interpretation of the practice prohibited in Art 102(a) in *United Brands* where the ECJ characterised the practice as the dominant undertaking having made use of the opportunities arising out of its dominant position in such a way as to reap trading benefits which it would not have reaped if there had been normal and sufficiently effective competition; *United Brands* (n 220) [249].

the disadvantage of its trading partners in a manner that would not be possible in competitive conditions, then it exploitatively abuses its position. The above suggestion of the expert group regarding dominance is also interesting since it implies that 'dominance' can be defined as the potential or capacity to exclude. Such an understanding could be utilised to create a sensible understanding of the prohibition of abuse of dominant position which unites exclusion with exploitation: exclusion would be dealt with at the stage of identifying dominance (by defining dominance as the capacity to exclude) and exploitation would be the 'abuse' element of the prohibition understood as disadvantaging the dominant undertaking's trading partners in ways that would not be possible *but for* the dominance. This understanding of exploitation and thus abuse under Article 102 will be consulted throughout this book to test its applicability and workability. The understanding of 'dominance' as potential or capacity to exclude will be returned to in chapter eight.

It is also noteworthy that, under this understanding, the disadvantages that can be seen as abusive exploitation are those that cannot be justified by commercial reasons and although the 'dominant undertaking's behaviour had to be judged by stricter standards than other undertakings', these standards are to be found in Article 102 itself. In other words, these undertakings do not have a 'special responsibility' over and above what they must do to comply with Article 102. Whether or not this is the same as the ECJ's expression of the 'special responsibility' of dominant undertakings is not entirely clear from the case law, which repeatedly mentions the 'special responsibility' without expressing much about its substance.[315] Finally, it is striking that this early understanding of 'dominance' as the capacity to exclude is extremely similar to the interpretation of 'monopoly' in the US under Sherman Act Section II, since monopoly there has been defined as 'the power to control prices or exclude competition' by the US Supreme Court.[316] Perhaps this can be seen as yet another piece of evidence to suggest that US antitrust law was indeed an example that was looked favourably upon by the Europeans in the early days of the Treaty, unlike the common argument which pictures the EU interpretation as strictly European by being ordoliberal.[317]

[315] 'Special responsibility' was first expressed in *Michelin I* (n 78).

[316] *United States v EI du Pont de Nemours & Co* 351 US 377, 391 (1956). According to Sherman Act Section II: '[e]very person who shall monopolize, or attempt to monopolize, or combine or conspire with any other person or persons, to monopolize any part of the trade or commerce among the several States, or with foreign nations, shall be deemed guilty of a felony'.

[317] For the argument that prohibiting abuse of a dominant position was very different from the discourse of US law see, eg, Gerber (n 1) 264.

VI IMPLICATIONS FOR ARTICLE 102[318]

The foregoing discussions of ordoliberalism, the *travaux préparatoires* and the early interpretation and understanding of the competition rules by the Commission have several implications for establishing what Article 102 actually is and what its aims are. The most basic but crucial point is that Article 102 does not prohibit a dominant position itself and this must be for a reason. The most plausible reason from the *travaux préparatoires* appears to be the concern for efficiency. The drafters were aware that Europe had to have strong undertakings to expand its economy; efficiency was of the utmost importance for both prosperity at home and competitiveness abroad. The drafters did not intend to prevent undertakings from becoming more efficient, even if this meant larger and dominant undertakings. That is the rationale for not prohibiting the domination of a market itself. Efficient undertakings – dominant or not – were necessary to increase Europe's wealth and to improve its place in the world economy.[319] The positive attitude towards mergers also shows that the accumulation of power was not perceived to be harmful per se. Indeed, the lack of merger control provisions in the EC Treaty demonstrates an explicit rejection by the drafters of such a proposition given that the ECSC Treaty contained provisions on merger control and control of mergers was also envisaged in the Spaak Report.[320]

This signifies the most important difference between the intent behind Article 102 and ordoliberalism: whereas efficiency was only a derived *result* of competition for ordoliberals, it was an *aim* for the drafters of the competition rules of the Treaty. Article 102 departs from classic ordoliberalism significantly by not prohibiting a dominant position itself, but only its abuse. A classic ordoliberal rule would have prohibited dominant positions, would have envisaged their divestiture and would have provided the control of conduct only for those dominant undertakings which could not be divested. For ordoliberals, conduct control becomes an option only when it is not possible to eliminate the dominant position itself.[321] The drafters of Article 102 obviously had the opportunity to contemplate an outright ban of dominant positions. Indeed, this was actually proposed by the French delegation during the negotiations. Nonetheless, it was rejected by the German delegation supposedly influenced by ordoliberalism.[322]

Article 102 is not ordoliberal from another prominent perspective as well. It was not intended to protect the (economic freedom of) competitors of the dominant

[318] To the extent that this section relies on material from section V.A–E, its findings were originally published in Akman (n 199).

[319] This perhaps explains why Art 102 was seldom enforced until the late 1960s. Indeed, Gerber argues that the concern during the foundational period that Art 102 might interfere with the objective of creating enterprises large enough to combat US multinationals diminished in the 1970s and Art 102 thus became an active area of enforcement; Gerber (n 27) 121.

[320] ECSC Treaty Art 66 and Spaak Report (n 203) 45.

[321] Gerber (n 1) 252.

[322] See text around n 233.

undertakings; it was intended to protect those who dealt with the dominant undertakings, namely the trading partners from the abuse of power. This is obvious from the statements of von der Groeben during the negotiations where he elaborated on the exclusion of rivals and found that exclusionary practices actually strengthened competition, and did not distort it – so long as they did not constitute 'unfair competition'.[323] What is striking is that the drafters did not perceive harming rivals as tantamount to harming competition. Indeed, their suggestion was that, if rules protecting *competitors* were to be included in the Treaty, this had to be done separately from the rules on competition, under rules on 'unfair competition'. Moreover, this is closely linked to not prohibiting the domination of a market itself since that would have meant prohibiting exclusion *per se* as harmful to competition which – according to von der Groeben – was not appropriate. Thus, the drafters of Article 102 intended the provision to prohibit merely the *exploitation* of those who dealt with dominant undertakings. The texts of Article 102 in French and German also support this view.[324] Similarly, the early understanding of dominance and abuse explained above show an interpretation of abuse as exploitation, whereas the potential for exclusion might be something to take into account when establishing dominance.[325]

Therefore, the propositions in the literature that the purpose of Article 102 is to ensure that the exercise of market power does not impair competitors' possibilities to succeed on the basis of superior business performance and that the provision protects competitors as part of the competitive process since the process of competition flows from the exercise of individual rights are questionable.[326] Similarly, the argument that its German drafters must have intended Article 102 to cover exclusionary abuses since the parallel debate in Germany concerning German competition law at the time focused on exclusionary abuses is not based on actual evidence from the negotiations.[327] The discussions at national level in Germany do not seem to have led to similar discussions during the drafting process of Article 102, but quite the contrary as far as the evidence this author has been able to find is concerned.[328] Moreover, as demonstrated above, the draft Bill in Germany that reflected the ordoliberal views (the Josten draft) was ultimately rejected at the German level.[329] This being the case at the national level, it is not obvious why ordoliberals might have had more influence at the European level. Finally, the lack of an intention to prohibit exclusion is also supported by the fact that the drafters had the example of the Sherman Act Section II which prohibits 'monopolisation' (ie, exclusion), but did not envisage such a prohibition in Article 102.

[323] See text to n 244.

[324] In the French and German texts, Art 102 prohibits 'abusive exploitation' ('*d'exploiter de façon abusive*' and '*missbräuchliche Ausnutzung*' respectively).

[325] See text to n 298.

[326] Eilmansberger (n 2) 129, 133; Schweitzer (n 2) 161–62.

[327] Schweitzer (n 2) 136–37.

[328] See text to n 244.

[329] See text around n 130. For other arguments as to why ordoliberals are unlikely to have had much influence at the European level, see Karagiannis (n 144) 183, 189, 231, 236.

Indeed, in the early years of implementation there was a dispute about whether Article 102 applied only to exploitative abuses or covered exclusionary abuses as well. For example, Joliet (later a judge of the ECJ) was of the view that Article 102 merely covered exploitative abuses; under the abuse theory of Article 102 – unlike the Sherman Act – the test of legality was *not* interference with other firms' freedom to compete and the use of 'exclusionary' practices to achieve and hold power, but rather whether there was monopolistic *exploitation* of the market.[330] Joliet reached this conclusion by studying the examples listed in Article 102 and finding that the main preoccupation of the Treaty was *not* the maintenance of a competitive system.[331] According to him, large size was considered an economic necessity, since the basic assumption underlying Article 102 was that monopolistic market 'structure' did not inevitably lead to monopolistic 'performance'. The reason why monopoly power as such was not condemned was because the Treaty assumed that this power would not be systematically utilised. Joliet noted that

> if Article [102] were to be applied to policies erecting barriers to entry and *consolidating* market domination, it is difficult to perceive why in such a case the market dominant position itself should not be dismantled, a consequence which is rejected by all.[332]

Although Joliet did not refer to the *travaux préparatoires* of the Treaty, the documents this author has found confirm his viewpoint. Thus, the ECJ judgment in *Continental Can* holding that Article 102 applies not only to exploitative practices, but also to exclusionary practices which strengthen the dominant position on the market,[333] appears to have been contrary to the intention of the drafters. It was indeed 'the apotheosis of the teleological method'.[334] As such, it has led to Article 102 being predominantly used for a purpose for which it was not designed.

What is ironic is that although the drafters wanted to protect those who dealt with dominant undertakings as trading partners, rather than their competitors, and their attitude was much more pro-business and pro-efficiency than an ordoliberal viewpoint, the resulting provision is almost counterintuitive. This is because Article 102 prohibits 'exploitative' abuse which is not only the most difficult to apply of the two types of abuse, but also the most intrusive one regarding the dominant undertaking's business practices since it gives the authorities leeway to set the terms of trade for the undertaking. Joliet has also emphasised this by finding that

[330] R Joliet, *Monopolization and Abuse of Dominant Position* (La Haye, Martinus Nijhoff, 1970) 250.
[331] ibid 131.
[332] ibid 252.
[333] *Continental Can* (n 78) [26]: 'As may further be seen from letters (c) and (d) of Article [102](2), the provision is not only aimed at practices which may cause damage to consumers directly, but also at those which are detrimental to them through their impact on an effective competition structure, such as is mentioned in Article 3 [(1)(g)] of the Treaty. Abuse may therefore occur if an undertaking in a dominant position strengthens such a position in such a way that the degree of dominance reached substantially fetters competition, ie, that only undertakings remain in the market whose behaviour depends on the dominant one'.
[334] Gerber (n 27) 116.

> [a]lthough the abuse theory approach might have been taken to avoid facing the decision of decreeing radical structural reorganization of markets and thus might have been inspired by a policy favourable to big business, it results . . . in the possibility of more administrative regulation which . . . might appear more antagonistic to a system of free enterprise than the Sherman Act.[335]

It is still puzzling to this author why Article 102 was couched in such vague terms even though Müller-Armack found abuse too 'shaky' a foundation and an infirm concept,[336] while von der Groeben did not think it possible to impose fines on dominant undertakings under Article 102 as long as no sufficiently detailed rules were laid for their conduct.[337] This almost implies that the provision was not intended to be enforced. Perhaps the answer lies somewhere among the *travaux préparatoires* not yet discovered.

As for the objective of Article 102, one is left with a provision that was supposed not to hamper the efficiency of big business, but at the same time protect those who dealt with it from the abusive use of power. What stands out from the *travaux préparatoires* is that there is constant mention of 'raising the standards of living' for the people of the Community. However, this may not necessarily refer to the concept of 'consumer welfare' in the technical economic sense of the term. This is because 'raising the standards of living' does not seem to have been used as a term of art during the negotiations. It appears to have been used as a general term to state the obvious aim of enhancing the living conditions of all people in the Community. Given the fact that Europe was still trying to recover from war, this is totally rational. In that context, 'people' meant everyone in the Community and it did not technically refer to 'consumers'.[338] Indeed, when the drafters used the term 'consumer', they did not actually mean 'consumer', but meant 'customer'.[339] Therefore, it can also be understood as a reference to 'total welfare' which would include the welfare of all, including producers and consumers.

This is reinforced by the fact that, unlike the discussions at the US Congress that adopted the Sherman Act, where monopolies were condemned for restricting output, raising prices and thereby earning extortionate profits at the expense of consumers,[340] the discussions concerning the prospective competition rules of the Treaty do not contain such remarks. Monopolies were mainly condemned for

[335] Joliet (n 330) 133.

[336] See text to nn 256 and 269.

[337] See text to n 265.

[338] 'Consumer' in its technical sense refers to any person acting for purposes outside her trade, business or profession when entering into a transaction.

[339] There are numerous examples of drafters' reference to 'consumers of atom energy' and 'consumers of ores and nuclear fuels' which demonstrate that they did not use the term in the technical sense. See, eg, *Entwurf des Protokolls der Konferenz der Aussenminister der Mitgliedstaaten der E.G.K.S.* (Paris am 20 und 21 Oktober 1956) 13–14 (Draft Protocol of the Conference of the Foreign Ministers of the Member States of the ECSC, 20–21 October 1956, Paris); *Exposé der Praesidenten* (n 202) 31; *Entwurf des Protokolls der Konferenz der Aussenminister der Mitgliedstaaten der E.G.K.S.* (Venedig, den 29 und 30 Mai 1956) 9 (Draft Protocol of the Conference of the Foreign Ministers of the Member States of the ECSC, 29–30 May 1956, Venice).

[340] See Lande (n 213) 88, 93, 94.

their inefficiency and specially their productive inefficiency, rather than the wealth transfers from consumers to producers that they caused. This is probably because, so long as there was no wealth to begin with, there was nothing to be shared between the producers and consumers. Hence, wealth had to be created by efficient undertakings in the first place. The drafters perhaps expected that increasing efficiency and competition would result in the benefits being passed on to the consumers as low prices since they saw high prices as the result of high costs and inefficiency. It is unclear from the *travaux préparatoires* what the attitude of the drafters would have been towards monopolies which did not pass on the benefits of increased efficiency to consumers. Nonetheless, if one tries to associate their position with a welfare standard, it stands closer to a total welfare standard than a consumer welfare standard. This is due to the strong emphasis on *productive* inefficiency since increasing productive efficiency would have increased *total* welfare, whereas preventing the wealth transfers would not have had any effect on total welfare but would have merely increased consumer welfare by redistributing existing wealth. The fact that the Treaty originally did not have a provision on consumer protection also supports their position being closer to 'total welfare' than 'consumer welfare'. This is not challenged by the existence of Article 101(3), which requires a fair share of the benefits arising from an otherwise anticompetitive practice falling foul of Article 101(1) to be passed on to consumers for the practice to be excepted from the prohibition. This will be elaborated on in chapter three.

Given that the drafters were greatly concerned with increasing efficiency and considered efficiency gains in the context of both Articles 101 and 102 but did not include an exception clause for such gains in Article 102, the most plausible explanation is that efficiency is imbedded in their concept of 'abuse'. Therefore, a *necessary* condition for conduct to be abusive should be a lack of increase in efficiency. This interpretation provides the Commission and the EU courts with a way of including efficiencies in their assessment under Article 102 without breaching the coherence or spirit of the provision. It also tallies with the understanding of abuse in the early days as practices that cannot be justified on commercial grounds and would not be possible but for the dominance of the undertaking. As the ECJ has not only stated that the system set in Article 102 for dominant positions does not recognise any exemption from the prohibition unlike Article 101(3),[341] but has also held that efficiencies can be taken into account even under Article 102,[342] the understanding of the drafters constitutes a suitable method for including efficiencies in the assessment. As such, the intent of the drafters provides the Commission with strong grounds to adopt a reformed and more economic approach to Article 102. It similarly provides the EU courts with the grounds to accept an assessment of efficiencies in their decisions should they wish to support a more economic

[341] *Continental Can* (n 78) [25].
[342] Case C-95/04 P *British Airways plc v Commission* [2007] ECR I-2331, [86].

approach to Article 102.[343] Thus, the arguments in the literature that adopting the 'consumer welfare' approach would imply a fundamental change in the goals of Article 102 and that Article 102 protects the competitive process itself flowing from the exercise of individual rights[344] are not backed by the provision itself as demonstrated by the intent of its drafters. Article 102 *can* be applied with a welfarist goal. The treatment of efficiencies in the context of Article 102 will be returned to in chapters three, seven and eight.

Moreover, it is illuminating that distributive concerns do not seem to have been included in competition rules. Competition rules were not discussed with an eye to their distributive results. Competition was to provide the basis for the division of income which was to be complemented with an effective social and incomes policy.[345] This perspective also finds support in Müller-Armack's 'social market economy', albeit expressed elsewhere than the *travaux préparatoires.* According to Müller-Armack – who was clearly prominent in the formulation of the competition rules – in a social market economy, efforts are made to achieve social progress by means of measures which are 'in conformity with the market'.[346] By this is meant measures which safeguard social welfare without interfering with the working of the market. Income creation in the free market system provides a solid basis for the redistribution of income by the state.[347] Income redistribution is brought about through welfare benefits, equalisation of pensions and so on. Indeed, Müller-Armack saw the justification of competition as a constant increase in *productivity.*[348] Rather than distort economic interrelationships by fixing prices and injecting purchasing power, it was deemed better to adjust undesirable disparities in incomes via a clearly defined income tax system.[349]

Müller-Armack's perception of competition and the social market economy may also explain the non-existence of a discussion of the wealth effects of monopolies on consumers. The results of competition were to be complemented by other policies specifically designed for income redistribution. Such redistribution was not supposed to be a part of competition policy. The aim of the competition rules was perceived in terms of increasing the productivity and efficiency of the producers and thus 'the size of the pie', rather than how this should be distributed

[343] Although the ECJ has adopted a 'teleological' method of interpretation, as confirmed by the ECJ, it does not act arbitrarily but judicially; it has to see that its interpretation reflects the intention of the parties to the Treaties and the *ratio legis* of the text (see Case 6/60 *Jean-E Humblet* v *Belgium* [1960] ECR 559, 575 and KPE Lasok, *Law & Institutions of the European Union* 7th edn (London, Butterworths, 2001) 165). In tracing the intention of the legislator, the Court *is* free to consult materials extraneous to the Treaty, such as the *travaux préparatoires*; Lasok, ibid. Therefore, there is legally no problem with the Court using the *travaux préparatoires* to base a modernised approach on. For examples of the Court and Advocates General using the *travaux préparatoires*, see Akman (n 199) fn 26.

[344] See Gerber (n 2) 50–51; Eilmansberger (n 2) 133; Schweitzer (n 2) 161.

[345] See above, text to n 293.

[346] A Müller-Armack, 'The Meaning of the Social Market Economy' in A Peacock and H Willgerodt (eds), *Germany's Social Market Economy: Origins and Evolution* (London, Macmillan, 1989) 84.

[347] ibid.

[348] ibid 85.

[349] A Müller-Armack, 'The Social Aspect of the Economic System' in W Stützel et al (eds), *Standard Texts on the Social Market Economy* (Stuttgart, Gustav Fischer, 1982) 18.

between consumers and producers. This may also explain why the *travaux préparatoires* are silent on the possibility of efficiency gains not being passed on to consumers. Even if they were not passed on as a result of the normal play of competition, the complementary income and social policies would pass these benefits onto consumers albeit in the form of welfare benefits, subsidies, etc.

What deserves elaboration is that the drafters do not appear to have considered or at least articulated the objectives of competition law in terms of the welfare standards which are commonly used today. They seem to have had the immediate concern of increasing the *efficiency* of Europe and its undertakings to be able to both make progress, improving the living standards of Europeans, and also compete with third countries. The welfare of consumers of Europe was obviously part of the aim of increasing the living standards of people. However, this does not mean that the drafters saw the aim of competition rules as that of increasing 'consumer welfare' in technical terms. What is important to note is that, given that Article 102 was intended to apply to *exploitative* abuses that directly harm the customers of dominant undertakings, the concern with the downstream market is apparent, albeit without emphasis on final consumers. Thus, Article 102 *can* accommodate a 'consumer welfare approach' in the technical sense and the provision itself does not need to be amended or reformed for this purpose. Indeed, it can even accommodate a 'total welfare approach'. The crucial issue is to give *efficiency* due weight as it appears to have been *the* rationale behind the whole exercise. This can only be done by recognising efficiencies as part of the assessment of 'abuse' under the provision. This would not bring about or require an 'efficiency defence' by the dominant undertaking; unlike the suggestion of the Commission, efficiencies would have to be considered ex officio as part of the 'abuse' test.[350] This has not been the way Article 102 has so far been implemented and this underlying ultimate aim of increasing efficiency of even dominant undertakings appears to have been somehow lost in the decisional practice and case law.

VII CONCLUSION

No legal provision can be properly understood outside the circumstances of its adoption, since only that context can explain why the provision was needed. The same goes for Article 102; it must be considered within the context of its foundation. This is not to deny the contributions of the Commission and the EU courts to the provision or the necessity of adapting the rule to the new conditions. Starting with the potential objectives of EU competition rules, this chapter has tried to fit Article 102 in the context that it belongs to see what it actually *is* and *can* be. For these purposes, the view that Article 102 has been influenced by ordo-

[350] 'Guidance' (n 35) [28], [30] suggesting the possibility of an 'efficiency defence' to be proved by the dominant undertaking.

liberalism is critical since that puts the norm in a certain context and implications about the rule follow from this placement. Contrary to the prevailing view in the literature, the chapter has sought to demonstrate that Article 102 was not envisaged as a classic ordoliberal norm. The fact that it does not prohibit the dominant position itself and the pervasive concern with efficiency throughout the negotiations are the most important reasons for this.

Moreover, the historical period leading up to the Treaties of Rome – including the negotiations of the ECSC Treaty and the political situation in Germany at the time – clearly demonstrate that it is over-simplistic and historically inaccurate to conclude that the EU competition rules were a product of German ordoliberal thought. This is historically inaccurate not least because of the great efforts of Jean Monnet which succeeded to include these rules in the ECSC Treaty *despite* the efforts of the German delegation. It is also inaccurate since ordoliberals did not succeed in having a competition law completely – or even mostly – in line with their thinking even in Germany, which makes it implausible that they were more successful abroad than at home. Furthermore, this chapter has tried to demonstrate that Article 102 itself was *not* intended to protect the (freedom of) competitors of dominant undertakings. There is evidence in the *travaux préparatoires* that the 'abuse' concept was not meant to cover 'exclusionary' conduct at all. Thus, one could conclude that it has perhaps been the application of the provision by the Commission and the EU courts that has been influenced by ordoliberalism which can be criticised for 'protecting competitors', but an assessment of whether the latter is the case is beyond the scope of this chapter. The question of whether 'welfare' is an objective in the jurisprudence on Article 102 is discussed in chapter three.

What is obvious is that the aim of 'market integration' has dominated the application of competition rules, including Article 102, in terms of objectives pursued. This cannot be criticised as such since the goal of a unified market was *the* central impetus for the 'new Europe'.[351] What can be questioned is whether *efficiency* which appears to have been the main concern of the drafters and perhaps seen as the *means* to achieve the objectives of the 'new Europe' has been given enough importance throughout this application process. This is important since the objective of market integration may at times conflict with efficiency[352] and eventually may come at the expense of inefficiencies in the organisation of production or distribution.[353]

This chapter has suggested that the intent of the drafters of Article 102 provides a basis for the Commission and the EU courts to adopt a more economic approach to Article 102, which is much to be desired. The arguments in the literature that adopting the consumer welfare approach would imply a fundamental change in the goals of Article 102 and that Article 102 cannot make consumer harm the ultimate test of anticompetitiveness do not find support in the provision itself as

[351] Gerber (n 1) 347.
[352] Monti (n 10) 1064; Neven (n 23) 118; Cseres (n 1) 255; Van den Bergh (n 5) 35; Motta (n 28) 23.
[353] Van den Bergh (n 5) 35.

demonstrated by the intent of its drafters.[354] Hence, what is required is merely a change in the application of Article 102 by the Commission and courts. What is guiding in this respect is that efficiency is already imbedded in Article 102. Thus, it would be a late but welcome recognition of this if the efficiency effects of allegedly abusive conduct were now considered under the provision. That efficiency was of the utmost importance for the drafters is in total conformity with the context of the provision's adoption. The whole purpose of having a common market was to expand the capacity of Europe's economy and efficient businesses – that could reach the optimum scale of production and reduce costs – were *necessary* for this. The *travaux préparatoires* demonstrate this clearly. This is also expressed by Hallstein – arguably another follower of ordoliberalism – who was the first president of the Commission: 'Every businessman today is aware of the fact that real competition based on efficiency is one of the basic aims of the Treaty'.[355] The understanding of abusive practices in the early days as practices that cannot be justified on commercial grounds also suggests that efficiency was understood to be part of the provision even at the very beginning of the application of the rule.

The issue of efficiency brings out the question of what was the ultimate aim of Article 102 as envisaged by its authors. Apart from the constant concern with increasing efficiency, it is not possible to determine another ultimate aim from the *travaux préparatoires*. Thus, one is left with an objective of increasing efficiency and a provision that prohibits 'exploitation' of those who deal with dominant undertakings. From this, one can infer that a *necessary* condition for 'exploitation' to occur is that the practice does not increase efficiency. In other words, conduct must be 'inefficient' to be abusive. The burden to prove this inefficiency would be on the competition authority/claimant and as such the undertaking would not have to prove efficiencies as a defence for its conduct.[356] Unfortunately, it is not possible to determine the *sufficient* conditions for exploitation from the *travaux préparatoires*, the historical context or the other discussions in the early days. Thus, it is not clear whether an increase in efficiency that outweighs the loss to consumers would be safe from infringing the provision and whether or not part of those efficiency benefits has to be passed on to consumers for the practice not to breach the provision. It is possible either that the drafters had presumed that, when the issue was the unilateral practice of an undertaking, these benefits would eventually be passed on or an increase in efficiency was sufficient, while the losses incurred by consumers would be compensated by other policies. Building on some of the historical findings, this study offers an understanding of 'abuse' with necessary and sufficient conditions in chapter eight.

[354] See Gerber (n 2) 50–51; Eilmansberger (n 2) 133; Schweitzer (n 2) 161.

[355] W Hallstein, *Europe in the Making* (trans C Roetter, London, George Allen & Unwin Ltd, 1972) 116.

[356] *cf* the 'Discussion Paper' (n 35) [77] according to which the burden to prove efficiencies should be on the undertaking. *Cf* 'Guidance' (n 35) [31] according to which the dominant undertaking must provide all the evidence necessary to demonstrate that its conduct is objectively justified. It then falls to the Commission to make the ultimate assessment.

It is also interesting that there was a suggestion in the early days to interpret exploitative abuse – at the time perceived as the only prohibited type of conduct – as the dominant undertaking receiving advantages to the disadvantage of its trading partners that would not be possible *but for* its dominance. In other words, practices that can be undertaken in competitive conditions as well would not be abusive. This understanding of abuse could be used to reach a workable model of the prohibition in Article 102. As will be discussed particularly in chapter eight, this might represent an understanding more modern than the Commission and the EU courts' current application of the provision.

What is still problematic for applying Article 102 in an economics-based way is that the vagueness of concepts such as 'exploitation' and 'abuse' do not provide a solid ground for the application of the provision in and of themselves. Nonetheless, one can conclude that Article 102 is capable of being applied in a manner consistent with both the 'consumer welfare' and the 'total welfare' standard. What must not be lost sight of is the explicit concern which lies underneath the whole idea of the common market and Article 102: efficiency.

The next part of this study turns to particular objectives in the context of Article 102, namely 'welfare' and 'fairness'. Thus, chapter three investigates the particular role 'welfare' has played in the enforcement of Article 102 and provides a critical look at the standard of harm in the application of Article 102 by the Commission and the EU courts. Chapter four subsequently discusses 'fairness' as an objective of Article 102 and elaborates on whether it is an appropriate goal for Article 102 to pursue.

II

Two Potential Objectives: 'Welfare' and 'Fairness'

3

Welfare in Article 102 TFEU

I INTRODUCTION

After a general discussion of objectives of competition law and policy with a special focus on 'welfare' in chapter one, chapter two assessed the context in which Article 102 was adopted from a historical viewpoint. Chapter two established that *efficiency* was of the utmost importance for the creators of the prohibition and that Article 102 *can* and *should* be applied with this objective of enhancing efficiency which underlies the whole European economic integration project. Chapter two also argued that this can be done by accepting a lack of increase in efficiency as a necessary condition for 'abuse'. This chapter turns to the provision of Article 102 itself and questions whether the objective of Article 102 is indeed welfare-based. This is examined by considering, inter alia, the application of the provision by the Commission and in particular the EU courts, alongside the Commission's policy declarations. The issue arises since although the legislative history clearly shows a preference for enhancement of efficiency and the Commission rhetoric demonstrates an apparent 'consumer welfare' objective, the case law and the decisional practice of the EU authorities are in stark contrast to this.

The term 'consumer welfare' has not only hardly ever been used in competition cases by the GC or the ECJ; in its *GlaxoSmithKline* judgment from 2009, the ECJ seems to have *rejected* prevention of harm to consumers as the single objective of the competition rules in favour of multiple interests being protected.[1] This is in sharp contrast with recent policy declarations of the Commission in which

[1] 'Consumer welfare' as a term has been used in Case T-168/01 *GlaxoSmithKline Services Unlimited v Commission* [2006] ECR II-2969 and Case T-201/04 *Microsoft Corp v Commission* [2007] ECR II-3601. In *Microsoft* the GC merely refers to the Commission decision using the term; ibid [41]. 'Consumer welfare' is also referred to in the Opinion of Advocate General Jacobs in Case C-53/03 *Synetairismos Farmakopoion Aitolias & Akarnanias (Syfait) and Others v GlaxoSmithKline plc and GlaxoSmithKline AEVE* [2005] ECR I-4609, [91], [92]; in the Opinion of Advocate General Kokott to dismissively refer to one party's argument in Case C-8/08 *T-Mobile Netherlands BV, KPN Mobile NV, Orange Nederland NV and Vodafone Libertel NV v Raad van bestuur van de Nederlandse Mededingingsautoriteit* [2009] ECR I-4529 and in the Opinion of Advocate General Trstenjak in Case C-209/07 *Competition Authority v Beef Industry Development Society Ltd and Barry Brothers (Carrigmore) Meats Ltd* [2008] ECR I-8637. On the dismissive usage by the ECJ (albeit without using the term 'consumer welfare') in *GlaxoSmithKline*, see Case C-501/06 *GlaxoSmithKline Services Unlimited v Commission* [2009] ECR I-9291, in particular [62]–[64].

'consumer welfare' has repeatedly been pronounced as an almost holy phrase in reference to the ultimate objective of EU competition rules, particularly during the modernisation process. Since the attempts of the Commission to modernise its application of Article 102 cannot succeed unless approved by the EU Courts, this contrast is significant. Moreover, it provokes the question of whether 'consumer welfare' has merely become a slogan and in some cases legitimatisation of what is done in the name of 'consumers' or whether it is a genuine concern. The fact that the Commission does not refer to 'consumer' in the sense of final-user which is the usual understanding of the term in consumer law and economics casts further doubt on the genuineness of the concern.[2] An overall assessment of the Commission's reform of its application of Article 102 is provided in chapter seven.

Unlike Article 101 which prohibits agreements, decisions and concerted practices which may affect trade between Member States and which 'have as their object or effect the prevention, restriction or distortion of competition' within the internal market, Article 102 merely states that 'any abuse by one or more undertakings of a dominant position within the internal market or in a substantial part of it shall be prohibited as incompatible with the internal market insofar as it may affect trade between Member States'. As such, Article 102 does not express a requirement of prevention, restriction or distortion of competition and thus does not stipulate the precise objective(s) or standard of harm of the provision in itself. However, since a dominant position itself is not prohibited, and as Protocol 27 to the Treaties stipulates that Article 3 TFEU includes 'a system ensuring that *competition* in the internal market *is not distorted*', it follows that there *must* be harm to something or someone for Article 102 to be applicable. In other words, the necessary *distortion of competition* must be established on the basis of harm to the protected value(s); it cannot be decided in the abstract since the meaning of distortion of competition is not self-obvious. 'Abuse' must be understood as a component of the prevention of distortion of competition as per Protocol 27 and it can mean harm to competition, harm to competitors, harm to consumers or a combination of these, to name a few. Moreover, whereas Article 101(3) has been interpreted as expressing the standard under Article 101 to be 'consumer welfare' by making exemption from the prohibition of Article 101(1) conditional on the consumers obtaining 'a fair share of the benefits', Article 102 does not contain such a clause.[3] Therefore, this chapter discusses not only the decisional practice on Article 102, but Article 101(3) to the extent that it is relevant for establishing whether the provision sets the standard as 'consumer welfare' for both of the competition rules in the Treaty.

[2] See, eg, Commission, 'Guidelines on the Application of Article 81(3) of the Treaty' [2004] OJ C101/97, [84]; 'DG Competition Discussion Paper on the Application of Article 82 of the Treaty to Exclusionary Abuses' (Brussels, December 2005) available at: ec.europa.eu/competition/antitrust/art82/discpaper2005.pdf, [55]. Throughout this volume, reference will be made to 'Guidelines on Article 101(3)' in line with the current numbering of the Treaty provisions, although at the time of adoption of the Guidelines, the relevant provision was 'Article 81(3)'.

[3] For the view that Art 101(3) sets the standard as 'consumer welfare', see text around n 17.

In the literature, on the one hand, it has been suggested that to counteract criticism that EU competition law 'protects competitors' would require among other things explicit proof of harm to consumers in all Article 102 cases.[4] It has been argued that although European competition law gradually assigns more weight to consumer welfare, its position does not yet resemble the same as in the US.[5] The Commission puts emphasis on considerations other than consumer welfare, like the openness of the market with as many players as possible.[6] It has similarly been noted that EU competition law does not require proof of harm to the consumer in order for either Article 101 or Article 102 to apply.[7] The direct actual or potential effect of conduct on 'consumer welfare' is generally not considered.[8]

On the other hand, it has also been suggested that Article 102 *cannot* make 'consumer harm' the ultimate test of anticompetitive conduct since Article 102 protects the 'institution' of competition, namely the 'competitive process' itself and this flows from the exercise of individual rights.[9] This implies that EU competition law is grounded in the belief that the undistorted competitive process will generally tend to maximise wealth and consumer welfare.[10] For example, Gerber has argued that accepting 'consumer welfare' as the goal of Article 102 would imply a fundamental change in the approach to Article 102.[11] This is because the central idea in Article 102 is arguably the concept of 'competitive distortion', according to which the starting proposition is that some firms have sufficient power to distort and thereby harm the 'competitive process'.[12] Since such distortions reduce the capacity of competition to produce wealth and benefit consumers, Article 102 should be used to deter such conduct and this 'competitive distortion' model has been used as a basis by the EU authorities for their entire conception of the role of Article 102.[13] Therefore, the purpose of the provision is suggested to be ensuring that the exercise of market power does not impair the

[4] JT Lang, 'Panel Discussion on Non-Pricing Abuses' in CD Ehlermann and I Atanasiu (eds), *European Competition Law Annual 2003: What is an Abuse of a Dominant Position?* (Oxford, Hart Publishing, 2006) 477. Lang argues that while this kind of proof could have been made in all Commission decisions based on Art 102, in practice this proof has not always been made explicitly; ibid.

[5] KJ Cseres, *Competition Law and Consumer Protection* (The Hague, Kluwer Law International, 2005) 294. The difference is arguably that efficiencies do not yet form such an inherent part of the European assessment of consumer welfare and competition analysis as they do in the US; ibid.

[6] ibid.

[7] P Marsden and P Whelan, '"Consumer Detriment" and its Application in EC and UK Competition Law' (2006) 27(10) *European Competition Law Review* 569, 576.

[8] ibid 584.

[9] T Eilmansberger, 'How to Distinguish Good from Bad Competition under Article 82 EC: In Search of Clearer and More Coherent Standards for Anti-competitive Abuses' (2005) 42 *Common Market Law Review* 129, 133; H Schweitzer, 'The History, Interpretation and Underlying Principles of Section 2 Sherman Act and Article 82 EC' in CD Ehlermann and M Marquis (eds), *European Competition Annual 2007: A Reformed Approach to Article 82 EC* (Oxford, Hart Publishing, 2008) 161.

[10] Eilmansberger (n 9) 133; Schweitzer (n 9) 161.

[11] DJ Gerber, 'The Future of Article 82: Dissecting the Conflict' in CD Ehlermann and M Marquis (eds), *European Competition Law Annual 2007: A Reformed Approach to Article 82 EC* (Oxford, Hart Publishing, 2008) 50–51.

[12] ibid 39.

[13] ibid.

competitors' possibilities to succeed or prevail on the market on the basis of superior performance.[14] Hence, a lack of consensus on objectives is pervasive at both the decisional and the academic level.

Thus, the aim of this chapter being to establish the role of '(consumer) welfare' in Article 102, section II first explores Article 101(3) since it arguably sets the standard of EU competition rules as 'consumer welfare' and it then examines the treatment of efficiencies under Article 102. This is to establish first, whether Article 101(3) sets a standard of 'consumer welfare' and if so, whether this implies the standard of Article 102 to be 'consumer welfare' as well. In this context, efficiencies are relevant since whether efficiencies resulting from otherwise anti-competitive conduct must be passed on to consumers can signify the standard. Section III presents a critical analysis of the Commission's and the EU courts' decisional practice on standard of harm to see whether the objective of Article 102 is 'consumer welfare' as practised by these authorities. Section IV concludes.

II ARTICLE 101(3), THE WELFARE STANDARD AND THE TREATMENT OF EFFICIENCIES UNDER ARTICLE 102

According to the ECJ both Articles 101 and 102 seek to achieve the same aim.[15] Although the ECJ in *GlaxoSmithKline* seems not to accept a single aim of 'consumer welfare' for these provisions, stating that the competition rules aim to protect not only the interests of competitors or of consumers, but also the structure of the market and thus competition as such,[16] this still leaves unanswered the question of what role 'consumer welfare' plays. This is because the ECJ also accepts that the protection of the interests of consumers *is* one of the aims of these rules. There is also the question of how to interpret Article 101(3) since it has been argued that the rationale behind this exemption rule in Article 101(3) is the objective of EU competition law to enhance 'consumer welfare' on the market.[17] This question is relevant for the purposes of Article 102 since the lack of a similar rule

[14] Eilmansberger (n 9) 133; Schweitzer (n 9) 161–62.

[15] Case 6/72 *Europemballage Corp and Continental Can Co Inc v Commission* [1973] ECR 215, [11], [25].

[16] *GlaxoSmithKline* (ECJ) (n 1) [63]. See similarly the earlier preliminary reference ruling of Case C-8/08 *T-Mobile Netherlands BV, KPN Mobile NV, Orange Nederland NV and Vodafone Libertel NV v Raad van bestuur van de Nederlandse Mededingingsautoriteit* [2009] ECR I-4529, [38].

[17] For the argument see, eg, J Bourgeois and J Bocken, 'Guidelines on the Application of Article 81(3) of the EC Treaty or How to Restrict a Restriction' (2005) 32(2) *Legal Issues of Economic Integration* 111, 119. For the argument that the exception in Art 101(3) suggests that the *core* objective of the provision is the protection of competition *in the interests of consumers*, see E Østerud, *Identifying Exclusionary Abuses by Dominant Undertakings under EU Competition Law: The Spectrum of Tests* (The Netherlands, Kluwer Law International, 2010) 25. For the argument that Art 101(1) involves a consumer welfare analysis and Art 101(3) concerns 'consumer protection' by the requirement of pass-on of a fair share of benefits to consumers, see C Townley, *Article 81 EC and Public Policy* (Oxford, Hart Publishing, 2009) particularly 263 *et seq.*

in Article 102 may have implications for establishing the objective of Article 102, if it is accepted that Article 101(3) sets a consumer welfare standard.

Article 101(3) only becomes applicable when a practice is found to be restrictive under Article 101(1). In applying Article 101(3), one must determine the procompetitive benefits produced by that practice and to assess whether these procompetitive effects outweigh the anticompetitive effects.[18] If this is the case, then the practice would not be in breach of Article 101 as a whole. Article 101(3) sets forth two positive and two negative cumulative conditions which make a practice breaching Article 101(1) exempt from the prohibition. The positive conditions are that the restrictive practice contributes to improving the production or distribution of goods or to promoting technical or economic progress *and* allows consumers a 'fair share' of the resulting benefit. The negative conditions are that the restrictive practice does not impose on undertakings concerned restrictions which are not indispensable to the attainment of these objectives *and* does not afford such undertakings the possibility of eliminating competition in respect of a substantial part of the products in question.

For the purposes of discovering the objective of EU competition rules, especially important is the condition that requires consumers to be allowed a 'fair share' of the resulting benefits from the restrictive practice for the practice to be exempt. It has been suggested that this particular requirement in Article 101(3) is based on a 'consumer welfare' consideration which cannot be explained from a neoclassical 'total welfare' perspective.[19] This is because it is under the consumer welfare standard that the competition authority takes into account *only* those benefits passed on to consumers; '[t]he treatment of efficiency gains is, therefore, an acid test in understanding the welfare standard being applied by a competition authority'.[20] Thus, it has been claimed to be a clear statement of the 'consumer welfare' standard.[21] As such, it has been argued that an equity-efficiency trade-off is always inherent in an analysis under Article 101(3).[22] Under this interpretation, European competition law does not allow the balancing of efficiency savings and distributive effects on consumers; to the European legislator, one Euro of consumer surplus is not equivalent to one Euro of producer surplus.[23]

[18] 'Guidelines on Article 101(3)' (n 2) [11].

[19] Cseres (n 5) 252–53. See also G Monti, 'Article 81 and Public Policy' (2002) 39(5) *Common Market Law Review* 1057, 1064–65.

[20] BR Lyons, 'Could Politicians be More Right than Economists? A Theory of Merger Standards' Revised Centre for Competition and Regulation Working Paper CCR 02-1 (15 May 2002) 1.

[21] ibid 2, fn 2.

[22] Cseres (n 5) 253.

[23] RJ Van den Bergh, 'The Difficult Reception of Economic Analysis in European Competition Law' in A Cucinotta, R Pardolesi and RJ Van den Bergh (eds), *Post-Chicago Developments in Antitrust Law* (Cheltenham, Edward Elgar, 2002) 43. Van den Bergh and Camesasca argue that although the explicit requirement of Art 101(3) that consumers receive a fair share of the resulting benefits makes it clear that gains incurred by producers do not offer an alternative profit justifying consumer losses, this does not imply that an economic analysis focusing on the effects on total welfare becomes superfluous. It merely necessitates an augmentation of the assessment by prescribing the inclusion of distributional aims; RJ Van den Bergh and PD Camesasca, *European Competition Law and Economics A Comparative Perspective* (Antwerpen, Intersentia-Hart, 2001) 67.

If this viewpoint is correct as a general principle of EU competition law, and if the holding of the ECJ that Articles 101 and 102 have the same aim is accepted, then the efficiency gains of unilateral conduct falling under Article 102 would have to be assessed in the same manner as well and 'total welfare' would not be applicable to Article 102 as a standard either. It has in fact been suggested that in the EU, the Treaty has already determined by way of Article 101(3) that the 'total welfare' standard is inapplicable.[24] As such, Article 101(3) provides a benchmark to test whether Article 102 also adopts the 'consumer welfare' standard if one accepts the proposition that Article 101(3) indeed sets the standard as 'consumer welfare'. Thus, the questions that are relevant for the purposes of Article 102 are: first, whether Article 101(3) mandates a consumer welfare standard; and, secondly, if it does, whether the same standard can and should be applicable to Article 102 in the same manner. The last question arises mainly due to the lack of a similar clause in Article 102 itself. Therefore, before one can decide whether the standard set in Article 101(3) also applies to Article 102, one must be explore why there is no clause similar to Article 101(3) in Article 102 and what the implications of this non-existence are. It should also be noted that the discussion here of whether the standard is 'consumer welfare' is not to exclude the possibility that the standard of harm under Articles 101 and 102 might not be welfare-based at all and this is investigated elsewhere in this book, for example, in chapter four on 'fairness' as a possible alternative objective of Article 102.

Finally, an inquiry into Article 101(3) is important also because during its recent modernisation attempt at Article 102, the Commission repeatedly expressed the necessity of taking into account efficiency gains under Article 102, as it is done under Article 101(3).[25] The former Competition Commissioner, under whose mandate the reform of Article 102 was undertaken, explicitly stated that although Article 102 does not expressly foresee the possibility of 'exempting' abusive behaviour because of efficiencies, 'we must find a way to include efficiencies in our analysis'.[26] Indeed, the reflection of Article 101(3) in the criteria for the 'efficiency defence' as elaborated on in the Commission Guidance and DG Competition Discussion Paper on exclusionary abuses almost suggests that an exemption clause under Article 102 limited to efficiencies is to be brought by the

[24] DJ Gifford and RT Kudrle, 'European Union Competition Law and Policy: How much Latitude for Convergence with the United States?' (2003) 48(3) *The Antitrust Bulletin* 727, 773. See also Cseres (n 5) 254 and Van den Bergh (n 23) 42. *Cf* O Odudu, 'Article 81(3), Discretion and Direct Effect' (2002) 23(1) *European Competition Law Review* 17, 19 who seems to be arguing that Art 101(3) is about 'total welfare' since he opines that 'Article [101](3) exists to enable us to consider total economic welfare by providing a mechanism where we can take productive efficiencies into account and consider the net consequences of an agreement'.

[25] See, eg, 'Discussion Paper' (n 2) [84]–[92] elaborating on the 'efficiency defence'; N Kroes, 'The Commission's Review of Exclusionary Abuses of Dominant Position' speech before the Korean Competition Forum organised on the occasion of the Fourth Annual Bilateral Meeting (Seoul, 26–27 June 2006) 9.

[26] See N Kroes, 'Preliminary Thoughts on Policy Review of Article 82' speech at the Fordham Corporate Law Institute (New York 23 September 2005) 5.

Commission application of that provision.[27] It should be noted that in its Guidelines on Article 101(3), the Commission has clearly adopted an approach which limits the first requirement of Article 101(3) to efficiency gains, to the exclusion of non-efficiency-related benefits.[28] This section will investigate three issues surrounding Article 101(3) insofar as they are relevant for providing insights for Article 102: first, the issue of lack of a provision similar to Article 101(3) in Article 102 and the implications of this; secondly, whether there is a pass-on requirement for efficiencies in Article 102; and thirdly, whether Article 101(3) indeed sets a standard of 'consumer welfare'.

A Why is there not an Equivalent of Article 101(3) in Article 102?

The first issue to be discussed is why there is not an equivalent of Article 101(3) in Article 102 and what the implications of this are. It has been suggested that since Article 102 has no exemption clause, the conflict between competition and productive or dynamic efficiency is assumed not to arise.[29] However, this contention must be examined in more detail as this absence of an exemption clause can be interpreted in one of three ways: (i) as an omission of the drafters; (ii) as a silent refusal; or (iii) as a silent acceptance since the clause already exists in Article 101. The last alternative is unlikely since, as a general principle, a clause that does not actually exist in a provision cannot be presumed to exist by way of transposition from another provision, due to considerations of legal certainty. Although Articles 101 and 102 are in the same Chapter of the TFEU, the drafters have not envisaged paragraph (3) of Article 101 as a common clause for both of the provisions as demonstrated by the difference in texts. By doing so, they have limited the applicability and effect of that clause to Article 101. Therefore, paragraph (3) of Article 101 cannot simply be transposed to Article 102 for the mere fact that it exists in Article 101.

Bearing in mind the different contexts to which both provisions are applicable (that is, unilateral versus multilateral conduct), it is more likely that the absence of a clause similar to paragraph (3) of Article 101 in Article 102 is also not an omission, but rather a silent refusal. The fact that the drafters have included such a provision in Article 101 shows that they were aware of the issue, but did not include it in Article 102. However, what must be examined is what the silent refusal actually means, that is whether it means that efficiencies are not relevant at all under Article 102 or whether they are already embedded in the concept of 'abuse' (it thus not being necessary or meaningful for the provision to 'exempt'

[27] See 'Guidance on the Commission's Enforcement Priorities in Applying Article 82 of the EC Treaty to Abusive Exclusionary Conduct by Dominant Undertakings' [2009] OJ C45/7, [28] *et seq* and 'Discussion Paper' (n 2) [84] *et seq.* On the Discussion Paper, see P Akman, 'Article 82 Reformed? The EC Discussion Paper on Exclusionary Abuses' [2006] (December) *Journal of Business Law* 816, 825–26.

[28] See 'Guidelines on Article 101(3)' (n 2) [48] *et seq.*

[29] J Pelkmans, 'Consumer Interests in the EC Competition Regime. An Economic Perspective' in M Goyens (ed), *EC Competition Policy and the Consumer Interest* Proceedings of the Third European Workshop on Consumer Law (Louvain-La Neuve, May 1984) (Louvain-La-Neuve, Cabay, 1985) 33.

efficient behaviour). The following seeks to further the findings of chapter two that the latter alternative is how Article 102 should be interpreted: lack of increase in efficiency should be accepted as a necessary condition for conduct to be abusive under Article 102. This is also in line with the other finding of chapter two that conduct that is 'normal commercial practice' for other undertakings on the market should not be found abusive when undertaken by a dominant undertaking. To demonstrate this argument it is necessary to investigate further the relation between Article 101(3), efficiencies and Article 102.

On the one hand, it has been proposed that Article 102 could incorporate the concept of Article 101(3) – by showing that a fair share of benefits is passed on to consumers – in a justification defence for otherwise exploitative conduct.[30] On the other hand, it has been argued that the abuse of a dominant position in the sense of Article 102 always comprises an unjustifiable violation of the Treaty and that is why Article 102 provides neither a legal defence nor an exemption procedure.[31] The abuse of a dominant position in the internal market or on a substantial part thereof is – without requiring any more conditions – forbidden, to the extent that trade between Member States can thereby be affected. The outlines of that common concept of competition can be described as follows in relation to Article 101 as well: paragraph (3) of Article 101 permits a certain restriction of competition on less than a 'substantial part of the market for the goods concerned' [subparagraph (b)], where indispensable [subparagraph (a)] to improvement in the production or distribution of goods or promotion of technical or economic progress, and as long as consumers are ensured a fair share of the resulting benefits.[32] This code of behaviour applicable to market groupings with less than a dominant position is arguably also directly relevant to the dominant position. From one standpoint, it represents the very assumptions of the Treaty drafters with regard to the necessity for economic concentration; from another, it provides the standard against which operations of a dominant position must be measured.[33] As such, the examples of abuse given in Article 102(a)–(d) are, seen in this light, merely cases which fail to fulfil either of the two 'positive conditions' of Article 101(3) or which come within the first 'negative condition' under subparagraph (a) of paragraph (3).[34]

[30] EM Fox, 'Monopolization and Dominance in the United States and the European Community: Efficiency, Opportunity, and Fairness' (1986) 61 *Notre Dame Law Review* 981, 1019.

[31] I Samkalden and IE Druker, 'Legal Problems Relating to Article 86 of the Rome Treaty' (1966) 3 *Common Market Law Review* 158, 164.

[32] ibid 166.

[33] ibid.

[34] According to this view, the second negative condition under subparagraph (b) would be inapplicable since the presence of a dominant position would already mean the 'elimination of competition in respect of a substantial part of the goods concerned'; Samkalden and Druker (n 31) 166. See L Gyselen, 'Abuse of Monopoly Power within the Meaning of Article 86 of the EEC Treaty: Recent Developments' in B Hawk (ed), *International Antitrust Law & Policy: Fordham Corporate Law 1989* (New York, Juris Publishing, 1990) 635 for the argument that 'objective justification' under Art 102 finds its counterpart in the first three requirements of Article 101(3). *Cf* Commission according to whom the existence of a 'dominant position' does not automatically mean 'substantial elimination' of competition; see 'Guidelines on Article 101(3)' (n 2) [106].

Indeed, according to the ECJ, that Article 102 does not have a clause akin to Article 101(3) can be explained by the fact that the system fixed in Article 102 for dominant positions – unlike Article 101(3) – does not recognise any exemption from the prohibition.[35] As such, Article 102 precludes any possible exception to the prohibition it lays down.[36] Although the position of the ECJ is correct in that Article 102 does not allow for any 'exemption', it nevertheless does not answer whether efficiencies are relevant and, if so, how they should be treated under Article 102.

Interestingly, the Commission Guidance and DG Competition Discussion Paper on exclusionary abuses almost repeat verbatim the conditions of Article 101(3) and the explanations thereof in the Guidelines on Article 101(3) for the proposed 'efficiency justification' under Article 102. Accordingly, the dominant undertaking must be able to show that the efficiencies brought about by the conduct concerned outweigh the likely negative effects on competition resulting from the conduct and therewith the likely harm to consumers that the conduct might otherwise have.[37] To establish this justification, the dominant undertaking must demonstrate that: the efficiencies are realised or likely to be realised as a result of the conduct concerned; the conduct concerned is indispensable to realise these efficiencies; the efficiencies outweigh any likely negative effect on competition and consumers; effective competition is not eliminated.[38] According to the previous Director General of DG Competition, efficiencies will be assessed in an integrated approach as part of an overall weighing of positive and negative effects of the conduct, like in mergers.[39] Yet, the basic assumption is that competition will benefit consumers and that limits on competition will normally harm consumers. This appears to be the view of the Commission as expressed in the Guidance as well: 'where there is no residual competition and no foreseeable threat of entry, the protection of rivalry and the competitive process outweighs possible efficiency gains'.[40]

Although it is welcome that the Guidance and the Discussion Paper elaborate on the treatment of efficiencies under Article 102 and attempt to include efficiencies in the assessment, the way they approach the issue is problematic. This is because, first, these documents are in effect introducing an 'exemption' or an 'exception' rule under Article 102, which is against both the letter of the provision and the case law of the EU courts.[41] An exemption rule does not exist in Article

[35] *Continental Can* (n 15) [25].

[36] Case T-51/89 *Tetra Pak Rausing SA v Commission* [1990] ECR II-309, [25].

[37] 'Discussion Paper' (n 2) [79] and 'Guidance' (n 27) [30].

[38] 'Discussion Paper' (n 2) [84] and 'Guidance' (n 27) [30].

[39] P Lowe, 'Consumer Welfare and Efficiency – New Guiding Principles of Competition Policy?' (13th International Conference on Competition and 14th European Competition Day, Munich, March 2007) 6.

[40] 'Guidance' (n 27) [30].

[41] See text around n 35. The Commission has already applied this approach to efficiencies in its *Intel* decision and has rejected the defence put forward by Intel in around six pages in a prohibition decision of over 500 pages; see *Intel* (COMP/C-3/37.990) Commission Decision 2009/C 227/07, 465–472 (summary of the decision can be found at [2009] OJ C227/13).

102 and therefore cannot be introduced without a Treaty amendment. The treatment of efficiencies as discussed in the Guidance and Discussion Paper is envisaged as a 'justification' that should be invoked by the dominant undertaking.[42] Thus, if adopted, it would work in a similar manner to Article 101(3). First, conduct would be found to prima facie breach Article 102 for being abusive and – only then – the undertaking could prove that efficiencies outweigh the likely negative effects. That is, if the *undertaking* does not prove the efficiencies, the conduct will be established to be abusive. However, as this mechanism simply does not exist in Article 102 itself – although it exists in Article 101 and thus must be an example of a silent refusal – the exemption rule cannot be imported into Article 102 as such. Secondly, the last condition proposed for the defence – namely that conduct does not eliminate effective competition – can mean that the proof of an 'efficiencies justification' under Article 102 is hardly ever possible since there is already an elimination of competition on the market due to the existence of a dominant position. As demonstrated by the *travaux préparatoires* of the negotiations of the Treaty, Article 102 indeed accepts and allows for this elimination.[43] Therefore, the elimination of competition should not be a consideration when assessing the efficiencies of conduct. It has indeed been argued that although the EU institutions have made clear that dominance does not necessarily mean that competition is 'substantially eliminated', since under Article 102 an efficiency defence would be raised in circumstances where the undertaking is already dominant *and* its conduct has been found to have an actual or likely exclusionary effect, for practical purposes, this may mean that competition is substantially eliminated.[44] Yet, even then, the conduct in question may still enhance 'consumer welfare' overall. Thus, there appears to be a logical contradiction between the substantive test for abuse and the availability of an efficiency defence since due to the addition of the 'elimination of effective competition' condition, the former seems to preclude the latter.[45]

Finally, there is a further problem with treating efficiencies as a 'justification' of conduct by a dominant undertaking that can be proven by the undertaking itself.[46] This is because the defence of 'objective justification' is in some ways a tautology despite the fact that it is established in case law that 'objective justification' can immunise from liability conduct that would otherwise be an abuse under Article 102.[47] The tautology is there since, as stated by Advocate General Jacobs, the

[42] 'Discussion Paper' (n 2) [77].

[43] See ch 2 this volume, text around fn 241.

[44] R O'Donoghue and AJ Padilla, *The Law and Economics of Article 82 EC* (Oxford, Hart Publishing, 2006) 233.

[45] ibid.

[46] See Rousseva for the argument that 'objective justification' has never been used and will most likely never be used as an efficiency justification in EU case law; E Rousseva, 'The Concept of "Objective Justification" of an Abuse of a Dominant Position: Can it Help to Modernise the Analysis under Article 82 EC?' (2006) 2(2) *The Competition Law Review* 27, 68.

[47] O'Donoghue and Padilla (n 44) 227 and case law cited ibid, fn 184. See also R Nazzini, 'The Wood began to Move: An Essay on Consumer Welfare, Evidence and Burden of Proof in Article 82 Cases' (2006) 31(4) *European Law Review* 518, 533 arguing that if behaviour is objectively justified, then it is

two-stage analysis suggested by the distinction between an abuse and its objective justification is somewhat artificial.[48] Article 102, in contrast with Article 101, does not contain a two-stage analysis for the exemption of conduct otherwise falling within its prohibition. The very fact that conduct is characterised as an 'abuse' suggests that a negative conclusion has already been reached, in contrast with the more neutral terminology of 'prevention, restriction, or distortion of competition' under Article 101.[49] Thus, as Advocate General Jacobs points out it is therefore more accurate to say that certain types of conduct on the part of a dominant undertaking do not fall within the category of abuse at all.[50]

This is how one should interpret the lack of an equivalent of Article 101(3) in Article 102 and this is how efficiencies should be included in the assessment therein: efficiencies should be taken into account in the definition and finding of 'abuse', rather than as a defence or justification.[51] There is no exemption rule for efficient conduct under Article 102 (unlike Article 101) because, as chapter two has demonstrated, the drafters of the Treaty did not intend to prohibit efficiency enhancing conduct of dominant undertakings by Article 102. It would not make sense for the drafters to consider efficiencies under Article 101, but not under Article 102. Indeed, the *travaux préparatoires* examined in chapter two demonstrate clearly that efficiency – and especially eliminating the productive inefficiency of dominant undertakings – was the foremost concern.[52] It also would not make sense for the drafters to be aware of possible efficiency benefits of otherwise anticompetitive practices while drafting Article 101, but not while drafting Article 102, given that unilateral practices (which are generally common business practice) are at least as likely as (if not more likely than) anticompetitive agreements that breach Article 101 to create efficiencies. Hence, Article 102 does not have an exemption rule because it assumes that conduct breaching the provision is not efficient since otherwise it cannot be an 'abuse'. Thus, inefficiency of conduct should be seen as a necessary condition for finding the practice abusive. Therefore, efficiencies should be considered ex officio by the competition authority before finding conduct abusive. O'Donoghue and Padilla similarly suggest that it should be for the plaintiff or competition authority to show that the anticompetitive effects outweigh efficiencies, as otherwise no abuse will have been proven.[53]

not abusive in the first place. For a detailed assessment of 'objective justification' under Art 102, see P Loewenthal, 'The Defence of "Objective Justification" in the Application of Article 82 EC' (2005) 28(4) *World Competition* 455.

[48] See Opinion of Advocate General Jacobs in *Syfait* (n 1) [72].

[49] ibid.

[50] ibid.

[51] See similarly Rousseva (n 46) 68–69 for the argument that efficiencies should be included in the concept of 'competition on the merits' or 'normal competition'.

[52] See ch 2 this volume, in particular section V.

[53] O'Donoghue and Padilla (n 44) 233. The authors argue that the dominant undertaking should simply bear the initial burden of producing colourable evidence to substantiate the efficiencies claimed. The legal burden should then shift to the plaintiff or the competition authority; ibid. *Cf* Rousseva (n 46) 70 arguing that efficiencies should be proved by the dominant undertaking even though they should form part of 'competition on the merits'.

Admittedly – and perhaps sometimes unfortunately – this is not how Article 102 has generally been interpreted by the Commission or the EU courts. The ECJ has adopted a 'teleological' approach construing Union acts in accordance with the broad system of Treaty aims and objectives.[54] As such, for example, the objective of market integration has trumped other concerns, like efficiency.[55] However, given that the *travaux préparatoires* of the Treaties show that increasing the efficiency of European undertakings was also a great concern in the establishment of the European Communities, there is no reason why even a 'teleological' interpretation could not include efficiency benefits in the analysis.[56] Indeed, considering the historical context within which the Treaties of Rome was adopted, increasing the performance and efficiency of European undertakings can even be deemed as the *reason* for including the competition rules in the Treaty.[57] Therefore, a teleological approach need not necessarily exclude – and perhaps would even require the inclusion of – efficiencies in the definition of 'abuse'.

B Is there a Pass-On Requirement for Efficiencies in Article 102?

The previous section established that the reason that Article 102 does not have a similar clause to Article 101(3) is because efficiencies are a part of the 'abuse' test in the former provision. The consequent question becomes that of whether or not efficiency gains have to be passed on to consumers in the context of Article 102 as Article 101(3) requires this for practices breaching Article 101(1). The issue is whether or not efficiency of conduct would imply a lack of abuse *only when* these efficiencies are passed on to consumers. It has been argued that since promoting efficiency (in the sense of total welfare) is a distinct concept in relation to increasing consumer surplus, a practice reducing the level of competition in the marketplace – if efficiency gains are not passed on to the consumers – is caught by the prohibition in Article 102.[58] In order to establish whether such a requirement of

[54] A Jones and B Sufrin, *EU Competition Law: Text, Cases and Materials* 4th edn (Oxford, OUP, 2011) 101.

[55] See ch 2 this volume, text around fn 28 for the discussion of the possible clash between market integration and efficiency.

[56] For the *travaux préparatoires*, see ch 2 this volume, in particular section V.

[57] eg, Goyder and Albors-Llorens argue that the principal reason for according so much importance to the value of procompetitive measures within the ECSC Treaty was the absence/imperfections of competition in the markets covered by the Treaty since these were felt to be the major weaknesses in industries that needed the spur of rivalry in order to achieve a higher level of performance; J Goyder and A Albors-Llorens, *Goyder's EC Competition Law* 5th edn (Oxford, OUP, 2009) 28.

[58] V Mertikopoulou, 'DG Competition's Discussion Paper on the Application of Article 82 of the EC Treaty to Exclusionary Abuses: The Proposed Economic Reform from a Legal Point of View' (2007) 28(4) *European Competition Law Review* 241, 243. The author nonetheless argues that if it could be shown that a certain foreclosure effect was counterbalanced by efficiency advantages passing through to and benefiting consumers and did not infringe the proportionality principle, the conduct under examination would probably not be found abusive even before the publication of the Discussion Paper. Thus, the efficiency argument is in essence incorporated in the notion of abuse; ibid 247.

pass-on can and/or should exist under Article 102 one should examine this requirement as it exists under Article 101(3).

According to the Commission Guidelines on Article 101(3), the concept of 'fair share' implies that the pass-on of benefits must at least compensate consumers for any actual or likely negative impact caused to them by the restriction of competition found under Article 101(1).[59] The analysis of pass-on to consumers requires a balancing of the negative and positive effects of a practice on consumers.[60] The net effect of the restrictive practice must at least be neutral from the point of view of those consumers directly or likely affected by the practice. If such consumers are worse off following the restrictive practice, the second condition of Article 101(3) is not fulfilled.[61] Moreover, the efficiencies generated by the restrictive practice within a relevant market must be sufficient to outweigh the anticompetitive effects produced by the practice within that *same* relevant market.[62] It has been argued that although in its past practice the Commission has generally assumed that consumers receive a fair share of any benefits as long as competition is not being or has not been eliminated, the new Guidelines on Article 101(3) have abandoned this presumption.[63] Indeed, the Guidelines on Article 101(3) explicitly state that since Article 101(3) only applies in cases where competition on the market is being appreciably restricted, there can be no presumption that residual competition will ensure that consumers receive a fair share of the benefits.[64]

Consumers do not have to receive a share of each and every efficiency gain identified under the first condition of Article 101(3).[65] It is enough that sufficient benefits are passed on to compensate for the negative effects of the restrictive practice since in that case consumers obtain a 'fair share' of the overall benefits. For example, if a restrictive practice is likely to lead to higher prices, consumers must be fully compensated through increased quality or other benefits. If the practice has both substantial anticompetitive and procompetitive effects, a careful analysis is required.[66] In the application of the balancing test it must be taken into account that competition is an important long-term driver of efficiency and innovation. More importantly, the Guidelines on Article 101(3) explain that undertakings that are not subject to effective competitive constraints, such as dominant undertakings, have less incentive to maintain or build on the efficiencies. Thus, there appears to be a built-in presumption that dominant undertakings are less likely than others to pass on the efficiency gains to consumers. Nonetheless, the Guidelines also accept as a general rule that if due to cost efficiencies undertakings in question can increase profits by expanding output, consumer pass-on may

[59] 'Guidelines on Article 101(3)' (n 2) [85].
[60] ibid [39].
[61] ibid [85].
[62] ibid [43].
[63] L Kjolbye, 'The New Commission Guidelines on the Application of Article 81(3): An Economic Approach to Article 81' (2004) 25(9) *European Competition Law Review* 566, 575.
[64] 'Guidelines on Article 101(3)' (n 2) [96].
[65] ibid [86].
[66] ibid [92].

occur.[67] Finally, the availability of new and improved products is accepted to constitute an important source of consumer welfare and so long as the increase in value stemming from such improvements exceeds any harm from a maintenance or an increase in price caused by the restrictive practice, consumers are better off than without the practice and the consumer pass-on requirement is normally fulfilled.[68]

With regard to types of benefits that can be considered under Article 101(3), cost savings that arise from the mere exercise of market power by the parties cannot be taken into account.[69] This bears elaborating on for the purposes of Article 102. The Guidelines on Article 101(3) give an example of such cost savings, namely those that arise from the exercise of market power, as those where undertakings agree to fix price or share markets, reduce output and thereby production costs. Such cost reductions are a direct consequence of a reduction in output and value and do not produce any procompetitive effects on the market. In particular, 'they do not lead to the creation of value through an integration of assets and activities'.[70] If this were to be implemented in the context of Article 102, it would mean that production cost savings which result from increased productive efficiency leading to creation of value *would be* legitimate considerations. Nonetheless, the later statement in the Guidelines on Article 101(3) according to which the causal link between the practice and the efficiencies must normally be direct and claims based on indirect effects are as a general rule too uncertain and too remote to be taken into account casts doubt on the possible acceptance of such efficiency gains.[71] This is apparent from the example given for indirect effects: in a case where it is claimed that a restrictive practice allows the undertakings concerned to increase their profits – enabling them to invest more in research and development to the ultimate benefit of consumers – although there may be a link between profitability and research and development, this link is generally not sufficiently direct to be taken into account under Article 101(3). Adapted to Article 102, this would imply that conduct of a dominant undertaking increasing its efficiency and profits – which may lead to increased research and development – would not be treated favourably. This is unfortunate given the importance of dynamic efficiencies in many markets and reflects a short-term focused approach to efficiency gains.

Nonetheless, it must be pointed out that in *GlaxoSmithKline*, the GC rightly held that the Commission's argument that there must be a 'direct' link between the restrictive clause and the gain in efficiency could not be accepted.[72] Accordingly, that distinction is not provided for in Article 101(3), which allows for the exemption of conduct producing an efficiency gain without distinction as to whether that effect is direct or indirect, and a distinction cannot in principle be drawn

[67] ibid [96].
[68] ibid [104].
[69] ibid [49].
[70] ibid.
[71] ibid [54].
[72] *GlaxoSmithKline* (GC) (n 1) [280].

where the Treaty draws no distinction. In accordance with the case law, any advantage in the form of a gain in efficiency must therefore be taken into account, provided that it is objective and appreciable and that its existence is proved convincingly.[73]

All in all, for the sake of consistency with the system under Article 101 and in light of the objective of the Commission's enforcement of Article 102, expressed as ensuring 'that dominant undertakings do not impair effective competition by foreclosing their competitors in an anti-competitive way, thus having an adverse impact on consumer welfare',[74] one could argue that efficiencies have to be passed on to consumers to be considered under Article 102.[75] This would also have to be the stance if one accepts that Article 101(3) sets the standard as consumer welfare and that both Articles 101 and 102 have the same objective. The ECJ also seems to have adopted a pass-on requirement, albeit one which is unclear as to its details and implementation. In its *British Airways* judgment the Court held that while assessing the economic justification of conduct by a dominant undertaking, it has to be determined whether the exclusionary effect arising from conduct which is disadvantageous for competition may be counterbalanced or outweighed by advantages in terms of efficiency which also benefit the consumer.[76] If the exclusionary effect of the conduct bears no relation to advantages for the market *and* consumers or if it goes beyond what is necessary in order to attain those advantages, that conduct must be regarded as an abuse. The ECJ repeated this position in its judgment in *TeliaSonera*.[77]

Nevertheless, it must be borne in mind that although the theory of balancing procompetitive and anticompetitive effects sounds straightforward, it might be anything but.[78] Arguably, the exercise is easy in theory: the amount of benefits (increased consumer welfare) is compared with the welfare loss caused by the exclusion of rivals (for example, reduced consumer surplus or deadweight loss) and whichever is larger determines the outcome. In practice, it may not be easy or even possible for a dominant undertaking to make such detailed assessments at the time it decides on its commercial strategy, specifically if it involves detailed knowledge of the effects of a particular practice on competitors and more generally on consumer welfare.[79] Thus, the dominant undertaking may not have the

[73] ibid.

[74] 'Guidance' (n 27) [19].

[75] As for merger control, Council Regulation (EC) No 139/2004 on the Control of Concentrations between Undertakings (EU Merger Regulation) [2004] OJ L24/1 has introduced 'efficiencies' explicitly into the legal framework, although it is not clear whether the Commission 'Guidelines on the Assessment of Horizontal Mergers under the Council Regulation on the Control of Concentrations between Undertakings' [2004] OJ C31/5 adopts a consumer welfare standard or a total welfare standard. Some paras (eg, [78], [79]) suggest that it is a consumer welfare test because efficiencies have to be passed on to consumers, whereas others (eg, [76]) suggest that it is a total welfare test by stipulating that efficiencies may outweigh potential harm to consumers; E Navarro, A Font, J Folguera and J Briones, *Merger Control in the EU: Law, Economics and Practice* 2nd edn (Oxford, OUP, 2005) 334–35.

[76] Case C-95/04 P *British Airways v Commission* [2007] ECR I-2331, [86].

[77] Case C-52/09 *Konkurrensverket v TeliaSonera Sverige AB* [2011] ECR I-00, [76].

[78] O'Donoghue and Padilla (n 44) 232.

[79] ibid.

necessary information to precisely identify and quantify the pass-on to consumers, not least because the subject matter is unilateral conduct. According to the Commission Guidance, the ultimate assessment of this will be made by the Commission, which will decide whether on a weighing-up of any apparent anti-competitive effects against any advanced and substantiated efficiencies consumer harm is likely to result. Yet, the Commission is also likely to suffer from similar informational deficiencies which would imply that efficiencies which by their nature are difficult to quantify (particularly dynamic efficiencies) will be disregarded in the assessment of 'abuse'.[80] For the purposes of this study's proposal of the conditions of 'abuse', direct pass-on of efficiency gains to consumers is indeed not required and the discussion of this is left for chapter eight.

In any case, even if efficiency gains have to be passed on to consumers to be legitimate, what should not be lost sight of is that limiting the assessment to only short-term effects of conduct may in the long term be detrimental to 'consumer welfare'. This is a direct implication of the necessity to interpret welfare not only in a static sense, but also in a dynamic context; in other words, future welfare matters as well as current welfare.[81] If 'consumer welfare' is adopted as the objective, one should consider this as that of maximising consumer surplus over time since otherwise by helping consumers today, one could hurt consumers tomorrow.[82] The Commission Guidance does not make any comments on the timing of the efficiencies or on whether dynamic efficiencies will be given the same weight as cost efficiencies; in fact, dynamic efficiencies are only expressed as an outcome of 'rivalry' on the market without which the dominant undertaking would lack the incentives to create and pass on efficiency gains.[83] Moreover, where there is no residual competition and no foreseeable threat of entry, the Guidance states that 'the protection of rivalry and the competitive process outweighs possible efficiency gains'.[84] This is unfortunate since not only the Guidance appears to imply the use of dynamic efficiencies as a factor *against* the dominant undertaking, it also represents a form-based approach with no economic or legal justification provided, particularly because it is unclear what 'protection of rivalry and the competitive process' means 'where there is no residual competition'.[85]

Such an unfortunate understanding of dynamic efficiencies can also be seen in the GC's judgment in *Microsoft*. In that case Microsoft put forward – as an objec-

[80] It has also been remarked that such a balancing exercise is neither useful nor necessary since either a given conduct represents competition on the merits in which case there is no reason to prohibit it or it is competition on the merits but forecloses the market in which case there is no place for balancing positive and negative effects since the conclusion is clear in that the behaviour is anticompetitive; D Waelbroeck, 'The Assessment of Efficiencies under Article 102 TFEU and the Commission's Guidance Paper' in F Etro and I Kokkoris (eds), *Competition Law and the Enforcement of Article 102* (Oxford, OUP, 2010) 125.

[81] M Motta, *Competition Policy: Theory and Practice* (Cambridge, CUP, 2004) 19.

[82] ibid.

[83] 'Guidance' (n 27) [30].

[84] ibid.

[85] See P Akman, 'The European Commission's Guidance on Article 102: From *Inferno* to *Paradiso*?'(2010) 73(4) *Modern Law Review* 605, 624.

tive justification of its conduct – the argument that it has made significant investment in designing the protocols which its competitors requested for interoperability and the success that its products has achieved represented the just reward; being obliged to supply this information to its competitors would reduce its incentives to invest in research and development.[86] The GC rejected this argument on the grounds that 'Microsoft merely put vague, general and theoretical arguments on that point'.[87] According to the GC, Microsoft merely stated that disclosure would eliminate future incentives to invest in the creation of more intellectual property 'without specifying the technologies or products to which it thus referred'.[88] However, given the inherent uncertainty in technological progress, innovation and thus dynamic efficiency, it is questionable how an undertaking can prove that it *will* innovate with the outcome of certain specific technologies or products to reach the threshold of credibility set by the GC. Moreover, the GC appears to have preferred the dynamic efficiency of the competitors of the dominant undertaking without subjecting the competitors to the same threshold: once the obstacle represented for Microsoft's competitors by the insufficient degree of interoperability was removed, those competitors would be able to offer products which would be distinguished from Microsoft's product with respect to parameters which consumers consider important.[89] What must be noted is that the threshold the Court has set for this condition to be satisfied is quite low since whether or not Microsoft's competitors would indeed offer 'new products' appears to have been based on the *assumption* that they would not have any interest in merely reproducing Microsoft's product and thus 'they will have no other choice, if they wish to take advantage of a competitive advantage over Microsoft and maintain a profitable presence on the market, than to differentiate their products from Microsoft's products'.[90] Hence, there appears to be a bias in favour of the dominant undertaking's competitors' incentives to invest and innovate against the dominant undertaking's incentives.[91] As adopted by the GC in *Microsoft* this appears to be an arbitrary distinction that distorts the equality between a dominant undertaking and its competitors without adequate justification since it is not obvious *why* the competitors' dynamic efficiency should be preferred over that of the dominant undertaking.

[86] *Microsoft* (n 1) [666], [670].
[87] ibid [698].
[88] ibid.
[89] ibid [656].
[90] ibid [658].
[91] ibid [636]–[37]. The GC treats Microsoft's incentives to innovate as irrelevant to the issue of the impact of the refusal to supply on the incentives of Microsoft's competitors; ibid [659]. As such, it is dealt with and refused as an 'objective justification' by the GC; ibid [697].

C Does Article 101(3) Set a Standard of 'Consumer Welfare'?

It should be reiterated that according to the ECJ, both Articles 101 and 102 pursue the same objective.[92] For the purposes of establishing the place of 'consumer welfare' in Article 102, one essential question is therefore whether the pass-on requirement in Article 101(3) indeed sets the standard as 'consumer welfare' for Article 101. There are two grounds on which it can be questioned whether Article 101(3) sets a consumer welfare standard: first, it has been argued that Article 101(3) merely requires that consumers must have a fair share of the 'resulting benefit' of the agreement in respect of which exemption is sought.[93] The cumulative nature of the conditions for the exception in Article 101(3) to be applicable means that provided that the agreement concerned leads to an improvement in production or distribution or technical or economic progress, some 'resulting benefit' for consumers is arguably inevitable.[94] Thus, the latter becomes a formality once the existence of the former is established. Therefore, assessment of the existence of resulting benefit for consumers has been noted to play no decisive role in the application of Article 101(3).[95] It has in fact been suggested that the conclusion could be drawn that the Commission treats the promotion of 'consumer welfare' as a consequence of the application of Article 101(3) rather than as a consideration affecting the content of this provision and the extent to which consumer interests are invoked.[96] What 'consumer benefit' exactly means under Article 101(3) has been decided by the Commission on a case-by-case basis and, despite this express recognition of consumer interests, this criterion has arguably not become a substantive right of consumers which could be defended by consumer associations.[97] Thus, it is not clear whether the requirement of pass-on to consumers suggests strongly enough that the standard under Article 101 is 'consumer welfare', since not only is it conceptually ambiguous, its practical relevance is also doubtful.

[92] *Continental Can* (n 15) [25].

[93] AC Evans, 'European Competition Law and Consumers: The Article 85(3) Exemption' (1981) *European Competition Law Review* 425, 429. Under the previous enforcement regulation, namely Regulation 17, the Commission had to grant an 'exemption' for Art 101(3) to be applicable since this provision was not directly applicable. Regulation 1 has abolished the exemption system in favour of an automatic 'exception' regime. See Council Regulation 17/62 Implementing Articles 85 and 86 EC Treaty [1962] OJ 13/204, Article 4 and Council Regulation (EC) No 1/2003 of 16 December 2002 on the implementation of the rules on competition laid down in Articles 81 and 82 of the Treaty [2003] OJ L1/1, Article 1.

[94] Evans, ibid, 431.

[95] ibid.

[96] A Evans, 'Article 85(3) Exemption: The Notion of "Allowing Consumers a Fair Share of the Resulting Benefit"' in M Goyens (ed), *EC Competition Policy and the Consumer Interest* Proceedings of the Third European Workshop on Consumer Law (Louvain-La Neuve, May, 1984 (Louvain-La-Neuve, Cabay, 1985) 108. See similarly E Buttigieg, *Competition Law: Safeguarding the Consumer Interest* (The Netherlands, Kluwer Law International, 2009) 128–29.

[97] Cseres (n 5) 256.

Secondly, it must be pointed out that the 'consumer' referred to in Article 101(3) does not necessarily refer to what is a 'consumer' for the purposes of consumer law.[98] This is clear from the *travaux préparatoires*, the original language versions of the Treaties of Rome and the Guidelines on Article 101(3).[99] According to the Guidelines on Article 101(3), the concept of 'consumer' encompasses all direct or indirect users of the products covered by the practice, including producers that use the products as an input, wholesalers, retailers and final consumers, namely natural persons who are acting for purposes outside their trade or profession.[100] Thus, it has been suggested that the requirement of a fair share for consumers can be seen as corresponding with the fourth requirement imposed by Article 101(3), in that sufficient remaining competitive pressure will ensure that the benefits arising from an agreement are actually passed on and do not just accrue with the parties to the practice.[101] As such, it only aims to ensure that the welfare gains (through increased efficiency) that are the result of the practice will also lead to an increase in social welfare, not necessarily consumer welfare.[102] This identification of 'consumer' as 'customer' has been called the 'Chicago trap' with the implication that final consumers do not always profit from a decision even when it is aimed at the improvement of consumers' welfare.[103]

It should be noted here that the Commission has indeed generally treated persons purchasing products of the parties to the restrictive practice as 'consumers' for the purposes of Article 101(3).[104] As such, the Commission has not allowed for the fact that the interests of the intermediate 'consumer' – the 'customer' – are not necessarily identical to those of the final consumer.[105] In particular, while the former will desire a product with which she may maximise her profits, the interests of the latter will revolve around the broad notion of 'satisfaction'. Therefore, the Commission's interpretation of the term 'consumers' in Article 101(3) would seem to have limited the extent to which principles appropriate to the needs of consumers in the ordinary sense of the word may be developed.[106] Moreover, how

[98] 'Consumer' in consumer law refers to any person who is acting for purposes outside her trade, business or profession when entering into a transaction. Equivalent terms would be 'end-user' and 'final customer'. See, eg, Council Directive 93/13/EEC on Unfair Terms in Consumer Contracts [1993] OJ L95/29, Article 2(b); Council Directive 2005/29/EC on Unfair Commercial Practices [2005] OJ L149/22, Article 2(a).

[99] eg, '*utilisateurs*' in the French version, '*utilizzatori*' in the Italian version and '*gebruikers*' in the Dutch version refer to 'users'. Although in the German version '*Verbraucher*' (consumer) is used, see *travaux préparatoires* of the Treaties on this usage of 'consumer' meaning 'customer' in ch 2 this volume, text around fn 339.

[100] 'Guidelines on Article 101(3)' (n 2) [84].

[101] H Vedder, 'Competition Law and Consumer Protection: How Competition Law can be used to Protect Consumers Even Better – Or Not?' [2006] *European Business Law Review* 83, 87.

[102] ibid 87.

[103] Cseres (n 5) 331.

[104] Evans (n 93) 429.

[105] For an explanation and discussion of the implications of the difference between 'consumer' and 'customer', see P Akman, '"Consumer" versus "Customer": The Devil in the Detail' (2010) 37(2) *Journal of Law and Society* 315.

[106] Evans (n 93) 429.

the term 'consumer' is interpreted by the competition authority or the courts should be decisive when one examines whether the terminological reference to 'consumer welfare' is merely a catchword which has nothing to do with the interests of end-users or whether it serves those interests directly or indirectly.[107] Therefore, all in all, it is doubtful whether Article 101(3) sets the standard and objective of Article 101 as 'consumer welfare' and even if it does, whether the 'consumer welfare' standard it sets is the appropriate one given the understanding of 'consumer' as 'customer' which would in most cases mean preferring the interests of buying firms over selling firms.[108] As a result, it is questionable whether Article 101(3) implies and/or necessitates the standard of EU competition law in general and of Article 102 to be 'consumer welfare'.

As a matter of fact, the Guidelines on Article 101(3) state that 'the ultimate aim of Article [101] is to protect the competitive process'.[109] Ultimately, the protection of rivalry and the competitive process is given priority over potentially procompetitive efficiency gains which could result from restrictive practices. Accordingly, the last condition of Article 101(3) recognises the fact that rivalry between undertakings is an essential driver of economic efficiency, including dynamic efficiencies in the shape of innovation. To be exempt, the restrictive practice must not afford the parties the possibility of substantially eliminating competition. Thus, elimination of competition is not accepted under Article 101. Although this is also the position in the Commission Guidance on Article 102 as mentioned above,[110] it raises concerns regarding its conformity with Article 102 since the fact that Article 102 does not prohibit a dominant position itself but only its abuse – as demonstrated also by the legislative history – shows that the elimination of competition to the extent that a dominant position exists *is* indeed allowed for under Article 102.[111] Therefore, contrary to the ECJ holding in *Continental Can*,[112] this may mean that the *specific* goals to be pursued by Articles 101 and 102 are different due to their different contexts. Nonetheless, it must also be pointed out that there might be a change of understanding at the EU authorities. In the past, the Commission had taken the view that elimination of competition could be equated

[107] Cseres (n 5) 332–33.

[108] For the latter point, see also J Farrell and ML Katz, 'The Economics of Welfare Standards in Antitrust' (2006) 2(2) *Competition Policy International* 3, 11–12 and Motta (n 81) 19–20 where the author argues that Art 101(3) and EU Merger Regulation (n 75) Article 2.1 *might* indicate that consumer welfare is *among* the ultimate objectives of EU competition law although he is not aware of any statement of the ECJ on this point or any Commission/Court decision where reliance on either standard has made a difference in practice.

[109] 'Guidelines on Article 101(3)' (n 2) [105].

[110] See above, text around n 43.

[111] *cf* Kroes (n 26) 5 where the previous Commissioner argues that this last condition of Art 101(3) must also be respected when applying Art 102 and, thus, there is a level of market power where efficiencies can no longer prevail over the long-term interest of protecting competition in the market. *Cf* also *Continental Can* (n 15) [24] where the ECJ held that competition cannot be eliminated. For the legislative history demonstrating that this was not the intention of the drafters of Art 102, see ch 2 this volume, text around fn 241.

[112] *Continental Can* (n 15) [25].

with dominance.[113] In contrast, in recent case law the GC has expressly held that elimination of competition is not the same as dominance.[114] Indeed, the Guidelines on Article 101(3) also state that Article 101(3) may be applicable to conduct of dominant undertakings since not all restrictive agreements concluded by a dominant undertaking constitute an 'abuse' of a dominant position.[115] Thereby, the Guidelines also accept that the existence of a 'dominant position' does not automatically mean the 'substantial elimination of competition' under Article 101(3). What is unfortunate is that the Guidelines do not elaborate on the treatment of efficiencies resulting from practices of dominant undertakings which are not necessarily restrictive agreements, but are practices, such as pricing decisions. Although this is understandable due to the scope of the Guidelines being limited to multilateral conduct, it is also not clear what criteria exist to distinguish between restrictive agreements of a dominant undertaking which would constitute 'abuse' of that position and which would not be abusive, albeit restrictive.

To summarise, the fact that there is not an equivalent of Article 101(3) in Article 102 suggests that efficiencies are part of the 'abuse' component of Article 102. For the sake of consistency with Article 101(3), one could argue that efficiencies should be passed on to consumers to be legitimate. Yet, there might be formidable practical problems with this, particularly in terms of proof. Moreover, even if one accepts that Article 101(3) sets the standard as 'consumer welfare', given the different contexts Article 101 and Article 102 are applied in (that is the former applies to multilateral, whereas the latter applies to unilateral conduct in different market structures), they may not necessarily have the same standard. Moreover, although a literal reading of Article 101(3) suggests that the pass-on requirement sets the standard as 'consumer welfare', it is disputable whether this is indeed the case, not least because 'consumer' in that provision does not refer to final consumers, which is the usual legal and economic understanding of the term. Hence, after this examination of the provisions of Articles 101(3) and 102, the next section investigates the practice of the Commission and the EU courts in terms of the standard of harm they apply in their decisional practice under Article 102.

III THE STANDARD OF HARM AND THE 'CONSUMER WELFARE' STANDARD: A CRITICAL LOOK AT THE APPLICATION OF ARTICLE 102 BY THE COMMISSION AND THE EU COURTS

It is unfortunately not possible to identify a coherent and unified approach to the standard of harm under Article 102. The legal concept of 'abuse' is sufficiently

[113] Kjolbye (n 63) 576.

[114] Joined Cases T-191/98, 212/98 and 214/98 *Atlantic Container Line (TACA)* [2003] ECR II-3275, [939] and Case T-395/94 *Atlantic Container Line* [2002] ECR II-875, [330].

[115] 'Guidelines on Article 101(3)' (n 2) [106]. According to the Guidelines the concept in Art 101(3) of elimination of competition in respect of a substantial part of the products concerned is an autonomous Union law concept specific to Art 101(3); ibid.

abstract and capacious to allow multiple conceptions of its goals.[116] Arguably, clashing images of the goals of the provision have caused uncertainty about the future of the law in this area and this impedes the capacity of European judges and administrators to apply the law consistently and effectively.[117] As such, it is not easy to determine whether and how 'consumer welfare' plays a role in the enforcement of EU competition rules and specifically Article 102. Although this is a question of objectives and is thus fundamental if enforcement is to serve the appropriate objectives, it is surprisingly unsettled. It has indeed been pointed out that given that one of the fundamental objectives of EU competition law relates to the maximisation of consumer welfare, it is undeniably odd that neither 'consumer benefit' nor 'consumer detriment' has been given comprehensive treatment under either hard or soft EU competition law.[118]

With regard to the standard of harm, there seem to be two important aspects: first, whether the finding of 'abuse' has to be based on (actual or likely) *effects* of the conduct or whether such an assessment is not necessary; and secondly, who or what is the subject on which harm (or harmful *effects*) must be demonstrated before a finding of infringement of Article 102 can be made. In other words, it must be determined whether it is harm to (or harmful *effects* on) competitors, competition or consumers that cause conduct to be abusive. Both limbs of this issue are directly related to the recent modernisation of the Commission's application of Article 102 which arguably sought to adopt an economic and effects-based approach.[119] This section deals with these two questions in turn on the basis of an assessment of the EU authorities' decisional practice.

A Are *Effects* Necessary for a Finding of Abuse?

The decisional practice is inconsistent on the necessity of anticompetitive *effects* under Article 102.[120] On the one hand, several cases indicate that there must be a concrete assessment of a practice's effects on the market before a finding of material adverse effect can be made.[121] On the other hand, there are cases which find

[116] Gerber (n 11) 37.

[117] ibid.

[118] Marsden and Whelan (n 7) 572.

[119] See, eg, Kroes (n 25) 5 stating that '[t]he exercise of market power must be assessed essentially on the basis of its effects on the market'.

[120] O'Donoghue and Padilla (n 44) 217.

[121] See, eg, Case T-65/89 *BPB Industries plc and British Gypsum Ltd v Commission* [1993] ECR II-389, [65]–[66], upheld on appeal in Case C-310/93 P *BPB Industries plc and British Gypsum Ltd v Commission* [1995] ECR I-865; Case T-65/98 *Van den Bergh Foods Ltd v Commission* [2003] ECR II-4563, upheld on appeal in Case C-552/03 P *Unilever Bestfoods (Ireland) Ltd (formerly Van den Bergh Foods Ltd) v Commission* [2006] 5 CMLR 27; Case T-83/91 *Tetra Pak International SA v Commission* [1994] ECR II-755, [151], upheld on appeal in Case C-333/94 P *Tetra Pak International SA v Commission* [1996] ECR I-5951. Similarly Commission decisions such as *ECS/AKZO* (Case IV/30.698) Commission Decision 85/609/EEC [1985] OJ L374/1, [86]; *Deutsche Post AG* (Case COMP/35.141) Commission Decision 2001/354/EC [2001] OJ L125/27, [37] *et seq.*

that anticompetitive *object* or *potential* restrictive *effects* are sufficient to prove an abuse.[122]

In *Deutsche Telekom* the ECJ held that for conduct to be abusive it *has to* have the *effect* of hindering the maintenance of the degree of competition still existing in the market or the growth of that competition and there *has to* be a *demonstration* of anticompetitive effect.[123] In this margin squeeze case, the relevant *effect* related to the possible creation of barriers for the growth of as efficient competitors' products.[124] Similarly, in *British Gypsum*, for example, the GC found that appraisal of the *effects* of exclusive purchasing commitments on the functioning of the market concerned depended on the characteristics of the market; it was thus necessary, in principle, to examine the *effects* of such commitments on the market in their specific context.[125] In *Van den Bergh* both the Commission and the GC considered the effects of the freezer-exclusivity agreements the dominant ice-cream manufacturer entered into with retailers. The GC held that the exclusivity clause had the *effect* of preventing the retailers from selling other brands of ice cream (even though there was demand for such brands) and of preventing competing manufacturers from gaining access to the relevant market.[126]

In contrast, there are also several cases where the effects of conduct were *not* deemed relevant, such as *Michelin II* and *Irish Sugar* where the GC held that, for the purposes of applying Article 102, establishing anticompetitive object and anticompetitive effect are one and the same thing.[127] Under this rationale, if it is shown that the object pursued by the conduct of a dominant undertaking is to limit competition, that conduct will also be liable to have such an effect.[128] Moreover, according to the GC, the *effect* referred to in the case law on Article 102 does not necessarily relate to the *actual* effect of the abusive conduct complained of; for the purposes of establishing an infringement of Article 102, it is sufficient to show that the abusive conduct of the dominant undertaking tends to restrict competition or, in other words, that the conduct is capable of having that effect.[129] Thus, not only are actual effects not necessary since *likely* effects are sufficient, given that anticompetitive *object* and effect are the same thing, even *likely* effects are *not* necessary for a finding of abuse if *object* is established.

[122] See Case T-203/01 *Manufacture francaise des pneumatiques Michelin v Commission* [2003] ECR II-4071, [239]; Case T-219/99 *British Airways plc v Commission* [2003] ECR II-5917, [293], upheld on appeal in *British Airways* (n 76); *Deutsche Telekom AG* (Case COMP/C-1/37.451, 37.578, 37.579) Commission Decision 2003/707/EC [2003] OJ L263/9, [179]–[80].

[123] Case C-280/08 *Deutsche Telekom AG v Commission* [2010] ECR 00, [251], [252].

[124] ibid [252].

[125] *British Gypsum* (GC) (n 121) [66]. See also Case T-61/89 *Dansk Pelsdyravlerforening v Commission* [1992] ECR II-1931, [99]; Case C-234/89 *Delimitis v Henninger Braeu* [1991] ECR I-935, [23], [28] *et seq.*

[126] *Van den Bergh* (GC) (n 121) [160].

[127] *Michelin II* (n 122) [241]; Case T-228/97 *Irish Sugar plc v Commission* [1999] ECR II-2969, [170], upheld on appeal in Case C-497/99 *Irish Sugar plc v Commission* [2001] ECR I-5333.

[128] *Michelin II* (n 122) [241]. See also Case T-340/03 *France Télécom SA (formerly Wanadoo Interactive SA) v Commission* [2007] 4 CMLR 21, [195], upheld on appeal in Case C-202/07 *France Télécom SA v Commission* [2009] ECR I-2369.

[129] *Michelin II* (n 122) [239]. Similarly *British Airways* (n 122) [293]; Case T-155/06 *Tomra Systems ASA and others v Commission* [2010] ECR II-00, [289].

These holdings of the GC are troubling since finding conduct abusive when it is capable of having an anticompetitive *effect* is very different from finding conduct abusive merely on the basis of alleged anticompetitive *object.* Unlike Article 101, Article 102 does not sanction anticompetitive object. This is in conformity with the nature of the provision; a dominant undertaking can only abuse its position if it *uses* its power abusively and it is not easy to contemplate how the undertaking can abusively use its power with merely having the object to do so without *actually* using its power. Oddly enough, the GC itself also stated that, unlike Article 101(1), Article 102 contains no reference to the anticompetitive object or anticompetitive effect of the practice referred to, but in the light of the context of Article 102, conduct will be regarded as abusive only if it *restricts* competition.[130] In fact, as in the example of predatory pricing, even if the undertaking has the *object* to restrict competition by predation, a failed attempt at predation would benefit consumers by reduced prices and, thus, the *effect* would not be anticompetitive under a 'consumer welfare' standard. It is difficult to see why such a practice which ultimately benefits consumers should be sanctioned as abuse. This, however, does not seem to be the understanding of the courts.

The courts have held on various occasions that when an undertaking actually implements practices with the *aim* of restricting competition, the fact that the result sought is not achieved is not enough to avoid the application of Article 102.[131] It has been suggested in the literature that certain decisions of European courts and wording in Commission guidelines suggest that an 'object or effect' test applies under Article 102 as well; there is a latent premise that certain kinds of behaviour are to be presumed abusive, such that the burden then shifts to the defendant to establish exceptional circumstances or objective justification.[132] Moreover, not only the object, but also the *intent* of the dominant undertaking appears to play a role in determining whether conduct is abusive.[133]

The policy of the Commission and the jurisprudence of the EU courts on Article 102 have indeed been long criticised for not being grounded in sound eco-

[130] *Michelin II* (n 122) [237]. Repeated in *Microsoft* (n 1) [867].

[131] *Irish Sugar* (GC) (n 127) [191]; *Michelin II* (n 122) [245]; *British Airways* (n 122) [297]; *Wanadoo* (GC) (n 128) [196]; *Deutsche Telekom* (n 123) [254].

[132] D Sinclair, 'Abuse of Dominance at a Crossroads – Potential Effect, Object and Appreciability under Article 82 EC' (2004) 25(8) *European Competition Law Review* 491, 497–98. In the context of Art 101, Odudu suggests that the justifications for object without effect being sufficient for liability under Art 101 are that, first, Art 101 is not only concerned with seeking out those who have caused restrictive effects, but with preventing restrictive effects from occurring and, secondly, failure to restrict competition after attempting to do so is a function of chance rather than choice and the choice is sufficient in itself; O Odudu, 'Interpreting Article 81(1): Object as Subjective Intention' (2001) 26(1) *European Law Review* 60, 71.

[133] Sinclair, ibid, 498–99. Eg, the test of predatory pricing in *AKZO* includes an intention based assessment; Case C-62/86 *AKZO Chemie BV v Commission* [1991] ECR I-3359, [70] *et seq.* See also *Tetra Pak II* (ECJ) (n 121) [41]. For the argument that the 'object' requirement in Art 101 can be satisfied by the *subjective intention* of the parties to the restrictive practice, see Odudu, ibid, 60, 70. *Cf* R Whish, *Competition Law* 6th edn (Oxford, OUP, 2009) 116 arguing that 'object' means not the subjective intention of the parties, but the objective meaning and purpose of the agreement considered in the economic context in which it is to be applied.

nomics as the traditional 'form-based' approach focused on the form of alleged abusive conduct is considered inferior to an 'effects-based' alternative.[134] This has led the Commission to review its application of Article 102. During this review which culminated in the Commission Guidance, it was repeatedly stated that enforcement of this provision should focus on conduct that has actual or likely restrictive *effects* on the market and so harms consumers.[135] The two main reasons for making this the priority were expressed as the necessity of enforcement agencies to be cautious about intervening in markets unless there is clear evidence that markets are not working well and the fact that enforcement agencies do not have unlimited resources which requires them to focus their efforts on what makes a real difference. The objective of Article 102 has thus been expressed as protecting competition on the market, not for its own sake, but rather as a means of enhancing consumer welfare and ensuring the efficient allocation of resources.[136] The Discussion Paper had also iterated the same goal.[137] The Commission Guidance which is the first and only official document of the European Commission concerning the application of Article 102, however, is more ambiguous on the ultimate objective of the provision and on the role of 'consumer welfare'. This is mainly because the Guidance is not so clear regarding the relationship between foreclosing rivals and adversely impacting consumer welfare since the way the Commission expresses its enforcement aim by stating that the concern is 'to ensure that dominant undertakings do not impair effective competition by foreclosing rivals in an anti-competitive way, thus having an adverse impact on consumer welfare' is equivocal.[138] It could be interpreted as a requirement to show likely adverse effect on consumer welfare in order to identify an abuse, or it could imply that the adverse impact on consumers is the expected consequence of foreclosing rivals in an anticompetitive way. However, under the latter interpretation, it is not certain how one should identify the *anticompetitiveness* of foreclosure and this would imply that it is *not* the effect on consumer welfare that signifies the anticompetitiveness of foreclosure. Although elsewhere in the Guidance, the Commission states that it is concerned with 'safeguarding the competitive process in the internal market and ensuring that undertakings which hold a dominant position do not exclude their competitors by other means than competing on the merits of the products or services they provide',[139] 'competition on the merits' is a

[134] Akman (n 27) 816. According to the EAGCP Report commissioned by EU DG Competition, an effects-based approach focuses on the presence of anticompetitive effects that harm consumers and is based on the examination of each specific case, based on sound economics and grounded on facts. An economics-based approach requires a careful examination of how competition works in each particular market in order to evaluate how specific company strategies affect consumer welfare; Report by the Economic Advisory Group for Competition Policy (EAGCP) 'An Economic Approach to Article 82' (July, 2005) available at ec.europa.eu/dgs/competition/economist/eagcp_july_21_05.pdf 2.

[135] See, eg, Kroes (n 26) 2; Kroes (n 25) 5; 'Discussion Paper' (n 2) [4].

[136] Kroes (n 26) 3; Kroes (n 25) 5.

[137] 'Discussion Paper' (n 2) [4], [54], [88].

[138] Akman (n 85) 614.

[139] 'Guidance' (n 27) [6].

vague concept.[140] An assumption of abuse based on it may result in the classification of some particular *conduct* as abusive, and therefore reduce the test to a form-based one; whenever the authority is faced with that particular conduct, it may assume that it is abusive.[141] Even if 'competition on the merits' is taken to mean competing on price, quality, etc, it remains without sufficient limiting principles.[142] All in all, it is not clear how much the Commission has actually modernised its understanding and approach to Article 102 to adopt an effects-based approach as a result of its review. This issue will be elaborated on further in chapter seven.

B On Whom or What should Harm (or Harmful *Effects*) be Demonstrated?

As for the second-limb of the question, namely on whom or what the anticompetitive *effects* of conduct must be observed for a finding of abuse, it is again not easy to discern a clear understanding. In the Discussion Paper, the test for the prohibition of exclusionary abuses in Article 102 was suggested to be one that looks for both actual/likely anticompetitive effects in the market *and* direct/indirect consumer harm.[143] This test required anticompetitive effects in the market *and* possible harm to consumers. In other words, they were not seen as one and the same thing unlike, for example, the EAGCP Report which perceived 'competitive harm' as 'harm to consumers'.[144] Moreover, although the avoidance of harm to consumers was seen as the ultimate concern of the provision,[145] the test proposed in the Discussion Paper did not seek proof of any actual or possible harm to consumers. Nowhere was it explained thoroughly how an assessment of the effects on consumers was to be made.[146] Thus, apart from the lip service paid to the adoption of an approach which is based on the likely effects on the *market*,[147] the stance of the Discussion Paper seemed to be almost an implicit assumption that exclusionary behaviour of a dominant undertaking necessarily harmed consumers and that the contrary could be proved by the undertaking as a defence.[148]

The Commission Guidance does not clarify the position much either. The central concept in the Guidance is 'foreclosure leading to consumer harm' which is seen as 'anticompetitive foreclosure' and as mentioned above, the role of effects

[140] See Jones and Sufrin (n 54) 369 for the argument that the enduring difficulty with Art 102 is where the courts and the Commission draw the line between anticompetitive conduct and competition on the merits. See also Whish (n 133) 189 for the same argument.

[141] Akman (n 27) 822–23.

[142] O'Donoghue and Padilla (n 44) 177.

[143] 'Discussion Paper' (n 2) [55].

[144] EAGCP Report (n 134) 7–9.

[145] 'Discussion Paper' (n 2) [4], [54]–[55], [88].

[146] Akman (n 27) 823.

[147] 'Discussion Paper' (n 2) [4].

[148] Akman (n 27) 824.

on 'consumer welfare' under this is not entirely clear.[149] Safeguarding the 'competitive process' and protecting an 'effective competitive process' are described as the aim of the Commission's enforcement activity.[150] Thus, it could be said that under the Commission's thinking it is effects on the *competitive process* that matter for a finding of abuse.

All in all, it will be the EU courts – ultimately the ECJ – that will have the last say on the standard of harm under Article 102; the Commission's aspired modernisation of application will not succeed unless the courts follow. Unfortunately, it is not at all clear from the case law so far whether the courts have any unified standard while applying Article 102 and it is especially doubtful whether they will adopt a properly defined 'consumer welfare' standard or require consumer harm to be demonstrated for a finding of abuse.

For example, in its recent *TeliaSonera* judgment the ECJ expressed the function of the competition rules in the Treaty as that of preventing 'competition from being distorted to the detriment of the public interest, individual undertakings and consumers, thereby ensuring the well-being of the European Union'.[151] The Court then interpreted this further to reiterate its oft-repeated holding from *Continental Can* that Article 102 must be interpreted as referring not only to practices which may cause damage to consumers directly, but also to those which are detrimental to consumers through their impact on competition.[152] Similarly, in *T-Mobile* and *GlaxoSmithKline*, the ECJ repeated the objective as that of protecting not only the immediate interests of individual competitors or consumers, but also of protecting the structure of the market and competition as such.[153] These judgments together suggest that there is a multiplicity of subjects on whom harmful effects can be demonstrated for establishing abuse. However, it should also be noted that although the first statement of the Court from *TeliaSonera* to include public interest, individual undertakings and consumers appears to imply a broad range of subjects the effects on which/whom might demonstrate abuse, the latter statement can be read as suggesting ultimate harm to consumers (albeit indirectly via harm to competition) as the benchmark for abuse. Therefore, it is not possible to reach a conclusion regarding whether an ultimate effect on consumers, even at a principle level, is necessary for a finding of abuse.

The holding of the Court in *T-Mobile* and *GlaxoSmithKline* and the holding in *Continental Can* and *TeliaSonera* and similar judgments can indeed be seen as potentially contradictory: whereas the former suggest an approach which has multiple subjects on which harm can be relevant, the latter create the impression that it is ultimately an impact on consumers that would establish abuse. An alternative method of interpretation which would remove the contradiction would be

[149] See above, text after n 137.
[150] 'Guidance' (n 27) [6].
[151] *TeliaSonera* (n 77) [22].
[152] *Continental Can* (n 15) [26]; *TeliaSonera* (n 77) [24]. See also *Deutsche Telekom* (n 123) [176] and Joined Cases C-468/06 to C-478/06 *Sot. Lélos kai Sia and Others* [2008] ECR I-7139, [68].
[153] *T-Mobile* (n 16) [38]; *GlaxoSmithKline* (ECJ) (n 1) [63].

to interpret *Continental Can* and *TeliaSonera* and the similar judgments stating that consumer harm can be direct or indirect as being applicable to only the cases in which consumer harm is an issue, and where consumer harm is not an issue, conduct can be still abusive if it has harmful effects on the rest of the subjects identified above by the Court. However, the stance of the Court on this is not clear enough and either interpretation may be correct. As such, the current state of the case law leaves much to be desired for the clarification of whom or what is to be protected from the harmful effects of a practice by a dominant undertaking.

Similar to the ECJ's approach of including multiple subjects on which harm can be relevant, the GC held in *Van den Bergh* that Article 102 prohibits a dominant undertaking from eliminating a competitor and from strengthening its position by recourse to means other than those based on 'competition on the merits'.[154] Further, it went on to find that '[t]he prohibition laid down in that provision is also justified by the concern not to cause harm to consumers'.[155] Thus, from the Court's expression, it is obvious that the concern not to cause harm to consumers is not the ultimate justification of Article 102, but it is *also* a legitimate concern.

Nevertheless, in an order suspending the Commission decision adopting interim measures in the *IMS Health* case, the GC expressed the *primary* purpose of Article 102 as that of preventing distortion of competition and especially of safeguarding the interests of consumers, rather than of protecting the position of particular competitors, and criticised the Commission for ignoring this purpose by equating the interests of competitors with the interests of competition.[156] Strikingly, the President of the ECJ held in the appeal of that order that this reasoning of the GC could *not* be accepted without reservation, in so far as it could be understood as excluding protection of the interests of competing undertakings from the aim pursued by Article 102, even though such interests cannot be separated from the maintenance of an effective competition structure.[157] It has been commented that by perspicuously contradicting precisely the passage in which the GC saw the main purpose of Article 102 as lying in safeguarding the 'interests of consumers', the President of the ECJ has thus interpreted Article 102 in terms of the traditional concept of the 'protection of competition'.[158] More important is perhaps that the President deemed the interests of competing undertakings as inseparable from the maintenance of 'effective competition'. Similarly, in *France Télécom (Wanadoo)*, against the argument of Wanadoo that consumers were not harmed by its pricing but on the contrary benefited from it, the GC itself repeated the above-mentioned holding of the ECJ in *Continental Can*; thus, lack of

[154] *Van den Bergh* (GC) (n 121) [157].

[155] ibid.

[156] Order of the President of the Court of First Instance of 26 October 2001 in Case T-184/01 R *IMS Health v Commission* [2001] ECR II-3103, [145].

[157] Order of the President of the Court of Justice of 11 April 2002 in Case C-481/01 *NDC Health GmbH & Co KG and NDC Health Corporation v Commission and IMS Health Inc* [2002] ECR I-3401, [84].

[158] M Dreher and M Adam, 'Abuse of Dominance under Reform – Sound Economics and Established Case Law' (2007) 28(4) *European Competition Law Review* 278, 280.

consumer harm was *not* deemed relevant.[159] The recent judgment of the ECJ in *GlaxoSmithKline*, in which the ECJ disagreed with precisely the finding of the GC that an object agreement could exist only to the extent that the agreement deprived final consumers of the advantages of effective competition,[160] appears to be further proof that the ECJ does not deem harmful effects on consumers as a necessary condition for infringement of the competition rules. This is particularly a cause for concern since, while rejecting consumer harm as the ultimate reason for intervention in a market, the ECJ is also justifying intervention on the grounds of protecting competitors, thus perhaps demonstrating a rejection of a potentially modernised economic effects-based approach in favour of a structuralist, form-based approach.

In the same vein, Advocate General Kokott argued in *British Airways* that Article 102, like the other competition rules of the Treaty, is not designed only or primarily to protect the immediate interests of individual competitors or consumers, but to protect the structure of the market and thus competition as such (as an institution) which has already been weakened by the presence of the dominant undertaking in the market.[161] In this way, consumers are also indirectly protected. The conduct of a dominant undertaking is not, therefore, to be regarded as abusive under Article 102 only when it has concrete effects on individual market participants, be they competitors or consumers.[162] The Advocate General held that it was sufficient to demonstrate that the conduct of a dominant undertaking is *likely* to make it *difficult* or impossible for its competitors to gain access to the market and for its business partners to choose between various sources of supply or business partners, unless there is an objective justification for it.[163] Where there is such a hindrance to remaining competition, it can be *assumed* that, indirectly, consumers are also disadvantaged. Thus, in the Advocate General's statement one can observe the line of thought proceeding from likely harm to competitors (by making access *difficult* or impossible) to likely harm to competition to likely harm to consumers. Indeed, the Advocate General expressed that for a finding of 'prejudice to consumers' under Article 102(b), it would be sufficient to prove that, without objective justification, the conduct of the dominant undertaking makes it difficult or impossible for its competitors to compete with it.[164] As such, it is clear that likely harm to consumers is presumed to follow likely harm to competition which is presumed to follow likely harm to competitors. The ECJ in the appeal of

[159] *Wanadoo* (GC) (n 128) [266].

[160] *GlaxoSmithKline* (GC) (n 1) [62].

[161] Opinion of Advocate General Kokott on 23 February 2006 in Case C-95/04 *British Airways plc v Commission* [2007] ECR I-2331, [68].

[162] ibid [69].

[163] ibid [87].

[164] ibid [89]. In the appeal, the ECJ held that in determining whether the discounts or bonuses constitute abuse, it first has to be determined whether they can produce an exclusionary effect, that is to say whether they are capable, first, of making market entry *very* difficult or impossible for competitors of the undertaking in a dominant position and, secondly, of making it more difficult or impossible for its co-contractors to choose between various sources of supply or commercial partners; *British Airways* (n 76) [68].

British Airways, repeated its above-mentioned holding that Article 102 is aimed not only at practices which may cause prejudice to consumers directly, but at those which are detrimental to them through their impact on an effective competition structure.[165] All in all, it is clear that the ECJ does not appear to be welcoming a requirement of effects on consumers as a condition for abuse under Article 102.

In the same vein, according to the Commission, Article 102 does *not* require it to be demonstrated that the conduct in question had any actual or direct effect on consumers: competition law concentrates upon protecting the market structure from artificial distortions because by doing so the interests of the consumer in the medium to long term are best protected.[166] A line of conduct of a dominant undertaking is abusive as soon as it runs counter to the purpose of protecting competition in the internal market from distortions as stipulated in Protocol 27. Therefore, what is to be proved is the mere *likelihood* of the conduct in question hindering the maintenance or development of competition still existing in the market by means other than competition on the merits, thereby prejudicing the goal of effective and undistorted competition in the internal market.[167]

A similar line of thought can be observed in the *Microsoft* judgment of the GC. In that case, while assessing whether Microsoft's refusal to supply interoperability information to its competitors was abusive, the GC held that

> [s]hould it be established . . . that the existing degree of interoperability does not enable developers of non-Microsoft work group server operating systems to remain viably on the market for those operating systems, it follows that the maintenance of effective competition on that market is being hindered.[168]

The GC found that this was indeed the case and Microsoft's refusal to supply the necessary interoperability information was an abuse of its dominant position.[169] Hence, the inability of Microsoft's competitors to remain viably on the market was deemed tantamount to effective competition being hindered. This is striking for the association of the position of competitors with the maintenance of effective competition. Moreover, the GC clarified that 'likely to eliminate competition' and 'risk of elimination of competition' are concepts used without distinction by the EU judicature to convey the same idea, namely that Article 102 does not apply only from the time when there is no more or practically no more competition on the market.[170] This is because if the Commission were required to wait until competitors were eliminated from the market or until their elimination was sufficiently imminent before being able to take action under Article 102, that

[165] *British Airways* (n 76) [106].
[166] ibid [264].
[167] Opinion of Advocate General Kokott in *British Airways* (n 161) [71]. The Advocate General found that the distinction between 'capable of having' and 'likely to have' is purely semantic; ibid [76].
[168] *Microsoft* (n 1) [229].
[169] ibid [421], [620], [712].
[170] ibid [561].

would clearly run counter to the objective of that provision.[171] That objective is 'to maintain undistorted competition on the common market and, in particular, to safeguard that competition that still exists on the relevant market'.[172] As a result, it is not necessary to demonstrate that all competition on the market would be eliminated since what matters is that the conduct in question is *liable* to or is *likely* to eliminate all effective competition on the market.[173] Moreover, the fact that the competitors of the dominant undertaking retain a marginal presence in certain niches on the market cannot suffice to substantiate the existence of such competition.[174] It is striking that the GC has *not* referred to the interests of consumers while expressing the objective of Article 102.

Although these findings of the GC suggest that the Court's understanding of 'effective competition' is closely related to how many viable competitors there are on the market, the Court did separately consider the interests of customers and consumers as well. As such, it found that the absence of interoperability had the effect of reinforcing Microsoft's competitive position, particularly because it induced consumers to use its work group operating system in preference to its competitors', even though its competitors' programmes offered features to which consumers attached great importance.[175] Thus, the limitation placed on 'consumer choice' by Microsoft's conduct was a factor in finding an abuse.[176] It should be noted that this understanding of 'choice' appears very closely related to the number of competitors on the market that offer competing products and, indirectly, protection of such choice might be equivalent to protection of competitors. This will be returned to in chapter seven.

Although the above-mentioned judgments mainly show a lack of direct concern with the existence of harm to consumers for conduct to be abusive, there are also examples from the case law where such harm was expressed as a requirement. One of these rare instances of the courts' referring directly to the 'welfare' of consumers, namely end-users, in the context of EU competition rules is found in the *Österreichische Postsparkasse AG* judgment of the GC. In that case the Court found that 'the ultimate purpose of the rules that seek to ensure that competition is not distorted in the internal market is to increase the well-being of consumers'.[177] As mentioned above, although later disagreed with by the ECJ, the GC repeated the same argument in *GlaxoSmithKline* by expressing that since the objective of the EU competition rules is to prevent undertakings, by restricting competition between themselves or with third parties, from reducing the 'welfare of the final consumer' of the products in question, it is necessary to demonstrate that the

[171] ibid.
[172] ibid.
[173] ibid [563].
[174] ibid.
[175] ibid [422].
[176] ibid [652].
[177] Joined Cases T-231/01 and T-214/01 *Österreichische Postsparkasse AG and Bank für Arbeit und Wirtschaft AG v Commission* [2006] ECR II-1601, [115].

limitation in question restricts competition 'to the detriment of the final consumer'.[178] Furthermore, the GC held that regarding the examination under Article 101(3), the Commission has a margin of discretion subject to a restricted judicial review, in weighing up the advantages expected from the implementation of the agreement and the disadvantages which the agreement entails for the 'final consumer' owing to its impact on competition.[179]

Another direct reference to 'consumer welfare' can be found in the Opinion of Advocate General Jacobs in *Syfait*, where it was argued that one possible consequence of prohibiting any restriction of supply by dominant pharmaceutical undertakings intended to limit parallel trade would be an incentive for such undertakings not to market their products in Member States where prices are fixed at a low level.[180] However, since the legal and moral obligations on undertakings might render it difficult for them to withdraw products already marketed in those states, more credibly, they might delay the launch of new products in those states. Hence, the levels of output and 'consumer welfare' generated by some pharmaceutical products would fall within the Union.[181] Similarly, the regulatory negotiation of prices in low-price Member States would almost certainly become difficult; there would be considerable pressure for prices to rise in those states if they were to be generalised, by the process of parallel trade, across the Union. Such price rises would again reduce output and 'consumer welfare' in the states where they occurred.[182]

The impact of conduct on consumers has been regarded in some other findings of abuse as well, such as the Italian railways case where the dominant national railway carrier in Italy (FS) refused to provide traction – an activity which it routinely performed – to a German railway undertaking (GVG).[183] This was found not to be justified by any objective reason and to protect FS's monopoly position in the downstream market for international passenger rail services between Basle

[178] *GlaxoSmithKline* (GC) (n 1) [171]. See also, ibid, [118]–[19]. The GC held that parallel trade is to be protected not as such, but in so far as it favours the development of trade, on the one hand, and the strengthening of competition, on the other hand, that is to say, in this second respect, in so far as it gives final consumers the advantages of effective competition in terms of supply or price; ibid [121]. Consequently, while it is accepted that an agreement intended to limit parallel trade must in principle be considered to have as its object the restriction of competition, that applies in so far as the agreement may be presumed to deprive final consumers of those advantages; ibid. The GC found that this presumption could not be made in this case; ibid [134]. The ECJ, however, rejected the interpretation of the GC to require harm to consumers for the agreement to be an object agreement as per Art 101; see *GlaxoSmithKline* (ECJ) (n 1) [63].

[179] *GlaxoSmithKline* (GC) (n 1) [244].

[180] Opinion of Advocate General Jacobs in *Syfait* (n 1) [90]–[91].

[181] ibid [91].

[182] ibid [92]. The Advocate General states that the conclusion he reaches, ie, that a restriction of supply by a dominant undertaking to limit parallel trade is not necessarily abusive, is highly specific to the pharmaceutical industry in its current condition and to the particular type of conduct at issue in the proceedings; ibid [100]–[01]. According to him, it is highly unlikely that any other sector would exhibit the characteristics which have led to this conclusion; ibid [102].

[183] *Georg/Ferrovie (GVG/FS)* (Case COMP 37.685) Commission Decision 27 August 2003 (unreported).

and Milan, namely the route on which GVG wanted to offer service.[184] It therefore constituted an abuse of a dominant position: FS's refusal to provide traction to GVG was found to eliminate a potential competitor and thereby hinder the growth of competition in the downstream market. This harmed *consumers* who would have benefited from alternatives to existing rail passenger services.

In the same vein, Advocate General Jacobs stated in *Oscar Bronner* that the primary purpose of Article 102 is to prevent distortion of competition – and in particular to safeguard the interests of consumers – rather than to protect the position of particular competitors.[185] It may therefore, for example, be unsatisfactory in a case in which a competitor demands access to a raw material in order to be able to compete with the dominant undertaking on a downstream market in a final product, to focus solely on the latter's market power on the upstream market and to conclude that its conduct in reserving to itself the downstream market is automatically an abuse. Such conduct would not have an adverse impact on consumers unless the dominant undertaking's final product is sufficiently insulated from competition to give it market power. Similarly, Advocate General Warner argued in *Commercial Solvents* that '[t]he consumer, after all, is interested only in the end product, and it is detriment to the consumer, whether direct o[r] indirect, with which Article [102] is concerned'.[186]

All in all, although there are references to 'consumer welfare' and 'harm to consumers' in some of the EU jurisprudence, it is not clear whether these references are merely catchphrases or whether they actually affect the decision reached. Moreover, there is not a consistent line of argument in practice; some decisions explicitly reject the necessity of considering effects on and harm to consumers, while some of them require such an assessment.

It has been argued that although harm to an 'effective competitive structure' has sometimes been mentioned as a possible alternative to direct consumer harm, the two concepts should amount to the same thing: unless there is consumer harm, there is no relevant harm to the 'structure of competition'.[187] Thus, there can be no case for intervention under competition law where there is harm to the competitive process, but none to consumers.[188] As argued in the EAGCP Report, the standard for assessing whether a given practice is detrimental to 'competition' or whether it is a legitimate tool of 'competition' should be derived from the effects of the practice on consumers.[189]

[184] ibid [145]. FS provided rail passenger transport service from Basle to Milan in cooperation with a Swiss undertaking; ibid [10].

[185] Opinion of Advocate General Jacobs in Case C-7/97 *Oscar Bronner GmbH & Co KG v Mediaprint Zeitungs- und Zeitschriftenverlag GmbH & Co KG* [1998] ECR I-7791, [58].

[186] Opinion of Advocate General Warner in Cases 6 and 7/73 *Istituto Chemioterapico Italiano Spa and Commercial Solvents Corp v Commission* [1974] ECR 223, 266.

[187] O'Donoghue and Padilla (n 44) 221; J Vickers, 'Abuse of Market Power' (2005) 115 *The Economic Journal* F244, F259.

[188] O'Donoghue and Padilla (n 44) 221–22.

[189] EAGCP Report (n 134) 8.

In the literature, it has thus been suggested that the standard for judging anti-competitive effects under Article 102 is (or should be) evidence of actual or likely consumer harm.[190] Ignoring such effects in favour of a legal presumption of effect as advocated in *Michelin II* is plainly inconsistent with the Commission's recent emphasis on an economic effects-based approach and the entire basis for the review of policy under Article 102.[191] In contrast to merger control, abuse of dominance cases involve situations in which the defendant is already in a dominant position. Thus, abuse of dominance usually concerns known present facts and established conduct in which case it should normally be possible to consider whether the market is consistent with potential exclusion or appears more consistent with a competitive environment.[192] In most cases, there should be relevant information regarding actual effects or, failing that, information on which reasonable assumptions as to future likely effects can be made.[193]

There would also be severe problems if statements by the Commission and the courts in *British Airways* and *Michelin II* that prima facie evidence of 'lack of adverse effect' can be ignored in favour of a presumption of effects were widely accepted.[194] There is no effective counter-thesis to this assumption; it can *always* be assumed that practices had an adverse effect on competitors if evidence of lack of effect is disregarded in favour of such an assumption.[195] This reasoning is circular and inconclusive:[196] it is circular in that conduct is said to be unlawful *only* because it ousts competitors, but if that is the reason, it cannot then be said that one does not need to look to see if it had that effect. It is inconclusive because legitimate competition can also result in competitors' exit.

The argument that one should look for evidence of effects of conduct is especially true when one considers that Article 102 ultimately prohibits 'exploitation' – exploitation must be observable; one cannot exploit without *actually* exploiting. Finding abuse in the mere *likelihood* of exploitation would not be consistent with Article 102: the fact that dominant position itself is not prohibited demonstrates that it is not the likelihood of exploitation that is abusive since that likelihood always exists as long as there is a dominant position. Conduct becomes abusive only when the dominant undertaking actually uses its power to 'exploit'. The presumption underlying Article 102 as proven by the lack of prohibition of dominance itself is that dominant undertakings may not always use their power to exploit.[197]

Another question rightly raised is that of what happens in cases where damage to consumers is direct and there is no (direct) effect on the structure of competi-

[190] O'Donoghue and Padilla (n 44) 219.
[191] ibid. See *Michelin II* (n 122).
[192] O'Donoghue and Padilla (n 44) 220.
[193] ibid.
[194] ibid. See *British Airways* (n 122); *Michelin II* (n 122).
[195] O'Donoghue and Padilla (n 44) 220.
[196] ibid.
[197] R Joliet, *Monopolization and Abuse of Dominant Position* (La Haye, Martinus Nijhoff, 1970) 131.

tion.[198] Haracoglou argues that although untested, it appears that the ambit of Article 102 is sufficiently wide to allow for an interpretation that would cover the situation where access to a product or service is restricted despite consumer demand and there is no apparent harm to competition; such a practice could be deemed to 'limit production, markets or technical development to the prejudice of consumers'.[199]

However, it must be remembered that Article 102 is not a provision of consumer law, but a provision of competition law. As also held by the EU courts, although Article 102 contains no reference to the anticompetitive object or anticompetitive effect of the practice referred to, in the light of the context of Article 102, conduct will be regarded as abusive only if it distorts competition.[200] Thus, mere consumer harm should not be sufficient for conduct to be abusive if it is not tied to some harm to competition or due to some conduct harming competition. Hence, neither mere harm to the process of competition nor mere consumer harm should be sufficient on its own for a finding of abuse: if the standard is 'consumer welfare', then harm to the competitive process and harm to consumers should be established for a finding of 'abuse' under Article 102. This would imply that there should be both exclusion and exploitation for conduct to be abusive, especially if harm to the competitive process is understood as harm to competitors which appears to be the position in the majority of the case law. This requirement of exploitation and exclusion to exist together will be further discussed in chapter eight within the context of the proposal of this study on the concept of 'abuse'.

IV CONCLUSION

This chapter investigated 'welfare' as an objective of Article 102 with emphasis on the application of and policy on that provision. Before investigating the decisional practice and the policy, this chapter examined Article 101(3) since that provision has been interpreted as setting the objective of EU competition rules as 'consumer welfare'. However, it has been demonstrated that it is not unequivocal that Article 101(3) sets a properly defined 'consumer welfare' standard, especially given that it refers to 'customers' and not necessarily 'consumers'. Moreover, the lack of an equivalent clause in Article 102 implies that Article 101(3) cannot be simply transposed into Article 102. This chapter argued that this absence of a similar clause is not due to a refusal of efficiency considerations in Article 102; rather, it is due to the accommodation of efficiency gains within the concept of 'abuse'. This

[198] I Haracoglou, 'Competition Law, Consumer Policy and the Retail Sector: The Systems' Relation and the Effects of a Strengthened Consumer Protection Policy on Competition Law' (2007) 3(2) *The Competition Law Review* 175, 204.

[199] ibid 204.

[200] *Michelin II* (n 122) [237]; *Microsoft* (n 1) [867].

therefore implies that inefficiency of conduct is a necessary condition for it to be abusive under Article 102.

As for the question of whether 'consumer welfare' is adopted as the standard of harm in the decisional practice, the answer is unfortunately not clear. This is because there does not appear to be a unified and coherent test applied by the Commission and the EU courts in finding behaviour of a dominant undertaking to constitute an 'abuse'. Currently, it is not even clear whether *effects* on consumers or the market are relevant or whether merely an anticompetitive *object* is sufficient. It is also not clear what the relation between the *likelihood* of anticompetitive effects with the *form* of conduct is. From the case law studied above, it is questionable whether the EU courts will modernise their application of Article 102 as per the call of the Commission and whether they will adopt a properly defined 'consumer welfare' standard. It is, however, also doubtful whether the Commission itself has a properly defined 'consumer welfare' standard which it in fact follows in its decisional practice. While the Commission may at times refer more explicitly to the consumer as the ultimate benefactor, the consideration of the consumer interest is often merely vague, in terms of considering it to be a natural consequence of 'harm to competition', rather than as a direct 'harm to consumers'.[201] Hence, what exactly 'consumer harm' consists of is not clear either.[202]

If the test adopted is 'consumer welfare', then it is important that the assessment takes into consideration the welfare of 'consumers' and not merely 'customers'. This is because, as demonstrated in chapter one, the adoption of a 'consumer welfare' standard rather than a 'total welfare' standard is not without conceptual and practical problems. Moreover, if applied in a manner that 'consumer' is equated with 'customer', this would pose the problem of possibly ignoring the effects on 'consumers' while taking into account the interests of some producers and not others. This is not an easily justifiable position and would also lead to perverse results where the interests of 'customers' are not aligned with those of 'consumers'.

For abusive conduct, it must also be recognised that once it is accepted that exploitation is a necessary part of 'abuse', mere likelihood of anticompetitive effects cannot suffice since this would not be consistent with the fact that Article 102 does not prohibit dominant position itself. By not prohibiting a dominant position itself, the provision clearly accepts that a dominant undertaking does not necessarily have to abuse its position. For abusive exploitation to occur therefore, the dominant undertaking has to *use* its power to exploit. The use of that power should be observable and thus demonstrable in terms of its *actual effects* since otherwise abuse would not have been proven. As will be further discussed in chapter eight, both harm to competition and harm to trading partners should exist for a finding of abuse.

[201] Haracoglou (n 198) 199.
[202] ibid 200.

This chapter has examined the role of 'welfare' as a potential objective of Article 102. The chapter has demonstrated that it is not possible to establish the objective of the provision as 'consumer welfare', particularly due to the jurisprudence of the ECJ. The next chapter therefore investigates whether the objective of the provision can – and if so, should – be 'fairness' since certain 'unfair' conduct is explicitly prohibited in Article 102 itself, which suggests that 'fairness' might be an objective more so than 'welfare'.

4

'Fairness' in Article 102 TFEU

I INTRODUCTION

Article 102 explicitly prohibits certain 'unfair' behaviour as abuse of a dominant position. The concept of 'fairness' underlies the Article 102 prohibition of imposing unfair prices or other unfair trading conditions, since prohibiting 'unfair' behaviour implies the existence of a 'fairness' conception.[1] 'Fairness' can also be thought to be implicitly referred to in the prohibition of 'discrimination', since equality – understood as the equal treatment of equal parties and the unequal treatment of unequal parties – can be considered as one understanding of the concept.[2] In other words, abuse of a dominant position by way of 'unfair' behaviour is prohibited and sanctioned by the TFEU itself. Yet, Article 102 does not define 'unfair' or 'fair', but merely gives examples of unfair practices.[3] This reference to 'unfair' conduct, its meaning and implications have not been subject to sufficient discussion by policy makers or academics. This is despite the fact that it is also stated in the Preamble of the TFEU that the removal of existing obstacles calls for concerted action in order to guarantee steady expansion, balanced trade and *fair* competition. Whatever the reason for the lack of discussion, the result is that the potential consequences of having a 'fairness' prescription in competition law have not been fully debated. It can be said that what is 'fair' or 'unfair' behaviour in EU competition law is not clear at all and that the 'fairness' concept has developed rather haphazardly. This is unfortunate since as an explicit component

[1] According to Art 102 'directly or indirectly imposing unfair purchase or selling prices or other unfair trading conditions' [subparagraph (a)] and 'applying dissimilar conditions to equivalent transactions with other trading parties, thereby placing them at a competitive disadvantage' [subparagraph (c)] are both prohibited as abuses of a dominant position. For the argument that 'unfair' in Art 102(a) merely means 'exploitative', see JT Lang, 'Fundamental Issues Concerning Abuse under Article 82 EC' paper presented at Annual Competition Policy Conference (Oxford, Regulatory Policy Institute, July 2005) available at: rpieurope.org/2005%20Conference/Temple_Lang_Abuse_under_article_82EC.pdf 28.

[2] Understanding 'fairness' as 'equality' dates back to Aristotle; Aristotle, *Nicomachean Ethics* (R Crisp ed and trans) (Cambridge, CUP, 2002) 1129a *et seq*. See Lang (n 1) 28 for the argument that unfairness is not relevant to Art 102(c) since it is written in wholly objective terms such as 'dissimilar conditions', 'equivalent transactions', 'competitive disadvantage'. However, the first two of these terms especially do not appear to be really objective. 'Dissimilar' as well as 'equivalent' are terms that can be defined in different ways by different people.

[3] The practices in Art 102 are not listed exhaustively, but are merely examples of 'abuse'; Case 6/72 *Europemballage Corp and Continental Can Co Inc v Commission* [1973] ECR 215, [26].

of the provision, it has to be decided whether achieving 'fairness' is and/or should be an objective of Article 102 and EU competition law and policy in general. If this is decided in the affirmative, then it is also imperative to make it explicit what this 'fairness' goal entails. Thus, the discussion of 'fairness' goes to the heart of the problem of what are the objectives of Article 102 and becomes particularly important once it is recognised that 'fairness' might clash with other potential objectives of the provision, such as 'welfare' and 'efficiency'. This study has thus far sought to demonstrate that, although welfarist goals *can* be adopted under Article 102 and the recent rhetoric of the Commission appears to prefer a 'consumer welfare' standard, the decisional practice of the EU authorities are much more ambiguous and to an extent unwelcoming of such an approach. Therefore, 'fairness' deserves elaboration in order to establish what its role is as an objective of Article 102 and as a component of the concept of 'abuse'. Understanding the 'fairness' element in the provision is thus essential for understanding the concept of 'abuse'. Similar to chapter three, this chapter discusses, inter alia, both the provision of and the decisional practice on Article 102 seeking to establish the role of 'fairness' in this context.

It has been commented that '[p]rinciples of fairness and justice are extraneous to competition law: the lion eats the deer'.[4] 'Fairness' as a policy object has indeed been defended by some and rejected by others in competition law circles.[5] Especially in the context of EU competition law, the role that 'fairness' plays is somehow doubtful as its content and scope have not been explored much in this area in contrast to other branches of law and even economics. This is particularly important in the context of the 'more economic approach' to Article 102 and the recent reform discussions claiming the objective of the provision to be 'consumer welfare'.[6] Introduction of welfarist objectives brings out the tension between

[4] M van der Woude, 'Unfair and Excessive Prices in the Energy Sector' in CD Ehlermann and M Marquis (eds), *European Competition Annual 2007: A Reformed Approach to Article 82 EC* (Oxford, Hart Publishing, 2008) 617.

[5] For the discussion see, eg, RH Bork, 'The Goals of Antitrust Policy' (1967) 57(2) *The American Economic Review* 242; KG Elzinga, 'The Goals of Antitrust: Other than Competition and Efficiency, What Else Counts?' (1977) 125 *University of Pennsylvania Law Review* 1191; EM Fox, 'The Modernization of Antitrust: A New Equilibrium' (1981) 66 *Cornell Law Review* 1140; RH Lande, 'Wealth Transfers as the Original and Primary Concern of Antitrust: The Efficiency Interpretation Challenged' (1982) 34 *Hastings Law Journal* 65; T Calvani, 'Rectangles and Triangles: A Response to Mr Lande' (1989) 58 *Antitrust Law Journal* 657; FM Scherer, 'Efficiency, Fairness and the Early Contributions of Economists to the Antitrust Debate' (1990) 29 *Washburn Law Journal* 243; TB Leary, 'Freedom as the Core Value of Antitrust in the New Millennium' (2000) 68 *Antitrust Law Journal* 545.

[6] See, eg, Commission, 'Guidelines on the Application of Article 81(3) of the Treaty' [2004] OJ C101/97, [13]; N Kroes, 'Preliminary Thoughts on Policy Review of Article 82' speech at the Fordham Corporate Law Institute (New York, 23 September 2005) 3; 'DG Competition Discussion Paper on the Application of Article 82 of the Treaty to Exclusionary Abuses' (Brussels, December 2005) available at: ec.europa.eu/competition/antitrust/art82/discpaper2005.pdf [4], [54], [55], [88]. See also 'Guidance on the Commission's Enforcement Priorities in Applying Article 82 of the EC Treaty to Abusive Exclusionary Conduct by Dominant Undertakings' [2009] OJ C45/7, where the Commission states the aim of its enforcement activity under Art 102 as ensuring that 'dominant undertakings do not impair effective competition by foreclosing their competitors in an anti-competitive way, thus having an adverse impact on consumer welfare' [19]. For the definition of 'consumer welfare' see ch1 this volume, text around fn 33.

'fairness' goals and 'efficiency' goals since what is deemed 'fair' may not always be 'efficient' or welfare-increasing and vice versa, as demonstrated throughout this study. In fact, commentators have argued that legal rules should be selected entirely with respect to their effects on the wellbeing (namely, 'welfare') of individuals and, thus, notions of 'fairness' should receive no independent weight in the assessment.[7] To be able to tackle the tension, the tension must first be made obvious and, to achieve this, one must first understand what 'fairness' may mean and what role it may play in the context of the prohibition of 'abuse' in Article 102.

When taking up office as the new EU Competition Commissioner in 2010, Joaquín Almunia expressed his vision for competition policy and stated that he 'see[s] competition policy as a means of strengthening our social market economy, and enhancing its efficiency and fairness'.[8] Similarly, he noted that unilateral conduct rules are important because they help in pursuing three goals: 'keeping markets open and fair, promoting innovation, and making sure that no harm is done to consumers'.[9] 'Fairness' is thus always there as an objective, next to 'efficiency' and preventing consumer harm, although these goals can at times clash with one another.

From an historical point of view, 'fairness' goals played important roles in competition law in Europe, arguably because the concept of 'abuse' is grounded in the idea of 'fairness'.[10] Looking at the development of competition law in Europe, it has been suggested that in the country where the idea of using law to protect the competitive process was developed in the 1890s, namely Austria, competition law was conceived as a way to encourage economic growth and competitiveness, but also to increase the perception of economic 'fairness' and reduce the antagonism between workers and ethnic groups.[11] As for the competition law of the EU, 'fairness' was arguably used in this context to integrate independent polities, since only where the market was perceived to be 'fair' would national decision makers have been willing to surrender some of their control over markets and allow economic integration.[12] Therefore, a level and so 'fair' 'playing field' for all market participants has been identified as an essential condition for integration of the European market.[13] It is worth repeating here that 'fair com-

[7] L Kaplow and S Shavell, *Fairness versus Welfare* (Cambridge, MA, Harvard University Press, 2002) 3–4.

[8] J Almunia, Mandate Statement, February 2010, available at: ec.europa.eu/commission_2010-2014/almunia/about/mandate/index_en.htm.

[9] J Almunia, 'Converging Paths in Unilateral Conduct' speech at the ICN Unilateral Conduct Workshop (Brussels, 3 December 2010) 3.

[10] DJ Gerber, 'Fairness in Competition Law: European and US Experience' presented at a conference on Fairness and Asian Competition Laws (Kyoto, 5 March 2004) available at: kyotogakuen.ac.jp/~o_ied/information/fairness_in_competition_law.pdf 6. See also MN Berry, 'The Uncertainty of Monopolistic Conduct: A Comparative Review of Three Jurisdictions' (2001) 32 *Law and Policy in International Business* 263, 310.

[11] Gerber (n 10) 6.

[12] ibid 9.

[13] ibid.

petition' during the negotiations of the Treaties of Rome has been used in the specific concept of referring to competition being free from state aid by the governments, which favours national undertakings.[14]

Although it is quite indisputable that 'fairness' is a part of Article 102, it is not clear what 'fairness' actually means under this provision. There appear to be two prongs to the inquiry: first, to whom the undertaking must be 'fair' and, secondly, what makes conduct 'fair' or 'unfair'. One interpretation of 'fairness' in this context is as fair behaviour towards competitors.[15] Another potential understanding is as 'fairness' towards trading partners of the dominant undertaking. Whereas the first would exclude consumers from an assessment of 'fairness', the latter would exclude competitors in general. A third view is that 'fairness' in competition law appears in both horizontal and vertical relations and thus includes competitors and trading partners. Gerber separates two basic forms of 'fairness' concerns in competition law as that of 'vertical' and 'horizontal', both of which are related to the use of power.[16] The vertical form appears in the relationship between buyers and sellers where, for example, an undertaking uses its monopoly power to raise prices to buyers above competitive levels and thus is 'unfair' to consumers. The horizontal form is the use of power to harm competitors where an economically powerful firm, for example, uses its power to block competitors from access to markets or to reduce their capacity to compete.[17] Obviously, this categorisation is more about the subject to whom the undertaking must be 'fair'. As such, it does not necessarily explain what is 'unfair', since it ultimately equates 'unfair' with 'anticompetitive' without defining either. Importantly, in the latter case of exclusion, it does not distinguish between anticompetitive exclusion and exclusion that might result from the efficiency and/or superiority of the dominant undertaking. Consequently, the question of what is 'unfair', and whether or not it always is or should be deemed 'anticompetitive', remains unanswered.

Importantly, these different interpretations of 'fairness' would result in different approaches. If 'fairness' is understood as 'fairness' towards competitors, it is met with the argument that competition law is supposed to protect competition, not competitors. Hence, 'fairness' becomes undesirable. Contrarily, if it is comprehended as 'fairness' towards customers/suppliers and if the protection of consumers is taken to be the central concern of Article 102, it can become part of the ultimate purpose.[18] This is one reason why it is crucial how 'fairness' is conceived. What is significant is that 'unfairness' is a broad enough concept to cover harm to competitors and harm to consumers. Thus, it can cover both 'exclusionary' and 'exploitative' conduct, in line with one of the main theses of this book that these should both exist for there to be an abuse.

[14] See ch 2 this volume,section V.B.iv.
[15] See, eg, Kroes (n 6) 3.
[16] Gerber (n 10) 2.
[17] ibid 2–3.
[18] For the point that protection of consumers is the ultimate aim, see Kroes (n 6) 3. See also 'Discussion Paper' (n 6) [4], [54], [55], [88].

Another reason why it is important to discuss 'fairness' is that, however interpreted, 'fairness' is a policy aim that would set limits to conduct on the market in order to provide 'fair' behaviour on the market. This could, nevertheless, result in the prevention or distortion of 'free competition' since the natural operation of the markets would be disrupted. In other words, allowing the limitation of the practices of competing undertakings on grounds of 'fairness' means that not all types of 'free competition' are good and desirable. As such, 'fairness' can be seen in conflict with the principle of 'free competition' underlying the chosen system of economy in the EU. This complicates the situation in the case of EU competition law and policy since the law itself entails a 'fairness' concept, but the policy concurrently seeks to achieve as much rigorous competition as possible.[19] Moreover, since Article 102 'is expressly aimed in fact at situations which clearly originate in contractual relations',[20] and since 'freedom of contract' is a fundamental principle of the laws of EU Member States and thus EU law,[21] scrutinising the transactions of dominant undertakings from a 'fairness' perspective directly sets limits to this freedom as well. As such, it is controversial, since as will be demonstrated in this chapter, scrutiny of contracts on 'fairness' grounds in national laws of the Member States is generally limited to exceptional circumstances, mainly due to the problems the concept brings along. Therefore, how much interference with 'freedom of contract' is justified on 'fairness' concerns arising from Article 102 deserves some elaboration.

Section II briefly examines the 'fairness' concept in 'ordoliberalism' as this school of thought is portrayed by many as providing the intellectual foundations of Article 102. Section III investigates EU case law in order to determine the 'fairness' concept applied by the Commission and the EU courts in the context of Article 102. As there does not appear to be a unique or coherent 'fairness' concept arising out of the jurisprudence of the EU authorities, section IV elaborates on various notions of 'fairness' in areas of law other than competition law. Since 'fairness' has been part of most legal traditions, albeit in different branches of law, and since competition law is closely related to some of these areas, in particular contract law and consumer law, how the concept is understood and operationalised in these subjects is thought to provide guidance to understanding what 'fairness' may mean in Article 102. Section V concludes.

[19] At the European Summit in Lisbon in 2005, the so-called 'Lisbon Agenda' aimed for the EU to become 'the most dynamic and competitive knowledge-based economy in the world'. This goal has perhaps become questionable with the removal of Art 3(1)(g)EC to Protocol 27 under the Lisbon Treaty, although it must be pointed out that the Protocol arts have the same value as Treaty arts.

[20] Case 85/76 *Hoffmann-La Roche & Co AG v Commission* [1979] ECR 461, [116].

[21] See, eg, Opinion of Advocate General Jacobs in Case C-7/97 *Oscar Bronner GmbH & Co KG v Mediaprint Zeitungs- und Zeitschriftenverlag GmbH & Co KG* [1998] ECR I-7791, [56] where he states that 'it is apparent that the right to choose one's trading partners and freely to dispose of one's property are generally recognised principles in the laws of the Member States, in some cases with constitutional status. Incursions on those rights require careful justification'. See also, Commission, 'A More Coherent European Contract Law: An Action Plan' COM (2003) 68 final (Brussels, 12 February 2003) [81], [93] and 'Discussion Paper' (n 6) [207] where this right is recognised for dominant undertakings as well.

II FAIRNESS AND ORDOLIBERALISM

Especially in the early development of the competition law tradition, calls for the enactment of these laws were often justified by reference to concepts of 'fairness' and 'justice'.[22] Beginning in Austria, where competition law in Europe was first developed, one of the means that competition law served was to increase the perception of economic 'fairness' and thus reduce antagonisms between various social groups.[23] Similarly, as explained in chapter two, in Germany, the scholars of 'ordoliberalism' tried to use law to protect market processes from distortion either by the public power of the state or by the private economic power of large firms.[24] Again, as explained in chapter two, the predominant view in the literature appears to be that Article 102 is intellectually grounded in 'ordoliberalism'.[25] This makes it important to analyse if 'fairness' played a role in ordoliberal competition policy and, if so, what it entailed, even though the predominant view has been challenged in chapter two on the basis of evidence from the legislative history and context of Article 102.

The actual basis of ordoliberal competition is deduced from an appreciation of law and justice based on contract which is contrary to the various concepts of utilitarianism.[26] A tension between 'freedom' and 'fairness' inevitably arises as a result of ordoliberal competition policy which has as its main aim the protection of 'economic freedom'. Ordoliberals have indeed argued that

> [f]ree competition must not be stopped on the erroneous grounds of alleged unfair practice. On the other hand, it must not be allowed to degenerate into truly unfair competition either. How the line is to be drawn between unfair and permissible competition, whether competition is restricted, whether competition is efficient or obstructive, whether or not price-cutting contradicts the principle of the system-all these issues can only be decided by investigations conducted by economists into the various states of the market. The colloboration of [law and economics], which in this respect still leaves much to be desired, is clearly essential.[27]

This paragraph shows that 'fairness' of competition is indeed part of the ordoliberal competition policy. Put into the context where the aim is the protection of economic freedom of market actors, it appears that the ordoliberal arguments on abuse of dominance are protection of the economic freedom of persons other

[22] DJ Gerber, Law and Competition in Twentieth Century Europe: Protecting Prometheus (Oxford, OUP, 1998) 419.

[23] Gerber (n 10) 6.

[24] ibid 7–8.

[25] See the references in ch 2 this volume, fn 1.

[26] W Möschel, 'Competition Policy from an Ordo Point of View' in A Peacock and H Willgerodt (eds), *German Neo-Liberals and the Social Market Economy* (London, Macmillan, 1989) 148.

[27] F Böhm, W Eucken and H Grossmann-Doerth, 'The Ordo Manifesto of 1936' in A Peacock and H Willgerodt (eds), *Germany's Social Market Economy: Origins and Evolution* (London, Macmillan, 1989) 24–25.

than the dominant undertaking. Therefore, the 'fairness' notion in ordoliberalism is very much 'fairness' towards competitors (perhaps coupled with a belief that this leads to good outcomes for everyone). 'Fairness' in this sense is used as a mechanism to ensure that the dominant undertaking does not use its power 'unfairly' to disadvantage its rivals. This implies that it is competitors and not competition that is protected, or at its best, competition is protected by way of protecting the competitors of the dominant undertaking. This is a helpful insight in understanding the source of the oft-levelled criticism that the EU authorities apply Article 102 in a manner which protects competitors not competition.[28]

In fact, one commentator has likened EU competition law to 'unfair competition law' due to the element of 'moral righteousness' in its enforcement.[29] As such, there are allegedly instances where a complainant presents to the Commission something that seems shocking in its 'unfairness', so that the Commission has a strong temptation to intervene on behalf of the party. This has been interpreted to suggest that even a sophisticated and senior competition agency may be readily distracted from 'competition law' into 'unfair competition law'.[30]

Yet, it must be noted that 'unfair competition law' is a separate body of law that deals with conduct between competitors and seeks to prevent dishonest and fraudulent rivalry in trade and commerce.[31] With 'unfair competition law' the emphasis is on the prevention of 'unfair' behaviour by market participants in trade.[32] It is not the government, but the parties themselves that are charged with the enforcement of 'unfair competition law'.[33] Competition law, on the other hand, contains a set of rules that provide states with the means to stop behaviour by market participants that is likely to distort competition, in the interest of the market as a whole.[34] With competition law, the emphasis is on *competition* as an economic entity that needs to be safeguarded.[35] Therefore, 'unfair competition law' purposely protects competitors, whereas competition law – regulated by Articles 101 and 102 in the EU – protects competition. The difference is crucial as the dictates of 'unfair competition law' may indeed clash with the dictates of 'competition law'. For example, 'unfair competition law' rules on price reductions and announcements may restrict price

[28] For the criticism see, eg, P Jebsen and R Stevens, 'Assumptions, Goals and Dominant Undertakings: The Regulation of Competition under Article 86 of the European Union' (1996) 64 *Antitrust Law Journal* 443, 459; J Kallaugher and B Sher, 'Rebates Revisited: Anti-Competitive Effects and Exclusionary Abuse under Article 82' (2004) 25(5) *European Competition Law Review* 263, 277; D Geradin, 'Limiting the Scope of Article 82 EC: What can the EU Learn from the US Supreme Court's Judgment in *Trinko* in the Wake of *Microsoft, IMS,* and *Deutsche Telekom*? (2004) 41 *Common Market Law Review* 1519, 1532; A Jones and B Sufrin, *EU Competition Law: Text, Cases and Materials* 4th edn (Oxford, OUP, 2011) 363.

[29] IS Forrester, Panel Discussion 5 in CD Ehlermann and LL Laudati (eds), *European Competition Law Annual 1997: Objectives of Competition Policy* (Oxford, Hart Publishing, 1998) 326.

[30] ibid.

[31] RW de Vrey, *Towards a European Unfair Competition Law* (Leiden, Martinus Nijhoff Publishers, 2006) 2–3.

[32] ibid 3, fn 8.

[33] ibid 3.

[34] ibid 2.

[35] ibid 2, fn 7.

competition between undertakings. The ECJ has indeed held that unfair competition law rules could restrict competition.[36]

For three reasons, 'unfair competition law' will not be studied further in this work: first, there is no European 'unfair competition law' in the sense of a uniform coherent set of regulations.[37] Secondly, the *travaux préparatoires* of the Treaties of Rome negotiations explicitly demonstrate that the drafters of Article 102 did not intend it to be about 'unfair competition law'.[38] In fact, the finding that the ordoliberal notion of 'fairness' concerned fair behaviour towards competitors is further proof that Article 102 was not envisaged as an ordoliberal rule. Finally, the Commission has lately been going to great lengths to express its aim as protecting competition rather than competitors.[39] The point being made here is that for ordoliberals, fairness of competition was an issue and it mainly implied fairness to competitors of the dominant undertaking, although the particulars of how far free competition can be restricted for reasons of fairness are not made clear. Such an understanding of 'fairness', however, albeit appropriate for 'unfair competition law', is problematic and at times perverse for the purposes of competition law, whose aim is to protect competition and not individual competitors. The next section investigates the decisional practice of the EU authorities on the issue of 'fairness' under Article 102.

III EU CASE LAW

Although the understanding of the authorities may naturally evolve over time, it is helpful to look at how 'fairness' has played a role in the case law so far to understand the 'fairness' notion behind Article 102. There are several instances in the decisional practice where the Commission and the EU courts have referred to the '(un)fairness' of conduct when finding it abusive. This section assesses both the questions of what and to whom the unfairness of a practice under Article 102 relates, in so far as this information can be extracted from the decisions. This section thus gives a non-exhaustive overview of cases where the conduct of a

[36] See Case C-126/91 *Schutzverband gegen Unwesen in der Wirtschaft eV v Yves Rocher GmbH* [1993] ECR I-2361, [22]. In this preliminary reference case, the compatibility of para 6e of the German Act Against Unfair Competition which prohibited eye-catching individual price comparisons with the EC Treaty was questioned. The ECJ found that '[a]s for the protection of fair trading, and hence of competition, it is important to note that correct price comparisons, prohibited by a rule of law of the kind at issue, cannot in any way distort the conditions of competition. On the other hand, a rule which has the effect of prohibiting such comparisons may restrict competition'; ibid. There are also instances of prohibition of sales at a loss in unfair competition laws of some EU Member States, such as France and Belgium which do not require market power of the seller. Similarly, German unfair competition law prohibits the impediment of individual competitors by 'deliberate' competitive action. For an explanation of all legal provisions, see F Henning-Bodewig, *Unfair Competition Law, European Union and Member States* (The Hague, Kluwer Law International, 2006) 84, 121, 136 respectively.

[37] Henning-Bodewig (n 36) xvi.

[38] See ch 2 this volume, text around fn 244.

[39] See Kroes (n 6) 3; 'Discussion Paper' (n 6) [54]; 'Guidance' (n 6) [6].

dominant undertaking was found to be an 'unfair trading condition' under Article 102(a) or where a general reference to 'unfairness' of the practice was made by the authorities. The abusive practices of 'unfair pricing' and 'discrimination' are studied at length separately in chapters five and six respectively.

An early example of the ECJ referring to 'unfair trading conditions' is found in *SABAM*, in which it was held that an abuse could consist in the fact that a dominant undertaking entrusted with the management of copyrights imposes on its members obligations which are not absolutely necessary for the attainment of its object and which thus encroach 'unfairly' on a member's freedom to exercise his copyright.[40] According to the ECJ, for this appraisal, account had to be taken of all the relevant interests to ensure a balancing between the requirement of maximum freedom for members to dispose of their works and the effective management of their rights by the undertaking.[41] As such, 'fairness' was about balancing the rights and obligations of contract parties. Thus, a condition going beyond what was *absolutely necessary* for the achievement of one party's objectives was an 'unfair' limitation of the freedom of the other party. In *GEMA*, basing its decision on this judgment of the ECJ, the Commission stated that the decisive factor in copyright collection cases was whether the collecting society's statutes exceed the limits absolutely necessary for effective protection (the 'indispensability test') and whether they limited the individual copyright holder's freedom to dispose of her work no more than need be (the 'equity test').[42] Thus, expressed as 'indispensability', the *absolute necessity* of a contract term was again seen as part of the test of 'fairness' of the dominant undertaking's behaviour. In both *SABAM* and *GEMA* 'fairness' was assessed in relation to the contracting parties of the dominant undertaking.

Another example is the *Ahmed Saeed* case in which the airline tariffs imposed by a dominant air carrier on other carriers were found to be abusive where such tariffs had to be regarded as 'unfair trading conditions of transport with regard to competitors or with regard to passengers'.[43] Therefore, the concern was with 'fairness' towards competitors and consumers. Such unfair conditions in *Ahmed Saeed* were found to be possible due to either the rate of tariffs imposed being excessively high or excessively low, or due to the exclusive application of only one tariff on a given route.[44] In another decision, imposition of conditions on competitors not imposed on oneself for the same operations, that is discrimination, was deemed an 'unfair' trading condition.[45] In other words, 'fairness' was understood as *equality* and as that towards competitors compared to oneself. Another

[40] Case 127/73 *Belgische Radio en Televisie v SV SABAM and NV Fonior* [1974] ECR 313, [15].

[41] ibid [8].

[42] *GEMA Statutes* (Case IV/29.971) Commission Decision 82/204/EEC [1982] OJ L94/12, [36].

[43] Case 66/86 *Ahmed Saeed Flugreisen and Silver Line Reisebüro GmbH v Zentrale zur Bekämpfung unlauteren Wettbewerbs eV* [1989] ECR 803, [42].

[44] ibid [43], [44].

[45] Case 311/84 *Centre Belge d'Etudes de Marche-Telemarketing (CBEM) v SA Compagnie Luxembourgeoise de Telediffusion (CLT) and Information Publicite Benelux (IPB)* [1985] ECR 3261, [24].

ECJ judgment found the charging of higher royalties to undertakings in one Member State than those charged in another to be an 'unfair' trading condition.[46] Hence, discrimination between customers was deemed to be 'unfair'.

In *DSD*, the Commission held that an 'unfair' commercial term exists where a dominant undertaking fails to comply with the principle of *proportionality*.[47] The Commission was referring to the ECJ judgment in *United Brands* where the Court had held that a possible counter-attack by a dominant undertaking had to be 'proportionate' to the threat taking into account the economic strength of the undertakings confronting each other.[48] Thus, 'fairness' appears to have been understood as that to the customers of the dominant undertaking in the sense that the interests of the contracting parties are balanced. In the same vein, in *Tetra Pak II*, contract clauses going beyond the recognised right of a dominant undertaking to protect its commercial interests were deemed 'unfair'.[49] Similar to the approach in *SABAM*,[50] this understanding of 'fairness' closely resembles fairness doctrines in contract law, such as 'inequality of bargaining power', as will be demonstrated below.[51] In *United Brands*, the ECJ had decided that a dominant undertaking could not stop supplying a long-standing customer who abides by regular commercial practice if the orders placed by that customer are in no way extraordinary.[52] Therefore, *arbitrariness* in the relationship with customers was also found to be the reason of the 'unfairness'.

In *Alsatel*, the unilateral fixing of the prices of supplements to the contract due to modifications and the automatic renewal of contract for 15 years (under certain circumstances) were found to be 'unfair' trading conditions.[53] In this case, it appears that the *oppressiveness* and *one-sidedness* of the contract for the customer were the cause of 'unfairness'. One other instance was the finding by the General Court (GC) that the criteria set by a dominant undertaking with regard to priority in meeting orders had to be objectively justified and had to observe the rules governing *fair competition* between economic operators.[54] Thus, here it is implied that there are indeed rules governing 'fair' competition and a dominant undertaking must obey them by treating its customers accordingly, in other words 'fairly'. Remarkably, the Commission has stated in its *ECS/AKZO* decision that

[46] Case 395/87 *Ministère Public v Jean-Louis Tournier* [1989] ECR 2521, [46].

[47] *DSD* (Case COMP D3/34493) Commission Decision 2001/463/EC [2001] OJ L166/1, [112].

[48] Case 27/76 *United Brands Co and United Brands Continental BV v Commission* [1978] ECR 207, [190].

[49] Case T-83/91 *Tetra Pak International SA v Commission* [1994] ECR II-755, [140], upheld on appeal in Case C-333/94 P *Tetra Pak International SA v Commission* [1996] ECR I-5951.

[50] *SABAM* (n 40).

[51] See below, text around nn 92 and 129.

[52] *United Brands* (n 48) [182].

[53] Case 247/86 *Alsatel v SA Novasam* [1988] ECR 5987, [10]. The case was a reference for a preliminary ruling concerning an obligation to deal exclusively with the installer of telephone systems regarding any modification of the installation.

[54] Case T-65/89 *BPB Industries plc and British Gypsum Ltd v Commission* [1993] ECR II-389, [94], upheld on appeal in Case C-310/93 P *BPB Industries plc and British Gypsum Ltd v Commission* [1995] ECR I-865.

> [a]ny unfair commercial practices on the part of a dominant undertaking intended to eliminate, discipline or deter smaller competitors would thus fall within the scope of the prohibition of Article [102] if the other conditions for its application were fulfilled.[55]

Thus, 'unfairness' towards smaller competitors was found capable of breaching the provision. In *Michelin II* a discount system applied by a dominant undertaking and which left it a considerable margin of discretion as to whether the dealer may obtain the discount was considered 'unfair' and found to be abusive.[56] It thus implies that 'fairness' requires *transparency*, *objectivity*, *certainty* and *limited discretion*. One of the Commission's arguments about the 'unfairness' of Michelin's practices in that case was that the payment of rebates by Michelin to the dealers were extremely late and the dealers were forced to enter into quantitative commitments to Michelin before they had even received the rebates for the previous year. Thus,

> [t]his was unfair not only because the dealers were placed in a weak psychological position during negotiations, but also because, during the negotiations, they were not able to base themselves on a reliable estimate of their cost prices and thus determine their business strategy freely.[57]

It is striking that the Commission has actually taken into account the presumed *psychological* positions of the dealers while assessing the 'fairness' of the practice. This again very much resembles the arguments made for the doctrine of 'inequality of bargaining power' in contract law as will be seen below.[58] It is, however, questionable how it can be determined and proved that one party was in a weak psychological position with standard judicial methods. Similarly, the Commission seems to view the customers, who in this case are firms and not final consumers, as being unable to make forecasts and organise their business, which demonstrates a rather paternalistic approach.[59] It is, nonetheless, noteworthy that it is once more 'fairness' to customers that is the concern.

In short, a brief look at the relevant decisions under Article 102 demonstrates that there is clearly a concept of 'fairness' being used while judging the 'abuse' part of the prohibition in some cases. It is equally clear, however, that there is not a single or coherent conception or test of 'fairness'. 'Fairness' has been understood as *absolute necessity*, *equality*, *proportionality*, *transparency*, *objectivity*, *certainty* and so on regarding the practices of dominant undertakings. In some cases, like *Michelin II*, 'fairness' also appears to have been used for purposes of tackling

[55] *ECS/AKZO* (Case IV/30.698) Commission Decision 85/609/EEC [1985] OJ L374/1, [74].

[56] Case T-203/01 Manufacture Francaise des Pneumatiques Michelin v Commission [2003] ECR II-4071, [141].

[57] *Michelin* (Case COMP/E-2/36.041/PO) Commission Decision 2002/405/EC [2002] OJ L143/1, [223].

[58] See below, text around nn 92 and 129.

[59] M Motta, 'Michelin II – The Treatment of Rebates' in BR Lyons (ed), *Cases in European Competition Policy: The Economic Analysis* (Cambridge, CUP, 2009) 39.

practices impairing 'market integration'.[60] As such, assessment of 'fairness' turns very much on the facts of the case and it seems as if 'fairness' has sometimes been used as an umbrella notion under which to condemn practices that the EU authorities would like to sanction under Article 102. An alternative interpretation could be that the Commission and courts have equated 'unfair' with 'anti-competitive' or 'abusive' without defining any of these and without elaborating on the criteria under which to assess the conduct. The vagueness of the concept naturally allows it to be used for different purposes in different contexts. Moreover, the way 'fairness' has been interpreted demonstrates similarities with how the concept is interpreted in other areas of law – such as contract law – specifically when reference is made to oppressiveness, one-sidedness and imposition of pressure on the other party by the dominant undertaking. In fact, this might imply that the practices decided to be abusive due to unfairness might signify contract law problems more than competition law problems. Furthermore, in the majority of the cases under scrutiny here, 'fairness' relates to the conduct of a dominant undertaking with its customers, rather than with its competitors. Even if this does not exclude the possibility that this concern is also related to preventing the exclusion of competitors which might follow the 'unfair' conduct towards customers, the direct concern appears to be with the 'fairness' of transactions entered into with trading partners. Consequently, section IV examines various notions of 'fairness' in law in the context of market transactions seeking to illuminate what 'fairness' may mean and what its implications may be in the context of Article 102.

IV NOTIONS OF 'FAIRNESS'

A In General

As the discussion of ordoliberalism and EU case law above demonstrates, the underlying question of what is meant by '(un)fairness' under Article 102 is left unanswered. Although there are hints regarding the *subject* of the concept – such as that it may mean 'fairness to competitors' or 'fairness to customers/suppliers' – the *content* of the concept is left vacuous. Since the decisional practice and the policy on Article 102 do not provide this content, and since competition law is intertwined with other areas of law, this section will investigate what 'fairness' may mean in a broader legal sense seeking insights into conceptualising 'fairness' under Article 102. The emphasis will be on how 'fairness' is interpreted with regard to market transactions, as this is directly relevant for competition law as well. This focus naturally brings to the fore contract law, and how 'fairness' is understood in contract law deserves elaboration.

[60] *Michelin II* (n 56) [66]. For 'market integration' as an objective of EU competition law and policy, see ch 2 this volume, section II.

The concept of 'abuse of a dominant position' indeed strongly resembles various perceptions of 'fairness' in contract law, such as 'inequality of bargaining power' and 'economic duress'. By sanctioning the imposition of prices and the application of various trading conditions, in many cases Article 102 essentially regulates the contracts of dominant undertakings. This is especially true for 'exploitation', since exploitation concerns the relation of the dominant undertaking with its trading partners. Yet, even for 'exclusion', the means to exclude can often be contracts, such as exclusivity agreements with customers that foreclose the market to competitors.[61] Indeed, according to the ECJ, Article 102 'is expressly aimed in fact at situations which clearly originate in contractual relations'.[62]

A word of caution is necessary. As contract law is an area regulated by the national laws of the Member States in the EU, the notions of 'fairness' are examined here without being jurisdiction specific to the extent possible, except for EU consumer law (constituting the main bulk of the European contract law *acquis*)[63] which is elaborated on separately. As will be seen, the underlying concern when scrutinising the 'fairness' of transactions usually appears to be the same across national laws. Therefore, this section first investigates 'fairness' notions in contract law in general along with the Principles of European Contract Law (PECL)[64] and the Draft Common Frame of Reference (DCFR)[65], then draws on the similar-

[61] For the argument that for contractual abuses under Art 102, such as vertical restraints, Art 102 can be discarded of by exclusive use of Art 101, see E Rousseva, 'Modernizing by Eradicating: How the Commission's New Approach to Article 81 EC Dispenses with the Need to Apply Article 82 EC to Vertical Restraints' (2005) 42 *Common Market Law Review* 587, 587.

[62] *Hoffmann-La Roche* (n 20) [116].

[63] T Wilhelmsson, 'Varieties of Welfarism in European Contract Law' (2004) 10(6) *European Law Journal* 712, 726; MW Hesselink, 'European Contract Law: A Matter of Consumer Protection, Citizenship, or Justice?' Centre for the Study of European Contract Law Working Paper Series No 2006/04, 4.

[64] 'Principles of European Contract Law' was prepared by the Commission on European Contract Law, a body of lawyers drawn from all the (then) Member States of the EC and chaired by Ole Lando. The Principles aim to serve as a basis for any future European Code of Contracts. They have been published as O Lando and H Beale (eds), *Principles of European Contract Law Parts I and II* (The Hague, Kluwer Law International, 2000). This was later supplemented with O Lando, E Clive, A Prum and R Zimmerman, *Principles of European Contract Law Part III* (The Hague, Kluwer Law International, 2003). Although PECL is not binding, it provides a legal foundation for measures taken and to be taken in the future by the organs of the EU and will assist both the organs of the Union in drafting measures and courts, arbitrators and legal advisers applying Union measures; ibid xxiii. As such, it represents the common core of the European systems or a progressive development from that common core; ibid xxiv.

[65] The 'Common Frame of Reference' (CFR) is a long-term project which aims at providing the European legislators (Commission, Council and European Parliament) with a 'toolbox' or a handbook to be used for the revision of existing and the preparation of new legislation in the area of contract law. This toolbox could contain fundamental principles of contract law, definitions of key concepts and model provisions. The 'Draft Common Frame of Reference' (DCFR) is a study commissioned by the Commission and prepared by the Study Group on a European Civil Code and the Research Group on EC Private Law (Acquis Group), based in part on a revised version of PECL. It provides principles, definitions and model rules of European private law and comprises ten books. At the time of writing, EU level discussions are continuing on the policy options for progress towards a European Contract Law for consumers and businesses. The text of DCFR can be found at ec.europa.eu/justice/policies/civil/docs/dcfr_outline_edition_en.pdf and the Commission Green Paper on policy options for progress towards a European Contract Law for consumers and businesses COM (2010) 348 final 1.7.2010 can be found at eur-lex.europa.eu/LexUriServ/LexUriServ.do?uri=COM:2010:0348:FIN:en:PDF.

ity of these with Article 102 and explains the implications of this before examining EU consumer law. It should be noted at the outset that at the time of writing, EU contract law is undergoing a major review by the EU authorities. For its part, EU consumer law *acquis* is reaching the conclusion of a similar review by the EU authorities.[66]

B Contract Law

In contract law, 'fairness' is mainly concerned with answering the question of who should get what and how in a transaction. As such, 'fairness' notions can generally be put under one blanket categorisation, which is that of 'substantive' and 'procedural' fairness. 'Substantive fairness' is used to express the 'fairness' of the terms and outcome of a bargain, whereas 'procedural fairness' refers to the process of obtaining the terms and outcome.[67]

'Substantive fairness' scrutinises the division of obligations and gains resulting from a transaction. This in itself may of course be one of the reasons why it is so hard to define what is 'fair'; it naturally includes value judgements which are almost always going to make one party win and another lose. This would occur especially in cases of judicial intervention where the court tries to divide these gains ex post faced with an allegation of an 'unfair' division. Indeed, most notions of 'fairness' reflect an ex post perspective on the situation under examination.[68] Nonetheless, even ex ante, since most people are self-interested, each party will want to have as big a share of the pie (ie, the gains from their trade) as possible and this might render anything less than that sub-optimal for that party. It has also rightly been pointed out that an ex post analysis may ignore important aspects of *ex ante* behaviour that may well be responsible for the ultimate result.[69] For example, contract law remedies that seem 'fair' ex post may tend to lead parties to adjust other contract terms ex ante and thus nullify or even reverse the apparent effect of the seemingly 'fair' rule or change parties' incentives to enter contracts or commit breaches in the first place.[70] Therefore, implementing a 'fairness' theory is difficult when parties have the freedom to alter 'fair' legal rules that do not maximise their expected gains.[71] Indeed, for business contracts, it has been

[66] For the argument that the substances of the review of these two closely connected areas of law are significantly disjunct, see MW Hesselink, 'The Consumer Rights Directive and the CFR: Two Worlds Apart?' (2009) 5(3) *European Review of Contract Law* 290. On the review of the consumer *acquis*, see below section IV.D.

[67] On 'substantive' and 'procedural' fairness in general, see SA Smith, 'In Defence of Substantive Fairness' (1996) 112 *Law Quarterly Review* 138.

[68] Kaplow and Shavell (n 7) 48.

[69] ibid 49.

[70] ibid.

[71] A Schwartz, 'Contract Theory and Theories of Contract Regulation' in E Brousseau and JM Glachant (eds), *Revue d'Economie Industrielle*, No Spécial, Économie des Contrats: Bilan et Perspective, No 92, (2eme et 3eme trimestre 2000) 101, 102, fn 3.

argued that contract law should facilitate efforts to maximise the contractual surplus (ie, the size of the pie) and do nothing else because firms *will* contract away from redistributive or 'fair' rules that do not maximise the joint surplus.[72] Since one party to a possible contract cannot ordinarily affect the other party's business opportunities, each potential contract partner will realise that its share of the maximum surplus the parties could generate jointly has already been fixed before any contract is signed. Therefore, each party will contract so as to maximise the size of the pie.[73] Furthermore, any division of ex post gains between business firms would be arbitrary since there is no legal or distributional principle that would permit a court to decide whether it is 'fair' to give the plaintiff or the defendant particular shares.[74] Business parties will contract out of 'fair', but 'inefficient' default rules.[75]

Some commentators have nevertheless considered 'fairness' in contract to mean 'adequacy in exchange', in the sense that the contract is not one-sided or imbalanced.[76] As such, one understanding of 'fairness' is the 'equal' split of a transaction's surplus between the parties[77] and, thus, a way of obtaining commutative justice (that is, not causing the unjust enrichment of one party at the expense of another).[78] The roots of this perspective may be traced back to Aristotle as for him, 'what is unjust is unfair, or unequal'.[79] According to Aristotle, in voluntary transactions parties should neither gain nor lose; what is 'just' in transactions is that each party has an equal amount both before and after the transaction.[80] Under this interpretation, a contract would be 'fair' when the gains and losses to one party from the contract are proportionate to those of the other party and neither party is enriched or impoverished in comparison with their situation before the transaction.

However, it is – to say the least – problematic to find a way to determine when the exchange is 'adequate' and when the terms are so 'one-sided' as to be identified as 'unfair'. It would require a tool to assess the 'adequacy' of the exchange;

[72] A Schwartz and RE Scott, 'Contract Theory and the Limits of Contract Law' (2003) 113 *Yale Law Journal* 541, 544, 546.

[73] ibid 554.

[74] Schwartz (n 71) 7, 10.

[75] ibid 10.

[76] See PS Atiyah, 'Contract and Fair Exchange' (1985) 34 *University of Toronto Law Journal* 1, 5, 6, 17; RD Petty and J Hamilton, 'Seeking a Single Policy for Contractual Fairness to Consumers: A Comparison of US and EU Efforts' (2004) 38(1) *The Journal of Consumer Affairs* 146, 146.

[77] O Bar-Gill and C Fersthman, 'Law and Preferences' (2004) 20 *The Journal of Law, Economics & Organization* 331, 338. For the argument that objective equivalence is meaningless and that this is a misinterpretation of Aristotle's commutative justice and Roman law, see MJ Golecki, 'Synallagma and Freedom of Contract – The Concept of Reciprocity and Fairness in Contracts from the Historical and Law and Economics Perspective' German Working Papers in Law and Economics No 18 (2003) available at: bepress.com/cgi/viewcontent.cgi?article=1070&context=gwp 2.

[78] E Brousseau, 'Did the Common Law Biased the Economics of Contract . . . and may it Change?' in B Deffains and K Thierry (eds), *Law and Economics in Civil Law Countries* (Amsterdam, Elsevier, 2001) 86–87.

[79] Aristotle (n 2) 1131a.

[80] ibid 1132b.

one would need something with which to measure the value of what each party receives. This appears to be very difficult, perhaps impossible, especially when it is accepted that value is subjective. This will be returned to in chapter five in the context of the prohibition of 'unfair pricing'.

Interpreting 'fairness' as 'equality' has also been criticised on the grounds that 'equality is an empty idea' since statements of equality 'logically entail and necessarily collapse into simpler statements of rights'.[81] According to this argument, equality is tautological. The entitlements people mistakenly attribute to the idea of equality all derive from external substantive rights and the idea of equality is logically indistinguishable from the standard formula of distributive justice that 'every person should be given his due'.[82] Without moral principles to determine 'which persons are alike', equality remains meaningless, a formula that can have nothing to say about how one should act.[83] Once the standard for treating some people alike is found, then equality becomes superfluous since the logical result of having a rule is applying that rule to all the cases that fall under it.[84]

Indeed, in general, contract law does not insist that bargains be 'fair' in the sense that the performances exchanged be of what others might call 'equal value'; it is commonly held that the parties are the best judges of the relative values to be exchanged.[85] This endorses the 'fairness' of voluntary transactions and demonstrates a faith in the ability of individuals to take care of their own interests by making informed and rational judgements.[86] This faith in individual autonomy and rationality fosters a belief in the 'fairness' of the distributive outcomes of a relatively uninhibited market.[87] As such, it endorses the principle of 'freedom of contract' (which is deemed to be 'the centrepiece of contract law in all Member States' of the EU), 'restrictions on [which] should only be envisaged where this could be justified for good reasons', according to the Commission.[88]

Yet, it has been argued that although the doctrine of *laesio enormis*[89] was either rejected by continental civil codes or accepted only in exceptional cases and that the common law starts from the position that the validity of a contract is entirely independent of the 'adequacy of the consideration', if one looks at what the courts are doing rather than what they say, one would realise that a party disadvantaged

[81] P Westen 'The Empty Idea of Equality' (1982) 95 *Harvard Law Review* 537, 542. According to Westen, 'equality' means the proposition in law and morals that 'people who are alike should be treated alike' and 'people who are unalike should be treated unalike'; ibid 539–40.

[82] ibid 542.

[83] ibid 547.

[84] ibid 547, 548 *et seq.*

[85] PECL Parts I–II (n 64) 261.

[86] H Collins, *The Law of Contract* 4th edn (London, Butterworths, 2003) 272.

[87] ibid.

[88] 'Action Plan' (n 21) [81], [93]. Similarly Opinion of Advocate General Jacobs in *Oscar Bronner* (n 21) [56].

[89] *Laesio enormis* (extraordinary injury) was a doctrine in Roman law according to which the price given in a contract by way of consideration had to be fair and reasonable or the contract might be rescinded; J Law (ed), *A Dictionary of Business and Management* (Oxford, OUP, 2006).

by a contract has a very good chance of being released from it if there is a manifest disproportion between what she is giving and what she is getting.[90] Indeed, many European legal systems refuse to uphold contracts which involve an obviously gross disparity in the value of the two performances when this appears to be the result of some bargaining weakness on one party *and* conscious advantage-taking on the other.[91]

For example, under the common law doctrine of 'inequality of bargaining power', the 'unfairness' of a bargain is deemed to result from the inequality of the bargaining powers of contracting parties.[92] The doctrine is especially relevant for the course of this study since Article 102 aims at regulating the abuse of a dominant position – that is abuse of market *power*. Described as 'a doctrine in search of content and substance' and one that '[a]fter almost a century of searching, . . . remains obscure',[93] inequality of bargaining power first requires an analysis of 'power'.

Power typically describes an ability to affect or obtain a preferred outcome.[94] It has three characteristics that are critical for any legal analysis of relative bargaining power: power is omnipresent (every actor has power of some kind and to some degree);[95] power is complex (it is highly situational and takes varied forms that may not be obvious to the observer); and power is dynamic (any power relationship can change dramatically and instantaneously).[96] Barnhizer has suggested that in any competitive system involving actors of varying levels of skill, with different needs, desires and goals, every scarce source including bargaining power will be subject to unequal distributions.[97] Thus, where the parties are free to bargain on some terms, nothing justifies a court in determining that what was or could have been bargained does not compensate for what was not.[98] Moreover, it has been argued that it is extremely difficult to define the scope of the inequality of bargaining power doctrine and without clearly-defined limits as – in all cases of

[90] H Kötz, European Contract Law Vol 1: Formation, Validity, and Content of Contracts; Contract and Third Parties (trans T Weir, Oxford, Clarendon Press, 1997) 10.

[91] PECL Parts I–II (n 64) 261.

[92] According to Collins, it is not sufficient that the parties enjoyed different degrees of bargaining power in the sense of better resources or an advantageous trading position due to possession of some scarce commodity; what is crucial is rather that the superior bargaining position was exploited in order to impose a disadvantageous transaction on the weaker party; Collins (n 86) 156.

[93] DD Barnhizer, 'Inequality of Bargaining Power' (2005) 76 *University of Colorado Law Review* 139, 201.

[94] ibid 155.

[95] Unless the parties are contracting in a state of emergency, duress or necessity, every party theoretically has the power to walk away from the proposed bargain and satisfy its needs or wants elsewhere; ibid, 180.

[96] ibid 142. Barnhizer also argues that because power is present in every relationship and every actor has some degree of power of some type, judicial intervention into private contracts cannot meaningfully turn on the determination that one party lacks power – no such situation exists or can exist; ibid 163. Thus, the determinative factor should be the quantities of bargaining power rather than the presence or absence of it; ibid 164.

[97] ibid 162.

[98] ibid 212.

substantive fairness examinations – it poses a direct threat to the freedom of contract doctrine.[99]

In any case, it would create too much uncertainty if a party could escape from a contract, even if it is disadvantageous to her, when there is no apparent reason why she did not look after her own interests better when agreeing.[100] Therefore, relief should arguably only be available when the party can point to some weakness, disability or need on her part to explain what happened.[101] Most continental European systems have rules permitting avoidance where one party deliberately takes advantage of the other's need or circumstances to obtain a very one-sided contract.[102] The common law and Scots law seem to give relief mainly in cases of abuse of a special relationship and grant it only under very limited conditions.[103] In English and Irish law, the doctrine of 'undue influence' also allows contracts to be set aside where there has been an 'unconscientious use of bargaining power arising out of necessitous circumstances of the weaker party'.[104] Although it may be true that here and there one finds traces of the old doctrine of *laesio enormis* and that there is a rooted sense that 'unfair' contracts should not be enforced, it is generally agreed in European legal systems that a contract is not 'unfair' simply because a party has agreed to pay too high a price.[105] This is particularly relevant for purposes of Article 102 since this provision does prohibit the imposition of 'unfair' prices by a dominant undertaking as 'abuse' which will be examined separately in chapter five.

The majority position in European systems, also followed by PECL and DCFR, requires one party to have taken advantage of the other's special weakness to obtain an 'unfair' contract or to 'unfairly exploit' the other party; it does not provide relief simply on the basis of a disproportion in value between the performances.[106] Article 4:109 of PECL adopts the principle that a contract which gives one party excessive advantage and which involves an 'unfair' advantage taking may be avoided or modified at the request of the disadvantaged party.[107] Thus, Article 4:109 of PECL applies where the advantage gained by one party is demonstrably excessive

[99] SN Thal, 'The Inequality of Bargaining Power Doctrine: The Problem of Defining Contractual Unfairness' (1988) 8 *Oxford Journal of Legal Studies* 17, 17. Thal distinguishes between inequality of bargaining power resulting from one party's strength and one party's weakness and argues that, for the doctrine to be relevant, it is essential that the inequality arises because of unusual *weakness* of bargaining on one side of the transaction. The issues of strength-based inequality are usually left to the legislature since an assessment of it requires an inquiry into the contestability of the market; ibid 30. It is worth pointing out that most transactions where there is an inequality of bargaining power will have one party stronger and one party weaker than the other. Thus, Thal's distinction might not be operational in most cases.

[100] PECL Parts I–II (n 64) 261.

[101] ibid 261–62.

[102] ibid 263.

[103] ibid.

[104] Collins (n 86) 148. See also PECL Parts I–II (n 64) 264.

[105] Kötz (n 90) 135.

[106] PECL Parts I–II (n 64) 265 and DCFR (n 65) Book II.-7:207.

[107] PECL, ibid, 261.

in comparison to the 'normal' price or other return in such contracts.[108] Unfortunately, what 'normal' price means is not defined in PECL.

Similarly, Article II.-7:207 of DCFR, interestingly entitled 'unfair exploitation', stipulates that a party may avoid a contract if, at the time of conclusion of the contract, the party was: (i) dependent on or had a relationship of trust with the other party; (ii) in economic distress or had urgent needs; (iii) improvident, ignorant, inexperienced or lacking in bargaining skill and the party knew or could reasonably be expected to have known this; and, (iv) given the circumstances and purpose of the contract, the other party exploited the first party's situation by taking an excessive benefit or grossly unfair advantage. It is striking that the title of this provision, 'unfair exploitation', is very similar to the literal prohibition of Article 102 in the German and French texts of the TFEU, namely 'abusive exploitation'. The DCFR rule can be criticised for not being clear enough regarding which of the conditions are cumulative and which are alternative (for example, whether dependency and economic distress are alternative or cumulative requirements) and for not defining what will constitute an excessive benefit or grossly unfair advantage. Nonetheless, similar to Article 4:109 of PECL, it is clear that it is more than a simple disproportion in value between the performances that renders the contract voidable. The question then becomes whether a position of dominance in itself can be seen as a position causing the dominant undertaking's practices to automatically fall under the scope of Article II.-7:207 of DCFR as per the dependency element of the provision. It is possible that dominance suffices for the element of dependency in this provision and 'abuse' under Article 102 can be interpreted as 'taking an excessive benefit or grossly unfair advantage'. This would imply that if this rule of DCFR is adopted by the EU or Member States as a binding principle, abusive conduct of dominant undertakings that arise in contractual relations can also be challenged under this rule. The problem, however, remains in DCFR not providing any guidance as to the interpretation of 'taking an excessive benefit or grossly unfair advantage'.

Another relevant provision is Article 4:110 of PECL which regulates 'unfair terms not individually negotiated' and imposes the sanction of voidability for such terms if, contrary to requirements of 'good faith' and 'fair dealing', they cause a significant imbalance in the parties' rights and obligations. Importantly, this provision excludes scrutiny of price regarding its 'fairness' or 'adequacy'. It is explicitly stated that judges and arbitrators may not judge the relation between the price and the main subject matter.[109] Consequently, Article 4:110 does not reintroduce the *iustum pretium* (fair price) doctrine of canon law.[110] Similarly, Book II.-Section 4 of DCFR regulates 'unfair terms' in not only business-to-consumer, but also business-to-business contracts and excludes scrutiny of price

[108] ibid 262.

[109] ibid 269.

[110] ibid. *Cf* MW Hesselink, 'Capacity and Capability in European Contract Law' (2005) 13(4) *European Review of Private Law* 491, 500–01, 507 arguing that a 'fair price' rule should be introduced in the internal market.

regarding its 'adequacy', so long as the term is drafted in plain and intelligible language.[111] This is in line with EU consumer law and most national laws of Member States and will be returned to under section IV.D.

Under Article 4:109 of PECL, the court may, if appropriate, adapt the contract in order to bring it into accordance with what might have been agreed had the requirements of 'good faith' and 'fair dealing' been followed.[112] According to the commentary in PECL, 'good faith' means honesty and 'fairness' in mind, which are subjective concepts.[113] 'Fair dealing' means observance of 'fairness' in fact which is an objective test.[114] What is again unfortunate is that 'fair dealing' is defined as 'fairness' in fact and 'fairness' remains undefined. According to Article 1:302 of PECL, 'reasonableness' is to be judged by what persons acting in good faith and in the same situation as the parties would consider to be 'reasonable'. As PECL appears to use 'unreasonable' and 'unfair' interchangeably,[115] 'fair' under PECL can also be understood as the behaviour that would be expected of persons in the same situation as the parties acting in 'good faith'. Nonetheless, this does not end the circularity of the argument since 'good faith' is also defined as 'honesty' and 'fairness'. It is therefore not exactly clear what is 'fair' under PECL.

DCFR also provides two definitions of 'unfair'; one for business-to-consumer and one for business-to-business contracts. Accordingly, in the business-to-consumer contracts, 'unfair' means that the term supplied by the business 'significantly disadvantages the consumer, contrary to good faith and fair dealing'.[116] In a business-to-business contract, the unfairness of a term forming part of standard terms of one party means that the term is of such a nature that its use 'grossly deviates from good commercial practice, contrary to good faith and fair dealing'.[117] DCFR in this regard is novel (and possibly controversial) because it suggests scrutiny of business-to-business contracts for the purposes of 'fairness'. Similar to Article II.-7:207 on unfair exploitation, these provisions would also provide additional legal grounds for consumers and businesses that have entered into contractual relations with dominant undertakings if 'unfairness' under these provisions is to be understood as being similar to 'unfairness' under Article 102. This would be the case to the extent that DCFR principles are accepted as binding. What is missing in DCFR again in terms operationalising the principles is guidance on how to understand and interpret 'significant disadvantage' and 'gross deviation from good commercial practice'. In contrast, a definition is provided for 'good faith and fair dealing' as 'a standard of conduct characterised by honesty, openness and consideration for the interests of the other party to the transaction or relationship in question'.[118] However, it is again not absolutely clear

[111] DCFR (n 65) Art II.-9.406.
[112] In DCFR, this is provided under the 'unfair exploitation' rule (Art II.-7:207).
[113] PECL Parts I–II (n 64) 115.
[114] ibid 115–16.
[115] See ibid 262.
[116] DCFR (n 65) Art II.-9:403.
[117] ibid Art II.-9:405.
[118] ibid Art I.-1:103.

what is to be understood by 'honesty' and 'consideration for the interests of the other party' in this context. As accepted by DCFR itself, these are 'open-ended concepts'.[119] Unfortunately, as such, they only provide limited means to help to interpret 'abuse' in Article 102.

Although European systems only exceptionally allow relief based on the grounds that the substance of the contract is 'unfair', all of them permit avoidance of a contract which has been obtained by 'unfair' *means* given certain circumstances.[120] In all systems, duress, fraud and (where applicable) abuse of circumstances are grounds for avoiding unilateral legal acts as well as contracts.[121] Thus, 'procedural fairness' appears to be commonly scrutinised. Indeed, it has been suggested that the only way to define 'fairness' is by focusing on the bargaining process and not the outcome; that is, by focusing on 'procedural fairness'.[122]

The notion of freedom of contract suggests that a party should only be bound by actions which were both voluntary, in the sense that the party was aware of what she was doing, and free, in the sense that she had some choice.[123] As such, 'duress' requires an illegitimate act performed by one party which causes the other to consent to the contract.[124] Duress is particularly relevant in the context of Article 102: one could argue, for example, that the existence of a dominant undertaking on the market results in a lack of alternatives for the contracting party and, therefore, a situation similar to duress arises, especially given the fact that most systems do not limit relief from duress to cases of threats of physical harm. In continental systems, relief is provided to cases of threats causing financial or moral harm, provided that the threat is illicit, and in English law this is recognised as 'economic duress'.[125] An answer to the question of whether the abuse of a dominant position is an example of duress or economic duress in competition law will be considered under section IV.C.

In short, contract law notions of 'fairness' refer to either the 'substantive fairness' or the 'procedural fairness' of a bargain. The former concerns the 'fairness' of the outcome reached, whereas the latter examines the 'fairness' of the procedure by which that outcome was reached. Deciding what is substantively 'fair' appears to be more controversial than deciding what is procedurally 'fair'. The interference with one of the party's autonomy by duress and similar conduct damages consent and deciding on this does not involve the court replacing its

[119] ibid 76.

[120] PECL Parts I–II (n 64) 263.

[121] ibid 228.

[122] Thal (n 99) 24. Hughes has also identified fairness as a procedural concept that guarantees an equal opportunity to all those who seek to participate in a particular undertaking; the concept being derived from the principles of equality and autonomy; EJ Hughes, 'The Left Side of Antitrust: What Fairness Means and why it Matters' (1994) 77 *Marquette Law Review* 265, 297. For the argument that what is a 'fair' outcome may depend on our views about 'fair' procedures and that the belief that it is possible to separate our ideas of 'fair' procedures from those of 'fair' results should be approached with caution, see Atiyah (n 76) 5.

[123] PECL Parts I–II (n 64) 257.

[124] Collins (n 86) 139.

[125] PECL Parts I–II (n 64) 260.

own judgement with that of the party. 'Substantive fairness', on the contrary, requires the court to replace its judgement with that of the party and, since the party's consent has not been interfered with, justifying such an assessment becomes harder and controversial. Whereas acceptance of party autonomy in a free market would require intervention into procedurally 'unfair' contracts, it would imply a lack of intervention into contracts that parties entered into freely. Moreover, deciding what is substantively 'fair' can easily become an arbitrary and subjective practice as there does not appear to be a universal understanding or definition of it. Thus, the following subsection examines the similarity of the various notions of 'fairness' studied so far with the 'fairness' concept under Article 102 and the implications of this.

C The Similarity of Fairness Notions in Contract Law with Article 102 and its Implications

'Fairness' as a concept of competition law does not have a generally accepted and clearly defined meaning and 'fairness' objectives in competition law take a variety of forms.[126] Arguably, at their core, they are based on the idea that dominant undertakings should not be allowed to use their economic power to distort market processes in their own favour at the expense of consumers and competitors. Arguably, 'fairness' is closely tied to the perceived role and legitimacy of markets in society.[127] This perception of 'fairness' is also very close to the definition of 'exploitation' provided in chapter two, as the dominant undertaking receiving advantages to the disadvantage of its trading partners that would not be possible but for its dominance.[128] Furthermore, this perception of 'fairness' in competition law is very similar to procedural fairness doctrines in contract law such as 'inequality of bargaining power', '(economic) duress' and 'undue influence' which will be dealt with in turn.

i Inequality of Bargaining Power

The aim of the 'fairness' notion in competition law and in contract law as served by the doctrine of 'inequality of bargaining power' seems to be the same, that is the protection of the weak from the stronger. It is deemed 'unfair' that 'the strong can push the weak to the wall'[129] and the courts may interfere to prevent or remedy this. Indeed, the ECJ decision in *United Brands* stating that '[e]ven if the possibility of a counter-attack [by a dominant undertaking] is acceptable that attack

[126] Gerber (n 10) 2.
[127] ibid.
[128] See ch 2 this volume, section V.F
[129] Lord Denning on the doctrine of 'inequality of bargaining power' in *Lloyds Bank Ltd v Bundy* [1975] QB 326, 336–37.

must still be proportionate to the threat taking into account the economic strength of the undertakings confronting each other'[130] seems to approve just this. In the same vein, the ECJ held in *Hoffmann-La Roche* that when deciding to pursue a case under Article 101 or Article 102, the Commission was entitled to take into account the nature of the reciprocal undertakings entered into under the contract and the competitive position of the various contracting parties.[131] Similarly, in *Courage v Crehan* – a case about the private enforcement of EU competition rules – the English Court of Appeal held that Article 102 was expressly directed at protection against consequences of unequal bargaining power.[132] Hence, the prohibition of abuse of a dominant position appears to draw the boundaries of 'fair' behaviour. It has actually been argued that '[t]he unfairness of the terms of the contract will inevitably provide crucial evidence of abuse of market position'.[133]

Although perhaps conceptually this similarity between 'abuse' and 'inequality of bargaining power' is 'good news', practically it might not be so. This is because the similarity implies that operationalising such a 'fairness' concept under Article 102 would bring along into competition law all the problems that the 'inequality of bargaining power' doctrine introduced into contract law as well. In other words, the difficulties with assessing power, the omnipresence of power, the doctrine rendering the law uncertain, direct interference with freedom of contract and so on would have to be dealt with. Not surprisingly, many criticisms of the application of Article 102 have indeed arisen from similar issues which have been grounds for criticising the doctrine of inequality of bargaining power in contract law. Moreover, the case of Article 102 in common law jurisdictions is even more problematic since 'the common law does not recognise the doctrine of inequality of bargaining power in commercial dealings'.[134] Thus, at least for common law, this is a doctrine that has been ultimately *rejected* by the courts for the problems it entails as demonstrated by, for example, the UK House of Lords (now Supreme Court) in *National Westminster Bank* which questioned the need for such a doctrine.[135]

Furthermore, one conclusion that the above discussions about the inequality of bargaining power leads to is that the doctrine could cause contracting parties to choose their prospective parties according to their relative bargaining power in

[130] *United Brands* (n 48) [190].

[131] *Hoffmann-La Roche* (n 20) [116].

[132] *Courage Limited v Crehan* [1999] ECC 455, [19]. In its preliminary reference ruling, the ECJ also held that the relative bargaining power of the parties could be taken into account when deciding whether a party to a contract breaching Art 101 (and thus void) can obtain damages from the other party to the exclusion of the principle that a litigant should not profit from her own unlawful conduct; Case C-453/99 *Courage Limited v Bernard Crehan and Bernard Crehan v Courage Limited and Others* [2001] ECR I-6297, [31]–[33].

[133] Collins (n 86) 280.

[134] Steyn LJ in *CTN Cash and Carry Ltd v Gallaher Ltd* [1994] 4 All ER 714, 716 commenting on *National Westminster Bank Plc v Morgan* [1985] AC 686.

[135] *National Westminster Bank*, ibid, 707–08. It should be noted that although a general doctrine of inequality of bargaining power is not accepted, there are specific instances in which the courts have intervened to set aside a contract which was, in the court's view, 'unfair'; E McKendrick, *Contract Law: Text, Cases and Materials*, 4th edn (Oxford, OUP, 2010) 688.

order to avoid a 'fairness' examination of the contract. Thus, it may change the nature of the prevailing contracting process if the understanding of 'bargaining power' is reduced to just the 'size' of a party, for example, a business. In that case, the 'big' players on a market would be deemed to have superior bargaining power and the 'small' ones inferior.[136] The result could be efficient or even collusive for the 'big' players, but not so efficient for the 'small' players that would have always to contract with other 'small' undertakings since their choice of contract parties and probably contract types would have been limited. Therefore, the mere fact that one party has more market share than the other should not, on its own, be sufficient to conclude that, as a result of this inequality, whatever agreement they reach is 'unfair'. There must be more than this; bargaining power should be understood as a more strategic and situational concept than one that depends on mere size. In the context of Article 102, for example, the likelihood of entry into the market would clearly be a directly relevant factor in establishing bargaining power.

It should also be questioned whether it is important that the same bargain would or would not have been deemed 'unfair' had there not been a disparity in the bargaining power of the parties. If the same contract when concluded between parties that have equivalent bargaining power against each other would not be 'unfair', then in the context of Article 102 this would mean that the conduct of a dominant undertaking contracting with another undertaking of substantial size will be subject to a different level of scrutiny than when it contracts with a smaller undertaking. This could result in the protection of certain undertakings rather than competition and cause disorder since the same contract – that is a contract with the same terms – would be subject to different treatment depending on whether the other party is as strong or weaker.[137]

ii Duress, Economic Duress and Undue Influence

The problems with the doctrine of inequality of bargaining power leads one to seek other interpretations of 'fairness' which might help to explain this concept in the context of Article 102. This similarity can be found in the procedural fairness doctrines of 'duress' (particularly 'economic duress') and 'undue influence', all of which deal with use of power. It has indeed been noted that the law addresses *structural* flaws through the law of competition, so that measures are taken to

[136] Although one may think that the concepts of 'bigness' and 'smallness' refer to the size of the undertaking on its own market relative to the other undertakings on that market, this is not necessarily so, since undertakings on the same market do not commonly contract with each other. Even though 'market share' is dependent on the market, the 'size' of the undertaking may be comparable across markets as well. The firm's turnover, reputation, capacity and so on may determine how 'big' it is. This would mean, eg, that a large upstream undertaking would have to find a large downstream undertaking (and a small upstream undertaking a small downstream undertaking) to contract with.

[137] Although the ECJ holding in *Hoffmann-La Roche* (n 20) [91] that 'abuse' is an 'objective' concept could oppose such an interpretation, the Court's holding in *United Brands* (n 48) that the dominant undertaking's counter-attack must be proportionate to the threat taking into account the economic strength of the other undertaking, would accommodate such an interpretation.

ensure that in relation to any one product sector no one producer can obtain a near-monopoly position.[138] Nevertheless, the law must also address particular types of *behaviour* which subvert the operation of a competitive market. Thus, the law of duress and undue influence arguably serves to identify those types of behaviour, drawing a boundary for unacceptable anticompetitive practices.[139] It is supplemented by competition law which also provides the possibility of injunctions against anticompetitive behaviour. Thus, Collins asserts that when economic resources are deployed to prevent equal competition, this anticompetitive practice will be prohibited and competition law provides an active remedy which permits the prevention of such practices.[140] At the same time, the private law of duress and undue influence serves to invalidate contracts which have been entered into under such conditions of 'unfair' competition.[141] Bringing contract and competition together, Collins seems to be arguing that the abuse of a dominant position would also be a case of duress or undue influence such that competition law is the *ex ante* measure prohibiting abuse, and the doctrine of duress and undue influence invalidating the contracts entered into ex post. Although this does not fit very well with the structure of Article 102 since 'abuse' can only occur after a certain conduct is carried out requiring the assessment to be made ex post, the essence of the argument deserves elaboration.[142]

a Duress and Economic Duress

In terms of establishing the relationship between the prohibition of 'duress' in contract law and 'abuse' under Article 102, first, it must be noted that the similarity mostly exists with 'economic duress' as opposed to 'duress to goods' or 'duress to person'.[143] Under the doctrine of 'economic duress' where the contract was made as the result of a threatened wrong (such as a breach of contract) and the party seeking relief gave in because she would suffer serious losses if the threat was carried out, and she had no alternative, the contract may be avoided.[144] In other words, it concerns situations in which one party uses her superior economic power in an illegitimate manner in order to compel the other party to enter into a contract or to agree to particular terms in the contract.[145] With economic duress, similar to abuse of a dominant position, the aim of the courts is to distinguish between agreements which are the result of 'mere commercial pressure' and those which are the consequence of unfair exploitation.[146]

[138] Collins (n 86) 155.
[139] ibid.
[140] ibid 156.
[141] ibid.
[142] *cf* L Lovdahl Gormsen, 'Article 82 EC: Where Are We Coming From and Where Are We Going To?' (2005) 2(2) *The Competition Law Review* 5, 25, fn 109 arguing that Art 102 is ex ante and ex post.
[143] This categorisation is based on UK contract law.
[144] PECL Parts I–II (n 64) 260.
[145] McKendrick (n 135) 628.
[146] E Peel, *Treitel on the Law of Contract* 12th edn (London, Sweet & Maxwell, 2007) 444.

Secondly, it must be accepted that dominance itself cannot be deemed 'duress'. In the words of Steyn LJ, '[t]he fact that the defendants were in a monopoly position cannot . . . by itself convert what is not otherwise duress into duress'.[147] For both duress and economic duress, there is a need for the consent of one of the parties to be vitiated or flawed as a result of the pressure from the other party: '[d]uress, whatever form it takes, is a coercion of the will so as to vitiate consent'.[148] Therefore, if dominance itself were accepted to form that pressure and vitiate consent, then all the contracts of a dominant undertaking could be voidable, which is not an acceptable position. It is not what Article 102 suggests either since that provision prohibits only the 'abuse' of a dominant position and not the dominant position itself.

If duress is perceived as the 'abuse' of power against the other party, then Article 102 could in essence resemble a prohibition of economic duress. It is questionable whether in instances of abuse of dominance, the consent of the other party is such vitiated or flawed as to make it an involuntary act.[149] Yet, it should be noted that at least in English law, the focus of judicial attention shifted away from the thought process of the victim (ie, coercion of the will) to the *nature* of the pressure applied by the other party.[150] The decision making process of the victim remains important for establishing the causal link between the pressure and the decision to enter into the contract.[151] Therefore, the question is whether the agreement would have been made at all or on the terms it was made but for the illegitimate pressure.[152] Therefore, in cases where 'abuse' under Article 102 involves illegitimate pressure whose practical effect is compulsion on or lack of a practical choice for the victim and this pressure is a significant cause inducing the victim to enter into the contract,[153] then it becomes clear that the concepts of 'abuse' and 'economic duress' are very similar. The element of lack of a practical choice in case of a dominant undertaking may be straightforward to establish, by nature of the existence of the dominant position. Similarly, given that abusive practices are prohibited by Article 102 (and their national equivalents), the threat to commit an act that would breach Article 102 can also be deemed to satisfy the illegitimacy condition. This is because a threat to commit an unlawful act, such as a tort or a crime, is

[147] *CTN Cash and Carry* (n 134) 716. Steyn LJ continues: '[t]he aim of our commercial law ought to be to encourage fair dealing between parties. But it is a mistake for the law to set its sights too highly when the critical inquiry is not whether the conduct is lawful but whether it is morally or socially unacceptable'; ibid 718.

[148] Lord Scarman in *Pao On v Lau Yiu Long* [1980] AC 614, 634. Lord Scarman's 'coercion of the will' theory has been subject to the criticism that duress does not 'vitiate' consent as the party entering *chooses* to enter into the contract to avoid the greater evil presented by the threat; McKendrick (n 135) 640.

[149] For the argument that, in the case of a monopoly, consent is a result of market failure, see MW Hesselink, 'Non-Mandatory Rules in European Contract Law' (2005) 1(1) *European Review of Contract Law* 43, 44, 46.

[150] McKendrick (n 135) 636.

[151] ibid.

[152] *Huyton SA v Peter Cremer GmbH* [1999] CLC 230, 250.

[153] For these elements of economic duress, see *DSND Subsea Ltd v Petroleum Geo-Services ASA* [2000] BLR 530, 545.

'illegitimate'.[154] Having said that, given that the list of practices in Article 102 is not exhaustive, there may be a counter-argument that ex ante and particularly for practices that have not been found abusive before, the mere threat to commit an act that is abusive under Article 102 does not automatically satisfy the illegitimacy condition. Yet, it should further be noted that the illegitimacy of a demand does not require the threat to commit an unlawful act to constitute economic duress. Economic duress can also exist where the threat is to do something lawful.[155] Thus, for example, even the threat not to contract if the threatener's terms are not accepted where the threatener is a monopoly, may be strongly coercive.[156] Therefore, the ultimate question of whether an abusive conduct is also an example of economic duress may turn on the question of causation if the lack of a practical choice and illegitimate pressure are accepted to exist in cases of 'abuse' of a dominant position.

Interestingly, in *Microsoft*, while finding the tying of the Windows operating system with Windows Media Player by Microsoft abusive, the GC identified the condition in Article 102(d) (ie, that the conclusion of contracts be made subject to acceptance by the other parties of supplementary obligations which by their nature or according to commercial usage have no connection with the subject of such contracts) as 'coercion'.[157] Thus, the inability of consumers and original equipment manufacturers to acquire the Windows operating system without simultaneously acquiring Windows Media Player was deemed as 'coercion' by the GC.[158] This is all the more interesting since the 'coerced' product was supplied without charge to consumers and consumers were free not to use Windows Media Player as they were not prevented from using substitute products.[159] Thus, there is support in the EU competition law case law that 'abuse' may indeed be very similar to 'economic duress' in contract law.

b Undue Influence

The prohibition in Article 102 can also be likened to the equitable doctrine of 'undue influence' in English law if one equates 'abuse' with 'taking advantage' of the other party. For 'undue influence' to arise, looking at the relationship between the parties is not enough. It must be proven that the transaction itself was wrongful in that it constituted an advantage taken of the person subject to influence

[154] *Universe Tankships of Monrovia v International Transport Workers Federation (The Universe Sentinel)* [1983] 1 AC 366, 401; McKendrick (n 135) 659.

[155] On duress in cases of threats of action not in themselves wrongful, see *Chitty on Contracts: General Principles* Vol 1, 30th edn (London, Sweet & Maxwell, 2008) 616 *et seq.*

[156] *Chitty on Contracts* (n 155) 617–18. This would be an exception to the general rule that refusal to contract does not normally constitute illegitimate pressure, at least in the absence of bad faith on the part of the party refusing to enter into the contract; see McKendrick (n 135) 660. For the general rule that there is no duty to contract *even in the case of a monopoly position*, see *CTN Cash and Carry* (n 134) 714.

[157] Case T-201/04 *Microsoft Corp v Commission* [2007] ECR II-3601, [961] *et seq.*

[158] ibid [961]–[62].

[159] ibid [969]–[70].

which is explicable only on the basis that undue influence was exercised to procure it.[160] Since the ECJ interprets dominance as 'a position of economic strength' which affords the undertaking the 'power to behave to an appreciable extent independently of its competitors, its customers and ultimately of the consumers',[161] one can think of 'abuse' as 'taking advantage' of such a position. This would again be very similar to the above-mentioned definition of 'exploitation' provided in chapter two.[162] Of the two types of undue influence – namely 'actual' and 'presumed' – abuse of a dominant position is more similar to actual undue influence since presumed undue influence requires the existence of a relationship of trust and confidence between the two parties to the contract.[163] This condition is likely not to be satisfied in cases of abuse of a dominant position. For actual undue influence, one party must induce the other party to enter into a transaction by actual pressure, which need not amount to duress.[164] Although common law now recognises economic duress, the concept of 'pressure' is still wider than that of 'duress' since undue influence can be exercised without illegitimate threats or any threats at all.[165] The party claiming actual undue influence has to show that such influence existed and was exercised, and that the transaction resulted from the influence.[166] Thus, the concept of 'abuse', if interpreted as the dominant undertaking using its 'influence' on the other party to acquire advantages for itself, can be deemed similar to the doctrine of actual undue influence.

To summarise, although not identical, there appear to be concepts in areas of law other than competition (such as 'inequality of bargaining power', 'economic duress' and 'undue influence') which may be of help in understanding Article 102 and especially the 'fairness' aspect of it. In common, they all point at one party using its stronger position vis-à-vis the other party to obtain terms that it could not have obtained without that disparity in power. Yet, all of these doctrines have brought with them into contract law difficulties that are not easily avoidable. These problems relate to assessing the relative powers of the parties; determining how this power affects the relation; deciding whether some terms in favour of the weaker party would balance the 'unfairness' of terms in favour of the stronger; establishing whether the mere inequality of power would render the contract 'unfair' and if not, what additional factor is required; determining how the tension with freedom of contract and legal certainty is to be resolved and so on. For competition law purposes, the 'fairness' idea behind Article 102 seems to resemble the doctrines of 'inequality of bargaining power', 'undue influence' and perhaps mostly 'economic duress', and thus raises similar questions which appear to result mainly from the vagueness of notions of 'fairness' and the lack of an objective test.

[160] Lord Scarman in *National Westminster Bank* (n 134) 704.
[161] *Hoffmann-La Roche* (n 20) [38].
[162] See ch 2 this volume, section V. F.
[163] For the two types of undue influence, see Peel (n 146) 447 *et seq.*
[164] ibid 447. The doctrine was established in equity when common law did not recognise any threats as duress beyond threats to the person; ibid.
[165] ibid.
[166] ibid.

All in all, if the similarity of 'fairness' in different areas of law with 'fairness' in Article 102 is accepted, then it becomes clear that it is not necessarily the competitors of the dominant undertaking that are to be protected due to their weakness when considering 'fairness' under Article 102. The subjects to be protected would be mainly those who deal with the dominant undertaking, namely its customers/suppliers. As such, one can argue that the 'fairness' concept in Article 102 is not the same as the 'fairness' concept in 'unfair competition law' or ordoliberalism, namely 'fairness' towards one's rivals. This interpretation would also be in conformity with the intent of the drafters of this provision, which demonstrates that it was envisaged to cover 'exploitative' abuses, but was not seen as an 'unfair competition law' provision.[167] It would also be in line with the definition of abuse provided in chapter two, which focuses on the dominant undertaking receiving advantages to the disadvantage of its trading partners that are only possible due to its dominant position. Some of the problems that exist in contract law may be alleviated for Article 102 due to the existence of a counterfactual in the case of the latter (ie, the *but for* situation) and due to one of the arguments of this study, namely that there should be harm to competition on top of exploitation before 'abuse' can be established. As a further inquiry into the regulation of the transactions between a stronger and a weaker party on 'fairness' grounds, the following subsection investigates EU consumer law and the concept of 'fairness' therein.

D EU Consumer Law

With the economic and social developments after the Second World War, mass consumption and mass production extended quickly, leading to a wide range of products and services.[168] Although the fulfilment of consumer needs improved considerably, consumers also found themselves in a position where their knowledge of and experience with goods and services could not keep up with the rapid speed of innovation.[169] The economic position of consumers was unequal in power as compared with the position of industrial producers who had substantial collective power and resources, and the former were not able to negotiate the terms of contracts or exercise their freedom of choice.[170] Market failures could not be corrected by the classical contract law instruments and the *caveat emptor* doctrine was criticised for reasons of 'fairness'; contractual relations had to be reshaped in order to improve the consumer's weak position.[171] As a result, consumer law developed.

[167] See ch 2 this volume, text around n 244. *Cf Continental Can* (n 3) [26] which held that the provision applies to exclusionary *as well as* exploitative practices.

[168] KJ Cseres, *Competition Law and Consumer Protection* (The Hague, Kluwer Law International, 2005) 152.

[169] ibid.

[170] ibid 153.

[171] ibid 153–55.

In fact, the main bulk of the European contract law *acquis* is related to consumer protection.[172] In the EU, consumer contracts are designated as an area separate from business contracts and the presumption appears to be that consumers have little or no choice regarding contract terms because of unequal bargaining power.[173] Thus, one of the aims of the EU has been to protect consumers against rogue traders, and 'fairness' finds it place in the instruments regulating this. Since 2004, EU consumer *acquis* has been undergoing a review with the aim of simplifying and completing the existing regulatory framework, in order to achieve a real business-to-consumer internal market.[174] The reason for the review has been expressed as the fragmented regulatory framework across the Union (which has resulted from the minimum-harmonisation clauses of the current Directives) leading to significant compliance costs for businesses wishing to trade cross-border, which in turn leads to reduced consumer welfare.[175] Eight of the Directives have gone under review and four of them were to be merged under a 'Directive on Consumer Rights'.[176] Although the Directive was drafted as one of maximum harmonisation, due to opposition from the Member States with higher levels of protection than that envisaged in the draft Directive (including the UK), the Commission seems to have given up on maximum harmonisation. As of the end of June 2011, following a deal between the three EU institutions (Commission, European Parliament and the Council of Ministers), the Directive has been adopted by the European Parliament.[177] Once the text is formally approved by the Council of Ministers, the transposition of the new rules into national laws is expected to take place before the end of 2013. The agreed text of the Directive adopts a minimum harmonisation approach and according to this text, some of

[172] Wilhelmsson (n 63) 726.

[173] Petty and Hamilton (n 76) 161–62. For the argument that EU consumer law is not about inequality of bargaining power between the business and consumer, but about information problems and asymmetries the consumers face, see S Grundmann, 'EC Consumer and EC Competition Law: How Related Are They? Examining the Existing EC Contract Law Sources' in H Collins (ed), *The Forthcoming EC Directive on Unfair Commercial Practices* (The Hague, Kluwer Law International, 2004) 211–12.

[174] Commission, 'Proposal for a Directive of the European Parliament and of the Council on Consumer Rights' COM (2008) 614 final (Brussels, 8 October 2008) 2.

[175] ibid.

[176] The Directives to be merged were: Council Directive 1999/44/EC on certain aspects of the sale of consumer goods and associated guarantees [1999] OJ L171/12; Council Directive 93/13/EEC on Unfair Terms in Consumer Contracts [1993] OJ L95/29; Directive 97/7/EC on the protection of consumers in respect of distance contracts [1997] OJ L144/19; Directive 85/577/EEC to protect the consumer in respect of contracts negotiated away from business premises [1985] OJ L372/31. The other four Directives under review were: Directive 1998/6/EC on consumer protection in the indication of the prices of products offered to consumers [1998] OJ L80/27; Directive 98/27/EC on injunctions for the protection of consumers' interests [1998] OJ L166/ 51; Directive 90/314/EEC on package travel, package holidays and package tours [1990] OJ L158/59; Directive 94/47/EC on the protection of purchasers in respect of certain aspects of contracts relating to the purchase of the right to use immovable properties on a timeshare basis [1994] OJ L280/ 83.

[177] See Press Release, 'Consumer Rights: 10 ways the new EU Consumer Rights Directive will give people stronger rights when they shop online' MEMO/11/450 (23 June 2011).

the Directives that were initially to be merged under this Directive are only amended, whereas some others have been repealed by the new Directive.[178]

i Unfair Contract Terms

Although it was among the crucial instruments that were subject to review, the EU Directive on Unfair Contract Terms remains unchanged except for a minor amendment by the Consumer Rights Directive.[179] The former Directive was adopted to ensure that contracts concluded with consumers do not contain 'unfair' terms as it was deemed necessary 'to fix in a general way the criteria for assessing the unfair character of contract terms'.[180] As one reason for adopting the Directive is stated as the possibility of distortions of competition due to the divergence of national laws on contract terms, this is another example of contract law and specifically 'fairness' intersecting with competition law.

According to the EU Directive on Unfair Contract Terms, 'a contractual term which has not been individually negotiated shall be regarded as unfair if, contrary to the requirement of good faith, it causes a significant imbalance in the parties' rights and obligations arising under the contract, to the detriment of the consumer'.[181] The 'unfairness' of a term shall be assessed, taking into account the nature of the goods or services and by referring to all the circumstances attending the conclusion of the contract and to all the other terms of the contract or of another contract on which it is dependent.[182] However, the assessment of the 'fairness' of terms shall relate neither to the definition of the main subject matter of the contract nor to the adequacy of the price and remuneration, on the one hand, as against the services or goods supplied in exchange, on the other, in so far as these terms are in plain intelligible language.[183] The sanction of an 'unfair' term is that such a term does not bind the consumer and the contract continues to bind both parties if it is capable of existing without the 'unfair' term.[184]

[178] The text of the Directive as adopted by the European Parliament can be found at europarl.europa.eu/sides/getDoc.do?type=TA&reference=P7-TA-2011-0293&language=EN&ring=A7-2011-0038. Directives 93/13/EEC and 1999/44/EC (n 176) are being amended to require Member States to inform the Commission about the adoption of specific national provisions in certain areas, and Directives 85/577/EEC and 97/7/EC (n 176) are being repealed.

[179] For the amendment, see above (n 178).

[180] EU Directive on Unfair Contract Terms (n 176) Preamble.

[181] ibid Art 3(1). Moreover, 'a term shall always be regarded as not individually negotiated where it has been drafted in advance and the consumer has therefore not been able to influence the substance of the term, particularly in the context of a pre-formulated standard contract. The fact that certain aspects of a term or one specific term have been individually negotiated shall not exclude the application of this Article to the rest of a contract if an overall assessment of the contract indicates that it is nevertheless a pre-formulated standard contract. Where any seller or supplier claims that a standard term has been individually negotiated, the burden of proof in this respect shall be incumbent on him'; Art 3(2).

[182] ibid Art 4(1).

[183] ibid Art 4(2).

[184] ibid Art 6(1). This prohibition was kept in almost exactly the same way in Chapter V of the draft Consumer Rights Directive, but does not exist at all in the text adopted by the European Parliament.

Consequently, for the 'fairness' test of the EU Directive on Unfair Contract Terms, the term must not have been individually negotiated, it must be contrary to the requirement of good faith and it must cause a significant imbalance in the parties' rights and obligations arising under the contract to the detriment of the consumer.[185] According to the Preamble of the Directive, in making an assessment of good faith, particular regard shall be had to the strength of the bargaining positions of the parties, whether the consumer had an inducement to agree to the term and whether the goods or services were sold or supplied to the special order of the consumer. Furthermore, the requirement of good faith may be satisfied by the seller or supplier where he deals fairly and equitably with the other party whose legitimate interests he has to take into account.[186]

The regulatory intentions of the EU Directive on Unfair Contract Terms have been criticised as being unclear.[187] Arguably, its priority could be to pave the way for standardised 'fair' consumer contracting in the internal market (as the 'market school' holds) or it could be to protect consumers' rights against various abuses of power by stronger contractors (as the 'welfarist school' holds).[188] It has been noted that 'a clause should be considered fair if it does not cause unfair surprise and if it represents a balance of risk against price that is acceptable to the margin of aware consumers'.[189] On the other hand, it has been noted that '[t]he Directive does not require consumer contracts to be substantively fair, but it does require them to be clear'.[190] Accordingly, '[w]hat matters primarily for [EU] contract law is consumer choice, not consumer rights'.[191]

[185] For an argument that the requirement of good faith in the Directive should not be read as an independent condition of fairness and that the test of unfairness should simply be whether the term in question causes a significant imbalance to the detriment of the consumer, see R Brownsword, G Howells and T Wilhelmsson, 'Between Market and Welfare: Some Reflections on Article 3 of the EC Directive on Unfair Terms in Consumer Contracts' in C Willett (ed), *Aspects of Fairness in Contract* (London, Blackstone Press, 1996) 28.

[186] eg, Lord Bingham has remarked that the requirement of good faith is one of fair and open dealing and fair dealing requires that a supplier should not, whether deliberately or unconsciously, take advantage of the consumer's necessity, indigence, lack of experience, unfamiliarity with the subject matter of the contract, weak bargaining position or any other factor listed in or analogous to those listed in Schedule 2 of the Regulations implementing the EU Directive on Unfair Contract Terms (n 176); *Director General of Fair Trading v First National Bank Plc* [2002] 1 AC 481, 494. However, it is questionable how a supplier can take advantage of the consumer 'unconsciously' since taking advantage should necessarily require consciousness as otherwise it can be negligence at the most. More controversially, if it is unfair even without deliberate advantage taking, then this would mean that the mere making of the contract would be contrary to good faith on its own when one party is in a weaker position.

[187] Brownsword, Howells and Wilhelmsson (n 185) 56.

[188] ibid. In this interpretation, the 'market school' would see the Directive as a vehicle for promoting fair standard forms in the European place whereas the 'welfarist school' would be more concerned that the Directive should protect weaker contracting parties, that are the consumers, ibid 27.

[189] H Beale, 'Unfair Contracts in Britain and Europe' (1989) 44 *Current Legal Problems* 197, 212. According to Lord Millett '[t]here can be no single test of unfairness; it is obviously useful to assess the impact of an impugned term on the parties' rights and obligations by comparing the effect of the contract with the term and the effect it would have without it', *First National Bank Plc* (n 186) 505.

[190] H Collins, 'Good Faith in European Contract Law' (1994) 14 *Oxford Journal of Legal Studies* 229, 238. He interprets 'substantive fairness' in this sense as that of the price, ibid.

[191] ibid 238.

What must be emphasised for the purposes of this study is that EU consumer law (and most Member States' national consumer protection legislation whose main objective is the protection of consumers) does *not* assess the 'fairness' or 'adequacy' of the price imposed on the consumer.[192] Traditionally, based on the ideology of the four freedoms, EU law has strongly emphasised the 'freedom of choice' of the European citizens and this emphasis has been reflected in the fairly market-rational starting points of EU consumer law.[193] The rational consumer is the dominant consumer image of EU consumer law.[194] As such, EU contract law is not interested in internally redistributive justice, that is, for example, in the general price/quality ratio of contracts, nor in externally redistributive justice, that is in promoting access and non-discrimination of economically less advantaged persons.[195]

Indeed, one could claim that EU contract law shows a relatively negative attitude towards attempts to achieve internally (between the consumer and business) redistributive welfarism through contractual regulation.[196] This is based on the thought that the relationship between the price and the performance of the contract has to be determined by the market mechanism and not through regulation.[197] As such, the EU Directive on Unfair Contract Terms explicitly excludes from its scope attempts to achieve internally redistributive goals.[198] It has actually been asserted that, the function of the EU is to promote a free market, not to ensure that this market is corrected in the light of distributive aims.[199] Accordingly, it has been suggested that the EU lacks a clear general mandate to pursue a scheme of 'fairness' or distributive justice in its regulation of trade.[200] This approach of EU consumer law is clearly in stark contrast with prohibiting 'unfair pricing' under Article 102(a), a topic which will be dealt with separately in chapter five.

ii *Unfair Commercial Practices*

Another EU instrument implementing a test of 'fairness' is the Unfair Commercial Practices Directive[201] concerning 'unfair business-to-consumer commercial practices' in the internal market. This Directive has been seen as 'one of the most

[192] The exceptions to the rule of not assessing the fairness of the main subject matter and the price are Austria, Denmark, Finland, Greece, Latvia, Luxembourg, Poland, Slovenia, Spain and Sweden. These countries have not transposed Art 4(2) of the EU Directive on Unfair Contract Terms and the unfairness control in these countries therefore also applies to the main subject and the price.

[193] Wilhelmsson (n 63) 726.

[194] ibid 727.

[195] ibid 732.

[196] ibid 728.

[197] ibid 728–29. See also *The Office of Fair Trading v Abbey National plc & Others* [2009] UKSC 6, [79], [80].

[198] Wilhelmsson (n 63) 729.

[199] Study Group on Social Justice in European Private Law, 'Social Justice in European Contract Law: A Manifesto' (2004) 10(6) *European Law Journal* 653, 660–61.

[200] ibid 661.

[201] Council Directive 2005/29/EC on Unfair Commercial Practices [2005] OJ L149/22.

significant pieces of legislation to emanate from Brussels in recent times'.[202] The Directive harmonises the laws of the Member States on 'unfair commercial practices' which directly harm consumers' economic interests and thereby indirectly harm the economic interests of legitimate competitors.[203] It adopts a maximum harmonisation approach (except for financial services and immovable property) and therefore Member States are not allowed to go above the protection provided in the Directive. As with the EU Directive on Unfair Contract Terms, this Directive refers to the appreciable distortions of competition and obstacles to the smooth operating of the internal market as a reason for its adoption.[204] Again, an important point for the purposes of this study is that by directly protecting consumers' economic interests from 'unfair business-to-consumer commercial practices', the Directive thereby 'indirectly protects legitimate businesses from their competitors who do not play by the rules in this Directive, and thus guarantees fair competition in fields coordinated by it'.[205]

The Unfair Commercial Practices Directive seeks to introduce a European conception of 'fairness' by introducing a general clause to cover all economic harm caused to consumers by 'unfair' practices.[206] This seems to confirm what can be derived from existing EU law where the formula appears in different forms, mostly as 'fair trading'.[207] Indeed, the term 'fair trading' can be found in various shapes and forms in the relevant secondary law, regulations and directives; the term is mentioned more than thirty times without the Community legislator providing a definition of 'fair trading' or 'fair commercial practices'.[208] No attempt appears to have been made by either the Advocates General or the ECJ to give shape to the term 'fair trading' and define its content.[209]

Article 5 of the Unfair Commercial Practices Directive prohibits 'unfair commercial practices' and defines an 'unfair' clause as one that (a) is contrary to the requirements of professional diligence, and (b) materially distorts or is likely to materially distort the economic behaviour[210] with regard to the product of the average consumer whom it reaches or to whom it is addressed, or of the average member of the group when a commercial practice is directed to a particular group

[202] G Howells, H Micklitz and T Wilhelmsson, *European Fair Trading Law: The Unfair Commercial Practices Directive* (Hamsphire, Ashgate, 2006) xiii. For the argument that the Directive brings more problems than it solves, see de Vrey (n 31) 76.

[203] Unfair Commercial Practices Directive (n 201) Recital 6. This raises the questions of who are 'legitimate' competitors and of who are 'illegitimate' ones.

[204] ibid Recital 3.

[205] ibid Recital 8.

[206] Howells, Micklitz and Wilhelmsson (n 202) xiii.

[207] ibid 83.

[208] ibid.

[209] ibid 84.

[210] 'To materially distort the economic behaviour of consumers' for the purposes of the Directive is defined as 'using a commercial practice to appreciably impair the consumer's ability to make an informed decision, thereby causing the consumer to take a transactional decision that he would not have taken otherwise'; Unfair Commercial Practices Directive (n 201) Article 2(e).

of consumers.[211] 'Professional diligence' for the purposes of the Directive is defined as 'the standard of special skill and care which a trader may reasonably be expected to exercise towards consumers, commensurate with honest market practice and/or the general principle of good faith in the trader's field of activity'.[212] It is thus defined by other concepts which also require defining such as 'standard of special skill and care', 'honest market practice', 'general principle of good faith', 'reasonable expectation' and so on. However, the Directive is silent on the meaning of these phrases.

Thus, there is a twofold test to be satisfied under the Unfair Commercial Practices Directive: to be deemed 'unfair', the conduct must be contrary to professional diligence and it must materially distort or be likely to materially distort the economic behaviour of the average consumer. This is not a very concrete test since it depends on what professional diligence would require under the circumstances. Inevitably, this requires the court to decide what can be 'reasonably' expected from the trader and it would especially be difficult in industries where there is no such thing as 'honest market practice' or a 'general principle of good faith'.

Indeed it has been argued that due to the deficient configuration of the concept of 'professional diligence' and the lack of Europeanised 'professional diligence', a European concept of 'fairness' has to rely on the second pillar of the test; the 'material distortion of the economic behaviour of the consumer' functions de facto and de jure as the decisive yardstick by which to assess 'unfair commercial practices'.[213] Moreover, since distortion has to be 'material', there seems to be a threshold which must be met in order to label a commercial practice 'unfair'.[214] However, a *potential* effect on the consumer's behaviour appears to suffice; the Directive does not establish a causal link between the commercial action and the consumer's behaviour.[215]

An important question is whether by introducing 'honest market practices' and 'good faith' in the definition of 'professional diligence', the Unfair Commercial Practices Directive in effect transposes extralegal or moral concepts from national laws of Member States to the EU level. One argument is that by providing the alternative basis of good faith or honest practices, the Directive makes clear that the actual business conduct may be corrected by extralegal criteria and this brings the general clause in line with national laws of those Member States which use terms like 'honest practices', 'good faith', '*bonos mores*' and so on.[216] On the other hand, it has been suggested that the true challenge of the Directive is to put the term 'fairness' into concrete form within a European context and that this requires the

[211] This being the general test, Unfair Commercial Practices Directive (n 201) Article 5(4) particularly prohibits unfair commercial practices which are misleading or aggressive as set out in Articles 6 and 7, and Articles 8 and 9 respectively.

[212] ibid Art 2(h).

[213] Howells, Micklitz and Wilhelmsson (n 202) 102.

[214] ibid.

[215] ibid.

[216] Henning-Bodewig (n 36) 60.

establishment of an autonomous concept of 'fairness'.[217] Only such an autonomous understanding would comply with the well-settled approach of the ECJ of not relying on how a legal term or concept is defined in a particular national legal system.[218] Although the Directive should not and cannot 'reinvent the wheel' and therefore the national concepts of 'fairness' still matter, the point is that national systems have been using different methods for controlling 'unfair commercial practices' – some are more market-based (such as 'market freedoms'), while others are more value-based (such as *bonos mores*).[219] The Directive does not provide much guidance in determining whether its notion of 'fairness' is morally bound or not.[220] However, every statement offered by the Commission shows that it intended to regulate 'unfair commercial practices' to break down barriers to intra-Union trade, and thus ethical and moral terms in a European concept of 'fairness' would jeopardise the achievement of this since they introduce non-market-related moral issues into the European law on 'unfair commercial practices'.[221] Therefore, the term 'fairness' as applied in the Directive should not be given a moral dimension which reaches beyond the market; 'fairness' is arguably a reflection of the concept of 'workable competition' and can be taken to mean 'universal economic clarity, unambiguousness and transparency in the sense of functioning competition'.[222]

It is surely appropriate to have a European notion of 'fairness' given that the Directive seeks to achieve maximum harmonisation and introduces a general clause on 'fair dealing' at the European level. It is also correct that the value-based understandings of 'fairness' stemming from national laws would impede harmonisation. However, the crucial question is what we mean by 'market-based fairness'. It is questionable whether the values that govern the market can be separated from non-market-related values. Since each concept controlling commercial practices starts from a particular moral premise,[223] it may be impossible to draw a line between market-based and non-market-based values. The result would be judging commercial practices through a moral lens, which would not only potentially distort incentives of undertakings to undertake commercial practices in the first place, but would also render the law uncertain.[224] This is the danger inherent in having a 'fairness' concept irrespective of the perspective from which it is interpreted. As seen from the doctrines studied above, 'unfair' can easily be understood as 'wrong'

[217] Howells, Micklitz and Wilhelmsson (n 202) 86.

[218] ibid. For the argument that the general clause prohibiting unfair commercial practices leaves considerable scope for traders to insist that their practices avoid dishonesty and are common in their line of business, see H Collins, 'Harmonisation by Example: European Laws against Unfair Commercial Practices' (2010) 73(1) *Modern Law Review* 89, 99.

[219] Howells, Micklitz and Wilhelmsson, ibid, 87.

[220] ibid.

[221] ibid 89–90.

[222] ibid 92–93. Collins argues that the 'mini general clauses' that prohibit misleading and aggressive practices eschew legal terminology such as good faith, good morals, honesty, etc and thus when judges and officials interpret them, the meaning of these provisions will not be weighed down or guided by national legal traditions; Collins (n 218) 117.

[223] Howells, Micklitz and Wilhelmsson (n 202) 87.

[224] See, eg, Steyn LJ's statement that introducing lawful act of duress in case of a refusal to contract would render the law too uncertain; *CTN Cash and Carry* (n 134) 719.

and deciding what is 'wrong' will almost always involve subjective value judgements. How much and to what extent commercial practices should be regulated according to their 'fairness' remains the ultimate question and is directly relevant for the purposes of interpreting the 'fairness' notion in Article 102. As such, how the ECJ interprets the 'fairness' of commercial practices under the Directive will determine the European concept of 'fairness' and will also provide guidance for Article 102. At the moment, this guidance does not exist.

To summarise, 'fairness' is directly regulated in EU consumer law which forms most of EU contract law. Importantly, even though the main purpose of this area of law is the protection of the consumer as the weaker party to the transaction, EU consumer law does not interfere with or assess the price in a contract on grounds of 'fairness', in strong contrast with Article 102(a). Nonetheless, since the regulation of 'fairness' of consumer transactions is directly relevant for the transactions a dominant undertaking enters into with consumers, how 'fairness' is interpreted in this area of law by EU authorities can – especially after the Unfair Commercial Practices Directive has brought a general duty not to trade unfairly – ultimately affect the interpretation of 'fairness' as part of the 'abuse' test under Article 102 as well. So far, the main commonality between these approaches appears to be the concern with the protection of the weaker party vis-à-vis the stronger party.

V CONCLUSION

Article 102 prohibits various 'unfair' practices as abuses of a dominant position. Neither the provision nor the EU jurisprudence defines what exactly is meant by 'unfair' under this prohibition. The difficulty in defining and operationalising 'fairness' or 'unfairness' does not appear to be peculiar to EU competition law and, even when a definition is provided, as has been done in some other areas of law, a significant element of inherent vagueness and arbitrariness is obvious.

There would appear to be two ways to interpret what 'fairness' means under Article 102. First, one can equate 'unfair' with 'anticompetitive', and thus (un)fairness would not mean anything other or more than '(anti)competitive'. In this case, the question would be merely that of defining 'anticompetitive', and one way of doing this might be to perceive unfairness as 'exploitation'. Alternatively, 'fairness' under Article 102 can refer to ensuring 'fair' competition and thus would imply a stand-alone policy objective to be pursued under the provision. In this case, the assessment of conduct would be done separately in terms of its 'anticompetitiveness' and its 'fairness'. It is the application of the provision under this second interpretation of 'fairness' that can be prone to criticism, for example, for protecting competitors rather than competition since seeking to achieve 'fair' competition can turn competition law into 'unfair competition law'. This latter interpretation – which appears to have been occasionally adopted by the EU authorities – can be perceived as the battle between 'fair' competition and 'free' competition.

'Fair' competition and 'free' competition are, however, different visions of what competition is and should be about. They are based on different assumptions. Moreover, they correspond to different perceptions that institutions have about the market and the role of law.[225] In promoting 'fair' competition, the law is supposed to bring order to a world which would otherwise fall into chaos, whereas in promoting 'free' competition order and rationality are already supposed to exist and the authorities are to limit their interventions to specific circumstances where markets do not provide a satisfactory solution by themselves.[226] This latter perspective considers consumers and businesses to be able to defend their interests by themselves, whereas the former assumes that undertakings and consumers would probably not behave rationally absent public intervention.[227] There may be a tension between 'fair' and 'free' competition as succinctly put by Judge Easterbrook of the US Court of Appeals:

> [m]y brethren want rivalry to be "fair" . . . Who says that competition is supposed to be fair, that we judge the behavior of the marketplace by the ethics of the courtroom? . . . When economic pressure must give way to fair conduct, . . . rivals will trim their sails. Fair competition is tempered competition.[228]

This tension is crucial in the EU since 'unfair' practices in competition are prohibited under Article 102, but the EU concurrently aimed to become 'the most dynamic and competitive' economy in the world by 2010.[229] Similarly, under 'Europe 2020' – namely the Union's strategy for the new decade – the objective is to turn the EU into a smart, sustainable and inclusive economy delivering high levels of employment, *productivity* and social cohesion.[230] In this strategy, competition policy plays the role of ensuring that markets provide the right environment for innovation.[231] Promoting innovation as much as possible, however, might not always coincide with promoting 'fairness', if this is to mean anything more than keeping the markets open (ie, anything other than 'free competition'). Consequently, interpreting 'fairness' under Article 102 as a stand-alone objective pursued by that provision, can result in a clash of policy goals.

Moreover, as the various 'fairness' notions studied above demonstrate, the issue of 'fairness' as an objective, especially 'substantive fairness', is one that is not fully resolved despite being queried for decades, for example, in contract law. This is mainly because the examination of bargains for their 'fairness' poses a threat to freedom of contract and the concept is too vague by itself to depend on for reaching consistent, objective and clear legal judgments. This shows that acceptance of

[225] P Nihoul, 'From Unfair Trading to Free Competition – Towards a New Organisation of Markets in the European Union' (2006) 17(1) *European Business Law Review* 23, 23.

[226] ibid.

[227] ibid 23, 28.

[228] *Fishman v Estate of Wirtz* 807 F2d 520, 577 (7th Cir 1986) (Easterbrook concurring in part and dissenting in part).

[229] European Summit (Lisbon, 2005).

[230] Commission, 'Europe 2020: A strategy for smart, sustainable and inclusive growth' COM (2010) 2020 (3 March 2010) 3.

[231] ibid 19.

'fairness' as a stand-alone objective in competition law would also bring along similar difficulties. It also points out another potential policy clash, since according to the Commission 'freedom of contract' should be the guiding principle of European contract law and 'restrictions on this freedom should only be envisaged where this could be justified for good reasons'.[232] The ultimate question would then be how much freedom of contract can be restricted to achieve 'fairness' by the competition rules.

With regard to Article 102, it must also be remembered that the subject is more often than not business-to-business transactions. Since, in the context of Article 102, undertakings would not be able to contract out of this provision, even if both parties wanted to, any artificial division of gains resulting from an ex post 'fairness' assessment under the provision would be permanent. This would first and foremost change the incentives to enter contracts *ex ante*. In addition, with regard to Article 102, there seems to be no examination of the properties of the exchange. The contract is not scrutinised as a whole regarding its 'fairness' and a finding of, for example, an 'unfair price' term suffices to declare an abuse of dominance. Nevertheless, there may be other provisions in the contract balancing the price term which will not be taken into consideration under the approach of Article 102, which is stricter than even EU consumer law in this respect.

Finally, even if one may not dislike giving courts some discretion by allowing them to base decisions on vague concepts such as 'fairness' in different contexts, this is not a desirable approach for competition law purposes. Such discretion in competition law, especially in Article 102 with regard to business-to-business transactions, would not only render the law uncertain, but would also endanger the certainty that businesses need, thereby increasing their risks. For businesses making hundreds of decisions at any time, including whether to invest and innovate, not knowing whether a court may decide that their practices are 'unfair' – without even an objective test of it – and thus void/voidable, creates a serious threat. Therefore, even if acceptable in different branches of law, an argument for 'fairness' in competition law is much harder to sustain. Thus, this study advocates an understanding of 'unfairness' simply as 'exploitation' without 'fairness' being a separate stand-alone objective. In line with the main argument of this book, such exploitation would need to be coupled with harm to competition which can demonstrate itself as 'exclusion' to breach Article 102.

The following part of this study seeks to demonstrate these findings further by showing that the concept of 'fairness' does not *function* effectively on its own, and to show the clash between stand-alone 'fairness' objectives and welfarist objectives. This is done by an examination of the specific prohibition of 'unfair pricing' under Article 102(a) in chapter five and of 'discrimination' under Article 102(c) in chapter six. These two practices – as will be seen in those chapters – are also good examples that demonstrate the problems with prohibiting 'exploitation' without separate harm to competition for competition law purposes.

[232] 'Action Plan' (n 21) [81], [93].

III

Conflicting Objectives in Practice: Two Case Studies

5

A Case Study on 'Fairness' Versus 'Welfare': 'Unfair Pricing' As an Abuse

I INTRODUCTION

Chapter four analysed the potential objective of 'fairness' in Article 102 TFEU. The imposition of an 'unfair' selling or purchasing price is one of the ways in which a dominant undertaking can abuse its dominant position in violation of Article 102. As such, it can be seen as an example of conduct that seeks to promote the 'fairness' objective. This chapter thus analyses 'unfair pricing' as an example of prohibited 'unfair' conduct under Article 102. It does so in order to achieve two objectives: first, it seeks to demonstrate that 'fairness' does not function effectively as a stand-alone objective in that provision; and secondly, it aims to assess 'unfair pricing' as an abusive practice in its own right since, apart from the issue of 'fairness', there are other problems related to and arising from the prohibition of 'unfair pricing' under Article 102. The problems are mainly the result of scrutinising the prices set in a market economy and the fact that such an assessment implies the regulation of prices by authorities rather than the market. Importantly, in the case of Article 102, the test on which such scrutiny will be based is ambiguous and can therefore lead to perverse outcomes in terms of both the operation of the market and the incentives of the undertakings in the market. As such, 'unfair pricing' is an example of abuse where 'fairness' goals potentially clash with 'welfare' goals. In this sense this chapter contributes to demonstrating this clash and its implications, which is one of the ongoing themes of this study. 'Unfair pricing' is also an example of abuse that demonstrates clearly the potential problems with prohibiting 'exploitation' on its own where there is no separate 'harm to competition'. Thus, a detailed examination of this particular type of abuse is an important inquiry for several reasons.

First, 'unfair pricing' is part of a provision whose application has recently been sought to be modernised and to date remains mostly vague without any clear substantive guidelines. As a result, it is still questionable what an 'unfair price' is under Article 102 and whether it is appropriate for the provision to sanction 'unfair pricing'. Secondly, with the direct enforcement of EU competition law before national competition authorities and courts, there may be a rise in the number of pricing cases. This rise is especially likely in private actions since 'unfair prices are good candidates for unhappy customers'.[1] Collective actions, if made available, would make this provision even more attractive, particularly in actions by consumers whose main piece of evidence in an alleged abuse case might be the price charged for the goods by the dominant undertaking.[2] Thirdly, even if 'unfair pricing' is not the alleged abuse, the 'fairness' or 'reasonableness' of price can become an issue in terms of the remedies to be imposed on dominant undertakings. For example, in 'refusal to supply' cases, the dominant undertaking would be expected to set 'fair' or 'reasonable' prices for the compulsorily supplied product.[3]

It must first be noted that Article 102 does not use terms such as 'excessive' or 'predatory'; rather, it prohibits 'unfair' prices and thus cannot be perceived as a shorthand, for example, for 'price above competitive level'.[4] This is important since most of the literature on this prohibition focuses on the subject of 'excessive' prices, which addresses only part of the prohibition in Article 102(a) and therefore does not adequately address the issue in full. By prohibiting 'unfair' prices, this provision is obviously based on the notion of 'fair price' which can be traced back to the medieval concept of *iustum pretium* (just price).[5] Indeed it has been

[1] M Motta and A de Streel, 'Excessive Pricing and Price Squeeze under EU Law' in CD Ehlermann and I Atanasiu (eds), *What is an Abuse of Dominant Position?* (Oxford, Hart Publishing, 2006) 92. The Commission itself does not seem to have given up on 'unfair pricing' as a potential abuse either as it has recently opened formal proceedings with respect to Standard and Poor's behaviour towards end users of International Securities Identification Numbers (ISINs) which allegedly constitutes 'unfair pricing'. See Press Release, 'Commission confirms sending of Statement of Objections to Standard & Poor's' MEMO 09/508 (19.11.2009). At the time of writing, Standard and Poor's have offered commitments to change their pricing policy and the Commission is market testing these commitments; see Press Release, 'Commission market tests Standard & Poor's commitments on international securities identification numbers' IP/11/571 (16 May 2011).

[2] At the time of writing, the Commission is undertaking a public consultation on 'collective redress' in the EU; see 'Towards a Coherent European Approach on Collective Redress' available at: ec.europa.eu/competition/consultations/2011_collective_redress/index_en.html.

[3] See, eg, *Microsoft* (Case COMP/C-3/37.792) Commission Decision 2007/53/EC [2007] OJ L32/23, [1008] requiring Microsoft to set 'reasonable' remuneration for information to be supplied to competitors. See also *NDC Health/IMS Health: Interim Measures* (Case COMP D3/38.044) Commission Decision 2001/165/EC [2002] OJ L59/18, [215] requiring IMS to licence its product at a 'reasonable' fee. For a discussion of problems with this approach, see D Geradin, 'Limiting the Scope of Article 82 EC: What can the EU Learn from the US Supreme Court's Judgment in *Trinko* in the Wake of *Microsoft, IMS*, and *Deutsche Telekom*?' (2004) 41 *Common Market Law Review* 1519, 1543–46.

[4] The usage is identical in most of the original language versions of the TFEU: French '*non équitables*', Italian '*non eque*', Dutch '*onbillijk*'. The German version prohibits '*unangemessen*' (inappropriate) prices. In any case, even if Art 102 had prohibited 'excessive' or 'above competitive level prices', since there is no objective definition or estimation of these either, problems set out in this chapter would have been applicable to 'excessive' or 'above competitive level' prices as well.

[5] See R de Roover, 'The Concept of the Just Price: Theory and Economic Policy' (1958) 18(4) *The Journal of Economic History* 418 and BW Dempsey, 'Just Price in a Functional Economy' (1935) 25(3) *The American Economic Review* 471 for an examination of 'just price'. See Gerber for the argument that one of the norms at the centre of the influence of *Ius Commune* was the just price norm which provided that for any transaction there was a 'just price' and significant deviation from that price could invalidate the transaction; DJ Gerber, *Law and Competition in Twentieth Century Europe: Protecting Prometheus* (Oxford, OUP, 1998) 34. According to Gerber, this firmly imprinted on European legal consciousness the idea that market transactions were subject to concepts of justice. This concept also focused attention on price in assessing whether transactions were 'just', and thus price became the central 'signal' or 'indicator' of economic justice; ibid. In general, a transaction was just if the price was just; ibid 35. For 'unfair competition law' see ch 4 this volume, text after fn 30.

argued that since the nineteenth century, the concept of 'fairness' implicit in the notions of 'just price' and 'usury' has been developed within the framework of 'unfair competition laws' which helped set the stage for the development of the 'abuse' concept.[6] This was a result of expanding the idea that legal processes could determine whether a price was 'fair' to include determination of whether particular business conduct was 'fair'.[7]

Contract law doctrines on 'fairness' – discussed in chapter four – demonstrate clearly how problematic it is to judge the substantive (un)fairness of a transaction and to determine whether the price is 'fair' in the sense that it is adequate or appropriate.[8] These are directly relevant and applicable in the area of competition law as well, where the issue is to decide whether the price in a transaction is 'unfair'. In fact, with the decline of natural law, the *iustum pretium* doctrine collapsed and since the eighteenth and nineteenth centuries commutative justice has been identified with whatever parties have freely agreed to, namely party autonomy.[9] Therefore, contract law generally avoids scrutinising the adequacy of price and limits itself to the assessment of 'procedural fairness'. This same difficulty translates into a challenge of finding what a 'fair' price is for any undertaking that is prohibited from charging an 'unfair' price.

The struggle in finding a 'fair price' is due, inter alia, to the impossibility of ascertaining an objective value for the subject of the transaction. This is because

> [t]he value of a thing is what it will produce, and admits of no precise standard. It must be in its nature fluctuating, and will depend upon ten thousand circumstances. One man in the disposal of his property may sell it for less than another would; he may sell it under pressure of circumstances, which may induce him to sell it at a particular time. Now, if [c]ourts . . . are to unravel all these transactions, they would throw everything into confusion, and set afloat all the [c]ontract of mankind.[10]

According to the argument about the imponderability of value, 'value may mean value to the parties', 'value on the market or from a "commercial point of view" ', or some 'absolute' or intrinsic value.[11] The third does not exist since value varies with time and place; the second is arguably irrelevant since it reflects the value which third parties put on a commodity. Thus, one is left with value to the parties themselves; but that is 'relative', 'subjective' and not discoverable without a 'psychological investigation' into their motives.[12] Moreover, it is precisely what the parties decided when they made the contract.[13] Furthermore, reviewing a bargain for 'fairness' of terms implies that an objective value can be placed on a

[6] DJ Gerber, 'Law and the Abuse of Economic Power in Europe' (1987) 62 *Tulane Law Review* 57, 61–62.

[7] ibid 61–62.

[8] See ch 4 this volume, section IV.B.

[9] MW Hesselink, 'Non-Mandatory Rules in European Contract Law' (2005) 1(1) *European Review of Contract Law* 43, 45, 53.

[10] Chief Baron Eyre in *Griffith v Spratley* (1787) 1 Cox Eq Cas 383, 388.

[11] J Gordley, 'Equality in Exchange' (1981) 69 *California Law Review* 1587, 1599.

[12] ibid 1599.

[13] ibid.

bargained-for performance, when one cannot know whether a party which has already rendered performance would have rendered it for any lesser price.[14] Finally, contract price is normally the most efficient price because permitting the price to be determined by the interaction of buyers and sellers will normally move it to the highest valued uses.[15]

These points are directly relevant for purposes of Article 102 so long as the alleged abusive price is 'imposed' in a transactional context which is likely to be the situation in most cases. Indeed, the ECJ has explicitly stated that Article 102 'is expressly aimed in fact at situations which clearly originate in contractual relations'.[16] However, despite the dislike for the 'fairness' review of price in other branches of law such as contract and consumer law, EU competition law carries an 'unfair price' prohibition in Article 102(a) and thus requires a proper test to be adopted for its application if the provision is to be kept in its current wording. Especially when Article 102 itself is taken into consideration, the real question appears to be whether there can be an 'unfair' price and, if so, how it can be distinguished from the 'fair' price.

Consequently, section II explains the scope of this chapter's inquiry, namely which 'unfair' prices are the subject of the discussion. Section III investigates the EU jurisprudence on 'unfair pricing' in order to demonstrate how the prohibition has been applied so far. Since there does not appear to be a coherent test of 'unfair pricing' arising from the EU jurisprudence, section IV elaborates on insights from behavioural economics on '(un)fair prices', thereby seeking a definition and test of 'unfair pricing' applicable to Article 102(a). This is justified also because the ECJ in its *United Brands* judgment explicitly refers to economics for determining when a price becomes unfair.[17] Furthermore, the 'fairness' of a price imposed by an undertaking on customers has indeed been subject to many studies in behavioural economics. Section V then illustrates the current academic debates on the abuse of 'unfair pricing' and sets out the suggestions in the literature for the application of the prohibition. Section VI seeks to further establish the problems with the prohibition of 'unfair pricing' under Article 102. Sections V and VI together demonstrate the potential problems from a welfare point of view that the prohibition of 'unfair pricing' can give rise to. Building on this, section VII proposes a

[14] MA Eisenberg, 'The Bargain Principle and its Limits' (1982) 95 *Harvard Law Review* 741, 745–46.

[15] ibid 746. Nevertheless, Eisenberg also argues that the 'market price' for a homogeneous good in a homogenous market is 'fair' since this would reflect the benefit the seller has conferred on the buyer, the seller's opportunity cost and also the seller's marginal cost; ibid 747. One of the reasons 'market price' is deemed fair is because the mechanism by which it is generated, ie, a perfectly competitive market, is generally regarded as a fair mechanism; ibid. He then proposes the adoption of a rule such that a merchant who offers a homogeneous commodity at a fixed price would be deemed to impliedly represent that the price is not strikingly disproportionate to that at which the commodity is normally sold in readily accessible marketplaces; ibid 780–81. However, it can be argued that this would be too much of a burden on merchants since the adoption of such a rule would ignore the differences in cost and impose a duty of monitoring at all times which could eventually foster collusion.

[16] See Case 85/76 *Hoffmann-La Roche & Co AG v Commission* [1979] ECR 461, [116].

[17] Case 27/76 *United Brands Co and United Brands Continental BV v Commission* [1978] ECR 207, [253].

new test for determining whether the price imposed by a dominant undertaking is 'unfair'. Section VIII concludes.

II SCOPE OF INQUIRY

For the purposes of competition law, 'unfair pricing' is generally understood in one of two ways. The first way in which the price can be thought to be 'unfair' is when it is discriminatory. Discrimination may occur when either a different price is given for equivalent transactions or the same price is given for non-equivalent transactions. Under EU competition law, this would fall under the prohibition common to Articles 101 and 102 of 'applying dissimilar conditions to equivalent transactions'. The 'unfairness' here is not about the *level* of the price, but is a reference to its being different in similar transactions or the same in dissimilar transactions. This should not be conceived as an 'unfair price' under Article 102(a) since the 'fairness' aspect of it says nothing about the *price* offered in each transaction as such; it merely dictates that similar parties should be treated similarly and different parties should be treated differently.

What is 'unfair' when a dominant undertaking imposes two different prices in equivalent transactions is not the price itself – it is the fact that the dominant undertaking *discriminates* between equivalent parties without any legitimate reasons.[18] The rationale behind this is more likely to be 'equality', rather than the notion of a certain 'fair price'. Thus, it should be dealt with under the prohibition of discrimination, not the prohibition of 'unfair pricing'. In other words, pricing cases where the dominant undertaking offers different prices for equivalent transactions or equivalent prices for non-equivalent transactions fall under the scope of Article 102(c), not Article 102(a), since the former is *lex specialis.* This is because when discrimination is sought to be prohibited, then the level of the different prices does not really matter; when it is the 'unfairness' of the price, then the level of the price matters. Of course, both may occur at the same time. For example, a different lower price may signal that, although the dominant undertaking is able to set such a low price, the fact that it has not done so in another similar transaction may be seen as an evidence of the excessiveness of the latter.[19]

[18] This is why Art 102(c) not only prohibits discrimination by use of price, but all types of discrimination in general. Although the letter of the provision also looks for the discrimination to put trading parties at a competitive disadvantage, it has been argued that neither the Commission nor the courts pay attention to this requirement, see A Jones and B Sufrin, *EU Competition Law: Text, Cases and Materials* 4th edn (Oxford, OUP, 2011) 538. This will be discussed below, this volume, ch 6.

[19] *cf* Motta and de Streel (n 1) 100 arguing that '[t]o prove unfair pricing, the Commission has to show that the prices are different without justification for the same service, and that both prices are profitable. To prove that prices are discriminatory, the Commission has to show that prices are different without justification, and that they place buyers at competitive disadvantage'. It is not possible to agree with this proposition since once the problem is identified as having 'different prices for the same service' it should fall under Art 102(c), which exactly deals with 'applying dissimilar conditions to equivalent transactions with other trading parties'. As discrimination is prohibited in subparagraph (c)

The second possibility for a price to be deemed 'unfair' is therefore when it is above or below a certain level. In other words, a price too high or too low compared with some benchmark can be thought to be 'unfair'. This understanding of 'unfair price' finds its expression in EU competition law in Article 102(a). It is the prohibition of this type of 'unfair price' that this chapter investigates.

A dominant undertaking can abuse its position by imposing an excessively high or excessively low selling or purchasing price if other conditions of Article 102 are met. This naturally requires the determination of a benchmark against which the price will be 'unfair'. The estimation of the 'unfair price' will depend on that level since prices above or below it will be excessively high or low respectively. Naturally, different levels should be estimated for these different types of 'unfair' prices. Excessively low *selling* prices would constitute 'predatory pricing' and although 'predatory pricing' has sometimes been dealt with under Article 102(a) as 'unfair pricing',[20] this chapter does not investigate 'predatory pricing' in itself. This is because low prices to customers do not 'exploit' them and a failed attempt at predation would actually benefit them; the possible 'unfairness' in predatory pricing is vis-à-vis competitors, not customers. Thus, 'predatory pricing' is not an 'unfair' practice in the sense of 'unfair' meaning 'exploitative' as per the definition of this book. However, exploitation can follow exclusion of other undertakings due to 'predatory pricing' of the dominant undertaking. In fact, under the thesis of this book, which is that exploitation and harm to competition (which may demonstrate itself as exclusion) should both be present before conduct can be deemed abusive, exploitation *should* follow exclusion for predation to be abusive. This would require the post-predation price to be 'unfair' and exploit the customers, in which case the practice would fall under the scope of this chapter.[21] Consequently, this chapter focuses on exploitative *and therefore* 'unfair' prices. Moreover, since there are no reported cases in EU jurisprudence in which Article 102 has been

specifically, it should be proved to be an abuse when conditions of that subparagraph are met, not (a). The difference is important since subparagraph (c) requires trading parties to be put at a 'competitive disadvantage' as a result of discrimination, whereas subparagraph (a) does not require any other assessment than finding the price to be 'unfair'.

[20] eg, in *Deutsche Telekom AG* (Case COMP/C-1/37.451, 37.578, 37.579) Commission Decision 2003/707/EC [2003] OJ L263/9 the Commission classified 'margin squeeze' which involved below-cost prices imposed by Deutsche Telekom as 'unfair pricing' under Art 102(a); ibid [1], [161]. This was upheld by both the General Court and the Court of Justice; see Case T-271/03 *Deutsche Telekom AG v Commission* [2008] ECR II-477 and Case C-280/08 *Deutsche Telekom AG v Commission* [2010] ECR I-00. Similarly, in *ECS/AKZO* (Case IV/30.698) Commission Decision 85/609/EEC [1985] OJ L374/1, the Commission considered 'predatory pricing' to be 'unfair' although it did not specify a certain paragraph of Art 102 while doing so; ibid [74], [80].

[21] Suffice to say that this would require proof of potential recoupment by the dominant undertaking, which is currently not a condition for predation to be abusive in the EU, unlike the position in the US. For the EU position, see Case C-202/07 *France Télécom v Commission* [2009] ECR I-2369, and for the US position, see *Brooke Group Ltd v Brown & Williamson Tobacco Corp* 509 US 209 (1993). For studies on predatory pricing see, eg, P Areeda and D Turner, 'Predatory Pricing and Related Practices Under Section 2 of the Sherman Act' (1975) 88 *Harvard Law Review* 697; PL Joskow and AK Klevorick, 'A Framework for Analyzing Predatory Pricing Policy' (1989) 89 *Yale Law Journal* 213; EM Fox, 'Price Predation – US and EEC: Economics and Values' in B Hawk (ed), *International Antitrust Law & Policy: Fordham Corporate Law 1989* (New York, Juris Publishing, 1990).

used for condemning an excessively low *purchasing* price imposed by a dominant undertaking, and since there is no fundamental distinction between the economic analysis and mechanism of buyer power and seller power,[22] the focus will be on exploitatively high *selling* prices which are 'unfair'. That said, the findings and suggestions of the chapter are applicable to both types of 'unfair' prices.

III EU CASE LAW ON 'UNFAIR PRICING'

The current EU approach to 'unfair pricing' is based on several different tests. Although there are not that many 'unfair pricing' cases at the EU level, the number is still enough to cause confusion. This section does not aim to provide an extensive study of each and every case, but rather seeks for an overarching principle.[23]

The practice of the Commission and the EU courts to date evidence a range of benchmarks against which prices have been compared in order to demonstrate 'unfairness'. These benchmarks include the costs of the dominant undertaking, prices charged by the dominant undertaking on other markets, the prices of competitors' products on the same market and the prices of competitors' similar products on other markets.[24] These comparators have either been used on their own or in conjunction with one another, depending on the information available in the case at hand.

The concept of 'unfair' prices has been used in the EU jurisprudence from the early days onwards. In *Parke Davis*, for example, the ECJ held that even though the sale price of a patent protected product may be regarded as a factor to be taken into account in determining the possible existence of an abuse, a higher price for the patented product as compared with the unpatented product does not necessarily constitute an abuse.[25] The ECJ repeated this in *Sirena v Eda* by stating that although the price level may not in itself necessarily suffice to disclose the abuse of a dominant position, if unjustified by any objective criteria and if particularly high, it may be a determining factor.[26] In *Volvo* and *Renault* the ECJ confirmed

[22] R O'Donoghue and AJ Padilla, *The Law and Economics of Article 82 EC* (Oxford, Hart Publishing, 2006) 639, 640. Excessively low pricing was argued in Case 298/83 *CICCE v Commission* [1985] ECR 1105, but rejected by the Commission and the ECJ on the facts of the case. The welfare effects of excessively low purchasing prices may, however, be different from those of excessively high prices if the dominant undertaking passed on the low input price to consumers: the effect on consumers would be neutral or benign, although sellers to the dominant undertaking would have been 'exploited'. If the low prices were not passed on to consumers, the principal effect would still only be a wealth transfer from input sellers to buyers which cannot be objectionable in itself under Art 102. Thus, a key factor of the 'anticompetitive' use of buyer power by too low purchase prices is a reduction in output; O'Donoghue and Padilla, ibid, 641.

[23] For such a study, see Motta and de Streel (n 1).

[24] See, ibid, 95 *et seq*. See also *Scandlines Sverige AB v Port of Helsingborg* (Case COMP/A.36.568/D3) Commission Decision 23 July 2004 (unreported) [170] *et seq*.

[25] Case 24/67 *Parke Davis and Co v Probel, Reese, Beintema-Interpharm and Centrafarm* [1968] ECR 71, 72.

[26] Case 40/70 *Sirena Srl v Eda Srl and Others* [1971] ECR 69, [17].

that charging 'unfair prices' for spare parts by a car manufacturer that refused to license its intellectual property rights might constitute abuse.[27] It must be noted though, these were cases arising out of issues of intellectual property rights and demonstrate the initial attempts of the Court to set out the relation between these rights and the abuse of a dominant position. What is noteworthy is that the ECJ in effect held that 'unfair pricing' is an abuse of such importance that it sets limits to the exercise of intellectual property rights.[28]

In *General Motors*, the ECJ used the expression 'excessive price' for the first time and decided that 'the imposition of a price which is excessive in relation to the economic value of the service provided' could be abusive under Article 102(a), even though in that case such abuse was not found contrary to the Commission's decision.[29] The leading case on the matter is *United Brands*, in which the ECJ set out the conditions for a price to be 'unfair', although in that case the Court held that the Commission had again not proved the existence of 'unfair' prices.[30] According to the test suggested in *United Brands* by the ECJ, 'charging a price that is excessive because it has no reasonable relation to the economic value of the product' would be an abuse of a dominant position.[31] Moreover, it was supposed that this excess could be determined objectively by looking at the amount of the profit margin.[32] A twofold test was proposed as follows. First, it should be determined whether the difference between the costs actually incurred and the price actually charged is excessive.[33] Secondly, if the answer to the first question is in the affirmative, then it should be assessed whether a price has been imposed which is either 'unfair' in itself or when compared to competing products.[34] In other words, the excessiveness of the profit margin does not in itself prove that the price is 'unfair' and the assessment of 'unfairness' is separate from the assessment of 'excessiveness'. The ECJ also appreciated 'the considerable and at times very great difficulties' in calculating production costs which may at times include discretionary apportionments of indirect costs and general expenditure.[35] The Commission similarly held that '[a]n infringement of Article [102](2)(a) of the [TFEU] exists where the price charged for a service is clearly disproportionate to the cost of

[27] Case 238/87 *AB Volvo Veng v Erik Veng (UK) Ltd* [1988] ECR 6211 and Case 53/87 *CICCRA v Renault* [1988] ECR 6039.

[28] See Jones and Sufrin (n 18) 534 for the argument that the idea that intellectual property rights owners are not entitled to extract the maximum rent from their monopoly position raises serious questions about the value of such rights.

[29] Case 26/75 *General Motors Continental NV v Commission* [1975] ECR 1367, [12], [20].

[30] *United Brands* (n 17) [267]. For a recent Commission Decision applying the test in *United Brands*, see *Scandlines* (n 24).

[31] *United Brands*, ibid, [250].

[32] ibid [251].

[33] For the argument that the test is single-staged, see Motta and de Streel (n 1) 96. However, the wording used by the Court is very clear in that it requires a two-staged examination. The Commission adopts this latter view as well in *Scandlines* (n 24) [149].

[34] *United Brands* (n 17) [252].

[35] ibid [254]. In the particular case, the Court held that there were no such problems; ibid.

supplying it'.[36] In short, this approach is mainly based on the comparison of the cost and the price of the product.[37] This appears to have been the test in *British Leyland* in which the fees charged by the car manufacturer British Leyland for national type approval certificates were 'unfair' as they were 'clearly disproportionate to the economic value of the service' and thus abusive according to the Commission and the ECJ.[38]

Of the other approaches, comparison of the dominant undertaking's allegedly abusive price with the price of the same product on other markets should be dealt with under the prohibition of discrimination. As stated above,[39] this is because such a comparison does not necessarily indicate anything about the 'unfairness' of the prices individually; it only demonstrates that the dominant undertaking has been 'unfair' by imposing different terms for similar transactions and thus has discriminated. Moreover, such an investigation would be extremely difficult in that it requires the perfect elimination of price differences resulting from the different characteristics of the different markets. In other words, if the difference in the properties of the markets is the reason for different prices, transactions would no longer be 'equivalent' and a sensible comparison could not then be made.

Comparison with the dominant undertaking's comparable products on the same market is the approach adopted by the Commission in cases of 'margin squeeze'. For example, in *Deutsche Telekom*, the margin between the wholesale price charged to competitors for access to the fixed network and the retail prices charged to end-users for access over local networks, was not sufficient enough to allow competitors to compete with Deutsche Telekom to provide end-user access over local networks. Deutsche Telekom was thus fined over €12 million for charging 'unfair' prices under Article 102(a).[40]

Comparison with other undertakings' prices may be done for the same market where abuse allegedly takes place or for a different market where similar products are offered by other undertakings. Prices of competitors on the same market could not be an appropriate benchmark most of the time, since if the market is dominated and thus competition is already impaired, then the prices of other undertakings on that market would not necessarily show what the price would be under competitive conditions. This was confirmed in *Deutsche Post AG – Interception of Cross-Border Mail*, where the Commission stated that, in a market open to competition, the normal test to be applied for 'fairness' of a price would

[36] *DSD* (Case COMP D3/34493) Commission Decision 2001/463/EC [2001] OJ L166/1, [111] upheld by the ECJ in Case C-385/07 *Der Grüne Punkt – Duales System Deutschland v Commission* [2009] ECR I-6155.

[37] See below (n 180) for an interpretation of the Commission's and courts' 'cost' concept which is problematic as it equates 'cost' with 'economic value'.

[38] Case 226/84 *British Leyland plc v Commission* [1987] 1 CMLR 185, [30]. The Court bases its judgment on the fact that the costs of issuing conformity certificates for right-hand drive and left-hand drive vehicles were not so different to justify the different higher fee for left-hand drive vehicles as compared with the fee for right-hand drive vehicles.

[39] See above, section II.

[40] *Deutsche Telekom AG* (n 20) [4], [199], [212]. This approach has been confirmed by the EU courts; see above (n 20).

be to compare the price of the dominant undertaking with the prices charged by its competitors.[41] However, since in that case Deutsche Post AG had a wide-ranging monopoly, such a comparison was not possible.[42] It should also be noted that if the comparator is a product (as opposed to, for example, a facility) and is produced at a non-trivial quantity, then the higher price of the dominant undertaking's product may not be used for abusive purposes since the demand of buyers deeming that price excessive could be met by the other undertaking. In other words, customers could switch to the comparison product, unless there are switching problems which would be a separate issue from the price's 'unfairness'.

Comparison with other undertakings' prices on other markets, as done in *SACEM*,[43] again risks comparing non-equivalent products since the competition authority and/or the courts would have to estimate how much of the price difference is due to different market characteristics. Moreover, it implicitly assumes that the price in the low-price market is a benchmark for the competitive price in the market where the alleged abuse took place.[44] Both of these problems can be insurmountable in practice for establishing whether the price is 'unfair'.

In short, there are several benchmarks used by the EU authorities in determining whether a price charged by a dominant undertaking is 'unfair'. All these benchmarks present various problems, both in terms of definition and assessment. Moreover, none of these benchmarks renders a coherent and objective test of finding price to be 'unfair'. The most logical starting point among the current approaches of looking for an 'excessive' 'unfair price' is represented by the first part of the *United Brands* test, which compares the price with the cost.[45] The second part of the test is more confusing than helpful. First, assessing whether the price is 'unfair in itself' merely duplicates the issue, since the question to be

[41] *Deutsche Post AG – Interception of Cross-Border Mail* (Case COMP/C-1/36.915) Commission Decision 2001/892/EC [2001] OJ L331/40, [159].

[42] ibid. In that case, the Commission compared the cross-border tariff with the domestic tariff of Deutsche Post AG instead; ibid [162].

[43] In that case, the ECJ, in a preliminary ruling, found that SACEM could be found to have charged unfair royalties as a result of a comparison between the royalties charged by SACEM in France and other copyright-management societies in other Member States if such a comparison could be made on a 'consistent basis'; Case 110/88 *François Lucazeau and others v Societe des Auteurs, Compositeurs et Editeurs de Musique (SACEM)* [1989] ECR 2811, [25]. The dominant firm is given the right to prove objective dissimilarities between the Member States to justify such a difference; ibid. However, this would require such a firm to be able to prove conditions of markets on which it is not active. Moreover, this would perversely encourage dominance since it would mean that being dominant on many markets is better than being dominant on one since in that way, the firm can eliminate the possibility of comparison with different markets. See also Case 30/87 *Bodson v Pompes Funèbres des Régions Libérées* [1988] ECR 2479 and Case 395/87 *Ministère Public v Jean-Louis Tournier* [1989] ECR 2521.

[44] O'Donoghue and Padilla (n 22) 618.

[45] See text to n 118 for an explanation why this method is also bound to fail. An interesting case is the leading UK case on excessive pricing, namely Case 1001/1/1/01 *Napp Pharmaceutical Holdings Ltd and Subsidiaries v Director General of Fair Trading* [2002] Comp AR 13 in which the Director General of Fair Trading used various comparisons – such as Napp's prices against those of its competitors, over time, across different markets and Napp's profitability across different markets and against that of its competitors – together to reach the conclusion that Napp had charged excessive prices for its sustained-release morphine in the community sector. This was approved by the Competition Appeal Tribunal; ibid [392]–[97].

answered is whether the price is 'unfair'. It merely restates the question and does not offer any guidance to find which price is 'unfair in itself' and which price is 'unfair', albeit not 'unfair in itself'. It implies that there are inherently 'fair' prices, which is an argument that must be rejected since both the concept of 'fairness' and the value of a good are subjective. Secondly, the possibility suggested in the second part of the test – that is the price being 'unfair' when compared with competing products – is similarly problematic, since if there are competing products, then the buyers should buy those competing products at a lower price. If the market is genuinely dominated (which should be the case for an infringement of Article 102), there would be a lack of meaningfully competing products and/or their price would not demonstrate what the price should be under more competitive conditions. In fact, if there are meaningfully competing products on the market, this would raise the question of whether dominance has been established correctly. Having said that, as the first part of the *United Brands* test also does not sufficiently answer when the price imposed by a dominant undertaking becomes 'unfair' (beyond pointing at the relevance of a price-cost comparison), the next section seeks insights from behavioural economics for interpreting 'unfairness' of prices under Article 102.

IV INSIGHTS FROM BEHAVIOURAL ECONOMICS ON '(UN)FAIR' PRICES

The ECJ in its *United Brands* judgment stated that economic theorists have thought of several ways to determine whether a price is 'unfair' other than looking at the profit margin and suggested that these may be of guidance in Article 102 cases.[46] This section thus seeks insights from economics on '(un)fair' prices. However, it must be noted that, unlike what the ECJ's reference might suggest, there is no general accepted definition in economics of what an '(un)fair' price is.[47] In fact, conventional economic theory is altogether unhelpful in this area since it is not concerned with 'fairness' or 'unfairness' of prices. Therefore, this section looks at behavioural economics (as the branch of economics under which studies into 'fairness' have been carried out), to determine whether there are any insights that can be useful for the purposes of the prohibition of 'unfair pricing' under Article 102.

The central insight that gave rise to modern economics is that the common good is well served by the free actions of self-interested agents in a market.[48] Almost all economic models assume that all people exclusively pursue their material self-interest and do not care about social goals per se.[49] Therefore a finding

[46] *United Brands* (n 17) [253].

[47] O'Donoghue and Padilla (n 22) 604.

[48] D Kahneman, JL Knetsch and R Thaler, 'Fairness and the Assumptions of Economics' (1986) 59 (October) *Journal of Business* S285, S286.

[49] M Rabin, 'Incorporating Fairness into Game Theory and Economics' (1993) 83(5) *The American Economic Review* 1281, 1281; E Fehr and KM Schmidt, 'A Theory of Fairness, Competition and Cooperation' (1999) 114(3) *The Quarterly Journal of Economics* 817, 817.

that people are not totally self-interested could challenge the deep-rooted assumptions and theories of economics. Indeed, in behavioural economics, 'fairness' is usually used as an explanation of behaviour that cannot be explained by the assumption of 'rationality' or 'self-interest'. In other words, certain behaviour that seems contrary to economists' expectations of rational self-maximising human behaviour is deemed to occur out of 'fairness' concerns. The implication of this finding is that people would take into account 'fairness' considerations when entering transactions and as a result, an undertaking might not be able to set the price as traditionally envisaged by economics, but have to take into account the possibility that an 'unfair price' could stop the customer from making a purchase. In the extreme, this would imply that there is no need for a competition law prohibition of 'unfair' prices since the potential reaction of customers should stop the undertaking from setting such prices. This finding, if accepted, would therefore be relevant for the prohibition of 'unfair pricing' in Article 102.

In one of the leading studies on the subject, Fehr and Schmidt have suggested that it is possible to explain the conflicting pieces of evidence (some of which show people are driven by 'fairness' considerations and some of which show that all people behave as if completely selfish), with a single simple model. This can arguably be done if it is assumed that – without even relaxing the rationality assumption – in addition to purely self-interested people, there is a fraction of people motivated by 'fairness' considerations.[50] The authors model 'fairness' as self-centred inequity aversion, in the sense that people resist inequitable outcomes – that is they are willing to give up some material pay-off to move in the direction of more equitable outcomes. This is 'self-centred' in that people do not care per se about inequity that exists among other people, but are interested in the 'fairness' of their own material pay-off relative to the pay-off of others.[51] The key insight of the literature is deemed to be that relative material pay-offs affect people's well-being and behaviour.[52] Moreover, it is assumed that individuals suffer more from inequality which is to their disadvantage than that which is to their advantage.[53]

Fehr and Schmidt's theory, however, begs the following question: if people are not concerned about being better off than others as much as they are concerned about being worse off, could this not be out of 'selfishness'?[54] Arguing that it is 'unfair' when one loses and not so 'unfair' when one wins still resembles self-interested behaviour. In fact, their approach would also imply that there are two 'fair' outcomes in the same transaction – one from the first party's point of view and the other from the second party's. This would inevitably leave any third party which has to choose one over the other basing the decision on grounds other than 'fairness'.

[50] Fehr and Schmidt, ibid, 818.

[51] ibid 819. Judgements on the fairness of outcomes are inevitably based on a kind of neutral reference outcome which is itself the product of complicated social comparison processes; ibid 820–21.

[52] ibid 821.

[53] ibid 823.

[54] 'Selfishness' here is used in the ordinary sense of the term, ie, concern for only oneself.

A common example used to support 'fairness' theories in behavioural economics is the 'ultimatum game'. The ultimatum game is a game used in experimental economics in which a proposer and responder bargain over the division of a fixed surplus. The proposer can offer the responder anything and, if the responder accepts the offer, the division is carried out accordingly and they both get their shares as agreed on; if the responder rejects the proposer's offer, they both get nothing.[55] Although the self-interest model predicts that the responder accepts anything above zero and is indifferent between accepting and rejecting an offer of zero, it has been argued that numerous experiments with different stakes and procedures seem to refute this proposition – the majority of offers seems to be in around 40–50 per cent and there are no offers below 20 per cent.[56]

Although these results have been interpreted as a preference for 'fairness', as has been pointed out, a 'fair' allocation in an ultimatum game could also be explained by the proposer's fear that the recipient might reject a small positive offer.[57] Moreover, when competition is introduced to the ultimatum game on the responder's side, the picture seems to totally change. The impossibility of preventing inequitable outcomes by individual players renders inequity aversion unimportant in equilibrium.[58] Fehr and Schmidt have claimed that competition rendered 'fairness' considerations irrelevant if, and only if, none of the competing players could punish the monopolist by destroying some of the surplus and enforcing a more equitable outcome.[59] The responder's willingness to reject a given offer decreases substantially as the number of competitors increases and this reduction is due to the impact of competition on responders' beliefs about their rivals' rejection behaviour. The higher the number of competing responders, the greater a given responder's probability belief that another responder will accept the offer.[60] In other words, when competition is introduced on the responder side, responders become more self-interested and know that if they do not accept the offer made, someone else most probably will.[61]

[55] At first sight, it appears as if the proposer has all the bargaining power against the responder as the responder has no power in determining the division of the surplus. However, since the responder is the one who actually has the power to decide whether there will be a deal or not, she is not in that weak a position. Hence, the inequality of bargaining power is the inequality with regard to the *content* of bargaining power that each party has, rather than one party having and the other lacking power. See ch 4 this volume, text around fns 92 and 129 for inequality of bargaining power in contract law.

[56] Fehr and Schmidt (n 49) 825–26.

[57] Kahneman, Knetsch and Thaler (n 48) S291; Rabin (n 49) 1284, fn 4.

[58] Fehr and Schmidt (n 49) 834.

[59] ibid 835.

[60] U Fischbacher, MC Fong and E Fehr, 'Fairness, Errors and the Power of Competition' (2009) 72(1) *Journal of Economic Behavior and Organization* 527, 528.

[61] Introducing competition on the proposer's side is argued to have just the opposite effect; a small amount of proposer competition causes a large increase in the proposer's rejection risk, thus the offer made by the proposer increases significantly compared with that in the ultimatum game with a single proposer, although the proposer still reaps a substantial share of the surplus; Fischbacher, Fong and Fehr, ibid, 540 *et seq*. What remains to be tested is the outcome when competition is introduced on both sides, which would be a more accurate reflection of reality.

Interestingly, Rabin has found that as material pay-offs become large, behaviour becomes dominated by material self-interest instead of 'fairness' concerns.[62] Rabin's definition of 'fairness' outcomes are the outcomes of people's liking to help those who help them and to hurt those who hurt them.[63] In other words, 'fairness' seems to be an expression of 'an eye for an eye and a tooth for a tooth'. In a later study, however, other authors have argued that, both in the high and the normal stake condition, 'fairness' concerns were strong enough to outweigh competitive forces and there was also no evidence of behaviour becoming generally more selfish at higher stake levels.[64]

In short, there is debate in this strand of literature regarding the effect on fairness concerns of both competition and the effect of the size of the stakes involved. What must be noted is that, if competition on the responder side or the size of the stake has an effect on the responders' acceptance or rejection of the offer, this would signify another weakness of the 'fairness' theory as modelled by these experiments: if the responders were rejecting offers because of 'fairness' reasons, then it should not matter for them how big the stakes are or whether someone else gets the surplus rejected by them or not. Their behaviour should be the same in both situations if motivated by 'fairness' reasons, as opposed to self-interest.

In fact, doubt has been cast on the assumption of individuals' 'preference for fairness' and therefore the studies mentioned so far – by a finding that when the direct link between actions and harmful outcomes to other people is eliminated – the subjects act significantly as more self-interested.[65] It has been shown that when the impact of the choice on the other party is unknown because pay-off information is hidden, subjects choose not to (costlessly) reveal this information and instead maximise their own pay-offs.[66] Thus, in a situation where choosing not to acquire information does not directly result in an unequal outcome, subjects essentially avoid an opportunity to behave altruistically.[67] According to this argument, the underlying motivation driving much of fair behaviour might be self-interest, coupled with a desire to maintain the illusion of not being selfish.[68] As a result, removing the transparency between one's actions and the outcomes to both parties creates a moral 'wiggle room' for the proposer to behave more selfishly.[69] In their experiments, Dana et al thus find that this moral wiggle room is

[62] Rabin (n 49) 1282, 1291. For a comment, proposing to adjust this proposition of Rabin's model, asserting that fairness gains importance again when stakes become *very very large*, see WR Nelson, 'Incorporating Fairness into Game Theory and Economics: Comment' (2001) 91(4) *The American Economic Review* 1180.

[63] Rabin (n 49) 1281.

[64] E Fehr, U Fischbacher and E Tougareva, 'Do High Stakes and Competition Undermine Fairness? Evidence from Russia' Institute for Empirical Research in Economics, University of Zurich Working Paper No 120 (July 2002) 2, 3.

[65] J Dana, RA Weber and JX Kuang, 'Exploiting Moral Wiggle Room: Experiments Demonstrating an Illusory Preference for Fairness' (2007) 33(1) *Economic Theory* 67, 69.

[66] ibid 74.

[67] ibid 75–76.

[68] ibid 68.

[69] ibid 69.

indeed utilised and that removing the transparency significantly decreases 'fair' behaviour.[70]

One must also note that in the experiments mentioned above, parties are not producing the surplus themselves – they are only dividing a surplus provided by the games' executors and they must be perfectly aware of the fact that none of them has more entitlement to the surplus than the other. In real life, however, people may think that they are entitled to more surplus than the others, even if that is not necessarily the case. Since the surplus is created by their transaction in real life, they may want to get as big a share of it as possible, perhaps actually believing that they are entitled to what they deem appropriate, and may not even think that they may be 'unfair' while doing that. Moreover, what they consider they may be entitled to might even change depending on which side of the transaction they are. In fact, there is evidence from behavioural studies that the 'endowment effect' implies that people place higher values on goods when they are to give up on them than they do when they are to acquire them.[71]

Outside the experimental realm, a different theory proposed to explain 'fairness' concerns in transactions is the principle of 'dual entitlement'. In a prominent study, Kahneman, Knetsch and Thaler argued that a principle of 'dual entitlement' governs community standards of 'fairness': transactors have an entitlement to the terms of the 'reference transaction' and firms are entitled to their 'reference profit'.[72] 'Reference transaction' is a relevant precedent that is characterised by a reference price or wage, and by a positive reference profit to the firm.[73] Market prices, posted prices and the history of previous transactions can serve as reference transactions.[74] Importantly, reference transaction provides a basis for 'fairness' judgements because it is 'normal', not necessarily because it is 'just'.[75] For this reason, for example, it is deemed 'unfair' by consumers for a firm to take advantage of an increase in its monopoly power by raising prices.[76] Nonetheless, people arguably adapt their views of 'fairness' to the norms of actual behaviour and, since terms of exchange that are initially seen as 'unfair' may in time become reference transaction, the gap between the behaviour that people consider 'fair' and the behaviour that they expect on the market tends to be rather small.[77] In terms of the prohibition in Article 102, 'dual entitlement' would imply that only some prices of a dominant undertaking would be 'unfair': it is only 'unfair' if a firm charges a price that – relative to the reference – realises a gain for the firm *at the expense* of its customers' entitlement. If, however, the firm does not gain *at the*

[70] ibid 78.

[71] See D Kahneman, JL Knetsch and RH Thaler, 'Experimental Tests of the Endowment Effect and the Coase Theorem' in CR Sunstein (ed), *Behavioural Law and Economics* (Cambridge, CUP, 2000).

[72] D Kahneman, JL Knetsch and R Thaler, 'Fairness as a Constraint on Profit Seeking: Entitlements in the Market' (1986) 76(4) *American Economic Review* 728, 729.

[73] ibid 729.

[74] ibid 730.

[75] ibid.

[76] ibid 735.

[77] ibid 731.

expense of the customer (for example, because the price is high as a result of a cost increase or the firm's profit increases without the customer's entitlement being infringed), the price would not be unfair. As such, dual entitlement provides useful insights into behaviour that can be deemed unfair and indeed has been used by this author elsewhere to operationalise the second stage of the *United Brands* test in terms of establishing which excessive prices are 'unfair'.[78]

Related to this is the suggestion that the utility of an action does not only depend on the material consequences of the action, but is also directly affected by the actions available to the decision maker.[79] It means that a decision maker can more easily enforce her preferred actions against opposition by secretly constraining the set of available actions or by pretending that certain actions are not available.[80] This would imply that if an undertaking can successfully disguise the set of, for example, available prices, then whatever price it sets may appear 'fair' to the consumer since it would seem like it had no other available actions to take, namely no other price to choose. Pretending and making the consumer believe that it has higher costs may be a way of doing this. This would at least in appearance be 'fair' under the principle of 'dual entitlement' as well, since the undertaking is allowed to pass on the cost increases, which would be protecting its own 'entitlement'.

Another model proposed in behavioural economics regarding unfair prices provides important insights for the prohibition in Article 102(a). In this model by Rabin, 'fairness' is considered in the context of monopoly pricing to investigate whether consumers may see conventional monopoly prices as 'unfair' and refuse to buy at such prices, even if the good is worth it in material terms.[81] If this were the case, then a profit-maximising monopolist would (have to) price its products below the level predicted by standard economic theory.[82] The competition policy implication of this would be that competition law and the enforcers of Article 102 need not worry about monopoly prices since the monopolist would not be able to charge monopolistic prices taking 'fairness' into account, if 'unfair' prices are deemed to correspond to monopoly prices in this context.

According to this model, any time the monopolist is not setting a price equal to its costs, the consumer thinks that the monopolist is being 'unfair', even if the price is equal to the consumer's reservation price or the consumer's valuation of the good.[83] Although this begs the question of why the consumer would think that any time the price is not set at cost, the monopolist is 'unfair' and would imply that the fairest equilibrium would be when the consumer has the whole surplus (which is a disputable position), the model still has important implications for

[78] See P Akman and L Garrod, 'When are Excessive Prices Unfair?' (2011) 7(2) *Journal of Competition Law & Economics* 403.
[79] A Falk, E Fehr and U Fischbacher, 'On the Nature of Fair Behavior' (2003) 41(1) *Economic Inquiry* 20, 25.
[80] ibid 25.
[81] Rabin (n 49) 1292.
[82] ibid.
[83] ibid.

Article 102.[84] According to the model, assuming that a monopolist has costs *c* per unit of production and a consumer values the product at *v*, the highest price a monopolist can set consistent with 'fairness' equilibrium is suggested to be given by z^* and this number is strictly less than *v* when $v>c$.[85] Thus, the highest equilibrium price possible is lower than the conventional monopoly price when 'fairness' is added to the equation and a monopolist interested in profit maximising should not set price at the 'monopoly price' because it should take consumers' attitudes towards 'fairness' as a given.[86] Hence, since the highest 'fair' monopoly price is lower than the consumer's valuation, trade does not occur even at a price equal to the consumer's valuation.[87]

More importantly, since the results of the model mean that the highest 'fair price' is found as a derivation of the consumer's valuation and the monopolist's costs, for every consumer who has a different valuation than the other, the highest 'fairness' equilibrium price z^* will be different. This is a problematic finding with regard to Article 102 since, if it is true, then there would be no way of establishing whether the *single* price the dominant firm has imposed was 'unfair', as the 'unfair price' would be a different price for different parties. If it is not possible to determine a single 'unfair price' for a single good and therefore a 'fair price', then it would seem inconsistent with legal certainty to deem the price an abuse of a dominant position: the undertaking must be able to know how it could price fairly if it does not want to abuse its position and must have a way of pricing 'fairly' when it actually seeks to. This is a particularly important finding since, as will be explained below, currently there is a move towards incorporating the customer's valuation in the concept of 'economic value' in EU decisional practice.[88] Furthermore, the model would suggest that the monopolist may indeed have to price discriminate to price 'fairly' (to be able to price in conformity with the other party's valuation of the good), which could result in another type of abuse under Article 102, namely discrimination by 'applying dissimilar conditions to equivalent transactions with

[84] The position is disputable, eg, because other authors give an example of a *very unfair* equilibrium by 'virtually all conceivable definitions of fairness' as the case where all of the gains from trade are reaped by one side of the market; Fehr and Schmidt (n 49) 829.

[85] According to the author z^*: $[2v^2-2cv+c]/[1+2v-2c]$; Rabin (n 49) 1292–93.

[86] ibid 1293.

[87] An alternative way of looking at the issue could be to argue for taking 'fairness' into account while the consumer is setting her valuation/reservation price. If it can be assumed that the consumer's valuation must somehow include fairness and the consumer must be setting her valuation after taking into account her criteria for 'fairness', there would be no need to look at fairness again from the monopolist's point of view. In other words, if we assume that fairness plays a role in consumer's determination of the reservation price, then at any price at *or below* that, the consumer would buy the good and the monopolist would only have to consider the consumer's reservation price/valuation and would not have to take fairness as a separate issue anymore. The monopolist would have to take into account only the reservation price and the fact that it is the highest price at which the consumer would buy the good. Then, the 'fair' price does not have to be below valuation, but the maximum can be at valuation. In this way, the reservation price would not only be a price above which the consumer is not willing to pay, but also a price below which the consumer *would* pay without deeming it unfair (Rabin assumes the reservation price is one above which the consumer is not willing to pay; Rabin, ibid, 1292).

[88] See below text around n 175.

other trading parties'. In short, an undertaking in a dominant position may be faced with a 'Catch-22' situation if this model holds, since it may have no other choice than to abuse its position whenever it sets a price.

In short, the main point of the findings of 'fairness' in behavioural economics is the consideration of 'fairness' and 'unfairness' from the perspective of the parties to the transaction. These studies argue for the existence of 'fair' and 'unfair' outcomes and prices, but base this on how the parties to a transaction perceive 'fairness'. This leads to 'fairness' and 'unfairness' becoming subjective concepts and as such limits the usefulness of the findings for legal purposes, since from a legal perspective, one party's subjective perception of 'fairness' cannot be meaningfully preferred over the other's due to equality before the law. Thus, the studies on 'fairness' of price in behavioural economics are useful for demonstrating possible understandings of 'fairness', but do not easily render legal or policy recommendations. Moreover, the implication of these models would be that a consistent approach within Article 102 cannot be operationalised regarding 'unfair pricing' in conformity with legal certainty and economics without the provision contradicting itself, since it would have to allow price discrimination. This would be the case under the current interpretation of discrimination in EU decisional practice, according to which different valuations of the parties do *not* render transactions non-equivalent and a lack of objective (cost) justification appears to suffice for a finding of discrimination.[89] With these insights from behavioural economics, section V sets out the academic debates on the 'unfair pricing' prohibition and various suggestions in the literature on how to apply it.

V SUGGESTIONS FROM THE LITERATURE ON OPERATIONALISING THE 'UNFAIR PRICING' PROHIBITION

Most of the literature on the prohibition of 'unfair pricing' under Article 102 has focused on 'excessive' prices without a separate discussion of 'unfairness' and is therefore incomplete in its assessment. This section tries to present some of the literature on this prohibition, including the few that have focused on 'unfairness' as well. The aim of reviewing this literature is to demonstrate the potential problems that arise when attempting to operationalise the prohibition of 'unfair pricing'.

In the literature, it has been argued that there are immensely complex problems inherent in the process of deciding whether a price is, in fact, abusive.[90] It has been

[89] See M Furse, 'Monopoly Price Discrimination, Article 82 and the Competition Act' (2001) 22(5) *European Competition Law Review* 149, 153; D Gerard, 'Price Discrimination under Article 82(c) EC: Clearing up the Ambiguities' in *Global Competition Law Centre Research Papers on Article 82 EC – July 2005* available at: www.coleurope.eu/template.asp?pagename=gclcresearch. For a further explanation see ch 6 this volume, text around fn 33.

[90] N Green, 'Problems in the Identification of Excessive Prices: The United Kingdom Experience in the Light of Napp' in CD Ehlermann and I Atanasiu (eds), *What is an Abuse of Dominant Position?* (Oxford, Hart Publishing, 2006) 80.

commented that to determine, with pinpoint accuracy, the precise margin which may be said to be 'reasonable' and thus non-abusive is an exercise fraught with difficulty.[91] Any policy seeking to detect and prohibit excessive prices in practice is likely to yield incorrect predictions and all these errors are costly.[92] In the standard terminology of decision theory, any legal standard for excessive pricing will result in 'false convictions' (or 'Type I' errors) and/or 'false acquittals' (or 'Type II' errors).[93] Therefore, a false conviction will result in over-enforcement of the provision by finding procompetitive conduct anticompetitive, whereas a false acquittal will result in under-enforcement by finding anticompetitive conduct procompetitive. In practice, no workable set of principles can avoid some of these errors, thus the issue is which type of error is more costly in balance.[94]

Arguably, the cost of a Type I error in excessive pricing cases is given by a reduction in the incentives to innovate and invest for undertakings that operate not only in the sectors where intervention takes place, but all throughout the economy, since evidence of false convictions would reduce the incentives to invest by reducing the expected rate of return on successful innovations.[95] In welfare terms, the cost of a Type I error is equal to the loss in consumer welfare resulting from the lack of introduction of valuable products for which there is potential demand.[96] The cost of a Type II error is the loss of consumer welfare that results from above-competitive prices, which is given by the sum of the wealth transfer from consumers to producers and the 'deadweight loss'.[97] It has been argued that firms need to mark up their variable costs in order to cover their fixed costs, fund new investments and innovate (that is, the cost of a Type I error is typically large) and that the ability of undertakings to sustain above-competitive prices is most often constrained by the possibility of entry (that is, the cost of a Type II error is small).[98] The ability of competition authorities and courts to distinguish between 'fair' and 'unfair' prices in practice is also very low.[99] The argument is that judicial errors that tolerate baleful practices are self-correcting, while erroneous condemnations are not.[100] Moreover, since there is no price-cost or profitability benchmarking rule that could be objective and efficient, it has been suggested that a per se legality approach to pricing should be adopted.[101] Nevertheless, there may still

[91] ibid 80–81. See also O'Donoghue and Padilla (n 22) 627.

[92] DS Evans and AJ Padilla, 'Excessive Prices: Using Economics to Define Administrable Legal Rules' (2005) 1(1) *Journal of Competition Law & Economics* 97, 99.

[93] ibid 113.

[94] O'Donoghue and Padilla (n 22) 625.

[95] Evans and Padilla (n 92) 114.

[96] ibid.

[97] ibid. This assessment is based on a 'consumer welfare' standard. Under a 'total welfare' standard, the cost of a Type I error would be larger and the cost of Type II error smaller, compared to the costs under the 'consumer welfare' standard; ibid 114, fn 82. For 'deadweight loss', see ch1 this volume, section II.B.i, Figure 1.

[98] Evans and Padilla, ibid, 118.

[99] ibid. What is worth noting is that the authors use 'fair' and 'unfair' as synonyms for 'efficient' and 'inefficient' respectively; ibid.

[100] FH Easterbrook, 'The Limits of Antitrust' (1984) 63(1) *Texas Law Review* 1, 3.

[101] Evans and Padilla (n 92) 111, 118.

be scope for the adoption of an interventionist approach towards excessive prices under some 'exceptional circumstances' which should exist cumulatively: (i) the firm enjoys a (near) monopoly position which is not the result of past investments or innovations and is protected by insurmountable legal barriers to entry; (ii) the prices charged widely exceed average total costs; and (iii) there is a risk that those prices may prevent the emergence of new goods and services in adjacent markets.[102]

It has similarly been remarked that although many forms of non-cost-related dominant undertaking pricing have the potential to adversely affect competition, economic efficiency and customers, taking a blanket stance against any one of those practices is not justified in economic terms and leads to the perverse effect of penalising and deterring procompetitive behaviour and harming consumer interests in many cases.[103] Instead, a much more focused approach to intervention against pricing behaviour is required.[104] The argument appears to be that the form-based rules used by the Commission fail to distinguish between procompetitive and anticompetitive behaviour and therefore the assessment should be done on the basis of the economic *effects* of conduct.

Another test proposed in the literature interprets 'unfair price' as price above the economic value of the product, which is deemed to mean above the 'normal competitive level'.[105] Therefore, a price is excessive when significantly above the effective competitive level.[106] In this approach, the competition authority is supposed to acquire cost data and compare them with the allegedly excessive price. It is only when it is too difficult to get these data, or in order to complement a cost analysis, that the authority may decide to compare competitors' prices and, more generally, compare the investigated prices with some benchmarked prices.[107] Consequently, the general presumption should be that market forces will over time reduce the market power of a dominant undertaking or at least oblige it to reduce price to prevent switching. That is, exploitative prices are deemed to be self-correcting because excessive prices will attract new entrants.[108] It must be noted that this explanation goes back to the 'Chicago School' of antitrust, accord-

[102] ibid 119–20.

[103] D Ridyard, 'Article 82 Price Abuses – Towards a More Economic Approach' in CD Ehlermann and I Atanasiu (eds), *What is an Abuse of Dominant Position?* (Oxford, Hart Publishing, 2006) 451.

[104] ibid.

[105] Motta and de Streel (n 1) 94. They take the 'normal competitive level' to be 'the minimum average cost', adopting the Commission's definition in the previous Guidelines on Vertical Restraints. A price below average costs would not be viable (and could not be taken as the competitive benchmark) since firms would not be able to cover their fixed costs if they set prices equal to marginal costs; ibid. It is worth noting that in the Guidelines, the Commission did not *conclusively* define the 'competitive level' as the 'minimum average total cost'. It stated that the 'competitive level' would *usually* be the 'minimum average total cost'; European Commission 'Guidelines on Vertical Restraints' [2000] OJ C291/01, [126]. In the most recent 'Guidelines on Vertical Restraints', there is no suggestion for establishing what the 'competitive level' might be; see European Commission, 'Guidelines on Vertical Restraints' [2010] OJ C130/1.

[106] Motta and de Streel, ibid

[107] ibid.

[108] ibid 108.

ing to which monopoly is self-destructive; monopoly prices will eventually attract entry.[109] It is also clear that the argument's strength is based on whether entry to the market is sufficiently easy or possible at all.

Like the previously suggested test, after arguing that excessive pricing is a very dangerous instrument to use in competition law, this second test also holds that there might be 'exceptional circumstances' that might justify the use of the prohibition. Thus, the following conditions must be met simultaneously to justify an excessive pricing action (as an exploitative use): (i) presence of high and non-transitory barriers to entry (in practice, the firm should enjoy a monopoly/near monopoly or control an essential facility whose position may not be contestable); and (ii) intervention should be limited to monopoly/near monopoly that is due to current or past exclusive or special rights. As a result, interventions would only be justified if they have no effect on investment incentives, or in other words, if monopoly (or near monopoly) was due to current or past legal protection.[110] If the dominant position has been attained in a market where entry was unrestricted, then competition law should not intervene on this ground.[111] Moreover, two additional conditions related to the institutional issues may have to be fulfilled for the antitrust action to be justified. First, there should not be effective ways for the competition authority to eliminate the entry barriers. Secondly, there should be no sector-specific regulator.[112]

Röller has also proposed that competition law action in cases of excessive pricing should be limited to cases where certain conditions are cumulatively satisfied.[113] First, there have to be significant entry barriers and the market should be unlikely to self-correct. If there are no entry barriers or if the market would self-correct, there is no compelling need to intervene. Secondly, if there are structural remedies available – such as removing the entry barriers, opening markets, liberalising and so on – then the proper policy would be advocacy in favour of these structural remedies, rather than ex post intervention. Similarly, such intervention would be warranted only if there is no regulatory agency or if the regulator does not operate effectively. Finally, action on grounds of exploitation is justified subject to the existence of 'gap cases' or 'mistakes'.[114] Therefore,

[109] Easterbrook (n 100) 2. For an explanation of the Chicago School and the 'Post-Chicago' School which grew as a reaction to the Chicago School, see ch 1 this volume, section III.A. For the argument that excessive prices do not attract entry and the 'self-correcting' reasoning should not serve to justify lack of intervention, see A Ezrachi and D Gilo, 'Excessive Pricing, Entry, Assessment, and Investment: Lessons from the *Mittal* Litigation' (2010) 76 *Antitrust Law Journal* 873, 879.

[110] Motta and de Streel (n 1) 109.

[111] ibid 110.

[112] ibid 111.

[113] LH Röller, 'Exploitative Abuses' in CD Ehlermann and M Marquis (eds), *European Competition Annual 2007: A Reformed Approach to Article 82 EC* (Oxford, Hart Publishing, 2008) 530 *et seq.*

[114] The author defines 'gap cases' as to refer to the enforcement 'gap' resulting from the fact that Art 102 applies only to firms that are already dominant and anticompetitive conduct that *leads* to a dominant position is not caught as an exclusionary abuse; ibid, 529. 'Mistakes' occur when, for some reason, a competition authority may not have effectively prosecuted an exclusionary abuse; ibid 529.

dominance should be the *result* of exclusionary conduct. If not, any anticompetitive conduct can be addressed by taking action to remedy the *exclusionary* abuse.

Another study that has focused on how to establish *which* excessive prices are unfair by using the abovementioned principle of dual entitlement suggests that only where the terms of trade between the customer and the firm are not sufficiently close to those of a reference transaction, and where the firm's profit is sufficiently larger than that in the reference transaction, the 'unfairness' of the price can be established.[115] However, even then, the reason for the larger profit of the firm would determine whether the price is unfair: only those prices resulting from the lack of competition (as opposed to those resulting from demand and supply conditions) should be deemed unfair under Article 102. Therefore, this test also seeks to ensure that the price is deemed unfair only in conditions where there will not be adverse effects on welfare, including dynamic efficiency concerns, from such a finding.[116]

In short, the recent debates in the literature all seem to point in one common direction: 'unfair pricing' should not be abusive unless there are exceptional circumstances, since the potential effects of a wrongful sanctioning of 'unfair pricing' might perversely affect future conduct of undertakings. Thus, there is a potential tension between 'fairness' and 'efficiency', in particular in the sense of future investment and innovation incentives. One of the most important exceptional circumstances validating intervention appears to be the existence of high barriers to entry into the market where the allegedly abusive price is charged. Thus, section VI takes the debate further by seeking to demonstrate the broader problems with the prohibition of 'unfair pricing' under Article 102.

VI IS THE PROHIBITION OF 'UNFAIR PRICING' INHERENTLY PROBLEMATIC?

A Problems with Consistency, Certainty and Welfare

Although a benchmark has been determined below which a dominant undertaking would not price its products except for predatory purposes, a similar benchmark has naturally not been found for excessively high pricing and probably cannot be found.[117] It cannot be found since unlike 'average variable cost' which can be somehow calculated by looking at the costs incurred for production

[115] See Akman and Garrod (n 78) 415 *et seq*. For 'dual entitlement' and 'reference transaction', see above text after n 72.

[116] For more on this, see Akman and Garrod, ibid, 420 *et seq*.

[117] In the EU the benchmark for 'predatory pricing' is 'average variable cost' and a price below this is presumed to be predatory. Price above 'average variable cost' but below 'average total cost' can be predatory if there is intent to predate; Case C-62/86 *AKZO Chemie BV v Commission* [1991] ECR I-3359, [70] *et seq*.

by the undertaking, there is no similar upper limit which would imply on its own that the price in itself is necessarily abusive. This is because there is no rational or natural upper bound to how much a seller can charge for its product as long as there is a buyer willing to pay that price. This is a result of the fact that a seller usually sells its products to many buyers. The cost of the product could be approximately determined and it may not be rational for the undertaking to go below that except for an intention to eliminate a competitor (ie, for predatory purposes). Such an assessment is not possible for excessiveness since the undertaking cannot know – as long as there is no price regulation – when the price becomes 'unfair' due to the lack of an objective 'unfairness' definition based on an objective benchmark. In other words, there is no natural upper bound on the valuation of a buyer and there is no good way to measure valuation except inference from what the buyer accepts to pay.

Moreover, even if such a benchmark is determined, it will always be arbitrary because there is no such price which is inherently 'fair' or 'unfair'. As mentioned above,[118] when assessing the excessiveness of price, the Commission and the EU courts have usually concentrated on the relation between the cost and price of a good. This approach is, however, doomed to fail in terms of legal consistency and business certainty. It does not allow for a consistent way of determining when a price is excessive since no one knows *exactly how much* the price can be above cost before it becomes 'unfair'.

Establishing what would be a 'reasonable' price by adding an acceptable profit margin to the actual costs of producing products is fraught with difficulties.[119] One difficulty is that it is unclear what the relevant 'cost' of producing products is, namely whether one should look at the historic costs involved in establishing a production line for goods or the cost that it would take to establish one at today's prices.[120] Although economic theory suggests that, in a competitive equilibrium, the price should equal the marginal cost of production, the problem lies in calculating the 'marginal' cost where there are common costs.[121] As a result, another problem is that it is difficult to apportion the common costs of a multi-product firm between its different products in order to determine whether it is making an 'unreasonable' profit in one particular market.[122] Moreover, in reality, virtually no market qualifies as perfectly competitive.[123] As such, pricing at perfectly competitive levels would yield overall losses in the short term and under-investment in the long term.[124] Thus, it would entail welfare losses. In any case, identifying the competitive price level is rarely possible in practice.[125] Further, there is no

[118] See above, text around n 33.

[119] R Whish, *Competition Law* 6th edn (Oxford, OUP, 2009) 709.

[120] ibid.

[121] O'Donoghue and Padilla (n 22) 614.

[122] Whish (n 119) 709.

[123] O'Donoghue and Padilla (n 22) 608.

[124] ibid 605.

[125] S Bishop and M Walker, *The Economics of EC Competition Law: Concepts, Application and Measurement* 3rd edn (London, Sweet & Maxwell, 2010) 43; Jones and Sufrin (n 18) 532.

necessary relationship between price-cost margins and the intensity of competition.[126] The fact that an undertaking is earning a large profit may be attributable to its superior efficiency over its rivals, rather than to its market power.[127] In such a case, too low a profit may reduce ex ante investment and harm consumers in the long run.[128] Therefore, especially in dynamic industries, prices need to be set significantly above cost to fund initial capital outlays and compensate for associated risk.[129] High profits may therefore be necessary to provide a return on the costs of innovation or to act as a spur to further innovation in dynamic markets.[130] In these instances, sanctioning high prices or profits by way of prohibiting 'unfair prices' would bring about losses in efficiency and welfare.

Moreover, when a competition authority or a court makes a finding and decides that a price is 'unfair', it implicitly announces that there is a 'fair' price. This is because for the undertaking to stop abusing its position, and thus for the infringement decision to be operational, the undertaking must know by how much to lower its price. In other words, if there is a price which can be called 'unfair', there must also be a price which can be called 'fair'. Since the undertaking cannot charge different prices without justification under Article 102(c), complying with both subparagraphs of Article 102 will ultimately mean having to set *one* price that is 'fair'. Consequently, when the authority or court holds that the price imposed by the dominant undertaking is 'unfair', it can be assumed that it has also decided on a 'fair price'. Otherwise, the decision would not be effective, since it is likely that, as a result of not being informed what the 'fair price' actually is, the undertaking can keep on breaching the provision by not reducing its price sufficiently. What is sufficient in such a case can only be made clear by the decision itself. Current Commission practice and jurisprudence indeed show such an approach. For example, in *British Leyland*, the Commission found that any fee of more than £50.00 for national type approval certificates was excessive.[131] A similar approach can be found in the Commission's decision in *Deutsche Post*[132] and the

[126] WJ Kolasky, 'What is Competition? A Comparison of US and European Perspectives' [2004] (Spring/Summer) *The Antitrust Bulletin* 29, 33.

[127] Whish (n 119) 709.

[128] O'Donoghue and Padilla (n 22) 605; Röller (n 113) 3.

[129] O'Donoghue and Padilla (n 22) 608. See also FM Fisher, 'Monopolization versus Abuse of Dominant Position: An Economist's View' in B Hawk (ed), *International Antitrust Law & Policy: Fordham Corporate Law 2003* (New York, Juris Publishing, 2004) 160; RJ Van den Bergh and PD Camesasca, *European Competition Law and Economics A Comparative Perspective* (Antwerpen, Intersentia-Hart, 2001) 259.

[130] Jones and Sufrin (n 18) 533.

[131] Although this amount was not spelled out in the decision (84/379/EEC [1984] OJ L207/11), it is found in a letter from the Commission to British Leyland, and British Leyland reduced its prices accordingly. Despite the fact that British Leyland's fees ranged from £25–£150, the Commission seems to have chosen £50 as the 'fair' amount. See *British Leyland* (n 38) 221 and ibid, 190 referring to the letter.

[132] *Deutsche Post AG – Interception of Cross-Border Mail* (n 41) [166]. In this case, the Commission decided that the price charged by Deutsche Post for incoming cross-border mail exceeded the average economic value of that service by at least 25%. The Commission chose the domestic tariff applied by Deutsche Post as the benchmark.

terminated proceedings against Deutsche Telekom,[133] in which rather speculative assessments were made regarding the 'fair' level of prices.

Yet, neither the courts nor the Commission have come up with a certain mark-up that would make the price 'unfair'. If they do, they would be price regulating by using 'competition' law. Price regulation is, however, the antithesis of the free market.[134] Moreover, it is questionable whether competition agencies have the competence to engage in classical price-and-profit utility-style regulation, since as generalist agencies, they lack the right people, the skill sets and adequate industry expertise.[135] This argument *a fortiori* holds for courts since they are even further removed from the markets than competition and regulatory agencies.

Further, a problem with using competition law to assume direct control over prices is that regulators are ill-placed to determine what price a competitive market would set for particular products, and by fixing a price they may even further distort the competitive fabric of the market.[136] In addition, there would be a need to determine different mark-ups for different industries since every industry is unique. It would also be necessary to constantly monitor and adjust the supposedly 'fair' price in accordance with dynamics of the market. Such fixing of price by the authority has therefore rightly been criticised on three grounds: (i) it is unorthodox because it amounts to regulating prices altogether; (ii) it is hardly workable because of the difficulty in determining what a 'fair price' is; and (iii) it is futile because a dominant undertaking charging an excessive price attracts new competitors and is thus committing suicide at short notice.[137] As a result, excessive prices may be procompetitive rather than anticompetitive because high prices may act as a signal to attract new competitors onto the market.[138] Therefore, intervention to reduce the profits of an incumbent might not only be unnecessary, but

[133] The Commission initiated proceedings against Deutsche Telekom AG following a complaint against the conditions imposed on third parties for access to Deutsche Telekom's infrastructures. A price survey that the Commission had carried out showed that the prices were not cost-orientated and found the price level to be 100% higher than on comparable competitive markets. Stating that '[a]lthough the Commission is not and does not wish to act as a price regulator', the Commission invited Deutsche Telekom to adjust its tariffs to real economic conditions. In the end, the Commission accepted a reduction of fees by 38% for access to the local network and 78% for access to the long-distance network and the proceedings were terminated (Commission, 'XXVIIth Annual Report on Competition Policy' (1997) point 77). One cannot help but wonder why the Commission accepted a reduction of only 38% if the charges were 100% higher than on the comparable markets. This clearly shows how arbitrary the assessment actually is.

[134] Jones and Sufrin (n 18) 531.

[135] W Blumenthal, 'Discussant Comments on Exploitative Abuses under Article 82 EC' in CD Ehlermann and M Marquis (eds), *European Competition Annual 2007: A Reformed Approach to Article 82 EC* (Oxford, Hart Publishing, 2008) 578. See also E Paulis, 'Article 82 EC and Exploitative Conduct' in CD Ehlermann and M Marquis (eds), *European Competition Annual 2007: A Reformed Approach to Article 82 EC* (Oxford, Hart Publishing, 2008) 517 and Report by the Economic Advisory Group (EAGCP) for Competition Policy 'An Economic Approach to Article 82' (July 2005) available at: ec.europa.eu/dgs/competition/economist/eagcp_july_21_05.pdf 11.

[136] Whish (n 119) 20.

[137] L Gyselen, 'Abuse of Monopoly Power within the Meaning of Article 86 of the EEC Treaty: Recent Developments' in B Hawk (ed), *International Antitrust Law & Policy: Fordham Corporate Law 1989* (New York, Juris Publishing, 1990) 601.

[138] Jones and Sufrin (n 18) 531; Röller (n 113) 3. *Cf* Ezrachi and Gilo (n 109).

could actually prolong the monopoly situation by blocking efficient market signals to potential entrants.[139] As such, the EU law on excessive pricing arguably has profound implications since it assumes that unfairly high pricing can be identified by courts and implies that courts are better mechanisms than markets to correct unfairly high pricing.[140] In contrast to the EU position, scrutiny of excessive pricing has been rejected by US courts which have highlighted the inherent uncertainty of a 'reasonable price' test.[141] Moreover, the strong scepticism towards the efficacy of government intervention and the difficulty in achieving optimal regulation due to information asymmetries have led to the belief that, even when markets are not competitive, the costs of such regulation are likely to outweigh its benefits.[142]

The EU approach is not in conformity with business certainty either. Even if it is accepted that exploitative pricing should be controlled, there is the difficulty of translating this policy into a sufficiently realistic legal test.[143] A legal rule condemning exploitative pricing needs to be cast in sufficiently precise terms to enable an undertaking to know on which side of legality it stands.[144] The subjectivity, inconsistency and uncertainty inherent in the concept of 'unfair price' does not allow the undertaking to formulate a pricing policy *ex ante* which it definitely can be sure is immune from an allegation of 'unfair pricing' by competition authorities or trading partners. In other words, in most of the cases the undertaking cannot know whether it is in safe grounds or not until it comes before the court. This in itself seems to be a questionable restriction on the freedom of the undertaking under such circumstances.

The result of the Commission and the EU courts not putting down generally applicable rules with regard to excessive pricing is to leave the undertakings in the dark. The undertaking has not only to estimate its costs for each of its products

[139] A Fletcher and A Jardine, 'Towards an Appropriate Policy for Excessive Pricing' in CD Ehlermann and M Marquis (eds), *European Competition Annual 2007: A Reformed Approach to Article 82 EC* (Oxford, Hart Publishing, 2008) 534.

[140] EM Fox, 'Monopolization and Dominance in the United States and the European Community: Efficiency, Opportunity, and Fairness' (1986) 61 *Notre Dame Law Review* 981, 992.

[141] S Kon and S Turnbull, 'Pricing and the Dominant Firm: Implications of the Competition Commission Appeal Tribunal's Judgment in the Napp Case' (2003) 24(2) *European Competition Law Review* 70, 84; MS Gal, 'Monopoly Pricing as an Antitrust Offense in the US and the EC: Two Systems of Belief About Monopoly?' [2004] (Spring/Summer) *The Antitrust Bulletin* 343, 352 *et seq*. See, eg, *US v Addyston Pipe & Steel Co* 85 Fed 271, 284 (6th Cir 1898), *aff'd* 175 US 211, 20 S Ct 96, 44 L Ed 136 (1899) where the court held that the 'reasonable price' test forces judges to 'set sail on a sea of doubt'. Similarly, see *US v L Cohen Grocery Co* 255 US 81 (1921) where the Supreme Court struck down Section 4 of the Lever Act as void for vagueness since it prohibited 'excessive price' and 'unjust or unreasonable' charges and rates. More recently, Justice Scalia has opined that the charging of 'monopoly' prices is not only 'not unlawful', but is 'an important element of the free-market system'; *Verizon Communications Inc v Law Offices of Curtis v Trinko LLP* 540 US 398, 407, 124 S Ct 872 (2004).

[142] Gal (n 141) 355 *et seq*; DW Carlton, RH Gertner and AM Rosenfield, 'Communication among Competitors: Game Theory and Antitrust' (1997) 5 *George Mason Law Review* 423, 425.

[143] Whish (n 119) 710.

[144] ibid. See similarly P Jebsen and R Stevens, 'Assumptions, Goals and Dominant Undertakings: The Regulation of Competition under Article 86 of the European Union' (1996) 64 *Antitrust Law Journal* 443, 505.

(which, as ECJ itself has admitted, is a very difficult task)[145], but also to decide on a mark-up which is 'fair' in relation to the economic value of the product. Moreover, it has to be aware of the fact that if its prices are above that 'fair price', as a result of its dominance, the competition on the market will be (even more) impaired. Without complete information on the market and competitors, asking an undertaking to do this when pricing each of maybe hundreds of products – when even the EU authorities cannot do it or test it most of the time – is unlikely to be functional.[146]

From the undertaking's point of view, unless there is an inevitably arbitrary and rigid rule which states that, for example, 'any price above *p* is unfair'[147] or 'any mark-up above *x* per cent is unfair', it will not know what a 'fair price' is. For the same reason, the undertaking will also not know when a price becomes 'unfair', and therefore will not have a way to distinguish between the two. Moreover, once it is accepted by the competition authority or courts that there is actually a 'fair price' for a product, then it must also be answered why one is only concerned with 'unfairness' when the price is imposed by a dominant undertaking. If it is the price that is 'unfair', then there should be no reason to not condemn an unfair price when it is charged by a non-dominant undertaking. If it is merely the *exploitation* of some parties that is to be prevented, it should not matter whether they are exploited by one undertaking or another. If the reason for being concerned only with the dominant undertaking's prices is 'because competition on the market would bring the price to the "fair" level if there is not a market dominating undertaking',[148] does this not imply that every price of a dominant undertaking is 'unfair'? This would, in turn, mean that dominance itself is recriminated. Moreover, it is hard to see the justification for allowing those parties to be exploited until competition actually brings the price down to the presumably 'fair' price.

B Inherent Irrationality?

Apart from all the consistency, certainty and welfare problems mentioned so far, the current EU approach also has two implications which are against economic

[145] *United Brands* (n 17) [254].

[146] Indeed, if the firm does believe that it prices its products fairly, and announces this in an advertisement such as 'All our prices are fair!', there may be a chance of this being found 'misleading'. In the UK, eg, the UK Code of Non-Broadcast Advertising, Sales Promotion and Direct Marketing (CAP Code) stipulates in Art 1.1 that all marketing communications should be legal, decent, honest and truthful. Moreover, marketers must hold 'documentary evidence to prove claims that consumers are likely to regard as objective and that are capable of objective substantiation' (Art 3.7). One wonders whether it would be ever possible to objectively substantiate a claim such as that of all prices being fair.

[147] For such a rule, see UK OFT Statement on 'Calculating Default Charges in Credit Card Contracts' April 2006 (oft.gov.uk/shared_oft/reports/financial_products/oft842.pdf) where it is determined that credit card default charges set above £12.00 are unfair unless there are exceptional factors; ibid 1.8–1.9.

[148] See S Blount, 'Whoever said that Markets were Fair?' [2000] (July) *Negotiation Journal* 237, 246 for the argument that there is nothing inherently and particularly 'fair' about the market price.

thinking and suggest that the prohibition is inherently irrational. First, according to economic theory, the price of a product will be above the willingness to accept (WTA) of the seller and below the willingness to pay (WTP) of the buyer. This proposition rests on the assumptions that: the parties are rational; the parties have perfect information; contracts are complete, fully binding; and there is a well-defined set of property rights. Freedom of contract builds directly on this and, as a rule, upholds the contracts that parties voluntarily enter into under these circumstances. In this system, the seller will only agree to sell if the price is above his WTA and the buyer will only buy if the price is below her WTP. The actual price can be anywhere in between these outer limits. In other words, if a buyer has bought something, then it can be assumed that it was below her WTP, since if it was not, trade should not have occurred. The ECJ's definition of an 'excessive price' as that which has no relation to economic value has indeed been rightly criticised on the grounds that the price must have reflected its value *to the buyer* since otherwise there would have been no sale.[149] Thus, with the current definition of 'unfair price' the prohibition becomes nonsensical and irrational.

Moreover, as long as all of the above-mentioned assumptions hold in a certain case, intervention in a contract on the basis of one party having paid an 'unfair price', that is for 'inadequacy of price', violates freedom of contract. Further, there is no way of deciding with certainty whether the price was 'unfair' since the buyer has actually paid that price and accepted the product in return. Thus, a holding by a competition authority or court that someone paid an 'unfair' price in a transaction simply denies this and tells the buyer that she paid a 'wrong' price and can ask for redemption. In other words, it assumes irrationality on the part of the buyer. This is a threat to freedom of contract since it limits what the parties can do, even though both parties must have been better off contracting as otherwise they would not have agreed to transact. As long as the price is below the WTP of the buyer and above the WTA of the seller, any agreement reached is also 'Pareto efficient' because there is no other way of making one party better off without making another worse off since they have reached an agreement on the terms of their exchange.[150] This would mean that, under these circumstances, any price between WTA and WTP has to be accepted as both 'fair' and Pareto efficient. It is 'fair' at least because there is no way of proving that it is 'unfair'. It is efficient because the parties have freely agreed to the division of the surplus practising their freedom of contract and, therefore, it is not possible to make one of them better off without making the other worse off. If two parties concluded a bargain at a certain price, wealth would have been increased (setting aside problems of externalities) because each has something she would rather have than what she gave up.[151]

Likewise, a finding by an authority that the price paid was 'unfair' distorts the agreed division of surplus and causes the will of the authority to supersede the will

[149] Fox (n 140) 993.
[150] For the 'Pareto principle', see ch 1 this volume, text after fn 9.
[151] RM Dworkin, 'Is Wealth a Value?' (1980) 9 *Journal of Legal Studies* 191, 197.

of the parties. Such a finding naturally gives one party broad powers to renegotiate *after* agreeing to a price. In contracting with an apparently dominant undertaking in a long-term relationship, the other party can threaten to have recourse to competition law to have the (already agreed) price reduced and in the process claim the 'fairness' of whatever level she wishes. The dominant undertaking cannot defend its position by claiming that the price was 'fair', for example, by arguing that it has only marked up the product at a certain percentage, since there is no such certain percentage to its knowledge. Furthermore, if there is not a case of only one undertaking offering a product without any substitutes, then the buyer who faces a price above her WTP at one undertaking should search the market to see if there is a price below her WTP. If there is no price on the market below her WTP, then she does not buy the product, an inevitable result of having a supply and demand curve. Buyers with a WTP below the price where the supply meets demand are left out of the market. In a market where there is not 'perfect competition', the only way to sell to everyone with a WTP below the equilibrium price but above the WTA of the seller is price discrimination, which is not allowed under competition law.[152] If in every case that a buyer is left out of the market because her WTP is not as high as the equilibrium price the price is called 'unfair', there would be no other way than discriminating between buyers for a firm to price its product in a fairer manner. Therefore, according to economic theory, given the assumptions, there can be no rational allegation of the price being 'unfair' as long as the buyer has actually paid that price.

Trebilcock's arguments on the relation between contract and competition law are illuminating here. He argues that the explanation for competition laws from an economic perspective conventionally focuses not on the *distributive* effects, but on the *allocative* effects of market power and their impact on consumer welfare in terms of consumers who have been *priced out* of the market through reductions in output.[153] Accordingly, these concerns do not implicate the welfare of immediate contracting parties who *remain in* the market. The welfare problem of monopolies is that the monopoly produces less than the efficient quantity of output, leaving consumers who value the good above the cost but less than the monopoly price out of the market.[154] Thus, monopolies are condemned as they leave some consumers priced out of the market who would not have been priced out if there was effective competition.

This explains one of the reasons why Article 102's prohibition of 'unfair pricing' cannot work properly. The provision allows intervention in contracts which

[152] In 'perfect competition', the price is given by the marginal cost of production which corresponds to the level of output which the market clears; O'Donoghue and Padilla (n 22) 605. For price discrimination, see ch 6 this volume.

[153] MJ Trebilcock, *The Limits of Freedom of Contract* (Cambridge, MA, Harvard University Press, 1997) 92. This holds true, except arguably if one views the consumer surplus appropriated from the ones that remain in the market as a proxy for socially wasteful rent-seeking investments by monopolists; ibid.

[154] NG Mankiw, *Principles of Economics* (Orlando, Dryden Press Harcourt Brace College Publishers, 1998) 318.

have already been entered into, giving the Commission and courts the ability to condemn ex post prices found in those contracts. In other words, it scrutinises the transactions with customers who remain in the market and have been able to buy the product – that is, customers who have *not* been priced out of the market. The current approach is thus focused on the wrong actors since they are not the immediate 'victims' of market power that competition law aims to protect in the first place (if the objective is the enhancement of 'consumer welfare' as advocated by the EU authorities).[155] This misplacement of focus is why the prohibition of 'unfair pricing' in the current approach is not rational and cannot function successfully. It disregards freedom of contract and the economic rule that trade occurs when price is below WTP of the buyer and above WTA of the seller. Moreover, it does not concern itself with the possible actual victims of an 'unfair' price who will have been excluded from the market due to the price. As a result, it does not serve the purposes of competition law either. This particular point will be returned to in section VII.

Nonetheless, by proving the assumptions mentioned above[156] to be false, one could argue for intervention into prices already agreed to without implying irrationality of the rule. In other words, if it can be proven that: there was not perfect rationality or information; or the contract is not complete or fully binding; or the property rights are not properly defined, then one can imagine a case where someone has paid a price that deserves intervention. This would usually mean that one party has entered into a contract which makes her worse off compared with her situation *ex ante*, but she nevertheless entered into such a contract since the assumptions did not hold.

For example, if the buyer is told by the seller that the product she is about to buy is brand new, although it is second-hand, the buyer would probably pay a price above her WTP for a second-hand product. In such a case trade occurs and one party pays a price above her genuine WTP due to misleading information. Another example would be where the parties do not have to fulfil their contractual duties simultaneously, that is when the transaction is not a simple quid pro quo. If the buyer enters into a contract for a custom-made order and the customer is supposed to pay once the order is completed, there can be situations in which either party can try to renegotiate the price, exploiting the situation of the

[155] See, eg, Commission, 'Guidelines on the Application of Article 81(3) of the Treaty' [2004] OJ C101/97, [13]; N Kroes, 'Preliminary Thoughts on Policy Review of Article 82' speech at the Fordham Corporate Law Institute (New York, 23 September 2005) 3; 'DG Competition Discussion Paper on the Application of Article 82 of the Treaty to Exclusionary Abuses' (Brussels, December 2005) available at: ec.europa.eu/comm/competition/antitrust/art82/discpaper2005.pdf [4], [54], [55], [88]. See also Joined Cases T-231/01 and T-214/01 *Österreichische Postsparkasse AG and Bank für Arbeit und Wirtschaft AG v Commission* [2006] ECR II-1601, [115]; Case T-168/01 *GlaxoSmithKline Services Unlimited v Commission* [2006] ECR II-2969, [171]. However, this is by no means settled on as *the* objective of EU competition rules; see, eg, the ECJ's statement in Case C-501/06 *GlaxoSmithKline Services Unlimited v Commission* [2009] ECR I-9291, [63] where the ECJ has held that the aim of EU competition rules is 'to protect not only the interests of competitors or of consumers, but also the structure of the market and, in so doing, competition as such'.

[156] See above, text before n 149.

other. In general, in a long-term contractual relationship where the contractual duties are fulfilled over time and/or not simultaneously, it is possible to imagine one party trying to change the price by threatening to hold up the other. Similarly, where one party is locked in to such a contract, if this lock-in effect has not been contracted out, the other party may try to exploit this by demanding a change in the price. However, in all these cases, although there is an extraction of surplus from one party by the other which the former would not have agreed to ex ante, these are all contractual malfunctions. The price is usually the most obvious way this malfunctioning would occur, but it is not the price which is 'unfair'. What can be argued to be 'unfair' is more the fact that one party can make the other one pay that price. In other words, it is the *procedure* that is unfair, as opposed to the *substance* of the contract. Therefore, such situations should be dealt with under contract law's rules on validity, enforcement or information disclosure, not under competition law rules. As seen in chapter four, there are indeed contractual doctrines such as 'economic duress' and 'undue influence' which are capable of dealing with such situations.

To sum up, the current approach towards 'unfair pricing' disregards freedom of contract as well as the principle that trade occurs only when the price is between WTA and WTP as long as the underlying assumptions hold. When the assumptions do not hold, then contract law is better equipped than competition law to deal with such failures.

The second implication of the Commission's and the EU courts' approach is that even when the buyer's perception of 'fairness' gets involved in economics, the findings of behavioural economics above[157] demonstrate that the 'fair price' is very closely related to the buyer's valuation of that product. In other words, the 'fair price' is a function of the buyer's valuation. Since every buyer can have a different valuation for the same product, this implies that there will be a different 'fair price' for each and every one of these different buyers. Consequently, there is no single 'fair price' for a single product. In other words, if the insights from economics examined above are included in the 'other ways' (which 'the economic theorists have not failed to think up')[158] of selecting the rules for determining whether the price is 'unfair', it would mean that the only approach that guarantees 'fairness' to all buyers is one which requires price discrimination, a practice which is prohibited in subparagraphs (c) of Articles 101 and 102. This would imply that there is a further problem with the rationality of Article 102 in general. However, this obviously depends on whether or not one accepts the findings of behavioural economics on the issue.

To summarise, one can argue that there is no price which is inherently and by its nature 'fair' or 'unfair'. When there are competition authorities and courts of 27 different judicial systems assessing whether a certain price is 'unfair', it would be of no surprise if each of them reached a different conclusion in almost identical

[157] See above, text around n 87.
[158] *United Brands* (n 17) [253].

cases at almost identical times. Moreover, sanctioning 'unfair pricing' is very likely to endanger business certainty, result in price regulation, violate freedom of contract, discourage investment/innovation and distort the natural working of the markets to name a few of the potential problems. Therefore, there are good reasons to scrap 'unfair pricing' as a stand-alone abuse from Article 102 since it is not capable of being properly enforced as it is currently defined.[159] This would not exclude price regulation *ex ante*, but would exclude price regulation ex post by use of Article 102. Given that a Treaty amendment is highly unlikely, if there is a wish to sanction the prices of dominant undertakings for public or private enforcement purposes – although the Commission does not want to 'normally' control or condemn the level of prices as such[160] – then it should be done in a manner which has consistency and enough rigidity so that not everyone can claim and prove 'abuse' – especially after having paid a price – on the grounds that the price was 'unfair'. Such a test of 'unfair pricing' is proposed in the section which follows.

VII A NEW TEST

Having established a range of problems that result from the prohibition of unfair prices in the previous two sections, it has been noted that there are good reasons to scrap this prohibition as a stand-alone abuse. Nonetheless, given that such an amendment is highly unlikely, this section proposes a new test which would render the prohibition operational in limited circumstances.

First, it must be borne in mind that prices falling in between WTA and WTP should be assumed 'fair' – at least for competition law purposes – for the above-mentioned[161] reasons. This leaves only prices below WTA and above WTP prone to scrutiny. Price below WTA of the dominant undertaking is tackled with the 'predatory pricing' test. Exploitatively high prices can occur only at levels above WTP of the customer of the dominant undertaking. In line with the scope of this chapter, this section focuses on exploitatively high selling prices.

Having prices above WTP appears counterintuitive at first sight since it requires the buyer to pay a price above her WTP, even though the rule is that trade does not occur if price is above the buyer's WTP. However, this is where dominance enters the scene: dominance of the seller has to have caused a party to pay a price above her WTP. The question then becomes how to determine that the buyer paid a price above her WTP after she has actually paid that price. Since Article 102

[159] This is also in conformity with the recommendations of the EAGCP Report (n 135) 10–11.

[160] See European Commission, 'XXIVth Annual Report on Competition Policy' (1994) [207] and n 162 below. See also *HOV SVZ/MCN* (Case IV/33941) Commission Decision 94/210/EEC [1994] OJ L104/34, [158]–[59] according to which 'it is not part of the Commission's duties to assess as such the level of prices charged by an undertaking or to decide which criteria should govern the setting of such prices'.

[161] See above, section VI.B.

is an ex post test, this is extremely difficult. That is why the application of Article 102 on alleged 'unfairness' of a price should be extremely difficult as well. In this context, a distinction has to be made between business-to-consumer transactions and business-to-business transactions.

A Business-to-Consumer Transactions

A distinction has to be made between business-to-consumer and business-to-business transactions since this study proposes that EU competition law should be silent about the mere 'unfairness' of the price found in business-to-consumer transactions for the following reasons.[162] The 'unfairness' of consumer contract terms is regulated in the EU under a separate Directive and this Directive explicitly leaves out the price of the contract.[163] The price of a contract is not examined with regard to its 'unfairness' in EU consumer law, whose sole purpose is indeed the effective protection of consumers. This is a natural result of the impossibility of assessing the 'fairness' of price and the lack of a meaningful benchmark, especially once the contract has been concluded. Nonetheless, if the price the consumer agrees to pay is still to be scrutinised in and of itself, then this should be done under consumer protection laws or by ex ante price regulation, not under competition law. Bearing in mind that assessing the 'unfairness' of the price in contracts is generally not accepted in the contract laws of most EU Member States,[164] competition authorities and courts should not be asked to do this either. At first glance, this argument may be thought to be against a 'consumer welfare standard', but it is not.

To begin with, it is not unequivocal whether Article 102 as a policy tool is a provision which aims to enhance 'welfare'.[165] Moreover, even if it is accepted that

[162] This is in line with the Commission declaration that '[t]he existence of a dominant position is not itself against the rules of competition. Consumers can suffer from a dominant company exploiting this position, the most likely way being through prices higher than would be found if the market were subject to effective competition. However, the Commission in its decision-making practice does not normally control or condemn the high level of prices as such. Rather it examines the behaviour of the dominant company designed to preserve its dominance, usually directed against competitors or new entrants who would normally bring about effective competition and the price level associated with it'; European Commission, 'XXIVth Annual Report on Competition Policy' (1994) [207].

[163] Council Directive 93/13/EEC on Unfair Terms in Consumer Contracts [1993] OJ L95/29 Article 4(2).

[164] O Lando and H Beale (eds), *Principles of European Contract Law Parts I and II* (The Hague, Kluwer Law International, 2000) 265.

[165] The 'Discussion Paper' (n 155) appears to favour a consumer welfare standard by stating that '[w]ith regard to exclusionary abuses the objective of Article 102 is the protection of competition on the market as a means of enhancing consumer welfare and of ensuring an efficient allocation of resources'; ibid [4]. The EAGCP Report (n 135) more explicitly adopts this view by asserting that '[a]n economic approach to Article 102 focuses on improved consumer welfare'; ibid 2. However, the 'Guidance on the Commission's Enforcement Priorities in Applying Article 82 of the EC Treaty to Abusive Exclusionary Conduct by Dominant Undertakings' [2009] OJ C45/7 is not so clear in expressing the objective as 'consumer welfare' and, more importantly, the ECJ's judgment in *GlaxoSmithKline* is quite clear in adopting multiple objectives (on the latter, see n 155). On the Guidance, see P Akman,

its purpose is to enhance 'consumer welfare', then this would mean that the more surplus given to the consumer, the better. Thus, the 'fairest' transaction would be the one in which the consumer gets to keep the whole surplus from trade. However, a 'fairness' theory that defines 'fairness' as one party reaping the whole gain from the transaction is very disputable.[166] In other words, 'fairness' does not fit well even with a consumer welfare standard; such a standard and the scrutiny of prices for this purpose need to be founded on other grounds. These grounds can be the high entry barriers to the market and the exclusion of competitors. Thus, in line with the general thesis of this book, the 'unfairness' of the price in business-to-consumer transactions is an example where 'exploitation' can be meaningfully scrutinised only when there is harm to competition as well. Admittedly, one has to have a benchmark for when business-to-consumer prices are high enough to be 'exploitative' and the test suggested below for business-to-business transactions – although in theory applicable – would not be helpful in this regard in practice. As mentioned above, this author has proposed a benchmark for business-to-consumer transactions elsewhere and therefore this will not be elaborated on further here.[167] The point made here is that the mere 'unfairness' of prices in business-to-consumer transactions on its own is not a competition law issue. What can be a competition law issue is the unfairness of price that leads to consumers not being able to make a purchase at all, that is the consumers being excluded from the market. This study suggests that establishing which consumers could have made a purchase but did not because the price was 'unfair' is an insurmountable task, not least due to the administrability and legal certainty implications it would have.[168] Thus, the new test of this study is limited to business-to-business transactions, which allow for establishing the potential exclusion issue with more certainty.

B Business-to-Business Transactions

Similar to business-to-consumer transactions, mere 'unfairness' of a price in business-to-business transactions should not be deemed as a competition law issue either. However, for these transactions, it is at least conceptually possible to distinguish those prices which might harm competition and those which might not: in business-to-business transactions, the test should be whether transacting at that certain price makes *business sense* for the party allegedly faced with an

'The European Commission's Guidance on Article 102 TFEU: From *Inferno* to *Paradiso*?' (2010) 73(4) *Modern Law Review* 605.

[166] See n 84 for the argument by Fehr and Schmidt that it is 'unfair' by virtually all definitions of fairness for one party to reap the whole surplus.

[167] See Akman and Garrod (n 78) and text around n 115 above.

[168] It is unlikely that an approach which has to establish the identity of consumers who would have made a purchase but did not with sufficient certainty will be administrable by a competition authority or a private claimant since the whole exercise would be speculative.

'unfair' price.[169] This provides a way of finding out whether the buyer paid a price above its WTP ex ante. As mentioned above, the current approach when assessing whether there has been abuse of a dominant position assesses whether a price has been charged 'that is excessive because it has no reasonable relation to the economic value of the product'.[170] To determine this, one first looks at the amount of profit margin and, if this is excessive, one then decides whether a price has been imposed which is either 'unfair' in itself or when compared with competing products.[171]

The new test offered here would work in the following way: when estimating whether there is, or is not, a reasonable relation between the price and the economic value of the product, instead of or in addition to comparing the cost and the price (an inquiry which only concentrates on the seller but does not question why the buyer agreed to that price), one would look at whether transacting at that price makes business sense for the buyer *ex ante*. Analysing it *ex ante* prevents contracting parties who realise after entering into the transaction that they actually have not made as good a deal as they expected from releasing themselves of the contractual duties, as long as this misjudgement cannot be attributed to the act(s) of the other party.

'Economic value' should be understood as the economic value of that product in that specific transaction for that specific buyer. This implies that a price then could be deemed 'unfair' only for a certain party in a certain transaction. This is a conclusion in conformity with the findings of behavioural economics illustrated above.[172] However, unlike some of those findings, the 'fairness' in this test is not a perception of one of the parties to the transaction which is bound to be subjective, but that of the decision maker which is an objective entity, in the sense that it is outside the relationship. As the adoption of this test would also answer the question whether a price has been imposed that is 'unfair in itself or in comparison with others', it in effect reduces the current twofold *United Brands* test to a single one when it is done instead of comparing the price and cost. It should be noted here that eliminating the price-cost assessment from the test would have the implication that a dominant undertaking might be found to abuse its position even when it charges a price at cost. Although such an approach might legally be possible within the context of Article 102 (since Article 102 does not mention anything other than the 'unfairness' of the price and since inefficiency of a dominant undertaking which would lead to high costs can also breach Article 102),[173] it would be a more interventionist approach than the alternative. Therefore, any policy that seeks to limit intervention can use the test proposed here as an addition to the price-cost comparison established in *United Brands*.

169 Although the test is expressed within the context of a transaction here, it should similarly be applicable to constructive refusal to deal cases where the dominant undertaking allegedly uses the price to refuse to deal with a potential customer.

170 *United Brands* (n 17) [250].

171 ibid [251], [252].

172 See above, section IV.

173 See ch 8 this volume, section V, for a discussion of these cases.

The proposed test allows the court to better differentiate between competitive and abusive use of bargaining power. Looking at a practice from only the dominant undertaking's point of view does not let the authority see clearly whether and how the power has been used. The way the transaction actually affects the trading party's business is one way of examining whether the position of the firm has been used for some type of 'abuse'. Some tendency towards such an approach can be seen in the Commission decision regarding the Swedish port of Helsingborg.[174] There it was alleged that the port operator had imposed excessive (and discriminatory) port charges to the ferry operators. Faced with the allegation of the complainant that the port charges do not reflect the actual costs borne by the operator (plus a reasonable profit) for the provision of the services, the Commission decided – after pointing out that the burden of proof is on itself – that while assessing the economic value of a product, 'non-cost related factors, especially as regards the demand-side aspects of the product/service concerned' should also be taken into account.[175] The cost-plus approach (allowing the firm to cover its costs plus a reasonable profit margin which is a predetermined percentage of costs) takes into account only the conditions of supply of the product.[176] Strikingly, the Commission argued that '[t]he demand-side is relevant mainly because customers are notably willing to pay more for something specific attached to the product/service that they consider valuable'.[177] Although this specific feature does not necessarily imply higher costs for the provider, nonetheless it is valuable for the customer and the provider, and thus increases the economic value of the product.[178] Therefore, economic value must be determined with regard to the particular circumstances of the case and take into account also non-cost related factors such as the demand for the product.[179] Demand side features in this sense means 'the valuation by the customers and consumers of the product/service'.[180] The

[174] *Scandlines* (n 24).
[175] ibid [226].
[176] ibid.
[177] ibid [227].
[178] ibid.
[179] ibid [232]. According to the Commission, the non-cost related factor in the case was the perfect location of the port which provided the shortest distance between Sweden and Denmark allowing the ferry-operators to operate a frequent short distance service; ibid [234].
[180] ibid [241]. This decision is particularly important because it shows a change of understanding in that the Commission does not argue that 'economic value' means only 'cost' which seems to have been the common practice of it and the courts so far. In the decision, the Commission refers to its letter holding the preliminary conclusion in the case. There the Commission treats 'opportunity costs' and 'sunk costs' as separate issues ('additional costs') other than 'costs actually incurred'; ibid [208]–[10]. This implies that 'costs actually incurred', ie, 'production costs', do not necessarily include the sunk costs and the opportunity costs of the firm. Unfortunately, it is stated at [212] that the Commission has substantially amended its assessment and no more explicit reference to 'opportunity costs' is made later on in the new assessment. Nonetheless, the decision makes it clear that the concepts generally used in Commission decisions and jurisprudence (ie, 'costs incurred' and 'production costs'), do not mean 'cost' in the economic sense, but rather in the accounting sense, since they do not include opportunity costs. The Commission does state that 'the cost of capital' (an opportunity cost) is not a cost counted for in the financial reports and therefore the costs allocation made by the Commission for the purposes of the decision, but should nevertheless be taken into account; ibid [224]. See *British Leyland* (n 38) [28]–[30] where the ECJ explicitly looks at the factors determining the cost of the service to find

Commission followed a similar line of thought when it rejected the complaint of Euromax which had alleged that IMAX was charging excessive rental fees for its projection systems to movie theatres.[181] According to the Commission, the value of the IMAX brand was a major feature of the system and had significant value to the theatre owner; thus, it had to be included in the assessment of the 'reasonable' fee.[182]

In the same vein, following *Scandlines*, the UK Court of Appeal in *Attheraces* held that the 'cost-plus' approach was only a first step in analysing 'economic value' and was not definitive.[183] In that case, Attheraces (ATR) – a supplier of websites, television channels and other audio-visual media relating to British racing used by bookmakers and punters – had alleged that the British Horseracing Board (BHB) had abused its dominant position on the market for the supply of pre-race data by charging excessively high 'unfair' prices. The Court of Appeal reversed the judgment of the trial judge which had found abuse of a dominant position since the prices charged by BHB were significantly in excess of the 'economic value' of BHB's pre-race data and not otherwise justified.[184] The 'economic value' of the data was to be measured by the cost to BHB of producing the data together with a reasonable return on that cost.[185] Disagreeing with the trial judge, the Court of Appeal held that exceeding cost-plus was a 'necessary, but in no way a sufficient, test of abuse of a dominant position' and the value of the pre-race data to ATR (ie, the customer) had to be taken into account in determining the 'economic value' of the pre-race data.[186] Moreover, in alignment with the new test suggested here, the Court of Appeal stated that the facts did not suggest that anybody downstream was going to go out of business as a result of the alleged abuse (ie, it made business sense); the case was about who was going to 'get their hands

that the price is disproportionate to the 'economic value'. In *General Motors* (n 29) the ECJ states that abuse may be found in the 'imposition of a price which is excessive in relation to the economic value of the service' and then decides that since General Motors brought its rates into line with the 'real economic cost' of the operation after the complaints, there is no abuse; ibid 12, 22. In *Deutsche Post AG – Interception of Cross-Border Mail* (n 41) the Commission found the prices to be '25% above the estimated average cost and the estimated economic value for that service' and hence, abusive; [162] (The Commission implies at [160] that 'average cost' includes 'a reasonable profit margin'). In the *Deutsche Post* decision 'average cost' is used interchangeably with 'economic value' at [162], [163]–[64], [166]. Although it is not clear from the judgment, this must also be why the ECJ in *United Brands* (n 17) compared the cost and the price of the product to see whether the price was excessive in relation to its 'economic value'; [250]–[51]. Contrarily, in *CICCE* (n 22), the ECJ upheld the Commission decision in which the Commission had found that 'abuse depended on the relationship between the cost and the economic value of the service provided' and that in the case of film broadcasting rights it was impossible to determine a yardstick valid for all films 'in view of the variety of potential criteria for assessing the value of films'; ibid [22]. Motta and de Streel also seem to agree that the 'economic value' of a product is the normal competitive level which is the minimum average cost of the firm; Motta and de Streel (n 1) 94.

[181] *Euromax v IMAX* (Case COMP/C-2/37.761) Commission Decision 25 March 2004 (unreported).

[182] ibid 8, 9, 10.

[183] *Attheraces Ltd v The British Horseracing Board Ltd* [2007] EWCA Civ 38, [207], [213].

[184] ibid [40].

[185] ibid.

[186] ibid [209], [218].

on ATR's revenues from overseas bookmakers'.[187] Although this could be thought to be 'unfair', this could not alone make it an abuse of BHB's dominant position since the principal object of Article 102 was the protection of consumers (in this case punters) and there was not sufficient evidence that competition in the market was being distorted by the demands made by BHB upon ATR.[188]

More recently, the ECJ seems to have possibly endorsed the assessment of the Commission in *Scandlines*: in a preliminary ruling the ECJ decided that the royalties paid to a collection society for the use of copyright protected musical works must be analysed with respect to the 'value of that use in the trade', and hence it may be adopting the more appropriate understanding of 'economic value' as suggested in *Scandlines*.[189] This holding of the ECJ, as well as the assessments of the Commission and the UK Court of Appeal (in *Scandlines* and *Attheraces* respectively) are in line with the test proposed here in that they examine the business of the buyer to decide what the 'economic value' is for that buyer.[190]

C The Operation of the New Test

The first step in the proposed test would be for the party which alleges the 'unfairness' of the price to prove that transacting at that price did not make any 'business sense' and/or could not be explained by any economic rationale, but it was still accepted. If transacting at that price makes any business sense for that buyer when the court/authority looks at the circumstances of that party's business, then no matter how excessive the profit margin of the dominant undertaking appears to be, the price should be presumed 'fair'. This is because in such a situation, the presumption that a buyer pays a price only below her WTP is reinforced by the fact that the price actually allows the buyer to carry on its business and thus makes business sense. In other words, if transacting at that price makes economic sense for the buyer, the price must have been below the buyer's WTP and thus 'fair'.

In this sense, the test proposed here is in conformity with the EU test for 'predatory pricing' as well. The latter looks at whether selling at such a low price has any economic rationale for the predator other than eliminating a competitor.

[187] ibid [214].

[188] ibid [215]. The Court approvingly also referred to *BHB Enterprises plc v Victor Chandler (International Limited)* [2005] EWHC 1074 (Ch), [56] at which the High Court stated that, in a case where unfair pricing is alleged, assessment of the *value* of the asset to both the seller and the buyer *must* be a crucial part of assessment (as opposed to simply the relation between price and *cost*). Similarly, see the Competition Appeal Tribunal judgment in *Albion Water* where it was held that in certain cases 'economic value' may exceed the cost of supply when there are additional benefits not reflected in the cost of supply; *Albion Water Ltd and Albion Water Group Ltd v Water Services Regulation Authority* Case No 1046/2/4/04 [2008] CAT 31, [7].

[189] See Case C-52/07 *Kanal 5 Ltd and TV4 AB v STIM* [2008] ECR I-9275, [36].

[190] *cf* M Furse, 'Excessive Prices, Unfair Prices and Economic Value: The Law of Excessive Pricing under Article 82 EC and the Chapter II Prohibition' (2008) 4(1) *European Competition Journal* 59, 82 arguing that the *problem* of defining 'economic value' by reference in part to demand-side factors is insurmountable.

Thus, predation implies sales at prices below WTA of the seller. The suggested test looks at the same issue from the buyer's perspective for an allegedly exploitative price. Thus, it assesses whether the buyer paid a price above its WTP. As such, the test examines whether transacting at that price makes any business sense for the buyer. If the price paid does not make any business sense, then the assessment moves on to the second step of the test.

In the second step, for the price to be found abusive, it has to be established that the price would not have made sense for an efficient and/or prudent business either. Thus, it has to be determined that the lack of business sense was not due to that certain buyer's inefficiency or lack of business judgement or similar reasons. In this way, inefficient or unsuccessful firms would be prevented from using the price of the transaction as a way of covering their losses later on. This is in conformity with the decision in *NALOO* where the Commission, in assessing the 'fairness' of the royalties, considered whether the price enabled efficient companies to make a profit.[191] However, the test here does not suggest the use of an efficient company as a benchmark in the first step since if it cannot be proved that the buyer that has already paid a price agreed to pay a price which did not make any business sense, then the price will be presumed 'fair'. Therefore, there will be no need to look at other actual or hypothetical efficient companies.

In case it is not established that the price would make business sense for an efficient company and it is proven that it did not make business sense for the actual buyer, then the price may be presumed 'unfair'. This would mean that something has gone wrong with the transaction so that the buyer has paid a price above the economic value of that product in that transaction. 'Economic value' in this sense is not the cost of product for the dominant undertaking, but the subjective value that such a product would have for the buyer in such a transaction. In other words, the court/authority has to take into account that, although the same product may not have been valued at a certain level by the same buyer in a relationship with another seller, there may have been legitimate business reasons to value it at that particular level in the relationship with this seller. In effect, it means that the WTP for the same product is different in different relationships. This may, for example, be due to the buyer making use of the relatively better terms in the contract other than the price or just the buyer's incentive to keep trading with the seller. The test would therefore require the price to be above even this possibly 'shifted' WTP. It would imply that there is a need for a situation akin to 'economic duress'. An efficient and prudent trader has made such a deal that there is no other way to explain why it would have accepted it, but for the abuse of power by the dominant firm.[192]

[191] Case C-172/01 *National Association of Licensed Opencast Operators (NALOO) v Commission* [2001] ECR II-515, [26] quoting Commission decision of 23 May 1991, [72].

[192] *cf* Case 6/72 *Europemballage Corp and Continental Can Co Inc v Commission* [1973] ECR 215, [27] where the ECJ held that there is no need for a causal link between dominance and abuse. See, eg, the decision of the Competition Tribunal of South Africa Case 13/CR/FEB04 (27 March 2007) *Harmony Gold Mining Company Ltd v Mittal Steel South Africa Ltd* [2007] ZACT 21, [151] in which case it was held that 'where the price appears to have no explanation other than the pure exercise of monopoly power', the price may be held to be not reasonable in relation to the economic value of the

Thus, in line with the thesis of this study on interpreting 'exploitation', this would imply that the dominant firm received advantages to the disadvantage of its trading partner that would not be possible but for its dominance. A position of mere dominance, especially under the EU standards, would hardly be enough for this to hold: the seller should be in a position of super-dominance, that is dominance reaching a monopoly, and/or should be providing essential facilities/inputs without which the buyer cannot conduct business.[193]

To establish that – although the buyer agreed to the price – the transaction does not make any business sense, it should be demonstrated that the buyer is not making any profits, but covering average variable costs before exiting the industry in the long run. Moreover, this would also imply that it has to be demonstrated that if the price comes down the buyer can expect to stay in business. In other words, paying the price would have to mean the ultimate elimination of that buyer from the market in the long run. Claiming that the price is 'unfair' just because the buyer cannot maximise its profits should not be enough to establish this. Therefore, imposing an 'unfair' price could be meaningfully sanctioned in competition law only if it has exclusionary potential – that is the potential exclusion of an efficient undertaking.[194] This potential for exclusion would indeed be what renders the price 'anticompetitive' and thus 'unfair'. Unlike most other exclusion cases, here the issue would be the exclusion of an undertaking that is in a vertical relationship with the dominant undertaking (ie, a customer of the dominant undertaking).

Trebilcock's distinction of situational and structural monopolies with regard to coercion in contract law is also worth discussing here. Trebilcock argues that, in a situational monopoly, it is the relatively fortuitous circumstances surrounding the interaction between the particular parties to the exchange that create the monopoly power that one of them opportunistically exploits in return for a quid pro quo that has no or negative social value or in respect of which the other party is induced to pay vastly more than the competitive or normal value of the

product. However, on appeal, this decision of the Tribunal has been overturned by the Competition Appeal Court for being purely structural and not examining the actual *level* of prices, profitability, etc; see Case No 70/CAC/Apr07. It should also be noted that s 8(a) of the South African Competition Act prohibits not 'unfair prices' but *excessive* prices as an abuse of a dominant position. For a discussion of the *Harmony* case, see C Calcagno and M Walker, 'Excessive Pricing: Towards Clarity and Economic Coherence' (2010) 6(4) *Journal of Competition Law & Economics* 891.

[193] See, eg, Tribunal, *Harmony* (n 192) [84], [121] where mere dominance was not deemed enough and 'super-dominance' was required for the existence of excessive pricing. Super-dominance was a necessary, but not sufficient condition; ibid [131]. However, as mentioned above at n 192, the *pure* structural approach has not been endorsed by the Competition Appeal Court. The proposal in this chapter is *not* a purely structural test.

[194] This is in conformity with the previous Commissioner Kroes's modernisation proposal for pricing abuses to be based on the premise that only the exclusion of equally efficient competitors be abusive; Kroes (n 155) 5. Similarly, it is in line with the 'Guidance' (n 165) [23] *et seq* which has adopted the 'as efficient competitor' test for price-based conduct. *Cf* J Kallaugher, 'Recent Developments under Article 82' Speech at IBC Advanced EC Competition Law Conference (Brussels, 7 November 2003) available at: www.lw.com/upload/pubContent/_pdf/pub867_1.pdf 19. For the 'as efficient competitor' test, see ch 7 this volume, section II.B.

services.[195] In situational monopolies, the reference point of one party is violated; the most obvious being the monopolist violating its own reference price in opportunistically taking advantage of the other.[196]

In contrast, in the case of structural monopolies, the market power is non-transitory, obtains against all parties in the market and is exogenous to and precedes the particular circumstances of the interaction between parties to a given exchange, 'which is arguably the appropriate focus of a theory of coercion in contract law where voluntariness is in issue'.[197] Unlike situational monopolies, there is competition on the demand side here and some rationing mechanism is necessary to allocate the resource among competing customers. Therefore, allocating the products on the basis of the price demanded, which reflects prior restrictions on output, will result in a misallocation of resources. This misallocation impacts, however, principally on the welfare of customers who are priced out of the market, rather than on those who remain in it. For the customers that remain in the market, the distributional implications are not systematic, but rather depend on the characteristics of customers and of suppliers, producers (shareholders) or workers.[198]

His conclusion is that such structural monopolies should be dealt with under competition law and in some cases with regulation because it is not clear that courts in two-party contractual disputes would be well advised to attempt to develop a parallel set of legal doctrines relating to coercion as a way of disciplining market power. The distributional and allocative implications of structural market power are too complex for contract law, unlike situational monopolies.[199] He suggests that private parties who wish to obtain redress from the exercise of structural market power use private competition law suits for relief; the cause of action here would turn not on concepts of coercion in exchange, but rather on injury from anticompetitive behaviour. This is because in such cases the issue is a problem of market failure, not contracting failure, and the normative reference point is a consumer or total welfare standard, not coercion or voluntariness in exchange.[200]

Although at first sight Trebilcock's proposition appears to rebut the explanations offered in this section, it actually reinforces them. His argument would work perfectly well where competition law – such as that of the US – prohibits 'monopolisation' itself, since in that case achieving the 'structural monopoly' by inappropriate conduct is prohibited and prevented from occurring. Contrarily, in a competition system like that of the EU, where having a dominant position itself is not recriminated but only its abuse is condemned, the test becomes an ex post test which looks at not only the unilateral use of power, but inevitably at the use of power in bilateral relations. Especially in 'unfair pricing' cases, this is problematic

[195] Trebilcock (n 153) 93.
[196] ibid 94.
[197] ibid 95.
[198] ibid.
[199] ibid.
[200] ibid 96.

exactly for the reasons Trebilcock puts forward: it intervenes in contracts already concluded, that is contracts with persons who remain in the market, not those who are priced out of the market. Therefore, only when it looks at relations with or impositions on persons left out of the market, then competition law would be doing something it is well equipped to do. In other words, the focus should be on the 'deadweight loss' resulting from the price.[201] In pricing cases, this would mean that only 'exclusionary' prices may be – somehow – meaningfully scrutinised with regard to their level. This is because such prices may have a distortive effect on competition, that is on the structure of the (usually downstream) market, by limiting entry or leading to exit which would not occur under more competitive circumstances. In other words, examining merely 'exploitative' prices in transactions already concluded can properly be done – if at all – at most in contract law since in that case, structural monopoly in a way becomes a situational monopoly once parties enter into the contract. Consequently, the current practice and case law finding prices in contracts already entered into 'unfair' is, as elaborated above,[202] against the nature of the process, and therefore cannot achieve the goal. The new test offered here – based on the concept of business sense – deals with this particular problem in its proof of business sense by, inter alia, the proof of imminent exclusion from the market.

To summarise, the examination of an allegedly 'unfair' price in a contract already concluded which is *only* exploitative should be left to contract law. Competition law should only look at allegedly 'unfair' prices that have exclusionary potential. The test would be whether it makes business sense for the buyer/an efficient buyer to accept such a price ex ante. This is in conformity with protecting competition since merely exploitative 'unfair' prices without any exclusionary potential do not necessarily mean possible harm to competition. One implication of the above is that it is probably easier to think of 'unfair pricing' as the result of an abuse of a dominant position, rather than a way in which abuse takes place. The source of the problem should therefore be sought elsewhere when the allegedly 'unfair' price implies that something is 'wrong' with the transaction or more likely with the market, such as the existence of insurmountable entry barriers.

VIII CONCLUSION

It has been argued that there are strong grounds for EU competition law and policy to abandon the scrutiny of the prices of dominant undertakings with regard to their 'unfairness' when sanctioning the abuse of a dominant position under Article 102. The most important reason for this is that 'fairness' is an inherently vague concept which to date has not been defined objectively; it is therefore not possible to determine with enough legal certainty when a price becomes 'unfair'.

[201] On 'deadweight loss', see ch 1 this volume, section II.B.i, Figure 1.

[202] See text around n 155.

It inevitably requires a value judgement and this leaves firms in the dark ex ante when they set prices. Even the 'special responsibility' of dominant firms imposed by the ECJ cannot be thought to require this because, for a legal system to have credibility, the boundaries of the responsibilities it imposes on persons should be drawn clearly.[203] A rule ordering the undertakings not to price unfairly, but not establishing – realistically – how they can price them 'fairly' lacks that clarity and credibility.

The choice between intervening on grounds of 'unfair pricing' and leaving the solution to the market (and thus to competition) involves a choice among competition policy regimes, as well as an inter-temporal trade-off.[204] If it were just a question of short-run versus long-run effects, one might be tempted to put the immediate gain of today's consumers above everything else with a 'consumer welfare' standard.[205] Yet, a policy intervention on such grounds requires the competition authority to actually determine what price it considers appropriate and how it should evolve over time – tasks for which it is not really qualified.[206] Moreover, if it is accepted that the goal is to enhance 'consumer welfare', such intervention drastically reduces and may even forego the chance to protect consumers in the future by competition rather than policy intervention.[207] This has succinctly been put by the previous Director General of the Commission's DG Competition:

> [h]igh prices certainly harm consumers in the short run. But is that a sufficient case for intervention by a competition authority? What if high prices would in the medium term attract entry and spur competition? If there are no high or insurmountable barriers to entry, it might well be that high prices are actually likely to be, on balance and with a longer term perspective, good for consumers. There is much more for consumers to gain through increased competition than a mere decrease in prices: competition brings more choice, scope for differentiation in quality, innovation, etc.[208]

Interestingly, in all EU cases where 'unfair pricing' is an issue, there is an additional practice other than 'unfair pricing' which is scrutinised; it is usually discrimination.[209] However, in some cases different practices – especially those impeding market integration – such as curbing of parallel trade,[210] refusal to supply,[211] creating

[203] The concept of 'special responsibility' refers to the duty of a dominant undertaking not to abuse its position; in *Michelin I* the ECJ held that an undertaking in a dominant position, irrespective of the reasons for which it has such a dominant position, has a special responsibility not to allow its conduct to impair genuine undistorted competition on the common market; Case 322/81 *NV Nederlandsche Banden-Industrie Michelin v Commission* [1983] ECR 3461, [57].

[204] EAGCP Report (n 135) 10–11.

[205] ibid 11.

[206] ibid.

[207] ibid.

[208] P Lowe, 'Consumer Welfare and Efficiency – New Guiding Principles of Competition Policy?' (13th International Conference on Competition and 14th European Competition Day, Munich, March 2007) 7–8.

[209] *United Brands* (n 17); *Deutsche Post AG – Interception of Cross-Border Mail* (n 41).

[210] *General Motors* (n 29).

[211] *United Brands* (n 17); *Deutsche Post AG – Interception of Cross-Border Mail* (n 41).

barriers to re-importations[212] or to free movement of goods[213] and so on have been condemned. This is an example of *substantive* fairness not being a good candidate for legal intervention in transactions. In other words, the natural incapability of courts to tell what is substantively 'unfair' – which has been for long accepted in contract law – now finds its expression in competition law. Since it is almost always impossible to assess the 'fairness' of the price, authorities and courts look for additional/other factors, such as distorting market integration or other abusive conduct which they do not have to assess from a 'fairness' perspective. This is perhaps why the Commission never even argues for an exclusive 'unfair pricing' allegation. Indeed, the Commission's concern is more likely to be engaged where it considers that a pricing practice could be 'exclusionary'.[214] One implication of this is that keeping 'unfair pricing' in Article 102 may distract other litigants, especially in private enforcement cases if they only claim 'unfairness' of the price without any other abuse allegations.

This chapter has also proposed that if 'unfair pricing' is to be kept as an example of abuse in Article 102, then it should be limited to prices with *exclusionary* potential as these are the prices which may have an adverse effect on competition. This should focus on business-to-business transactions and the test should be whether transacting at that price makes business sense for the non-dominant party. While doing this, 'economic value' should be understood as that for the buyer, rather than the cost for the seller. Mere *exploitative* prices found in already concluded contracts without exclusionary potential should be left for contract law or *ex ante* regulation. Such an approach offers a more coherent and sensible alternative to the current haphazard treatment of 'unfair pricing' under EU competition law.

The next chapter investigates another example of prohibiting an 'unfair' practice (ie, discrimination) and its potential implications for the tension between 'fairness' and 'welfarist' objectives.

[212] *British Leyland* (n 38).

[213] *Renault* (n 27); Case 78/70 *Deutsche Grammophon Gesellschaft mbH v Metro-SB-Grossmarkte GmbH & Co KG* [1971] ECR 487.

[214] R Whish, 'Recent Developments in Community Competition Law 1998/99' (2000) 25(3) *European Law Review* 219, 231.

6

A Case Study on 'Fairness' Versus 'Welfare': 'Discrimination' as an Abuse*

I INTRODUCTION

'Discrimination' may easily be conceived as 'bad' in a society which upholds ideals such as 'equality' and 'fairness'. This may be a natural result of discrimination usually being discussed in racial, sexual or religious contexts. Transposed on to the competition law arena, however, this conception may lead to perverse outcomes. Indeed, 'discrimination' may sound benign, for example, to an economist who understands it as a common business practice with ambiguous effects on 'welfare'. One area in which this difference can give rise to tension is the practice of discrimination by a dominant undertaking under EU competition law. This is because Article 102(c) prohibits dominant undertakings from 'applying dissimilar conditions to equivalent transactions with other trading parties, thereby placing them at a competitive disadvantage'. This provision has come to be known as the prohibition of discrimination. What is important is that although the idea of 'treating equals alike and unequals unalike' and prohibiting discrimination can be thought to be grounded in 'fairness', its dictates may not always be 'welfare enhancing' or even 'fair', if one adopts a more nuanced understanding of 'fairness'.[1] It has indeed been argued that the shift to 'protection of competition rather than competitors' should eliminate the view that price discrimination by a dominant undertaking is per se abusive.[2] The question is therefore whether the perceived 'unfairness' of discrimination means that it is also anticompetitive, or whether one should require more, such as separate harm to competition in order

* Some of the issues in this chapter have been discussed in the narrower context of discrimination between consumers in P Akman, 'To Abuse, or not to Abuse: Discrimination between Consumers' (2007) 32 *European Law Review* 492.

[1] The clash between 'fairness' and 'welfare' may be more complicated than this if one also understands 'consumer welfare' as representing a 'fairness' viewpoint by favouring the welfare of consumers over the welfare of undertakings. For such a characterisation, see DJ Gifford and RT Kudrle, 'The Law and Economics of Price Discrimination in Modern Economies: Time for Reconciliation?' (2010) 43 *University of California, Davis Law Review* 1235, 1241, fn 21.

[2] M Lorenz, M Lubbig and A Russell, 'Price Discrimination, A Tender Story' (2005) 26(6) *European Competition Law Review* 355, 355.

to prohibit such conduct. In this sense, whether or not there is meaningful harm to competition can possibly be decided by looking at whether there is exclusion and/or harmful effects on 'welfare'. As such, following on from chapter five on 'unfair pricing', this chapter demonstrates another instance of the potential clash between 'fairness' and 'welfare' objectives and seeks to propose a reconciliation. It also demonstrates the potential problems with prohibiting mere 'exploitation' without separate harm to competition if one interprets the 'unfairness' of discrimination as its being 'exploitative'.

Particularly in the literature, Article 102(c) has generally been interpreted as being limited to discrimination directed at other undertakings. This is based on the provision requiring discrimination to place the dominant undertaking's 'trading parties' at a 'competitive disadvantage'. The literature has thus mainly progressed on the premise that Article 102(c) applies to discrimination against other undertakings, as a result of which competition is distorted due to the potential exclusionary effects of the practice.[3] This is in contrast to the economics literature, in which discrimination (particularly price discrimination) is generally examined as practised *between consumers* and the welfare effects are studied accordingly.[4] This author has argued elsewhere that discrimination between *consumers* also falls under the scope of the prohibition,[5] an argument which (admittedly) has not yet been tested before the EU courts.[6] This chapter therefore aims to demonstrate the challenge of reconciling 'fairness' and 'welfare' objectives, particularly with an economic effects-based approach in light of insights from the economics literature on the practice of discrimination regardless of the subjects of the practice. It thus elaborates on how it can be ensured that competition law does not prohibit discrimination in cases where economics suggests it to be potentially welfare enhancing.

Discrimination – notably price discrimination – is practised in many industries.[7] It has been noted that there are three main reasons why competition policy

[3] See, eg, A Jones and B Sufrin, *EU Competition Law: Text, Cases and Materials* 4th edn (Oxford, OUP, 2011) 389, 538; R O'Donoghue and AJ Padilla, *The Law and Economics of Article 82 EC* (Oxford, Hart Publishing, 2006) 554 *et seq*; C Graham, *EU and UK Competition Law* (Harlow, Pearson, 2010) 158.

[4] Nonetheless, price discrimination and its welfare effects have also been studied in the context of intermediate markets. See, eg, ML Katz, 'The Welfare Effects of Third-Degree Price Discrimination in Intermediate Good Markets' (1987) 77 *American Economic Review* 154 and DP O'Brien and G Shaffer, 'The Welfare Effects of Forbidding Discriminatory Discounts: A Secondary Line Analysis of Robinson-Patman' (1994) 10 *Journal of Law, Economics & Organization* 296.

[5] 'Consumer' in this ch is understood as any person who is acting for purposes outside her trade, business or profession when entering into a transaction. Equivalent terms would be 'end-user' and 'final customer'. For the same usage see, eg, Council Directive 93/13/EEC on Unfair Terms in Consumer Contracts [1993] OJ L95/29 Article 2(b); Council Directive 2005/29/EC on Unfair Commercial Practices [2005] OJ L149/22 Article 2(a).

[6] See P Akman, 'To Abuse, or not to Abuse: Discrimination between Consumers' (2007) 32 *European Law Review* 492.

[7] See S Bishop, 'Delivering Benefits to Consumers or Per Se Illegal? Assessing the Competitive Effects of Loyalty Rebates' in *The Pros and Cons of Price Discrimination* (Swedish Competition Authority, 2005) 65 on price discrimination. See also OFT Assessment of Conduct (draft competition law guideline for consultation) (414a) April 2004, [3.3] for the argument that price discrimination

may be concerned with price discrimination: first, price discrimination may be 'exploitative' of final consumers where it reduces consumer and/or total welfare; secondly, it may be 'exclusionary' where it puts the dominant undertaking's rivals or its customers' rivals at a disadvantage leading to their exit or competing less aggressively; and finally – particularly in the EU – it may be seen as segmenting the markets against the 'internal market' imperative.[8] Indeed, it should be noted that discrimination might have been adopted as an abuse to prevent the segmentation of the European markets and therefore to contribute to the achievement of the 'internal market'.[9] In fact, in the early days of the drafting of the Treaties of Rome, discrimination was an issue so important for the drafters that it was prohibited in a separate provision.[10] It has similarly been suggested that when the Treaties were signed in 1957, many economists objected to discrimination as distorting markets upstream or downstream and foreclosing competitors, and others objected on grounds of 'fairness' to competitors, and this accounts for Article 102(c).[11] However, it has also been noted that, if firms in an industry are selling absolutely undifferentiated products, these firms cannot price discriminate and, in nearly every real-world competitive market, products are differentiated to some degree; each firm's product has some unique characteristics that distinguish it from the products of competitors.[12] Thus, each seller in a typical real market has the potential ability to price discriminate, because inter-seller competition will not eliminate price differences.[13]

As product differentiation is normal and pervasive in real-world markets, price discrimination can be expected to be normal and pervasive as well: price discrimination arguably often exists in extremely competitive markets.[14] Once a firm is selling a somewhat differentiated product and thus faces a negatively sloped demand it can, and frequently does, engage in price discrimination.[15] This implies that not only should one discuss how 'fairness' can be reconciled with 'welfare'

occurs frequently and in a wide range of industries, including industries where competition is effective. On this last point, see also WJ Kolasky, 'What is Competition? A Comparison of US and European Perspectives' [2004] (Spring/Summer) *The Antitrust Bulletin* 29, 34.

[8] M Armstrong, 'Price Discrimination' in P Buccirossi (ed), *Handbook of Antitrust Economics* (Cambridge, MA, MIT Press, 2008) 433.

[9] For a recent example of discrimination leading to segmentation of the internal market, see *Swedish Interconnectors*, a decision in which the Commission opened formal proceedings against the Swedish electricity Transmission System Operator (Svenska Kraftnät) for limiting export transmission capacity on Swedish interconnectors to neighbouring countries, thereby favouring consumers in Sweden over consumers in neighbouring EU or EEA Member States by reserving domestically produced electricity for domestic consumption. The case was closed by the Commission making the commitments offered by Svenska Kraftnät binding. See COMP Case No 39351 *Swedish Interconnectors* (14 January 2010) a summary of which can be found at [2010] OJ C142/28.

[10] See ch 2 this volume, text to fn 226 and fn 226.

[11] V Korah, 'Modernisation of Article 82' speech delivered at I Lisbon Conference on Competition Law and Economics (Lisbon, 3–4 November 2005) 6.

[12] B Klein and JS Wiley Jr, 'Competitive Price Discrimination as an Antitrust Justification for Intellectual Property Refusals to Deal' (2003) 70 *Antitrust Law Journal* 599, 609.

[13] ibid 610.

[14] ibid.

[15] ibid 611.

objectives regarding this practice, one must also question whether discrimination should be an abuse at all due to the ubiquity of the practice as normal commercial conduct in many markets including competitive ones. Accepting the definition of 'abusive exploitation' offered in this study as the dominant undertaking advantaging itself to the disadvantage of its trading partners in ways that would not be possible *but for* its dominance would also suggest that conduct so commonly practised is difficult to characterise as being impossible *but for* the dominance of the undertaking.[16] Once discrimination is accepted as a practice widely practised in competitive markets, then its prohibition by a provision such as Article 102(c) becomes perverse where the prohibition itself can prevent intensified competition when the practice is welfare enhancing.

This potential perverse outcome is important, since not only a dominant undertaking's trading partners (other traders), but also their consumers could bring legal suits once it is accepted that the provision can cover discrimination in business-to-consumer practices as well. With the emphasis recently placed on 'private enforcement' by the EU institutions and with the introduction of class actions a possibility,[17] consumers could make use of this particular provision in the future using both national and EU competition law given that discrimination is a very common practice. For example, a dominant rail company charging different ticket prices to a professional and to a student for the same train journey, could be challenged as an 'abuse', provided other conditions of the provision are met. Other undertakings could include airlines, mobile network operators, petrol stations, supermarkets, postal service providers, pharmaceutical companies and gas and electricity suppliers that practise discrimination either by charging uniform or differential prices to different consumers. Compared with a situation where the enforcement of the provision is limited to business-to-business transactions, a situation where the enforcement of Article 102(c) includes business-to-consumer transactions may prove particularly complicated and difficult. This would mostly occur in cases where some consumers gain and others lose from discrimination, and where the competition authority/court faces a trade-off between the interests of these consumer groups. Thus, these are important concerns that have to be considered while trying to reconcile the possible clash between 'fairness' and 'welfare'.

This chapter is divided into three substantive sections. Section II sets out the definitional and operational issues regarding the prohibition of discrimination under Article 102 TFEU, along with the possible consequences of different definitions in law and economics. It establishes that the requirement of 'competitive disadvantage' that is found in the text of Article 102(c) has almost been read out of the provision and this has serious implications for establishing the correct scope for the prohibition. Although this chapter considers discrimination under

[16] For the definition of 'abusive exploitation' see ch 2 this volume, section V.F.

[17] See current Commission public consultation on 'collective redress' in the EU; 'Towards a Coherent European Approach on Collective Redress' available at: ec.europa.eu/competition/consultations/2011_collective_redress/index_en.html.

Article 102 in general, it concentrates on 'price discrimination' as a common and obvious practice of it. In section III, the chapter questions whether discrimination *should* be an abuse from the perspective of 'welfare' and 'fairness'. This is because there are strong economic findings that suggest that the prohibition of discrimination itself in many instances can have perverse welfare outcomes. Section IV then elaborates on how the clash between 'fairness' and 'welfare' can be reconciled. Section V concludes.

II DEFINITIONAL ISSUES AND THE OPERATION OF THE PROHIBITION UNDER ARTICLE 102 TFEU

A Definitional Issues

Discrimination – in the context of competition law and policy – is a practice inherently difficult to define since it is necessary to determine the conditions under which two transactions may be deemed equivalent and thus comparable. In addition, it requires the assessment of the criteria which render the treatment of the two transactions dissimilar. For example, it must be decided whether the sales of two rail tickets to two consumers for the same journey by the same company are equivalent transactions, even though the sales occur at different times or even though the willingness to pay of one consumer is higher than the other's. As will be seen below, for the purposes of competition law, the potential tension between law and economics arises straight away with the definition of 'discrimination' and it is perhaps fair to say that so far neither of these disciplines has been able to construe discrimination satisfactorily enough for a consistent application across the board in conformity with legal certainty. It should also be noted that, although it may not be obvious at first glance – and although they may not have always been treated as such by the EU authorities under Article 102(c) – practices such as selective price cutting, bundling, target rebates and margin squeeze are also, essentially, examples of price discrimination. Therefore, discrimination covers a broad range of practices that have been found to be abusive under Article 102.[18]

Article 102 does not define discrimination; rather, it bans the application of dissimilar conditions to equivalent transactions with different trading parties, thereby placing them at a competitive disadvantage. This has been interpreted to include, in addition, the similar treatment of dissimilar transactions.[19] Hence, when it is determined that two transactions are equivalent (non-equivalent), then the undertaking should treat these transactions similarly (dissimilarly). As for economics, the study of discrimination has mainly concentrated on 'price

[18] See Armstrong (n 8) 434–37 for the classification of these as discriminatory practices.

[19] Case 13/63 J *Italian Republic v Commission* [1963] ECR 165 in the context of ECSC Treaty and *Van den Bergh Foods Limited* (Case IV/34.073, IV/34.395 and IV/35.436) Commission Decision 1998/531/EC [1998] OJ L246/1, [76].

discrimination'. The definition of it appears to be problematic in this discipline as well. For example, in the Economic Advisory Group on Competition Policy (EAGCP) Report commissioned by DG Competition, price discrimination is defined as 'charging different prices for different units and/or to different customers'.[20] A different definition is the ability to set prices so that the difference between average prices and average costs varies between different sales of either the same good or closely related goods.[21] The practice has also been described as making two sales at two different rates of return; two sales are discriminatory when they have different ratios of price to marginal cost.[22] Whereas the EAGCP Report's definition is closer to Article 102(c), the more common approach in economics appears to be treating only the differences that are not due or proportionate to cost differences as 'discrimination'.[23] For the purposes of this study, this definition is adopted for economic discrimination. Thus, in the example above, charging a higher price to the commuter on the train who had the ticket delivered to her home rather than picking it up at the station would not be economically discriminatory so long as the price difference reflects this cost difference. In the same manner, charging the same price to both commuters regardless of this cost difference would be economically discriminatory. Finally, it must be mentioned that for discrimination to be possible, the firm must have market power (although as will be seen below there is dispute regarding this condition) and the ability to both sort customers and prevent arbitrage or resale of the goods.[24]

In contrast to the common economic definition, some decisions under Article 102(c) imply that the provision is broad enough to cover *any difference* in treatment of similar transactions as discriminatory, without establishing, for example, that the difference is due to a difference in costs. Conduct can then be *defended* by an 'objective justification' (such as cost differences) by the undertaking. Indeed, the Commission has held in its *Portuguese Airports* decision that '[t]here must be

[20] Report by the EAGCP 'An Economic Approach to Article 82' (July 2005) available at: ec.europa.eu/dgs/competition/economist/eagcp_july_21_05.pdf 30. It is nevertheless conceded that this simple definition raises tricky issues when, for example, different customers involve different costs; ibid 30, fn 21.

[21] J Church and R Ware, *Industrial Organization* (Singapore, Irwin McGraw-Hill, 2000) 160.

[22] H Hovenkamp, *Federal Antitrust Policy: The Law of Competition and its Practice* 3rd edn (Minnesota, Thomson/West, 2005) 572.

[23] See, eg, Tirole: 'there is no price discrimination if differences in prices between consumers exactly reflect differences in the costs of serving these consumers'; J Tirole, *The Theory of Industrial Organization* 9th edn (Cambridge, MA, MIT Press, 1997) 133–34. 'Price discrimination' can take one of three forms: first-degree, second-degree and third-degree. 'First-degree' (perfect) price discrimination refers to the situation when the firm has perfect information on the willingness to pay of each consumer. Thus, the firm can charge each consumer a price equal to her willingness to pay. In 'second-degree' price discrimination, a firm cannot identify the customers between whom it would like to discriminate. By the use of self-select mechanisms, however, the firm may induce consumers to sort themselves in a way that allows additional surplus to be extracted. 'Third-degree' price discrimination or market segmentation is when the firm is aware of willingness to pay across groups, but not within a group and charges different prices to different groups. See in general, Church and Ware (n 21) 161–62.

[24] HR Varian, 'Price Discrimination' in R Schmalensee and R Willig (eds), *Handbook of Industrial Organization* Vol 1, 2nd edn (Amsterdam, Elsevier, 1990) 599; Church and Ware, ibid, 160. For the disagreements on the requirement of market power, see below text after n 88.

an objective justification for any difference in treatment of its various clients by an undertaking in a dominant position'.[25] Similarly in *Aéroports de Paris* the GC held with regard to the policy of the airport manager ADP that 'the Commission was justified in inferring from the difference in rates of the fees demanded from the groundhandlers by ADP that ADP was imposing discriminatory fees, unless it justified that difference in treatment by objective reasons'.[26] Moreover, it was found that 'in the event of disparity, it is for ADP to justify the reasons for and correctness of the differences in the rates of fee applied to different groundhandlers operating at Orly and Roissy-CDG airports'.[27] The GC also held in *Tetra Pak II* regarding Tetra Pak's differential pricing of machines that '[i]n the absence of any argument by the applicant which might provide objective justification for its pricing policy, such disparities were unquestionably discriminatory'.[28] Likewise in the US, to prove price discrimination under the Robinson-Patman Act, one needs to show only a 'price difference'.[29]

This difference in defining discrimination (ie, equating any 'differential' treatment with 'discrimination') can potentially affect the procedure and, particularly, the burden of proof. In the case law, 'objective justification' is a defence possible for any allegedly abusive conduct and the burden of proving it is on the dominant undertaking in the sense of providing all the necessary evidence to demonstrate that the conduct under scrutiny is objectively justified.[30] However, when the economic definition is adopted, the burden to prove that, for example, the difference in prices is not due to a difference in costs, would be on the Commission since only then would the practice be 'discriminatory'. Under the current interpretation (similar to the Robinson-Patman Act), the burden is on the dominant undertaking to demonstrate that the allegedly abusive different (or uniform) prices are justified and thus should not be prohibited. Therefore, if the undertaking cannot

[25] *Portuguese Airports* (Case IV/35.703) Commission Decision 1999/199/EC [1999] OJ L69/31, [27].

[26] Case T-128/98 *Aéroports de Paris v Commission* [2000] ECR II-3929, [201], upheld on appeal in Case C-82/01 *Aéroports de Paris v Commission* [2003] 4 CMLR 12.

[27] *Aéroports de Paris v Commission* (GC), ibid, [202].

[28] Case T-83/91 *Tetra Pak International SA v Commission* [1994] ECR II-755, [207], upheld on appeal in Case C-333/94 P *Tetra Pak International SA v Commission* [1996] ECR I-5951.

[29] *FTC v Anheuser-Busch, Inc* 363 US 536, 549, 80 S Ct 1267, 1274 4 L Ed2d 1385 (1960): 'a price discrimination within the meaning of that provision is merely a price difference'. The defendant can then claim a 'cost justification' defence to show that the different prices were not discriminatory. Nonetheless, it is noteworthy that, unlike EU competition law, the Robinson-Patman Act does not prohibit charging the *same price* for dissimilar transactions. See Hovenkamp (n 22) 581 for the argument that it is a misnomer to call the Robinson-Patman Act a 'price discrimination' statute since it directly condemns price *differences*, and only indirectly and haphazardly reaches economic discrimination. The ironic result has been to force many sellers to engage in true economic price discrimination by charging the same price to different groups of buyers, even though costs of serving them differ; ibid 587.

[30] See 'Guidance on the Commission's Enforcement Priorities in Applying Article 82 of the EC Treaty to Abusive Exclusionary Conduct by Dominant Undertakings' [2009] OJ C45/7 [31]. *Cf* 'DG Competition Discussion Paper on the Application of Article 82 of the Treaty to Exclusionary Abuses' (Brussels, December 2005) available at: ec.europa.eu/competition/antitrust/art82/discpaper2005.pdf, [77] which had placed the *legal* burden to prove the defence on the dominant undertaking.

convince the Commission of this justification, the Commission can find abuse on the basis of mere differential (or uniform) pricing without having proved the prices to be economically discriminatory.[31] This is a consequence of the legal test being two-staged in that it first asks whether the prices are *different* and if so, whether this can be objectively justified, as opposed to the single-staged economic test which questions whether the price-cost ratios – that is the profit margins in two equivalent transactions – are different and thus *discriminatory.*

In the context of EU competition law, the adoption of the economic definition of discrimination may at first glance be problematic since the competition authority may not be able to assess the costs of the dominant undertaking before and without alleging that the differential (or uniform) pricing is abusive. It can only observe the occurrence of differential (or uniform) pricing and cannot establish without further investigation whether the differential (or uniform) pricing is economically discriminatory (ie, not due or proportionate to cost differences). Since the dominant undertaking would have the relevant cost information, placing the *evidentiary* burden to provide that information may be the more feasible and efficient approach. Yet, the legal burden should remain with the Commission. Abuse should only be established when there is enough evidence to prove that the differential (or uniform) prices are also economically discriminatory. Finding an infringement based on the mere observance of differential (or uniform) pricing can result in unduly requiring the dominant undertaking to justify its whole pricing policy. The difficulty of assessing the costs of the dominant undertaking for the competition authority should not be overstated either since such an assessment underlies many if not most types of allegations of abuse.[32]

In short, bringing together the legal and economic interpretations for the purposes of competition law, 'discrimination' can be defined as the application of dissimilar conditions to equivalent transactions or equivalent conditions to dissimilar transactions without objective justification. This definition clearly hinges on what renders the transactions and the conditions applied to them 'equivalent', and what constitutes 'objective justification'. A systematic framework answering these questions does not currently exist in EU competition law and is out of this chapter's scope. Nevertheless, it is worth noting that what is apparent in discrimination cases to date is that it is the criteria relating to the *transaction*, rather than to the party engaged in the transaction, that matter.[33] Although it has been argued that the Commission should broaden the notion of objective justification under

[31] See P Loewenthal, 'The Defence of "Objective Justification" in the Application of Article 82 EC' (2005) 28(4) *World Competition* 455, 456 for the argument that none of the EU courts has ever applied this defence in favour of a dominant undertaking alleged to have infringed that provision by the Commission, although the defence has been mentioned in almost all of the cases.

[32] This is particularly the case where the approach to exclusionary abuse is based on an 'as efficient competitor' test as the Commission seems to have adopted in the Guidance for price-based conduct, since that assessment requires an examination of the costs of the dominant undertaking; see 'Guidance' (n 30) [23] *et seq.*

[33] M Furse, 'Monopoly Price Discrimination, Article 82 and the Competition Act' (2001) 22(5) *European Competition Law Review* 149, 153.

Article 102(c) and accept that conditions specific to the customer could render transactions 'dissimilar',[34] the wording of Article 102(c) and the decisional practice focus on 'transactions' being equivalent, and objective justification has so far usually been understood as cost-related justifications. Customer-specific conditions have therefore generally not been regarded as possible objective justifications.[35] This is potentially problematic since it would imply that the 'willingness to pay' of different customers would not provide justification for their differential treatment. Although it has been noted that the customer and her demand function are an inseparable part of the transaction,[36] the law has not made clear to date the extent to which it would be permissible for a dominant undertaking to discriminate between customers based on their demand for the product or their ability to bargain effectively. This is important since the extent to which a monopolist can actually practise price discrimination if arbitrage is restricted depends on the information it has about the willingness of consumers to pay.[37] The Commission's recent statement that conceptualised discrimination between customers by making those customers with a higher willingness to pay and fewer switching possibilities pay a higher price than others as 'direct exploitation'[38] demonstrates a stance against such a position. Indeed, in one case, albeit without taking a formal decision due to reaching an agreement with the undertaking, the Commission found Deutsche Telekom AG's business customer tariffs discriminating in favour of its business customers vis-à-vis residential customers potentially abusive.[39] The Commission argued that while competition was growing in the recently liberalised markets such as business and data services, other areas such as access to end customers would mostly remain closed for a while and, in this period, there was a risk that incumbent telecommunications operators might restructure tariffs to *exploit* the difference between the different 'price elasticities'

[34] D Gerard, 'Price Discrimination under Article 82(c) EC: Clearing up the Ambiguities' in *Global Competition Law Centre Research Papers on Article 82 EC – July 2005*, 133 available at: www.coleurope.eu/template.asp?pagename=gclcresearch.

[35] See also Gerard, ibid, 120. In *United Brands* the possible justifications for price discrimination were cited as difference in transport costs, taxation, customs duties, the wages of the labour force, the conditions of marketing, the differences in the parity of currencies and the density of competition; Case 27/76 *United Brands Co and United Brands Continental BV v Commission* [1978] ECR 207, [228]. It is only very recently that the Commission has started paying attention to buyer-specific reasons and, thus, the buyer's valuation. This can be seen in the arguments of the Commission against the unfair pricing allegations in *Scandlines Sverige AB v Port of Helsingborg* (Case COMP/A.36.568/D3) Commission Decision 23 July 2004 (unreported).

[36] Furse (n 33) 153. See also Geradin and Petit arguing that it is not clear whether differences in *elasticity of demand* can render transactions non-equivalent under the terms of Art 102(c); D Geradin and N Petit, 'Price Discrimination under EC Competition Law: Another Antitrust Doctrine in Search of Limiting Principles?' (2006) 2(3) *Journal of Competition Law & Economics* 479, 486.

[37] Church and Ware (n 21) 161.

[38] 'Discussion Paper' (n 30) [141].

[39] 'Commission Reaches Agreement with German Authorities Concerning Conditions for DT's New Business Customer Tariffs' press release IP/96/543 (25 June 1996). The Commission thus required Deutsche Telekom AG to offer trial rebates to domestic customers before the new business customer tariffs entered into force. As such, residential customers were expected to benefit from rebates introduced in parallel with the rebates for business customers.

in these different markets.[40] Thus, this approach demonstrates clearly the tension and conflict between practices which might be deemed 'unfair' for being exploitative but which might at the same time be efficient and potentially welfare-enhancing. It also demonstrates the disjoint between the EU authorities' approach and not only business practice, but also the treatment of common business practices under economics, since under both of these, the customers' willingness to pay and elasticity of demand are fundamentally important for the practice of discrimination. This will be further elaborated on below in sections III.A and III.C.

In general, one can conclude that different costs may render transactions dissimilar and provide an objective justification for their different treatment. On the other hand, the nationalities of different parties do not render transactions dissimilar and do not justify their different treatment, as this has been condemned in many cases.[41] Apart from these situations, it is not possible to reach general conclusions on what would and would not be abusive discrimination under EU competition law as it currently stands. The next subsection discusses the operation of the prohibition as practised by the EU authorities. In particular it focuses on the requirement of 'competitive disadvantage', as this requirement has implications regarding the types of discriminatory practices covered by Article 102(c).

B The 'Competitive Disadvantage' Requirement and the Operation of the Prohibition in Practice

In competition law, discrimination is generally thought to result in either 'primary' or 'secondary' line injury to competition. Primary line injury prejudices the dominant undertaking's competitors by having exclusionary effects, whereas secondary line injury impacts on the downstream markets.[42] As such, primary line injury harms competition between the dominant undertaking and its rivals, while secondary line injury causes distortion of downstream competition among the discriminating undertaking's customers or third parties. In a dynamic context with the possibility of strategic behaviour, price discrimination can have negative effects on welfare if it is used as an instrument for predatory pricing or for other exclusionary practices that eliminate competition and thereby allow the price-discriminating firm to subsequently raise price above competitive levels, thus causing primary line injury.[43] Similarly, price discrimination can lead to secondary line injury, for example, by affecting the outcome of competition between

[40] 'Elasticity of demand' is the percentage change in the quantity demanded divided by the corresponding percentage change in its price; D Begg, S Fischer and R Dornbusch, *Economics* 2nd edn (Maidenhead, McGraw-Hill, 2003) 41.

[41] See, eg, Case 7/82 *Gesellschaft zur Verwertung von Leistungsschutzrechten mbH (GVL) v Commission* [1983] ECR 483; *Portuguese Airports* (n 25); *Aéroports de Paris v Commission* (GC) (n 26).

[42] Jones and Sufrin (n 3) 388.

[43] D Ridyard, 'Exclusionary Pricing and Price Discrimination Abuses under Article 82 – An Economic Analysis' [2002] *European Competition Law Review* 286, 288.

the firms who rely on the price-discriminating firm for some raw material or input.[44]

In the legal literature, Article 102(c) has been interpreted as being concerned with discrimination causing secondary line injury.[45] Subsequently, Article 102(c) has been understood as banning discrimination between the downstream customers of the dominant undertaking, thereby distorting competition between them.[46] It has been argued that the reference to the placing of the dominant firm's trading parties at a 'competitive disadvantage' clearly indicates that the parties Article 102(c) seeks to protect are the customers of the dominant player and not its competitors.[47] This requirement makes the finding of a discriminatory abuse dependent on the finding of a downstream market on which these firms compete.[48] It has thus been noted that the rationale of Article 102(c) might have been quite close to the primary rationale behind the Robinson-Patman Act, which was to protect competition on the downstream market and, more specifically, small purchasers against large purchasers.[49] As mentioned above,[50] this author has already argued elsewhere that the discrimination between consumers also falls within the scope of Article 102(c) and this issue will not be discussed further herein. Therefore, in the rest that follows it is assumed that both discrimination between undertakings and consumers are covered by Article 102(c).

For the purposes of establishing *when* discrimination will breach Article 102, an important requirement is found in subparagraph (c) itself. Article 102(c) bans the application of dissimilar conditions to equivalent transactions by a dominant undertaking with other trading parties 'thereby placing them at a competitive disadvantage'. Therefore, the requirement of placing trading partners at a 'competitive disadvantage' can be thought to be *the* factor distinguishing discrimination that can be a competition issue from that which cannot be. In fact, in the context

[44] ibid 288.

[45] Jones and Sufrin (n 3) 389; SM Lage and R Allendesalazar, 'Community Policy on Discriminatory Pricing: A Practitioner's Perspective' in CD Ehlermann and I Atanasiu (eds), *What is an Abuse of Dominant Position?* (Oxford, Hart Publishing, 2006) 341; Geradin and Petit (n 36) 487; Gerard (n 34) 132 argues that primary line injury should be dealt with under Art 102(b); M Waelbroeck, 'Price Discrimination and Rebate Policies under EU Competition Law' in B Hawk (ed), *International Antitrust Law & Policy: Fordham Corporate Law 1995* (New York, Juris Publishing, 1996) 160.

[46] Jones and Sufrin (n 3) 443. Support for this can also be implicitly found in Case 6/72 *Europemballage Corp and Continental Can Co Inc v Commission* [1973] ECR 215 where the ECJ held that '[a]s may further be seen from letters (c) and (d) of Article [102] (2), the provision is not only aimed at practices which may cause damage to consumers directly, but also at those which are detrimental to them through their impact on an effective competition structure, such as is mentioned in Article 3 [(1)(g)] of the [EC] Treaty', [26]. In other words, the ECJ interpreted Art 102(c) as a provision aimed at the protection of a competitive structure and not direct protection of consumers. However, at the time of the judgment the ECJ was trying to establish that Art 102 was not limited to exploitative practices, but also covered exclusionary conduct, and the consequent application of subparagraph (c) does not demonstrate loyalty to this initial holding. Thus, it should not be treated as ruling out the inclusion of consumers in the scope of the provision.

[47] Geradin and Petit (n 36) 487.

[48] ibid.

[49] ibid 487–88.

[50] See above, text around n 5.

of the Robinson-Patman Act, it has been argued that a 'significant but unwarranted competitive disadvantage' (defined as effectively lacking access to substitute sources of supply) should be how one interprets the requirement of 'injury to a competitor' to ensure that the Act catches those injuries that also lead to harm to competition.[51] However, this is not a clear-cut issue regarding Article 102(c).

First, it is not clear what is meant by 'competitive disadvantage' in the provision. If this is comprehended as broad enough to cover 'exploitation' of some trading parties, then discrimination can be thought to place some consumers at a competitive disadvantage when some of them are, for example, paying higher prices compared with others or to what they would pay under non-discriminatory pricing. As a result of such conduct, some consumers may be able to consume less of other products since a bigger part of their income would be spent on purchasing at the discriminatorily high price as compared with similarly placed consumers paying the lower price. In this case, there would not be an obvious competitive disadvantage. An alternative understanding of 'competitive disadvantage' would be to interpret it as a change in the structure of competition on the market. However, the Commission has already held that discrimination can be abusive even if there is no effect on the structure of competition. The Commission stated in its *1998 Football World Cup* decision that

> [w]hile the application of Article [102] often requires an assessment of the effect of an undertaking's behaviour on the structure of competition in a given market, its application in the absence of such an effect cannot be excluded. Consumers' interests are protected by Article [102], such protection being achieved either by prohibiting conduct by dominant undertakings which impairs free and undistorted competition or which is direct[ly] prejudicial to consumers. Accordingly, and as has been expressly recognised by the Court of Justice [in Continental Can], Article [102] can properly be applied, where appropriate, to situations in which a dominant undertaking's behaviour direct[ly] prejudices the interests of consumers, notwithstanding the absence of any effect on the structure of competition.[52]

Hence, once it is accepted that there is no need to affect the structure of competition and that directly prejudicing the interests of consumers is sufficient for discrimination to be abusive, the requirement of 'competitive disadvantage' loses its practical importance. This is because when discrimination puts some customers (suppliers) at a competitive disadvantage, this can be expected to lead to a change on the structure of the downstream (upstream) competition since some of the customers (suppliers) will not be able to compete as effectively as they could. Therefore, the lack of an impact on the structure of competition might imply that the requirement of competitive disadvantage is not satisfied. Indeed, taking a more literal approach, one commentator has suggested that the use of 'thereby' in

[51] See AI Gavil, 'Secondary Line Price Discrimination and the Fate of *Morton Salt*: To Save It, Let It Go' (1999) 48(4) *Emory Law Journal* 1057, 1069.

[52] *1998 Football World Cup* (Case IV/36/888) Commission Decision 2001/12/EC [2000] OJ L5/55, [100].

subparagraph (c) suggests that it is *presumed* that a competitive disadvantage flows from the application of 'dissimilar conditions'.[53]

Moreover, the decisional practice in this area has progressed in a way that almost removed the requirement since it has rarely been attended to.[54] For this reason, there is relatively little analysis in the case law to date of what constitutes meaningful competitive disadvantage between customers.[55] However, the ECJ has elaborated on the requirement in its *British Airways* judgment and seems to read the requirement back into the provision by stating that for subparagraph (c) to be applicable, there must be a finding not only that the behaviour of the dominant undertaking is discriminatory, 'but also that it tends to distort that competitive relationship, in other words to hinder the competitive position of some of the business partners of that undertaking in relation to others'.[56]

Whether the judgment in *British Airways* reads the 'competitive disadvantage' requirement back into the provision and thus restricts the scope of subparagraph (c) to discrimination that distorts the competitive relationship between the dominant undertaking's trading partners remains to be seen. What should be noted is that in many decisions, this requirement played no role in terms of establishing the existence or absence of abuse. For example, in *United Brands*,[57] the practice of United Brands charging different prices for Chiquita bananas that reflected the retail prices in the Member State of the ripener/distributor had been found discriminatory, even though the ripeners/distributors from different Member States were not in competition with one another and 'greengrocers in Ireland certainly did not compete with those in Germany'.[58] Indeed, once the markets were partitioned across national lines, different prices could no longer create a competitive disadvantage among distributors/ripeners since these traders could not compete with each other internationally due to the partitioning.[59] The ECJ appears to have *assumed* that the different prices would place certain ripeners/distributors at a competitive disadvantage.[60] It has been suggested that if the firm is faced with a market which is partitioned independently from its action, one could argue that the transactions are not equivalent, at least for buyers who evaluate the transactions in terms of resale opportunity and are faced with different opportunities

[53] M Furse, *Competition Law of the EC and UK* 6th edn (Oxford, OUP, 2008) 346.

[54] R Whish, *Competition Law* 6th edn (Oxford, OUP, 2009) 752; Jones and Sufrin (n 3) 538; Waelbroeck (n 45) 160.

[55] JT Lang and R O'Donoghue, 'Defining Legitimate Competition: How to Clarify Pricing Abuses under Article 82EC' (2002) 26 *Fordham International Law Journal* 83, 115.

[56] Case C-95/04 P *British Airways plc v Commission* [2007] ECR I-2331, [144]. In *British Airways*, it was competition between travel agents that were downstream in comparison to British Airways that was distorted as a result of British Airways' discriminatory practices. More recently, the GC has followed this approach in upholding the Commission's decision in *Clearstream*; see Case T-301/04 *Clearstream Banking AG and Clearstream International SA v Commission* [2009] ECR 00, in particular [192]–[94].

[57] *United Brands* (n 35).

[58] Jones and Sufrin (n 3) 545.

[59] Geradin and Petit (n 36) 523.

[60] *United Brands* (n 35) [233].

in the various markets.[61] It has thus been suggested that the judgment in *United Brands* appears more similar to laws which aim to protect existing competitors rather than competition.[62]

Similarly, in *Corsica Ferries I* the operator of the port of Genoa was found to have abused its dominant position by applying dissimilar tariffs to maritime transport undertakings depending on whether they operated services between Member States or between national ports (insofar as trade between Member States were affected).[63] It has been rightly argued that, in that case, the domestic and international shipping lines were not competing with each other.[64] In the same vein, very little or no attention has been paid to the requirement of 'competitive disadvantage' by the Commission and/or courts in the *1998 Football World Cup*,[65] *Deutsche Post – Interception of Cross-Border Mail*,[66] *Portuguese Airports*,[67] *Hoffmann-La Roche*,[68] *Tetra Pak II*[69] and *Alpha Flight Services/Aéroports de Paris*[70] decisions. In fact, for example in *Hoffman-La Roche*, by finding the dominant undertaking's fidelity rebates conditioned on its customers purchasing all or a large part of their requirements from itself abusive under Article 102(c), the ECJ appears to have used this provision as a means of protecting Hoffmann-La Roche's competitors as it was mainly concerned with the effects of the rebates impeding the firm's competitors from selling to the dominant undertaking's customers.[71] This implies that although the provision is about the prohibition of secondary-line effects, it has been used to sanction primary-line effects which have been considered to be exclusionary.[72] This can be interpreted as a consequence of the disappearance of the 'competitive disadvantage' requirement in the decisional practice.

The Commission elaborated on this issue in *BdKEP – Restrictions on Mail Preparation* and found that Deutsche Post's interpretation of the concept of 'com-

[61] LZ Di Valgiurata, 'Price Discrimination under Article 86 of the EEC Treaty: The *United Brands* Case' (1982) 31 *International Comparative Law Quarterly* 36, 53.

[62] ibid 53.

[63] Case C-18/93 *Corsica Ferries Italia Srl v Corpo dei Piloti del Porto do Genova* [1994] ECR I-1783, [45].

[64] Jones and Sufrin (n 3) 545; Whish (n 54) 752.

[65] *1998 Football World Cup* (n 52).

[66] *Deutsche Post AG – Interception of Cross-Border Mail* (Case COMP/C-1/36.915) Commission Decision 2001/892/EC [2001] OJ L331/40.

[67] *Portuguese Airports* (n 25).

[68] The ECJ circumvents Hoffmann-La Roche's proposition that the fidelity rebates do not put customers at a competitive disadvantage by holding that, under the circumstances, it cannot be accepted that the rebates are not of importance to customers and that, since the structure of competition on the market is already weakened due to the existence of a dominant undertaking, any further weakening of the structure of competition may constitute abuse; Case 85/76 *Hoffmann-La Roche & Co AG v Commission* [1979] ECR 461, [122]–[23].

[69] *Tetra Pak II* (n 28).

[70] *Alpha Flight Services/Aéroports de Paris* Commission Decision (Case IV/35.613) Commission Decision 1998/1417/EC [1998] OJ L230/10.

[71] Gifford and Kudrle (n 1) 1274.

[72] ibid 1274–75.

petitive disadvantage' was too restrictive.[73] It held that the wording of Article 102(c) covered three types of discrimination, the first two being exclusionary and the last one exploitative. Accordingly, the customer of the dominant undertaking may be placed at a competitive disadvantage either vis-à-vis the dominant undertaking itself; or in relation to other customers of the dominant undertaking; or the customer suffers commercially in such a way that his or her ability to compete on whichever market is impaired. The first and third possibilities do not require a competitive relationship between the two comparator groups.[74] Moreover, regarding the exploitative type of abuse covered by Article 102(c), the Commission remarked that

> numerous precedents demonstrate that both the Commission and the Courts apply a broad interpretation of this provision, condemning dominant undertakings for exploitative discrimination between customers who are not competing on the same market.[75]

Thus, once it is accepted that there is no need for a competitive relationship between the undertaking's customers for discrimination to be abusive, it would follow that discrimination can fall under Article 102 as an 'exploitative' practice without demonstrating a competitive disadvantage.[76] To the extent that this practical removal of the 'competitive disadvantage' requirement leads to a lack of showing of harm to competition, as opposed to mere harm to some trading partners, that is it leads to sanctioning of mere 'exploitation', it raises concern from both an economical and legal perspective. This is because it broadens the scope of a prohibition that is deemed to deserve limited enforcement, if it is to be enforced at all.[77] Thus, the following section will discuss whether discrimination should be an abuse under Article 102.

III SHOULD DISCRIMINATION BE AN ABUSE UNDER ARTICLE 102 TFEU?

The question of whether discrimination should be an abuse under Article 102 arises because, according to economics, discrimination is a practice with ambiguous effects on total and consumer welfare. As such, it is argued that the welfare effects of discrimination require a case-by-case analysis and that a blanket prohibition of

[73] *BdKEP – Restrictions on Mail Preparation* (Case COMP/38.745) Commission Decision 20 October 2004 (unreported) [93].

[74] ibid.

[75] ibid [95].

[76] See similarly Gerard arguing that discrimination among final consumers who do not compete with each other may also give rise to an issue of exploitation; Gerard (n 34) 122, fn 68. Nonetheless, he further notes that the Commission should make clear that price discrimination might constitute an abuse under Art 102(c) only to the extent that it results in a distortion of competition among the dominant undertaking's trading parties; ibid 107.

[77] See, eg, O'Donoghue and Padilla (n 3) 602 arguing for a limited enforcement. See also O'Brien and Shaffer (n 4) 298 arguing that forbidding intermediate price discrimination leads to higher prices for all buyers and that the Robinson-Patman Act *reduces* welfare.

discrimination is not justified.[78] Some commentators have indeed asked *why* discrimination could be an abuse of a dominant position. There are a number of potential answers. A slightly cynical view would arguably say that this prohibition stems from a human desire for simple rules.[79] Alternatively, one might posit that, like any other form of discrimination, price discrimination is inherently 'unfair'.[80] From a political-economical perspective one could be tempted to argue that a ban on price discrimination actually benefits the industry by reducing competitive pressure.[81]

It has also been suggested that, in practice, it will be rare that a profit-maximising firm will have the ability or incentive to charge different prices to comparable customers to such an extent that competition between those customers will be significantly distorted.[82] The only clearly identifiable situation under EU competition law in which the non-discrimination principle would apply (and for which none of the valid defences would be available) is argued to be where a state-owned or controlled company charges different prices to domestic and foreign buyers for protectionist reasons.[83] In contrast, it is difficult to visualise a situation in which a company that was not state-owned would have an interest in charging significantly different prices in genuinely similar transactions to customers that were in competition with one another.[84]

Regardless of the arguments about why it does not make sense to have a prohibition of discrimination in Article 102, the prohibition exists and therefore the potential conflict between 'welfare' (which is arguably the objective it should seek to achieve) and 'fairness' (which is possibly the grounds for the prohibition of discrimination) must be elaborated on. Thus, in the text that follows, using a law and economics approach, 'fairness' and 'welfare' will be assessed as possible criteria for establishing whether discrimination should or should not be a type of abuse.

A Welfare

Although the standard of harm under Article 102 is still not unambiguous, at least the current tendency appears to be one towards a 'consumer welfare' standard. This can mainly be seen in documents such as the EAGCP Report, the DG

[78] Ridyard (n 43) 291; Lang and O'Donoghue (n 55) 111; M Armstrong, 'Recent Developments in the Economics of Price Discrimination' in R Blundell, W Newey and T Persson (eds), *Advances in Economics and Econometrics: Theory and Application: Ninth World Congress* (Cambridge, CUP, 2006) 100.

[79] TP Gehrig and R Stenbacka, 'Price Discrimination, Competition and Antitrust' in *The Pros and Cons of Price Discrimination* (Swedish Competition Authority, 2005) 137.

[80] ibid.

[81] ibid 138.

[82] Lang and O'Donoghue (n 55) 87.

[83] ibid.

[84] ibid 120.

Competition Discussion Paper and, to a lesser extent, in the Commission Guidance. Particularly in the EAGCP Report, which recommended the adoption of an economic and effects-based approach to Article 102, the focus was explicitly on the improvement of consumer welfare.[85] As such, the standard for assessing whether a conduct was legitimate competition or anticompetitive had to be derived from the effects of the practice on consumers.[86] Similarly, in the Discussion Paper, the objective of Article 102 with regard to exclusionary abuses was expressed as the 'protection of competition on the market as a means of enhancing consumer welfare and of ensuring an efficient allocation of resources'.[87] Finally, in the Guidance Paper – the only official document representing the Commission's position – although it is more subtly expressed than a single objective of 'consumer welfare', the aim of the Commission's enforcement activity regarding exclusionary conduct is expressed as ensuring that dominant undertakings do not impair effective competition by foreclosing their rivals in an anticompetitive way, 'thus having an adverse impact on consumer welfare'.[88]

In terms of the assessment of discrimination in economics (which is clearly important for establishing its effects on 'welfare'), there are differing opinions as to whether the ability to discriminate is proof of market power. Some have argued that price discrimination is correctly understood as providing evidence of market power, although competitive price discrimination – the possibility that a market could be characterised simultaneously by price discrimination and free entry – could break the link between market power and anticompetitive effect, on a demonstration that entry is easy.[89] Yet, some have also argued that discriminatory pricing is a normal phenomenon, and certainly is not by itself sufficient evidence of market power.[90] It has been noted that price discrimination is perfectly consistent with competition, just not with perfect competition, and although it implies

[85] EAGCP Report (n 20) 2. The EAGCP Report emphasises the need to concentrate on the effects of conduct, rather than its form; ibid 3.

[86] ibid 7–9.

[87] 'Discussion Paper' (n 30) [4], [54]. The 'Discussion Paper' concentrates on exclusionary abuses and leaves out discriminatory practices which it appears to deem as neither exclusionary nor exploitative; ibid [3].

[88] 'Guidance' (n 30) [19].

[89] JB Baker, 'Competitive Price Discrimination: The Exercise of Market Power without Anticompetitive Effects (Comment on Klein and Wiley)' (2003) 70 *Antitrust Law Journal* 643, 644. Yet, that possibility does not break the link antitrust law correctly makes between price discrimination and market power; ibid. Similarly for an argument that the ability to price discriminate demonstrates that the firm has a certain amount of market power, see Hovenkamp (n 22) 573. For an empirical example of price discrimination demonstrating market power albeit the lack of it showing lower consumer surplus (as competition leads firms to segment the market further) in the Spanish local TV industry, see R Gil and D Riera-Crichton, 'Price Discrimination and Competition in Two-Sided Markets: Evidence from the Spanish Local TV Industry' IESE Business School, University of Navarra Working Paper WP-894 (January 2011).

[90] WJ Baumol and DG Swanson, 'The New Economy and Ubiquitous Competitive Price Discrimination: Identifying Defensible Criteria of Market Power' (2003) 70 *Antitrust Law Journal* 661; B Klein and JS Wiley, 'Market Power in Economics and in Antitrust: Reply to Baker' (2003) 70 *Antitrust Law Journal* 655, 655; P Muysert, 'Price Discrimination – An Unreliable Indicator of Market Power' (2004) 25(6) *European Competition Law Review* 350, 350.

that price is above marginal cost, this has no bearing on a firm's potential to harm competition.[91] It has also been suggested that it is actually competition, rather than its absence, that in many cases serves to impose discriminatory pricing, since it is scale economies in general and repeated sunk costs in particular that force firms in the affected industries, if they operate in competitive markets, to adopt prices that are discriminatory and exceed marginal costs.[92] Arguably, firms cannot avoid these practices wherever such prices are feasible (ie, because customers or sales can be divided up effectively without risk of arbitrage).[93] Such firms may be able to persistently indulge in *uniform* pricing *only if* they possess the sort of monopoly power that forecloses such competition and enables them to obtain abundant earnings.[94] In markets where entry is quick and easy, discriminatory prices generally will be the only way for firms to generate revenues that cover costs.[95] This would imply that it is actually *uniform* pricing which is implicitly imposed on dominant undertakings by the prohibition of discrimination that is in fact potentially harmful. Thus, this might further imply that the prohibition of discrimination in Article 102 is perverse. In fact, as will be seen below, there are instances in which it is *uniform* pricing as opposed to discriminatory pricing that will have harmful effects on welfare, for example, by leading to higher prices.

According to economics, discrimination can either reduce or increase consumer welfare; its effects on welfare are therefore ambiguous.[96] The economic studies – which generally concentrate on price discrimination in final goods markets – find that the welfare effects depend mainly on whether discrimination causes output to increase or decrease.[97] For example, in industries with fixed and common costs, such as airlines, hotels and cinemas, discrimination can be beneficial as it can lower the price to *all* users of the service due to the costs being spread over more customers.[98] An important class of cases in which the total output effect and the overall welfare effect is more likely to be positive is where price discrimination leads to the opening up of new markets.[99] However, as stated by Motta, '[e]conomic theory shows that price discrimination unambiguously reduces welfare only when it does not raise total output, whereas the sign of

[91] JC Cooper, L Froeb, DP O'Brien and S Tschantz, 'Does Price Discrimination Intensify Competition? Implications for Antitrust' (2005) 72 *Antitrust Law Journal* 327, 357.

[92] Baumol and Swanson (n 90) 662.

[93] ibid.

[94] ibid.

[95] ibid 671.

[96] See, eg, M Armstrong and J Vickers, 'Price Discrimination, Competition and Regulation' (1993) 41 *Journal of Industrial Economics* 335, 336; Gerard (n 34) 105; A Perrot, 'Towards an Effects-based Approach of Price Discrimination' in *The Pros and Cons of Price Discrimination* (Swedish Competition Authority, 2005) 168.

[97] See R Schmalensee, 'Output and Welfare Implications of Monopolistic Third-Degree Price Discrimination' (1981) 71 *American Economic Review* 242 and HR Varian, 'Price Discrimination and Social Welfare' (1985) 75 *American Economic Review* 870, 871 for the argument that, in general, output and welfare may increase or decrease when price discrimination is allowed, although an increase in output remains a necessary condition for welfare increase.

[98] Muysert (n 90) 353; Kolasky (n 7) 34.

[99] Armstrong and Vickers (n 96) 336.

welfare change is ambiguous in all other cases'.[100] Accordingly, depending on the informational and strategic context, the various forms of price discrimination may have very different effects on consumer surplus, as well as on producer surplus.[101] As a result, the welfare effects of price discrimination require a case-by-case analysis.[102]

Moreover, it has also been noted that the effects of discrimination in intermediate markets are not necessarily the same as those in final markets.[103] The models of final good markets are therefore inappropriate for the analysis of intermediate good markets.[104] There are two fundamental differences between final and intermediate good markets. First, in an intermediate market, unlike a typical final good market, the buyers' demands for the product are interdependent.[105] Secondly, buyers of inputs often have the ability to integrate backward into supply of the good.[106] In fact, intermediaries such as retailers compete in different ways, but a key component of competition, at least for retailers of a reasonable size, is the vigorous negotiations retailers have with suppliers.[107] Each retailer hopes to gain a competitive edge over its retail competitors by extracting a better deal from its suppliers and this competitive negotiation process plays a key role in forcing down the profits of upstream suppliers and bringing down prices for consumers.[108] If a dominant supplier is not allowed to price discriminate, each retailer realises that any deal it extracts from this supplier will also be available to its competitors, and thus retailers have less incentive to negotiate vigorously.[109] At the same time, the supplier realises that any deal it offers to one retailer will have to be given to all, and thus it has less incentive to give any retailer a price cut.[110] The likely result is higher prices for all, the suppliers keeping a greater share of monopoly profits, and less pressure on the supplier to enhance its productivity.[111] Since lower marginal payments translate into lower retail prices, consumers stand to

[100] M Motta, *Competition Policy: Theory and Practice* (Cambridge, CUP, 2004) 496. Hovenkamp argues that even when price discrimination increases output, it may be exclusionary and in contrast where it does not increase output, it may attract entry to the market due to the higher prices charged by the discriminating firm; see Hovenkamp (n 22) 294.

[101] Perrot (n 96) 168. See also Lowe who argues that while some consumers will pay a higher price and others will pay a lower price, collectively consumers will have to pay more to finance the extra profits obtained by the supplier and to cover the extra costs of supporting the price discrimination scheme. Therefore, consumer welfare will in general decline unless it can be clearly shown that otherwise the lower priced market(s) would not be served at all and therefore the price discrimination will lead to an undisputable increase of output. It is only in the latter case that consumer welfare may actually increase; P Lowe, 'Current Issues of EU Competition Law: The New Competition Enforcement Regime' (2004) 24 *Northwestern Journal of International Law & Business* 567, 583.

[102] Geradin and Petit (n 36) 483; Lage and Allendesalazar (n 45) 17.

[103] Katz (n 4) 155; O'Brien and Shaffer (n 4) 297.

[104] Katz (n 4) 155.

[105] ibid.

[106] ibid.

[107] A Fletcher, 'The Reform of Article 82: Recommendations on Key Policy Objectives' speech at the Competition Law Forum (Brussels, 15 March 2005) 2.

[108] ibid.

[109] ibid.

[110] ibid.

[111] ibid.

gain and on balance social welfare rises as well, and prohibiting intermediate price discrimination leads to higher marginal input prices for all buyers.[112] The model implies that, *ceteris paribus*, provisions such as the Robinson-Patman Act *unambiguously* reduce welfare and this is independent of both the degree of asymmetry among the downstream firms as well as their idiosyncratic bargaining powers.[113]

For business-to-business discrimination, it has also been noted that a manufacturer or supplier has no interest in destroying competition among its own distributors or dealers, which would injure itself as well as the smaller dealers and customers.[114] In fact, a manufacturer might use differential pricing in order to create incentives at the dealer level, forcing dealers to perform better.[115] Therefore, it has been argued that a prerequisite to secondary-line recovery should be a showing that the supplied market is not performing competitively, and that dealer buying power, rather than manufacturer reward, explains the price discrimination under consideration.[116]

Regarding discrimination in final good markets, it has similarly been noted that even though price discrimination can be seen as a way in which the firm can extract some of the unexploited consumer surplus and the deadweight loss, and thus increase its profits, consumers may not be worse off with such strategies.[117] For example, when discrimination expands output so that customer segments that would otherwise be excluded are served, it might stimulate profits so as to enable investment projects that would not otherwise be taken; returns from discrimination then may encourage firms to invest more.[118] This would obviously also have the direct effect of serving those customers who would otherwise be priced out of the market. Furthermore, economics also shows that in some cases the effects of discrimination between consumers are not easily determined and may boil down to an assessment of the curvature of total demand for the products. This will be demonstrated below in the context of spatial price discrimination since it is important for the purposes of operationalising the prohibition under Article 102.

The products of spatial competitors are differentiated in their physical location or in their products' attributes.[119] So 'spatial competition' in this sense would cover the competition between any differentiated products and is not limited to physical space as such. In an important class of spatial models and many real-world markets, the consumers to whom one firm would like to raise price – its strong market – are another firm's weak market to which it would like to lower

[112] O'Brien and Shaffer (n 4) 298.

[113] ibid.

[114] H Hovenkamp, 'The Robinson-Patman Act and Competition: Unfinished Business' (2001) 68 *Antitrust Law Journal* 125, 137. See similarly Bishop (n 7) 79.

[115] Hovenkamp, ibid, 137.

[116] ibid 139.

[117] Church and Ware (n 21) 157.

[118] Gehrig and Stenbacka (n 79) 134.

[119] Cooper, Froeb, O'Brien and Tschantz (n 91) 328.

price ('best-response asymmetry').[120] When this asymmetry exists, the equilibrium outcome of spatial competitors reacting to each other's discriminatory price reductions may be lower prices for all consumers and lower profits for all firms, compared with an equilibrium in which all firms offer uniform pricing to all consumers.[121] It has been suggested that the welfare effects of deterring competitive spatial discrimination are not ambiguous; deterrence of it *unambiguously* harms consumers and to the extent that legislation such as the Robinson-Patman Act induces oligopolists to choose uniform pricing rather than spatial price discrimination, it helps them achieve the outcome they would choose jointly if the competition laws allowed such collusion.[122]

A necessary condition for 'competitive spatial price discrimination' to obtain is that each firm's strong market is at least one other firm's weak market, and vice-versa. Thus, competitive spatial price discrimination should be distinguished from another common sort of price discrimination that arises when firms agree on which consumer groups are strong markets and which are weak markets ('best-response symmetry'). The latter results in discrimination in the form of pricing strategies, such as movie discounts for students, early-bird dinner specials, or higher airfares for business travellers, and does not necessarily result in more intense competition than uniform pricing. Thus, when firms agree on which customers are strong markets (and which are weak), all firms have an incentive to offer higher prices to the same group of customers.[123]

When firms agree on which markets are weak and which are strong, the effects of price discrimination are harder to determine. Since firms agree on the customers to whom they raise and lower price, competitive reactions to rivals may reinforce the initial responses of higher and lower prices. The net overall effect of price discrimination on welfare is determined by the degree to which prices increase for strong-market consumers and fall for weak-market consumers, which in turn depends on the curvature, the own-price elasticity, and the cross-price elasticity of demand.[124]

From a competition law and policy perspective, apart from the possible incapability of competition authorities and courts to assess sufficiently the relevant parameters, such a situation would also require one to make trade-offs between different consumer groups. Thus even if all the price elasticities can be estimated accurately enough, and the aggregate welfare effect of discrimination found to be positive because the negative effects on some consumers are outweighed by the positive effects on other consumers, economics and public policy may still clash. This is because one has to weigh the losses of consumers in low-elasticity markets against the gains of those in high-elasticity markets and of the producer.[125] Price

[120] ibid.
[121] ibid 328–29.
[122] ibid 332.
[123] ibid 329.
[124] ibid 343.
[125] Tirole (n 23) 139.

discrimination redistributes income away from the low-elasticity groups towards consumers in the high-elasticity groups and the monopolist, but the low-elasticity groups are often (but not always) the richer consumers.[126] However, there can also be situations where, for example, it is the poorer consumers whose welfare will be reduced or it may be one of the poorer Member States of the EU whose welfare will be reduced and this is outweighed by an increase in the welfare of richer consumers or a richer Member State. Allowing discrimination under such circumstances may be much more controversial than the contrary scenario. Bearing in mind that the EU does not merely pursue economic objectives, but also social ones, this may cause problems. Thus, the assessment of 'welfare' effects may inevitably lead to an assessment of 'fairness', which will be discussed in the next subsection.

B Fairness

'Fairness' does not provide a straightforward answer to the question of whether discrimination should be an abuse under Article 102. This is because whether discrimination is 'unfair' or not depends on how one understands 'fairness' and there is no universal definition of 'fairness'. Similar to the findings in chapters four and five, 'fairness' does not provide clear-cut answers in the context of 'discrimination' either. When 'fairness' is understood as the equal treatment of equals (and the unequal treatment of unequals), the EU ban on discrimination described as 'applying dissimilar conditions to equivalent transactions' on its face appears 'fair' and, thus, legitimate.[127] Therefore, with regard to price discrimination, 'fairness' understood as 'equality'[128] would result in uniform prices for equivalent purchases. In the train example, different prices paid by the professional and the student for the same journey would be discriminatory and 'unfair' so long as the purchases can be deemed equivalent. Whether or not the different status of the commuters renders the transactions non-equivalent is a different question, but once the focus is on the transaction rather than the parties, and once it is decided that the transactions are equivalent, then the different prices would be 'unfair'. If, however, 'fairness' is understood from a distributional perspective, it would be 'fair' for the commuter with the lower income to pay a lower price for the ticket than the one with the higher income. This would imply that a *ban* on discrimination such as the prohibition in Article 102 would be 'unfair' since it would prevent the offering of lower prices to lower income consumers.

[126] ibid.

[127] For the argument that a standard such as the equal treatment of parties in similar positions is not helpful for antitrust since '[i]f the parties are really equally situated, the market will treat them equally, for that will be the most profitable way to treat them'; see RH Bork, 'The Goals of Antitrust Policy' (1967) 57(2) *American Economic Review* 242, 253.

[128] See P Westen, 'The Empty Idea of Equality' (1982) 95 *Harvard Law Review* 537 for the argument that 'equality' is meaningless as a benchmark.

The 'fairness' assessment of discrimination is a markedly peculiar issue due to the perception of 'fairness' as 'equality'. For example, universal service obligations tend to insist on 'equal treatment', according to which all consumers should be offered the same price even in spite of possible large cost differentials.[129] In other words, although the costs differ and thus the obligation of, for instance, national pricing in universal services requires discrimination in economic terms, this is not condemned by law due to other social policy objectives.[130] An interesting example is postal services, since even though it would cost more to run a post office in a rural area, charging a higher price reflecting the higher costs to the consumers in the rural area compared with the price of the same service at urban branches would probably be perceived as 'unfair', at least by the consumers in the rural area.

Indeed, a standard argument for banning price discrimination posits that every consumer should pay the same price for comparable transactions; in particular, this fairness notion implies that the price should not depend on the valuation of the buyers, or any other characteristic.[131] In this sense, the 'equal price' doctrine does not imply equal market access and it favours high-valuation customers, which in many cases tend to be the wealthier customers.[132] In contrast, one might define fairness in terms of equal market access and, under this fairness notion, customers with valuations exceeding marginal production costs should be allowed to engage in trade and participate in sharing the surplus: in markets with market power, this necessarily means that low-valuation customers will have to pay lower prices than high-valuation customers.[133] Thus, fairness per se may not be a sufficient reason for banning price discrimination.[134] Even among the simple fairness notions of 'equal price', 'equal access' and 'equal split of surplus', only the first concept seems to be consistent with uniform pricing, while the remaining two notions seem to require discriminatory pricing.[135]

In fact, it has been argued that with oligopolistic competition the availability of schemes for individualised prices catch firms in a classical 'prisoner dilemma' trap and any legal interpretation of 'fairness' as a support for a ban on price discrimination would solve the industry's coordination problem and allow them to implement uniform pricing schemes.[136] This is because the competing firms would have a strong joint incentive to create mechanisms so as to coordinate the pricing rules applied by all of them and, essentially, any mechanism which is able to coordinate the pricing rules to uniform prices would be equivalent to a collusive device.[137] A

[129] EAGCP Report (n 20) 30, fn 21.

[130] See Council Directive 2002/22/EC on Universal Service and Users' Rights Relating to Electronic Communications Networks and Services [2002] OJ L108/51.

[131] Gehrig and Stenbacka (n 79) 140.

[132] ibid.

[133] ibid 140–41.

[134] ibid 141.

[135] ibid.

[136] ibid 144.

[137] ibid.

ban on discrimination such as the one in Article 102 would therefore provide firms with a convenient mechanism to extract a larger fraction of the consumer surplus.[138] Given that it is not uncommon that a finding of dominance in the EU is made at levels of market share around 40 per cent and the subsequent possibility of finding single firm dominance in oligopolistic markets, this is a potential implication of the ban in Article 102; the ban, then, might actually facilitate collusion.

Moreover, the notion that two customers should pay the same price regardless of their degree of preference for the product – as marked by the price they are willing to pay (ie, elasticity of demand) and regardless of their bargaining power on 'fairness' grounds – has been criticised as having nothing to do with competition or the efficient allocation of resources.[139] It has been noted that prohibiting price discrimination on the grounds of 'unfairness' to those consumers who have to pay a higher price may end up making these very consumers worse off.[140] Furthermore, it has been argued that the 'fairness' or 'unfairness' of price discrimination is necessarily based on a local assessment of distributive effects and there is no way of telling whether such local assessment is consistent with global concerns for distribution either.[141] Such global concerns can hardly be made the subject of antitrust proceedings under a rule of law and therefore it seems advisable to assess price discrimination less in terms of 'fairness' and more in terms of procompetitive and anticompetitive effects.[142] All in all, it is particularly unclear whether 'fairness' arguments support uniform prices or discriminatory price schemes with individualised prices.[143]

As discussed in chapter four, 'fairness' as an objective has arguably played a prominent role in the context of Article 102 due to the 'ordoliberal' influences.[144] Article 102's prohibitions of unfair pricing, unfair trading conditions and discrimination are undoubtedly related to a certain (undefined) notion of 'fairness'. Nonetheless, the pursuance of a stand-alone 'fairness' objective may not be appropriate, particularly with a modern economic effects-based approach.[145] In this context, it is noteworthy that the ban on discrimination is somewhat different from the other types of 'unfair' conduct prohibited by Article 102. This is because, as demonstrated in chapters four and five, the other types of unfair behaviour described there cannot even be objectively defined and thus their prohibition poses a greater risk to legal certainty and freedom of contract than the ban on

[138] ibid.

[139] Lage and Allendesalazar (n 45) 344.

[140] EAGCP Report (n 20) 32.

[141] ibid.

[142] ibid.

[143] Gehrig and Stenbacka (n 79) 133.

[144] See, in general, DJ Gerber, 'Fairness in Competition Law: European and US Experience' presented at a Conference on Fairness and Asian Competition Laws (Kyoto, 5 March 2004) available at: .kyotogakuen.ac.jp/o_ied/information/fairness_in_competition_law.pdf 6. See ch 4 this volume, section II.

[145] See, eg, N Kroes, 'Preliminary Thoughts on Policy Review of Article 82' speech at the Fordham Corporate Law Institute (New York, 23 September 2005) 3.

discrimination.[146] Thus, the ban on 'unfair pricing' and 'unfair trading conditions' – which reflects a 'substantive fairness' ideal in competition law – remains as an almost unenforceable piece of law.

The ban on discrimination is different from the ban on 'unfair pricing' or 'unfair trading conditions' because 'discrimination' can at least be defined to a greater extent than the former. This is because the ban in Article 102(c) does not *directly* use a 'fairness' prescription. Although it is not always easy to assess which transactions, conditions and/or parties are equivalent, once (or if) this is determined, the ban on discrimination can be operationalised. In other words, the current understanding of discrimination as the unequal treatment of equals (and the equal treatment of unequals) can be enforced more easily than a ban on 'unfair pricing'. Surely, this requires the authority to decide what renders the transactions non-equivalent and when the different treatment of equivalent transactions is acceptable. Whether this is desirable depends again to a great degree on how one understands 'fairness' and includes it as an objective in competition law.

The best example of what place 'fairness' should be given in deciding whether discrimination should be prohibited can be found in price discrimination. Since price is seen as a tool by which the dominant undertaking exploits its power to earn more profits, price discrimination is also considered to be 'unfair' because some people pay more for the product in question than others.[147] Moreover, economic analysis has put a lot of weight on the exploitative effects of price discrimination allowing the dominant undertaking to earn more profits.[148] Economic analysis has also stressed that distribution of output across consumers tends to be inefficient if different consumers pay different prices and presumably put different valuations on the last units they purchase.[149]

Furthermore, if people's 'fairness' conceptions depend on interpersonal comparisons, as suggested in the literature,[150] then a different price paid by another person in an equivalent transaction could result in an 'unfairness' perception and this may cause a loss of utility for the consumer who has paid the higher price. For price comparisons, when the degree of similarity between the comparative transactions is relatively high, buyers have little differential information to explain a

[146] eg, as demonstrated in ch 5 this volume, even though 'unfair' pricing by a dominant undertaking is an abuse, the application of the provision has so far not been able to define what an 'unfair' price actually is. This inability is not even limited to competition law; 'fair price' has been quested ever since the middle ages without success. A body of law much older than competition law, namely contract law, has failed to answer the question of what an unfair price is and therefore has rightly ceased asking it; see ch 4 this volume, section IV.B. In general see, eg, R de Roover, 'The Concept of the Just Price: Theory and Economic Policy' (1958) 18(4) *The Journal of Economic History* 418 and BW Dempsey, 'Just Price in a Functional Economy' (1935) 25(3) *American Economic Review* 471 for an examination of 'just price'.

[147] EAGCP Report (n 20) 31.

[148] ibid.

[149] ibid; M Armstrong and J Vickers, 'Competitive Price Discrimination' (2001) 32(4) *RAND Journal of Economics* 579, 582.

[150] See, eg, L Xia, KB Moore and JL Cox, 'The Price Is Unfair! A Conceptual Framework of Price Fairness Perceptions' (2004) 68 *Journal of Marketing* 1, 6.

price discrepancy.[151] Thus, the consumers expect or believe that they are entitled to equal prices, and they are likely to judge the price discrepancy as 'unfair'.[152] Therefore, a high degree of transaction similarity leads to a high perception of price unfairness.[153] For example, if a commuter on the train finds out that the person sitting next to her has paid a much lower price for exactly the same journey, the following feeling of having been treated 'unfairly' may lead her to switch to another type of transport instead; this may or may not be desirable and/or efficient depending on the circumstances.

Although 'equality' and 'equal treatment' may be more easily acceptable in policy and law than differential treatment, from an economic point of view, as discussed above,[154] uniformity can also constitute discrimination. Indeed, the 'fair price' may actually *require* discrimination. This can be derived from the insights from behavioural economics discussed in chapter five, and particularly from the model of Rabin.[155] The key insight is that the 'fair' price depends on the consumer's valuation of the product.[156] The result of this is that since consumers' valuations of the same product would in most cases be different, the 'fair price' would also differ from one consumer to another depending on the consumer's valuation. Hence, there is not a single 'fair price' but there are different individually 'fair' prices. This necessitates different prices to be offered to different people for the same product – namely discrimination. In other words, this economic insight would mean that the 'fair price' is actually 'discriminatory' in competition law terms. For EU competition law, the implication is a Catch-22: a dominant undertaking can comply with either subparagraph (a) or (c) of Article 102 but not both, since only discriminatory prices can be 'fair' if these economic models are accepted. If the undertaking does not discriminate and complies with Article 102(c), then its prices may inevitably fall foul of Article 102(a).[157] Other than the absurdity of this outcome, it would also imply that the prohibition in subparagraph (c) not only potentially fails under a welfare test, but also fails under a fairness test.

To summarise, 'fairness' supports equivocal conclusions depending on the interpretation of the concept regarding the inclusion of discrimination under Article 102. The insight from economics is that discrimination is a practice that should be assessed with regard to its effects on 'welfare', rather than from a 'fairness' perspective. The next subsection demonstrates some instances of this clash

[151] ibid 3.

[152] ibid 4.

[153] ibid.

[154] See above, text around n 22.

[155] See M Rabin, 'Incorporating Fairness into Game Theory and Economics' (1993) 83(5) *American Economic Review* 1281, discussed in ch 5 this volume, text around fn 81.

[156] See ch 5 this volume, text around fn 83.

[157] Although this conclusion depends on whether the difference between the valuations of consumers would render the transactions non-equivalent and thus outside the scope of Art 102(c), that question has not been answered. In other words, whether customer-specific reasons would provide an objective justification for the ban on discrimination is not yet clear but, as so far construed, it is the criteria relating to the transactions rather than the party that matters. See above, text around n 35.

between 'fairness' and 'welfare' with examples from decisional practice at the national level.

C Fairness versus Welfare

Although 'fairness towards consumers' is perhaps the most easily acceptable understanding of 'fairness' under Article 102 when a 'consumer welfare standard' is pursued, this understanding of fairness can clash with the objective of 'welfare' in certain circumstances. For example, the most extreme case of price discrimination (ie, 'perfect price discrimination' being as efficient as perfect competition in maximising output and 'total welfare'), nevertheless minimises 'consumer welfare' as the producer reaps the whole surplus. Similarly, where 'fairness' is understood as 'fairness towards competitors' this can lead to losses in consumer and total welfare by protection of inefficient competitors. Commentators have given the example of selective price cutting on this point: where Article 102(c) is used to prohibit selective price cutting when the price is not predatory, they do so in pursuit of a policy of 'fairness' to competitors of the favoured customer which comes at the expense of consumer and total welfare.[158] Thus, there may be a conflict between 'fairness' and 'welfare', alongside a conflict between different types of 'welfare' and different understandings of 'fairness'.

This possible conflict between 'welfare' (understood as 'efficiency') and 'fairness' has been argued in front of the UK Competition Commission (CC) during its investigation regarding the 'termination charges' of some mobile network operators (Vodafone, O2, T-Mobile and Orange).[159] In the investigation, the termination charges of the named operators were found to be excessive and 'unfair'. Moreover, the alleged use of Ramsey pricing (which is an example of price discrimination in that prices are set in relation to elasticities rather than costs), where higher termination charges were used to subsidise customer acquisition costs and the (cheaper) price of outbound mobile phone calls, was deemed to produce adverse distributional effects.[160] The CC found it 'unfair' that fixed-line customers who call mobiles should subsidise mobile phone subscribers.[161] The CC held that Ramsey pricing[162] might be thought to lead to distributional 'unfairness' since

[158] Gifford and Kudrle (n 1) 1280.

[159] 'Vodafone, O2, Orange and T-Mobile: Reports on References under section 13 of the Telecommunications Act 1984 on the charges made by Vodafone, O2, Orange and T-Mobile for terminating calls from fixed and mobile networks' 2003 available at: www.competition-commission.org.uk/rep_pub/reports/2003/475mobilephones.htm#full. A 'termination charge' is a wholesale charge made by one telecommunications operator to another for connecting calls to a phone on its network; ibid [2.2].

[160] ibid [2.400].

[161] ibid [2.399].

[162] Although economic theory states that in competitive markets, prices will be set equal to marginal costs, it is also recognised that where there are fixed or common costs to be recovered, setting price equal to marginal cost would leave firms making losses. To cover these costs, prices need to rise above marginal costs and one approach is to require less price-sensitive customers or products for which

fixed-to-mobile and off-net callers – whose demand is thought to be relatively price-inelastic – would pay for mobile call termination well in excess of the costs which their calling activity causes the mobile network operators to incur.[163] This is not only an instance of the practice of discrimination between consumers being scrutinised by the competition authority of a Member State and being found against public interest,[164] but is also an example of 'fairness' considerations playing a prominent role in such a case in the clash with 'efficiency' arguments.

Moreover, it also points out the trade-off issue. One of the arguments of the mobile network operators in that case was that, because most people had a mobile phone, what they lost in high termination charges they gained in low access and outgoing call charges.[165] The Office of Telecommunications (OFTEL) (now OFCOM) countered that although these people may be the same in some cases, there was a significant number of people for whom the adverse effect could be important.[166] Even if the proportion of the population adversely affected was quite modest, for example around 10 per cent, this would be a large amount of people (around five million). Moreover, OFTEL believed that the people most adversely affected were those without a mobile phone – around 15 per cent of the population – and this group had a disproportionate number of elderly and low-income people in it. The CC held that it was not necessary to decide whether fixed line-only or mobile-only customers would be the more advantaged or disadvantaged by a price control on termination charges.[167] All those who have both a fixed line and a mobile phone would suffer a detriment to the extent that they use their fixed line instead of their mobile phone to call a mobile phone or make more off-net calls to mobiles than they receive. The group of payphone users who called mobiles but did not own mobile phones themselves were also found to contribute 'unfairly' to funding the mobile network operators' customers through high termination charges.

The CC explicitly held that although the investigated pricing structure may, in theory, be an efficient way to recover fixed and common costs, there are other considerations that it believed should be taken into account in assessing whether a particular pricing structure operated in the public interest.[168] One of these other considerations was whether the pricing structure was *equitable* as among different

demand is less elastic to bear a greater proportion of the common costs and more price-sensitive customers or products for which demand is more elastic to bear a smaller portion of these costs. This pricing structure is sometimes referred to as 'Ramsey pricing'; ibid [2.214].

[163] ibid [2.510]. In any case, the CC found that the mobile network operators currently did not [2.434] (except possibly for time-of-day variations) and would likely not [2.446] set Ramsey prices regarding termination charges.

[164] Each mobile network operator was found to have a monopoly of call termination on its network; ibid [2.147].

[165] ibid [2.390].

[166] ibid [2.391].

[167] ibid [2.399].

[168] ibid [2.402].

telecommunications users.[169] The CC did not agree with Vodafone's argument that efficiency considerations had to be elevated above those of equity.[170] Thus, the CC recommended the use of price caps on the termination charges of the mobile network operators under investigation.

Similarly, OFGEM, the British energy regulator in introducing a non-discrimination requirement on energy retailers appears to have preferred achieving 'fairness' in the sense of apparently protecting vulnerable consumers at the expense of leading to higher prices for *all* consumers in the long run.[171] What would have been the outcome of these cases had they occurred in the EU remains debatable, but there is a high probability that they would have been decided differently under an approach excluding 'fairness' as a distinct policy objective.

In a case similar to that decided by the CC, the Czech Republic Supreme Court affirmed the national competition authority's decision to fine Eurotel – the third largest Czech mobile operator – around €1.6 million for charging its mobile phone users a higher price for calls made to Èeský Mobil (CM) than T-Mobile.[172] Even more interestingly, the Swedish Competition Authority lodged an action against TeliaSonera – the Swedish incumbent telecoms operator – for abusing its dominant position by selectively targeting customers who have left the company for a competing operator by offering them advantageous terms if they returned to TeliaSonera. The terms which aimed to entice customers back to TeliaSonera included a reduced reconnection fee and reduced prices on low-cost calling plans.[173]

In another case, the CC found the practice of geographical price discrimination of some supermarkets which consisted of charging lower prices to consumers in some localities to be against the public interest.[174] As another example of scrutiny of discrimination between consumers, the practice of varying prices in different geographical locations in the light of local competitive conditions, such variation not being related to costs as carried on by some supermarkets, was found to distort competition.[175] The conduct, when carried out by Safeway, Sainsbury and

[169] Nevertheless, the CC found that the data was insufficiently robust by itself to support conclusions leading to action regarding the distributional arguments. Yet, it held that the fixed network operators' customers unfairly bore the costs of the distorted pricing structure and this was an important element of the argument that action should be taken to reduce the termination charges; ibid [2.428]. For the judicial review judgment upholding the CC's decision, see *R (on the application of T-Mobile, Vodafone, Orange) v The Competition Commission* [2003] EWHC 1566 Admin, particularly [120]–[24].

[170] Vodafone, O2, Orange and T-Mobile Report (n 159) [2.514].

[171] See M Hviid and C Waddams Price, 'Non-discrimination Clauses in the Retail Energy Sector' ESRC Centre for Competition Policy Working Paper 10-18 (November 2010).

[172] P Nosek, I Šime ek and KŠ Balaštík, 'Current Developments in Member States: Czech Republic' (2006) 2(1) *European Competition Journal* 195, 198.

[173] M Johnsson, 'Current Developments in Member States: Sweden' (2006) 2(1) *European Competition Journal* 253, 255.

[174] 'Supermarkets: A Report on the supply of groceries from multiple stores in the United Kingdom' 2000 [1.6] available at: www.competition-commission.org.uk/rep_pub/reports/2000/446super.htm#full.

[175] ibid.

Tesco, who had market power, operated against the public interest because their customers tended to pay more at stores that did not face particular competitors than they would if those competitors had been present in the area.[176] The practice distorted competition in the retail supply of groceries in that it tended to focus some element of price competition into localities where particular lower-priced competitors were present and away from other areas; it also contributed to the position that a majority of grocery products were not fully exposed to competitive pressure.[177] The CC held that

> [t]o the extent that consumers who shop in each of these supermarket fascias pay more for their groceries in some areas than in others, and to the extent that cost variations do not account for the differences, the practice has obvious adverse effects because it discriminates between different consumers. Some consumers pay more than they otherwise would, but only because certain competitors are not present in their area.[178]

It is striking that the CC reached this decision despite its recognition that some prices were set *in response to* regional and local factors such as average local incomes or local customer price sensitivity.[179] In other words, lower prices in the low-income areas were nevertheless found to be against the public interest merely because they did not reflect costs, although uniform prices would have resulted in low-income groups paying higher prices.[180]

Interestingly, in its home credit market investigation the CC had to deal with the argument of some credit providers that 'fairness requires a single pricing policy' since 'it would not be fair to offer different terms to neighbours', justifying national pricing of home credit products.[181] In contrast to its findings in the supermarkets investigation mentioned above, the CC treated the *lack* of *differential* pricing regardless of the presence of competing offers in localities as a sign of a *lack* of competition.[182] Similarly, the lack of price variation for different types of customers was seen as demonstrating a lack of competition.[183] What is not clear from these statements is whether discrimination in its economic sense was being

[176] Nonetheless, recognising that it is unusual, the CC did not recommend any remedies for the identified adverse effects of this practice in the light of the overall finding that the market is generally competitive; ibid [1.8].

[177] ibid [2.406].

[178] ibid [2.407]. The CC found that only those supermarkets having the largest market shares at the national and regional levels, and with a large number of stores of significant size, were likely to have sufficient market power such that their actions would be capable of operating against the public interest. Thus, the practice was found to clearly operate against the public interest when practised by a major party; ibid [2.328], [2.408].

[179] ibid [2.403].

[180] The CC states elsewhere in the Report that '[i]f costs vary on a regional basis, then uniform pricing implicitly entails consumers in low-cost areas cross-subsidizing consumers in high cost areas. This may imply a socially undesirable redistribution of income from low- to high-income areas (if low-cost areas coincide with low-income areas)'; ibid [7.129].

[181] 'Home Credit Market Investigation' Final Report, 30 November 2006 [6.39], [6.48] *et seq*, available at: www.competition-commission.org.uk/rep_pub/reports/2006/fulltext/517.pdf.

[182] ibid [6.26]–[6.28].

[183] ibid [6.29] *et seq*.

condemned or encouraged since the discussion is mostly expressed in terms of 'price variation' which may or may not economically constitute discrimination.

What must be pointed out on the basis of these cases is that there are two very different scenarios in which 'fairness' and 'welfare' may clash as a result of a discriminatory practice: in some cases, discrimination leads to lower income customers paying a higher price (such as in the termination-charges case) or discrimination leads to lower income customers paying a lower price (such as in the supermarkets case). Although the former can be explicable on the basis of 'fairness' and although, as a *policy choice*, 'fairness' may be preferred to efficiency, it is very difficult to see how the latter scenario is explicable on the basis of 'fairness', since although customers pay different prices for the same services, it is the lower income group that benefits from it. For example, it has been argued that the general effect of the *United Brands* decision is clear in that it redistributes income away from consumers in the poorer regions of Europe and toward consumers in the richer regions.[184] Thus, a crude understanding of 'fairness' as 'equality' is therefore problematic since not only does it lead to objectionable outcomes from different perspectives of 'fairness', it also comes at the cost of possible efficiency gains.

What these national cases also signify is that, once it is accepted that Article 102 is also applicable to business-to-consumer conduct, similar cases are bound to occur more frequently, bringing with them the risk of prohibiting discrimination which may be welfare enhancing. In other words, telecommunications operators, supermarkets, transport operators, petrol stations and so on may be challenged for their discriminatory pricing structures by unhappy consumers. Indeed, a quiet condemnation of Ramsey pricing, for example, has already occurred at the EU level in *British Leyland* where it was held that the different fees charged by British Leyland for conformity certificates allegedly depending on whether the applicant was a dealer or a private individual was abusive.[185] The difference was not based on the cost, but on the consideration that the trader which was carrying out a transaction for gain could be required to pay a higher fee that a private individual. In other words, British Leyland was charging a different fee depending on the willingness to pay of the customers, that is, the elasticity of demand. However, this was not deemed legitimate by the ECJ. Interestingly, this was abusive, even though it was consumers paying lower prices and businesses paying higher prices.

The reason that such enforcement has not occurred more widely could be that, reinforced by the lack of class actions, private enforcement has so far not been an important part of EU competition law enforcement in general. On the contrary, the enforcement of the US Robinson-Patman Act, for example, has mainly been by way of private actions.[186] Thus, one wonders what would have been the

[184] W Bishop, 'Price Discrimination under Article 86: Political Economy in the European Court' (1981) 44 *Modern Law Review* 282, 288–89.

[185] Case 226/84 *British Leyland plc v Commission* [1987] 1 CMLR 185, [29].

[186] WE Kovacic, 'The Modern Evolution of US Competition Policy Enforcement Norms' (2004) 71 *Antitrust Law Journal* 377, 413–14.

outcome if the UK consumers claimed from Tesco damages consisting of the difference between what they paid at the higher-priced stores and what they would have paid at the cheaper-priced stores. The consequences and welfare effects of such increased litigation would mainly depend on the merits of individual cases and could result in socially wasteful over-intervention. Moreover, given that economics demonstrates ambiguous welfare effects, and that these effects may be dependent on demand characteristics, it may not be possible for the courts to overcome the technicalities involved to reach a decision in conformity with an effects-based approach that would also provide sufficient legal certainty while avoiding perverse welfare effects.

IV RECONCILIATION

This chapter has so far demonstrated that an outright ban on discrimination is not justified without a consideration of its effects on welfare. In other words, it must be ensured that competition law does not prevent discrimination that is welfare-enhancing particularly if the objective is enhancing consumer welfare. If the objective is based on 'fairness', it should be ensured that competition law only prevents discrimination where the lack of doing so would breach a well-established conception of 'fairness'. As demonstrated so far, this may be far from easy and it might be better for competition law to focus on 'welfare' since as seen in chapters four and five 'fairness' does not render itself to rational and operational rules that also provide the undertakings with sufficient legal certainty. This is particularly noteworthy in the area of discrimination where only one understanding of 'fairness' (ie, 'equal price') would actually support a ban on discrimination, but there is no authority to support this understanding of 'fairness' over any other potential interpretations such as 'equal access'. Therefore, there is a very strong case for preferring 'welfare' over 'fairness' as the benchmark in this area.

At first glance, the most plausible way of ensuring that discrimination that is welfare-enhancing or at least welfare-neutral is not prohibited appears to be by recourse to the 'objective justification' defence. Using this defence established in the case law, the dominant undertaking can prove that its conduct is objectively justified, and thus does not constitute abuse. Moreover, as mentioned above,[187] in many cases the Commission and the EU courts have implicitly or explicitly found that any *differential* treatment of trading parties should be objectively justified by the dominant undertaking to escape the prohibition of Article 102. Nonetheless, the understanding of this defence in the Commission Guidance raises serious problems for this defence in the area of discrimination. This is because the Guidance states that a dominant undertaking can justify its practice by demonstrating either that its conduct is 'objectively necessary' or that it produces 'sub-

[187] See above, text around n 25.

stantial efficiencies that outweigh any anticompetitive effects on consumers'.[188] For both of these defences, according to the Guidance, the conduct in question must be indispensable for the goal pursued or the efficiencies claimed by the dominant undertaking.[189]

The implication of this is that, if the Commission adopts this understanding of objective justification for discriminatory abuses as well,[190] discrimination by a dominant undertaking can hardly be defended as an 'objective necessity' or even as a practice leading to efficiencies. This is because such a practice of price discrimination will seldom be 'indispensable': the undertaking can always price non-discriminatorily.[191] The perverse result of this can be that although discrimination could increase (consumer) welfare, the undertaking would not be able to defend such a practice merely because it was not an 'indispensable' action. Moreover, for the efficiency defence as elaborated on in the Guidance to be applicable, conduct must first cause likely harm to consumers. This is obvious from the explanation of indispensability: conduct being indispensable to the realisation of the efficiencies means that there are 'no less anti-competitive alternatives to the conduct that are capable of producing the same efficiencies'.[192] Thus, it is assumed that conduct is anticompetitive when the application of the *defence* comes into question. The defence is therefore not appropriate in the case of discrimination since discrimination which arguably enhances consumer welfare would not be likely to harm consumers and thus would not be anticompetitive under a consumer welfare standard in the first place. Therefore, 'objective justification' as interpreted by the Commission is not an adequate tool to ensure that welfare-enhancing discrimination is not prohibited under Article 102.

The inapplicability of the 'objective justification' defence implies that the types of discrimination which do not reduce welfare should not constitute abuse to begin with. In other words, the assessment should be done in the definition and finding of 'abuse'. Since the burden of proving abuse is on the Commission, it must establish that discrimination reduces welfare before it sanctions it. The lesson from economics is that discrimination should not be found abusive merely because some consumers are deemed to be 'exploited' by paying higher prices than others. For example, if price discrimination increases output by sales to consumers who would have been left out of the market under uniform pricing and there is no decrease in welfare, then this should be considered 'legitimate' or 'normal' competition. The undertaking should not be punished only because its

[188] 'Guidance' (n 30) [28].

[189] ibid [28], [30].

[190] The Guidance does not elaborate on 'discrimination' as a type of abusive practice, although it covers practices such as 'margin squeeze' and 'bundling' which involve discrimination.

[191] One exception to this can be thought as geographical price discrimination in cases where the different conditions in different geographical areas objectively necessitate different terms to be applied in order for all markets to be served.

[192] See 'Guidance' (n 30) [30].

practice was not 'indispensable'.[193] The same would be true for discrimination aimed at covering fixed and common costs of the undertaking by expanding output. The comparative benchmark, that is the counterfactual, would be the case under non-discriminatory pricing.[194] Even when the undertaking has no purpose other than maximising its profits, so long as this does not cause a *decrease* in consumer welfare – if the standard of harm is 'consumer welfare' – compared with non-discriminatory pricing, it should not be deemed abusive.

Although this approach to an extent ignores the abovementioned[195] trade-off issue in that *some* consumers may be paying higher prices than they would under non-discriminatory pricing as a result of discrimination, the only objective assessment in conformity with legal certainty is to look at consumer welfare in the aggregate. If discrimination results in *some* consumers being 'exploited' and these are consumers worthy of more protection than the ones benefiting from discrimination, then that protection can be provided by other means, such as *ex ante* regulation or consumer law, as a reflection of an explicit policy choice. Thus, the trade-off problem for competition law would be resolved by choosing the welfare of consumers in general. This is because if the undertaking's conduct is on the whole not harmful to consumers, then it should not be punished for having caused harm to *some* consumers. In fact, one prominent commentator has argued that due to the formidable amount of information that a competition authority needs in order to determine when price discrimination is likely to enhance or decrease welfare, one rule of thumb can be to presume that price discrimination aimed at final consumers should be permitted.[196] Moreover, where there is only harm in the form of 'exploitation' of some consumers and there is no separate harm to competition such as 'exclusion', this also raises the issue discussed throughout this study, namely that of there being possibly a lack of harm to competition in such cases which should mean that no competition law issue exists.

In this vein, it has been argued that price discrimination should be analysed under an 'effects-based' approach rather than under a form-based approach, where the former focuses on the existence of harm to competition and consists in analysing the potential exclusionary effects of the practice.[197] This approach would result in less emphasis put on the exploitative effects of discrimination since either exploitation comes from a (legal) monopoly position, a situation that calls for regulation rather than competition policy, or it is due to barriers to entry or exclu-

[193] For the argument that efficiencies should be included in the assessment of whether competition is 'normal', ie 'competition on the merits' or not, see E Rousseva, 'The Concept of "Objective Justification" of an Abuse of a Dominant Position: Can it help to Modernise the Analysis under Article 82 EC?' (2006) 2(2) *The Competition Law Review* 27, 68–69. On the treatment of efficiencies, see also this volume ch 7, section II.C and ch 8, section IV.

[194] According to the GC, in order to be lawful, the protection of the commercial position of an undertaking in a dominant position must be based on criteria of economic efficiency and consistent with the interests of consumers; Case T-228/97 *Irish Sugar plc v Commission* [1999] ECR II-2969, [189], upheld on appeal in Case C-497/99 *Irish Sugar plc v Commission* [2001] ECR I-5333.

[195] See above, text around nn 125 and 165.

[196] Armstrong (n 8) 460.

[197] Perrot (n 96) 183.

sionary practices, for which the approach described here is applicable.[198] This would imply that one must not only focus on the effects of discrimination on welfare, but also scrutinise the potential effect of discrimination on entry and exit.[199]

An example of where discrimination can distort competition due to its foreclosure effects is in the cases where the dominant undertaking uses non-price related practices (such as refusal to supply) to disadvantage its customers that are also its potential competitors.[200] Thus, reading back the 'competitive disadvantage' requirement into Article 102(c) should lead to discrimination being prohibited in these types of cases where the prohibition can raise welfare by enabling an as efficient competitor to enter the market.[201] In these cases, one can establish both 'exploitation' (for example, by the customer paying too high a price for the input) and 'exclusion' (for example, by an efficient undertaking having to leave the market). For all other cases, the assessment of the effects of discrimination can be far less straightforward and a demonstration of harm to trading partners coupled with harm to competition appears to be one way of ensuring that welfare-enhancing discrimination is not prohibited. Such an approach would also be in line with the general thesis of this book in that both exploitation and exclusion should exist before a practice can be found to breach Article 102. The fact that it is only welfare-reducing discrimination that would be prohibited under this approach also implies that conduct is only prohibited when it is inefficient. As will be seen in chapter eight, a lack of increase in efficiency is another condition of abuse under the proposal of this study.

V CONCLUSION

This chapter sought to demonstrate that although discrimination is prohibited under Article 102(c) as an abuse, this prohibition can have perverse effects not only from a welfare point of view, but also from a fairness point of view under a range of interpretations of 'fairness'. This brings along a serious possibility of over-intervention into the practices of private law entities, threatening their freedom of contract, particularly because the practice is one with ambiguous welfare effects according to economics. In fact, according to economics, the effects of discrimination should be analysed on a case-by-case basis which appears far different from the approach of the EU authorities, which seems to deem any differential treatment of the trading partners of a dominant undertaking as 'discrimination'. On the other hand, it is again this ambiguity of the effects of discrimination that may justify its ban, particularly when it is 'exploitative' of some trading partners. As a result, the competition authority may have to not only

[198] ibid.
[199] ibid 179.
[200] See, eg, *Clearstream* (n 56).
[201] For the formal demonstration of this, see Armstrong (n 8) 458–59.

choose between 'fairness' and 'welfare', but also make trade-offs between the interests of different consumer groups or even different types of 'welfare'.

The prohibition can become particularly important if there is an increase in private enforcement, since prohibiting mere differential treatment by a dominant undertaking where it is not economically discriminatory and/or economically welfare-decreasing would clearly be undesirable due to the over-intervention it would imply. In certain cases, given that discrimination increases welfare, its sanctioning would indeed be perverse. Where 'consumer welfare' is accepted as the main objective of policy, the solution that discrimination is not found abusive unless the Commission (or the claimant) can prove a *decrease* in consumer welfare (for example, by proving that output does not (sufficiently) increase) appears to be an appropriate approach. This can be seen as the 'exploitation' element of abuse. This should, however, be coupled with a scrutiny of the potential foreclosure effects (ie, exclusionary effects) of discrimination since mere harm to trading partners without harm to competition should not be sanctioned under competition law. This would conversely also imply that mere harm to competitors without an examination of the effects of the conduct on customers/suppliers should not lead to the prohibition of the practice either, since the harm to competitors may not necessarily harm competition as it may simply be due to the inefficiency of the competitors.

The next part of this study seeks to achieve two aims. Chapter seven establishes the current state of the Commission's enforcement of Article 102, after its 'reform' of its approach in the recent years. It also demonstrates the problems that still remain under this 'reformed' approach. As such, chapter seven aims to fully establish the current position before chapter eight puts forward the proposal of this study on how the concept of 'abuse' should be interpreted in the context of Article 102. This is done by suggesting the necessary and sufficient conditions for an interpretation of 'abuse' that is in line with both the historical roots of Article 102 and modern economic thinking.

IV

Modernising the Approach to 'Abuse'

7

The 'Reformed' Approach to 'Abuse'

I INTRODUCTION

Following on from a discussion of the potential objectives of the prohibition in and the enforcement of Article 102 in chapters one to four, and from a practical demonstration of the clash between two of these objectives in chapters five and six, this chapter examines the recent 'reform' of the Commission's approach to 'abuse'. The next chapter (chapter eight) will, in turn, propose a modern approach to 'abuse' which follows from the culmination of the findings of this study. The aim of the current chapter is therefore to establish fully the current position over which this study's proposed modern approach is sought to be an improvement.

The Commission's rethinking of its approach to Article 102 started in the 2000s and, as has been mentioned earlier in this study, involved the publication of a Discussion Paper by DG Competition (preceded by an EAGCP Report commissioned by the Commission) and of a Guidance document by the Commission.[1] This chapter does not aim to provide a detailed assessment of either of these documents, but merely seeks to display the highlights of these documents which are relevant for a modernised approach to the concept of 'abuse'.[2] It is worth noting

[1] 'DG Competition Discussion Paper on the Application of Article 82 of the Treaty to Exclusionary Abuses' (Brussels, December 2005) available at: ec.europa.eu/competition/antitrust/art82/discpaper2005.pdf; Report by the Economic Advisory Group (EAGCP) for Competition Policy 'An Economic Approach to Article 82' (July, 2005) available at ec.europa.eu/dgs/competition/economist/eagcp_july_21_05.pdf; 'Guidance on the Commission's Enforcement Priorities in Applying Article 82 of the EC Treaty to Abusive Exclusionary Conduct by Dominant Undertakings' [2009] OJ C45/7. For earlier discussions on some particular points in these documents see, eg, ch 3 this volume, text around fns 26, 83, 134 and ch 6 this volume, section IV.

[2] For a detailed discussion of these documents see, eg, on the Discussion Paper: P Akman, 'Article 82 Reformed? The EC Discussion Paper on Exclusionary Abuses' [2006] (December) *Journal of Business Law* 816 and on the Guidance: J Killick and A Komninos, 'Schizophrenia in the Commission's Article 82 Guidance Paper: Formalism Alongside Increased Recourse to Economic Analysis' (2009) (February-I) *Global Competition Policy*; Y Katsoulacos, 'Some Critical Comments on the Commission's Guidance Paper on Art 82 EC' (2009) (February-I) *Global Competition Policy*; P Akman, 'The European Commission's Guidance on Article 102TFEU: From *Inferno* to *Paradiso*?'(2010) 73(4) *Modern Law Review* 605; G Monti, 'Article 82 EC: What Future for the Effects-Based Approach?' (2010) 1(1) *Journal of European Competition Law & Practice* 2; M Motta, 'The European Commission's Guidance Communication on Article 82' (2009) 30(12) *European Competition Law Review* 593.

that the Commission's scope of revision has been limited to exclusionary abuses; exploitative abuses were left outside of its scope.

This chapter first sets out the Commission's aspired reform of its approach concerning 'abuse' under Article 102 in section II by introducing the relevant documents, the proposed standard for price-based exclusionary conduct (the 'as efficient competitor' test) and the treatment of objective necessity and efficiencies in the analysis. In section III, it turns to the question of whether an economic effects-based approach is inherently problematic for reasons of certainty, administrability and judiciability. This question is addressed since there are criticisms of this approach in the literature on these grounds. Section IV then considers the issue of 'choice', since although the use of this concept is not new in EU competition law, the use of this concept by the Commission under its 'reformed' approach particularly deserves elaboration due to the possible implication of protection of *choice* as protection of *competitors*. Section IV therefore seeks to demonstrate that the issue of choice can become the litmus test for establishing whether the EU authorities adopt a more economic approach with a welfare-based standard or whether their approach is more in line with a structuralist approach that seeks to protect the competitors of a dominant undertaking. Section V concludes.

II THE COMMISSION'S 'REFORM' OF ITS APPROACH TO 'ABUSE'

A In General

The Commission has advocated adopting a more economic approach to 'abuse' under Article 102 and this process has revolved around 'exclusionary' abuse. Former Commissioner Kroes, under whose mandate the review was undertaken, expressed the reasoning for focusing on exclusionary abuse as it being 'wise in [their] enforcement policy to give priority to so-called exclusionary abuses, since exclusion is often at the basis of later exploitation of customers'.[3] This focus on exclusionary conduct to the exclusion of 'exploitative' abuse is paradoxical as it raises the question of why the emphasis is not on exploitative abuse if exclusionary abuses are problematic *because* they ultimately exploit consumers.[4] This paradox follows from the fact that the main objection to an undertaking with market power is its ability to *exploit* its position in a way that would not be possible for an

[3] N Kroes, 'Tackling Exclusionary Practices to Avoid Exploitation of Market Power: Some Preliminary Thoughts on the Policy Review of Article 82' in B Hawk (ed), *International Antitrust Law and Policy: Fordham Corporate Law Institute Annual Proceedings 2005* (New York, Juris Publishing, 2006) 384.

[4] See BR Lyons, 'The Paradox of the Exclusion of Exploitative Abuse' in *The Pros and Cons of High Prices* (Swedish Competition Authority, 2007) 65.

undertaking on a competitive market.[5] This is particularly important for a standard based on consumer welfare since exploitative practices *directly* harm customers of a dominant undertaking in comparison with exclusionary practices that may indirectly harm customers. Thus, under the thesis of this study, namely that exploitation and exclusion must exist together before 'abuse' can be established, the approach of the Commission is significantly incomplete. Nevertheless, this section will examine the 'modernisation' process, which the Commission's approach to Article 102 has undergone, as the outcome of the process establishes the status quo which this study seeks to improve on by its proposed approach to 'abuse'.

Both the policy and the practice of the Commission and the jurisprudence of the EU courts on Article 102 have been subject to criticism over the years for not being grounded in sound economics and for protecting competitors instead of competition.[6] The 'economic approach' to Article 102 with an 'effects-based' methodology was foremost supported in the EAGCP Report, but was also portrayed as the overall motivation of the Commission's reform, in line with the Commission's preceding reform of Article 101 and merger control.

Under an 'effects-based' approach a case would be assessed on the basis of the anticompetitive effects generated by conduct, as opposed to the form of the conduct.[7] According to the EAGCP Report, the main concern should be the improvement of 'consumer welfare' and the standard for assessing conduct should be derived from the effects of the practice on consumers; thus, the aim would not even be the 'protection of competition' but the prevention of anticompetitive effects that harm consumers.[8] The application of this approach requires the competition authority to explain in each case the harm for consumers from the conduct and to indicate the precise consumer welfare effects.[9] The authority must establish a consistent and verifiable economic account of significant competitive harm and also consider whether the practice can be seen as legitimate

[5] A Jones and B Sufrin, *EU Competition Law: Text, Cases and Materials* 4th edn (Oxford, OUP, 2011) 359.

[6] For various criticisms, see among others EM Fox, 'Monopolization and Dominance in the United States and the European Community: Efficiency, Opportunity, and Fairness' (1986) 61 *Notre Dame Law Review* 981; P Jebsen and R Stevens, 'Assumptions, Goals and Dominant Undertakings: The Regulation of Competition under Article 86 of the European Union' (1996) 64 *Antitrust Law Journal* 443; B Sher, 'The Last of Steam-Powered Trains: Modernising Article 82' (2004) 25(5) *European Competition Law Review* 243; J Kallaugher and B Sher, 'Rebates Revisited: Anti-Competitive Effects and Exclusionary Abuse under Article 82' (2004) 25(5) *European Competition Law Review* 263; D Waelbroeck, 'Michelin II: A Per Se Rule against Rebates by Dominant Companies?' (2005) 1(1) *Journal of Competition Law & Economics* 149; C Ahlborn and AJ Padilla, 'From *Fairness* to *Welfare*: Implications for the Assessment of Unilateral Conduct under EC Competition Law' in CD Ehlermann and M Marquis (eds), *European Competition Annual 2007: A Reformed Approach to Article 82 EC* (Oxford, Hart Publishing, 2008); Jones and Sufrin, ibid, 363–64.

[7] EAGCP Report (n 1) 3.

[8] ibid 8–9.

[9] ibid 8–9, 10.

competitive conduct.[10] As such, the EAGCP's proposed approach would mainly focus on entry barriers and competitive harm arising from exclusionary behaviour.[11] Although this approach might at first glance appear to contradict the thesis of this study (which requires both exploitation and exclusion to exist), it does not in fact do so: what is required as anticompetitive *effects* on consumers under the EAGCP approach can easily be conceptualised as 'exploitation'. In fact, as per the thesis of this study, this should be the way to interpret 'abuse' in line with Article 102 itself; this will be further elaborated on in chapter eight.

In comparison with the EAGCP Report, the DG Competition Discussion Paper and the Commission Guidance that followed the EAGCP Report can both be seen as disappointments regarding the level of vigour and enthusiasm for a single objective of 'consumer welfare'. For example, according to the Discussion Paper, the test for the prohibition of exclusionary abuses is one that looks for both actual or likely anticompetitive effects on the market and direct or indirect consumer harm; thus, unlike the EAGCP Report, 'competitive harm' and 'harm to consumers' were not seen as one and the same thing.[12] Similarly, although the avoidance of harm to consumers was seen as the ultimate concern of the provision, the test proposed in the Discussion Paper did not seek proof of any actual or possible harm to consumers; nowhere was it explained how an assessment of the effects on consumers is to be made.[13] Indeed, the stance of the Discussion Paper appeared to be one that implicitly *assumed* that exclusionary behaviour necessarily harmed consumers and the contrary could be proved by the dominant undertaking as a defence, despite the lip service paid to the adoption of an effects-based approach.[14]

In the same vein, the Commission Guidance on enforcement priorities in applying Article 102 to exclusionary conduct does not unambiguously adopt an effects-based approach with a consumer welfare standard.[15] According to the Guidance, the aim of the Commission's enforcement activity regarding exclusionary conduct is

> to ensure that dominant undertakings do not impair effective competition by foreclosing their competitors in an anti-competitive way, thus having an adverse impact on consumer welfare, whether in the form of higher price levels than would have otherwise prevailed or some other form such as limiting quality or reducing consumer choice.[16]

In turn, the Guidance defines 'anticompetitive foreclosure' as a situation where effective access of actual or potential competitors to supplies or markets is hampered or eliminated as a result of the dominant undertaking's conduct, whereby the dominant undertaking is likely to be in a position to profitably increase prices

[10] ibid 13.
[11] ibid 3.
[12] Akman (2006) (n 2) 823.
[13] ibid. See 'Discussion Paper' (n 1) [4], [54]–[55], [88] for the concern with harm to consumers.
[14] Akman (2006) (n 2) 824. See 'Discussion Paper' (n 1) [4] for the effects-based approach.
[15] For the argument that it does not set priorities either, see Akman (2010) (n 2) 610.
[16] 'Guidance' (n 1) [19].

to the detriment of consumers.[17] Although this is welcome in that the Commission accepts that a market can be foreclosed by a dominant undertaking without this being anticompetitive (ie, not every exclusion of a competitor is anticompetitive) the precise relationship between foreclosing rivals and adversely impacting consumer welfare is unclear.[18]

The way that the Commission expresses its enforcement aim by stating that the concern is to ensure that dominant undertakings do not impair effective competition by foreclosing rivals in an anticompetitive way, *thus* having an adverse impact on consumer welfare, is equivocal.[19] It could mean either that one has to show likely adverse effect on consumer welfare in order to identify an abuse *or* that the adverse impact on consumers is the *expected consequence* of foreclosing rivals in an anticompetitive way.[20] If it is the latter, it is not certain how one should identify the anticompetitiveness of foreclosure since it would not be tantamount to the adverse impact on consumers.[21] Early in the Guidance it is stated that the Commission is concerned with 'safeguarding the competitive process in the internal market and ensuring that undertakings which hold a dominant position do not exclude their competitors by other means than competing on the merits of the products or services they provide'.[22] However, 'competing on the merits' is a vague concept and even if it is taken to mean competing on price, quality, etc, remains without sufficient limiting principles.[23] It is therefore unfortunate that the Guidance is not clear enough on perhaps the most crucial issue regarding the enforcement of Article 102 – the basis on which a practice is to be found abusive.[24]

It is worth noting that when the Guidance refers to detriment to consumers or anticompetitive foreclosure, it only refers to *likely* harm or foreclosure and not actual.[25] Added to this is the fact that the Commission does not explain what type of evidence is relevant for this assessment of *likely* effects; thus, the assessment remains as a speculative exercise.[26] Moreover, although it is welcome that the Commission intends to assess 'abuse' by comparing the actual or likely future situation (with the dominant undertaking's conduct in place) with an appropriate counterfactual (such as the absence of the conduct in question), the Guidance is silent on *how* this counterfactual will be interpreted.[27] In other words, it is unclear whether the Commission will find abuse, for example, even if in the

[17] ibid. In the Guidance, the expression 'increase prices' is used as a shorthand for the various ways in which the parameters of competition, such as prices, output, innovation, the variety or quality of goods or services, can be influenced for the profit of the dominant undertaking and to the detriment of consumers; ibid [11].

[18] Akman (2010) (n 2) 613–14.

[19] ibid 614. See 'Guidance' (n 1) [19] for the enforcement aim.

[20] Akman, ibid.

[21] ibid.

[22] 'Guidance' (n 1) [6].

[23] R O'Donoghue and AJ Padilla, *The Law and Economics of Article 82 EC* (Oxford, Hart Publishing, 2006) 177.

[24] Akman (2010) (n 2) 614.

[25] See, eg, 'Guidance' (n 1) [19], [20].

[26] Akman (2010) (n 2) 615.

[27] ibid.

counterfactual, consumer welfare would be as much (harmed) as in the actual scenario.[28] Very disappointingly, the Guidance also includes a statement that

> [t]here may be circumstances where it is not necessary for the Commission to carry out a detailed assessment before concluding that the conduct in question is likely to result in consumer harm. If it appears that the conduct can only raise obstacles to competition and that it creates no efficiencies, its anti-competitive effect may be inferred.[29]

By accepting that there may be conduct whose anticompetitive *effect* may be inferred without any detailed assessment, and that there may be unilateral conduct which can 'only raise obstacles to competition' without this being confirmed by an assessment of *effects*, the Commission turns its alleged economic effects-based approach on its head and devalues the references to 'consumer welfare' in the Guidance as the appropriate enforcement standard.[30]

B The Standard for Price-Based Exclusionary Conduct: The 'As Efficient Competitor' Test

The Discussion Paper and the Guidance both adopt the so-called 'as efficient competitor' test as the standard of abuse for price-based exclusionary conduct.[31] This is not a novelty for EU competition law since the ECJ had already adopted this test in its *AKZO* judgment on predatory pricing, as indeed the Guidance acknowledges.[32] The ECJ has also approvingly elaborated on the 'as efficient competitor' test in two recent judgments, namely *Deutsche Telekom* and *TeliaSonera*.[33] Thus, according to the Guidance, the Commission will *normally* only intervene to prevent anticompetitive foreclosure where the conduct concerned has been or is capable of hampering competition from competitors that are as efficient as the dominant undertaking.[34] This test basically asks the question whether the dominant undertaking itself would be able to survive the (exclusionary) conduct if *it* were the target of its own conduct.[35] It should be noted that although this test is technically capable of being applied to non-price-based conduct as well, the Guidance does not provide a general test for non-price-based conduct. Thus, at least at face value, the Guidance limits the 'as efficient competitor' test to price-based conduct.

[28] ibid.

[29] 'Guidance' (n 1) [22]. The same statement can be found in the 'Discussion Paper' (n 1) [60].

[30] Akman (2010) (n 2) 615.

[31] For the Discussion Paper, see 'Discussion Paper' (n 1) [63] *et seq* and for the Guidance, see 'Guidance' (n 1) [23].

[32] 'Guidance' (n 1) [23] and see Case C-62/86 *AKZO Chemie BV v Commission* [1991] ECR I-3359, [72].

[33] See Case C-280/08 *Deutsche Telekom v Commission* [2010] ECR I-00, [177], [253] and Case C-52/09 *Konkurrensverket v TeliaSonera Sverige AB* [2011] ECR I-00, [39], [40], [63]. Both of these cases related to the abuse of margin squeeze.

[34] 'Guidance' (n 1) [23].

[35] 'Discussion Paper' (n 1) [66].

It should also be noted that the 'as efficient competitor' test is *not* intended to be applied in all cases of price-based exclusionary conduct. According to the Commission, 'in certain circumstances a less efficient competitor may also exert a constraint which should be taken into account when considering whether particular price-based conduct leads to anti-competitive foreclosure'.[36] The Commission's approach can lead to the protection of inefficient competitors and clashes with its alleged economic effects-based approach. This is because the Guidance states that to prevent anticompetitive foreclosure, intervention is only appropriate, where *as efficient* competitors can be hampered which implies that only *then* the conduct would be abusive.[37] Yet, when explaining that intervention may also be justified to protect inefficient competitors, it is stated that this is the case where *in the absence of abuse*, those competitors may enhance their efficiency. Therefore, what abuse means and how abuse is to be proved when the competitors are not as efficient as the dominant undertaking remains unclear.[38] In fact, some commentators have already noted that the Commission's stance has a hint of an 'efficiency offence'.[39]

To assess whether even a hypothetical competitor as efficient as the dominant undertaking would be likely to be foreclosed by the dominant undertaking's conduct, the Commission will examine cost and sales prices, and in particular whether the dominant undertaking is engaging in below-cost pricing.[40] Indeed, the test of predation – whether or not the dominant undertaking is pricing below cost – appears to have become the baseline for all price-based exclusionary conduct due to the adoption of the 'as efficient competitor' test.[41] One obvious problem with such an approach, however, is the difficulty of distinguishing low prices which would benefit consumers from predatory prices that would harm them in the future.[42] Another obvious problem with the test is that under many national laws, information on cost is treated as a business secret which implies that private litigants will certainly not be able to collect the necessary cost information.[43] This would imply a serious impediment for private cases if the test of predation is adopted for all price-based exclusionary conduct, and the Commission's approach appears to suggest that this is the case.

There are other problems with the Commission's 'as efficient competitor' test as well. One logical problem with the test is that it is based on the level of

[36] 'Guidance' (n 1) [24].

[37] Akman (2010) (n 2) 616.

[38] ibid.

[39] See Killick and Komninos (n 2) 6; D Waelbroeck, 'The Assessment of Efficiencies under Article 102 TFEU and the Commission's Guidance Paper' in F Etro and I Kokkoris (eds), *Competition Law and the Enforcement of Article 102* (Oxford, OUP, 2010) 123.

[40] 'Guidance' (n 1) [25].

[41] That predation seems to have become the baseline for price-based exclusionary conduct can be seen in the Guidance's approach to '(conditional) rebates' that are granted to customers to reward them for a particular form of purchasing behaviour; see Akman (2010) (n 2) 617, fn 63.

[42] Akman (2010) (n 2) 617.

[43] W Wurmnest, 'The Reform of Article 82 in the Light of the "Economic Approach"' in MO Mackenrodt, B Conde Gallego and S Enschelmaier (eds), *Abuse of Dominant Position: New Interpretation, New Enforcement Mechanisms?* (Berlin, Springer-Verlag, 2008) 18.

efficiency of the dominant undertaking and therefore ignores the fact that the dominant undertaking may be inefficient due to the 'quiet monopoly life' that it leads.[44] As such, this might lead to a problem similar to the cellophane fallacy.[45] Thus, a rival who cannot compete with the dominant undertaking because it is as efficient (or rather, as *inefficient*) as the dominant undertaking will be protected by the Commission's test even though its lack of success against the conduct of the dominant undertaking may be simply due to its *inefficiency*. This would also imply that Article 102 would prohibit conduct that excludes (inefficient) competitors who might not have been excluded had they been objectively efficient as opposed to as efficient as a dominant undertaking that might be objectively *inefficient*. This means that the enforcement of Article 102 would reward and therefore promote inefficiency. The test would therefore make more sense if the question to be asked were whether the conduct of the dominant undertaking would exclude *an efficient competitor* or one that is *at least as efficient* as the dominant undertaking.[46] This has to an extent been recognised by the ECJ in its *Deutsche Telekom* judgment, where the Court expressed the test as being about excluding competitors who are 'at least as efficient as the dominant undertaking itself'.[47] However, the ECJ elsewhere in the same judgment and later in *TeliaSonera* expressed the same test as one of excluding 'equally efficient' competitors.[48] Given that the protection of inefficient competitors of the dominant undertaking clashes with the alleged modernisation of the application of Article 102, this is more than a semantic issue and needs clarification by the EU authorities.[49]

There are two further problems with the approach of the Guidance to the 'as efficient competitor' test. Both of these problems relate to the cost benchmarks

[44] See Hicks, stating that the best of all monopoly profits is a quiet monopoly life; JR Hicks, 'Annual Survey of Economic Theory: The Theory of Monopoly' (1935) 3(1) *Econometrica* 1, 8. 'Quiet monopoly life' refers to X-inefficiency; for an explanation of which, see ch 1 this volume, fn 63.

[45] 'Cellophane fallacy' refers to a difficulty with the SSNIP (hypothetical monopolist) test used for establishing the relevant market in a competition inquiry: the SSNIP test asks the question whether a hypothetical monopolist would find it profitable to make a small but significant non-transitory increase in the current price of the product under investigation. If the answer is in the affirmative, then the product under investigation *itself* constitutes the relevant product market as it implies that the product does not face any significant competition from other products. The 'cellophane fallacy' refers to the problem that the SSNIP test might give a negative answer to this question where the undertaking is already dominant and is therefore already charging monopoly prices. In this case, it would lead to a too-wide market definition which might lead to a finding of no dominance for the undertaking in question. The US Supreme Court has arguably failed to recognise this in *United States v El du Pont de Nemours & Co* 351 US 377 (1956); see M Motta, *Competition Policy: Theory and Practice* (Cambridge, CUP, 2004) 105 and 102–03 for a general explanation of the SSNIP test.

[46] See Akman (2006) (n 2) 823.

[47] *Deutsche Telekom* (n 33) [253].

[48] ibid [177], [250], [252]; *TeliaSonera* (n 33) [39].

[49] It should be noted, however, that one criticism of the as efficient competitor test is also that sometimes less efficient competitors can also exert pressure on the dominant undertaking and for that reason should be protected, although the test would exclude their protection. For this point see, eg, J Vickers, 'Abuse of Market Power' in P Buccirossi (ed), *Handbook of Antitrust Economics* (Cambridge, MA, MIT Press, 2008) 427; D Riziotis, 'Efficiency Defence in Article 82 EC' in MO Mackenrodt, B Conde Gallego and S Enschelmaier (eds), *Abuse of Dominant Position: New Interpretation, New Enforcement Mechanisms?* (Berlin, Springer-Verlag, 2008) 112–13.

that the Commission is adopting to operationalise the test.[50] The first relates to the fact that according to the Guidance, the Commission – where available – will use information on the costs of the dominant undertaking itself, but if reliable information on those costs is not available, the Commission may use the cost data of competitors or other comparable reliable data.[51] This means that the Commission can decide that a certain undertaking abused its position by making sales below the cost of its competitors or as compared with 'other comparable reliable data', whatever they might be.[52] Such an approach of finding that a dominant undertaking has breached the law by charging prices below another undertaking's costs is not legitimate and has already been stated to be unacceptable by the GC in *Deutsche Telekom*.[53] There, the GC stated that it follows clearly from the case law that the abusive nature of a dominant undertaking's pricing practices is determined, in principle, on the basis of its own charges and costs, rather than on the basis of the situation of actual or potential competitors.[54] This is because 'any other approach could be contrary to the general principle of legal certainty' since

> [i]f the lawfulness of the pricing practices of a dominant undertaking depended on the particular situation of competing undertakings, particularly their cost structure – information which is generally not known to the dominant undertaking – the latter would not be in a position to assess the lawfulness of its own activities.[55]

Thus, the legality of the Commission's approach – as well as its legitimacy – is questionable as it might be in breach of a fundamental principle of EU law, namely legal certainty.[56] The ECJ in the appeal of *Deutsche Telekom* confirmed the approach of the GC.[57] Yet, in its later judgment in *TeliaSonera* the ECJ appears to have qualified this rule: it cannot be ruled out that the costs and prices of competitors may be relevant to the examination of the pricing practice at issue, particularly where the cost structure of the dominant undertaking is not precisely identifiable for objective reasons and so on.[58] Thus, according to the ECJ,

> account should as a general rule be taken primarily of the prices and costs of the undertaking concerned . . . Only where it is not possible, in particular circumstances, to refer to those prices and costs should those of its competitors on the same market be examined.[59]

[50] For a detailed discussion of these two problems, see Akman (2010) (n 2) 617–20, on which this paragraph is based.
[51] 'Guidance' (n 1) [25].
[52] This is explicitly stated for, eg, the abuse of 'margin squeeze'; 'Guidance' (n 1) [80], fn 9. See Akman (2010) (n 2) 617 for a discussion.
[53] Akman (2010) (n 2) 617.
[54] Case T-271/03 *Deutsche Telekom AG v Commission* [2008] ECR II-477, [188].
[55] ibid [192].
[56] See Hofmann on the principle of legal certainty in EU law; HCH Hofmann, 'Negotiated and Non-Negotiated Administrative Rule-Making: The Example of EC Competition Policy' (2006) 43 *Common Market Law Review* 158, 162 *et seq.*
[57] *Deutsche Telekom* (n 33) [196]–[204].
[58] *TeliaSonera* (n 33) [45].
[59] ibid [46].

This holding of the ECJ that in certain circumstances the prices and costs of the competitors of the dominant undertaking can be used as a benchmark to establish abuse is problematic since, as stated by the ECJ itself, '[w]hile a dominant undertaking knows what its own costs and charges are, it does not, as a general rule, know what its competitors' costs and charges are'.[60] Therefore, the ECJ finding in *TeliaSonera* potentially breaches the rule of legal certainty and implies a situation for dominant undertakings in which it will be impossible for them to establish ex ante whether their conduct is within the boundaries of the law or not (without colluding with their competitors). This is clearly a problematic situation that requires reconsideration by the EU authorities by way of adopting possibly an alternative approach to abuse in such cases which provides sufficient ex ante legal certainty to dominant undertakings.

The second *potential* problem with the cost benchmarks in the Guidance is that the Commission appears to be introducing new cost levels under its 'as efficient competitor' test and departing from the case law of the EU courts on 'predatory pricing', which is the main area in which this test has been applied.[61] According to the Guidance, the cost benchmarks that the Commission is likely to use under the 'as efficient competitor' test are average avoidable cost (AAC) and long-run average incremental cost (LRAIC).[62] Failure to cover AAC implies that the dominant undertaking foregoes profits in the short term and that an as efficient competitor cannot serve the targeted customers without making a loss.[63] Failure to cover LRAIC means that the dominant undertaking is not recovering all the attributable fixed costs of production and that an equally efficient competitor could be foreclosed from the market.[64] The Commission seems to be substituting these benchmarks with those established in the case law, namely average variable cost (AVC) and average total cost (ATC).[65] This substitution is problematic since AAC will not always be the same as AVC and LRAIC will not always be the same as ATC.[66] The implication of introducing new benchmarks is a change in the dominant undertakings' freedom to set prices compared with the situation with the benchmarks traditionally used. By making prices that would not be found presumptively abusive under the traditional benchmark (AVC), to be found presumptively abusive under the new benchmark (AAC), the Commission effectively increases the lower level below which prices are presumed to be predatory and thus

[60] *Deutsche Telekom* (n 33) [202].

[61] See Akman (2010) (n 2) 619–20.

[62] 'Guidance' (n 1) [26]. AAC is the average of the costs that could have been avoided if the company had not produced a discrete amount of (extra) output, ie, the amount allegedly the subject of abusive conduct; see 'Guidance (n 1) [26] n 2.

[63] Guidance (n 1) [26].

[64] ibid.

[65] See Case C-62/86 *AKZO Chemie BV v Commission* [1991] ECR I-3359, [71], [72]; Case T-83/91 *Tetra Pak International SA v Commission* [1994] ECR II-755, [148], [149]. AVC is the average of the costs that vary directly with the output of the undertaking and ATC is the average of all the variable and fixed costs; see 'Discussion Paper' (n 1) [64].

[66] See Akman (2010) (n 2) 619 for a full discussion and 'Guidance' (n 1) [26], fn 2 and [64], fn 3 for examples in the Guidance as to when these cost benchmarks will not coincide.

decreases the undertakings' freedom to price low.[67] This is perverse since low prices to customers are generally seen as the foremost beneficial and desirable effect of competition and the Commission's approach can hamper this by punishing low prices.[68] In contrast, the new upper level (LRAIC) is below the traditional upper level (ATC) and thus the level below which prices will be found abusive with additional evidence of intent to eliminate a competitor is decreased, to the undertakings' advantage.[69] The changing of these cost benchmarks means that the Commission is effectively changing the scope of abusive pricing behaviour and what will be found (not) to breach Article 102.[70] Whether the Commission can legally do so requires elaboration.

On the one hand, one can argue that employing these cost benchmarks to establish which prices are abusive is an exercise that 'entails a complex economic assessment' on the part of the Commission and that the Commission must therefore be afforded a broad discretion.[71] It could be argued that whether or not prices are abusive (for example, by being predatory) is ultimately an exercise based on economic theories and falls under the Commission's discretion for interpretation.[72] On the other hand, one could also argue that by changing the cost benchmarks, the Commission departs from established case law since there can be cases where, for example, LRAIC is below ATC and the dominant undertaking charges a price between LRAIC and ATC.[73] Given that the ECJ has established that prices between ATC and AVC *must* be considered abusive if they are part of a plan for eliminating a competitor,[74] by using LRAIC as the upper level and not finding such a price abusive, the Commission would derogate from the jurisprudence.[75] The legal consequences of this departure require a broader discussion of the relationship between soft-law (the Guidance) and jurisprudence. Such a discussion is outside the scope of this section.[76] Suffice it to say that the position of case law as a source of EU law is debatable since case law is not even always considered as a source of law and there is no doctrine of precedent in EU law, which means that the ECJ can depart from a previous judgment.[77] This implies that even if the Guidance departs from the jurisprudence with this change

[67] Akman, ibid, 619.
[68] ibid 619.
[69] ibid 619–20.
[70] ibid 620.
[71] ibid. On the discretion of the Commission concerning such issues see Case T-340/03 *France Télécom SA (formerly Wanadoo Interactive SA) v Commission* [2007] ECR II-107, [129].
[72] Akman (2010) (n 2) 620.
[73] ibid.
[74] *AKZO* (n 65) [71], [72]; *Tetra Pak II* (n 65) [148], [149].
[75] Akman (2010) (n 2) 620.
[76] For this broader discussion, see Akman, ibid, 624 *et seq.*
[77] At least from a formal point of view, the ECJ's role is limited to applying and interpreting the written law and thus the ECJ's jurisprudence cannot itself constitute a separate source of law; see L Selden, *Soft Law in European Community Law* (Oxford, Hart Publishing, 2004) 58 and the references therein. For the discussion of the doctrine of precedent, see A Arnull, 'Owning up to Fallibility: Precedent and the Court of Justice' (1993) 30 *Common Market Law Review* 247, 248, 262; KPE Lasok, *Law & Institutions of the European Union* 7th edn (London, Butterworths, 2001) 171.

in cost benchmarks, this in itself may not mean that it is unlawful; unless the ECJ decides that the Guidance goes against the Treaty and/or other rules of law, the Court can approve the change in the methodology if the Commission's new interpretation of cost benchmarks is raised in front of it in a dispute.[78]

C 'Objective Necessity' and 'Efficiencies'

As part of the general approach to exclusionary conduct, the Guidance includes a short discussion of 'objective necessity' and 'efficiencies' as claims of a dominant undertaking that can justify its practice.[79] The Guidance reiterates the case law on 'objective justification' and states that the Commission will examine claims put forward by a dominant undertaking that its conduct is justified.[80] A dominant undertaking can demonstrate that its conduct is either objectively necessary or produces substantial efficiencies which outweigh any anticompetitive effects on consumers.[81] This is a *defence* by the dominant undertaking and 'the Commission will assess whether the conduct in question is indispensable and proportionate to the goal allegedly pursued by the dominant undertaking'.[82]

Although it is welcome that, in line with an economic effects-based methodology, the Commission recognises that efficiencies must be taken into account in deciding whether conduct is abusive under Article 102, there are problems with the approach. First, the Commission does not explain what the counterfactual is for the assessment. The Guidance is silent as to the alternative situation with which the comparison will be made for the dominant undertaking's conduct to be found (in)dispensable and (dis)proportionate.[83] Secondly, the Commission states that a dominant undertaking can demonstrate that its conduct 'produces substantial efficiencies which outweigh any anti-competitive effects on consumers'.[84] The problem with this approach is that the Commission is requiring the dominant undertaking to guarantee that *no* net harm to consumers is *likely* to arise due to the efficiencies,[85] when the Commission itself only proves *likely* anticompetitive foreclosure.[86] Therefore, in cases where the Commission does not prove effects on consumers or actual foreclosure to find abuse, the undertaking is left with the burden to defy a position that the Commission has not actually established in its allegation and/or finding of abuse.[87] In such cases, the undertaking's duty is closer to establishing whether or not conduct is abusive – the burden of

[78] Akman (2010) (n 2) 627.
[79] See 'Guidance' (n 1) [28] *et seq.*
[80] ibid [28].
[81] ibid.
[82] ibid.
[83] Akman (2010) (n 2) 620–21.
[84] 'Guidance' (n 1) [28].
[85] ibid [30].
[86] Akman (2010) (n 2) 621.
[87] ibid.

proving which is on the *Commission* – than providing a 'defence' to a sufficiently established allegation of abuse, if the standard is 'consumer welfare'.[88] Moreover, the requirement that the dominant undertaking demonstrates that there will be no net harm to consumers begs the question of 'no net harm compared with what?': is the counterfactual the scenario in which the dominant undertaking does not engage in the practice in question at all or is it, for example, the scenario in which the dominant undertaking engages in the practice(s) alternative to the investigated conduct?[89] These are left unanswered and the Guidance is incomplete in its treatment of the issue.

The Commission also appears to treat efficiencies under Article 102 as equivalent to efficiencies in merger cases. Although in EU merger control one can legitimately require proof of anticipated efficiencies that can be placed alongside proof of anticipated harm (due to the analysis being *ex ante*), such an approach may be inappropriate when the assessment is ex post, as in cases of abuse.[90] Under an ex post assessment, the Commission will *not* have proven abuse without proving harm to consumers, if the objective is 'consumer welfare' as it claims. However, if it has proven (likely) harm to consumers, proving that there is no (likely) net harm to consumers would be rebutting the proof of abuse and not providing a justification for the conduct.[91] Since Article 102 involves an ex post assessment where *past* conduct is examined – unlike the ex ante merger control – a *prospective* proof of efficiencies to guarantee that no harm to consumers is likely to arise is nonsensical.[92] Article 102 prohibits the *abuse* of a dominant position and does not give the Commission the authority to control *ex ante* the conduct of a dominant undertaking to ensure that it benefits consumers; if the standard for abuse is prohibiting conduct harmful to consumers, then the claimant bears the burden to prove that the conduct harms or can harm consumers.[93] This burden cannot be shifted to the dominant undertaking to prove that there is no harm to consumers resulting from its behaviour. Article 102 should not be seen as a tool to *maximise* welfare: '[f]ailure to maximize consumer well-being cannot be the litmus test of abuse'.[94] The standard – if it is to be based on welfare – should be about *preventing decreases* in welfare, the burden to prove which is on the claimant.

How efficiencies can be included under Article 102 requires discussion and as already discussed in chapter three, there are two possible routes for this: either a defence can be included in the assessment in a similar manner to Article 101(3) or efficiencies can be integrated into the concept of 'abuse'. The former is problematic

[88] ibid. See Council Regulation (EC) No 1/2003 of 16 December 2002 on the implementation of the rules on competition laid down in Articles 81 and 82 of the Treaty [2003] OJ L1/1, Article 2 on burden of proof.

[89] Akman (2010) (n 2) 621.

[90] ibid.

[91] ibid.

[92] ibid.

[93] ibid.

[94] See J Vickers, 'A Reformed Approach to Article 82 EC and the US Practice: An Overall Appreciation' in CD Ehlermann and M Marquis (eds), *European Competition Law Annual 2007: A Reformed Approach to Article 82 EC* (Oxford, Hart Publishing, 2008) 241.

since inserting the equivalent of Article 101(3) into Article 102 would require a Treaty amendment and, as elaborated on earlier in this study, the latter is the correct approach in line with the provision of Article 102 itself.[95] The Commission, however, appears to have chosen the former approach and the Guidance provides very similar criteria to those in Article 101(3) for the efficiency defence under Article 102, although the burden of proof differs, as discussed below.[96]

According to the Guidance, to establish an efficiency defence, the dominant undertaking will be expected to demonstrate, with a sufficient degree of probability, and on the basis of verifiable evidence that: (i) the efficiencies have been or are likely to be realised as a result of the conduct; (ii) the conduct is indispensable for realising these efficiencies; (iii) the likely efficiencies brought about by the conduct outweigh any likely negative effects on competition and consumer welfare in the affected markets; and (iv) the conduct does not eliminate effective competition by removing all or most existing sources of actual or potential competition.[97] These four cumulative conditions are almost identical to the conditions in Article 101(3) which must be satisfied for conduct breaching Article 101(1) to be excepted from the prohibition.[98]

The method of introducing a defence similar to Article 101(3), however, would be the inferior method of dealing with efficiencies, in comparison with *incorporating* efficiencies in the concept and finding of 'abuse'. This is because a defence does not expressly exist in Article 102; furthermore, the fact that exception criteria exist in Article 101(3) but not the former strengthens the argument that they cannot simply be read into it by the enforcer.[99] It has been argued earlier in this study that this omission in Article 102 is not a silent refusal of efficiencies since efficiency was one of the main concerns, if not the main concern, of the drafters of Article 102.[100] This means that there is support inherent in Article 102 to include efficiencies in the assessment. Given that the drafters were greatly concerned with increasing efficiency and considered efficiency gains in the context of both provisions but did not include an exception clause for such gains in Article 102, a plausible (if not the most plausible) explanation is that efficiency is imbedded in the concept of 'abuse'.[101] This would mean that the lack of increase in efficiency resulting from the conduct should be established by the Commission in order to prove the existence of abuse. In fact, it has also been suggested that introducing an efficiency *defence* contradicts the ECJ's definition of 'abuse' as conduct different from those governing 'normal competition . . . based on a trader's performance'; this definition implies that conduct based on performance (ie, efficient behav-

[95] See ch 3 this volume, text around fn 51. This is also the approach in line with the legislative history; see ch 2 this volume, section VI.

[96] See below, text to n 104.

[97] 'Guidance' (n 1) [30].

[98] The main difference being that Art 101(3) itself is not just limited to 'efficiencies'. See Akman (2010) (n 2) 622.

[99] Akman, ibid.

[100] See ch 2 this volume, section VI and ch 3 this volume, text around fn 51.

[101] See ch 2 this volume, sections V and VI.

iour) is legitimate and therefore does not need to be *defended* to prove that it is legitimate.[102] As it stands, the Guidance muddles what the Commission has to assess to prove abuse and what the undertaking has to prove as a defence, which shows that separating the assessment of 'abuse' from 'efficiencies', as advocated by the Guidance, is not operational.[103]

Regarding the burden of proof, according to the Guidance, it is incumbent on the dominant undertaking to provide all the evidence necessary to demonstrate that the conduct is objectively justified.[104] It then falls to the Commission to ultimately assess whether the conduct is objectively necessary and whether 'based on a weighing-up of any apparent anti-competitive effects against any advanced and substantiated efficiencies', it is likely to result in consumer harm.[105] In this way, the efficiency defence which is being introduced appears to differ from Article 101(3), as the burden of proving the conditions thereof is on the undertaking claiming its benefit.[106] With Article 102, the ultimate legal burden of proof (as opposed to the burden of producing evidence) is placed on the Commission.[107] The GC has also established in *Microsoft* that it is for the dominant undertaking to raise a plea of objective justification and support it with arguments and evidence, after which it falls to the Commission 'where it proposes to make a finding of an abuse . . . to show that the arguments and evidence relied on by the dominant undertaking cannot prevail and, accordingly, that the justification . . . cannot be accepted'.[108] Since it is *likely* anticompetitive effects that the Commission is concerned with, how a weighing-up of *likely* effects with *likely* efficiencies can be realistically made remains unclear; the assessment is completely speculative.[109] Moreover, the Commission does not explain what sort and how much of efficiencies can outweigh what sort and how much of anticompetitive effects. Furthermore, as argued above efficiency should be incorporated in the definition of 'abuse' itself and it should be the Commission's burden to establish that

[102] Waelbroeck (n 39) 121–22. For this definition of 'abuse' by the ECJ, see Case 322/81 *Michelin v Commission* [1982] ECR 3461, [70].

[103] See Akman (2010) (n 2) 623 and 623, fn 103 for a demonstration of this using the example of the assessment of 'refusal to supply' in the Guidance demonstrating that what the Guidance deems as possible efficiencies to be proved by the dominant undertaking seem to be identical to the conditions the lack of which the Commission would have to determine in order to establish consumer harm. According to the Guidance, consumer harm may arise where competitors of the dominant undertaking are prevented from bringing innovative products/services to the market and/or where follow-on innovation is likely to be stifled; 'Guidance' (n 1) [87].

[104] 'Guidance' (n 1) [31].

[105] ibid.

[106] Regulation 1/2003 (n 88) Article 2.

[107] See E Rousseva, *Rethinking Exclusionary Abuses in EU Competition Law* (Oxford, Hart Publishing, 2010) 385. Rousseva treats the 'efficiency defence' as an 'affirmative defence' as opposed to a mere 'defence' although this point might be debateable. See AI Gavil, 'Secondary Line Price Discrimination and the Fate of *Morton* Salt: To Save It, Let It Go' (1999) 48(4) *Emory Law Journal* 1057, 119 *et seq* on the distinction between a 'defence' and an 'affirmative defence'.

[108] Case T-201/04 *Microsoft Corp v Commission* [2007] ECR II-3601, [1144].

[109] Akman (2010) (n 2) 623–24.

conduct does not increase efficiency before finding abuse.[110] Under such an approach, if the Commission fails to *disprove* the evidence brought by the dominant undertaking that its conduct is efficient and/or fails otherwise to prove that the conduct is inefficient, it will not have proven 'abuse'. As such, 'efficiency' would not be a 'defence' by the dominant undertaking, but 'inefficiency' would be an inherent component of proving that conduct is abusive in the first place. The treatment of efficiency will be returned to in chapter eight.

A final problem with the efficiency defence lies in the relation between rivalry and efficiencies, since according to the Commission, 'the protection of rivalry and the competitive process outweighs possible efficiency gains'.[111] Similarly, 'exclusionary conduct which maintains, creates or strengthens a market position approaching that of a monopoly can normally not be justified on the grounds that it also creates efficiency gains'.[112] These arguments demonstrate not a commitment to an economic effects-based approach, but a formalistic approach based on the size of the undertaking in question.[113] Moreover, by stating that conduct that *creates* a position approaching monopoly cannot be justified, the Commission clashes with the provision of Article 102, which does not prohibit a dominant *position* regardless of the size of this position. In fact, the Commission's statement, taken at face value, would imply that innovations that lead to patents, etc automatically lead to a situation that cannot be justified since the achievement of a patent by one undertaking will exclude the others from the same market. This would be a perverse outcome. Furthermore, by prioritising the 'protection of rivalry' and 'the competitive process' over efficiencies, it departs from the consumer welfare standard it advocates and moves closer to an ordoliberal approach.[114] It is equivocal as well since it begs the question of what 'protection of rivalry and the competitive process' means 'where there is no residual competition.'[115]

III IS AN ECONOMIC, EFFECTS-BASED APPROACH INHERENTLY PROBLEMATIC?

A question that has been raised during the Commission's rethinking of its approach to Article 102 is whether a more economic, effects-based approach would bring problems that should be avoided. One potential problem relates to the issue of whether an effects-based approach would make the law impossible to enforce (ie, unadministrable), particularly for the non-specialist courts with judges who are not trained in economics. Another potential issue is whether such

[110] See above, text around n 99.
[111] 'Guidance' (n 1) [30].
[112] ibid.
[113] Akman (2010) (n 2) 624.
[114] ibid.
[115] ibid.

an approach is problematic for merely focusing on effects and disregarding the form of conduct altogether. A related concern is whether adopting an effects-based approach would bring uncertainty since assessments would be done on a case-by-case basis. The separate issue of whether objectives based on economic concepts, such as consumer welfare and efficiency, are legally possible under the framework of Article 102 has already been discussed in chapter two and is therefore outside the scope of this section.

Interestingly, the previous Director General of DG Competition commented that beyond the question of principle as to how consumer welfare should be defined in a given case, there might be operational difficulties in applying a more effects-based approach under Article 102.[116] Arguably, since the dominant undertaking has better access to the relevant information than a complainant or the Commission, it is challenging to gauge in a specific case the consequences, efficiencies or others, of a challenged practice. Thus, it is suggested that as possible elements of a plausible economic theory of harm, one use proxies and presumptions when applying Article 102 to make enforcement more practical and swift. Consequently, it has been suggested that a pure effects-based approach can be too costly in terms of enforcement.[117] This is not understandable since the Commission itself has been promoting an effects-based approach and, as seen earlier in this study,[118] one reason for this is the necessity to focus the efforts of enforcement agencies on what makes a real difference, particularly given that they do not have unlimited resources. Thus, arguments like this render it difficult to establish how committed the Commission is to an effects-based approach to Article 102. However, the argument itself, namely that an effects-based approach may bring insurmountable enforcement difficulties deserves further elaboration.

It has indeed been argued in the literature that a full effects-based approach presents important shortcomings, such as decision costs which involve costs of information gathering and processing, since it is impossible to perform a thorough competition analysis of all commercial practices.[119] It has also been suggested that although an effects-based approach is welcome in that it reduces the risk of over-regulation and of chilling competition which may result from a form-based approach, the practicability of the effects-based approach is challenging.[120] Arguably, the move from a form-based approach to an effects-based approach

[116] P Lowe, 'Consumer Welfare and Efficiency – New Guiding Principles of Competition Policy?' (13th International Conference on Competition and 14th European Competition Day, Munich, March 2007) 8.

[117] ibid.

[118] See ch 3 this volume, text after fn 135.

[119] I Lianos, 'Categorical Thinking in Competition Law and the "Effects-Based" Approach in Article 82 EC' in A Ezrachi (ed), *Article 82 EC: Reflections on its Recent Evolution* (Oxford, Hart Publishing, 2009) 21.

[120] A Ezrachi, 'The Commission's Guidance on Article 82 EC and the Effects Based Approach – Legal and Practical Challenges' in A Ezrachi (ed), *Article 82 EC: Reflections on its Recent Evolution* (Oxford, Hart Publishing, 2009) 53.

creates uncertainty as to the relevant benchmarks to establish abuse and their limiting principles.[121] It is said that part of the uncertainty is unavoidably linked to the shift from one analytical framework to another and part of it stems from the open-ended and novel nature of some parts of the Commission Guidance.[122] Consequently, it has been suggested that a form-based rule may be preferred to an effects-based rule for reasons of predictability, judiciability and enforcement efficiency.[123]

The issue of certainty is indeed important, although a move towards an effects-based approach can hardly be argued to lead to less certainty than the current position. This is because one cannot suggest that the thus far adopted form-based approach to Article 102 provides any meaningful certainty for undertakings. The reasons for this are manifold. First, it has never been made clear by the EU courts what *the* ultimate objective of the prohibition of Article 102 actually is. Although the courts have sometimes provided a list of objectives, it still remains unclear what the ultimate purpose of this prohibition is. Therefore, currently there is inherent uncertainty in the enforcement of Article 102, since the ultimate purpose of any enforcement action – which must be derived from the ultimate purpose of the provision – is unclear. Secondly, there is no general test or criteria approved by the EU courts that establish what exactly distinguishes abusive conduct from conduct that is not abusive. Thus, even under a form-based approach, the general criteria that render one form of conduct abusive and another form of conduct non-abusive are non-existent. Given that the list of abusive practices in Article 102 is non-exhaustive, there is clearly an issue of uncertainty for dominant undertakings for practices that have not yet been sanctioned by the EU authorities even with a form-based approach.[124] Thirdly, with dominance being found at market share levels of around 40 per cent, there is even uncertainty for an undertaking in terms of knowing that it *is* dominant and subject to Article 102. None of this is to say that an effects-based approach would provide more certainty than a form-based approach. The point being made here is that there is currently not sufficient certainty in this area of law anyway (perhaps other than that the Commission is more likely to win an Article 102 appeal than lose it). Therefore, it is questionable whether the move towards an effects-based approach would lead to less certainty than the *status quo* and this is open to debate.[125]

[121] ibid. For the argument that a comprehensive economic analysis of every case risks reducing legal certainty and increasing the costs of enforcing the law, see E Østerud, *Identifying Exclusionary Abuses by Dominant Undertakings under EU Competition Law: The Spectrum of Tests* (The Netherlands, Kluwer Law International, 2010) 9.

[122] Ezrachi (n 120) 53.

[123] WH Roth, 'The "More Economic Approach" and the Rule of Law' in D Schmidtchen, M Albert and S Voigt (eds), *The More Economic Approach to European Competition Law* (Tübingen, Mohr Siebeck, 2010) 51.

[124] For the point that the list is not exhaustive, see Case 6/72 *Europemballage Corp and Continental Can Co Inc v Commission* [1973] ECR 215, [26].

[125] See, eg, Katsoulacos and Ulph arguing that legal certainty might indeed be best achieved by effects-based procedures provided that the test is based on factors that are known to firms and that the rule is made transparent; Y Katsoulacos and D Ulph, 'Optimal Enforcement and Decision Structures

Other commentators have criticised the effects-based approach from the point of compatibility with the Treaty. As such, it has been questioned whether the more economic approach can be properly integrated with basic legal values and the peculiar aims of competition policy assigned by the Treaty.[126] One commentator has argued that a pure effects-based approach *cannot* be accommodated under the current legislative framework: according to this argument, one must not ignore the rationale that made adoption of Article 102 necessary.[127] It is suggested that a dominant firm has a 'special responsibility' not to abuse its position precisely because its unilateral behaviour bears an inherent risk for the market structure, competitors, customers and ultimately consumers, since its impact and incidence determine the rules of the game.[128] Hence, consumers are arguably best served by a competition policy towards exclusionary conduct featuring both form-based and effects-based elements.[129] An open-ended, effects-based analysis of potentially exclusionary unilateral conduct is alleged to be not just problematic, but most likely counterproductive.[130]

One problem with this argument is that it is not clear what the relation is between the rationale that made the adoption of Article 102 necessary and the concept of 'special responsibility'. This is because, first, the 'special responsibility' of dominant undertakings is *not* found in Article 102 itself. Secondly, the prohibition of 'abuse' rather than the dominant position itself in the provision shows that the drafters actually *accepted* the 'inherent risk' resulting from the existence of such positions. Therefore, it is difficult to rationalise adopting an approach that justifies a form-based approach on the basis of Article 102 itself.

Another potential problem with the more economic approach is arguably that it is not justiciable, and this will benefit big firms to the disadvantage of smaller firms when it comes to litigation: there will be a war of experts and, with the help of law firms, economic and legal experts, the big firms will benefit from the approach by escaping the application of the law.[131] In fact, the more economic

for Competition Policy: Economic Considerations' in F Etro and I Kokkoris (eds), *Competition Law and the Enforcement of Article 102* (Oxford, OUP, 2010) 78. See also Art and Colomo noting that, due to the deference granted to the Commission by the EU courts and the vagueness of the criteria used for identifying 'abuse', legal precedents in Art 102 cases have little practical relevance for subsequent cases; that is, legal certainty already suffers under the existing approach; JY Art and PI Colomo, 'Judicial Review in Article 102 TFEU' in F Etro and I Kokkoris (eds), *Competition Law and the Enforcement of Article 102* (Oxford, OUP, 2010) 105.

[126] L Borlini, 'Methodological Issues of the "More Economic Approach" to Unilateral Exclusionary Conduct' (2009) 5(2) *European Competition Journal* 409, 415.

[127] V Mertikopoulou, 'DG Competition's Discussion Paper on the Application of Article 82 of the EC Treaty to Exclusionary Abuses: The Proposed Economic Reform from a Legal Point of View' (2007) 28(4) *European Competition Law Review* 241, 250. See in general, ch 2 this volume, section V on the intent of the drafters.

[128] Mertikopoulou, ibid, 250.

[129] GJ Werden, 'Competition Policy on Exclusionary Conduct: Toward an Effects-Based Analysis?' (2006) 2 (Special Issue) *European Competition Journal* 53, 53.

[130] ibid 62.

[131] ILO Schmidt, 'The Suitability of the More Economic Approach for Competition Policy: Dynamic vs Static Efficiency' (2007) 28(7) *European Competition Law Review* 408, 410–11.

approach has been suggested to be not pro-consumer, but in favour of big business.[132]

It is indeed the case that competition laws directly concern an economic concept, namely 'competition on the market', and therefore more than any other area of law, they raise issues of the relations between legal principles and economics.[133] Economics contributes to the interpretation of the law at two different levels: first, by providing a framework of analysis for 'competition' and its features and, secondly, by playing an important role in developing the rules of decision which render it possible to evaluate whether certain conduct is illegal.[134] In terms of devising the decisional rules, if a practice is prohibited per se, it means that its analysis under a legal and economic viewpoint shows that it is restrictive of competition in the generality of cases.[135] When a practice is not immediately seen as anticompetitive, then further economic analysis may help the decisional process by defining whether one should start from a presumption of illegality or legality and also by defining the criteria on which it can be evaluated to be restrictive.[136] The decision on these, in turn, depends on the paradigm of analysis of competition that is followed: if one follows a paradigm of competition based on 'perfect competition', then it will be the structural aspects of the market that will be considered in order to evaluate whether the practice deviates from its desirable outcome.[137] If, on the other hand, one adopts the paradigm of competition based on 'incentives and dynamic features of a market', then it will be the actual or presumed effects that the practice would end up having on the market that matter.[138]

It is indeed true that in the increasingly complex area of competition litigation, courts *need* the assistance of economic experts to acquire specialised information which is, otherwise unavailable to them.[139] However, this should not mean that the judge/jury should conform to the expert's opinion; not only is there a risk that the expert could favour one of the litigants, there is also the possibility that there will be conflicting expert opinions.[140] The latter arguably occurs because '[t]he possibility of an objective economic truth could be questioned'.[141] The shift to a more economic approach, in turn, brings with it the increased likelihood that judges will be confronted with economic analysis and will have to make use of economic expertise.[142] According to Lianos, the EU courts' implicit reliance on

[132] ibid 411.
[133] A Pera, 'Changing Views of Competition, Economic Analysis and EC Antitrust Law' (2008) 4(1) *European Competition Journal* 127, 131.
[134] ibid.
[135] ibid 134.
[136] ibid.
[137] ibid.
[138] ibid.
[139] I Lianos, '"Judging" Economists: Economic Expertise in Competition Law Litigation: A European View' in I Lianos and I Kokkoris (eds), *The Reform of EC Competition Law* (The Netherlands, Kluwer Law International, 2010) 190.
[140] ibid 191.
[141] ibid.
[142] ibid 235.

economic authority may produce some shortcomings such as the economic theories resting on assumptions for which there is no consensus in economic theory.[143] Another problem is said to be that these theoretical models are generally based on poor and, at best, inconclusive empirical analysis.[144] This absence of empirical evidence and/or consensus between economists may lead the judge to ignore economic expertise or base her choice of economic theory on extra-economic grounds, such as the degree of compatibility of assumptions and first principles with the objectives and the context of the particular competition law system.[145]

All in all, it appears that there are arguments in the literature suggesting that a more economic effects-based approach will inherently bring problems that should be avoided. In response, other commentators argue that this is not necessarily the case. For example, Motta succinctly responds to these criticisms of a more economic, effects-based approach to Article 102 on three grounds. First, the ease of administrability can easily be used to support not just a 'very-interventionist' approach as in the EU, but also a 'fully non-interventionist' approach as in the US.[146] Thus, a request in favour of easy-to-administer rules can also be satisfied with a laissez faire approach to Article 102 which would imply that the EU approach thus far developed as interventionist and form-based is not the only possible easy-to-administer approach. In fact, Motta approvingly refers to Kovacic's argument that the laissez faire approach of the US is the outcome of the Chicago School's substantive arguments coupled with the Harvard School's stress on *administrability* – the need for simple rules that any judge can administer without having to deal with complex economic matters.[147] This point does not seem to have been picked up by any of the critics of the effects-based approach and the stance seems to be a presumption that any approach that is administrable because it is form-based is also an interventionist approach. This, as Motta argues, is not necessarily the case. Therefore, a plea for a form-based approach should also establish the grounds for rejecting a non-interventionist approach such as an approach based on per se legality.

Secondly, Motta notes that although it may make sense to use simple rules in circumstances which admit no or very rare exceptions (such as hard-core price fixing cases), in the case of Article 102 economic theory does not provide such indications about whether false positives (finding firms guilty of abuse when they are innocent) or false negatives (finding firms innocent when they are guilty of abuse) are more likely.[148] Moreover, there is no empirical support for either position.[149] This is perhaps one of the most important points about the correct

[143] ibid 244.
[144] ibid 245.
[145] ibid 246.
[146] Motta (n 2) 595.
[147] See Motta, ibid, referring to WE Kovacic, 'The Intellectual DNA of Modern US Competition Law for Dominant Firm Conduct: The Chicago/Harvard Double Helix' (2007) 1(1) *Columbia Business Law Review* 1. See ch 1 this volume, section III.A for a discussion of Chicago and Harvard schools of antitrust.
[148] Motta, ibid.
[149] ibid.

approach to Article 102 and this is what makes it so difficult to administer Article 102. This can also be said to be a potential weakness of the more economic approach, although that is not how Motta interprets it. The reason that this can be seen as a weakness of the more economic approach is that, *because* the current state of economics does not provide universal and non-fact-dependent rules for unilateral conduct, it is difficult to use it as the ultimate basis for decision making. This, however, raises a question not just of using an economic, effects-based approach, but a much more fundamental question of whether a prohibition such as that in Article 102 should exist *at all.* This latter question is one of *legitimacy* and not operation: if this is an area of law that must be informed by economics and economics suggests no universal rules at all which can be used to operationalise a prohibition of unilateral conduct (in contrast to, for example, hard-core price-fixing), then the legitimacy of the prohibition itself becomes questionable. This is only exacerbated by the fact that this ambiguity results in a failure to provide sufficient legal certainty to businesses that might be subject to the rule. Thus, it could be said that the recent discussion of a possible move towards a more economic, effects-based approach has simply revealed that the emperor had not been wearing any clothes for over 50 years.

Thirdly, Motta argues that although legal certainty should be sought, economics can also be used to provide simple and easy-to-administer rules.[150] Thus, the question is really one of how well the rules are grounded in economics and not one of whether the rules should be replaced by discretion on a case-by-case basis depending on whatever is thought to be desirable in economic terms.[151] However, as stated above and noted by Motta himself, the economics of unilateral conduct are far from providing universal rules at the moment and therefore it is difficult to argue that it leads itself to simple and easy-to-administer rules. This is not to say that a form-based approach would be better since to be legitimate, such an approach should also be based on sound economic theory and with a non-exhaustive list of prohibited practices, a form-based approach is not likely to provide certainty for all cases either. Indeed it has been argued that *because* most abuses are mostly normal and legal behaviour for non-dominant undertakings, the legality of a given conduct by a dominant undertaking should almost always depend on an analysis of efficiencies and effects of the practice on competition.[152] Thus, the desirability of a move towards an effects-based approach raises a far more important issue than whether the approach should be based on effects or form of conduct: as mentioned above, it challenges the ultimate *existence* of the prohibition in Article 102 and not just the enforcement of it, due to this lack of sufficiently strong economic underpinnings. For the purposes of this section, it can therefore be concluded that an economic, effects-based approach is no more inherently problematic than a form-based approach to Article 102.

[150] ibid.

[151] See Motta, ibid, 596 referring to J Vickers, 'Abuse of Market Power' (2005) 115 (June) *The Economic Journal* F244.

[152] Waelbroeck (n 39) 120.

IV CHOICE: THE PROBLEM WITH THE 'REFORMED' APPROACH?

One issue that is particularly important for establishing whether the approach to Article 102 is indeed modernised to embrace a more economic effects-based approach is the treatment of 'choice' in the analysis. This is because 'choice' is included by the Commission in its understanding of 'consumer welfare'. For example, according to the Guidance, an adverse impact of a dominant undertaking's conduct on consumer welfare can take the form of higher price levels than would have otherwise prevailed or some other form such as 'limiting quality' or 'reducing consumer choice'.[153] Moreover, the Guidance states that an undertaking which is capable of profitably increasing prices above the competitive level for a significant period of time can be considered 'dominant'.[154] Importantly, the Guidance uses the expression 'increase prices' to include power to maintain prices above the competitive level and as a shorthand for the various ways in which parameters of competition – such as prices, output, *innovation*, the *variety* or *quality* of goods or services can be influenced for the profit of the undertaking and to the detriment of consumers.[155]

Increasing price levels – in the literal sense – is indeed a relatively straightforward component of a consumer welfare standard. In fact, an increase in price and a reduction in output is perhaps the most straightforward explanation of any anticompetitive practice as it demonstrates the lack of effective competition.[156] However, the issue of limiting *quality* or *variety* and reducing *consumer choice* is far from straightforward and has serious potential implications for the approach to Article 102. Particularly how the reduction of 'choice' is treated in this sense can become the litmus test for establishing whether the approach is based on effects and/or consumer welfare at all. This is because 'choice' might end up becoming the new word for 'competitor' depending on how one understands and interprets it. This might in turn mean that the standard becomes that of protecting the freedom of competitors of a dominant undertaking to exist on the market. This would be closer to an ordoliberal approach than to an economic, effects-based approach.

It must be noted that, although it is the elasticity of demand facing an individual firm that is of interest for the application of competition law, the usual starting point for a competition law inquiry is finding the products that provide an effective competitive constraint on the price and other terms of supply of the product under investigation.[157] This is said to be a sensible approach since the elasticity of demand depends partly on the degree to which consumers are willing

[153] 'Guidance' (n 1) [19].
[154] ibid [11].
[155] ibid.
[156] On 'effective competition' see, eg, S Bishop and M Walker, *The Economics of EC Competition Law: Concepts, Application and Measurement* 3rd edn (London, Sweet & Maxwell, 2010) 27.
[157] ibid 84.

to switch to alternative suppliers following a relative price increase.[158] In most industries, products are not homogenous and 'product differentiation' exists where different consumers have different preferences for the various product offerings.[159] 'Horizontal product differentiation' relates to differences in preferences of consumers, while 'vertical differentiation' relates to differences in quality.[160] Given that the Guidance refers to limiting quality and reducing consumer choice separately, it can be argued that the statement about reducing consumer choice relates to 'horizontal differentiation' and that the statement about quality relates to 'vertical differentiation'.[161]

Economists suggest that the overall economic effect of product differentiation is the softening of the degree of price competition between firms since this differentiation makes the residual demand curve of each firm less elastic: the sales of a firm setting a price slightly above the price of other firms do not necessarily fall to zero.[162] In fact, a price above marginal cost can and will be sustained under product differentiation.[163] This is in contrast with, for example, markets with homogenous products where an increase in the price of one firm's products relative to others will result in consumers switching to other suppliers since the products are identical.[164] This implies that '[d]iversity prevents unbridled competition for customers'.[165] Thus, if 'choice' is understood in the sense of product differentiation, then a tension becomes apparent: the existence of 'choice' itself might imply the existence of market power.[166] This casts doubt on the use of 'choice' in the sense of product differentiation in the Guidance as a component of 'consumer welfare', since it appears counter-intuitive: the Guidance statement is about *prevention* of the abusive exercise of market power by a reduction in 'choice' whereas product differentiation is an indicator of the existence of market power. Thus, if 'choice' had been used in the sense of product differentiation, one would have expected it to be mentioned as part of the test of establishing dominance and not as part of that establishing abuse (the test for which in fact suggests that the *restriction* of choice can be abusive). In fact, it appears that the Commission is using the term 'variety' in its definition of dominance to imply the idea of product differentiation as accepted in economics.[167] This suggests that the Commission is using the concept of 'choice' (and 'quality') in a different sense than product differentiation (and 'variety').

In fact, it should also be noted that if the standard for abuse is indeed based on a welfare standard, the welfare loss from a monopoly – that is the deadweight loss

[158] ibid.
[159] ibid 85.
[160] ibid.
[161] See 'Guidance' (n 1) [19].
[162] Bishop and Walker (n 156) 85.
[163] J Tirole, *The Theory of Industrial Organization* (Cambridge, MA, The MIT Press, 1988) 277.
[164] Bishop and Walker (n 156) 85.
[165] Tirole (n 163) 277.
[166] This is not to say that there will be no competition at all between different suppliers; see Bishop and Walker (n 156) 85.
[167] See 'Guidance' (n 1) [11] and above, text around n 159 on product differentiation.

– can be measured empirically by estimating the demand curve and the marginal-cost curve.[168] This would imply that 'choice' (between products and qualities) is already taken into account at the point of defining the market and the demand function. When looking for the products that exercise a competitive constraint on the products under scrutiny (ie, when trying to define the relevant market), one looks at both demand-side and supply-side substitutability.[169] Demand-side substitution takes place when consumers switch from one product to another in response to a change in the relative prices of the products.[170] In fact, the possibility of demand-side substitution provides an immediate and effective disciplinary force on the suppliers of any given product.[171] Whether or not *enough* consumers will switch is dependent, inter alia, on consumers' preferences and this presents itself in the utility function of consumers, which becomes the demand function for the relevant product market. Thus, 'choice' in the sense of consumers' preferences for different products (and qualities) is already taken care of in the demand function. This implies that, for competition law and policy purposes, taking choice into account at a later stage again, when establishing the existence or absence of abuse, would be counting choice twice as a value in the analysis. The necessity of this with a consumer welfare standard is highly questionable and the fact that 'consumer' in EU competition law means 'customer' aggravates this: the analysis begs the question why the existence of choice per se for the customers of a dominant undertaking that might be other businesses should be taken into account in the analysis twice when every other value (such as price and output) is only taken into account once. Such an approach valuing choice per se is indeed closer to a structuralist ordoliberal approach than to a consumer welfare standard. In fact, if one looks at the hitherto EU jurisprudence it appears that 'choice' might simply be another word for 'competitor' and the preservation of 'choice' might simply mean the preservation of rivals on the relevant market.

Cases that mention preserving more 'choice' for the customer or finding conduct of a dominant undertaking to be abusive due to a reduction in 'choice' can potentially be interpreted as protecting competitors since more choice appears to be the result of more rivals existing on the market. The practice of 'tying' is a good example here. When an undertaking dominant in one market attempts to increase its market share in a market in which it is not dominant by tying the sale of its product in the first market to the sale of the product in the second market, customers have no 'choice' but to purchase *both* products from the dominant undertaking.[172] This would be the case when customers have little opportunity to choose alternative suppliers in the first market where there is a dominant undertaking whose position approaches that of a monopoly.[173] This is said to hurt the

[168] Tirole (n 163) 68.
[169] Motta (n 2) 103.
[170] Bishop and Walker (n 156) 118.
[171] ibid.
[172] E Buttigieg, *Competition Law: Safeguarding the Consumer Interest* (The Netherlands, Kluwer Law International, 2009) 217.
[173] ibid.

consumer indirectly because consumer *choice* will suffer: if the effect of tying is to drive out competitors from the market by preventing their sales or entry to the market, the outcome for the consumer will be fewer alternative suppliers on the market.[174] This seems to have been the approach in cases such as *Napier Brown*,[175] *Hilti*[176] and *Tetra Pak II*,[177] where the limitation on the customer's choice of supplier for the tied product was found to be abusive.[178] This has also been recognised in some older decisions in the US, such as *Loew's Inc* and *Northern Pacific Railway*, where the Supreme Court held that the buyers were forced to forego their free choice between competing products as a result of tying.[179]

More recently in *Microsoft* the Commission's evaluation of the tying of Windows Media Player to the Windows Operating System appears to have been based not on actual effects on exclusion and consumer welfare, but on prospective long-term effects on the possibility of choice for consumers, which in turn is related to the evolution of the *market structure*.[180] Lianos argues that although in *Microsoft* the GC noted that consumer choice would be affected if rival products of equal or better quality could not compete on equal terms, the Court interpreted this as requiring only the preservation of the market access of competitors, without requiring that the claimant produce evidence that the excluded competitors are indeed producing or are likely to produce better products.[181] Thus, consumer choice seems to be equated with the preservation of competitive rivalry on the marketplace.[182] In turn, this rivalry can easily be thought to depend on the *number* of undertakings providing these different products that make up the 'choice'. Yet, the number of competitors in a market does not always provide a good indication of the level of competition; if price competition is vigorous, then even two competitors can be enough for there to be effective competition.[183] Similarly, if entry and exit were costless and very easy, then even a monopolist might be unable to increase prices as the mere threat of entry would keep prices low.[184]

Exclusivity agreements are another example of conduct which the EU authorities have examined by focusing on the restriction of choice.[185] The basic objection to an exclusivity agreement under Article 102 is that the customer is prevented

[174] ibid 219–20.

[175] *Napier Brown – British Sugar* (Case IV/30.178) Commission Decision 88/518/EEC [1988] OJ L284/41.

[176] Case T-30/89 *Hilti v Commission* [1994] ECR II-1439.

[177] *Tetra Pak II* (n 65).

[178] See Østerud (n 121) 84–88.

[179] See Buttigieg (n 172) 219 referring to *US v Loew's Inc* 371 US 38 (1962) 45 and *Northern Pacific Railway Co v US* 356 US 1 (1958) 6.

[180] Pera (n 133) 161.

[181] Lianos (n 119) 28 referring to *Microsoft* (n 108) [652].

[182] ibid [664].

[183] Bishop and Walker (n 156) 64.

[184] ibid 65.

[185] Exclusivity agreements are obligations that require customers to purchase specific products exclusively from a particular supplier; see Østerud (n 121) 63.

from buying products from competitors of the dominant undertaking.[186] The condemnation of exclusivity by the EU courts has stressed that these agreements restrict the customers' freedom of choice and this in turn denies other producers access to the market.[187] Examples of such reasoning can be found in cases such as *Suiker Unie*,[188] *Hoffmann-La Roche*,[189] *Michelin I*[190] and *Michelin II*,[191] where exclusivity agreements or rebates ensuring exclusivity were found abusive for restricting the customer's choice of supply.[192] More recently, the Commission has elaborated on choice in its *Intel* decision, where one of the main issues was the rebates Intel was offering to its customers (original equipment manufacturers) conditional on exclusivity. The Commission found that foreclosing an as efficient competitor of the dominant undertaking

> would thereby deprive final consumers of the choice between different products which the Intel trading partner would otherwise have chosen to offer were it to make its decision solely on the basis of the relative merit of the products and unit prices offered by Intel and its competitors.[193]

Similarly, in elaborating on 'reduction of consumer choice' as a component of harm to competition and consumers, the Commission held that

> [t]hrough a variety of rebates which were tailored for each [original equipment manufacturer], Intel was able to use the tool of conditional rebates that were capable of inducing loyalty and thereby limiting consumer choice and foreclosing the access of competitors to the market.[194]

Without going into the merits of the Commission's arguments on choice on the particular facts of *Intel*, one can nonetheless observe that the reduction in consumer choice is clearly treated as part of the test of 'abuse'.

One commentator has indeed argued that the EU courts have given a very narrow meaning to 'consumer harm' and this concept has become associated with the limitation of consumers' choice to source the product from different suppliers.[195] In turn, this narrow interpretation makes it easy to find consumer harm,

[186] Østerud, ibid.

[187] ibid 65.

[188] Joined Cases 40/73 *Coöperatieve Vereniging Suiker Unie UA and others v Commission* [1975] ECR 1663, [517]–[28].

[189] Case 85/76 *Hoffmann-La Roche v Commission* [1979] ECR 461, [89].

[190] Case 322/81 *NV Nederlandsche Banden-Industrie Michelin v Commission* [1983] ECR 3461, [73].

[191] Case T-203/01 *Manufacture française des pneumatiques Michelin v Commission* [2003] ECR II-4071, [110].

[192] Østerud (n 121) 63–64, 71–73. See also more recently Case T-155/06 *Tomra Systems ASA and others v Commission* [2010] ECR II-00, [209]; *Deutsche Telekom* (n 33) [175], [182]; *TeliaSonera* (n 33) [28].

[193] *Intel* (Case COMP/C-3/37.990) Commission Decision 2009/C 227/07 [2009] OJ C227/13, [1154]. The relevant product was microprocessors, known as Central Processing Units (CPUs) of the x86 architecture. The CPU is a key component of any computer, both in terms of overall performance and cost of the system; it is often referred to as a computer's 'brain'; ibid [106] *et seq.*

[194] *Intel*, ibid [1598].

[195] L Lovdahl Gormsen in 'Antitrust Marathon II' (2008) 4(1) *European Competition Journal* 213, 242.

since whenever a competitor is excluded from the market, it means that there is one fewer supplier and one can wonder whether this is a disguised form of protecting competitors.[196] It has also been argued that when trying to achieve *economic freedom* in the market, the harmful effects of foreclosure are competitors' reduced choice of customers and customers' reduced choice of suppliers.[197] Such a protection of economic freedom can be associated with ordoliberalism (examined in chapter two), which perceives the main aim of competition policy as the protection of economic freedom.[198] In contrast, from a welfare point of view, choice is only valued if it leads to a better and more efficient outcome for consumers; choice would not be valued in itself.[199]

Another point to be made is that if the concern of the EU authorities is 'choice', in the sense of firms investing and innovating to create new products for consumers as opposed to the number of competitors on a market, then the focus of their inquiry should be *dynamic* efficiencies. In contrast, the Commission's more economic approach is mainly based on microeconomics, industrial organisation and game theory, all of which are of a static nature.[200] The Commission does not seem to demonstrate any concrete positive stance towards dynamic efficiencies in its decisions or policy documents. Yet, it is mainly technical progress in a changing, dynamic environment characterised by product and process innovations that makes competition preferable to other, centralised economic systems.[201] Having said that, although what one should strive for is dynamic and not primarily static efficiency, dynamic efficiency has not yet been clearly defined, whereas static efficiency has, in terms of price and quantities under perfect competition and a static equilibrium.[202] Dynamic competition, in contrast, is a *process* with uncertain results and therefore one cannot measure how 'good' or 'bad' performance is.[203] This implies that there will be measurement problems for an approach focused on 'choice' in the sense of innovation and new products, but this in itself cannot be a justification for equating 'choice' with the *number* of competitors that produce different products on the same market. This is because the number of competitors in itself cannot meaningfully signify the existence of choice and/or competition on any given market.

The problem with equating choice with the number of competitors and finding a reduction in the number of competitors to be a reduction of choice and therefore to be an abuse is that it protects competitors instead of competition. Effective consumer choice is *not* about requiring the maximum number of options; competition law prevents business conduct that *artificially* limits the natural range of

[196] ibid 242.
[197] L Lovdahl Gormsen, *A Principled Approach to Abuse of Dominance in European Competition Law* (Cambridge, CUP, 2010) 119.
[198] See ch 2 this volume, section III for ordoliberalism and protection of economic freedom.
[199] Lovdahl Gormsen (n 197) 121.
[200] Schmidt (n 131) 408.
[201] ibid.
[202] ibid.
[203] ibid.

options in the market and thereby seeks to preserve a *sufficient* array of options.[204] 'Artificial' in this sense is the direct reduction of options without the mediating agency of consumer choice as opposed to reduction through the ordinary workings of the market (for example, as a result of firms exiting the market due to lack of innovation or inefficiency).[205] Similarly, it *cannot* be said that the larger the number of firms in the industry the higher the welfare, particularly as firms have to incur fixed costs.[206] The presence of fixed costs implies a trade-off: a higher number of firms entails more competition and lower prices which increase consumer surplus and allocative efficiency, but it also entails a duplication of fixed costs which reduces productive efficiency.[207] This implies that a policy aimed at maximising the *number* of firms in a given industry would be unsound and that competition policy should be about defending competition, not competitors.[208] Indeed some studies show that where entry is free, there exists a positive relationship between the toughness of competition and industrial concentration since firms have to cover fixed set-up costs and anticipate lower profits when competition is tougher.[209] This would imply that markets where competition is toughest might not be associated with the highest welfare since at the equilibrium, fewer firms will co-exist.[210]

Regarding the relationship between innovation (ie, dynamic efficiency leading to *actual* choice in the form of new products) and competition, although competition pushes firms to invest in order to improve their position relative to their competitors, this cannot be generalised to conclude that the more competition there is in a market the more likely that firms will innovate.[211] Neither theoretical nor empirical research on the link between market structure and innovation is conclusive, although an intermediate position (where there is some competition but also high enough market power resulting from innovation) might be the most conducive to innovation.[212] This is because firms' incentives to innovate are not only determined by the existence of competition, but also by the possibility of appropriating the results of their investment.[213] Too strong competition implies reduced appropriability and in turn reduced incentives to invest and innovate.[214] Thus, it is the prospect of enjoying some market power that pushes firms to use more efficient technologies, improve product quality or introduce new product

[204] NW Averitt and RH Lande, 'Consumer Choice: The Practical Reason for both Antitrust and Consumer Protection Law' (1998) 10 *Loyola Consumer Law Review* 44, 46.
[205] ibid 46, fn 4.
[206] Motta (n 45) 51.
[207] ibid 51.
[208] ibid 51–52.
[209] See Motta, ibid, 52, fn 32 referring to C d'Aspremont and M Motta, 'Tougher Competition or Lower Concentration: A Trade-Off for Antitrust Authorities?' in G Norman and JF Thisse (eds), *Market Structure and Competition Policy: Game-Theoretic Approaches* (Cambridge, CUP, 2000).
[210] Motta, ibid.
[211] ibid 56, 57.
[212] ibid 57.
[213] ibid.
[214] ibid.

varieties.[215] All in all, as its approach currently stands, it is impossible to demarcate the Commission's understanding of 'choice' from the number of 'competitors' on a given market and it is highly questionable that choice (either in the Commission's decisions or in the Guidance) refers to the outcome of dynamic competition. How the EU authorities treat the issue of 'choice' in their future actions will indeed reveal what their actual standard of harm is and particularly whether they have adopted a consumer welfare standard based on harmful effects of conduct on consumers.

V CONCLUSION

This chapter has sought to analyse the current position of the Commission's approach to Article 102 in light of the recent 'reform' to which the Commission aspired. It is noteworthy that this process has been limited to exclusionary abuses and has mainly focused on price-based conduct for which the Guidance has suggested a general standard based on the 'as efficient competitor' test. This leaves exploitative abuse without any discussion and non-price-based exclusionary conduct without a general standard.

This state of affairs is far from ideal. First, the Commission cannot simply 'do away' with the *fact* that Article 102 prohibits exploitative abuse and even if the Commission itself can prioritise its enforcement of exclusionary abuse cases, other claimants might have different priorities. For example, for private claimants such as customers, an action based on exploitative abuse might be much more attractive or might be the only option. Yet, the Commission has not provided any guidance thus far in the reform process on how Article 102 could or should be operationalised in dealing with these cases. Although EU competition law as such is not subject to private enforcement before the EU courts, the silence of the Commission can adversely impact private enforcement in front of the national courts: it can be a potential disincentive for private litigants, not least because of a lack of understanding about *how* exploitation is prohibited by the national equivalents of Article 102. Given that the Commission would like to enhance private enforcement of EU competition rules, one would have expected it to at least provide some guidance on the operation of exploitative abuses to facilitate these potential cases of 'unhappy' trading partners of dominant undertakings. There may also be a related problem for *national courts* that would have to decide on private claims of exploitative abuse under the national equivalents of Article 102 since there is no Commission or EU court guidance on how to apply Article 102 in these cases. This is only exacerbated by the demonstrations in this study of how mere exploitation on its own might not signify harm to competition, even though exploitation should be present before conduct can be found abusive. Thus, there

[215] ibid 64.

must be limiting principles for exploitation as a component of 'abuse' and, as yet, these are not provided by the Commission or the EU courts.

Secondly, the current situation is not ideal as the Commission has failed to set out a general standard for non-price-based exclusionary conduct. The lack of a general standard for non-price-based conduct is problematic because it creates an artificial separation of price-based conduct from non-price-based conduct. This is despite the fact that there is no obvious reason at a principle level why they should be treated differently. Although the potential elimination of a competitor at least as efficient as the dominant undertaking from the market *can* conceptually become the test for non-price-based conduct as well, the Guidance does not adopt such an approach for reasons unknown.

This chapter has also sought to demonstrate that the approach of the Commission to the issue of efficiencies under Article 102 is problematic as it appears to treat these as part of a defence on the part of the dominant undertaking. It has been argued here that efficiencies should be considered as part of establishing abuse in the first place and not as a defence. Similarly, the inclusion of choice by the Commission in its understanding of 'consumer welfare' is also potentially problematic as thus far there seems to be no separation of the existence of 'choice' from the existence of 'competitors'. This implies that by arguably protecting choice, the EU authorities are protecting competitors. This would in turn imply that nothing has been reformed thus far, as the main criticism towards the EU authorities' application of Article 102 was that they protect competitors instead of competition. Therefore, how the EU authorities understand and treat choice in their future decisions is of particular importance for establishing whether they indeed adopt a more economic, effects-based approach with a consumer welfare standard.

The next and final substantive chapter of this study will propose an alternative, modern approach to the concept of 'abuse' under Article 102. It will bring together the arguments thus far made in this book and propose an approach in line with a more economic, effects-based approach to Article 102 that also embraces the historical roots of the provision.

8

A New Approach to 'Abuse'

I INTRODUCTION

This chapter proposes a modern approach to the concept of 'abuse' in Article 102 by bringing together the main arguments thus far made in this study. It seeks to offer an approach in line with both modern economic thinking and the historical roots of the provision. Starting with a discussion of possible objectives of competition law and policy in chapter one, this study identified the proposition that competition law and policy is not just about outcomes, but also the process as the best starting point concerning the appropriate objectives of Article 102.[1] In the context of that particular provision, an effects-based approach aiming to enhance consumer welfare should imply that it is detriment to consumers that is connected to harm to competition that makes conduct abusive. This means that both exploitation and exclusion should be present before conduct is found abusive and that, therefore, fusion of exploitation and exclusion is necessary.[2] This chapter seeks to elaborate further on these elements of the proposed approach to the concept of 'abuse' in Article 102.

Other than exploitation and exclusion, this study has also demonstrated (particularly in chapters two, three and seven) that efficiencies have to be considered as part of the 'abuse' test. Within the current text of Article 102, this appears to be the most appropriate way of incorporating efficiencies into the assessment. In fact, chapter two has demonstrated that efficiency was one of the main concerns of the drafters of Article 102 and that efficiency underlies the whole European market integration objective.[3] This implies that efficiencies *should* be incorporated in the concept of abuse. This chapter seeks to also further elaborate on this additional requirement of the proposed approach to the concept of 'abuse' in Article 102.

To be clear, then, in incorporating these findings, this chapter proposes that the components of 'abuse' with a modern approach to Article 102 should be: (i) exploitation; (ii) exclusion; and (iii) a lack of an increase in efficiency. These

[1] This point is made in J Farrell and ML Katz, 'The Economics of Welfare Standards in Antitrust' (2006) 2(2) *Competition Policy International* 3; see ch 1 this volume, section III.D for a discussion.

[2] This author has made this point earlier in P Akman, 'The Role of Exploitation in Abuse under Article 82 EC' (2009) 11 *Cambridge Yearbook of European Legal Studies* 165.

[3] See ch 2 this volume, section V.

three components make up cumulatively the *necessary and sufficient* conditions for conduct to be found abusive. For a start, the 'exploitation' element proves harm to consumers. With a consumer welfare approach, this would be the proof of a relevant reduction in consumer welfare. This condition is therefore in line with the more economic, effects-based approach. This condition is also in line with the historical roots of Article 102, since these demonstrate a clear concern with the prevention of 'exploitation' as the subject matter of Article 102.[4] This implies that requiring demonstration of 'exploitation' would not actually result in a change in the law, but rather in the recognition of the true nature of the law of abuse of a dominant position. Thus, even if consumer welfare is not accepted as the objective of Article 102, loyalty to the provision itself necessitates exploitation to be part of the concept of 'abuse'. Additionally, the 'exclusion' element shows distortion of competition and thereby satisfies the Protocol 27 requirement that a system ensuring that competition in the internal market is not distorted.[5] It also ensures that the approach proposed here accommodates the fact that Article 102 has mainly been interpreted as a prohibition of exclusionary practices in the decisional practice. The requirement that both 'exploitation' and 'exclusion' exist before conduct can be found abusive implies that prohibiting either without the other does not make sense for competition law purposes. Finally, the element of 'a lack of an increase in efficiency' recognises that efficiency was a fundamental concern underlying the adoption of Article 102 and ensures that conduct that is efficiency-enhancing and/or is normal commercial practice is not prohibited. The rest of this chapter elaborates on these three components in turn, and provides an evaluation of the new approach.

The layout of this chapter is as follows. Section II discusses why exploitation is necessary and why prohibiting exploitation where there is no exclusion is not appropriate. Section III flips the issue on its head and demonstrates why exclusion should be prohibited, but only where there is also exploitation. Section IV explains the necessity of incorporating efficiencies in the assessment of abuse. Section V evaluates the new approach by considering its advantages and limitations. Section VI concludes.

II EXPLOITATION AS A NECESSARY CONDITION

There is no doubt that Article 102 prohibits exploitation. First, this is obvious from the provision itself, which is concerned with unfair prices; unfair trading conditions; discrimination between *trading partners*; making the conclusion of contracts subject to acceptance by the *other parties* of supplementary obligations;

[4] See ch 2 this volume, section V.C and in particular text to fn 244.

[5] 'Protocol (No 27) on the Internal Market and Competition' annexed to the TEU and TFEU contains the same statement which was found in Art 3(1)(g) EC prior to the entry into force of the Treaty of Lisbon. See n 52 for the text of the provision.

and limitation of production, markets or technical development *to the prejudice of consumers.*[6] All of these named practices relate to the conduct of a dominant undertaking that will take place in its relationship with its *customers* (or *suppliers*). Even the prohibition of limitation of production, markets or technical development – which has been argued to be the part of Article 102 that prohibits exclusion[7] – is not about exclusion, but exploitation: it explicitly requires the conduct to be to the prejudice of *consumers.* Secondly, the legislative history of the provision examined in chapter two explicitly contains statements to the effect that the prohibition in Article 102 is about conduct aimed at trading partners of the dominant undertaking, not competitors.[8] Thus, the text of the provision is indeed supported by the intention of the drafters of the provision, which demonstrates the main concern as that of preventing exploitation. Thirdly, the French and German texts of Article 102 literally prohibit 'abusive exploitation'.[9] Indeed, as mentioned in chapter two, by studying the examples in Article 102, Joliet concluded in the 1970s that the prohibition merely covered exploitative abuses: under the abuse theory of Article 102 – unlike with the Sherman Act – the test of legality was *not* interference with other firms' freedom to compete or the use of exclusionary practices to achieve and hold power, but rather whether there was monopolistic *exploitation* of the market.[10] Joliet's view, however, was ultimately rejected by the ECJ in *Continental Can* where the Court held that Article 102 applies *not only* to exploitative abuse *but also* to exclusionary practices.[11] In chapter two, it was suggested that this was a misreading of Article 102 which led to Article 102 being predominantly used for a purpose for which it was not designed.[12] For the purposes of this section, suffice it to say that it is not questionable that the provision of Article 102 applies to exploitation. This is one reason why exploitation should be made a necessary condition for a finding of abuse in the enforcement of Article 102, namely loyalty to the provision itself. This remains so regardless of the objective that the EU authorities adopt in their enforcement of Article 102; exploitation is *required* by the provision.

A more 'contemporary' reason why exploitation should be a necessary condition of abuse is that it is exploitation that shows harm to someone other than 'competitors' in the context of Article 102. This is particularly important for an effects-based approach with a consumer welfare standard: exploitation can and should be used as the test of harmful effects of conduct that would qualify the conduct as abusive. Since this chapter argues that exclusion is also a necessary

[6] Note that the term 'consumers' means 'customers'; see ch 2 this volume, text around fn 338 and ch 3 this volume, text around fn 98.

[7] See, eg, R O'Donoghue and AJ Padilla, *The Law and Economics of Article 82 EC* (Oxford, Hart Publishing, 2006) 196 *et seq.*

[8] See ch 2 this volume, text around fn 244.

[9] In the French and German texts, Art 102 prohibits '*d'exploiter de façon abusive*' and '*missbräuchliche Ausnutzung*' respectively.

[10] R Joliet, *Monopolization and Abuse of Dominant Position* (La Haye, Martinus Nijhoff, 1970) 250.

[11] See Case 6/72 *Europemballage Corp and Continental Can Co Inc v Commission* [1973] ECR 215, [26].

[12] See ch 2 this volume, text around fn 330.

condition of abuse, the proposal regarding exploitation would imply that exploitation is sanctioned when it is related to exclusion, as a reason or a result thereof. As argued throughout this book, a definition of exploitative abuse as 'the receiving of advantages by the dominant undertaking to the disadvantage of its trading partners that would not be possible but for its dominance' is apt to catch those exploitative practices that are the result of the undertaking's dominant position on the market. It should be noted that this particular interpretation would imply a departure from the ECJ's judgment in *Continental Can*, which established that it was possible to abuse a dominant position without actually exercising or relying on market power.[13] This implies that under the case law there is no causation requirement in Article 102 between the dominant position and its abuse.[14] It is suggested here that requiring this causal link between the dominant position and its abuse is crucial for the correct interpretation of 'exploitation' and to ensure that only those practices that are possible because of the dominance of the undertaking in question are challenged. Otherwise, without the causal link, the prohibition would come very close to a recrimination of the dominant position itself. It must also be noted that it has been remarked that, for a model based on consumer or total welfare, there is no 'exclusionary' violation and that the only type of violation is 'exploitation'.[15] This is not the proposal of this study; it is argued here that exploitation and exclusion must *both* be present for a violation of Article 102 to occur. This is so even if the ultimate aim of prohibiting exclusion is the prevention of exploitation; as will be demonstrated below in section III, exclusion must remain part of the test to delineate competition law problems from contract law and consumer protection law problems. In other words, not all exploitative practices should be a matter of concern for competition law.

A related, further reason why exploitation should be necessary before conduct is found abusive is that, absent exploitation, it is difficult to see *why* the exclusion of a dominant undertaking's competitors is prohibited.[16] In fact, one could argue that the whole reason for the Commission to rethink its approach to Article 102 (as elaborated on in chapter seven) was the fact that there was not sufficient demonstration of harm to consumers in its decisions on exclusionary conduct, which made it also subject to the criticism that it is protecting competitors and not competition. A good example that demonstrates this is the practice of 'tying', a practice which is prohibited by Article 102(d) and which occurs when an undertaking supplies a product on the condition that the customer obtains something else from it as well.[17] For instance, in *Hilti*, the Commission found that Hilti, an undertaking dominant in the supply of patented nail guns, abused its position by supplying patented cartridge strips only to those purchasing its non-patented

[13] *Continental Can* (n 11) [27].

[14] See R Whish, *Competition Law* 6th edn (Oxford, OUP, 2009) 201–02.

[15] EM Fox, 'What is Harm to Competition? Exclusionary Practices and Anticompetitive Effect' (2002) 70 *Antitrust Law Journal* 371, 372.

[16] Akman (n 2) 181.

[17] A Jones and B Sufrin, *EU Competition Law: Text, Cases and Materials* 4th edn (Oxford, OUP, 2011) 454.

nails.[18] Similarly, in *Tetra Pak II*, the tying of the supply of non-aseptic packaging machines to the supply of cartons that the machines filled was found abusive by the Commission.[19]

Some commentators interpret both *Hilti* and *Tetra Pak II* as being driven by concerns about the structure of the market, rather than the extraction of monopoly profits or the protection of consumers.[20] They argue that in these cases the concern was with the ability of smaller firms to compete, which represents a policy not so much about efficiency and free competition as the protection of small firms and competitors.[21] This criticism implies that when there is no 'exploitation' in the form of harmful effects on customers, the prohibition of exclusionary conduct results in protecting competitors rather than competition. However, what is also clear from these cases is that exploitation by imposing certain contract terms on a trading partner can be abusive if it is the result of dominance.[22] For example, in *Hilti* the problem was expressed as that of the dominant undertaking leaving 'the consumer with no choice over the source of his nails and as such abusively exploit[ing] him'.[23] Exploitation was also a matter of concern in *Microsoft*, where the GC characterised as 'coercion' the conclusion of contracts being made subject to the acceptance of supplementary obligations having no connection with the subject of such contracts.[24] This coercion existed even though the coerced product was supplied without charge to consumers and consumers were free not to use Windows Media Player as they were not prevented from using substitute products.[25] Exploitation thus *flows from* exclusion that tying entails in the form of lack of customer choice, the unavailability of products separately, and from pressure exerted on the customer through the promise of favourable treatment to customers who purchase both products.[26] Indeed, in *Hilti*, for example, immediately following the above statement about exploitative abuse, the Commission also stated that Hilti's policies, in addition, 'all have the object or effect of excluding independent nail makers who may threaten the dominant position Hilti holds'.[27] Hence, exploitation and exclusion, according to the Commission, went hand in hand in this case. Yet, it should be noted that the concept of exploitation in *Hilti* is not necessarily the same as the concept as defined in this study; it is unclear what advantages the dominant undertaking was receiving from its practice *to the disadvantage* of its customers. It appears that it was mainly the reduction of 'choice'

[18] *Eurofix-Bauco v Hilti* Commission Decision (Case IV/30.787 and 31.488) 88/138/EEC [1988] OJ L65/19, [74]–[75].

[19] *Elopak Italia/Tetra Pak* Commission Decision (Case IV/31.043) 92/163/EEC [1992] OJ L72/1, [117]. Customers were also tied to obtain all maintenance and repair services and spare parts from Tetra Pak.

[20] Jones and Sufrin (n 17) 462.

[21] ibid.

[22] Akman (n 2) 182.

[23] *Hilti* (n 18) [75].

[24] Case T-201/04 *Microsoft Corp v Commission* [2007] ECR II-3601, [961] *et seq.*

[25] ibid [969]–[70].

[26] Jones and Sufrin (n 17) 517–18.

[27] *Hilti* (n 18) [75].

between different suppliers for the customers, but this reduction in choice appears also to have been taken as proof of exclusion.[28] The problems with an approach focusing on an undefined 'choice' objective have already been examined in chapter seven and will not be discussed further here.[29]

Given that a necessary condition for abuse is exploitation, one must also elaborate on *how* exploitative effects should be deemed to exist. Currently in EU competition law, an (exclusionary) abuse can be found in the mere likelihood of adverse effects and a demonstration of actual effects of conduct is not necessary.[30] However, this position cannot be transposed to the condition of 'exploitation', as per the 'abuse' concept of this study. 'Exploitation' must be observable; for abusive exploitation to occur, the dominant undertaking has to *use* its power to exploit.[31] Finding abuse in the mere *likelihood* of exploitation would not be consistent with Article 102 either; the fact that a dominant position itself is not prohibited demonstrates that it is *not* the likelihood of exploitation that is abusive: that likelihood always exists as long as there is a dominant position.[32] Conduct becomes abusive *if and only if* the dominant undertaking actually *uses* its power to 'exploit'. The presumption underlying Article 102 (as proven by not prohibiting dominance itself) is that dominant undertakings may not always use their power to exploit.[33] It follows that the use of that power should be observable and thus demonstrable in terms of its *actual effects*, as otherwise abuse would not have been established.[34]

A related issue is the determination of the entity *on whom* the exploitative effects should be observable. The exploitation that is necessary under Article 102 should be understood as either exploitation directly of final consumers or exploitation of trading partners. It should be noted that the interests of final consumers and other customers of the dominant undertaking might not always be aligned.[35] Therefore, if a policy choice is made to adopt a (properly defined) 'consumer welfare' standard, then the 'exploitation' that ultimately makes conduct abusive under Article 102 should be deemed to be that of the *final consumer*. This author has argued elsewhere that there are many instances in which the conduct of a dominant undertaking will have opposite effects on customers and final

[28] Another oft-cited issue with the *Hilti* case is the narrowness of the Commission's market definition which held that nails, nail guns and cartridges were each separate markets; see, eg, Jones and Sufrin (n 17) 308.

[29] See ch 7 this volume, section IV.

[30] See, eg, Opinion of Advocate General Kokott on 23 February 2006 in Case C-95/04 *British Airways plc v Commission* [2007] ECR I-2331, [71]; Case T-203/01 *Manufacture francaise des pneumatiques Michelin v Commission* [2003] ECR II-4071, [239], [241]; Case T-340/03 *France Télécom SA (formerly Wanadoo Interactive SA) v Commission* [2007] ECR II-107, [195]–[97].

[31] Akman (n 2) 187.

[32] ibid.

[33] Joliet (n 10) 131.

[34] Akman (n 2) 187.

[35] See P Akman, '"Consumer" versus "Customer": The Devil in the Detail' (2010) 37(2) *Journal of Law and Society* 315 for a discussion of the instances in which the impact of a dominant undertaking's conduct on the interests of consumers and customers differ.

consumers.[36] In cases where this happens, one must justify why the interests of an intermediate undertaking must be preferred *for its own sake* over the interests of final consumers or even those of the dominant undertaking. There might be scenarios where the exploitation of trading partners will indeed demonstrate a distortion of competition, for example, if they lead to the ultimate exclusion of certain customers (suppliers) from the market, leading to elimination of competition on the downstream (upstream) market. A practice of 'unfair pricing' satisfying the conditions of the new test proposed in chapter five can have such an impact depending on the conditions of the downstream market.[37] What is important to reiterate is that if the objective is consumer welfare, then mere exploitation of customers that do not necessarily have the same or similar harmful effects on consumers might not demonstrate the necessary or sufficient harm to be abusive. Indeed, such conduct can even benefit consumers.[38] Similarly, conduct that benefits intermediate customers can harm consumers and may warrant prohibition for this reason.[39] A recent example of this can be seen in the *Intel* case where the dominant undertaking was basically making payments to intermediate customers to delay the launch of Intel's competitors' products.[40] Thus, customers might have benefited from the conduct in the form of additional profits, even though consumers might have been exploited in a manner that would satisfy the condition of exploitation. Therefore, in cases where the practice directly involves trading partners, a careful and holistic analysis of the downstream and/or upstream markets might become necessary to establish where the harm lies. The second condition of the proposal of this chapter, namely that there exists exclusion as well as exploitation, can indeed help in such cases to demarcate harm that is relevant for competition law purposes from harm that is not relevant.

In sum, this section has argued that exploitation should be made a necessary condition for abuse in the enforcement of Article 102. One current problem, however, is that since the focus in the decisional practice has thus far been on exclusionary conduct, the *Continental Can* judgment has also led to the misinterpretation of exploitative abuse. Where exploitation has been found abusive in the case law, as demonstrated in chapters four, five and six in the context of fairness, unfair pricing and discrimination, there is often no separate showing of harm to competition.[41] One need only think of cases such as *British Leyland*,[42] *1998 Football World Cup*[43] and *BdKEP*[44] where certain price-based and other practices were

[36] ibid 326–42.

[37] See ch 5 this volume, section VII for the new test.

[38] See Akman (n 35) 331–37 for examples of conduct harmful to intermediate customers but beneficial for consumers.

[39] See ibid 337–42.

[40] *Intel* (Case COMP/C-3/37.990) Commission Decision 2009/C 227/07 [2009] OJ C227/13, in particular [580] *et seq.*

[41] See also Akman (n 2) 169.

[42] Case 226/84 *British Leyland plc v Commission* [1987] 1 CMLR 185.

[43] *1998 Football World Cup* (Case IV/36/888) Commission Decision 2001/12/EC [2000] OJ L5/55.

[44] *BdKEP – Restrictions on Mail Preparation* (Case COMP/38.745) Commission Decision 20 October 2004 (unreported).

found 'unfair' and thus were perhaps 'exploitative' of the customer, although it was not necessarily obvious how these were harmful to *competition*.[45] Without this separate showing of harm to competition in the form of, for example, exclusion, some of these practices appear more like contract law problems than competition law problems. Indeed, some authors have suggested that if a dominant undertaking can exploit its customers for a significant period of time, there must be something wrong with the *market*.[46] It has thus been argued that exploitation should only be sanctioned when significant barriers to entry exist.[47] In other words, only where there is (potential) foreclosure of the market and (potential) exclusion of competition, does exploitation become a concern for competition law. An analogy with the US might be useful here: the implication of not requiring separate harm to competition in the EU would imply that there would be no 'antitrust injury' in the sense of the requirement in US antitrust law.[48] Thus, the next section discusses exclusion as a necessary condition for conduct to be abusive. Exclusion is immediately relevant as it can demonstrate the 'harm to competition' with which exploitation must be coupled in order for a competition law issue to be present.

III EXCLUSION AS A NECESSARY CONDITION

Exclusion should be accepted as another necessary condition for conduct to be found abusive under Article 102. This is despite the fact that, as demonstrated in chapter two, the intention of the drafters of Article 102 was to merely prohibit exploitation by Article 102.[49] The reason for requiring exclusion is that the provision of Article 102 was envisaged as part of the Chapter on 'rules on competition' in the Treaty, as opposed to, for example, rules on consumer protection. In fact, consumer protection rules did not even exist in the EEC Treaty as adopted in

[45] See, this volume, ch 4 section III, ch 5 section II and ch 6 section II.B for a discussion of these and similar cases.

[46] Jones and Sufrin (n 17) 363.

[47] See M Motta and A de Streel, 'Excessive Pricing and Price Squeeze under EU Law' in CD Ehlermann and I Atanasiu (eds), *What is an Abuse of Dominant Position?* (Oxford, Hart Publishing, 2006); LH Röller, 'Exploitative Abuses' in CD Ehlermann and M Marquis (eds), *European Competition Annual 2007: A Reformed Approach to Article 82 EC* (Oxford, Hart Publishing, 2008); P Akman and L Garrod, 'When are Excessive Prices Unfair?' (2011) 7(2) *Journal of Competition Law & Economics* 404. See also BR Lyons, 'The Paradox of the Exclusion of Exploitative Abuse' in *The Pros and Cons of High Prices* (Swedish Competition Authority, 2007) whose argument somewhat differs regarding the conditions for intervention.

[48] Akman (n 2) 169. In the US, for private plaintiffs to recover damages from breaches of competition law, '[p]laintiffs must prove *antitrust* injury, which is to say injury of the type the antitrust laws were intended to prevent and that flows from that which makes defendants' acts unlawful. The injury should reflect the anticompetitive effect either of the violation or of anticompetitive acts made possible by the violation'; *Brunswick Corp v Pueblo Bowl-O-Mat, Inc* 429 US 477, 489 (1977). Consequently, without proving anticompetitive *effects*, harm to competition (which may then give rise to a claim for damages) will not be proven.

[49] See ch 2 this volume, text after fn 244.

1957. Moreover, the drafters of Article 102 also adopted the provision in Article 3(f) EEC.[50] According to this provision, the activities of the Community included 'the institution of a system ensuring that competition in the common market is not distorted'.[51] This provision is now found in Protocol 27, which is annexed to the TEU and TFEU.[52] Article 102 is part of the rules that make up the system which ensures that competition in the internal market is not distorted. Therefore, it is distortion of competition in the internal market that Article 102 seeks to prevent. Exploitation on its own does not demonstrate this distortion. This is because the relation between the practices listed in Article 102 and the harm to competition is not obvious; it is not self-evident what makes these practices anti-competitive, over and above simply damaging the trading partners' interests. Hence, there must be a limiting principle that establishes what makes those exploitative practices of a dominant undertaking a competition law issue, as opposed to a contract law or consumer law issue.

If one recalls the examples of abuse of unfair pricing and discrimination elaborated on in chapters five and six, as was explained therein, although these are typical exploitative practices, they only seem to signify a competition law problem when there is exclusion as well.[53] This implies that there must be *harm to competition* other than mere harm to trading partners. Indeed, the EU courts – at least the GC – have also recognised this by stating that although Article 102 contains no reference to the anticompetitive object or effect of the practice referred to, in the light of the context of Article 102, conduct will be regarded as abusive *only if it restricts competition*.[54] This 'restriction of competition' or 'harm to competition' can potentially be established in one of two ways within the context of Article 102.

One way to incorporate the requirement of 'harm to competition' into Article 102 is to use the provision of Protocol 27. The ECJ indeed appears to have tried to do this already as far back as 1973 with its *Continental Can* judgment. Notably, it decided that

> [a]s may further be seen from letters (c) and (d) of Article [102](2), the provision is not only aimed at practices which may cause damage to consumers directly, but also at those which are detrimental to them through their impact on an effective competition structure, such as is mentioned in Article 3[(1)(g)] of the Treaty. Abuse may therefore occur if an undertaking in a dominant position strengthens such a position in such a way that the degree of dominance reached substantially fetters competition, ie, that only undertakings remain in the market whose behaviour depends on the dominant one.[55]

[50] Art 3(f) EEC became Art 3(g) EC with the adoption of the Treaty of Maastricht in 1993 and Art 3(1)(g) EC with the entry into force of the Treaty of Amsterdam in 1999.

[51] With the Treaty of Maastricht this provision was amended by deletion of the words 'the institution of'.

[52] Protocol 27 states that the internal market as set out in Art 3 TEU 'includes a system ensuring that competition is not distorted'.

[53] See this volume, ch 5, particularly sections II and VI, and ch 6, particularly sections II.B and IV.

[54] *Michelin II* (n 30) [237]; *Microsoft* (n 24) [867].

[55] *Continental Can* (n 11) [26].

Further, according to the ECJ, 'if Article 3[(1)(g)] provides for the institution of a system ensuring that competition in the common market is not distorted, then it requires a fortiori that competition must not be eliminated'.[56]

This author has argued elsewhere that the ECJ's finding in this decision that Article 102 applies to exclusionary practices which *strengthen* the dominant position on the market was contrary to the intention behind Article 102 and, in fact, led to this provision being predominantly used for a purpose for which it was not designed.[57] The lack of competition due to the *existence* of a dominant undertaking was accepted by the drafters, contrary to the ECJ's holding in *Continental Can.*[58] Both of these findings are obvious not only from the legislative history, but also from the fact that there are no merger control provisions in the Treaty. Thus, power per se is not what is sought to be prohibited by the competition rules in the Treaty. What was and is prohibited by Article 102 is the reduction in competition which results from the *utilisation* of the power of dominant undertakings; it is *not* the lack of competition that is the result of the *existence* of dominance and it is *not* the lack of competition that results from the *strengthening* of dominance. It is the harm to competition that results from or in the exploitation of the trading partners of the dominant undertaking that Article 102 is meant to prohibit.

Thus, the ECJ appears to have confused two things in *Continental Can*: the issue of whether Article 102 applies to *mere* exclusion by which an undertaking strengthens or reaches a dominant position and the issue of whether harm to competition (in the shape of exclusion) is necessary for the exploitative practices listed in Article 102 to be abusive. This study argues that although this separate harm to competition is necessary, the ECJ's linking of Article 3(1)(g) EC with Article 102 in the manner it did in *Continental Can* was not appropriate since it exceeded the purpose. It exceeded the purpose not least because it created a separation between exclusionary conduct and exploitative conduct by finding that conduct that is *merely* exclusionary can be abusive. Conduct that is not exploitative is *not* prohibited by Article 102. The ECJ's judgment was also unfortunate because it led to the understanding that Article 102 was a provision concerned with the exclusion of the *competitors* of the dominant undertaking. The examples in Article 102 and the legislative history clearly demonstrate that the provision is concerned with the *trading partners* of the dominant undertaking. Thus, the harm to competition that can be conceptualised as 'exclusion' should not have been primarily understood as the exclusion of competitors. This exclusion should be understood as 'exclusion of competition' so as to also include the exclusion of trading partners of the dominant undertaking from the markets on which they are active.

A better way of incorporating the 'harm to competition' requirement into Article 102 by using Protocol 27 [Article 3(1)(g) EC] would be to accept that, due

[56] ibid [24].

[57] See P Akman, 'Searching for the Long-Lost Soul of Article 82EC' (2009) 29(2) *Oxford Journal of Legal Studies* 267, 296 and ch 2 this volume, text around fn 330.

[58] See Akman (n 57) 286 and ch 2 this volume, text around fn 242.

to the existence of the requirement in Protocol 27 that competition is not distorted, the concept of abuse in Article 102 *only* covers exploitation that results from or is in some other way related to harm to competition. This harm to competition can be deemed to exist where there is exclusion of competition, in the form of exclusion of trading partners or competitors of the dominant undertaking. This does not imply that exclusion automatically or on its own establishes that the conduct is anticompetitive or abusive. It is anticompetitive exclusion coupled with exploitation that does not lead to an increase in efficiency (as per the final condition of this study's proposal) that makes conduct abusive. The possible tests for establishing whether exclusion is anticompetitive are returned to below.[59]

Other than using Protocol 27, there is one more possible way to incorporate 'harm to competition' into the assessment that is required under Article 102. This is by an interpretation of 'dominance' as the potential or capacity to exclude. Indeed, this might be how the drafters of Article 102 envisaged the provision to operate. This is because, as demonstrated in chapter two, in some early discussions of Article 102, dominance appears to have been understood as the capacity to exclude.[60] Indeed, this has been discussed in the modern literature as a method of establishing dominance as well. The 'power to exclude' has been suggested as an alternative type of market power to that defined as 'pricing power'.[61] Whereas the dominant undertaking's raising of its own price corresponds to 'pricing power', its raising of the costs of its rivals corresponds to 'power to exclude'.[62] Thus, commentators distinguish between 'the power to control price profitably, directly by restraining one's own output' (classical or Stiglerian market power) and 'exclusionary power' (Bainian market power) which occurs where a firm can raise its rivals' costs and thereby reduce their ability to compete or exclude them from the market altogether.[63] Bishop and Walker argue that there are instances where there are differences between these two types of market power and, on occasions, thinking primarily in terms of exclusionary power simplifies the analysis.[64] This is particularly the case when consumers may be harmed in more ways than just by higher than competitive prices, such as when the ability of competitors to introduce new products is limited.[65] This notion of exclusionary power is arguably also consistent with the ECJ's definition of 'dominance', which holds that dominance involves the power to act independently of competitors.[66]

[59] See below, text after n 79.

[60] See ch 2 this volume, section V.F.

[61] S Bishop and M Walker, *The Economics of EC Competition Law: Concepts, Application and Measurement* 3rd edn (London, Sweet & Maxwell, 2010) 91.

[62] Bishop and Walker, ibid, referring to TG Krattenmaker, RH Lande and SC Salop, 'Monopoly Power and Market Power in Antitrust Law' (1987) 76 *The Georgetown Law Journal* 241.

[63] Bishop and Walker, ibid, 92.

[64] ibid.

[65] ibid 92.

[66] ibid. Krattenmaker et al also note this to be the 'monopoly power' definition of the Supreme Court in Sherman Act Section II cases; Krattenmaker, Lande and Salop (n 62) 246–47. One definition of 'dominance' by the ECJ is a 'position of economic strength enjoyed by an undertaking which enables it to prevent effective competition being maintained on the relevant market by affording it the power

Incorporating the 'harm to competition' element into Article 102 by using the concept of 'dominance' has the advantage of loyalty to the provision of Article 102 itself: although Article 101 has an explicit requirement of 'prevention, restriction or distortion of competition' for it to be applicable, Article 102 does not have this requirement. Yet, logic suggests that this requirement should be in Article 102 since it is a rule on competition just like Article 101; both rules are found in the Chapter on 'rules on competition' in the Treaty. Given that in some original languages, as mentioned above,[67] it is 'exploitative abuse' that is prohibited, this requirement of harm to competition that may result from exclusion is unlikely to be found in the concept of 'abuse'. This would imply that it is indeed possible that the drafters assumed this harm to competition to be incorporated into the concept of 'dominance'. If so, their envisaged provision would work like this: an undertaking that is dominant because it has the capacity to exclude harms competition in violation of Article 102 if it exploits its position by disadvantaging its trading partners in a manner that is only possible due to its position of dominance. Thus, exclusion would be dealt with at the stage of establishing dominance and exploitation would be dealt with at the stage of establishing abuse. This would mean that 'abuse' is only exploitative and exclusion is not a type of abuse, but a precondition of exploitation being abuse. Indeed, with an understanding of dominance as the power to exclude, it is the exclusionary conduct that creates the market power under scrutiny, and not the other way around.[68] This approach would also do away with the need to 'import' the requirement of harm to competition from a provision external to Article 102, such as Protocol 27.

There are two problems, however, with establishing exclusionary conduct by way of establishing dominance. The first is that, although this approach would fit well into a system like that of the US where *monopolisation* is a breach of antitrust law and exploitation by a monopolist that achieved its monopoly without anticompetitive means is not,[69] achieving a position of dominance is not illegal under Article 102. This is so regardless of the methods of achieving dominance. There must be an *abuse* of that dominant position and one cannot abuse a position that one does not yet have. Thus, even where the power to exclude is actually used and dominance is achieved by way of exclusionary conduct, sanctioning this type of exclusion alone would be tantamount to prohibiting dominance against the letter of the provision. Therefore, where the power to exclude has been used and the

to behave to an appreciable extent independently of its competitors, customers and ultimately of its consumers'; Case 27/76 *United Brands and United Brands Continental BV v Commission* [1978] ECR 207, [65].

[67] See n 9 above.

[68] Krattenmaker, Lande and Salop (n 62) 255.

[69] See E Elhauge and D Geradin, *Global Competition Law and Economics* (Oxford, Hart Publishing, 2007) 234. *Cf* Krattenmaker, Lande and Salop (n 62) 260–61 for the argument that it is only the exercise of lawfully acquired Stiglerian market power that can be exercised without breaching Sherman Act Section II, whereas a firm that lawfully acquired Bainian market power does not have unbridled licence to exercise it. Accordingly, a firm lawfully may exercise Bainian market power only if the resulting power over price is more than offset by gains in efficiency; ibid 261.

dominance has been achieved as a result of exclusionary conduct, this alone cannot be sanctioned by using Article 102. Yet, an approach that reduces exclusion to the stage of establishing dominance should be expected to prohibit such conduct (ie, the achievement of dominance by exclusion) because exclusion (or harm to competition) will not be dealt with at any other stage of the assessment. Hence, there would be a conceptual anomaly if the power to exclude and exclusionary abuse are not seen as separate concepts.

Secondly, such an approach would go against the case law of the EU courts and the recent policy declarations of the Commission. It would go against the case law of the EU courts since the predominance of judgments on Article 102 concerns exclusionary *conduct* over and beyond the establishing of dominance. Incorporating exclusion into dominance would in effect mean that there is no exclusionary *conduct* that can be abusive. Although this might have indeed been the intention behind Article 102 it is highly unlikely that the EU jurisprudence will move in this direction, and overrule over 50 years of case law. Although this author's proposed approach also departs from the case law by, for example, requiring actual exploitation and causation, the degree of change required in these instances is very different from that in the case of limiting exclusion to the establishing of dominance. Moreover, there is less textual support in the provision itself for limiting exclusion to dominance than requiring exploitation and causation. This approach is unlikely to be accepted by the Commission as well since recently in its Guidance, the Commission defined dominance in the Stiglerian sense and not the Bainian one. According to the Guidance, an undertaking can be regarded as dominant if it is capable of profitably increasing prices above the competitive level for a significant period of time.[70] Thus, the indicator of market power is the ability to increase price, *not* the ability to exclude competition. This can indeed be seen as the victory of the Chicago School of antitrust in Europe: power over price is the usual focus of the Chicago School,[71] whereas power to exclude may be thought to be more in line with the Harvard or the post-Chicago School of antitrust.[72] For these reasons this study suggests that the 'harm to competition' requirement is read into Article 102 on the basis that this is a rule on competition and also that Protocol 27 dictates a system ensuring that competition is not distorted in the internal market. This implies that the early understanding of dominance as power to exclude (discussed in chapter two) should not be adopted in the modern approach to Article 102.

One final issue that has to be discussed is *whose* exclusion matters and *how* one should establish exclusion that is relevant for determining harm to competition. First, exclusion and thus 'harm to competition' can be at the level of the production chain that the dominant undertaking is active on or at the downstream (upstream) level, consisting of the customers (suppliers) of the dominant undertaking.[73] Thus,

[70] 'Guidance on the Commission's Enforcement Priorities in Applying Article 82 of the EC Treaty to Abusive Exclusionary Conduct by Dominant Undertakings' [2009] OJ C45/7, [11].

[71] Krattenmaker, Lande and Salop (n 62) 249.

[72] For these schools of antitrust, see ch 1 this volume, section III.A.

[73] Akman (n 2) 176.

it can be horizontal or vertical foreclosure. As demonstrated in chapter five in the context of unfair pricing, exclusion does not have to be the exclusion of competitors of the dominant undertaking.[74] It can be the exclusion of the customers (or suppliers) of the dominant undertaking. Similarly, in the context of discrimination in chapter six, it was seen that it is discrimination that has the potential to exclude some customers of the dominant undertaking to the disadvantage of others that can be deemed to be a competition law problem.[75] In all cases where the issue is vertical exclusion, this should be understood as the exclusion of efficient undertakings. Thus, the dominant undertaking's exploitative practices would be either the reason or the outcome of the exclusion of its efficient customers (or suppliers). For example, if the issue is refusal to supply customers, then this refusal should exclude efficient undertakings from the market in ways that would not be possible for the dominant undertaking but for its dominance. This is similar to the ECJ's holding in *Oscar Bronner* in that the criterion for exclusion when an undertaking is refused access by the dominant undertaking is the exclusion of an undertaking with similar efficiency to the dominant undertaking and not the actual undertaking which made the request, which might be operating on a much smaller scale.[76]

The exclusion that harms competition can be that of competitors of the dominant undertaking at the horizontal level as well. What is important to note is that harm to competitors cannot be assumed to lead to harm to competition because harm to competitors is a necessary but not sufficient condition for establishing anticompetitive exclusion.[77] In fact, exclusion of competitors is how the majority of EU jurisprudence has conceptualised harm to competition under Article 102, although this has also been the source of criticism that the EU practice 'protects competitors, not competition'.[78]

The issue of *how* exclusion that demonstrates harm to competition is to be established is a thorny one and one on which there is no consensus in the literature or in practice. The first point to be made is that, unlike exploitation, which has to be *actual* exploitation, exclusion can be potential or actual in the context of an abuse under Article 102. This is because actual exploitation demonstrates that something has *already* gone wrong with the market and, so long as a convincing story of exclusion can be provided that explains the exploitation, the first two requirements of the test of abuse will have been met. There are no grounds to treat exploitation that will result in exclusion (ie, where exclusion is potential) and exploitation that results from exclusion (ie, where exclusion is actual) differently. In a sense, the proof of exploitation implies that there is already some harm that has occurred; exclusion is necessary to establish that this harm is of relevance

[74] See ch 5 this volume, section VII.

[75] See ch 6 this volume, section IV.

[76] See Case C-7/97 *Oscar Bronner GmbH & Co KG v Mediaprint Zeitungs- und Zeitschriftenverlag GmbH & Co KG* [1998] ECR I-7791, [46], [47]. In this preliminary reference case, Oscar Bronner – a competitor of Mediaprint on the daily newspapers market – requested and was refused access to the home-delivery network of Mediaprint.

[77] Bishop and Walker (n 61) 234.

[78] For the criticism, see the literature in ch 7 this volume, fn 6.

for competition law. Potential exclusion can suffice to demonstrate the existence (or the lack) of this relevance for competition law. In this aspect, the proposal of this chapter is in line with the EU case law that has on various occasions held that the *capability* of restricting competition is sufficient for conduct to be abusive.[79]

Several tests have been suggested in the literature for establishing anticompetitive exclusion. These tests are mainly aimed at establishing the exclusion of competitors, but can potentially be applied in cases of vertical exclusion as well. They include the 'profit sacrifice test' ('the but for test'), the 'no economic sense test' and the 'as efficient competitor test', among others.[80] The 'profit sacrifice test' is based on the assumption that a firm would not rationally engage in exclusionary conduct unless it considers that any short-term profit sacrifice will be less than the expected gains as a result of exclusion or deterred entry.[81] Although the test is said to have some initial appeal, it also raises questions such as what the benchmark is for assessing sacrifice and whether the test is a substantive standard or a standard to assess intent.[82] The 'no economic sense test' asks whether conduct would have been expected to be profitable apart from any gains that conduct may produce through eliminating competition.[83] One criticism of this test is that, in practice, it would be extremely difficult to assess whether a course of conduct made sense only if competitors were eliminated on the basis of business plans, which will be the best evidence of a company's options.[84] The 'as efficient competitor test', as discussed in chapter seven, is based on the premise that 'exclusionary conduct' is conduct that excludes an equally efficient undertaking.[85] Problems with this test are argued to be that there are circumstances where entry of less efficient rivals can improve total welfare because the gain in allocative efficiency through lower

[79] See, eg, *Michelin II* (n 30) [239]; Case T-219/99 *British Airways v Commission* [2003] ECR II-5917, [293].

[80] See O'Donoghue and Padilla (n 7) 184 *et seq* for a discussion of these tests. O'Donoghue and Padilla treat the 'consumer welfare test' as a separate and individual test. This study has dealt with 'consumer welfare' as a broader objective than a particular test of exclusionary conduct, in the sense that, for example, the 'as efficient competitor' test can also have an ultimate consumer welfare standard. This would imply that the exclusion of competitors as efficient as the dominant undertaking is not allowed *because* such conduct is presumed to lead to a decrease in consumer welfare. Thus, this author understands 'consumer welfare' as a broader concept than a test for exclusionary conduct.

[81] ibid, 185.

[82] J Vickers, 'Abuse of Market Power' in P Buccirossi (ed), *Handbook of Antitrust Economics* (Cambridge, MA, MIT Press, 2008) 424. It has also been suggested that sacrificing short-run profits to exclude rivals typically reflects socially desirable investments, whereas undesirable conduct that excludes rivals normally does not require any sacrifice of short-run profits; see E Elhauge, 'Defining Better Monopolization Standards' (2003) 56 *Stanford Law Review* 253, 255, 271 *et seq.* See also SC Salop, 'Exclusionary Conduct, Effect on Consumers, and the Flawed Profit-Sacrifice Standard' (2006) 73 *Antitrust Law Journal* 311 criticising the test.

[83] GJ Werden, 'Identifying Exclusionary Conduct under Section 2: The "No Economic Sense" Test' (2006) 73 *Antitrust Law Journal* 413, 414.

[84] O'Donoghue and Padilla (n 7) 188. For the argument that the test does not make sense for exclusive dealing, see JM Jacobson and SA Sher, '"No Economic Sense" Makes No Sense for Exclusive Dealing' (2006) 73 *Antitrust Law Journal* 779.

[85] O'Donoghue and Padilla, ibid, 189. See ch 7 this volume, section II.B.

prices can outweigh the loss in productive efficiency through higher costs.[86] In essence, all these tests seek to identify the situations in which conduct is inefficient and so is ultimately harmful to consumers, as opposed to promoting efficient conduct that yields consumer benefits over time.[87] Therefore, the differences between them should arguably not be overstated.[88]

The Commission in its Guidance has clearly adopted the 'as efficient competitor' test for price-based conduct, as was discussed in chapter seven.[89] The Guidance does not explicitly adopt a general test for non-price-based conduct. Yet, on occasions, in the discussion of such conduct, it can be seen that the concern with at least some of these practices is also the exclusion of as efficient competitors.[90]

This study does not attempt to achieve the 'unattainable objective' of elaborating a rule for exclusionary conduct that is both totally precise and perfectly administrable.[91] It does not deem it necessary either. This is because, under the proposal of this study, exclusion is only one of three necessary and sufficient conditions. Moreover, by making actual exploitation a necessary condition of abuse, this study indirectly shifts the focus of the inquiry from exclusion to exploitation since exclusion is only necessary to establish which exploitation is a matter of concern for competition law and which exploitation is not. Therefore, what test is used for establishing exclusion is not at the core of the proposal and any decisional error that the choice of test leads to could potentially be corrected by the other two stages of the proposal. In a way, each condition of the proposal is a safeguard against errors that might be made in establishing one of the other conditions.

Having said that, as a general principle, the rule that it is only the exclusion of undertakings that are at least as efficient as the dominant undertaking that should be a concern for competition law appears to be a good starting point. Although the exclusion of undertakings that are not as efficient as the dominant undertaking can also, in limited circumstances, harm competition, this can be taken care of by the use of a rebuttable presumption: it can be presumed that it is only the exclusion of undertakings that are at least as efficient as the dominant undertaking that is to be prevented by the enforcement of Article 102. If the Commission or the claimant believes that in a particular case the exclusion of undertakings that are less efficient than the dominant undertaking also harms competition, then by proving this on the facts of the particular case, they can rebut the presumption. The point that has to be reiterated is that exclusion is only one (necessary) third of the story. The next section turns to the last condition of 'abuse', which is the requirement that the dominant undertaking's conduct does not increase efficiency.

[86] Vickers (n 82) 427.

[87] O'Donoghue and Padilla (n 7) 185.

[88] ibid.

[89] See ch 7 this volume, section II.B.

[90] This can be seen in the examples of 'conditional rebates' at 'Guidance' (n 70) [41] and 'multi-product rebates' in the context of 'tying and bundling' at 'Guidance', ibid [59].

[91] See E Rousseva, *Rethinking Exclusionary Abuses in EU Competition Law* (Oxford, Hart Publishing, 2010) 351 for the argument that the only consensus is on this objective being unattainable.

IV A LACK OF AN INCREASE IN EFFICIENCY AS A NECESSARY CONDITION

The final condition for conduct of a dominant undertaking to be abusive is for conduct not to lead to an increase in efficiency. In other words, conduct that leads to a (non-trivial) increase in efficiency and thus has an efficiency explanation should not be found abusive. This assessment of increase in efficiency can be made by comparing the situation with the allegedly abusive conduct in place and the situation without the dominant undertaking's conduct in place, taking also into account the alternative conduct that the undertaking would possibly undertake if its investigated conduct is found abusive. The requirement of a lack of an increase in efficiency serves two purposes: first, it enables an interpretation of 'abuse' in line with the intent behind Article 102 and more broadly the intent behind the market integration imperative; and, secondly, it ensures that conduct that is otherwise normal and legitimate business practice is not prohibited.

Chapter two demonstrated that, for the drafters of the Treaties of Rome, efficiency was of the utmost concern not only when drafting the competition rules, but also when deciding why the European markets had to be merged.[92] The whole idea behind the merging of the European markets was to increase the efficiency of European undertakings so that economic progress could be made and Europe could compete with forces like the US and the USSR.[93] The lack of merger control provisions in the Treaty is further evidence that European undertakings' getting more efficient, even by getting 'bigger', was desirable for the founding fathers. It was also demonstrated in chapters three and seven that including efficiencies in the assessment of abuse by way of an objective justification was not appropriate.[94] The assessment there led to the conclusion that efficiencies should be part of establishing abuse, as opposed to a defence on the part of the dominant undertaking. This section thus elaborates on this requirement of a lack of an increase in efficiency as part of proving the conduct to be abusive.

The relevant efficiencies that can prevent conduct being abusive can be productive, allocative or dynamic efficiencies.[95] The reasoning behind the requirement is that if the dominant undertaking's conduct increases its efficiency by reducing its costs, increasing its output or introducing new or better products, it should be seen as legitimate business practice. One issue here is whether these efficiencies would have to be passed on to consumers to be legitimate. It has been argued in chapter three that, for the sake of consistency with Article 101(3), this could be required.[96] The ECJ has also stated in *British Airways* that, while assessing the economic justification of conduct by a dominant undertaking, it has to be deter-

[92] See ch 2 this volume, particularly sections V.B.i and V.B.ii.

[93] See ch 2 this volume, text around fn 205.

[94] See this volume, ch 3, text around fn 50 and ch 7, section II.C.

[95] For different types of efficiency and their role in competition law and policy see ch 1 this volume, section II.B.

[96] See ch 3 this volume, text around fn 74.

mined whether the exclusionary effect arising from conduct which is disadvantageous for competition may be counterbalanced or outweighed by advantages in terms of efficiency which also benefit the consumer.[97] If the exclusionary effect of the conduct bears no relation to advantages for the market *and* consumers, or if it goes beyond what is necessary in order to attain those advantages, that conduct must be regarded as an abuse.[98] The ECJ repeated this position in its judgment in *TeliaSonera* as well.[99] This is likely to be how the EU authorities will expect efficiencies to be demonstrated by dominant undertakings in the future. There are, however, a number of problems with this approach.

First, as mentioned in chapter three, there are difficulties in establishing whether pass-on will occur and thus in undertaking the necessary balancing exercise which considers advantages from efficiency and disadvantages from exclusion.[100] Secondly, dynamic efficiencies in particular are very difficult to establish affirmatively before they realise. A strict pass-on requirement can have the unfortunate outcome of removing dynamic efficiencies from the assessment altogether. Given that dynamic efficiencies are arguably the most important type of efficiency,[101] this would have serious negative long-term consequences. Thirdly, it is not obvious that Article 102 itself requires pass-on of efficiencies to consumers. This is despite the fact that Article 101(3) does so. Thus, one can infer that in the context of Article 102 this is not required either because, when the issue is unilateral conduct, it is presumed that a certain element of pass-on is inevitable, or because consumers could be compensated with different policies. Indeed, according to the economics literature, even with a monopoly, an increase in efficiency *will* be passed on.[102] For these reasons, for the purposes of operationalising the proposal of this study, it is argued here that the requirement of a lack of an increase in efficiency should not also include an assessment of whether the efficiencies are passed on to consumers. Increasing the efficiency of a dominant undertaking is desirable for the whole economy regardless of the particular positive effects on particular consumers. The assessment necessary to establish whether the efficiencies will be passed on to consumers does not take into account the possibility that the efficiencies that the dominant undertaking receives can be used to the benefit of the economy by new investments and innovations whose

[97] *British Airways* (n 30) (ECJ) [86].

[98] ibid.

[99] Case C-52/09 *Konkurrensverket v TeliaSonera Sverige AB* [2011] ECR I-00, [76].

[100] See ch 3 this volume, text around fn 78.

[101] See JF Brodley, 'The Economic Goals of Antitrust: Efficiency, Consumer Welfare, And Technological Progress' (1987) 62 *New York University Law Review* 1020, 1025. Similarly, see FM Scherer, 'Antitrust, Efficiency, and Progress' (1987) 62 *New York University Law Review* 998, 1002, 1026 and ch 1 this volume, section II.B for a general discussion.

[102] A reduction in marginal cost (ie, an increase in efficiency) will lead to a lower price even under monopoly since if the marginal cost curve shifts down, it would intersect the marginal revenue curve lower down. This would imply greater output and thereby lower price; Bishop and Walker (n 61) 32 and 32, fn 37. Some authors argue that the pass-on will be at least 50% of the cost savings; see JA Hausman and GK Leonard, 'Efficiencies from the Consumer Viewpoint' (1999) 7(3) *George Mason Law Review* 707, 708–09, 727.

effects go beyond the consumers of the particular product under investigation. The only efficiency that should not be taken into account in this context is the cost savings that the dominant undertaking achieves merely from a reduction in its output which leads to the abusive conduct.[103] It should be noted that not requiring the efficiencies to be passed on to consumers would bring the test closer to a 'total welfare' standard rather than a 'consumer welfare' standard; the latter standard would require efficiencies to be passed on to consumers for conduct not to be abusive.[104] As argued in chapter two, the legislative history of Article 102 suggests that the position of the drafters of the provision was closer to a total welfare standard than a consumer welfare standard.[105] However, if the choice is made to adopt the consumer welfare standard (which is the current apparent tendency of the Commission), then one might require an explicit demonstration of the efficiencies being passed on. It should still be noted that, not requiring separate proof of pass-on and thus moving closer to a total welfare approach, can bring the EU and US laws on unilateral conduct closer to each other. This is based on the findings of recent research which demonstrates that when applying Sherman Act Section II, the US courts have adopted a total welfare approach and not a consumer welfare approach.[106] Studying the Section II case law, Meese argues that conduct that enhances total welfare by increasing the efficiency of the dominant undertaking does not breach Section II, regardless of the effects of conduct on the welfare of customers.[107] If this interpretation of the US doctrine is accepted, then adopting the approach proposed in this chapter would narrow the gap between the EU and US laws on unilateral conduct, thereby providing more consistency and legal certainty for undertakings subject to the law on both sides of the Atlantic.[108]

In terms of operationalising this requirement, the legal burden to prove that conduct is not efficiency-enhancing would be on the Commission (or the claimant). The only burden that can be placed on the undertaking would be the initial burden of producing plausible evidence to substantiate the efficiencies.[109] As this issue has already been elaborated in chapter seven, it will not be discussed further

[103] This is in line with the Commission's position on Art 101(3). See Commission, 'Guidelines on the Application of Article 81(3) of the Treaty' [2004] OJ C101/97, [49].

[104] See ch 1 this volume, section III.B.

[105] See ch 2 this volume, text after fn 337.

[106] See AJ Meese, 'Debunking the Purchaser Welfare Account of Section 2 of the Sherman Act: How Harvard Brought Us to a Total Welfare Standard and Why We Should Keep It' (2010) 85(3) *New York University Law Review* 659.

[107] ibid 703, 709, 710, 736.

[108] On the differences between the EU and US approaches see, eg, DL Meyer, 'The Development and Communication of Competition Law Standards Applicable to Single-Firm Exclusionary Conduct: A Perspective Based on US Experience' in CD Ehlermann and M Marquis (eds), *European Competition Annual 2007: A Reformed Approach to Article 82 EC* (Oxford, Hart Publishing, 2008); J Vickers, 'Speaking Note, Panel II' in CD Ehlermann and M Marquis (eds), *European Competition Annual 2007: A Reformed Approach to Article 82 EC* (Oxford, Hart Publishing, 2008); B Hawk, 'Article 82 and Section 2: Abuse and Monopolizing Conduct' in (2008) 2 *Issues in Competition Law and Policy* 871 (ABA Section of *Antitrust Law* 2008).

[109] O'Donoghue and Padilla (n 7) 233.

here.[110] Suffice it to note that this would require the Commission and the EU courts to change their understanding of efficiencies as an 'objective justification' that has to be proved by the dominant undertaking.

This requirement of a lack of an increase in efficiency also ensures that conduct which is normal commercial practice, and which is possible for undertakings that are not dominant as well, is not found abusive. This is in line with some early understandings of abuse of dominance and particularly with that of von der Groeben, who was one of the drafters of Article 102.[111] This is also a natural consequence of the definition of 'abuse' as conduct that would not be possible but for the dominance of the undertaking. Thus, if a certain practice is available to and commonly practised by non-dominant undertakings as well, then it should mean that such conduct is not abusive. Abusive practices are those that are only possible as a result of the position of dominance that the undertaking enjoys. This would also imply that the boundaries of the 'special responsibility' of a dominant undertaking are drawn by the prohibition of Article 102 itself. In other words, the 'special responsibility' that dominant undertakings have is to not distort competition *by way of* abusing their positions. This means that dominant undertakings do not have a special responsibility over and beyond that of not abusing their positions of dominance. Thus, the concept of 'special responsibility' is another tautology in the context of Article 102 since it should not mean anything more than that dominant undertakings should not abuse their positions *by way of* undertaking abusive conduct that breaches Article 102.[112] Having completed the discussion of the elements of the proposed concept of 'abuse', the next section evaluates this proposed approach by considering its advantages and limitations.

V EVALUATION OF THE NEW APPROACH

The new approach to abuse which fuses exploitation and exclusion and requires a demonstration of a lack of an increase in efficiency has several advantages over the current approach. The first advantage is that it enables one to distinguish the exploitative practices of a dominant undertaking that distort competition from those that should not fall within the ambit of competition law. Some examples

[110] See ch 7 this volume, text around fn 102.

[111] See ch 2 this volume, section V.F. It has similarly been argued by a prominent author in the US that for the application of Sherman Act Section II that where alleged exclusionary conduct does have an efficiency justification, and can succeed in furthering monopoly power only to the extent that the monopolist has successfully improved its own efficiency, then that alone suffices to make the conduct legal without further inquiry into its possibly adverse effects on overall market efficiency; Elhauge (n 82) 320.

[112] For 'objective justification' being a tautology, see O'Donoghue and Padilla (n 7) 227; Opinion of Advocate General Jacobs in Case C-53/03 *Synetairismos Farmakopoion Aitolias & Akarnanias (Syfait) and Others v GlaxoSmithKline plc and GlaxoSmithKline AEVE* [2005] ECR I-4609, [72]; R Nazzini, 'The Wood began to Move: An Essay on Consumer Welfare, Evidence and Burden of Proof in Article 82 Cases' (2006) 31(4) *European Law Review* 518, 533.

from EU case law that found the inefficiency of a dominant undertaking to be abusive demonstrate the importance of this.

In one of these cases, namely *Port of Genoa*, the statutory monopoly with the exclusive right to organise dock work at the port of Genoa refused to use modern technology. This led to the performance of services taking longer than necessary and to an increase in costs.[113] A customer of the dominant undertaking demanded compensation for the damage it suffered as a result of the delay, and the case was referred to the ECJ for a preliminary ruling. The ECJ held that the conduct of, inter alia, refusing to have recourse to modern technology which results in an increase in costs of the operations and a prolongation of the time required for their performance is a potential breach of Article 102.[114] In this case, there was clearly no exclusionary *conduct* and the issue was the exploitation of the customer due to the inefficiency of the dominant undertaking. Similarly, in *Klaus Höfner* the ECJ held that a state employment agency with the monopoly of employment procurement for business executives, abuses its position when it is clearly not in a position to satisfy demand for its services.[115] The issue was again not exclusion, but rather exploitation due to the inefficiency of the dominant undertaking to the prejudice of its trading partners. In another case, *British Telecommunications*, the Commission held that the maintenance of obsolete systems through measures taken by a dominant undertaking was an abuse as it limited technical development to the prejudice of consumers.[116] Finally, in *P & I Clubs* the Commission expressly stated that there would be an abuse under Article 102(b) TFEU by way of 'exploitation' where an association that provided marine insurance offered only a single level of cover that left a very substantial share of the demand unsatisfied.[117] Yet, it was not for the Commission to decide on the level of cover to be offered; the Commission might only intervene if there was clear and uncontroversial evidence that a very substantial share of the demand was being deprived of a service which it manifestly needed.[118]

The implication of these cases is that 'inefficiency' of a dominant undertaking can be an abuse: the 'prejudice to trading partners', in these cases, is the result of a limitation of production, markets or technical development by the dominant undertaking which would not be possible but for the dominance of the undertaking.[119] This is in line with the concept of exploitation in this study. What is sought to be sanctioned by the prohibition of this exploitation is the 'quiet monopoly

[113] Case C-179/90 *Merci convenzionali porto di Genova SpA v Siderurgica Gabrielli SpA* [1991] ECR I-5889, [19].

[114] *Port of Genoa* (n 113) [18]–[20].

[115] Case C-41/90 *Klaus Höfner and Fritz Elser v Macrotron GmbH* [1991] ECR I-1979, [31].

[116] *British Telecommunications* (Case IV/29/877) Commission Decision 82/861/EEC [1982] OJ L360/36, [34].

[117] *P&I Clubs, IGA and P&I Clubs, Pooling Agreement* (Case IV/D-1/30.373 and IV/D-1/37.143) Commission Decision 1999/329/EC [1999] OJ L125/12, [128].

[118] ibid [128].

[119] Akman (n 2) 178.

life' and, thus, the productive inefficiency of the dominant undertaking.[120] Hence, in this case, one would have exploitation and a lack of an increase in efficiency as per the concept of abuse proposed in this chapter. Yet, what is questionable is (since it is the lack of competition that makes the 'quiet monopoly life' possible for the dominant undertaking) whether or not mere inefficiency of the dominant undertaking should be deemed abusive without any separate harm to competition, such as exclusion. In line with the proposal of this chapter, without this separate demonstration of harm to competition, such instances should not be found to breach Article 102. Therefore, the proposal of this study would ensure that in these cases, there is harm to competition, and thus a competition law issue.

The same applies to cases mentioned in chapter four on 'fairness', such as *SABAM*,[121] *GEMA*,[122] *DSD*[123] and *Tetra Pak II*[124] where 'unfair trading conditions' were found abusive.[125] In these cases the issue was when trading conditions became unfair and abusive. Thus, it is clear that these cases were mainly concerned with the exploitation of the trading partners of the dominant undertaking and not necessarily with exclusion: the underlying assumption seems to be that these clauses would not be possible but for the dominance. Yet, similar to the abovementioned cases, it is not obvious what the competition law issue was and why and when the unfairness of these contract clauses became a competition law issue.[126] The proposal of this study would again ensure that there is a competition law issue in these cases, cases which are mainly based on an assessment of 'unfairness'. Thus, the fusion of exploitation and exclusion would ensure that there is harm to competition, similar to the 'antitrust injury' requirement of the US, in exploitative abuse cases.[127]

The second advantage of the proposed approach, related to requiring exclusion in cases of exploitation, is that if exploitation were scrutinised on its own, then there would be a problem of appropriate remedies. This is because sanctioning pure exploitation would almost inevitably require the scrutiny of the terms, in particular the price term of the contracts of a dominant undertaking.[128] Yet, tackling prices directly is problematic and undesirable since there is the problem of identifying what is an 'unfair price', as well as the problem of the apt remedy, namely that of what is the 'fair price'.[129] Consequently, competition authorities do not like acting as price regulators; 'price regulation is the antithesis of the free

[120] As put by Hicks, '[t]he best of all monopoly profits is a quiet life' which expresses the inefficiency that would result from the monopolist not being pressured to reduce its costs and maximise its productive efficiency; JR Hicks, 'Annual Survey of Economic Theory: The Theory of Monopoly' (1935) 3(1) *Econometrica* 1, 9.

[121] Case 127/73 *Belgische Radio en Televisie v SV SABAM and NV Fonior* [1974] ECR 313.

[122] *GEMA Statutes* (Case IV/29.971) Commission Decision 82/204/EEC [1982] OJ L94/12.

[123] *DSD* (Case COMP D3/34493) Commission Decision 2001/463/EC [2001] OJ L166/1.

[124] Case T-83/91 *Tetra Pak International SA v Commission* [1994] ECR II-755, [140].

[125] See ch 4 this volume, section III for the facts of the cases.

[126] Akman (n 2) 181.

[127] ibid 182.

[128] ibid 185.

[129] See ch 5 this volume, sections V and VI.A in general.

market' and is better restricted to ex ante regulation in the case of natural or legal monopolies.[130] The scrutiny of mere 'exploitation' by competition authorities may require them to act as regulators, a task for which they are unlikely to be the appropriate bodies.[131] The fusion of exploitation and exclusion should resolve the remedy problem by enabling the competition authority to use sanctions aimed at exclusion, which are remedies they commonly use and for which they are indeed the appropriate institutions.

The third advantage of the proposed approach is that, by requiring exploitation in the form of harm to trading partners in every Article 102 case, not only does one remain loyal to the provision itself, but one also adopts a more modern position than the current approach. This is because requiring exploitation in each case implies that it is not possible to protect merely the competitors of a dominant undertaking, which has been the main criticism towards the thus far EU decisional practice. The requirement of exploitation would ensure that there is harm to trading partners (and ultimately consumers) of the dominant undertaking that justify an intervention relating to its practices. Particularly with a consumer welfare approach, this would signify the necessary harmful effects on consumers and their welfare. This implies that were cases such as *Hilti*,[132] *Tetra Pak II*,[133] *British Airways*,[134] *Michelin I*[135] *and Michelin II*,[136] and *Wanadoo*[137] reconsidered under the approach proposed here, different outcomes might be reached since in all of these cases there is a lack of demonstration of actual harm to trading partners (and ultimately consumers).

A related, fourth advantage is that, by requiring a demonstration of a lack of an increase in efficiency, the new approach would embrace the economic underpinnings of modern competition law. Incorporating a lack of an increase in efficiency has the advantage of avoiding an artificial construction of Article 102 by a transposition of Article 101(3) into this provision as a defence.[138] Accepting efficiency as part of the assessment also represents an improvement over adopting objectives such as 'fairness', since 'fairness' does not have the objective or predictive characteristics of 'efficiency'.[139]

Another advantage of requiring exploitation alongside exclusion is that since there is a great deal of controversy surrounding how to establish exclusion that harms competition, and since all the tests thus far proposed in the literature have

[130] Jones and Sufrin (n 17) 531.
[131] Akman (n 2) 185.
[132] *Hilti* (n 18).
[133] *Tetra Pak II* (n 124).
[134] *British Airways* (GC) (n 79) and *British Airways* (ECJ) (n 30).
[135] Case 322/81 *NV Nederlandsche Banden-Industrie Michelin v Commission* [1983] ECR 3461.
[136] *Michelin II* (n 30).
[137] *Wanadoo* (n 30).
[138] This appears to be the Commission's proposed approach as discussed earlier in ch 7, this volume, text around fn 96.
[139] KG Elzinga, 'The Goals of Antitrust: Other than Competition and Efficiency, What Else Counts?' (1977) 125 *University of Pennsylvania Law Review* 1191, 1213.

been criticised for being suboptimal,[140] establishing harm to trading partners can be another safeguard against decision errors. For example, it has been argued that the as efficient competitor test – the test currently favoured by the Commission – is problematic since it would often be impossible for firms to apply any version of this test when attempting to conform their conduct to the requirements of the law in the real world.[141] This is because doing so would require firms to know a great deal about their rivals and their ability to respond in the marketplace.[142] The requirement of exploitation can remedy such potential problems with the test for exclusion: the dominant undertaking may be in a better position to know whether its conduct harms its trading partners since it will be directly involved in the practices towards its trading partners.

Similarly, the as efficient competitor test arguably renders ambiguous results in some instances, and this is problematic. For example, it has been noted that in the presence of scale economies, it is theoretically possible for a dominant undertaking, through exclusive dealing to profitably exclude from the market a rival whose costs are nowhere higher than its own.[143] This is because each customer would *individually* do better to accept than reject an exclusive contract with the dominant undertaking at a price just below the unit cost at the small-scale of the rival, even if that price is substantially above the unit cost of the large-scale dominant undertaking.[144] In contrast, it would be in the *collective* interest of the customers to deal with the rival at a large scale, but none will do so individually due to the diseconomies of its small scale.[145] This is a form of raising rivals' costs.[146] Thus, '[t]he dominant firm can thereby exploit to its advantage, but to the detriment of customers and efficiency, the coordination problem of the customers – a strategy of divide and rule'.[147] It is clear that such a practice falls squarely within the concept of abuse as defined in this study: conduct is exploitative, exclusionary and inefficient. However, it is not obvious how the 'as efficient competitor' test would apply in such a case, since the competitor is *overall* as efficient but is less efficient in supplying each individual customer due to its lack of scale economies.[148] This is therefore an example of how inefficient exclusion can be profitable for the dominant undertaking, although this theory is only applicable where the proportion of the market foreclosed would significantly affect scale economies.[149] It has also been suggested that loyalty inducing rebates, though less restrictive than exclusive dealing, have the potential to similarly engender a foreclosing

[140] See above, text after n 79.
[141] AD Melamed, 'Exclusive Dealing Agreements and Other Exclusionary Conduct – Are there Unifying Principles?' (2006) 73 *Antitrust Law Journal* 375, 388.
[142] ibid 388.
[143] Vickers (n 82) 428.
[144] ibid.
[145] ibid.
[146] ibid.
[147] ibid. See also Elhauge (n 82) 284 on collective action problems.
[148] Vickers, ibid, 428.
[149] ibid.

effect.[150] Thus, the proposal of this study can remedy the potential problem in the operation of the as efficient competitor test, as such conduct would breach Article 102 if the proposal is accepted.

Regarding the limitations of the proposed approach, it should be noted that as with any test that seeks to establish a general rule, this test should not be treated as a panacea. There may be problematic cases where the test will not be as helpful as it is in other cases. As economic knowledge improves, any test can be improved. The test proposed here is based on some fundamental principles which are unlikely to lose their importance and relevance, so long as Article 102 is kept in its current wording.

It is also acknowledged that the proposed approach requires a change in the case law of the EU courts on four issues: causation between the dominant position and abuse; actual effects of conduct on the market; the 'special responsibility' of dominant undertakings; and incorporating efficiency into the definition of 'abuse'. The proposal of this study necessitates a causal link between the dominant position and the conduct, in that abusive conduct is one which would not be possible but for the dominance of the undertaking. As mentioned above,[151] this is not the position of the ECJ. Similarly, by requiring *actual* exploitation, the proposal requires there to be *actual* effects on the market before conduct can be found abusive. This, again, departs from the jurisprudence of the ECJ.[152] In the same vein, the proposal in effect implies that dominant undertakings do not have a 'special responsibility' as envisaged by the ECJ, over and above that of not entering into practices that are prohibited in Article 102 itself. Finally, the proposal incorporates efficiency into the finding of abuse, as opposed to treating efficiency as an objective justification that has to be proved by the undertaking as a 'defence'.[153] As a result, under the proposal, the legal burden to establish that conduct is not efficiency-enhancing would be on the claimant, as otherwise abuse will not be proven.

These departures from the case law bring the approach closer to the text of Article 102 itself. The lack of a necessity to show causation or actual effects as well as the existence of a special responsibility both represent the outcome of an extremely broad interpretation of Article 102 by the ECJ. It is difficult to find support for any of these in the text of Article 102 itself. Similarly, efficiency of conduct has largely been ignored in the jurisprudence even though the legislative history and context of Article 102 clearly demonstrate a strong concern for enhancing efficiency. Therefore, the proposed approach offers a plausible alternative to the current approach, which has introduced requirements alien to Article 102 and ignored requirements that are found in the provision itself. Consequently, there is little certainty in this area of the law as the jurisprudence currently stands. By adopting an understanding that is loyal to the provision itself, the proposed

[150] ibid.
[151] See above, text to n 14.
[152] See above, text to n 30.
[153] On objective justification, see above, text to n 94.

approach can provide more certainty for undertakings, enforcers and those subject to abusive practices. Given that there is no doctrine of precedent in EU law, there is no legal problem in terms of adopting the proposed approach.[154] Not only is there not a problem, one could argue that the correct reading of Article 102 *requires* exploitation to exist before conduct can be found abusive. Similarly, the legislative history demonstrates that efficiency *should* be taken into account in all Article 102 cases before abuse can be established. All in all, the proposed approach presents an improvement over the current approach to Article 102, while respecting the boundaries and the nature of the provision itself.

VI CONCLUSION

The EU decisional practice has thus far focused on 'exclusion' when establishing breach of Article 102. Moreover, the decisional practice has displayed a particularly narrow understanding of exclusion as the exclusion of *competitors* of the dominant undertaking (as opposed to exclusion that leads to the foreclosure of the *market*). This chapter proposed a modern approach to abuse in which exclusion is only one of three requirements; accordingly, exclusion has to be complemented with exploitation and with a demonstration that conduct does not increase efficiency. This modern approach has been proposed on the basis of the text and the historical context of Article 102, as well as current economic thinking on unilateral conduct.

There is some indication that the Commission might be moving towards the approach proposed here. For example, according to the Guidance,

> tying may lead to less competition for customers interested in buying the tied product, but not the tying product. If there is not a sufficient number of customers who will buy the tied product alone to sustain competitors of the dominant undertaking in the tied market, the tying can lead to these customers facing higher prices.[155]

Moreover, efficiencies that might relate to tying such as reduction in transaction costs for customers and savings on packaging and distribution costs for suppliers, as well as potential innovation, will also be taken into account in the assessment of the practice.[156] Such an assessment falls squarely within the concept of 'abuse' as proposed in this study from a *substantive* point of view: in an abusive tying practice, as explained in the Guidance, there would be exploitation of customers, exclusion of competing suppliers and a lack of an increase in efficiency.[157] Although the Guidance is promising in this regard, it is not possible to say that it

[154] For the lack of a doctrine of precedence in the EU, see A Arnull, 'Owning up to Fallibility: Precedent and the Court of Justice' (1993) 30 *Common Market Law Review* 247, 248, 262.

[155] 'Guidance' (n 70) [55].

[156] ibid [62].

[157] The proposal of this study *procedurally* departs from the Guidance's approach since it incorporates efficiencies into the assessment of abuse.

wholly embraces the test proposed in this study since, for example, it does not require actual exploitation of trading partners for conduct to be abusive. As discussed extensively in chapter seven, there are also many other instances in which the Guidance displays weaknesses.[158]

However, more worrying than the Commission, which at least *appears* to be intent on modernising its approach to Article 102, is the approach of the EU courts, particularly the ECJ. As recently as late 2010, in its *Deutsche Telekom* judgment, the ECJ has simply held that short term consumer *detriment* is acceptable – and in fact, must be effected – to prevent exclusion of competitors from the market.[159] In this margin squeeze case, the ECJ confirmed that a dominant undertaking that has no control over its regulated wholesale access prices has to *increase* its retail prices to final consumers, so that competitors who are at least as efficient as the dominant undertaking can compete for their custom.[160] This is because the margin squeeze

> has the effect that consumers suffer detriment as a result of limitation of the choices available to them and, therefore, of the prospect of a longer-term reduction of retail prices as a result of competition exerted by competitors who are at least as efficient in that market.[161]

Using Article 102 to impose an obligation on dominant undertakings to increase prices to the detriment of final consumers – and inviting perhaps cartel-like behaviour to the market by using the dominant undertaking's price as an umbrella – is, to say the least, bizarre and extremely worrying. Its legality on the face of a provision that requires *exploitation* of trading partners for breach is also highly questionable if the ECJ considers itself still bound by the Treaty provisions.[162] Where the genuine problem is the regulated nature of the wholesale access prices, a decision resulting in final consumers paying more for the same service, is perverse.

The ECJ judgment in *Deutsche Telekom* demonstrates clearly how far the current approach is from an economic, effects-based approach as propagated by the Commission. This is only exacerbated by other recent declarations of the ECJ that the function of the competition rules is to prevent competition from being distorted 'to the detriment of the public interest, individual undertakings and consumers, thereby ensuring the well-being of the European Union'.[163] Protection of values such as 'public interest', 'individual undertakings' and to a degree an unidentified 'well-being of the European Union' represents an approach and

[158] See, eg, ch 7 this volume, text around fns 19, 29, 36.

[159] Case C-280/08 *Deutsche Telekom v Commission* [2010] ECR I-00, [182].

[160] ibid [183].

[161] ibid [182].

[162] According to the ECJ itself, the ECJ does not act arbitrarily but judicially and it has to ensure that its interpretation reflects the intention of the parties to the Treaties and the *ratio legis* of the text; see Case 6/60 *Jean-E Humblet v Belgium* [1960] ECR 559, 575. See also KPE Lasok, *Law & Institutions of the European Union* 7th edn (Butterworths, London, 2001) 165.

[163] *TeliaSonera* (n 99) [22].

thinking going not forward, but backwards. These are vague standards based on vague concepts. The vaguer the standard the less legitimate enforcement becomes. As the law currently stands, enforcement of Article 102 appears to be approaching the outer boundaries of legitimacy that is expected of legal rules. It is hoped that the approach proposed here will contribute to remedying this deficiency in legitimacy.

Conclusion

This book has identified various problematic issues concerning the prohibition of abuse of a dominant position in the EU. Some of these problems arise from the vagueness of Article 102 itself and some of these problems arise from its application thus far by the Commission and the EU courts. After inquiring into the potential objectives of Article 102, this book has established that the application of the provision has been inconsistent and incoherent. This leads to the boundaries of this legal provision not being sufficiently known to those undertakings that might be subject to the law before they enter into various practices. Without sufficiently clear objectives that are also followed in practice, and without sufficient modern economic thinking underlying the relevant enforcement policy, the application of Article 102 raises a serious question of legitimacy. No one quite seems to know what exactly Article 102 should be doing, although this does not seem to stop anyone from enforcing it. There is a plethora of opinion on what the aim of the provision and its enforcement should be. There is, however, no sign of consensus: even between the Commission and the ECJ there seems to be an ocean of differing opinions. Some recent judgments of the ECJ, such as *GlaxoSmithKline*,[1] *Deutsche Telekom*[2] and *TeliaSonera*,[3] indeed suggest that the Commission and the ECJ might be moving in opposite directions in their thinking on what the ultimate purpose of the rule is.

This book has argued that on too many occasions the enforcement of Article 102 has introduced concepts and ideas into this area of law that have gone beyond the text of and the intent behind the provision. If this had had the effect of rendering the rule better due to more legal certainty or due to achieving more justice, this could have been acceptable. Unfortunately, these concepts and ideas have made the law neither more certain nor more just. In fact, they have moved the law further away from sound economic thinking and from the recognition of the fact that, when the subject matter is unilateral conduct, the cost of false positives can be formidable. Moreover, when the subject matter is unilateral conduct, the onus to establish that the practice is harmful should be higher than that in the case of, for example, hard-core cartels: although it is well-established that a hard-core cartel will by and large be harmful, the same cannot be said at all regarding unilateral

[1] Case C-501/06 *GlaxoSmithKline Services Unlimited v Commission* [2009] ECR I-9291.
[2] Case C-280/08 *Deutsche Telekom v Commission* [2010] ECR I-00.
[3] Case C-52/09 *Konkurrensverket v TeliaSonera Sverige AB* [2011] ECR I-00.

practices. The unilateral practices that are condemned under Article 102 are generally practices adopted independently by many other businesses, due to the practices making business sense. Therefore, the extent of the onus on the claimant in an abuse of a dominant position case should be more demanding than that in a hard-core cartel case. This should imply a robust and stringent scrutiny of the effects of the practice on the market. It is not possible to suggest that this has been the attitude of the EU authorities thus far in the area of unilateral conduct.

In seeking to contribute to remedying the current deficiency in legitimacy and certainty, this book has proposed a modern approach to the concept of 'abuse'. This approach posits that there are three *necessary and sufficient* conditions of 'abuse': exploitation, exclusion and a lack of an increase in efficiency. Even though the new approach departs from the jurisprudence on occasions, it remains loyal to the provision itself and incorporates the current economic thinking in the area of unilateral conduct. The approach is also based on some fundamental principles that are unlikely to lose their importance so long as Article 102 is kept in its current wording. One of these fundamental principles is that the provision of Article 102 is one that seeks to prevent exploitation of the trading partners of the dominant undertaking. The focus of inquiry must therefore be on establishing exploitation. Another fundamental principle is that enhancement of efficiency underlies not only Article 102, but also the entire European integration project. Efficiency must therefore be part of establishing 'abuse' and not a 'defence' for otherwise abusive conduct. It is ironic that the case for including exclusionary practices in the scope of Article 102 is actually the hardest to make, yet the application of this provision has mainly been one of sanctioning exclusionary conduct. Exclusion is relevant for establishing which exploitative practices of a dominant undertaking are a competition law problem and therefore can be sanctioned by Article 102. In a way, exclusion is secondary to exploitation in the assessment since if there is no exploitation, there is no relevant harm.

Having said all that, new economic thinking can of course improve the approach in the future by bettering our understanding as to which unilateral practices are anticompetitive and which are not. Until that day comes, the approach proposed here can be adopted as an improvement over the current approach of the EU authorities, an approach which is nearing the outer boundaries of legitimacy.

Bibliography

Adams W and Brock J, 'Antitrust and Efficiency: A Comment' (1987) 62 *New York University Law Review* 1116.

Ahdar R, 'Consumers, Redistribution of Income and the Purpose of Competition Law' (2002) 23(7) *European Competition Law Review* 341.

Ahlborn C and Grave C, 'Walter Eucken and Ordoliberalism: An Introduction from a Consumer Welfare Perspective' (2006) 2(2) *Competition Policy International* 197.

Ahlborn C and Padilla AJ, 'From *Fairness* to *Welfare*: Implications for the Assessment of Unilateral Conduct under EC Competition Law' in CD Ehlermann and M Marquis (eds), *European Competition Annual 2007: A Reformed Approach to Article 82 EC* (Oxford, Hart Publishing, 2008).

Akman P, 'Article 82 Reformed? The EC Discussion Paper on Exclusionary Abuses' [2006] (December) *Journal of Business Law* 816.

—— 'To Abuse, or not to Abuse: Discrimination between Consumers' (2007) 32 *European Law Review* 492.

—— 'Searching for the Long-Lost Soul of Article 82EC' (2009) 29(2) *Oxford Journal of Legal Studies* 267.

—— 'The Role of Exploitation in Abuse under Article 82 EC' (2009) 11 *Cambridge Yearbook of European Legal Studies* 165.

—— '"Consumer" versus "Customer": The Devil in the Detail' (2010) 37(2) *Journal of Law and Society* 315.

—— 'The European Commission's Guidance on Article 102TFEU: From *Inferno* to *Paradiso*?'(2010) 73(4) *Modern Law Review* 605.

Akman P and Garrod L, 'When are Excessive Prices Unfair?' (2011) 7(2) *Journal of Competition Law & Economics* 40.

Amato G, *Antitrust and the Bounds of Power* (Oxford, Hart Publishing, 1997).

Andriychuk O, 'Rediscovering the Spirit of Competition: On the Normative Value of the Competitive Process' (2010) 6(3) *European Competition Journal* 575.

Areeda P and Turner D, 'Predatory Pricing and Related Practices under Section 2 of the Sherman Act' (1975) 88 *Harvard Law Review* 697.

Aristotle, *Nicomachean Ethics* (R Crisp ed and trans) (Cambridge, CUP, 2002).

Armstrong M, 'Recent Developments in the Economics of Price Discrimination' in R Blundell, W Newey and T Persson (eds), *Advances in Economics and Econometrics: Theory and Application: Ninth World Congress* (Cambridge, CUP, 2006).

—— 'Price Discrimination' in P Buccirossi (ed), *Handbook of Antitrust Economics* (Cambridge, MA, MIT Press, 2008).

Armstrong M and Vickers J, 'Price Discrimination, Competition and Regulation' (1993) 41 *Journal of Industrial Economics* 335.

—— 'Competitive Price Discrimination' (2001) 32(4) *RAND Journal of Economics* 579.

Arnull A, 'Owning up to Fallibility: Precedent and the Court of Justice' (1993) 30 *Common Market Law Review* 247.

Art JY and Colomo PI, 'Judicial Review in Article 102 TFEU' in F Etro and I Kokkoris (eds), *Competition Law and the Enforcement of Article 102* (Oxford, OUP, 2010).

Atiyah PS, 'Contract and Fair Exchange' (1985) 34 *University of Toronto Law Journal* 1.

Averitt NW and Lande RH, 'Consumer Choice: The Practical Reason for both Antitrust and Consumer Protection Law' (1998) 10 *Loyola Consumer Law Review* 44.

Baker JB, 'Competitive Price Discrimination: The Exercise of Market Power without Anticompetitive Effects (Comment on Klein and Wiley)' (2003) 70 *Antitrust Law Journal* 643.

—— 'Competition Policy as a Political Bargain' (2005) 73(2) *Antitrust Law Journal* 483.

Bar-Gill O and Fersthman C, 'Law and Preferences' (2004) 20 *The Journal of Law, Economics & Organization* 331.

Barnhizer DD, 'Inequality of Bargaining Power' (2005) 76 *University of Colorado Law Review* 139.

Baumol WJ and Swanson DG, 'The New Economy and Ubiquitous Competitive Price Discrimination: Identifying Defensible Criteria of Market Power' (2003) 70 *Antitrust Law Journal* 661.

Beale H, 'Unfair Contracts in Britain and Europe' (1989) 44 *Current Legal Problems* 197.

Begg D, Fischer S and Dornbusch R, *Foundations of Economics* 2nd edn (Maidenhead, McGraw-Hill, 2003).

Berghahn VR, *The Americanisation of West German Industry 1945–1973* (Leamington Spa, Berg, 1986).

Berry MN, 'The Uncertainty of Monopolistic Conduct: A Comparative Review of Three Jurisdictions' (2001) 32 *Law and Policy in International Business* 263.

Bishop S, 'Delivering Benefits to Consumers or Per Se Illegal? Assessing the Competitive Effects of Loyalty Rebates' in *The Pros and Cons of Price Discrimination* (Swedish Competition Authority, 2005).

Bishop S and Walker M, *The Economics of EC Competition Law: Concepts, Application and Measurement* 3rd edn (London, Sweet & Maxwell, 2010).

Bishop W, 'Price Discrimination under Article 86: Political Economy in the European Court' (1981) 44 *Modern Law Review* 282.

Blount S, 'Whoever said that Markets were Fair?' [2000] (July) *Negotiation Journal* 237.

Blumenthal W, 'Discussant Comments on Exploitative Abuses under Article 82 EC' in CD Ehlermann and M Marquis (eds), *European Competition Annual 2007: A Reformed Approach to Article 82 EC* (Oxford, Hart Publishing, 2008).

Böhm F, 'The Non-State ("Natural") Laws Inherent in a Competitive Economy' in W Stützel et al (eds), *Standard Texts on the Social Market Economy* (Stuttgart, Gustav Fischer, 1982).

Böhm F, Eucken W and Grossmann-Doerth H, 'The Ordo Manifesto of 1936' in A Peacock and H Willgerodt (eds), *Germany's Social Market Economy: Origins and Evolution* (London, Macmillan, 1989).

Bork RH, 'Legislative Intent and the Policy of the Sherman Act' (1966) 9 *Journal of Law and Economics* 7.

—— 'The Goals of Antitrust Policy' (1967) 57(2) *American Economic Review* 242.

—— *The Antitrust Paradox: A Policy at War with Itself* (New York, Basic Books Inc, 1978).

Borlini L, 'Methodological Issues of the "More Economic Approach" to Unilateral Exclusionary Conduct' (2009) 5(2) *European Competition Journal* 409.

Bourgeois J and Bocken J, 'Guidelines on the Application of Article 81(3) of the EC Treaty or How to Restrict a Restriction' (2005) 32(2) *Legal Issues of Economic Integration* 111.

Bredimas A, *Methods of Interpretation and Community Law* (Amsterdam, North-Holland Publishing, 1978).
Brodley JF, 'The Economic Goals of Antitrust: Efficiency, Consumer Welfare, And Technological Progress' (1987) 62 *New York University Law Review* 1020.
Brousseau E, 'Did the Common Law Biased the Economics of Contract . . . and may it Change?' in B Deffains and K Thierry (eds), *Law and Economics in Civil Law Countries* (Amsterdam, Elsevier, 2001).
Brownsword R, Howells G and Wilhelmsson T, 'Between Market and Welfare: Some Reflections on Article 3 of the EC Directive on Unfair Terms in Consumer Contracts' in C Willett (ed), *Aspects of Fairness in Contract* (London, Blackstone Press, 1996).
Buttigieg E, *Competition Law: Safeguarding the Consumer Interest* (The Netherlands, Kluwer Law International, 2009).
Calcagno C and Walker M, 'Excessive Pricing: Towards Clarity and Economic Coherence' (2010) 6(4) *Journal of Competition Law & Economics* 891.
Calvani T, 'Rectangles and Triangles: A Response to Mr Lande' (1989) 58 *Antitrust Law Journal* 657.
Carlton DW, Gertner RH and Rosenfield AM, 'Communication among Competitors: Game Theory and Antitrust' (1997) 5 *George Mason Law Review* 423.
Chitty on Contracts: General Principles vol 1, 30th edn (London, Sweet & Maxwell, 2008).
Church J and Ware R, *Industrial Organization* (Singapore, Irwin McGraw-Hill, 2000).
Clark JM, 'Toward a Concept of Workable Competition' (1940) 20 *American Economic Review* 241.
Coleman JL, 'Efficiency, Utility and Wealth Maximization' (1980) 8 *Hofstra Law Review* 509.
Collins H, 'Good Faith in European Contract Law' (1994) 14 *Oxford Journal of Legal Studies* 229.
—— *The Law of Contract* 4th edn (London, Butterworths, 2003).
—— 'Harmonisation by Example: European Laws against Unfair Commercial Practices' (2010) 73(1) *Modern Law Review* 89.
Cooper JC, Froeb L, O'Brien DP and Tschantz S, 'Does Price Discrimination Intensify Competition? Implications for Antitrust' (2005) 72 *Antitrust Law Journal* 327.
Cooter R and Ulen T, *Law and Economics* 4th edn (Boston, Pearson Addison Wesley, 2004).
Craig P and de Burca G, *EU Law: Text, Cases and Materials* 4th edn (Oxford, OUP, 2008).
Cseres KJ, *Competition Law and Consumer Protection* (The Hague, Kluwer Law International, 2005).
—— 'The Controversies of the Consumer Welfare Standard' (2007) 3(2) *The Competition Law Review* 121.
D'Aspremont C and Motta M, 'Tougher Competition or Lower Concentration: A Trade-Off for Antitrust Authorities?' in G Norman and JF Thisse (eds), *Market Structure and Competition Policy: Game-Theoretic Approaches* (Cambridge, CUP, 2000).
Dana J, Weber RA and Kuang JX, 'Exploiting Moral Wiggle Room: Experiments Demonstrating an Illusory Preference for Fairness' (2007) 33(1) *Economic Theory* 67.
De Roover R, 'The Concept of the Just Price: Theory and Economic Policy' (1958) 18(4) *The Journal of Economic History* 418.
De Vrey RW, *Towards a European Unfair Competition Law* (Leiden, Martinus Nijhoff Publishers, 2006).
Dempsey BW, 'Just Price in a Functional Economy' (1935) 25(3) *American Economic Review* 471.

Di Valgiurata LZ, 'Price Discrimination under Article 86 of the EEC Treaty: The *United Brands* Case' (1982) 31 *International Comparative Law Quarterly* 36.

Dibadj R, 'Saving Antitrust' (2004) 75 *University of Colorado Law Review* 745.

Diebold W, *The Schuman Plan: A Study in Economic Cooperation 1950–1959* (New York, Council of Foreign Relations, 1959).

Drauz G, 'Unbundling *GE/Honeywell*: The Assessment of Conglomerate Mergers under EC Competition Law' in B Hawk (ed), *International Antitrust Law & Policy: Fordham Corporate Law 2001* (New York, Juris Publishing, 2002).

Dreher M and Adam M, 'Abuse of Dominance under Reform – Sound Economics and Established Case Law' (2007) 28(4) *European Competition Law Review* 278.

Duchêne F, 'Robert R Bowie, Interview with F Duchêne, Washington, 12 May 1987' Historical Archives of the European Union.

—— 'George Ball, Under-Secretary of State in the Kennedy and Johnson Administrations, Interview with F Duchêne, Library Place, Princeton, 10 August 1987' Historical Archives of the European Union.

Duhamel M and Townley PGC, 'An Effective and Enforceable Alternative to the Consumer Surplus Standard' (2003) 26(1) *World Competition* 3.

Dworkin RM, 'Is Wealth a Value?' (1980) 9 *Journal of Legal Studies* 191.

Easterbrook FH, 'The Limits of Antitrust' (1984) 63(1) *Texas Law Review* 1.

Eilmansberger T, 'How to Distinguish Good from Bad Competition under Article 82 EC: In Search of Clearer and More Coherent Standards for Anti-competitive Abuses' (2005) 42 *Common Market Law Review* 129.

Eisenberg MA, 'The Bargain Principle and its Limits' (1982) 95 *Harvard Law Review* 741.

Elhauge E, 'Defining Better Monopolization Standards' (2003) 56 *Stanford Law Review* 253.

Elhauge E and Geradin D, *Global Competition Law and Economics* (Oxford, Hart Publishing, 2007).

Elzinga KG, 'The Goals of Antitrust: Other than Competition and Efficiency, What Else Counts?' (1977) 125 *University of Pennsylvania Law Review* 1191.

Engelsing F, Marsden P and Möller D (primary authors), 'A Bundeskartellamt/Competition Law Forum Debate on Reform of Article 82: A "Dialectic" on Competing Approaches' (2006) 2 (Special Issue) *European Competition Journal* 211.

Erhard L, 'Confusion of Thoughts on the Question of the Economic Order' article in *Die Neue Zeitung* of 23 June 1947 in L Erhard, *The Economics of Success* (trans JA Arengo-Jones and DJS Thomson, London, Thames and Hudson, 1963).

—— 'Ten Theses in Defence of the Anti-Cartel Legislation' 10 July 1952 in L Erhard, *The Economics of Success* (trans JA Arengo-Jones and DJS Thomson, London, Thames and Hudson, 1963).

—— 'The Aims of the Law Against Restrictions on Competition' speech in the German Federal Parliament, 24 March 1955 in L Erhard, *The Economics of Success* (trans JA Arengo-Jones and DJS Thomson, London, Thames and Hudson, 1963).

Eucken W, 'What Kind of Economic and Social System?' in A Peacock and H Willgerodt (eds), *Germany's Social Market Economy: Origins and Evolution* (London, Macmillan, 1989).

—— 'The Competitive Order and its Implementation' (trans C Ahlborn and C Grave) reprinted in (2006) 2(2) *Competition Policy International* 219.

Evans A, 'Article 85(3) Exemption: The Notion of "Allowing Consumers a Fair Share of the Resulting Benefit"' in M Goyens (ed), *EC Competition Policy and the Consumer Interest,*

Proceedings of the Third European Workshop on Consumer Law (Louvain-La Neuve, May 1984) (Louvain-La-Neuve, Cabay, 1985).

Evans AC, 'European Competition Law and Consumers: The Article 85(3) Exemption' (1981) *European Competition Law Review* 425.

Evans DS and Padilla AJ, 'Excessive Prices: Using Economics to Define Administrable Legal Rules' (2005) 1(1) *Journal of Competition Law & Economics* 97.

Evans P, 'Assessing Consumer Detriment' (2007) 28(1) *European Competition Law Review* 26.

Ezrachi A, 'The Commission's Guidance on Article 82 EC and the Effects Based Approach – Legal and Practical Challenges' in A Ezrachi (ed), *Article 82 EC: Reflections on its Recent Evolution* (Oxford, Hart Publishing, 2009).

Ezrachi A and Gilo D, 'Excessive Pricing, Entry, Assessment, and Investment: Lessons from the *Mittal* Litigation' (2010) 76 *Antitrust Law Journal* 873.

Falk A, Fehr E and Fischbacher U, 'On the Nature of Fair Behavior' (2003) 41(1) *Economic Inquiry* 20.

Farrell J and Katz ML, 'The Economics of Welfare Standards in Antitrust' (2006) 2(2) *Competition Policy International* 3.

Farrell J and Shapiro C, 'Horizontal Mergers: An Equilibrium Analysis' (1990) 80(1) *American Economic Review* 107.

Faull J, 'Panel Discussion 1, Competition Policy Objectives' in CD Ehlermann and LL Laudati (eds), *European Competition Law Annual 1997: Objectives of Competition Policy* (Oxford, Hart Publishing, 1998).

Fehr E and Schmidt KM, 'A Theory of Fairness, Competition and Cooperation' (1999) 114(3) *The Quarterly Journal of Economics* 817.

Fehr E, Fischbacher U and Tougareva E, 'Do High Stakes and Competition Undermine Fairness? Evidence from Russia' Institute for Empirical Research in Economics University of Zurich Working Paper No 120 (July 2002).

Fels A and Edwards G, 'Working Paper' in CD Ehlermann and LL Laudati (eds), *European Competition Law Annual 1997: Objectives of Competition Policy* (Oxford, Hart Publishing, 1998).

Fischbacher U, Fong MC and Fehr E, 'Fairness, Errors and the Power of Competition' (2009) 72(1) *Journal of Economic Behavior and Organization* 527.

Fisher FM, 'The Social Costs of Monopoly and Regulation: Posner Reconsidered' (1985) 93(2) *The Journal of Political Economy* 410.

—— 'Monopolization versus Abuse of Dominant Position: An Economist's View' in B Hawk (ed), *International Antitrust Law & Policy: Fordham Corporate Law 2003* (New York, Juris Publishing, 2004).

Fletcher A, 'The Reform of Article 82: Recommendations on Key Policy Objectives' speech at the Competition Law Forum (Brussels, 15 March 2005).

Fletcher A and Jardine A, 'Towards an Appropriate Policy for Excessive Pricing' in CD Ehlermann and M Marquis (eds), *European Competition Annual 2007: A Reformed Approach to Article 82 EC* (Oxford, Hart Publishing, 2008).

Forrester IS, Panel Discussion 5 in CD Ehlermann and LL Laudati (eds), *European Competition Law Annual 1997: Objectives of Competition Policy* (Oxford, Hart Publishing, 1998).

Fox EM, 'The Modernization of Antitrust: A New Equilibrium' (1981) 66 *Cornell Law Review* 1140.

—— 'Monopolization and Dominance in the United States and the European Community: Efficiency, Opportunity, and Fairness' (1986) 61 *Notre Dame Law Review* 981.

Fox EM, 'Price Predation – US and EEC: Economics and Values' in B Hawk (ed), *International Antitrust Law & Policy: Fordham Corporate Law 1989* (New York, Juris Publishing, 1990).
—— 'What is Harm to Competition? Exclusionary Practices and Anticompetitive Effect' (2002) 70 *Antitrust Law Journal* 371.
Fox EM and Sullivan LA, 'Antitrust – Retrospective and Prospective: Where Are We Coming From? Where Are We Going?' (1987) 62 *New York University Law Review* 936.
Furse M, 'Monopoly Price Discrimination, Article 82 and the Competition Act' (2001) 22(5) *European Competition Law Review* 149.
—— *Competition Law of the EC and UK* 6th edn (Oxford, OUP, 2008).
—— 'Excessive Prices, Unfair Prices and Economic Value: The Law of Excessive Pricing under Article 82 EC and the Chapter II Prohibition' (2008) 4(1) *European Competition Journal* 59.
Gal MS, 'Monopoly Pricing as an Antitrust Offense in the US and the EC: Two Systems of Belief About Monopoly?' [2004] (Spring/Summer) *The Antitrust Bulletin* 343.
Gavil AI, 'Secondary Line Price Discrimination and the Fate of *Morton Salt*: To Save It, Let It Go' (1999) 48(4) *Emory Law Journal* 1057.
Gavil AI, Kovacic WE and Baker JB, *Antitrust Law in Perspective: Cases, Concepts and Problems in Competition Policy* 2nd edn (Minnesota, Thomson/West, 2008).
Gehrig TP and Stenbacka R, 'Price Discrimination, Competition and Antitrust' in *The Pros and Cons of Price Discrimination* (Swedish Competition Authority, 2005).
Geradin D, 'Limiting the Scope of Article 82 EC: What can the EU Learn from the US Supreme Court's Judgment in *Trinko* in the Wake of *Microsoft*, *IMS*, and *Deutsche Telekom*? (2004) 41 *Common Market Law Review* 1519.
Geradin D and Petit N, 'Price Discrimination under EC Competition Law: Another Antitrust Doctrine in Search of Limiting Principles?' (2006) 2(3) *Journal of Competition Law & Economics* 479.
Gerard D, 'Price Discrimination under Article 82(c) EC: Clearing up the Ambiguities' in *Global Competition Law Centre Research Papers on Article 82 EC – July 2005*.
Gerber DJ, 'Law and the Abuse of Economic Power in Europe' (1987) 62 *Tulane Law Review* 57.
—— 'Constitutionalizing the Economy: German Neo-Liberalism, Competition Law and the "New" Europe' (1994) 42 *American Journal of Comparative Law* 25.
—— 'The Transformation of European Community Competition Law?' (1994) 35(1) *Harvard International Law Journal* 97.
—— *Law and Competition in Twentieth Century Europe: Protecting Prometheus* (Oxford, OUP, 1998).
—— 'Fairness in Competition Law: European and US Experience' presented at a conference on Fairness and Asian Competition Laws (Kyoto, 5 March 2004).
—— 'The Future of Article 82: Dissecting the Conflict' in CD Ehlermann and M Marquis (eds), *European Competition Law Annual 2007: A Reformed Approach to Article 82 EC* (Oxford, Hart Publishing, 2008).
Gifford DJ and Kudrle RT, 'European Union Competition Law and Policy: How much Latitude for Convergence with the United States?' (2003) 48 (3) *The Antitrust Bulletin* 727.
—— 'The Law and Economics of Price Discrimination in Modern Economies: Time for Reconciliation?' (2010) 43 *University of California, Davis Law Review* 1235.
Gil R and Riera-Crichton D, 'Price Discrimination and Competition in Two-Sided Markets: Evidence from the Spanish Local TV Industry' IESE Business School, University of Navarra Working Paper WP-894 (January 2011).

Gillingham J, *Coal, Steel, and the Rebirth of Europe, 1945–1955* (Cambridge, CUP, 1991).
Goldschmidt N and Berndt A, 'Leonhard Miksch (1901–1950): A Forgotten Member of the Freiburg School' (2005) 64(4) *American Journal of Economics and Sociology* 973.
Golecki MJ, 'Synallagma and Freedom of Contract – The Concept of Reciprocity and Fairness in Contracts from the Historical and Law and Economics Perspective' German Working Papers in Law and Economics No 18 (2003).
Gordley J, 'Equality in Exchange' (1981) 69 *California Law Review* 1587.
Goyder DG, *EC Competition Law* 4th edn (Oxford, OUP, 2003).
Goyder J and Albors-Llorens A, *Goyder's EC Competition Law* 5th edn (Oxford, OUP, 2009).
Graham C, *EU and UK Competition Law* (Harlow, Pearson, 2010).
Grauer MC, 'The Use and Misuse of the Term "Consumer Welfare": Once More to the Mat on the Issue of Single Entity Status for Sports Leagues under Section 1 of the Sherman Act' (1989) 64 *Tulane Law Review* 71.
Green N, 'Problems in the Identification of Excessive Prices: The United Kingdom Experience in the Light of Napp' in CD Ehlermann and I Atanasiu (eds), *What is an Abuse of Dominant Position?* (Oxford, Hart Publishing, 2006).
Grundmann S, 'EC Consumer and EC Competition Law: How Related Are They? Examining the Existing EC Contract Law Sources' in H Collins (ed), *The Forthcoming EC Directive on Unfair Commercial Practices* (The Hague, Kluwer Law International, 2004).
Gyselen L, 'Abuse of Monopoly Power within the Meaning of Article 86 of the EEC Treaty: Recent Developments' in B Hawk (ed), *International Antitrust Law & Policy: Fordham Corporate Law 1989* (New York, Juris Publishing, 1990).
Hallstein W, *Europe in the Making* (trans C Roetter, London, George Allen & Unwin Ltd, 1972).
Haracoglou I, 'Competition Law, Consumer Policy and the Retail Sector: The Systems' Relation and the Effects of a Strengthened Consumer Protection Policy on Competition Law' (2007) 3(2) *The Competition Law Review* 175.
Harberger A, 'Monopoly and Resource Allocation' (1954) 44 *American Economic Review* 77.
Hausman JA and Leonard GK, 'Efficiencies from the Consumer Viewpoint' (1999) 7(3) *George Mason Law Review* 707.
Hawk B, 'Article 82 and Section 2: Abuse and Monopolizing Conduct' in (2008) 2 *Issues in Competition Law and Policy* 871 (ABA Section of *Antitrust Law* 2008).
Heitzer, B, Statement from President of the Bundeskartellamte on European Competition Day (Paris, 18–19 November 2008).
Henning-Bodewig F, *Unfair Competition Law, European Union and Member States* (The Hague, Kluwer Law International, 2006).
Hesselink MW, 'Capacity and Capability in European Contract Law' (2005) 13(4) *European Review of Private Law* 491.
—— 'Non-Mandatory Rules in European Contract Law' (2005) 1(1) *European Review of Contract Law* 43.
—— 'European Contract Law: A Matter of Consumer Protection, Citizenship, or Justice?' Centre for the Study of European Contract Law Working Paper Series No 2006/04.
—— 'The Consumer Rights Directive and the CFR: Two Worlds Apart?' (2009) 5(3) *European Review of Contract Law* 290.
Heyer K, 'Welfare Standards and Merger Analysis: Why not the Best?' (2006) 2(2) *Competition Policy International* 29.
Hicks JR, 'Annual Survey of Economic Theory: The Theory of Monopoly' (1935) 3(1) *Econometrica* 1.

Hicks JR, 'The Foundations of Welfare Economics' (1939) 49(196) *The Economic Journal* 696.

Hofmann HCH, 'Negotiated and Non-Negotiated Administrative Rule-Making: The Example of EC Competition Policy' (2006) 43 *Common Market Law Review* 158.

Hovenkamp H, 'Distributive Justice and the Antitrust Laws' (1982) 51 *George Washington Law Review* 1.

—— 'Antitrust Policy After Chicago' (1985) 84 *Michigan Law Review* 213.

—— 'The Robinson-Patman Act and Competition: Unfinished Business' (2001) 68 *Antitrust Law Journal* 125.

—— *Federal Antitrust Policy: The Law of Competition and its Practice* 3rd edn (Minnesota, Thomson/West, 2005).

Howells G, Micklitz H and Wilhelmsson T, *European Fair Trading Law: The Unfair Commercial Practices Directive* (Hamsphire, Ashgate, 2006).

Hughes EJ, 'The Left Side of Antitrust: What Fairness Means and why it Matters' (1994) 77 *Marquette Law Review* 265.

Hviid M and Waddams Price C, 'Non-discrimination Clauses in the Retail Energy Sector' ESRC Centre for Competition Policy Working Paper 10-18 (November 2010).

Jacobs MS, 'An Essay on the Normative Foundations of Antitrust Economics' (1995) 74 *North Carolina Law Review* 219.

Jacobson JM and Sher SA, '"No Economic Sense" Makes No Sense for Exclusive Dealing' (2006) 73 *Antitrust Law Journal* 779.

Jebsen P and Stevens R, 'Assumptions, Goals and Dominant Undertakings: The Regulation of Competition under Article 86 of the European Union' (1996) 64 *Antitrust Law Journal* 443.

Joffe RD, 'Antitrust Law and Proof of Consumer Injury' (2001) 75 *St John's Law Review* 615.

Johnsson M, 'Current Developments in Member States: Sweden' (2006) 2(1) *European Competition Journal* 253.

Joliet R, *Monopolization and Abuse of Dominant Position* (La Haye, Martinus Nijhoff, 1970).

Jones A and Sufrin B, *EU Competition Law: Text, Cases and Materials* 4th edn (Oxford, OUP, 2011).

Joskow PL and Klevorick AK, 'A Framework for Analyzing Predatory Pricing Policy' (1989) 89 *Yale Law Journal* 213.

Just RE, Hueth DL and Schmidtz A, *The Welfare Economics of Public Policy: A Practical Approach to Project and Policy Evaluation* (Cheltenham, Edward Elgar, 2004).

Kahneman D, Knetsch JL and Thaler RH, 'Fairness and the Assumptions of Economics' (1986) 59 (October) *Journal of Business* S285.

—— 'Fairness as a Constraint on Profit Seeking: Entitlements in the Market' (1986) 76(4) *American Economic Review* 728.

—— 'Experimental Tests of the Endowment Effect and the Coase Theorem' in CR Sunstein (ed), *Behavioural Law and Economics* (Cambridge, CUP, 2000).

Kallaugher J, 'Recent Developments under Article 82' speech at IBC Advanced EC Competition Law Conference (Brussels, 7 November 2003).

Kallaugher J and Sher B, 'Rebates Revisited: Anti-Competitive Effects and Exclusionary Abuse under Article 82' (2004) 25(5) *European Competition Law Review* 263.

Kaplow L and Shavell S, *Fairness versus Welfare* (Cambridge, MA, Harvard University Press, 2002).

Karagiannis Y, 'Preference Heterogeneity and Equilibrium Institutions: The Case of European Competition Policy' (PhD thesis, European University Institute, Florence, 2007).

Katsoulacos Y, 'Some Critical Comments on the Commission's Guidance Paper on Art 82 EC' (2009) (February-I) *Global Competition Policy*.

Katsoulacos Y and Ulph D, 'Optimal Enforcement and Decision Structures for Competition Policy: Economic Considerations' in F Etro and I Kokkoris (eds), *Competition Law and the Enforcement of Article 102* (Oxford, OUP, 2010).

Katz ML, 'The Welfare Effects of Third-Degree Price Discrimination in Intermediate Good Markets' (1987) 77 *American Economic Review* 154.

Kaysen C and Turner DF, *Antitrust Policy: An Economic and Legal Analysis* (Cambridge, MA, Harvard University Press, 1971).

Kiljanski K, '"Pass-on" in Merger Efficiency Defence' (2003) 26(4) *World Competition* 651.

Killick J and Komninos A, 'Schizophrenia in the Commission's Article 82 Guidance Paper: Formalism Alongside Increased Recourse to Economic Analysis' (2009) (February-I) *Global Competition Policy*.

Kjolbye L, 'The New Commission Guidelines on the Application of Article 81(3): An Economic Approach to Article 81' (2004) 25(9) *European Competition Law Review* 566.

Klein B and Wiley JS, 'Competitive Price Discrimination as an Antitrust Justification for Intellectual Property Refusals to Deal' (2003) 70 *Antitrust Law Journal* 599.

—— —— Market Power in Economics and in Antitrust: Reply to Baker' (2003) 70 *Antitrust Law Journal* 655.

Kolasky WJ, 'What is Competition? A Comparison of US and European Perspectives' [2004] (Spring/Summer) *The Antitrust Bulletin* 29.

Kon S and Turnbull S, 'Pricing and the Dominant Firm: Implications of the Competition Commission Appeal Tribunal's Judgment in the Napp Case' (2003) 24(2) *European Competition Law Review* 70.

Korah V, 'Modernisation of Article 82' speech delivered at I Lisbon Conference on Competition Law and Economics (Lisbon, 3–4 November 2005).

Kötz H, *European Contract Law Vol 1: Formation, Validity, and Content of Contracts; Contract and Third Parties* (trans T Weir, Oxford, Clarendon Press, 1997).

Kovacic WE, 'The Modern Evolution of US Competition Policy Enforcement Norms' (2004) 71 *Antitrust Law Journal* 377.

—— 'The Intellectual DNA of Modern US Competition Law for Dominant Firm Conduct: The Chicago/Harvard Double Helix' (2007) 1(1) *Columbia Business Law Review* 1.

Krattenmaker TG, Lande RH and Salop SC, 'Monopoly Power and Market Power in Antitrust Law' (1987) 76 *The Georgetown Law Journal* 241.

Kroes N, 'Preliminary Thoughts on Policy Review of Article 82' speech at the Fordham Corporate Law Institute (New York, 23 September 2005).

—— 'Tackling Exclusionary Practices to Avoid Exploitation of Market Power: Some Preliminary Thoughts on the Policy Review of Article 82' in B Hawk (ed), *International Antitrust Law and Policy: Fordham Corporate Law Institute Annual Proceedings 2005* (New York, Juris Publishing, 2006).

—— 'The Commission's Review of Exclusionary Abuses of Dominant Position' speech at the Korean Competition Forum organised on the occasion of the Fourth Annual Bilateral Meeting (Seoul, 26–27 June 2006).

—— Exclusionary Abuses of Dominance – The European Commission's Enforcement Priorities' speech at the Fordham University Symposium (New York, 25 September 2008).

Kronman AT, 'Wealth Maximization as a Normative Principle' (1980) 9 *Journal of Legal Studies* 227.

Lage SM and Allendesalazar R, 'Community Policy on Discriminatory Pricing: A Practitioner's Perspective' in CD Ehlermann and I Atanasiu (eds), *What is an Abuse of Dominant Position?* (Oxford, Hart Publishing, 2006).

Lancaster K, 'The Economics of Product Variety: A Survey' (1990) 9(3) *Marketing Science* 189.

Lande RH, 'Wealth Transfers as the Original and Primary Concern of Antitrust: The Efficiency Interpretation Challenged' (1982) 34 *Hastings Law Journal* 65.

—— 'Chicago's False Foundation: Wealth Transfers (Not Just Efficiency) Should Guide Antitrust' (1989) 58 *Antitrust Law Journal* 631.

Lando O and Beale H (eds), *Principles of European Contract Law Parts I and II* (The Hague, Kluwer Law International, 2000).

Lando O, Clive E, Prum A and Zimmerman R, *Principles of European Contract Law Part III* (The Hague, Kluwer Law International, 2003).

Lang JT, 'Fundamental Issues Concerning Abuse under Article 82 EC' paper presented at Annual Competition Policy Conference (Oxford, Regulatory Policy Institute, July 2005).

—— 'Panel Discussion on Non-Pricing Abuses' in CD Ehlermann and I Atanasiu (eds), *European Competition Law Annual 2003: What is an Abuse of a Dominant Position?* (Oxford, Hart Publishing, 2006).

Lang JT and O'Donoghue R, 'Defining Legitimate Competition: How to Clarify Pricing Abuses under Article 82EC' (2002) 26 *Fordham International Law Journal* 83.

Lasok KPE, *Law & Institutions of the European Union* 7th edn (London, Butterworths, 2001).

Law J (ed), *A Dictionary of Business and Management* (Oxford, OUP, 2006).

Leary TB, 'Freedom as the Core Value of Antitrust in the New Millennium' (2000) 68 *Antitrust Law Journal* 545.

Leibenstein H, 'Allocative Efficiency vs X-Efficiency' (1966) 56 *American Economic Review* 392.

Lianos I, 'Categorical Thinking in Competition Law and the "Effects-Based" Approach in Article 82 EC' in A Ezrachi (ed), *Article 82 EC: Reflections on its Recent Evolution* (Oxford, Hart Publishing, 2009).

—— '"Judging" Economists: Economic Expertise in Competition Law Litigation: A European View' in I Lianos and I Kokkoris (eds), *The Reform of EC Competition Law* (The Netherlands, Kluwer Law International, 2010).

Loewenthal P, 'The Defence of "Objective Justification" in the Application of Article 82 EC' (2005) 28(4) *World Competition* 455.

Lorenz M, Lubbig M and Russell A, 'Price Discrimination, A Tender Story' (2005) 26(6) *European Competition Law Review* 355.

Lovdahl Gormsen L, 'Article 82 EC: Where Are We Coming From and Where Are We Going To?' (2005) 2(2) *The Competition Law Review* 5.

—— 'Antitrust Marathon II' (2008) 4(1) *European Competition Journal* 213.

—— *A Principled Approach to Abuse of Dominance in European Competition Law* (Cambridge, CUP, 2010).

—— 'Why the European Commission's Enforcement Priorities on Article 82 EC should be Withdrawn' (2010) 31 *European Competition Law Review* 45.

Lowe P, 'Current Issues of EU Competition Law: The New Competition Enforcement Regime' (2004) 24 *Northwestern Journal of International Law & Business* 567.

—— 'Preserving and Promoting Competition: A European Response' 2006 (2) (Summer) *EC Competition Policy Newsletter* 1.

—— 'Consumer Welfare and Efficiency – New Guiding Principles of Competition Policy?' (13th International Conference on Competition and 14th European Competition Day, Munich, March 2007).

—— 'The Commission's Current Thinking on Article 82' BIICL Annual Trans-Atlantic Antitrust Dialogue (15 May 2008).

Lutz FA, 'Observations on the Problem of Monopolies' in A Peacock and H Willgerodt (eds), *Germany's Social Market Economy: Origins and Evolution* (London, Macmillan, 1989).

Lyons BR, 'Could Politicians be More Right than Economists? A Theory of Merger Standards' Revised Centre for Competition and Regulation Working Paper CCR 02-1 (15 May 2002).

—— 'The Paradox of the Exclusion of Exploitative Abuse' in *The Pros and Cons of High Prices* (Swedish Competition Authority, 2007).

Maier-Rigaud F, 'On the Normative Foundations of Competition Law: Efficiency, Political Freedom and the Freedom to Compete' (5th Academic Society for Competition Law (ASCOLA) Conference on the Goals of Competition Law, Bonn, May 2010) (forthcoming in the ASCOLA Competition Law series by Edward Elgar).

Majumdar A, 'The Role of a Consumer Harm Test in Competition Policy' (2008) 20(2) *Loyola Consumer Law Review* 144.

Mankiw NG, *Principles of Economics* (Orlando, Dryden Press Harcourt Brace College Publishers, 1998).

Marenco G, 'The Birth of Modern Competition Law in Europe' in A von Bogdandy, PC Mavroidis and Y Mény (eds), *European Integration and International Co-ordination: Studies in Honour of Claus-Dieter Ehlermann* (The Hague, Kluwer Law International, 2002).

Marsden P and Whelan P, '"Consumer Detriment" and its Application in EC and UK Competition Law' (2006) 27(10) *European Competition Law Review* 569.

Marshall A, *Principles of Economics: An Introductory Volume* 8th edn (London, Macmillan and Co, 1920).

McDonnell BH and Farber DA, 'Are Efficient Antitrust Rules Always Optimal?' (2003) 48(3) *The Antitrust Bulletin* 807.

McKendrick E, *Contract Law: Text, Cases and Materials* 4th edn (Oxford, OUP, 2010).

Meese AJ, 'Debunking the Purchaser Welfare Account of Section 2 of the Sherman Act: How Harvard Brought Us to a Total Welfare Standard and Why We Should Keep It' (2010) 85 *New York University Law Review* 659.

Melamed AD, 'Exclusive Dealing Agreements and Other Exclusionary Conduct – Are there Unifying Principles?' (2006) 73 *Antitrust Law Journal* 375.

Mertikopoulou V, 'DG Competition's Discussion Paper on the Application of Article 82 of the EC Treaty to Exclusionary Abuses: The Proposed Economic Reform from a Legal Point of View' (2007) 28(4) *European Competition Law Review* 241.

Mestmäcker EJ, 'The Development of German and European Competition Law with Special Reference to the EU Commission's Article 82 Guidance of 2008' in LF Pace (ed), *European Competition Law: The Impact of the Commission's Guidance on Article 102* (Cheltenham, Edward Elgar, 2011).

Meyer DL, 'The Development and Communication of Competition Law Standards Applicable to Single-Firm Exclusionary Conduct: A Perspective Based on US Experience' in CD Ehlermann and M Marquis (eds), *European Competition Annual 2007: A Reformed Approach to Article 82 EC* (Oxford, Hart Publishing, 2008).

Monti G, 'Article 81 and Public Policy' (2002) 39(5) *Common Market Law Review* 1057.

—— 'Article 82 EC: What Future for the Effects-Based Approach?' (2010) 1 (1) *Journal of European Competition Law & Practice* 2.

Möschel W, 'Competition Policy from an Ordo Point of View' in A Peacock and H Willgerodt (eds), *German Neo-Liberals and the Social Market Economy* (London, Macmillan, 1989).

Motta M, *Competition Policy: Theory and Practice* (Cambridge, CUP, 2004).

—— 'Michelin II – The Treatment of Rebates' in BR Lyons (ed), *Cases in European Competition Policy: The Economic Analysis* (Cambridge, CUP, 2009).

—— 'The European Commission's Guidance Communication on Article 82' (2009) 30(12) *European Competition Law Review* 593.

Motta M and de Streel A, 'Excessive Pricing and Price Squeeze under EU Law' in CD Ehlermann and I Atanasiu (eds), *What is an Abuse of Dominant Position?* (Oxford, Hart Publishing, 2006).

Müller-Armack A, 'The Social Aspect of the Economic System' in W Stützel et al (eds), *Standard Texts on the Social Market Economy* (Stuttgart, Gustav Fischer, 1982).

—— 'The Meaning of the Social Market Economy' in A Peacock and H Willgerodt (eds), *Germany's Social Market Economy: Origins and Evolution* (London, Macmillan, 1989).

Muysert P, 'Price Discrimination – An Unreliable Indicator of Market Power' (2004) 25(6) *European Competition Law Review* 350.

Navarro E, Font A, Folguera J and Briones J, *Merger Control in the EU: Law, Economics and Practice* 2nd edn (Oxford, OUP, 2005).

Nazzini R, 'The Wood began to Move: An Essay on Consumer Welfare, Evidence and Burden of Proof in Article 82 Cases' (2006) 31(4) *European Law Review* 518.

Nelson WR, 'Incorporating Fairness into Game Theory and Economics: Comment' (2001) 91(4) *American Economic Review* 1180.

Neven DJ, 'Working Paper' in CD Ehlermann and LL Laudati (eds), *European Competition Law Annual 1997: Objectives of Competition Policy* (Oxford, Hart Publishing, 1998).

Neven DJ and Röller LH, 'Consumer Surplus vs Welfare Standard in a Political Economy Model of Merger Control' (2005) 23 *International Journal of Industrial Organization* 829.

Ng YK, *Welfare Economics: Towards a More Complete Analysis* (Hampshire, Palgrave Macmillan, 2004).

Nihoul P, 'From Unfair Trading to Free Competition – Towards a New Organisation of Markets in the European Union' (2006) 17(1) *European Business Law Review* 23.

Nosek P, Šimeček I and Balaštík KŠ, 'Current Developments in Member States: Czech Republic' (2006) 2(1) *European Competition Journal* 195.

O'Brien DP and Shaffer G, 'The Welfare Effects of Forbidding Discriminatory Discounts: A Secondary Line Analysis of Robinson-Patman' (1994) 10 *Journal of Law, Economics & Organization* 296.

O'Donoghue R and Padilla AJ, *The Law and Economics of Article 82 EC* (Oxford, Hart Publishing, 2006).

Odudu O, 'Interpreting Article 81(1): Object as Subjective Intention' (2001) 26(1) *European Law Review* 60.

—— 'Article 81(3), Discretion and Direct Effect' (2002) 23(1) *European Competition Law Review* 17.

Ogus AI, *Regulation: Legal Form and Economic Theory* 2nd edn (Oxford, Hart Publishing, 2004).

Okun AM, *Equality and Efficiency: The Big Tradeoff* (Washington, DC, The Brookings Institution, 1975).

Oliver HM, 'German Neoliberalism' (1960) 74(1) *The Quarterly Journal of Economics* 117.

Orbach BY, 'The Antitrust Consumer Welfare Paradox' (2010) 7(1) *Journal of Competition Law & Economics* 133.

Østerud E, *Identifying Exclusionary Abuses by Dominant Undertakings under EU Competition Law: The Spectrum of Tests* (The Netherlands, Kluwer Law International, 2010).
Pardolesi R and Arnando L, 'Single-Firm Conduct: A Discipline in Search of Itself (Try with Google?)' Working Paper (2010).
Paulis E, 'Article 82 EC and Exploitative Conduct' in CD Ehlermann and M Marquis (eds), *European Competition Annual 2007: A Reformed Approach to Article 82 EC* (Oxford, Hart Publishing, 2008).
Peel E, *Treitel on the Law of Contract* 12th edn (London, Sweet & Maxwell, 2007).
Pelkmans J, 'Consumer Interests in the EC Competition Regime. An Economic Perspective' in M Goyens (ed), *EC Competition Policy and the Consumer Interest* Proceedings of the Third European Workshop on Consumer Law (Louvain-La Neuve, May 1984) (Louvain-La-Neuve, Cabay, 1985).
Pera A, 'Changing Views of Competition, Economic Analysis and EC Antitrust Law' (2008) 4(1) *European Competition Journal* 127.
Perrot A, 'Towards an Effects-based Approach of Price Discrimination' in *The Pros and Cons of Price Discrimination* (Swedish Competition Authority, 2005).
Petty RD and Hamilton J, 'Seeking a Single Policy for Contractual Fairness to Consumers: A Comparison of US and EU Efforts' (2004) 38(1) *The Journal of Consumer Affairs* 146.
Pittman R, 'Consumer Surplus as the Appropriate Standard for Antitrust Enforcement' (2007) 3(2) *Competition Policy International* 205.
Posner RA, 'The Social Costs of Monopoly and Regulation' (1975) 83(4) *The Journal of Political Economy* 807.
—— 'The Value of Wealth: A Comment on Dworkin and Kronman' (1980) 9 *Journal of Legal Studies* 243.
—— *Economic Analysis of Law* 4th edn (Boston, Little, Brown and Company, 1992).
—— *Antitrust Law* 2nd edn (Chicago, The University of Chicago Press, 2001).
—— 'Antitrust in the New Economy' (2001) 68 *Antitrust Law Journal* 925.
Price CM, *Welfare Economics in Theory and Practice* (London, Macmillan, 1977).
Rabin M, 'Incorporating Fairness into Game Theory and Economics' (1993) 83(5) *American Economic Review* 1281, 1281.
Ridyard D, 'Exclusionary Pricing and Price Discrimination Abuses under Article 82 – An Economic Analysis' [2002] *European Competition Law Review* 286.
—— 'Article 82 Price Abuses – Towards a More Economic Approach' in CD Ehlermann and I Atanasiu (eds), *What is an Abuse of Dominant Position?* (Oxford, Hart Publishing, 2006).
Riziotis D, 'Efficiency Defence in Article 82 EC' in MO Mackenrodt, B Conde Gallego and S Enschelmaier (eds), *Abuse of Dominant Position: New Interpretation, New Enforcement Mechanisms?* (Berlin, Springer-Verlag, 2008).
Röller LH, 'Exploitative Abuses' in CD Ehlermann and M Marquis (eds), *European Competition Annual 2007: A Reformed Approach to Article 82 EC* (Oxford, Hart Publishing, 2008).
Ross TW and Winter RA, 'The Efficiency Defense in Merger Law: Economic Foundations and Recent Canadian Developments' (2005) 72 *Antitrust Law Journal* 471.
Roth WH, 'The "More Economic Approach" and the Rule of Law' in D Schmidtchen, M Albert and S Voigt (eds), *The More Economic Approach to European Competition Law* (Tübingen, Mohr Siebeck, 2010).
Rousseva E, 'Modernizing by Eradicating: How the Commission's New Approach to Article 81 EC Dispenses with the Need to Apply Article 82 EC to Vertical Restraints' (2005) 42 *Common Market Law Review* 587.

Rousseva E, 'The Concept of "Objective Justification" of an Abuse of a Dominant Position: Can it Help to Modernise the Analysis under Article 82 EC?' (2006) 2(2) *The Competition Law Review* 27.

—— *Rethinking Exclusionary Abuses in EU Competition Law* (Oxford, Hart Publishing, 2010).

Salop SC, 'Exclusionary Conduct, Effect on Consumers, and the Flawed Profit-Sacrifice Standard' (2006) 73 *Antitrust Law Journal* 311.

—— 'Question: What is the Real and Proper Antitrust Welfare Standard? Answer: The *True* Consumer Welfare Standard' (2010) 22(3) *Loyola Consumer Law Review* 336.

Samkalden I and Druker IE, 'Legal Problems Relating to Article 86 of the Rome Treaty' (1966) 3 *Common Market Law Review* 158.

Schaub A, 'Working Paper' in CD Ehlermann and LL Laudati (eds), *European Competition Law Annual 1997: Objectives of Competition Policy* (Oxford, Hart Publishing, 1998).

Scherer FM, 'Antitrust, Efficiency, and Progress' (1987) 62 *New York University Law Review* 998.

—— 'Efficiency, Fairness and the Early Contributions of Economists to the Antitrust Debate' (1990) 29 *Washburn Law Journal* 243.

Schmalensee R, 'Output and Welfare Implications of Monopolistic Third-Degree Price Discrimination' (1981) 71 *American Economic Review* 242.

Schmidt ILO, 'The Suitability of the More Economic Approach for Competition Policy: Dynamic vs Static Efficiency' (2007) 28(7) *European Competition Law Review* 408.

Schulze R and Hören T (eds), *Dokumente zum Europäischen Recht Band 3 Kartellrecht (bis 1957)* (Berlin, Springer-Verlag, 2000).

Schumpeter JA, *Capitalism, Socialism and Democracy* 5th edn (London, George Allen & Unwin, 1976).

Schwartz A, 'Contract Theory and Theories of Contract Regulation' in E Brousseau and JM Glachant (eds), *Revue d'Economie Industrielle,* No Spécial, Économie des Contrats: Bilan et Perspective, No 92 (2eme et 3eme trimester, 2000).

Schwartz A and Scott RE, 'Contract Theory and the Limits of Contract Law' (2003) 113 *Yale Law Journal* 541.

Schweitzer H, 'The History, Interpretation and Underlying Principles of Section 2 Sherman Act and Article 82 EC' in CD Ehlermann and M Marquis (eds), *European Competition Annual 2007: A Reformed Approach to Article 82 EC* (Oxford, Hart Publishing, 2008).

—— 'Recent Developments in EU Competition Law (2006–2008): Single-firm Dominance and the interpretation of Article 82' (2009) (2) *European Review of Contract Law* 175.

Selden L, *Soft Law in European Community Law* (Oxford, Hart Publishing, 2004).

Sher B, 'The Last of Steam-Powered Trains: Modernising Article 82' (2004) 25(5) *European Competition Law Review* 243.

Sinclair D, 'Abuse of Dominance at a Crossroads – Potential Effect, Object and Appreciability under Article 82 EC' (2004) 25(8) *European Competition Law Review* 491.

Smith A, *An Inquiry into the Nature and Causes of the Wealth of Nations* (E Cannan (ed) Chicago, The University of Chicago Press, 1976).

Smith SA, 'In Defence of Substantive Fairness' (1996) 112 *The Law Quarterly Review* 138.

Sosnick SH, 'A Critique of Concepts of Workable Competition' (1958) 72 *Quarterly Journal of Economics* 380.

Study Group on Social Justice in European Private Law, 'Social Justice in European Contract Law: A Manifesto' (2004) 10(6) *European Law Journal* 653.

Thal SN, 'The Inequality of Bargaining Power Doctrine: The Problem of Defining Contractual Unfairness' (1988) 8 *Oxford Journal of Legal Studies* 17.

Tirole J, *The Theory of Industrial Organization* (Cambridge, MA, The MIT Press, 1988).

—— *The Theory of Industrial Organization* 9th edn (Cambridge, MA, MIT Press, 1997).

Townley C, *Article 81 EC and Public Policy* (Oxford, Hart Publishing, 2009).

Trebilcock MJ, *The Limits of Freedom of Contract* (Cambridge, MA, Harvard University Press, 1997).

Tullock G, 'The Welfare Costs of Tariffs, Monopolies, and Theft' (1967) 5(3) *Western Economic Journal* 224.

Van den Bergh RJ, 'The Difficult Reception of Economic Analysis in European Competition Law' in A Cucinotta, R Pardolesi and RJ Van den Bergh (eds), *Post-Chicago Developments in Antitrust Law* (Cheltenham, Edward Elgar, 2002).

Van den Bergh RJ and Camesasca PD, *European Competition Law and Economics: A Comparative Perspective* (Antwerpen, Intersentia-Hart, 2001).

Van den Doel H and van Velthoven B, *Democracy and Welfare Economics* 2nd edn (Cambridge, CUP, 1993).

Van der Woude M, 'Unfair and Excessive Prices in the Energy Sector' in CD Ehlermann and M Marquis (eds), *European Competition Annual 2007: A Reformed Approach to Article 82 EC* (Oxford, Hart Publishing, 2008).

Van Hook JC, *Rebuilding Germany: The Creation of the Social Market Economy, 1945–1957* (Cambridge, CUP, 2004).

Van Horn R, 'Chicago's Shifting Attitude Toward Concentrations of Business Power (1934–1962)' (2011) 34 *Seattle University Law Review* 1527.

Varian HR, 'Price Discrimination and Social Welfare' (1985) 75 *American Economic Review* 870.

—— 'Price Discrimination' in R Schmalensee and R Willig (eds), *Handbook of Industrial Organization* Vol 1, 2nd edn (Amsterdam, Elsevier, 1990).

Vatiero M, 'The Ordoliberal Notion of Market Power: An Institutionalist Reassessment' (2010) 6(3) *European Competition Journal* 689.

Vedder H, 'Competition Law and Consumer Protection: How Competition Law can be used to Protect Consumers Even Better – Or Not?' [2006] *European Business Law Review* 83.

Vickers J, 'Abuse of Market Power' (2005) 115 *The Economic Journal* F244.

—— 'A Reformed Approach to Article 82 EC and the US Practice: An Overall Appreciation' in CD Ehlermann and M Marquis (eds), *European Competition Law Annual 2007: A Reformed Approach to Article 82 EC* (Oxford, Hart Publishing, 2008).

—— 'Abuse of Market Power' in P Buccirossi (ed), *Handbook of Antitrust Economics* (Cambridge, MA, MIT Press, 2008).

—— 'Speaking Note, Panel II' in CD Ehlermann and M Marquis (eds), *European Competition Law Annual 2007: A Reformed Approach to Article 82 EC* (Oxford, Hart Publishing, 2008).

Von der Groeben H, 'Die Wettbewerbspolitik als Teil der Wirtschaftspolitik im Gemeinsamen Markt' Rede vor dem Europäischen Parlament in Strassburg am 16. Juni 1965 ('Competition Policy as Part of the Economic Policy in the Common Market' speech before the European Parliament (Strasbourg, 16 June 1965)).

Waelbroeck D, 'Michelin II: A Per Se Rule against Rebates by Dominant Companies?' (2005) 1(1) *Journal of Competition Law & Economics* 149.

Waelbroeck D, 'The Assessment of Efficiencies under Article 102 TFEU and the Commission's Guidance Paper' in F Etro and I Kokkoris (eds), *Competition Law and the Enforcement of Article 102* (Oxford, OUP, 2010).

Waelbroeck M, 'Price Discrimination and Rebate Policies under EU Competition Law' in B Hawk (ed), *International Antitrust Law & Policy: Fordham Corporate Law 1995* (New York, Juris Publishing, 1996).

Werden GJ, 'Competition Policy on Exclusionary Conduct: Toward an Effects-Based Analysis?' (2006) 2 (Special Issue) *European Competition Journal* 53.

—— 'Identifying Exclusionary Conduct under Section 2: The "No Economic Sense" Test' (2006) 73 *Antitrust Law Journal* 413.

—— 'Consumer Welfare and Competition Policy' in J Drexl, W Kerber and R Pozsun (eds), *Competition Policy and the Economic Approach* (Cheltenham, Edward Elgar, 2011).

Westen P, 'The Empty Idea of Equality' (1982) 95 *Harvard Law Review* 537.

Whish R, 'Recent Developments in Community Competition Law 1998/99' (2000) 25(3) *European Law Review* 219.

—— *Competition* Law 6th edn (Oxford, OUP, 2009).

Wilhelmsson T, 'Varieties of Welfarism in European Contract Law' (2004) 10(6) *European Law Journal* 712.

Willgerodt H and Peacock A, 'German Liberalism and Economic Revival' in A Peacock and H Willgerodt (eds), *Germany's Social Market Economy: Origins and Evolution* (London, Macmillan, 1989).

Williamson OE, 'Economies as an Antitrust Defense: The Welfare Trade-Offs' (1968) 58 *American Economic Review* 18.

—— 'Economies as an Antitrust Defense Revisited' (1977) 125 *University of Pennsylvania Law Review* 699.

Winch DM, *Analytical Welfare Economics* (Harmondsworth, Penguin, 1971).

Witkowski H, *Zur Missbrauchsaufsicht über Preise marktbeherrschender Unternehmen* (Frankfurt, Peter Lang, 1981).

Wurmnest W, 'The Reform of Article 82 in the Light of the "Economic Approach"' in MO Mackenrodt, B Conde Gallego and S Enschelmaier (eds), *Abuse of Dominant Position: New Interpretation, New Enforcement Mechanisms?* (Berlin, Springer-Verlag, 2008).

Xia L, Moore KB and Cox JL, 'The Price Is Unfair! A Conceptual Framework of Price Fairness Perceptions' (2004) 68 *Journal of Marketing* 1.

Zimmer D, 'On Fairness and Welfare: The Objectives of Competition Policy (Comment)' in CD Ehlermann and M Marquis (eds), *European Competition Law Annual 2007: A Reformed Approach to Article 82 EC* (Oxford, Hart Publishing, 2008).

Index

www.ingramcontent.com/pod-product-compliance
Ingram Content Group UK Ltd.
Pitfield, Milton Keynes, MK11 3LW, UK
UKHW020259051026
15470UKWH00024B/1848/J